Sustainability through Participation?

Legal Aspects of Sustainable Development

Series Editor

David Freestone

This series publishes work on all aspects of the international legal dimensions of the concept of sustainable development. Its aim is to publish important works of scholarship on a range of relevant issues including conservation of natural resources, climate change, biodiversity loss and the role of international agreements, international organizations and state practice.

VOLUME 27

The titles published in this series are listed at *brill.com/lasd*

Sustainability through Participation?

Perspectives from National, European and International Law

By

Birgit Peters and Eva Julia Lohse

BRILL | NIJHOFF

LEIDEN | BOSTON

Open Access publication of this book was funded by DFG (2019), grant no. 414063758.

The Library of Congress Cataloging-in-Publication Data is available online at https://catalog.loc.gov
LC record available at https://lccn.loc.gov/2023008151

Typeface for the Latin, Greek, and Cyrillic scripts: "Brill". See and download: brill.com/brill-typeface.

ISSN 1875-0923
ISBN 978-90-04-50937-5 (hardback)
ISBN 978-90-04-50938-2 (e-book)

This book is printed on acid-free paper and produced in a sustainable manner.

Printed by Printforce, the Netherlands

Contents

Series Editor's Preface

This volume, edited by Eva Julia Lohse and Birgit Peters, is the twenty-seventh volume in the Brill Nijhoff series on *Legal Aspects of Sustainable Development* published under my General Editorship. The aim of this series is to publish works at the cutting edge of legal scholarship that address both the practical and the theoretical aspects of this important concept.

I am very pleased to be able to include this book in the series. It is the result of an innovative collaboration between younger scholars from Argentina, Germany, Italy, Kenya, Norway and South Africa, who during the period 2018–2022 met initially at workshops in Bayreuth and Trier and latterly, during the COVID pandemic, virtually.

In the ongoing quest for sustainable development, which has found its most recent iteration in the 2015 UN Sustainable Development Goals (SDGs), the need for public participation is commonly flagged as an essential requirement, As the Editors remind us the origins of this idea can perhaps be traced to the influential Brundtland Report of 1987 that suggested that the participation of the public affected, as well as of further stakeholders, would ensure the recognition of the common interests that sustainable development was to protect. Principle 10 of the Rio Declaration begins by emphasising that 'Environmental issues are best handled with participation of all concerned citizens, at the relevant level ..."

The overarching objective of this ambitious work, therefore, is to unpack the requirements of effective participation and to ask from a legal perspective - whether, and if so, how sustainability can be achieved through participation in the multi-level governance structures of international, supranational and national law. The resulting research questions are complex and multifaceted and as the Editors themselves again suggest the answers are indeed "neither obvious nor trivial."

This book breaks new ground. It provides a wealth of insights and unrivalled perspectives on participation as a means to further sustainable development from a legal perspective, in the multi-level environment of international, European and national law. I am certain it will merit a warm reception.

David Freestone
Washington DC

Acknowledgements

The present book is the fruit of a collaboration between younger researchers from Argentina, Germany, Italy, Kenya, Norway, South Africa (SustaiNet), on questions of sustainability and participation, during 2018–2022. The network SustaiNet was facilitated with the generous support of the Deutsche Forschungsgemeinschaft (DFG), grant no. 414063758. The aim of the network was to research the specific connection between sustainability and participation, and its legal framework and structures. The book summarizes the findings of the encounters of the members of the network and additional authors, who contributed further insights, in Bayreuth and Trier, in person and – due to the Covid pandemic – digitally.

We owe thanks Roberto Caranta, Elena Fasoli and Matthias Goldmann, who formed part of the advisory board of SustaiNet, for their invaluable comments and contributions at the workshop in Bayreuth. We also wish to thank the two anonymous reviewers for their helpful comments on the book outline, as well as Beth Derr and everyone at Brill for their patience and continuous advice during the process of the final manuscript.

Birgit Peters and Eva Julia Lohse
Trier and Bayreuth, May 2023

Tables and Figures

Tables

Figures

Notes on Contributors

Daniele Brombal, Ph.D.
is an Associate Professor at the Department of Asian and North African Studies of Ca' Foscari University Venice, where he teaches courses on China's society, politics, and environmental governance and co-directs the master programme in environmental humanities. His research focuses on institutional change for sustainability in China and along the new Silk Roads.

Julius Buckler, PD Dr.
is a Postdoc and Lecturer at the University of Bayreuth (Germany). His research focuses, inter alia, on the economic aspects of EU Law, particularly in the regulated industries.

Federica Cittadino, Ph.D.
is a Senior Researcher at the Institute for Comparative Federalism, Eurac Research, Bolzano, Italy. She holds a Ph.D. in International Studies, University of Trento. She is an expert of Environmental Law, with a particular focus on Biodiversity and Climate Change Law, environmental governance in multi-level systems, environmental participation, environmental litigation, and environmental justice.

Cristina Fraenkel-Haeberle, Prof. Dr.
is a Coordinator of the research programme European Administrative Space at the German Research Institute for Public Administration and Professor for Public Law at the German University of Administrative Sciences Speyer (Germany).

Giacomo Gattinara, Ph.D.
is a Member of the Legal Service of the European Commission and a former Legal Secretary at the Court of First Instance of the European Communities. He holds a Ph.D. in International Public and EU Law (La Sapienza, Rome), LL.M. in European Community Law (College of Europe, Bruges), LL.M. and MA in European Competition Law (King's College, London), D.e.s.s. (Institut Universitaire International de Luxembourg et Université Robert Schuman de Strasbourg).

Louis Kotzé, Prof. Dr. Dr.
is a Research Professor at the Faculty of Law, North-West University, South Africa, and Senior Professorial Fellow in Earth System Law at the University of

Lincoln, United Kingdom. His research focus lies at the interface of Global Environmental Constitutionalism, Law and the Anthropocene, and Earth System Law.

Eva Julia Lohse, Prof. Dr.
is a Full Professor of Public, European and Comparative Law at the University of Bayreuth, Germany, and Director of the Research Centre for the Law of Sustainable Development at Bayreuth. She holds a LL.M. in Comparative and EU Law (University of Kent, Canterbury) and is co-founder of SustaiNet.

Emma Mitrotta, Ph.D.
is an Environmental Law Consultant who collaborates with the Eurac Research Institute for Comparative Federalism on issues relating to the role of local actors in multi-level environmental governance. She holds a Ph.D. in International Studies (University of Trento) for her research on the involvement of local communities and sub-national entities in the protection and management of transboundary natural resources. Her research interests include the protection of biodiversity and its transboundary dimension, public participation in multi-level environmental governance, and local sustainable development.

Magnus Noll-Ehlers, Ph.D.
is a Member of the Legal Service of the European Commission. He works in the team in charge of the internal market for goods, energy and environment and holds a Ph.D. in EU Law (Goethe University Frankfurt).

Omondi R. Owino, Dr.
is a Expert on Environmental Law, Climate Change Law, Energy Law, and Natural Resources Law. He leads the Environment, Energy and Climate Change Law department at Acorn Law Advocates-LLP, Nairobi (Kenya) where he is a partner. He is a Senior Lecturer at JKUAT School of Law, Nairobi and, amongst others, reporter for the Sabin Centre for Climate Change Law. He holds a Dr. jur degree in international environmental law from Universität Bayreuth, Germany; an LLM degree from University of Dar es Salaam and an LLB degree from Moi University, Kenya. He is a visiting fellow of the Bayreuth University Africa Multiple Cluster of Excellence in Germany.

Birgit Peters, Prof. Dr.
is a Professor of Public Law, International and European Law at University of Trier, Faculty of Law and co-founder of "SustaiNet". Her current research projects tackle "Law and Nature", International and European Climate Change

Law and Litigation, and the interplay of Human Rights and Environmental/ Climate Change Law.

Margherita Paola Poto, Prof. Dr.
is a Professor of Administrative Law at the Department of Management, University of Turin, Italy; Research Professor, Faculty of Law, UiT the Arctic University of Norway.

Violeta S. Radovich, Prof. Dr.
is a Professor and Researcher at UNDEF (Universidad Nacional de la Defensa), Escuela de Guerra Naval. She is Assistant Researcher at CONICET (Argentine Council on Scientific and Technical Research) and UBA, School of Law, Instituto de Investigaciones Jurídicas y Sociales Ambrosio L. Gioja and holds a Ph.D. in Maritime Law and LL.M. in Environmental Law from UBA (Universidad de Buenos Aires).

Michael Riegner, Prof. Dr.
is an Assistant professor of Public International Law and International Administrative Law at Erfurt University. He holds a Ph.D. in law (Humboldt University Berlin), an LL.M. (New York University) and studied law in Passau and Geneva. His published research covers International Institutional Law, human rights, Global Administrative Law, as well as Comparative Constitutional Law and development in the Global South.

Angela, Schwerdtfeger, Prof. Dr.
is a Professor of Law and Chairholder of the Chair of Public Law at Georg August University Göttingen (Germany). Her main areas of interest include European, International and Comparative Administrative Law with a special focus on Environmental and Climate Change Law. She leads various research projects on Environmental and Climate Change Law as well as on public participation.

Paolo Turrini, Dr.
is an Associate Professor of International Law at the Faculty of Law of the University of Trento, Italy. His main fields of expertise are International Economic Law (he co-edited a book on Investment Law in Latin America, published by Brill) and the Law of Natural Resources, especially Water Law.

Matthias, Uffer, Dr.
works at the Federal Administrative Court of Switzerland, in areas such as Financial Market Law, Competition Law and Agricultural Law. He studied law in

Bern (2006–2011), and Leuven. His dissertation (2019) deals with the conflict of fundamental rights and ethical dilemmas in the context of threats to life. Other research interests include law and creativity, the regulation of new technologies, political rights and competition law.

Matthias Valta, Prof. Dr.
is a Full Professor of Public Law and Tax Law at Heinrich Heine University Duesseldorf. His main fields of research are International and European Tax Law, Public International Law and the Law of Public Finance.

Paola Villavicencio-Calzadilla, Ph.D.
is an Associate Research Fellow at the Tarragona Centre for Environmental Law Studies, Rovira i Virgili University, Spain, and Extraordinary Research Fellow at the Faculty of Law, North-West University, South Africa. Her main areas of interest include Climate Change Law and human rights, climate justice, climate litigation, SDGs and the ecocentric/rights of nature paradigm.

Introduction: “Sustainability through Participation? – National, Supranational and International Legal Perspectives”

Eva Julia Lohse and Birgit Peters

1 Introduction

Since the 1980s, the concept of sustainability, or sustainable development,[1] has dominated global, supranational and national contexts. In 2015, in its 2030 Agenda for Sustainable Development, the United Nations General Assembly (UNGA) approved no less than 17 sustainable development goals (SDGs), ranging from the elimination of poverty (goal 1) to creating partnerships for sustainable development (goal 17).[2] The decision aimed to ‘foster the organisational operationalisation and integration of sustainability and, therefore, to address the current and forthcoming stakeholder needs and ensure a better and sustainable future for all, balancing the economic, social and environmental development’.[3] In the current climate emergency, achieving sustainability and the SDGs, enabling the world to transition into a future in harmony with nature,[4] seems more pressing than ever. If sustainability addresses our common future, the required transformation to achieve sustainability will not be realised without the proper engagement of all relevant members of society. In fact, as principle 10 of the Rio Declaration, and many subsequent instruments adopted since then[5] have emphasised: ‘Environmental issues are best handled with participation of all concerned citizens, at the relevant level.

---

1 As sustainability and sustainable development are used interchangeably in many international, supranational and national contexts, this book will also use both terms synonymously. Individual authors may however, refer to particular conceptualizations in their specific context.

2 UNGA. Transforming our world: the 2030 Agenda for Sustainable Development, Resolution adopted by the General Assembly, A/RES/70/1, 25 September 2015.

3 Luis M Fonseca, José P Domingues and Alina M Dima, ‘Mapping the Sustainable Development Goals Relationships’ [2020] in Sustainability, 12(8) 3359 <https://www.mdpi.com/2071-1050/12/8/3359> (last accessed 19 October 2022).

4 United Nations Environmental Programme, Report of the World Commission on Environment and Development, Our Common Future, UNEP/GC.14/13, 14 April 1987, summary, para. 30.

5 For a recent example, see the Regional Agreement on Access to Information, Public Participation and Justice in Environmental Matters in Latin America and the Caribbean, 4 March 2018, entered into force 21 May 2021, UNTS No. 56654, 22 April 2021, Art. 7.

DOI:10.1163/9789004509382_002

At the national level, each individual shall have appropriate access to information concerning the environment that is held by public authorities, including information on hazardous materials and activities in their communities, and the opportunity to participate in decision-making processes. States shall facilitate and encourage public awareness and participation by making information widely available. Effective access to judicial and administrative proceedings, including redress and remedy, shall be provided.'[6] But how exactly can participation result in more sustainable future(s) for all? On the basis of which legal rules and processes?

Thoughts and legal conceptualisations of sustainability, or what is perceived as sustainability, such as rules tackling the protection and conservation of exhaustible natural resources, have been around possibly since the early antiquity.[7] Many historical resource conservation or nature protection schemes around the globe – national or international – aimed to preserve exhaustible natural resources for future use.[8] In Western Europe, the motivation of a society to agree on those schemes was often led by economic reasons, i.e. utilitarian. Preservation schemes aiming at the protection of nature for its own good have only been recorded from the 20th century onwards. Sometimes, preservation schemes included the recognition of local stakeholders, such as neighbours or indigenous populations, yet, often without truly including their views in the law- or decision-making processes.

These early manifestations of the connection between sustainability and participation experienced a powerful transformation with the international establishment of the principle of 'sustainable development' in 1987.[9] Only then was 'sustainable', 'sustained', 'sustainability' or 'sustainable development' introduced as distinct legal and political notion, with a distinct meaning comprising three pillars: economic development, environmental protection and the protection of current and future generations.[10] Numerous supranational and national legal instruments refer to the concept of sustainability or sustainable development today.[11] Several national and international judicial decisions

6 UNGA, report of the United Nations Conference on Environment and Development. UNDoc. A/Conf.151/26 (Vol. I), 12 August 1992.

7 Jacobus A Du Pisani, 'Sustainable development–historical roots of the concept' [2006] in: Environmental Sciences 3(2) 83, 84.

8 Cf: Pacific Fur Seals Arbitration, 15 August 1893, RIAA, XXVIII, 263–276.

9 United Nations Environmental Programme, Report of the World Commission on Environment and Development – Our Common Future, 14 April 1987, para 27.

10 Ibid, para 27.

11 E.g. in the Rio Declaration on Environment and Development 1992, respectively in the conventions and their protocols passed in the course of this conference: Framework

have taken into account the criterion of sustainability or sustainable development in the assessment of varying claims.[12]

In many of these legal instruments, the participation of civil society in national and supranational decision-making is presented as one of the major means in achieving sustainability or sustainable development.[13] The report 'Our Common Future', prepared in 1987 by the Norwegian Prime Minister Gro Harlem Brundtland for the United Nations Conference on Environment and Development, is central for this connection. It emphasised that sustainable development can best be achieved when political systems ensure effective participation in public decisions and a democratic co-determination at the international level.[14] As the report stated, only participation of the public

---

Convention on Climate Change (UNFCCC) 1992; UNTS, vol. 1771, 107 ff.; Kyoto Protocol to the United Nations Framework Convention on Climate Change 1997; UNTS, vol. 2303, 162; Biodiversity Convention 1992. UNTS, vol. 1760, 79ff; Besides, the concept can be found in: Convention on Access to Information, Public Participation in Decision Making and Access to Justice in Environmental Matters 1998, UNTS, vol. 2161, p. 447; Johannesburg Declaration on Sustainable Development and Plan of Implementation 2002, UN Doc A/CONF.199/20, 2002, para 31–32; UN Conference on Sustainable Development, Rio+20, The Future we want 19 June 2012. UN Doc. A/CONF. 216/L.1, para 226; Paris Convention 2015, UN Doc FCCC/CP/2015/L.9/Rev.1, art. 3 ter; Preamble TEU, art. 11 TEU, art. 21 TEU; art. 37 EU Charter of Fundamental Rights.

12 See esp.: Pacific Fur Seals Arbitration, 15 August 1893, RIAA, XXVIII, 263–276; International Court of Justice, *Gabčíkovo Nagymaros* (Hungary v. Slovakia) (1998), para 78; WTO AB, United States-Import Prohibition of Certain Shrimp and Shrimp Products, WTO Doc. WT/DS58/AB/R; Supreme Court of the Philippines, *Oposa et al. v. Fulgencio S. Factoran, Jr. et al.* (1993), G.R. no 101083; *S Jagannath vs Union of India & Ors* (1996), available at https://indiankanoon.org/doc/507684/ (last accessed 30 September 2022); Sustainable development – together with intergenerational equity – is also invoked in a recent case pending before the National Green Tribunal of India, see *Pandey v. India*, available at <https://climate-laws.org/geographies/india/litigation_cases/pandey-v-india> (last accessed 19 October 2022).

13 Cf. Preamble and art. 14, European Parliament and Council Directive 2000/60/EC of 23 October 2000 for establishing a framework for Community action in the field of water policy. OJ L-327 of 22 December 2000, 1, (Water Framework Directive); Preamble of the Aarhus Convention. For the social science literature, see esp.: Fleury/ Petit/ Dobremez/ Schermer/ Kirchengast/ de Ros/ Magnani/ Struffi/ Mieville-Ott/ Roque, *Mountain Research and Development* [2008] p. 226; Ghai/ Vivian, *Grassroots Environmental Action* [2014]; Meadowcroft, *Governance for Sustainable Development: The challenge of Adapting Form to Function* [2004] p. 162; Narayan, *Environmentally Sustainable Development Occasional Paper Series* [1994]; Newig, in: *Communication, Cooperation, Participation. Research and Practice for a sustainable Future* [2007] p. 51; *Warburton*, Community and Sustainable development [2013].

14 UNEP, Report of the World Commission on Environment and Development – Our Common Future [14 April 1987], para 28.

affected, as well as of further stakeholders, would ensure the recognition of the common interests that sustainability was to protect.[15] Ultimately, the report suggested, public projects of high-level impact on the environment should be subjected to public approval and, possibly, referenda.[16]

In a similar vein, many national and international regulations referring to sustainability today include references to the participation of stakeholders or the public.[17] In (national and international) environmental law, in particular, this turn towards participation marks the so-called 'turn to human rights'.[18] It focuses on the rights of individuals to information, participation and access to justice in environmental decision-making. These so-called procedural environmental rights[19] have been recognised in two important regional conventions, the Aarhus Convention and the Escazú Agreement. Both have had a major influence on environmental decision-making processes within their regional scope of application. In Europe, it is fair to conclude that the Aarhus Convention has transformed national and European administrative decision-making processes, not only in the field of the environment. Participation has also gained particular relevance in the climate change context. We find allusions to participation in the United Nations Framework Convention on Climate Change.[20] The Paris Agreement regards participation as a central element in achieving the 1.5–2 degree temperature goal.[21] In addition, the growing body of climate litigation can be regarded as supporting participation in the climate change context.[22] Other fields of law, such as international finance, or international

15 Our Common Future, 14 April 1987, ch 2, para 77.

16 Our Common Future, 14 April 1987, ch 2, para 78.

17 In addition to the preamble of the Convention, which commends public participation on all decision-making levels, art. 6 (8) of the Paris Agreement demands that states shall promote public participation in the implementation of the national contributions. Art. 14 (1) of the European Water Framework Directive requires the "active participation of all interested bodies".

18 Birgit Peters, 'Unpacking the Diversity of Procedural Environmental Rights: The European Convention on Human Rights and the Aarhus Convention' [2018] in: Journal of Environmental Law 1 30(1), 2–7; cf. the reports of the 2012 appointed UN Special Rapporteur on Human Rights and the Environment at: <http://www.ohchr.org/EN/Issues/Environment/SREnvironment/Pages/Annualreports.aspx> (last accessed 19 October 2022).

19 Birgit Peters, 'Unpacking the Diversity of Procedural Environmental Rights: The European Convention on Human Rights and the Aarhus Convention' [2018] in: Journal of Environmental Law 1 30(1), 2.

20 Art 4 I i UNFCCC.

21 Arts 6 IV a, Art. 7 VIII b, 12 Paris Agreement.

22 Compare: <http://climatecasechart.com/> (last accessed 19 October 2022) IPCC 6th Assessment Report, Working Group 3, SPM 3.3; 13.4.2.

biodiversity, also refer to participation as a means of achieving sustainability, or sustainable development.

Finally, participation in sustainability contexts does not only refer to human participation. A growing body of legislation and litigation, in particular in South America, as well as in India, New Zealand and the Philippines, evidences that the non-human world must also be included in rules and regulations about sustainability.[23]

However, contrary to their usage in other disciplines, such as the social and political sciences,[24] in law the relationship between sustainability or sustainable development and participation in law has remained sketchy. Which sustainability must be achieved by participation? And by which kinds of participation? Which procedures must be observed? Who must or should be considered to participate? The questions result, as the meaning of both 'sustainability' and 'participation' are commonly perceived to be unclear. A considerable body of scholars have highlighted that sustainable development, or sustainability does not amount to a legal principle. It merely describes an evolving international norm.[25] Moreover, the lack of clarity on the term sustainability or 'sustainable development' as a legal concept, has led legal scholars to question the practicality and usefulness of the concept in addressing current global ecological challenges and crises.[26] Legal accounts of participation and, in particular, its role as a means to achieve sustainability or sustainable development have remained equally opaque. Participation is sometimes discussed as

---

23 IPCC 6th Assessment Report, Working Group 3, SPM 3.3; 13.4.2; Annalisa Savaresi, Juan Auz, 'Climate Change Litigation and Human Rights: Pushing the Boundaries' [2019] in: Climate Law, 9(3), 244–262.

24 Cf. esp.: Barral, European Journal of International Law [2012] p. 377; Fleury/ Petit/ Dobremez/Schermer/ Kirchengast/ de Ros/ Magnani/ Struffi/ Mieville-Ott/ Roque, in: *Mountain Research and Development* [2008] p. 226; Ghai/ Vivian, *Grassroots Environmental Action* [2014]; Giddings/ Hopwood/ O'Brien, in: *Sustainable Development,* [2002] p. 187 ff.; Hagiwara, *The Principle of Integration in Sustainable Development Through the Process of Treaty Interpretation* [2013]; Meadowcroft, *Governance for Sustainable Development: The challenge of adapting form to function* [2004], p. 162; Narayan, in: *Environmentally Sustainable Development Occasional Paper Series* [1994]; Ostrom/ Schroeder/ Wynne, *Institutional Incentives and Sustainable Development* [1993].

25 See the summary in: Duncan French in: M. Fitzmaurice, D. M Ong and P. Merkouris, *Research Handbook on International Environmental Law* (Research handbooks in international law, Second edition, Edward Elgar Publishing 2021), 54 et seq., 66.

26 Jorge E Viñuales, 'The rRse and Fall of Sustainable Development' [2013], in: Review of European, Comparative & International Environmental Law 3 22(1); Iglesias Pérez, Hernández Márquez (Hrsg), *Rethinking Sustainable Development in terms of Justice*, Newcastle upon Tyne 2018.

an alternative[27] and on other occasions as a manifestation of sustainability or sustainable development.[28] Furthermore, the discussion is mostly focussed on environmental matters – disregarding both the fact that sustainability has also an economic or financial aspect and that societies from the global South have different approaches to both concepts due to different needs and historical contingencies.

2 Main Aim and Research Question of This Book

The main question addressed in this book is whether, and if so, how sustainability can be achieved through participation in the multi-level governance structures of international, supranational and national law. Though it may seem straight forward, the answer to this question is neither trivial nor obvious. An answer first requires a clarification of the concept of sustainability, in the relevant fields of law looked at in this book. Elements of the concept of sustainability exist as separate principles, such as the principle of sovereignty over natural resources,[29] sustainable use, resource management or the responsibility for future generations.[30] Sustainability may also find expression in specific obligations and prohibitions (such as to refrain from fishing during particular months of the year). Do they always express the same standard of sustainability within the same legal order and across legal orders? Second, and most importantly, authors need to clarify whether and how participation can serve as a means of achieving sustainability. How can sustainability be achieved through participation? More specifically, by which kinds of participation or by whom? How do the concepts of sustainability and participation interconnect at all? What specific participatory rights are essential in furthering the aim of sustainability? Does the term 'sustainability through participation' describe specific substantive or procedural rules, standards, principles and programmes? If so, how are those standards enforced?

---

27 Ibid, 5.

28 Marie-Claire C Segger and others, 'Prospects for Principles of International Sustainable Development Law after the WSSD: Common but Differentiated Responsibilities, Precaution and Participation' [2003] in: Review of European Community & International Environmental Law 12(1), 54, 64 f.; Taís Ludwig, 'The Key to Engaging with the SDGs: Utilizing Rio Principle 10 to Successfully Implement the UN Sustainable Development Goals' [2017] in: Sustainable Development Law & Policy 16(2), 7.

29 Cf. principle 2 United Nations Commission on Environment and Development, Rio Declaration on Environment and Development 1992. 31 ILM 874 [1992].

30 Cf. principle 3 Rio Declaration (fn. 18).

This book addresses the foregoing questions both in environmental and in economic law, i.e. the two core fields of law featured in the Brundtland report.[31] Spanning such diverse fields of law, this book further investigates whether there are common legal conceptions, which both concepts of sustainability and participation express, across legal subject areas and jurisdictional boundaries.

3 Aim, Approach and Methodology of the Book

Taking an exclusive legal perspective, the book primarily assesses the legal conceptualisations of participation, which have, have not, or perhaps ought to have been formulated to achieve sustainability in the multi-level-governance structures of international, supranational and national law. The book simultaneously looks at and compares the particular rights, obligations or other legal manifestations (principles, soft law, procedural obligations, etc.) commonly associated with or leading to sustainability through participation in the above-mentioned governance structures.

In doing so, the book seeks to clarify, whether and how sustainability may indeed be achieved through participation. In specifically addressing participation as a means of sustainability, the book provides a valuable addition to the existing literature on the legal ramifications of sustainability and participation.

The book follows an inductive, functional-comparative and multi-level approach. First and foremost, an inductive, bottom-up view on sustainability and participation allows authors to perceive the specific interconnections of sustainability and participation. In particular, this approach aids in understanding how individual norms or even judgments in various subject areas and jurisdictions seek to realise set objectives. A functional-comparative[32] approach enables authors to examine the specific legal characteristics, rights, obligations and further legal conceptualisations of participation in sustainable development across various fields of law.

A multi-level perspective on sustainability and participation, is emphasised in the book for various reasons. First, sustainability or sustainable development can only be assessed by taking into account the multiple jurisdictional layers, in which the above stated objectives ultimately become relevant. Conceptualisations of sustainability appeared for the first time in national jurisdictions,

31 See principle 10 United Nations Commission on Environment and Development, Rio Declaration on Environment 1992. 31 ILM 874 [1992].

32 See Ralf Michaels in: Reimann/Zimmermann (eds), *The Oxford Handbook of Comparative Law* (OUP 2006), 339–382.

namely, to ensure the conservation of exhaustible natural resources like wood, wild animals, minerals, or coal. Ultimately, they inspired the establishment and the spread of sustainable development at the international level. Until recently, standards for sustainability and participation have mostly been set at the international and European levels. Nevertheless, modern versions of sustainability and participation found in national constitutions and administrative law conceptualisations across the world, could impact on the further reform of established views on sustainability and participation at the international and regional levels. Finally, special attention needs to be drawn to the EU. This is because the EU is one of the most coherent and economically integrated economic regional organisations in the world and the standards developed by and within the EU contribute to a certain view on sustainability and participation. Such views are then reflected at the level of the member states.

The inductive, functional, multi-level analysis of sustainability and participation provided by this book shall, ultimately provide what we call the legal answer to sustainability through participation. It shall:

a clarify why participation can or cannot function as a means to achieve sustainability or sustainable development, and in which areas of law;
b identify potential legal obligations of the state, the authorities or of private actors possibly resulting from the pledge of sustainability through participation, and finally;
c compare the different approaches and conceptualisations of participation in sustainability, across multiple levels of law and legal governance, and subject areas. To this end, the book encourages further theoretical reflection on participation and sustainability, and particularly the interconnections between them.

Against the foregoing backdrop, the proposed book enriches and makes a valuable contribution to the existing literature on sustainable development and participation. There is currently *no publication,* which tackles participation as a means to further sustainable development from a legal perspective, in the multi-level environment of international, European and national law.[33] Authors have not yet dwelled on the question posed by this book; whether and how sustainability is, can and should be achieved through participation. Additionally, the book addresses the interconnection between the two concepts of sustainability and participation in a variety of areas of economic and

33 Klaus Bosselmann, *The Principle of Sustainability: Transforming Law and Governance* (Second edition, Taylor & Francis; Routledge 2017); Hans C Bugge and C. Voigt, *Sustainable Development in International and National Law* (The Avosetta Series, 8, Europa Law Publishing 2008)

environmental law. The present book tackles novel and thus far neglected areas of law, where the combination of sustainability and participation appears truly problematic.[34] Finally, the book takes a legal analytical perspective (inductive and functional-comparative) to address the question of sustainability through participation.[35] It therefore hopes to give some definite answers on whether, sustainability and participation, and which of their various legal concretions either reinforce or conflict with one another.

4 Overview and Outline of the Contributions in the Book

The first part of the book introduces the overall theme of this work and its fundamental context. *Birgit Peters* draws some conclusions about the international historical dimension of sustainability and participation. Amongst others, she shows in further detail how the Brundtland report regarded participation as one of the key processes in achieving sustainable development.[36] After uncovering the key characteristics of sustainability and participation in that report, she turns to the international historical dimension of sustainability, showing that sustainability slowly developed from rules aiming at resource protection for future (human) use, to more eco-centred institutional arrangements concerned with nature, species and area protection. She concludes that the particular understanding of sustainability through participation established in the Brundtland Report has no international precedent.

The following chapter by *Louis Kotzé and Paola Villavicencio-Calzadilla* then refers to other-than-human[37] participation as a part of sustainability in the Anthropocene. The authors contextualise how sustainability must consider other than human conceptualisations in order to be true to the preservation of the environment for coming generations. They outline that participation of the non-human world in decisions concerning the environment is key for achieving sustainability. They discuss the participation of nature from the angle of representation and guardianship, drawing on a comparative approach, with examples from Latin America.

---

34 In fiscal law, it is argued that participation threatens parliamentary autonomy.

35 In particular Bugge and Voigt (n 34), were more open in their analytical approach.

36 See Birgit Peters, 'The Historical Perspective', in this book, section 2.3.

37 Seb O'Connor and Jasper O Kenter, 'Making Intrinsic Values Work; Integrating Intrinsic Values of the More-than-human World through the Life Framework of Values' [2019] in: Sustainability Science, 14(5) 1247 <https://link.springer.com/article/10.1007/s11625-019-00715-7> (last accessed 19 October 2022).

The second part of the book is concluded by the complimentary chapters of *Eva Lohse* and *Daniele Brombal* who illustrate national conceptualisations of sustainability and participation in Europe, Latin America, Africa and Asia, in particular, China. *Eva Lohse* tries a macro-comparison: sustainability is used in legal orders with different backgrounds with varying foci. Domestic law is directly applicable and therefore the gateway for inter- and supranational provisions and their effective implementation. Yet, the 'green' leg, i.e. environmental protection and responsibility for future generations, is central with economic, social or cultural elements added into the balancing process. Participatory instruments are frequently linked to the ecological leg, but sometimes also to indigenous rights. They seem to be most effective if attributed to local communities, municipalities or indigenous groups. *Lohse* highlights the potential of rights-based approaches found in several jurisdictions. *Daniele Brombal* complements this macro-comparison with a detailed description of public participation in China's environmental impact assessment. He shows that public participation is seen as a means to support sustainable decision-making, but at the same time, political and social developments and enforcement gaps might hinder the realisation of its full potential. By this, he gives a vivid account on the possibilities and difficulties of public participation in an authoritarian regime that until recently was not too much concerned about the protection of the environment or sustainable development. Nevertheless, he also demonstrates that participation is used as a means of legitimising decisions. Moreover, environmental impact assessment as a corner stone of the green leg of sustainability can look back at more than 20 years of existence.

The third part of the book then tackles the European perspective on sustainability and participation. Since the introduction of environmental law as a policy field for the Union in 1972, the EU has passed extensive legislation in the field of the environment. In addition, the EU acceded to the Aarhus Convention, the leading international agreement establishing binding standards on participation in environmental decision-making, which lead to the fact that the directly applicable individual rights contained in that agreement are applicable at the level of primary union law (i.e. the Treaty on the European Union (TEU) and the Treaty on the Functioning of the European Union (TFEU)). Moreover, since the Lisbon Treaty, sustainability is an essential crosscutting principle influencing this, and other policy areas of the EU.[38] EU environmental

38 Art. 191 TFEU, Art. 11 TFEU.

law is also the only area of European law where member states are allowed to adopt stricter standards at the national levels.[39]

The contribution of *Magnus Noll-Ehlers* and *Giacomo Gattarina* provides an introductory overview over the role and importance of sustainability and participation in EU Law. The authors explain the complex web of international and supranational rules that have developed in this area. Additionally, they turn to important findings of the international treaty body and judiciary organs, like the Aarhus Compliance Committee (ACC) and the Court of Justice of the European Union (CJEU) and elaborate on the further clarification that those judicial organs have contributed, mostly on participation, at the level of EU law.

The concurring contribution by *Cristina Fraenkel-Haeberle* complements this overview by drawing attention to the national implementation of this framework, concentrating, amongst others, on the varying approaches that national jurisdictions have taken in addressing the complexities at the national level. She focuses on the three approaches known for the implementation of EU rules at the national level: minimal implementation, gold plating and spill over. She illustrates how these three approaches have played out and been used by member states in the area of European environmental law: In particular, the implementation of procedural environmental provisions of the Aarhus Convention has led to the broadening of transparency and participatory legislation at the level of the member states.[40]

The following chapters in part three address sustainability and participation in – until today – neglected areas of law, such as in state aid (*Julius Buckler*), the law of public finance (*Matthias Valta*) and in EU competition law (*Matthias Uffer*).

Julius Buckler vividly illustrates how sustainability and participation are concepts alien to state aid law, which primarily concerns subsidies of member states to companies and enterprises. Nonetheless, the concepts are tightly interwoven within this field of European law. He shows this firstly, by highlighting that sustainability may be recognised as an objective justifying the granting of state aid, turning to renewable energy as an example. Secondly, he illustrates that participation plays an important role when considering the rights of third parties in individual State aid procedures. There is a certain

39 Art. 193 TFEU.

40 See Fraenkel-Haeberle, 'Impact of Supranational Concepts of Participation and Sustainability on National Administrative Law' in this book, section 2.1.

potential for participatory procedures under the Aarhus regulation.[41] It would, nonetheless, require that the relevant Commission decision was in breach of EU environmental rules.

Matthias Valta adds a comparative perspective on sustainability and (less) participation in relation to government debt. His chapter takes the reverse approach to most other authors: he asks the seemingly heretical question whether less participation in public finance leads to more sustainability. Exploring the approaches to limitations on debt in Germany and Portugal (within the EU framework) he reaches a first definition of sustainability as the capacity to incur and pay back debt on the capital market,[42] and further rather critically reflects the missed opportunity to a greening of the economy and the connection to inter-generational justice, thereby introducing a further aspect of sustainability. He then draws the attention to various ways of participation – indirect on parliamentary level as well as direct in the form of referenda and municipal participatory budgets – in order to demonstrate that only in an ideal world more participation leads to more financial sustainability.

Matthias Uffer shows in his appraisal of EU competition law, how competition law can realise all three dimensions of sustainability, the environmental, economic and social. Uffer also illustrates that competition law has long strived for purity, leaving it 'relatively unresponsive to expectations emanating from public interests'. Still, he argues, certain environmental effects should also be taken into account at the level of competition law, such as CO2 emissions or prohibitions concerning waste disposal or the trade in chemicals. He adds, participation can play a role in competition law, as it furthers the participation of market actors. In addition, competition law is usually adopted by national parliaments, and thus in a democratic and therefore participatory process. The main part of his chapter then muses on which rules of EC competition law are the most apt and open to interpretations furthering environmental sustainability. He identifies four paths through which this could be done: by enforcing art 101 and 102 TFEU, by declaring art. 101 TFEU inapplicable to conduct which serves sustainability objectives, by defining environmental benefits as 'efficiencies' under art 101(3) TFEU and fourthly, by discontinuing certain investigations. He concludes that participation was relevant in furthering the functioning of those solutions.

41 EP and Council Regulation (EC) 1367/2006 of 6 September 2006 on the application of the provisions of the Aarhus Convention on Access to Information, Public participation in Decision-making and Access to Justice in Environmental Matters to Community institutions and bodies [2006] OJ L264/13.

42 Matthias Valta, 'The Law of Public Finance' in this book.

The fourth and final part of the book will then draw to the conceptualisations of sustainability and participation at the level of international law, and thus regard the modern home of sustainability. This part will feature an introductory chapter by *Angela Schwerdtfeger*, who turns to the human rights dimension of sustainability and participation. She illustrates that public participation is rooted in the human rights dimension of environmental protection and an element of realising the human right to a clean healthy and sustainable environment. At the level of rights, sustainable development was a symbiosis between the right to development and the right to an adequate environment. The function of participation, however, depended on the underlying context and legal instrument, by which it was guaranteed. Whereas the Aarhus Convention underlines the procedural character of participation, the newly adopted Escazú agreement promoted participation as a self-standing, individual right.

In the following chapter, *Federica Cittadino* and *Emma Mittrotta* discuss the distinct and particular role that sustainability has assumed in international biodiversity law. They examine the rules of the Convention on Biological Diversity (CBD), the Convention on Wetlands of International Importance (Ramsar Convention) and the Convention for the Protection of World and Natural Heritage. In their description of sustainability, they rely on an integrative approach (economic, environmental, social) modelled after the Brundtland report and also focus on issues of inter- and intragenerational justice. They address participation as a guiding principle of international law, which is included in several international treaties and agreements on environmental law. *Cittadino and Mittrotta* analyse whether the two terms (and similar notions like 'wise use' in the Ramsar Convention) are used consistently in the three conventions on biodiversity – highlighting that all conventions follow more or less a three-pronged approach of 'sustainable development' that includes the eradication of poverty and is not limited to the conservation of nature or the environment. The underscore that all conventions contain participatory elements, however mostly in the form of access to information and involvement in decision-making. Both the CBD and the Ramsar Convention lay their focus on indigenous and local communities – a fact that is also observed in other chapters. Participation is used as an important tool to reach conservation and sustainable management of biodiversity, therefore putting obligations and responsibility not only on state-actors but also on individuals and communities.

Omondi R. Owino considers the role and importance of sustainability and participation in the ever more important area of international climate change law. He draws on the concept of hybrid multilateralism to achieve climate sustainability, which he understands as the participation of non-state and sub-national actors as complementors to state party climate commitments. He draws on the example of international cooperative initiatives to flesh out participation and its causal effect for sustainability in climate governance. He highlights that participation in climate governance also suffers from congestion, over-saturation and asymmetries and thus needs further coordination and ordering to be effective. Hence, decision-making processes under the Paris Agreement still need further adaptation to counter some of these problems.

In a consecutive chapter, *Violeta Radovich* draws attention towards the not so apparent rules on sustainability and participation in the law of the high seas. Again, the main focus lies on participation of indigenous and local communities. She highlights the presumably added value of involvement of those non-state actors for conservation and sustainable use of the high seas in an ocean-centred system of governance in an international climate change regime, claiming a shift to eco-centrism. The chapter is thereby linked to other chapters,[43] which also describe a shift to more eco-centric approaches, earth law and a growing responsibility of indigenous and local communities. She discusses the draft BBNJ Treaty (UNCLOS binding legal instrument for the conservation and sustainable use of marine biological diversity of areas beyond national jurisdiction), which specifically includes rules on participation of indigenous and local communities, from the perspective of whether those rules fulfil general criteria for effective participation (like inclusiveness, influence on the final decision, and accountability of decision-makers). The important criteria for meaningful participation in environmental decision-making – and this is the focus of sustainable ocean governance – is that it goes beyond mere consultation and allows for co-decision-making. She regards them to be partially fulfilled in the draft BBNJ Treaty.

The following chapter by *Michael Riegner* explores the increasing importance of sustainability and participation in the law of the World Bank. He illustrates, amongst others, how sustainability and participation have shaped the self-conception and perception of the World Bank from the mid-1980s and served as conditionalities on recipient states. In addition, sustainability and participation have become standards, which may also be invoked by non-state actors against the World Bank. He however cautions that the established framework of sustainability and participation, which can be derived from the

---

43 Louis Kotzé and Paola Villavincencio-Calzadilla, 'Re-imagining Participation in the Anthropocene: The Potential of the Rights of Nature Paradigm' in this book; Federica Cittadino and Emma Mitrotta, 'The Case of Biodiversity Protection', in this book; Eva Julia Lohse, 'Comparative Administrative Law Perspectives – Europe, Latin-America, Africa', in this book.

practices of the bank, contains its own deficits, in particular, as it is built on a functional and managerial logic which is unable to unleash the emancipatory potential of both concepts.

Finally, *Paolo Turrini* explores the growing importance of sustainability and participation in international investment law, and the consequences of the lack of substantive rules of participation in this area of international law. He points to the possibility that current investment law and policy might hamper sustainable development. He outlines that hitherto, sustainability and participation have been addressed as a multitude of differing rules concerning social standards, labour rights, health, environmental protection and a variety of participatory standards. However, those rules and standards remain generally unconnected such that the potential of sustainability and participation cannot be fully realised.

The book concludes with a chapter by *Margherita Paola Poto*. She highlights that sustainability and participation are very much rooted in the Western tradition of environmental law, and anthropocentric at their core. In order to become meaningful concepts to address the current environmental crises, they need to be rethought and recaptured as part of a multilevel and polycentric governance model, which includes indigenous epistemologies and kinship perspectives. This could counter-balance the current perception of sustainability and participation and contribute to a more holistic understanding of environmental law centered around the "concept of ecology and health of rights of the planet and its inhabitants, and of collective duties to respect both"[44].

Bibliography

Barral V, 'Sustainable Development in International Law: Nature and Operation of an Evolutive Legal Norm' (2012) 23(2) European Journal of International Law 377.

Bosselmann K, *The Principle of Sustainability: Transforming Law and Governance* (2nd edn, Routledge 2017).

Bugge H C and Voigt C (eds), *Sustainable Development in International and National Law* (The Avosetta Series, 8 Europa Law Publishing 2008).

Du Pisani J A, 'Sustainable Development–Historical Roots of the Concept' (2006) 3(2) Environmental Sciences 83.

Felipe Pérez B, Martínez Hernández L and Iglesias Márquez D (eds), *Rethinking Sustainable Development in Terms of Justice* (Cambridge Scholars Publishing 2018).

Fitzmaurice M, Ong D M and Merkouris P, *Research Handbook on International Environmental Law* (Research Handbooks in International Law series, 2nd edn, Edward Elgar Publishing 2021).

44 Poto, 'Conclusions', in this book, section 4.

Fleury P and others, 'Implementing Sustainable Agriculture and Rural Development in the European Alps' (2008) 28(3/4) Mountain Research and Development 226–232.

Fonseca L M, Domingues J P and Dima A M, 'Mapping the Sustainable Development Goals Relationships' [2020] in Sustainability 12(8) 3359 <https://www.mdpi.com/2071-1050/12/8/3359> last accessed 19 October 22.

Ghai D and Vivian J M (eds), *Grassroots Environmental Action, Peoples's Participation in Sustainable Development* (Routledge 2014).

Giddings B, Hopwood B and O'Brien G, 'Environment, Economy and Society : Fitting them together into Sustainable Development' (2002) 10(4) Sustainable Development 187.

Hagiwara K, *The Principle of Integration in Sustainable Development Through the Process of Treaty Interpretation*, Master's thesis (University of Ottawa 2013).

Ludwig T, 'The Key to Engaging with the SDGs: Utilizing Rio Principle 10 to Successfully Implement the UN Sustainable Development Goals' (2017) 16(2) Sustainable Development Law & Policy 26.

Meadowcroft J, 'Participation and Sustainable Development: Modes of Citizen, Community and Organisational Involvement' in Lafferty W M (ed) *Governance for Sustainable Development: The Challenge of Adapting Form to Function* (Edward Elgar 2004) 191–220.

Michaels R, 'The Functional Method of Comparative Law' in Reimann M and Zimmermann R (eds), *The Oxford Handbook of Comparative Law* (OUP 2006) 339–382.

Newig J, 'Does Public Participation in Environmental Decisions Lead to Improved Environmental Quality' (2007) 1 Communication, Cooperation, Participation 51.

Ostrom E, Schroeder L and Wynne S, *Institutional Incentives and Sustainable Development: Infrastructure Policies in Perspective* (Avalon Publishing 1993).

O'Connor S and Kenter J, 'Making Intrinsic Values Work; Integrating Intrinsic Values of the More-Than-Human World through the Life Framework of Values' (2019) 14(5) Sustainability Science 1247.

Peters B, 'Unpacking the Diversity of Procedural Environmental Rights: The European Convention on Human Rights and the Aarhus Convention' (2018) 30(1) Journal of Environmental Law 1.

Savaresi A and Auz J, 'Climate Change Litigation and Human Rights: Pushing the Boundaries' (2019) 9(3) Climate Law 244.

Segger M-C C and others, 'Prospects for Principles of International Sustainable Development Law after the WSSD: Common but Differentiated Responsibilities, Precaution and Participation' (2003) 12(1) Review of European Community & International Environmental Law 54.

Viñuales J E, 'The Rise and Fall of Sustainable Development' (2013) 22(1) Review of European, Comparative & International Environmental Law 3.

Warburton D (ed), *Community and Sustainable Development* (Taylor & Francis Group; Routledge 2013).

PART 1

Fundamentals

CHAPTER 1

The Historical Perspective

Birgit Peters

1 Introduction

Research investigating the historical provenance of sustainability, or sustainable development and participation is notoriously difficult.[1] This is due to two underlying problems: Firstly, although precursors of both concepts have been around since early antiquity, both notions are relatively new. They entered common and especially international environmental language only in the 1970s and 1980s, when the Club of Rome, and thereafter Gro Harlem Brundtland, published their reports on the "Limits to Growth"[2] and "Our Common Future"[3]. Secondly, sustainability, as well as participation, are not concepts applicable to any one particular scientific field. Instead, sustainability and participation are commonly used as a reference framework for various areas of research and science. They span the humanities, in particular the social sciences, such as political sciences, history, developmental studies and law, economics, but also the natural sciences, such as geography, biology or climatology.

Therefore, any attempt to trace the provenance of both concepts encounters methodological and disciplinary difficulties. *Klippel and Otto* have labelled the methodological problems as arbitrariness trap and anachronism trap. The arbitrariness trap describes the problem that because sustainability is found in so many aspects of human behaviour, its meaning often refers to not more than long-term-viability of human action and planning.[4] The anachronism trap highlights the problem that sustainability, as well as participation, were coined only recently, ie from the 1970s onwards. Therefore, enquiries into the historical imprints of sustainability or participation predating those dates will

1 The present chapter will refer to sustainability and sustainable development interchangeably.

2 Donella H Meadows, *The limits to growth: A report for the Club of Rome's project on the predicament of mankind* (A Potomac Associates book, 12th edn, Universe Books 1973).

3 United Nations Environmental Programme, Report of the World Commission on Environment and Development, Our Common Future, UNEP/GC.14/13, 14.04.1987; Jeremy Caradonna, *Sustainability: A history* (First paperback edition, Oxford University Press 2014// 2016), 3.

4 Diethelm Klippel and Martin Otto, 'Nachhaltigkeit und Begriffsgeschichte' in Wolfgang Kahl (ed), *Nachhaltigkeit als Verbundbegriff* (Recht der nachhaltigen Entwicklung vol 2. Mohr Siebeck 2008) 42.

 | DOI:10.1163/9789004509382_003

be looking for traces of historical concepts, which had yet not been used.[5] Thus, only *Ersatz* conceptualisations can be identified, which may not reflect every ramification of sustainability, or participation, which is in use today.

What is more, the history of sustainability (and participation) can also be told in various ways and from various disciplinary perspectives, resulting in different narratives. Often, this is due to the individual focus of the relevant discipline involved. Political and social scientists have addressed the history of sustainability referring to perceptions about progress, historical change,[6] (economic) development and ecological thought.[7] Economists have addressed the aspect of growth.[8] Historians have described the concept as interaction of law and nature and culture[9] or concerning the relationship of progress, resource consumption and ecological awareness.[10] Legal scholars, in turn, addressed the nascence of the rules associated with both sustainability and participation during the world conferences for environment and development, starting with the Stockholm conference in 1972.[11] All those approaches take a particular view on sustainability and participation, and they may very well leave out certain important perspectives. For example, they often exclude holistic views on advancement and progress,[12] or the insight that economic development and growth are neither linear, nor need they be.[13]

---

5 ibid 41.

6 Jacobus A Du Pisani, 'Sustainable development–historical roots of the concept' (2006) 3(2) Environmental Sciences 83; Desta Mebratu, 'Sustainability and sustainable development: historical and conceptual review' (1998) 18(6) Environmental Impact Assessment Review 493, 497 ff.

7 Du Pisani (n 6)

8 Enric Tello-Aragay and Gabriel Jover-Avellà, 'Economic History and the Environment: New Questions, Approaches and Methodologies' in Mauro Agnoletti (ed), *The basic environmental history* (Environmental history vol 4. Springer 2014), 31.

9 Christopher Schliephake, Natascha Sojc and Gregor Weber, 'Einleitung' in Christopher Schliephake, Natascha Sojc and Gregor Weber (eds), *Nachhaltigkeit in der Antike: Diskurse, Praktiken, Perspektiven* (Geographica Historica vol 42. Franz Steiner Verlag 2020); Caradonna (n 3), 12, 14, 16.

10 Du Pisani (n 6), 86.

11 Peter H Sand, *The history and origin of international environmental law* (The international library of law and the environment 1, Edward Elgar 2015); Katja Gehne, 'Historische Grundlagen des Nachhaltigkeitsbegriffs' in Wolfgang Kahl (ed), *Nachhaltigkeit als Verbundbegriff* (Recht der nachhaltigen Entwicklung vol 2. Mohr Siebeck 2008), 11; Klippel and Otto (n 4), 41 (with reservations regarding the feasibility of this approach).

12 Mebratu (n 6), 498.

13 ibid, 495; Donald Hughes, *An Environmental History of the World* (Routledge 2001), 39, referring to the Egyptian culture, which perceived the processes of nature as operating in cycles.

It is difficult to overcome these problems as they are inherent in any historical assessment of concepts that were coined only recently and involving many disciplines. This, however, does not render those assessments moot. Research addressing the historical legal roots of sustainability and participation can take into account that there may be alternative understandings of both the historical sources and their interpretation. As such, this can provide insights into regulating the relationships and dependencies which sustainability nowadays addresses, ie actors, institutions of sustainability and participation, the relation of man toward nature, about perceptions of nature, nature conservation, preservation. These insights can then inform modern legal conceptualisations of sustainability and participation, which still need further addressing.[14] Historical insights can therefore highlight problematic issues and inform about potential obstacles, which any modern version of sustainability and participation will encounter; and identify ways of how they can be overcome.

Though many historical assessments have been made to evaluate national rules associated with sustainability (and participation),[15] inquiry into sustainability and participation in early international environmental agreements has not yet been undertaken.[16] This is surprising, given that the concept was in fact coined at the international level.[17] In particular the Brundtland report formulated some distinct features of sustainable development and participation. According to the report, sustainability had to be regarded as process enabling and guaranteeing both future, human needs oriented environmental decision-making, in which information and prior participation of interested and affected parties were necessary elements.[18]

The present chapter therefore asks whether the relationship between sustainability and participation can be traced back to early international environmental law and practice. To address this question, this chapter will describe and analyse the international precursors and rules addressing sustainability and participation, predominantly in early international environmental treaty law. The chapter begins with a delineation and contextualisation of the particular notion of sustainability and participation formulated in the 1987 Brundtland report. This is followed by an overview of the existing historical

---

14 See this chapter, section 2.1, below.

15 See the literature and footnotes assessed in section 2 of this chapter.

16 A very rough scheme of the historical roots of sustainability provides Duncan French 'Sustainable Developmnet' in Malgosia Fitzmaurice, David M Ong and Panos Merkouris, *Research handbook on international environmental law* (Research handbooks in international law, Edward Elgar 2010), 52 ff.

17 United Nations Environmental Programme, Report of the World Commission on Environment and Development, Our Common Future, UNEP/GC.14/13, 14.04.1987.

18 See this chapter, section 2.1 below.

literature on sustainability and participation focusing on national regulations and rules. After this recap of the concept's scope described by national law, part two will analyse the international material. This analysis encompasses the period starting from 1868 to 1950 and thus covers an analysis of the provisions of next to 40 early environmental agreements. The University of Oregon Database of International Environmental Agreements[19] and the series International Protection of the Environment[20] were used as sources to identify relevant environmental agreements. In addition, reference is made to historical environmental findings, such as prominent court rulings, where applicable.[21] The analysis of the international material is structured around common themes of sustainability and participation that emerged from the analysis of the national sources. In particular, the chapter will focuses on rules concerning animal and livestock protection, institutionalized international animal and livestock protection, nature protection and nature conservation. A final, fourth part concludes this chapter.

2 Sustainability through Participation: The 1987 Brundtland Report

The Report of the World Commission on Environment and Development – Our Common Future, edited by former Norwegian Prime Minister Gro Harlem Brundtland, is often referred to as the inauguration of "sustainable development" at the international level.[22] And indeed, whereas the report was not the first declaration on the world environment – it was preceded by the Stockholm declaration of 1972, which highlighted the importance of improving the world's environment for future generations[23] – it is the first publication of an international institution utilising the term "sustainable development" when dealing with vital international environmental obligations of states.[24]

19 https://iea.uoregon.edu, last accessed 6 March 2023.

20 Bernd Rüster and Bruno Simma, *International Protection of the Environment* (series) (Oceana Publications, Inc. 1975).

21 Mostly those compiled by Cairo A R Robb, *International Environmental Law Reports: Early Decisions* (International Environmental Law Reports 1, Cambridge University Press 1999).

22 Ulrich Grober, *Deep roots - a conceptual history of 'sustainable development'* (*Nachhaltigkeit*) (Wissenschaftszentrum Berlin für Sozialforschung, Discussion Paper, No. P 2007-002, Berlin 2007), 3, 5.

23 Gehne (n 11), 30; United Nations Conference on the Human Environment, Stockholm, 16.06.1972, Declaration on the Human Environment, UNGA 2994/XXVII, 2995/XXVII and 2996/XXII, 15.12.1972, principle 1.

24 The Stockholm Declaration mentioned only the preservation of Earth's capacity "to produce vital renewable resources" (Principle 3); the "responsibility of man to wisely manage

Although many international instruments defined sustainable development after 1987, the Brundtland report has remained the international document, which comprehensively unfolded central aspects of the concept that are still applicable today.

2.1 *Sustainability, or Sustainable Development*

Not surprisingly, the report was a product of its time. It was informed by the writings and conferences about the limits of growth, degrowth, and also sustainability, which had been concluded and convened nationally, and internationally, roughly since the Club of Rome had published its treatise on the Limits to Growth in 1972.[25] In the Limits to Growth, the authors had introduced the idea that the world economy could not be based on an endless reservoir of resources[26] and suggested a world system that was "1. *Sustainable* without sudden and uncontrollable collapse; and 2. capable of satisfying the basic material requirements of all of its people".[27] Hence, the term sustainability was in use well before the Brundtland report.[28]

Very similar to the Club of Rome authors, the Brundtland report defined sustainability as living within the self-perpetuating limits of the environment[29] and sustainable development as development, which "meets the needs of the present without compromising the ability of future generations to meet their own needs."[30] The report focused on economic development, or "economic growth".[31] It acknowledged that economic growth and development had limits. The report explicitly stated sustainable development hinged on the "idea of limitations imposed by the state of technology and social organisation on the

---

the heritage of wildlife" (Principle 4), the non-exhaustion of non-renewable resources (Principle 5).

25 Caradonna (n 3), 17, 136 ff. Compare: James C Coomer, *Quest for a sustainable society: Woodlands Conference on Growth Policy* (Pergamon Press 1979); Meadows (n 2). See also Samuel H Ordway, 'Possible Limits of Raw-Material Consumption' in Libby Robin, Sverker Sörlin and Paul Warde (eds), *The Future of Nature: Documents of Global Change* (Yale University Press 2013), 31–35.

26 Meadows (n 2), 23; James C Coomer, 'Introduction: The Nature of the Quest for a Sustainable Society' in James C Coomer (ed), *Quest for a Sustainable Society: Woodlands Conference on Growth Policy* (Pergamon Press 1979), 9.

27 Meadows (n 2), 158. Emphasis added.

28 Compare Coomer, 'Introduction: The nature of the Quest for a Sustainable Society' (n 25), 1.

29 Compare Coomer (n 25), 1, 9.

30 Our Common Future, 14.04.1987, summary, para 27.

31 Our Common Future, 14.04.1987, summary, para 28.

environment's ability to meet present and future needs."[32] More particularly, the Brundtland report referred to the "limitations imposed by the present state of *technology* and *social* organisation *on environmental resources* and by the *ability of the biosphere* to absorb the effects of human activities."[33]

The limits of the world's biosphere were central to the concept of sustainable development in the Brundtland report. This was also due to the fact that, and perhaps even more so than in previous writings, the Brundtland report was formulated under the shadow of several large and catastrophic environmental disasters and crises with global impacts: the 1976 Seveso chemical catastrophe, the 1984 Bhopal pesticide plant explosion and the 1986 Chernobyl nuclear desaster in the former Soviet Union (now Ukraine).[34] These incidences lent support to the view that almost every ecological disaster had transboundary and international implications. The Brundtland report framed the concerns raised over those tragedies as interlocking international crises. Therefore, it highlighted that global economic and environmental developments were interwoven phenomena, especially in the age of a beginning globalisation.[35] Present generations lead unsustainable lives, using up the world's resources and future generations – with "no financial or political power" –[36] had no vote in this and thus they could not "challenge our decisions".[37]

In addition, the Brundtland report underscored the point that sustainable development rested not only on the concept of limitations, but also on the "concept of needs, in particular essential needs of the world's poor".[38] At the time, the needs concept was trending at international level. Also the Club of Rome had highlighted that human "basic material requirements" be recognised.[39] At the level of the United Nations, the needs concept figured prominently in the so called Cocoyoc Declaration on "Patterns of Resource Use, Environment and Development Strategies" of 1974.[40] However, developing and

32 Our Common Future, 14.04.1987, ch 2, para 1.

33 Our Common Future, 14.04.1987, summary, para 27. Emphasis added.

34 Compare Gehne (n 11), 27.

35 Our Common Future, 14.04.1987, summary, para 15. "Ecology and economy are becoming ever more interwoven – locally, regionally, nationally, and globally – into a seamless net of causes and effects."

36 Our Common Future, 14.04.1987, summary, para 25.

37 Our Common Future, 14.04.1987, summary, para 25.

38 Our Common Future, 14.04.1987, ch 2, para 1.

39 Meadows (n 2).

40 UNGA, the Cocoyoc Declaration adopted by the participants in the UNEP/UNCTAD Symposium on "Patterns of Resource Use, Environment and Development Strategies" (Second Committee), 1 November 1974, UN Doc. A/C.2/292, 1 and 2.

developed countries alike contested that understanding.[41] Whereas the former feared an intervention in their inner affairs, the latter were concerned over who defined what basic needs were.[42] In the end, the strategy was discontinued at UN level.[43] Nonetheless, a needs-based understanding of sustainability continued to live on in academia. In the third Woodlands conference 1979 J. C. Coomer explained, "The central question is not so much technological, but how one may more directly relate physical, economic and social growth to the actual needs of people. It is not a management of the environment; it is rather, a management of those myriad activities that impact on the environment."[44] This view on sustainability also prevailed in in the concept of sustainable development formulated in the Brundtland Report.

Despite the strong emphasis of the Brundtland report on the underlying and entangled ecological, social, technological and environmental crises, the report did not propose a sustainable development formula. Neither did it define sustainable development in clear cut terms. In this, it differed from the Club of Rome report, which had introduced sustainability as a the state of a global equilibrium, in which population growth is stabilised, non-renewable resources are consumed less, economic preferences of society had shifted toward services and pollution had been reduced,[45] such that population levels and capital were physically maintainable.[46] Rather, the authors of the Brundtland report were convinced that sustainable development could have different preconditions in different settings and societies of the world.[47] Accordingly, the report emphasised that "sustainable development is not a fixed state of harmony, but rather *a process of change* in which the exploitation of resources, the direction of investments, the orientation of technological development, and institutional change are made consistent with future as well as present needs."[48]

41 Gehne (n 11).
42 ibid
43 ibid, 23.
44 Coomer (n 25), 6. Emphasis added.
45 Meadows (n 2).
46 Ibid.
47 Our Common Future. 14.04.1987, ch 1, para 51. "No single blueprint of sustainability will be found, as economic and social systems and ecological conditions differ widely among countries. Each nation will have to work out its own concrete policy implications. Yet irrespective of these differences, sustainable development should be seen as a global objective."
48 Our Common Future, 14.04.1987, summary, para 30. Emphasis added.

The focus on sustainability as a process deserves particular attention. Like growth theory in economics, the proceduralisation of (international) environmental law or the general distinction between substantive and procedural environmental rules was a phenomenon, which European and North-American academics discussed intensely on a more general and theoretical level right about the time the Brundtland report was published.[49] At that time, international environmental law stated mostly broad obligations, which needed further specification.[50] More particularly, many basic provisions of international environmental law, such as the duty not to cause harm, did not describe obligations of result, but of obligations of conduct.[51] Procedural rules therefore formed the "parameters and settings for legal interaction"[52] which described how these broad obligations of conduct ought to be fulfilled.

The Brundtland report described a number of procedures and mandates, which led to realisation of sustainable development. For example, the term was to be understood as a mandate for national and international lawmakers. At the international level, this meant the adoption of a universal declaration for environmental protection and a subsequent convention, as well as "procedures for avoiding or resolving disputes on environment and resource management issues".[53] Furthermore, the report emphasised, that sustainability, or sustainable development, should move beyond the traditional field of "command and control" regulation of environmental law, and move into procedures that dominate both the private and public sector. Hence, it should be "built into taxation, prior approval procedures for investment and technology choice, foreign trade incentives, and all components of development policy",[54]

49 Gunther Teubner, *Dilemmas of Law in the Welfare State* (de Gruyter 1988); Rudolf Wiethölter, 'Proceduralization Of The Category Of Law' (2011) 12(1) German Law Journal 465, 472, www.cambridge.org/core/article/proceduralization-of-the-category-of-law/4175046E8901DD561DDD15B448629A03; Rudolf Wiethölter, 'Materialization and Proceduralization in Modern Law' in Gunther Teubner (ed), *Dilemmas of Law in the Welfare State* (de Gruyter 1988); Günther Handl and others, 'The environment: International rights and responsibilities' (1980) 74 Proceedings of the Annual Meeting (American Society of International Law) 223, 221.

50 United Nations Conference on the Human Environment, Stockholm, 16.06.1972, Declaration on the Human Environment, UNGA 2994/XXVII, 2995/XXVII and 2996/XXII, 15.12.1972.

51 Such as the duty to prevent harm/not to cause damage to the transnational environment, Handl and others (n 48), 224; see also: Jutta Brunnée, 'Procedure and Substance in International Environmental Law' (2020) Publications of The Hague Academy of International Law 75

52 Brunnée (n 51).

53 Our Common Future, 14.04.1987, summary, para 97.

54 Out Common Future, 14.04.1987 ch 2, para 79.

thus serving as a cross-sectoral principle that resonated in the rules of neighbouring fields. According to the report, sustainable development should be understood in a very broad sense. It described a strategy to "promote harmony among human beings and between humanity and nature."[55]

2.2 *Participation (for Sustainable Development)*

Most interestingly, the report emphasised that decision-making regarding sustainability required certain procedures to be in place, which took economic, societal, environmental and technological implications into account. The report highlighted: "Sustainability requires the enforcement of wider responsibilities for the impacts of decisions. This requires changes in the legal and institutional frameworks that will enforce the common interest. …."[56] This recognition of common interests required "community knowledge and support, which entails greater public participation in the decisions that affect the environment. This was best secured by decentralizing the management of resources upon which local communities depend, and giving these communities an effective say over the use of these resources. It would also require promoting citizens' initiatives, empowering people's organisations, and strengthening local democracy."[57]

Hence, the report viewed public participation as not only relevant to those affected communities and public associations, but also as key to representing common interests in environmentally sensitive decision-making. The report also highlighted additional ways in which common interests could be defended in those decisions. For example, by public inquiries and hearings, and by granting access to information, to enable informed decision-making by the public.[58] The report also added that "When the environmental impact of a proposed project is particularly high, public scrutiny of the case should be mandatory and, wherever feasible, the decision should be subject to prior public approval, perhaps by referendum."[59] After all, the Brundtland report identified several, very concrete suggestions for participation in environmental decision-making as procedures which could be employed to ensure sustainable development.

Obviously, the informed reader will recognise those suggestions in later international articulations and regulations about environmental decision-making:

55 Our Common Future, 14.04.1987, ch 2, para 81.
56 Our Common Future, 14.04.1987, ch 2, para 76.
57 Our Common Future, 14.04.1987, ch 2, para 77.
58 Our Common Future, 14.04.1987, ch 2, para 78.
59 Our Common Future, 14.04.1987, ch 2, para 78.

they are, for example, contained in principle 10 of the Rio Declaration,[60] in the Aarhus Convention[61] negotiated five years after the report, or the even more recent Escazú Agreement.[62] The Aarhus Convention and the Escazú Agreement appear as two of the most literal interpretations of those recommendations at the international level. Nonetheless, even those comprehensive treaties on participatory rights do not include the suggestions on prior public approval or referenda for projects of high environmental impact as identified by the Brundtland report. Given the general focus of the literature on the Rio Declaration and the Aarhus and Escazú agreements,[63] it is however, remarkable that those very concrete suggestions for public participation in environmental decision-making were not highlighted earlier.

2.3 *Sustainability through Participation: Key Features Highlighted by the Brundtland Report*

The Brundtland report formulated sustainability, or sustainable development, as a broad concept promoting harmony between humanity and nature, concentrating on human needs, and the preservation of natural resources for future generations. The report perceived sustainability as a "a process of change" addressing not only ecology, but investment, technological development, and institution building.[64] Accordingly, the report envisaged policies and rules promoting sustainable development be formulated as processes. Although international and national law-making in environmental matters could promote those procedures, the Brundtland report stressed that sustainable development should be built into all relevant fields of law, technology, economics, ecology and society.

The report regarded participation in environmental decision-making as crucial in achieving sustainable development. In view of this, the report made some very concrete suggestions on how participation should be realised. For

60 Principle 10, UNGA, Report of the United Nations Conference on Environment and Development Rio de Janeiro, 12 August 1993, A/CONF.151/26 (Vol. I).

61 United Nations Economic Commission for Europe (UNECE) Convention on Access to Information, Public Participation in Decision-making and Access to Justice in Environmental Matters (Aarhus Convention), entered into force 30 October 2001 in the Danish city of Aarhus, 2161 UNTS 447.

62 Regional Agreement on Access to Information, Public Participation and Justice in Environmental Matters in Latin America and the Caribbean (Escazú Agreement), entered into force 22 April 2021 in the Costa Rican city of Escazú, C.N.196.2018 TREATIES-XXVII.18 of April 2018.

63 See Aarhus Convention (n 61); Escazú Agreement (n 62) above.

64 Our Common Future, 14.04.1987, summary, para 30. Emphasis added.

example: including affected communities and their organisations, informing those affected by environmental decisions, granting access to information, conducting inquiries and hearings in decision-making processes, and introducing mandatory procedures of approval, or referenda, if the environmental impact of the project was perceived to be particularly high.

3 Early Roots: Overview of Some Early European Rules Tackling Sustainability and Participation

As emphasised in the introduction to this chapter, there are many assessments, which trace sustainability or sustainable development and participation[65] throughout history. They differ according to the discipline and perspective involved[66] and cover different time spans.[67] In order to provide a framework for the assessment of sustainability and participation in international environmental law, the following paragraphs will briefly summarise some of the main historical findings about national legal rules associated with sustainability and participation, starting with early antiquity. The focus is on European rules, as sustainability emerged as a reaction to unsustainable, North-American and European colonial industrial societies.[68]

3.1 *Sustainability*

Numerous writings have highlighted that sustainability as a term was coined in German and Swedish forestry laws, in the early 18th century.[69] It is here, where "sustainability", or rather the adjective "sustained" (translated from the German word "nachhaltend") was mentioned for the first time. *Von Carlowitz*, a German official working for the Ministry of Mining in Saxony, used it in his treatise on forestry and the conservation of forests. As forests had been

65 Gehne (n 11), 44–45.

66 For example, assessments highlight growth, development, progress or change, depending on the underlying discipline and perspective. Compare: Mebratu (n 6), 506 f, 511; Carl Mitcham, 'The concept of sustainable development: its origins and ambivalence' (1995) 17(3) Technology in society 311, 313.

67 Christopher Schliephake, Natascha Sojc and Gregor Weber (eds), *Nachhaltigkeit in der Antike: Diskurse, Praktiken, Perspektiven* (Geographica Historica 42, Franz Steiner Verlag 2020).

68 Caradonna (n 3), 20.

69 Grober (n 22), 2, 3.

considerably depleted in Saxony for the benefit of mining, he cautioned that forests be cultivated "sustainably" to yield wood over the years to come.[70]

Despite this referral to the term "sustainability", rules dealing with the depletion of non-exhaustible natural resources and the prohibition of their degradation are probably as old as humanity. As *Mebratu* pointed out: "...hazards of pollution, deforestation, land degradation, and chemical food adulteration ... have dogged humanity, to a greater or lesser extent, for most of its existence."[71] In light of this, especially in Europe, historians identified a plethora of sources concerned with the prevention of harm, the preservation of livestock or the preservation of freshwater from pollution, or the fight against the further decimation of forests, to name but a few important examples.[72]

Neighbour laws were among the first that forbade harming another's territory.[73] Deforestation was a problem already in early antiquity.[74] Plato, for example, had suggested certain institutions and regulations to prevent deforestation in Athens.[75] Similarly, Roman rules on usufruct of woods contained the rule that an usufruct on woods could only be exercised if the wood be reforested.[76] Also rules on the preservation of certain livestock date back to the Roman age. In Roman law, an usufruct on a flock of animals entailed the rule that a beneficiary of the usufruct could not acquire ownership of the new-born. Rather, new-born animals should first be considered as a replacement for the deceased to keep flock numbers steady.[77] Medieval rules did not address the

---

70 "Wird derhalben die größte Kunst, Wissenschaft, Fleiß, und Einrichtung hiesiger Lande darinnen beruhen, wie eine sothane Conservation und Anbau des Holzes anzustellen, daß es eine continuriliche beständige und nachhaltende Nutzung gebe weil es eine unentbehrliche Sache ist, ohne welche das Land in seinem Effe nicht bleiben mag". Hans C von Carlowitz, *Sylvicvltvra Oeconomica* (Braun 1713) 105; see eg Grober (n 22), 4.

71 Mebratu (n 6), 495.

72 For an overview: Günter Heine, 'Umweltbezogenes Recht im Mittelalter' in Bernd Herrmann (ed), *Umwelt in der Geschichte: Beiträge zur Umweltgeschichte* (Kleine Vandenhoeck-Reihe vol 1544. Vandenhoeck & Ruprecht 1989), 120, 122; Joachim Radkau, *Natur und Macht: Eine Weltgeschichte der Umwelt* (Beck 2000), 166 f; Heike Bilgenroth-Barke, *Kriminalität und Zahlungsmoral im 16. Jahrhundert* (Edition Ruprecht 2010), 120 ff; Donald Hughes, *Environmental Problems of the Greeks and Romans* (Johns Hopkins University Press 2014), 85 f, 102 f.

73 See, for an example: John L Innes, 'Sustainable forest management - from concept to practice' in John L Innes and Anna V Tikina (eds), *Sustainable forest management: From concept to practice* (The Earthscan forest library, First published. Routledge an imprint of the Taylor & Francis Group earthscan from Routledge 2017), 9.

74 Caradonna (n 3), 23.

75 Hughes (n 13), 64.

76 Digesten 7, 1, 10 - 12 pr.

77 Digesten 7, 1, 68 pr. 2.

preservation of woods in a similar way.[78] Yet, in the early 14th century, work and rules on reforestation developed in the German city of Nuremberg and quickly spread throughout Europe.[79] Also rules on wildlife, for example, recognizing the reproductive cycle of fish, are known from the 14th century.[80] The same applies to rules regulating bird-hunting.[81]

Concerning the preservation of freshwater, Aristotle argued that freshwater should be preserved (and separated from irrigation water, for example).[82] Around 300 BC, Athens punished "water theft" and a Water Commissioner was a part of the city government.[83] Specific regulations for the preservation of freshwater are known since the 13th century.[84] In 1231, King Friedrich II enacted a Sicilian law forbidding the throwing of toxic plants into lakes and other freshwater resources because they poisoned the fish and also humans drinking from it.[85] In 1302, Nuremberg enacted a law forbidding the emptying of general waste into the local river. At the same time, the town passed laws which forbade clothes being washed in the river. The town also prohibited the emptying of hard dirt into the river.[86]

An institutionalised form of water resource management and protection has existed since the early Middle Ages in the form of dike, dam or pond[87] commissions or associations, for example in the Netherlands, and Germany.[88] Those commissions or associations were collectives of users that were obliged to collectively decide and financially contribute to the maintenance of dams,

78 Innes (n 73), 9 illustrating the 1217 Charter of the Forest of England, which did not address the future preservation of English woods.

79 Wolfgang Stromer von Reichenbach, '600 Jahre Nadelwaldsaat, die Leistung des Peter Stromer von Nürnberg' in Georg Sperber, Die Reichswälder bei Nürnberg, aus der Geschichte des ältesten Kunstforstes (Frankenverlag 1968), 25.

80 Heine (n 72), 123; Gustav Hermann Zeller, Sammlung der württembergischen Regierungsgesetze (Fues 1841), 133.

81 Antiquarische Gesellschaft in Zürich, Die Zürcher Stadtbücher des 14. Und 15. Jahrhunderts (vol 1. Verlag von S Hirzel 1906), 146.

82 Hughes (n 13), 60.

83 ibid, 60.

84 Heine (n 72), 114.

85 ibid, 114.

86 ibid, 114.

87 On this compare Joseph Bongartz, 'Miszellen. Zur Geschichte der Dürener Papierindustrie' (1904) 78 Annalen des Historischen Vereins für den Niederrhein 142, 144.

88 Pieter Hendrik Gallé, 'Protected existence; characteristic legal features concerning water control during the Middle Ages in the south-west Netherlands and main elements in the history of dike management in this area (1200–1963)' in Pieter Hendrik Gallé, Beveiligd bestaan. Grondtrekken van het middeleeuwse waterstaatsrecht in Zuid-West Nederland en hoofdlijnen van de geschiedenis van het dijksbeheer in dit gebied (1200–1963) (1963), 372.

dikes or joint water resources. In the latter case, this was done for the for the benefit of (paper) mills that had been established on their shore.[89]

Rules on the conservation of nature, nor only for utilisation but for further enjoyment by humans were developed at the beginning of the 19th century in the epoch of nature-romanticism in North-America and Europe.[90] With a growing awareness of the "beauty" of nature, the first nature reserves were declared. The first German nature reserve was the so called dragon rock, a very popular viewpoint on the river Rhine, established in 1836 to safeguard the area from quarrying.[91] In North America, the Yosemite Park, established in 1864, was the first national park.[92] Only a little later, national initiatives to protect natural objects as natural monuments around Europe[93] and national, European and international associations for nature protection were founded.[94]

While the aforementioned rules evince different approaches to nature protection and preservation, sustainability is also concerned with the preservation of resources for coming and future generations. Those concerns were addressed in historical writings mostly from the beginning of the industrial age. Authors discussed the detrimental effects of uncontrolled human influence and behaviour on nature and natural resources, as well as on economic development.[95] Malthusian concern about the unlimited population growth in Europe is a case in point.[96] Also the responsible use and conservation of exhaustible natural resources – in particular coal – for future use became an issue.[97] Jevons, researching the "coal question" therefore questioned the use of alternative energies, imports and the resulting economic losses, if coal reserves were exhausted in the British Isles.[98]

89 Bongartz (n 87), 145.

90 Gottfried Zirnstein, *Ökologie und Umwelt in der Geschichte* (Ökologie und Wirtschaftsforschung vol 14, 2nd edn. Metropolis-Verlag 1996), 212 f.

91 ibid, 212.

92 ibid, 213.

93 ibid, 224 f.

94 Raf de Bont, '"Primitives" and Protected Areas: International Conservation and the "Naturalization" of Indigenous People, ca. 1910–1975' (2015) 76(2) Journal of the History of Ideas 215, 219.

95 Caradonna (n 3), 62.

96 Thomas R Malthus, *First Essay on Population* (Macmillan 1798, reprinted 1926).

97 Consider, for example: William S Jevons, *The Coal Question: An Inquiry Concerning the Progress of the Nation, and the Probable Exhaustion of our Coal Mines* (vol 69, 2nd edn. Macmillan 1866); Du Pisani (n 6), 86.

98 William S Jevons and Paul Warde, 'The Coal Question (1865)' in Libby Robin, Sverker Sörlin and Paul Warde (eds), *The Future of Nature: Documents of Global Change* (Yale University Pres 2013), 79 f.

Summing up, early rules associated with sustainability, or sustainable development, address different environmental aspects and serve different aims. Not only do they aim to preserve non-exhaustible natural resources for future utilisation and exploitation, they also address environmental problems, such as pollution. Finally, some of these rules aim at the conservation of nature's natural beauty. Concerning implementation management and organisation of those regimes, one can differentiate between the classic law and order approach and collective, institutionalised decision-making.

The exclusively anthropocentric character of those rules and underlying aims is unmistakable. Even the rules dealing with nature conservation addressed the conservation of the beauty of nature, as perceived by humans. This illustrates that the early rules on sustainability do not differ much from the notion of sustainability introduced by the Brundtland report. The concept of sustainable development presented in that report was mainly concerned with the continued availability and utility of nature and natural resources for future generations and thus is anthropocentric in character.[99] This is underscored by the needs approach and the focus on economic development.

3.2 *The Role of Participation in Historical National Rules on Sustainability*

It is clear that in the early conceptualisations of sustainability, participation, very broadly perceived as the involvement in public decision-making, does not play a major role. With regard to the national level, there are two main contexts, which may connect sustainability and participation: neighbour rights; and institutionalised participation. Neighbour participation, which has been traced back to the early 18th century,[100] concerns a defined group of humans, who are immediately affected by decisions that have an impact on the environment.[101] The main aim of provisions involving neighbours in decision-making, was to secure and respect established or historic rights of affected neighbours in administrative decision-making processes.[102] Securing community interests or public scrutiny of the relevant decisions, as the Brundtlandt report emphasised,[103] was not an aim outlined in those rules. By contrast, the

99 Compare: Gehne (n 11), 31.

100 Pascale M Cancik, 'Die Erfindung der Beteiligung im Verwaltungsverfahren' in Wolfgang Hoffmann-Riem (ed), *Innovation und Recht – Recht und Innovation* (Mohr Siebeck 2016); Pascale M Cancik, *Verwaltung und Öffentlichkeit in Preußen: Kommunikation durch Publikation und Beteiligungsverfahren im Recht der Reformzeit* (Mohr Siebeck 2007)

101 Cancik, 'Die Erfindung der Beteiligung im Verwaltungsverfahren' (n 100), 112.

102 ibid, 112.

103 See this chapter, section 2, above.

institutionalised settings of the medieval dike, dam, pond or river associations already foresaw the participation of affected communities and allowed for public scrutiny. Dike associations usually entailed the compulsory membership of all affected users to a water resource or dam. This secured community interests, in the sense that Brundtland envisaged, yet only on a particular matter.

4 Historical Traces of Sustainability and Participation at the International Level

The late 19th century and the early 20th century mark the beginning of early international environmental multilateralism.[104] Like the early national rules on environmental protection and sustainability, early international environmental agreements concerned aspects of transboundary pollution, or the pollution of common resources, (institutionalised) protection schemes for natural resources, in particular for hunting and fishing, and, about half a century later, also the protection of nature itself. Whereas they are often referred to as lending expression to good neighbourliness in international law,[105] they also exhibit early conceptualisations of what later crystallised into sustainability, or sustainable development. This is illustrated further in the following paragraphs.

4.1 *Animal (Stock) Conservation and Preservation for Future Use*

There are a variety of historical treaties dealing with the preservation and conservation of animal stocks for future use. A very early agreement addressing those issues is the 1875 Convention between Baden and Switzerland Concerning Fishing in the Rhine.[106] Already the preamble formulated the overall goal of the convention to *preserve* and reproduce fish in the Rhine and the Lake Constance, especially by regulating ways in which fish may be caught. In this regard, the Convention provided in art 1 that fish may not be caught by barriers

---

104 Peter H Sand, 'Introduction' in Peter H Sand (ed), *The history and origin of international environmental law* (The international library of law and the environment vol 1. Edward Elgar 2015), xiii.

105 ibid, XIII.

106 Convention Between Baden and Switzerland Concerning Fishing in the Rhine and its Influxes as well as in Lake Constance, signed on 25 March 1875 in Basel, Martens, Nouveau recueil général de traités et autres actes relatifs aux rapports de droit international, deuxième série, vol 2, 60, 64. Followed by two Declarations Dated November 30/December 5, 1875, and a Convention Between the two Initial Parties and Alsace-Lorraine, Mulhouse summary and original text (additional Convention and final protocol 1884).

introduced into the river that span more than half of the river's breadth. In a later protocol to the agreement, fishing was prohibited, if nets were not wide enough.[107] Follow-up agreements on fishing in the Rhine and Lake Constance prohibited fishing conducted by permanent means introduced and anchored in the river which spanned more than half of the breadth of the river.[108] Many other agreements concluded thereafter dealt with the prohibition and regulation of fishing. In the treaty concerning fishing in the river Tourneå of 1897, Russia, Sweden and Finland restricted salmon fishing in the river.[109] Only local populations and persons holding a right to usufruct, granted by at least two parties of the agreement, were allowed to fish.[110] Yet, even in that case, fishing rights needed to be exercised in conformity with the conditions of the treaty, which forbade, for example, fishing with more than eight fixed apparatuses.[111] But agreements did not only foresee bans and prohibitions for livestock preservation. The treaty concerning the Jan Mayen Seal Fishery of 1876 set up a temporal hunting ban, prohibiting and fining the fishing of seals during certain parts of the year in the area of Jan Mayen Island.[112]

Consecutive agreements combined the two previous approaches (the restriction of methods and a temporal hunting ban) providing for a framework of species conservation. The Convention for the Preservation for the Fur Seal and Sea Otter in the North Pacific Ocean and Bering Sea is a case in point. It was modelled after a proposal formulated by the arbiter of the Pacific Fur Seals

---

107 Art 2, Convention between Austria-Hungary, Baden, Bavaria, Liechtenstein Switzerland and Wurttemberg, Decreeing Uniform Regulations for Fishing in Lake Constance, Including a Final Protocol, signed on 5 July 1893 in Bregenz, ST/LEG/SER.B/12 403.

108 Art 1, Convention between Switzerland, The Grand Duchy of Baden, And Alsace-Lorraine, Establishing Uniform Provisions on Fishing in the Rhine and Its Tributaries, Including Lake Constance, With Final Protocol, signed on 18 May 1887 in Lucerne, ST/LEG/SER.B/12, 397.

109 Art 1, Convention Between Russia And Sweden And Norway, Regulating The Salmon Fishery In The Tornea, signed on 23 February 1897 in Parry, The Consolidated Treaty Series, vol 184, 229.

110 Art 4, Convention Between Russia And Sweden And Norway, Regulating The Salmon Fishery In The Tornea, 1897.

111 ibid, art 6, "1. il ne sera pas permis d'établir des appareils fixes de pêche qu'au nombre de 8 tout au plus, et leur emplacement, ainsi que l'étendue seront déterminés d'un commun accord par les hautes Parties contractantes à la suite d'un examen préalable effectué par des experts. Toutefois au printemps jusqu'à l'époque où la pêche, au moyen d'appareils fixes, aura commencé, il sera permis d'employer aussi d'autres engins servant à la pêche du saumon et du poisson dit «taimen», dont l'emploi est admis par le règlement en vigueur;"

112 Treaty concerning the Jan Mayen Seal Fishery, British Order in Council of 28 November 1876, The Seal Fishery Act, 1875, 38 Vict. c. 18.

Arbitration[113] – a famous arbitration dealing with species conservation – and was signed by all relevant parties in 1911. The arbitration concerned a dispute between the USA and the UK about territorial claims and exclusive rights in the hunting of seals in the Bering Sea. The parties requested that the arbiters adjudicate and declare the territorial boundaries of Russia and the United States and fishing rights of the two states in the Bering Sea, under general international law as well as under a treaty of 1825 concluded between the UK and Russia. The parties had also asked the arbiter to set up further rules and regulations to regulate the hunting of fur seals in the Bering Sea.[114] In response to the questions posed by the parties, the arbiters firstly found that Russia, as the former owner of Alaska, owned no further rights in the Bering Sea. Secondly, the territorial rights of the new owner of Alaska, the USA, did not extend beyond the three-mile limit. Thirdly, therefore, in order to settle the claims of the parties to hunt seals in the Bering Sea, the arbiters drew up a conservation scheme for the seals, which would then serve to preserve the seal population in the Bering Sea.[115] As part of that scheme, the arbiters declared a particular island in the Bering Sea as sanctuary for the pacific fur seals,[116] introduced a hunting ban for particular months of the year,[117] and restricted the manner of hunting fur-seals to licensed fishermen,[118] who used particular boats and designated equipment for the hunt.[119]

Multiple conventions with the aim of preserving certain species addressed either fishing or hunting. The Convention Respecting Measures for the Preservation and Protection of the Fur Seals in the North Pacific Ocean of 1911 prohibited pelagic sealing[120] and the sale of seal products belonging to seals

---

113 Award of the Arbitral Tribunal established under the Treaty signed in Washington, on the 29th of February 1892, between United States and Her Majesty the Queen of United Kingdom of Great-Britain and Ireland, decision of 15 August 1893, Reports of International Arbitral Award ('RIAA') ST/LEG/RIAA/28, 263–276. See French (n 16); 'Man saved from deportation after pollution plea in French legal "first"' *The Guardian* (12 January 2021) www.theguardian.com/world/2021/jan/12/bangladeshi-man-with-asthma-wins-france-deportation-fight last accessed 12 January 2021.

114 RIAA, (N 113), 267.

115 ibid, 270.

116 ibid, Art 1.

117 ibid, Art 2.

118 ibid, Art 4.

119 ibid, Arts 3, 6.

120 Entered into force on 15 December 1911 in Washington, [1913] Australian Treaty Series (ATS) No. 6. Art. 1 of the Treaty.

originating from these waters.[121] The Agreement regarding the regulation of plaice and flounder[122] relied on a temporal hunting ban prohibiting the fishing of plaice in certain months.[123] In addition, certain methods of fishing such as trawl fishing[124] were banned and minimum sizes of fish were agreed upon.[125] Also a later agreement on plaice regulated the minimum sizes of fish that may be caught.[126]

The Convention for the Regulation of Whaling of 1931, entered into force in 1935,[127] established a killing ban for the, albeit limited, number of whales subject to its regulation.[128] A further agreement dealing with whaling, the International Agreement for the Regulation of Whaling of 1937,[129] forbade the killing or hunting of specified whales, which measured below certain lengths, as well as of calves and suckling whales.[130] While it also established hunting bans and prohibitions, the convention did not include catch limits.[131]

Rules defining allowable catch and catchment methods can be found in many other regional fishing conventions concluded thereafter.[132] Also protected areas were established as a method to guarantee species conservation. The Convention between Denmark, Norway and Sweden Concerning the

---

121 ibid, Art 4

122 Agreement between Denmark, Free City of Danzig, Germany, Poland and Sweden, Regarding the Regulation of plaice (Pleuronectes Platessa) and Flounder (Pleuronectes Flesus) Fishing in the Baltic Sea, 1929, File S648bis/78/48 - No.2679 Treaties Collection Vol 115.

123 ibid, Art 2.

124 ibid, Art 3.

125 ibid, Art 4.

126 Art 2, Convention between Denmark, Norway and Sweden, Concerning the Preservation of Plaice and Dab in the Skagerrak, Kattegat and Sound, with Final Protocol, signed on 6 September 1937 and entered into force on 23 March 1938, 186 League of Nations Treaty Series (LNTS) 419 (No. 4326).

127 Convention for the Regulation of Whaling, entered into force on 16 January 1935, adopted on 24 September 1931 in Geneva, 155 LNTS 349 (No. 3586). https://iea.uoregon.edu/MarineMammals/engine/Documents/0-1394-1399.htm last accesssed on 6 March 2023.

128 ibid, Art 4.

129 International Agreement between South Africa, USA, Argentina, Australia, Canada, Germany, UK, Ireland, Mexico, New Zealand, Norway, For the Regulation of Whaling, entered into force on 1 July 1937 in London, 190 LNTS 79 (No. 4406).

130 Ibid, Arts 5, 6.

131 Jochen Braig, 'Whaling' (2013 Max Planck Encyclopedia of Public International Law, para 3.

132 Compare Arts 5, 8, 9, Convention for the Regulation of the Meshes of Fishing Nets and the Size Limits of Fish, concluded on 5 April 1946 and entered into force on 5 April 1953, 231 UNTS 199 (No. 3221).

Preservation of Plaice in the Skagerak, Kattegat and Sound established a protected zone in which the plaice could reproduce and hatch.[133]

Where multilateral agreements on stock preservation were missing, states could – by way of customary international law – unilaterally pass fishing limitations to ensure preservation of the fish stocks. This was confirmed by the Permanent Court of International Justice (PICJ) in the North Atlantic Coast Fisheries Case.[134] In its judgment, the Court held that states, where granted with fishing rights, could pass fishing restrictions, as long as they were appropriate and necessary for the preservation of fisheries and allowed for an equitable and fair regimen that did not disadvantage fishermen from either party.[135]

Regarding the diverse methods and rules aiming at species preservation, it is safe to conclude that by that time, the protection and preservation of individual species by rules, inter alia defining fixed quotas, hunting methods, protected areas or a however defined sustained yield[136] was established international practice. Those rules were adopted with the aim to conserve the relevant species for future human use and consumption. And, adoption of the rules mostly became necessary because the species had been decimated by human behaviour (hunting, fishing) in the first place.

4.2 *Institutionalized Livestock and Nature Protection*

Institutionalized livestock and nature protection transpires as another approach to sustainability from early international treaty practice. Agreements foresaw the design and set up of designated institutions to oversee the protection and preservation of species, natural environments and the implementation of rules with that aim. An early example is the treaty of Versailles, which internationalised, amongst others, the river Oder,[137] and established the International Commission for the River Oder to administer the rights of the riparian and non-riparian states parties.[138] The International Convention

133 Convention between Denmark, Norway and Sweden, Concerning the Preservation of Plaice in the Skagerrak, Kattegat and Sound, signed on 31 December 1932 and entered into force on 22 June 1933, 139 LNTS 189 (No. 3210).

134 PERMANENT COURT OF ARBITRATION (PCA) (PICJ), North Atlantic Coast Fisheries Case (USA v. Great Britain), decision of 7 September 1910, 11 RIAA 167.

135 IBID 189.

136 See: Grober, (n 22), 7.

137 Arts 332–337, Treaty of Versailles (Treaty of peace with Germany), adopted on 28 June 1919 and entered into force on 10 January 1920, LNTS No. 37.

138 On the legality of the establishment of this commission compare: PCA (PICJ), Case Relating to the Territorial Jurisdiction of the International Commission of the River Oder, Publication of the Permanent Court of International Justice Series A – No 23 (1929), 26–29.

for the Regulation of Whaling of 1946,[139] established a Commission[140] tasked with the proper conservation of whale stocks and the orderly development of the whaling industry.[141] It was competent to set up moratoria and maximum catches, to define hunting methods and regulating gear. Accordingly, the Commission was equipped with a whole range of powers[142] to "sustain exploitation in order to give an interval for recovery to certain species of whales".[143] Also later amendments to the 1946 Whaling Convention included and referred to thoughts that became part and parcel of the principle of sustainable development. A 1949 addition to the preamble, for example, highlighted "the interest of the nations of the world in *safeguarding for future generations* the great natural resources represented by the whale stocks."[144]

Subsequent conventions, such as the Agreement for the Establishment of a General Fisheries Council for the Mediterranean[145] or the Convention for the Establishment of an Inter-American Tropical Tuna Commission included similar provisions.[146] They institutionalise the protection of the resource in concern and underscored its sustainable use. The amended preamble to the Agreement for the General Fisheries Council for the Mediterranean, underlined that the states parties were "determined to ensure the long-term conservation and sustainable use of living marine resources and marine ecosystems in the area of application." It also recognized the "economic, social and nutritional benefits deriving from the sustainable use of living marine resources in the area of application".[147] Furthermore, when describing the functions of the Council, the agreement provided, in its art III: "The purpose of the Commission shall be to promote the development, conservation, rational management

139 International Convention for the Regulation of Whaling, signed on 2 December 1946 and entered into force on 10 November 1948, 161 UNTS 72 (No. 2124), https://archive.iwc.int/pages/download.php?ref=3607&size=&ext=pdf&k=&alternative=-1&usage=-1&usagecomment= last accessed on 6 March 2023.

140 ibid, Art III, 1.

141 ibid, compare the preamble of the Convention; Braig (n 131), para 9.

142 ibid, art V, 1. Emphasis added.

143 ibid, Preamble; Compare: French 'Sustainability' in Fitzmaurice, Ong and Merkouris (n 16), 52.

144 ibid, Preamble. Amendment, entered into force on 11 October 1949, 161 UNTS 100. Emphasis added.

145 Agreement for the Establishment of General Fisheries Council for the Mediterranean, signed on 24 September 1949 and entered into force on 20 February 1952, 126 UNTS 237 (No. 1691).

146 Convention for the Establishment of an Inter-American Tropical Tuna Commission (IATTC), signed on 31 May 1949 and entered into force 1950, 80 UNTS 3 (No. 1041).

147 Agreement for the Establishment of a General Fisheries Council for the Mediterranean, (n 145), Preamble.

and best utilisation of living marine resources, as well as the *sustainable development of aquaculture* in the Region…"[148]

The Preamble to the Inter-American Tropical Tuna Commission underscored the "mutual interest in maintaining the populations of … tuna … in the eastern Pacific Ocean by reason of continued use have come to be of common concern … and to facilitate maintaining the populations of these fishes at a level which will permit *maximum sustained catches* year after year…"[149] The general purpose of the Tuna Commission was to assess the abundance of tuna of the kind regulated by the convention and collect information relating to the populations of those fishes.[150] Moreover, the Commission was commissioned with studying "methods and procedures for maintaining and increasing the populations of fishes covered by the Convention."[151] Also the preamble of the International Convention for the Northwest Atlantic Fisheries of 1949 referred to the overall aim to "make possible the maintenance of the maximum sustained catch".

After all, by that time, the establishment of international institutions to determine "maximum sustained catches" had become an accepted method of resource and nature preservation. In comparison to previous approaches, which defined the methods or schemes to achieve a sustained yield in the international treaty itself, institutionalised protection offered a more flexible way of monitoring the reproduction and vulnerability of the species in question. It empowered the respective institutions to adapt their actions for preservation and protection to the actual facts on the ground, ie to stock size and conditions. Still the preservation of stocks for future human consumption was the main aim of institutionalized protection schemes.

4.3 *Nature Protection from Harm/Pollution*

There are a number of international awards and treaties dealing with pollution prevention. Concerning international treaties, the Provisions Relating to the Belgian-German Frontier Established by a Boundary Commission Composed of Representatives of the United Kingdom, France, Italy, Japan, Belgium and Germany following the Provisions of the Treaty of Versailles provide an early example.[152] Those provisions explicitly dealt with the water resources in the

---

148 ibid, Art III, 1. Emphasis added.

149 Convention for the Establishment of IATTC, (n 146), Preamble. Emphasis added.

150 ibid, Art II, 1.

151 ibid, Art II, 3.

152 Treaty of Versailles, (n 137)

Belgian-German border region and most particularly, with a dam built in 1909 in that region. The provisions prohibited pollution in the area of precipitation of that dam, as well as the construction of any facility, which could lead to such pollution.[153] In addition, the Provisions prohibited the deterioration of the water resources in that area.[154]

An example, which lead to the crystallisation of an international customary rule dealing with transboundary pollution of natural resources, is the famous *Trail Smelter* arbitration of 1941.[155] The *Trail Smelter* arbitration dealt with the emissions from a smelter in Canada that caused environmental degradation and harm in US territory, especially of forests. In the case, the arbiter established that States are responsible for transnational environmental damage, if the emissions could be attributed to a certain public or private enterprise under the control of the State.[156] The case serves as a leading example for the customary no harm rule in international environmental law.[157]

4.4 *Nature Conservation and Preservation as an Aim in Itself*

Probably the most controversial rules on nature conservation are those that establish the conservation of certain natural resources as an aim in itself. They often evince a utilitarian, anthropocentric and colonial[158] approach, which was to preserve nature for the benefit of man. It ran counter to ecocentric conservationist approaches, where nature is protected as an aim in itself.[159] One of the first conventions – sometimes hailed as the "world's first international environmental agreement"[160] – which is representative of that approach, is the Convention Designated to Ensure the Conservation of Various Species

153 No 2, Provisions Relating to the Belgian-German Frontier Established by a Boundary Commission Composed of Representatives of the United Kingdom, France, Italy, Japan, Belgium and Germany, signed and entered into force on 6 November 1922, 3897 IEA.

154 ibid, No 4.

155 *Trail Smelter Arbitration*, Award, 11 March 1941, 3 RIAA 1905.

156 *ibid*, 1965.

157 Subsequent international cases which affirmed that rule are: ICJ, *Legality of the Threat of Nuclear Weapons*, Advisory Opinion, 8 July 1996, ICJ Reports 1996, para 29; ICJ, *Gabčíkovo-Nagymaros Project* (*Hungary* v *Slovakia*), Judgment, 25 September 1997, ICJ Reports 1997, para 53; ICJ, *Certain Activities Carried out by Nicaragua in the Border Area* (*Costa Rica v Nicaragua*) *and Construction of a Road in Costa Rica along the San Juan River* (*Nicaragua v Costa Rica*), Judgment, 16 December 2015, ICJ Reports 2015, para 162

158 Sigrid Boysen, Die postkoloniale Konstellation (Mohr Siebeck 2021), 47.

159 Sand (n 104); Zirnstein (n 90), 210.

160 Boysen (n 158).

of Wild Animals in Africa, which are Useful to Man or Inoffensive.[161] As may already be derived from the title of the convention, the treaty had an entirely utilitarian objective. Art II para 1 of the treaty addressed the protection only of those animals "whose protection, whether owing to their usefulness or their rarity and threatened extermination, may be considered necessary by each Government."[162] In addition, art II para 2 prohibited the hunting and destruction of young animals of those species. Hence, the protection and preservation of animals was only intended, as far as these animals were considered useful or soon extinct, two terms, which give much room for further interpretation and controversy. Another treaty with a similar utilitarian but still conservationist approach is the Convention for the Protection of Birds Useful to Agriculture of 1902.[163] It foresaw the preservation of an enumerated list of "birds useful to agriculture", and installed a hunting and killing ban for those birds, as well as of their "nests, eggs and broods."[164]

Right about that time, the topic of genuine nature preservation and concerns for the common natural heritage gained momentum.[165] States concluded the Founding Treaty for a Consultative Commission for the International Protection of Nature,[166] a scientific lobbying organisation for the global protection of nature. The Commission was founded upon the initiative of the Swiss Paul Sarasin,[167] who headed the commission for the protection of natural monuments in Switzerland.[168] According to the treaty, the mandate of the Commission concerned the international protection of nature,[169] the collection of data relative to the international protection of nature, as well as the promulgation

---

161 Convention between the United Kingdom, Germany, Spain, Congo, France, Italy and Portugal, Designed to Ensure the Conservation of Various Species of Wild Animals in Africa, which are Useful to Man or Inoffensive (the London Convention of 1900), concluded and signed on 19 May 1900, it never entered into force, British Parliamentary Papers, 1900, Cd 101., vol 56, 825–837.

162 ibid, Art II, para 1.

163 Convention between Austria, Belgium, France, Germany, Greece, Hungary, Liechtenstein, Luxembourg, Monaco, Netherlands, Norway, Poland, Portugal, Spain, Sweden, Switzerland, For the Protection of Birds useful to Agriculture (the 1902 Paris Convention), concluded on 19 March 1902 in Paris and entered into force on 6 December 1905, Amtliche Sammlung (Schweizerische Eidgenossenschaft) Ausgabe 22 611; IUCN ELC, 08.2005.

164 ibid, Art 1.

165 Sand, (n 104).

166 Acte de Fondation d'une Commission Consultative Pour La Protection Internationale De La Nature, signed 1913 in Berne, Ruster and Simma, vol IV, 1631ff.

167 Bont (n 94), 219.

168 Zirnstein (n 90), 225.

169 Acte Foundation (n 166), Art 1.

of the protection of nature at international level.[170] Hence, in addition to an overall approach to general nature conservation, the treaty foresaw an institutionalised approach to nature protection.

The Commission for the International Protection of Nature was a predecessor to the International Union for the Conservation of Nature (IUCN), the now largest non-governmental organisation for the conservation of nature, with observer status in many international organisations. IUCN's Statutes were concluded in 1948.[171] Already the preamble to the IUCN Statutes included language commonly associated with sustainable development. It called for the realisation of man's "close dependence upon those natural resources and recognize the need both for the preservation of these resources and for exploiting them only with careful management in such a way as to conduce to the future peace, progress and prosperity of mankind."[172] Also, art I, which defined the objects of the Union, highlighted the "conservation of natural resources with a view to their wise utilization."[173] The preservation of (natural) resources for future use looms prominently behind those formulations, although sustainability, or sustainable development, is not used as a reference framework.

A very early treaty concerned with the international protection of a particular world region was the Spitzbergen Treaty. It established an international regime for the exploitation of the natural resources of the island of Spitzbergen, rendering Norway sovereign rights over Spitzbergen. At the same time, it guaranteed other States parties equal access and non-discrimination rights, similar to the mandate system of the League of Nations.[174] To that end, the treaty instituted Norway as administrator of that island and conferred her with the competence to institute "measures to ensure the preservation and, if necessary, the re-constitution of the fauna and flora of the said region, and their territorial waters".[175]

Natural parks as a means of nature conservation were established about a decade later, starting with the Convention Relative to the Preservation of

170 ibid, Art 6, No 1 a und 2.

171 Statutes Of The International Union For Conservation Of Nature And Natural Resources, 5 October 1948, as amended in September 1958.

172 ibid, Preamble.

173 ibid, Art I, 1 lit b.

174 Christopher R Rossi, 'A unique international problem: The Svalbard Treaty, equal enjoyment, and terra nullius: Lessons of territorial temptation from history' (2016) 15 Washington University Global Studies Law Review 93, 97.

175 Art 2, Treaty concerning the Archipelago of Spitsbergen, signed on 9 February 1920 in Paris and entered into force on 14 August 1925, 2 LNTS 7 (No. 41).

Fauna and Flora in their Natural State of 1933.[176] It addressed the natural fauna and flora (in Africa), which were in danger of extinction or permanent injury,[177] by way of establishing national parks and natural reserves.[178] The convention called upon states to guarantee as little disturbance as possible,[179] which, according to popular opinion at that time, included disturbance by resident (Massai) populations![180] The Convention on Nature Protection and Wildlife Preservation in the Western Hemisphere[181] of 1940 pursued a similar approach. It foresaw the establishment of national parks as means to preserve natural habitats, fauna and flora[182] and established a hunting, killing and capturing ban on species present in those natural parks.[183] Similar to the 1933 convention, the 1940 convention continued some of the nature romanticism, which underpins the natural park movement, by providing for "strict wilderness" in those parks.[184]

Finally, the General Agreement on Tariffs and Trade (GATT), concluded in 1947, defined a new chapter in nature and resource protection. It saw nature and resource protection as a cross-sectoral topic and task, which reached into fields other than environmental law, and which was to be fulfilled by other fields and areas of law. Its art XX included a general exception, which recognized the protection of human, animal or plant life or health,[185] as well as the conservation of exhaustible natural resources.[186] The cross-sectoral approach to sustainability is an idea highlighted in the Brundtland report. Yet, it had been voiced long before its publication. Only in those late environmental agreements, the protection of nature as an end in itself had found its way into international environmental regulation.

---

176 Convention between Belgium, Egypt France, India, Italy, Portugal and South Africa, Spain, Sudan, Tanzania, United Kingdom, Relative to the Preservation of Fauna and Flora in their Natural State, Annex and Protocol, signed on 8 November 1933 in London and entered into force on 14 January 1936, 172 LNTS 241 (No. 3995).

177 ibid, Art 1.

178 ibid, Art 3.

179 ibid, Art 4.

180 See: Boysen (n 158,) 49.

181 Convention on Nature Protection and Wild Life Preservation in the Western Hemisphere, signed on 12 October 1940 in Washington and entered into force 1942, 161 UNTS 193 (No. 485).

182 ibid, Art II.

183 ibid, Art.III.

184 ibid, Art IV.

185 Art XX lit b, General Agreement on Tariffs and Trade (GATT), signed on 30 October 1947 in Geneva and entered into force on 1 January 1948, 55 UNTS 187 (No. 814).

186 ibid, Art XX li. g.

4.5 *The Role of Participation Procedures in Early International Agreements*

There are few instances which evidence the existence of participation procedures in early international environmental agreements. If procedures exist, they mostly address either indigenous, ancestral or small scale fishing or hunting rights and exempt the respective communities from the protection schemes established by the agreements. The following examples may illustrate this: already the Pacific Fur Seals Arbitration foresaw an exemption for indigenous populations from the protection regimen established in the award.[187] Also the Convention Respecting Measures for the Preservation and Protection of the Fur Seals in the North Pacific Ocean of 1911 allowed for exceptional hunting by indigenous populations, with traditional measures (canoes) etc.[188] Likewise, the International Convention for the Regulation of Whaling also included an exception for "aborigines dwelling on the coasts of the territories of the High Contracting Parties".[189] Those aborigines were permitted to whale given that they only utilized "native craft propelled by oars or sails",[190] did not carry firearms, were not employed by other persons, and were not contracted to whale by third persons.[191] Finally, the Spitzbergen Treaty foresaw certain hunting privileges for occupiers of law with recognised title to that land.[192]

Sometimes, participation was also deliberately non-existent, although there clearly were communities, which should have been involved either the

187 RIAAA (N 113), 271, Art 8. "The regulations contained in the preceding articles shall not apply to Indians dwelling on the coasts of the territory of the United States or of Great Britain, and carrying on fur seal fishing in canoes or undecked boats not transported by or used in connection with other vessels and propelled wholly by paddles, oars or sails and manned by not more than five persons each in the way hitherto practised by the Indians, provided such Indians are not in the employment of other persons and provided that, when so hunting in canoes or undecked boats, they shall not hunt fur seals outside of territorial waters under contract for the delivery of the skins to any person."

188 Convention respecting Measures for the Preservation and Protection of the Fur Seals in the North Pacific Ocean (n 120), Art 4 provides: "It is further agreed that the provisions of this Convention shall not apply to Indians, Ainos, Aleuts, or other aborigines dwelling on the coast of the waters mentioned in Article 1, who carry on pelagic sealing in canoes not transported by or used in connection with other vessels, and propelled entirely by oars, paddles or sails, and manned by not more than five persons each, in the way hitherto practiced and without the use of firearms; provided that such aborigines are not in the employment of other persons, or under contract to deliver the skins to any person."

189 International Convention for the Regulation of Whaling (n 139), Art 3.

190 ibid, Art 3, para 1.

191 ibid, Art 3, paras 2–4.

192 Treaty concerning the Archipelago of Spitsbergen (n 175).

decision-making procedures that lead to the international agreement, or in subsequent pronouncements concerning nature protection and conservation. The rules on nature reserves and nature parks are a case in point.[193] Here, rules on indigenous participation are missing, either in the negotiations, or in the agreements themselves, mostly because of the fact that those indigenous communities were either considered as a disturbing factor, or as part of the natural environment, which needed to remain as untouched as possible.[194] However, as the provisions addressing indigenous hunting rights evidence, indigenous populations were also considered an object of protection,[195] and the rules aimed to preserve their natural lifestyles. Both approaches are controversial for their colonial and presumptive approach to indigenous life.

Finally, there is no international parallel to the institutionalised protection schemes developed for dams and dikes at national levels. Although there was an increasing number of international treaties which foresaw institutionalised protection and preservation of nature and natural resources, through international commissions, or trustees like Norway, those commissions and frameworks only enabled the recognition of the interests of states parties to the relevant agreement. They did not include rules that enabled participation of communities or individuals affected by their decisions.

5 Conclusion

Historical international agreements contain a number of elements and considerations associated with and identified as sustainability or sustainable development in the Brundtland report. They show that sustainability or sustainable development, is not a concept which was born at the time of writing of the report. Sustainability, or sustainable development, has a long history in national and international rules on resource preservation and protection and nature protection. Even the term "sustained" was used in international agreements long before the report. As others have shown in their assessments of sustainability or sustainable development at the national levels, the chapter demonstrated that sustainability also transpires from early international rules dealing with resource and species preservation. In particular, it is central to rules that address either their future availability or existence, establishing and

193 Bont (n 94).
194 ibid, 231 ff.
195 ibid.

prohibitions and bans, addressing and preventing harm, or defining protected areas, establishing protection schemes, or international institutions concerned with those tasks. The chapter showed, nonetheless, that rules and regulations associated with sustainability have evolved over time. Whereas early rules primarily addressed the anthropocentric aim of making natural resources available for future human use, later protection also aimed to protect nature for its inherent worth, and therefore included more ecocentric considerations. However, the chapter also highlighted, that even more ecocentric considerations can be problematic. Moreover, due to their select rules and scope of application, they fail to embrace more holistic, or adequate protections of nature and the worlds biosphere.

Despite those early traces of sustainability, the early international environmental agreements scrutinised in this chapter fall short of rules that precede the particular role and importance of participation, which the Brundtland report outlines. Given the scarce rules associated with participation, early international environmental agreements predating the report could not have served as a blueprint for the particular role that the report foresaw for participation in sustainability. Thus, further research must identify the whereabouts of the particular connection of sustainability and participation, which the report evinces.

Bibliography

Bilgenroth-Barke H, *Kriminalität und Zahlungsmoral im 16. Jahrhundert* (Edition Ruprecht 2010).

Bongartz J, 'Miszellen. Zur Geschichte der Dürener Papierindustrie' (1904) 78(jg) Annalen des Historischen Vereins für den Niederrhein 142.

Bont R de, '" Primitives" and Protected Areas: International Conservation and the" Naturalization" of Indigenous People, ca.1910–1975' (2015) 76(2) Journal of the History of Ideas 215.

Boysen S, *Die postkoloniale Konstellation: Natürliche Ressourcen und das Völkerrecht der Moderne* (Jus Publicum Band 296, Mohr Siebeck 2021).

Braig J, 'Whaling' (2013) 2013 Max Planck Encyclopedia of Public International Law.

Brunnée J, 'Procedure and Substance in International Environmental Law' [2020] Publications of The Hague Academy of International Law 75.

Cancik P, *Verwaltung und Öffentlichkeit in Preußen: Kommunikation durch Publikation und Beteiligungsverfahren im Recht der Reformzeit* (Mohr Siebeck 2007).

Cancik P, 'Die Erfindung der Beteiligung im Verwaltungsverfahren' in Wolfgang Hoffmann-Riem (ed), *Innovation und Recht – Recht und Innovation* (Mohr Siebeck 2016).

Caradonna J, *Sustainability: A history* (First paperback edition, Oxford University Press 2014// 2016).

Carlowitz HC von, *Sylvicvltvra Oeconomica: Oder Haußwirthliche Nachricht und Naturmäßige Anweisung Zur Wilden Baum-Zucht Nebst Gründlicher Darstellung, Wie zu förderst durch Göttliches Benedeyen dem allenthalben und insgemein einreissenden Grossen Holz-Mangel, Vermittelst Säe-Pflantz- und Versetzung vielerhand Bäume zu prospiciren, auch also durch Anflug und Wiederwachs des so wohl guten und schleunig anwachsend, ... Alles zu nothdürfftiger Versorgung des Hauß-Bau-Brau-Berg- und Schmeltz-Wesens, und wie eine immerwährende Holtz-Nutzung, Land und Leuten, auch jedem Hauß-Wirthe zuunschätzbaren grossen Auffnehmen, pfleglich und füglich zu erziehlen und einzuführen, Worbey zugleich eine gründliche Nachricht von den in Churfl. Sächß. Landen Gefundenen Turff Dessen Natürliche Beschaffenheit, grossen Nutzen, Gebrauch und nützlichen Verkohlung* (Braun 1713).

Coomer JC, 'Introduction: The nature of the Quest for a Sustainable Society' in James C Coomer (ed), *Quest for a sustainable society: Woodlands Conference on Growth Policy* (Pergamon Press 1979).

Coomer (ed), *Quest for a sustainable society: Woodlands Conference on Growth Policy* (Pergamon Press 1979).

Du Pisani JA, 'Sustainable development–historical roots of the concept' (2006) 3(2) Environmental Sciences 83.

Galle PH, 'Protected existence; characteristic legal features concerning water control during the Middle Ages in the south-west Netherlands and main elements in the history of dike management in this area (1200–1963)' [1963] Beveiligd bestaan; grondtrekken van het middeleeuwse waterstaatsrecht in Zuid-West Nederland en hoofdlijnen van de geschiedenis van het dijksbeheer in dit gebied (1200–1963) 1963, 372 pp.

Gehne K, 'Historische Grundlagen des Nachhaltigkeitsbegriffs' in Wolfgang Kahl (ed), *Nachhaltigkeit als Verbundbegriff* (Recht der nachhaltigen Entwicklung vol 2. Mohr Siebeck 2008).

Grober U, 'Modewort mit tiefen Wurzeln - Kleine Begriffsgeschichte von "sustainability" und "Nachhaltigkeit"' [2003] Jahrbuch Ökologie 167.

Grober U, *Deep roots - a conceptual history of 'sustainable development' (Nachhaltigkeit)* (gGmbH, Wissenschaftszentrum Berlin für Sozialforschung tr 2007-002, DEU; Berlin 2007).

Handl G and others, 'The environment: International rights and responsibilities' (1980) 74 Proceedings of the Annual Meeting (American Society of International Law) 223.

Heine G, 'Umweltbezogenes Recht im Mittelalter' in Bernd Herrmann (ed), *Umwelt in der Geschichte: Beiträge zur Umweltgeschichte* (Kleine Vandenhoeck-Reihe vol 1544. Vandenhoeck & Ruprecht 1989).

Hughes D, *An Environmental History of the World* (Routledge 2001).

Hughes D, *Environmental Problems of the Greeks and Romans* (Johns Hopkins University Press 2014).

Innes JL, 'Sustainable forest management - from concept to practice' in John L Innes and Anna V Tikina (eds), *Sustainable forest management: From concept to practice* (The Earthscan forest library, First published. Routledge an imprint of the Taylor & Francis Group earthscan from Routledge 2017).

Jevons WS, *The Coal Question: An Inquiry Concerning the Progress of the Nation, and the Probable Exhaustion of our Coal Mines* (vol 69, 2nd edn, Macmillan 1866).

Klippel D and Otto M, 'Nachhaltigkeit und Begriffsgeschichte' in Wolfgang Kahl (ed), *Nachhaltigkeit als Verbundbegriff* (Recht der nachhaltigen Entwicklung vol 2. Mohr Siebeck 2008).

Malthus TR, *First Essay on Population* (Macmillan 1798, reprinted 1926).

Meadows DH, *The limits to growth: A report for the Club of Rome's project on the predicament of mankind* (A Potomac Associates book, 12th edn, Universe Books 1973).

Mebratu D, 'Sustainability and sustainable development: historical and conceptual review' (1998) 18(6) Environmental Impact Assessment Review 493.

Mitcham C, 'The concept of sustainable development: its origins and ambivalence' (1995) 17(3) Technology in society 311.

Ordway SH, 'Possible Limits of Raw-Material Consumption' in Robin, Libby, 1956- (ed), *The Future of Nature: Documents of Global Change/ edited by Libby Robin, Sverker Sörlin, Paul Warde* (New Haven: Yale University Press, [2013] 2013).

Radkau J, *Natur und Macht: Eine Weltgeschichte der Umwelt* (Beck 2000).

Robb CAR, *International Environmental Law Reports: Early Decisions* (International Environmental Law Reports 1, Cambridge University Press 1999).

Robin L, 1956- (ed), *The Future of Nature: Documents of Global Change/ edited by Libby Robin, Sverker Sörlin, Paul Warde* (New Haven: Yale University Press, [2013] 2013).

Rossi CR, 'A unique international problem: The Svalbard Treaty, equal enjoyment, and terra nullius: Lessons of territorial temptation from history' (2016) 15 Washington University Global Studies Law Review 93.

Sand PH, 'Introduction' in Peter H Sand (ed), *The history and origin of international environmental law* (The international library of law and the environment vol 1. Elgar 2015).

Sand PH (ed), *The history and origin of international environmental law* (The international library of law and the environment 1, Elgar 2015).

Schliephake C, Sojc N and Weber G, 'Einleitung' in Christopher Schliephake, Natascha Sojc and Gregor Weber (eds), *Nachhaltigkeit in der Antike: Diskurse, Praktiken, Perspektiven* (Geographica Historica vol 42. Franz Steiner Verlag 2020).

Schliephake C (eds), *Nachhaltigkeit in der Antike: Diskurse, Praktiken, Perspektiven* (Geographica Historica 42, Franz Steiner Verlag 2020).

Stromer von Reichenbach, '600 Jahre Nadelwaldsaat, die Leistung des Peter Stromer von Nürnberg' 1968 Die Reichswälder bei Nürnberg, aus der Geschichte des ältesten Kunstforstes 25.

Tello-Aragay E and Jover-Avellà G, 'Economic History and the Environment: New Questions, Approaches and Methodologies' in Mauro Agnoletti (ed), *The basic environmental history* (Environmental history Volume 4. Springer 2014).

Teubner G (ed), *Dilemmas of Law in the Welfare State* (de Gruyter 1988).

Wiethölter R, 'Materialization and Proceduralization in Modern Law' in Gunther Teubner (ed), *Dilemmas of Law in the Welfare State* (de Gruyter 1988).

Wiethölter R, 'Proceduralization Of The Category Of Law' (2011) 12(1) German Law Journal 465.

Zirnstein G, Ökologie und Umwelt in der Geschichte (Ökologie und Wirtschaftsforschung Bd. 14, 2. erw. und überarbeitete Aufl. Metropolis-Verlag 1996).

CHAPTER 2

Re-imagining Participation in the Anthropocene: The Potential of the Rights of Nature Paradigm

Paola Villavicencio-Calzadilla and Louis Kotzé

1 Introduction

The Anthropocene inaugurates a new regulatory reality that requires a fundamental rethink of how our socio-regulatory institutions facilitate participation (and by implication representation) in the numerous governance processes that affect all constituents of a vulnerable living order, and which includes both human and non-human beings. While numerous laws at the international, regional and domestic levels laudably offer humans an opportunity to have a say in the environmental governance processes that affect their health and wellbeing, these laws, by their purpose and design, are predominantly anthropocentric and exclusively aimed at promoting human interests.[1] The legal means to facilitate participation in environmental governance therefore remain, on balance, mostly geared towards promoting human interests and to facilitating human representation in these processes. The Anthropocene's deepening socio-ecological dilemma exists,[2] in part, precisely because we have not sufficiently cared for a vulnerable human *and* non-human world.[3]

Our basic proposal is that the hitherto ignored voices of the non-human world and its interests must be more fully present and represented in our anthropocentric socioregulatory institutions. The Anthropocene, therefore, urges an opening up of the anthropocentrically embedded notion of participation in law and governance processes to also include more-than-humans, if law and governance is to more fully respond to the differentially distributed vulnerabilities of the *entire* living order, including non-human vulnerability. This could be accomplished through the rights of nature paradigm. This

1 See, for an overview, Thomas Beierle, *Democracy in Practice: Public Participation in Environmental Decisions* (Routledge 2002).

2 A dilemma that has itself been created as a result of predatory forms of anthropocentric development that law facilitates. See Louis Kotzé, 'International Environmental Law and the Anthropocene's Energy Dilemma' (2019) 36 EPLJ 437.

3 Clive Hamilton, 'The Anthropocene as Rupture' (2016) 3 The Anthropocene Review 93.

paradigm embraces and responds to the concerns, rights, needs and interests of the non-human world. While there are several examples of rights of nature provisions emerging around the world, it is perhaps most clearly evident in Latin American countries.

In this chapter we make out a case in support of opening up the notion of participation to also include within its strict anthropocentric remit the concerns of non-humans, by drawing on the rights of nature paradigm.[4] We do so, first, by briefly reflecting on the new socio-ecological reality of the Anthropocene, its deepening socio-ecological crisis, and its multiple patterns of differentially distributed vulnerability, which we believe collectively demand better care for the non-human world. We then interrogate why a rights of nature based approach could be a viable option, in theory, to extend participation opportunities to the non-human world. The next part analyses several examples from Latin American countries where rights of nature provisions are being used, or at least have the potential to be used, to facilitate participation of the non-human world in the governance processes that affect their health, integrity and wellbeing. Our discussion shows that new ways to enable participation for non-humans in the context of rights of nature are mostly facilitated through innovative measures that enable humans to act as guardians and representatives of nature in formal law and governance processes. While these measures have their own limitations and pitfalls, they hold out considerable promise for law and governance to offer the non-human world better protection in the Anthropocene epoch.

2 The Anthropocene's Vulnerable Living Order[5]

Humans are pushing the earth system into an unpredictable and unstable state. We have left the Holocene epoch – a relatively harmonious interglacial

4 Other related studies focus, among others, on how the rights of nature paradigm could counter the stifling hegemonic closures and oppression of the vulnerable living order that are being occasioned by the neoliberal sustainable development principle in international environmental law. See eg, Louis Kotzé and Sam Adelman, 'Environmental Law and the Unsustainability of Sustainable Development: A Tale of Disenchantment and of Hope' (2022) Law & Critique, <https://doi.org/10.1007/s10978-022-09323-4> last accessed 12 September 2022.

5 This part draws on Louis Kotzé, 'The Anthropocene, Earth System Vulnerability and Socio-ecological Injustice in an Age of Human Rights' (2019) 10 JHRE 62.

state – and are entering the Anthropocene; a new geological epoch.[6] As a trope, the Anthropocene illuminates the acute socio-ecological decay that we now observe. Weather patterns are changing and extreme weather events are occurring more frequently and causing vast disruptions and displacement; biodiversity is lost at an unprecedented rate and species are becoming extinct; soil, water and air pollution is rampant, evidenced by global plastics pollution; and deadly zoonic diseases, such as Covid-19 that are caused by improper human interference in human-animal relationships, are on the rise.[7] These intertwined ecological disruptions impact an increasingly vulnerable living order (which is itself interconnected and interdependent) and they contribute to exacerbate an uneven world order that is characterized by continuing "forms of eco-violence, economic predation and the unparalleled imposition of precarity on humans and non-humans alike".[8]

The Anthropocene trope abandons the idea that the Earth "somehow provides a stable ground on which the social or human world is constructed",[9] and instead exposes the extraordinary degree of planetary harm that has historically been caused, is currently being caused, and will be caused in future, by some powerful humans.[10] In doing so, the Anthropocene trope clearly reveals the vulnerability of the entire living order: we (humans and non-humans) are all vulnerable in the Anthropocene. We are vulnerable because of oppressive forms of human mastery that are exercised by some privileged, hierarchically superior, humans at the expense of an oppressed human and non-human world on which humans depend to sustain an unsustainable neoliberal growth-without-limits metabolism that feeds of a vulnerable living order.[11]

6 Will Steffen, Paul J Crutzen and John R McNeill, 'The Anthropocene: Are Humans Now Overwhelming the Great Forces of Nature?' (2007) 36 Ambio 614.

7 See, among others, United Nations Environment Programme (UNEP), 'Global Environment Outlook 6: Healthy Planet Healthy People' (UNEP 2019), https://wedocs.unep.org/handle/20.500.11822/27539;jsessionid=6397789F9F41D2F33A1D6791D926ECC0 last accessed 28 March 2022.

8 Anna Grear, 'Legal Imaginaries and the Anthropocene: "Of" and "For"' (2020) 31 Law & Critique 351.

9 Gerard Delanty and Aurea Mota, 'Governing the Anthropocene: Agency, Governance, Knowledge' (2017) 20 EJST9.

10 Frank Biermann, '"Earth System Governance" as a Crosscutting Theme of Global Change Research' (2007) 17 Global Environmental Change 326.

11 Sam Adelman, 'The Sustainable Development Goals, Anthropocentrism and Neoliberalism' in Louis Kotzé and Duncan French (eds), *Sustainable Development Global Goals: Law, Theory and Implementation* (Edward Elgar 2018).

The Anthropocene's crisis of human hierarchy enables us to see that its differentially distributed patterns of vulnerability do not exclusively apply to humans, but also to non-humans.[12] The prevailing view has been that:

> The embodied existence of individuals is, to a large extent, encompassed by vulnerability. While our embodied existence has generally been viewed as coterminous with the surrounding biophysical environment, the conceptualization of vulnerability has most often focused on human susceptibility to external harms posed by our biophysical or social environments.[13]

Harris elaborates that "[H]umans are dependent not only on one another but [also] on a series of trans-human systems, and this interdependence is a source of resilience and vulnerability".[14] In this view, "humans are vulnerable not only because they age, become ill, and die, but because their survival depends on complex macro- and micro-ecologies — all of which are, in turn, vulnerable to harm".[15] The Anthropocene trope therefore illuminates the "agentic entanglement [of humans] with a planetary field of radically distributed, multiplicitous agentic forces".[16] The agentic entanglement that characterizes the Anthropocene means that the 'fate of humanity', will be determined as much by planetary integrity and the extent to which a stable earth system can support life, as it will be by humanity itself. In short, our vulnerability, while *differentiated* because not everyone is equally vulnerable, is ultimately also *shared*.

Departing from such an 'enlarged' notion of a differentially distributed shared vulnerability, we propose 'earth system vulnerability' as the context for rethinking participation of non-humans in the Anthropocene. Earth system vulnerability is a concept that potentially embraces the social-human *and* ecological elements of a disrupted earth system, explicitly emphasising the stakes of the Anthropocene and the fact that human vulnerability is ontologically intertwined with non-human vulnerability.[17] Because it relates

12 For example, Martha Fineman, 'The Vulnerable Subject: Anchoring Equality in the Human Condition' (2008) 20 Yale JL & Feminism 1.

13 Huey-li Li, 'Rethinking Vulnerability in the Age of Anthropocene: Toward Ecologizing Education' (2017) 67 Educational Theory 435.

14 Angela Harris, 'Vulnerability and Power in the Age of the Anthropocene' (2014) 6 Washington and Lee Journal of Energy, Climate, and the Environment 98.

15 Ibid at 98.

16 Grear, n 8, at 358.

17 Anna Grear, 'The Vulnerable Living Order: Human Rights and the Environment in a Critical and Philosophical Perspective' (2011) 2 JHRE 23.

to human-social and ecological elements and considerations, an all-inclusive earth system vulnerability perspective better responds to the vulnerability of non-human entities and to the interdependent nature of human-non-human systems and their shared vulnerability. This all-embracing conception of vulnerability in a planetary context means that:

> [v]ulnerability can be understood as *intrinsic* to the intercorporeality offered by [an] alternative ontology, for we can understand vulnerability as an irreducible incident of physical embodiment—and as a general condition of biotic materiality. A full emphasis upon our thoroughly incarnate materiality ... allows us to acknowledge what we share, not only with other human beings, but with the living order itself - a certain *affect-ability* emerging from biomateriality itself.[18]

The idea of earth system vulnerability dissolves cartesian dualisms and epistemologies of mastery by reconnecting humans with a hitherto externalised, submissive and compliant 'nature' that can be 'managed', shaped, exploited and used as 'resources' by promethean humans.[19] Such a recognition is occurring consequent on an awareness, that is foregrounded by the Anthropocene tope, of the power of humans in transforming the earth system and the realisation that how we use this awareness will shape planetary futures and the future of *all* life, not only our own.[20] As Dryzek says:

> The Anthropocene ... does not just amplify existing ecological concerns: it changes their content by putting humans at the centre of causal processes in the Earth system. In highlighting the vulnerability of the character of the system on which we depend to human action, it also confirms that this system is not something out there demanding limited and occasional attention. Rather, human-induced instability means this system is a key player in how human history will unfold.[21]

---

18 Ibid at 43.

19 Sam Adelman, 'Epistemologies of Mastery' in Anna Grear and Louis Kotzé (eds), *Research Handbook on Human Rights and the Environment* (Edward Elgar 2015).

20 William Clark, Paul Crutzen and Hans Schellnhuber, 'Science for Global Sustainability: Towards a New Paradigm' in Hans Schellnhuber *et al* (eds), *Earth System Analysis for Sustainability* (MIT Press 2004).

21 John Dryzek, 'Institutions for the Anthropocene: Governance in a Changing Earth System' (2016) 46 British Journal of Political Science 937.

When considered in the context of the Anthropocene, earth system vulnerability "prompts new calls for thought and action that can imagine different relationships between geologic time, the cultural logics of capital and accumulation, and the ontological realities of our species-being".[22] These new "calls for thought and action" are also deeply *ethical*, as Burdon suggests:

> there has never been a time when human history and the history of the Earth were so intertwined. Attempts to grapple with this insight cannot be resolved through scientific questioning alone and ought to give rise to an appreciation of the uniqueness and integrity of each component of the Earth system (humans included) and the world as a relational whole.[23]

The implications of such a realization and the need for new imaginations have the potential to significantly disrupt law, and particularly environmental law. Among others, human law will arguably have to be more sensitive and responsive to the shared vulnerability of the entire living order. One way to do so is to discard assumptions of human mastery that anthropocentric law still underwrites.[24] As we will show below, this endeavour lies precisely at the heart of the rights of nature paradigm.

3 Rights of Nature: A Non-anthropocentric Approach to Address the Socio-ecological Crisis

We have argued above that law will have to be more focused on protecting non-humans, not because such an endeavour would benefit humans, but because it must adhere to an ethical obligation to address earth system vulnerability in its widest sense by extending juridical care to law's non-traditional subjects. We already see encouraging signs of what is possible in this regard emerging around the globe in the form of rights of nature in several countries.[25] Mostly stemming from indigenous laws and cosmovisions, and their altogether more

---

22 Donna Houston, 'Crisis is Where we Live: Environmental Justice for the Anthropocene' (2013) 10 Globalizations 439.

23 Peter Burdon, 'Rethinking Global Ethics in the Anthropocene' in Peter Burdon, Klaus Bosselmann and Kirsten Engel (eds), *The Crisis in Global Ethics and the Future of Global Governance: Fulfilling the Promise of the Earth Charter* (Edward Elgar 2019).

24 Shawkat Alam *et al* (eds), *International Environmental Law and the Global South* (CUP 2015).

25 Eg Roderick Nash, *The Rights of Nature: A History of Environmental Ethics* (University of Wisconsin Press 1989).

embracing onto-epistemologies of care, such alternative framings offer valuable examples of how law could discard the human as its main concern while at once being more sensitive to the vulnerability concerns of the entire living order. Law that embraces the vulnerability concerns of non-humans could offer possible pathways to counter the destructive power of privileged humans that exploit the non-human world for selfish gain. This could facilitate a new understanding of relationality, of "co-becoming in a relational world", that is based on the premise that "Not only are all beings – human, animal, plant, process, thing or affect – vital and sapient with their own knowledge and law, but their very being is constituted through relationships that are constantly re-generated."[26]

While in some countries groundbreaking legislation has been adopted for the recognition and protection of rights of nature, in others an emerging jurisprudence built on ecocentric rightsbased approaches to environmental protection is changing the legal status of non-human living entities such as rivers, mountains and forests. As a result, nature has been recognised in several countries as a legal subject with enforceable rights.[27] This paradigm shift confirms that non-human living entities have intrinsic value and can no longer be viewed as objects of property, or mere service and resource providers; they must instead be considered as vulnerable subjects of law that deserve special legal protection that could also be facilitated through rights. Rights of nature are especially flourishing in several Latin American countries such as Ecuador, Bolivia, and Colombia, which have all recognized nature as a subject of rights that is entitled to legal protection. For the purpose of this chapter, we will focus on these three countries.

Ecuador is at the forefront in terms of promoting and recognising rights of nature at the constitutional level.[28] In 2008, the country adopted a new constitution that incorporates indigenous worldviews and that recognizes the inextricable link between human beings and nature. By accounting for the need to (re)define the humannature dichotomy and to move away from an anthropocentric orientation of law generally and of rights specifically, the Constitution embraces an ecocentric ontology and extends its protection of

26 Bawaka Country *et al*, 'Co-becoming Bawaka: Towards a Relational Understanding of Place/Space' (2016) 40 Progress in Human Geography 455.

27 For a summary of those countries, see Harmony with Nature United Nations, 'Rights of Nature Law and Policy' (*Harmony with Nature*, date unknown), www.harmonywithnatureun.org/rightsOfNature/ last accessed 28 March 2022.

28 For a thorough analysis of the Ecuadorian case, see: Louis Kotzé and Paola Villavicencio Calzadilla, 'Somewhere between Rhetoric and Reality: Environmental Constitutionalism and the Rights of Nature in Ecuador' (2017) 6 TEL 401.

rights in favour of nature or Mother Earth (*Pachamama*), which is now considered a legal subject and holder of enforceable rights. The Ecuadorian Constitution, which also recognizes a traditional environmental human right,[29] was the first constitutional text in the world to formally adopt a rights of nature provision. The Constitution provides that "[n]ature shall be the subject of those rights that the Constitution recognizes for it" and affirms that nature has the inherent rights to exist, to maintain and regenerate its vital cycles, structures, functions and evolutionary processes, as well as to be restored in case of damage, independently of any damage (and compensation) owed to persons who may have been affected.[30] According to the Constitution, these rights are of "equal importance" when compared to other (human) rights.[31]

Bolivia does not offer an explicit constitutional provision providing for rights of nature in the same way as Ecuador does.[32] However, the Bolivian Constitution adopted in 2009 provides for an environmental right that includes non-humans that

> everyone has the right to a healthy, protected, and balanced environment. The exercise of this right must be granted to individuals and collectives of present and future generations, as well as to *other living things*, so they may develop in a normal and permanent way.[33]

Consequent on this provision, the formal recognition of nature as a bearer of rights was achieved through subsequent legislative reforms, notably with the adoption of two statutes that are rooted in indigenous thought: (i) the Law of the Rights of Mother Earth (*Ley de Derechos de la Madre Tierra*),[34] and (ii) the Framework Law of Mother Earth and Integral Development for Living Well (*Ley Marco de la Madre Tierra y Desarrollo Integral para Vivir Bien*).[35] The Law of the Rights of Mother Earth enumerates specific rights to which nature is entitled and the obligations and duties of the State, and society more broadly,

---

29 Constitution of the Republic of Ecuador (Constitución Política de la República del Ecuador) [Ecuador], 20 October 2008, Official Registry No 449, at art 14.

30 Ibid at arts 10, 71 and 72.

31 Ibid at art 11(6).

32 Eg Paola Villavicencio Calzadilla and Louis Kotzé, 'Living in Harmony with Nature? A Critical Appraisal of the Rights of Mother Earth in Bolivia' (2018) 7 TEL 397.

33 Constitution of the Plurinational State of Bolivia (Constitución Política del Estado (CPE) Plurinacional de Bolivia) [Bolivia], 7 February 2009, at art 33 (own emphasis).

34 Law 071 of the Rights of Mother Earth (Ley de Derechos de la Madre Tierra, Ley N° 71) 21 December 2010, Gaceta Oficial de Bolivia núm 2370, 5 págs.

35 Framework Law 300 of Mother Earth and Integral Development for Living Well (Ley Marco de la Madre Tierra y Desarrollo Integral para Vivir Bien, Ley N° 300) 15 October 2012, Gaceta Oficial, núm 431NEC, 61 págs.

to ensure respect for these rights. Thus, Mother Earth,[36] who takes on the character of a collective subject of public interest,[37] has the rights to life and diversity, to maintain and regenerate her life cycles and structures, and to be restored.[38] The *Framework Law of Mother Earth and Integral Development for Living Well* reaffirms nature's rights and highlights the importance to promote an integral form of development in harmony with Mother Earth. This is important because this law lays the foundation for the design of environmental policies in Bolivia and serves as a framework law under which other sectoral laws, such as those dealing with energy or mining, must operate. Moreover, this law enjoys preferential application over other laws dealing with natural resources and their extraction, and it must guide sectoral legislative developments at all levels of the state (national, departmental and municipal).

The case of Colombia shows that rights of nature can be recognised not only exclusively through legislative channels, but also through judicial endeavours. Unlike Ecuador and Bolivia, no legislation on rights of nature has been adopted in Colombia so far. However, tribunals in the country have ruled in favour of non-human entities through groundbreaking decisions. This has changed these entities' legal status by recognising them as rights-bearing subjects, and it is setting important precedents for rights of nature in Colombia and around the world. In 2016, for example, the Colombian Constitutional Court drew international attention when it issued a landmark judgment recognizing a river – the Atrato River – and its basin and tributaries as a "subject of rights" (*sujeto de derechos*); a status traditionally reserved for natural persons and legal entities.[39] The decision was issued on the basis of a constitutional 'tutela' injunction (*acción de tutela*) that was brought in 2015 by a nongovernmental organization and several indigenous communities against various agencies of the Colombian government. They sought to obtain an order from the court for the effective protection of their fundamental rights, which were allegedly

36 Mother Earth is defined as "a dynamic living system comprising an indivisible community of all living systems and living organisms, interrelated, interdependent and complementary, which share a common destiny" (Law 071 of the Rights of Mother Earth, n 34, at art 3).

37 Ibid at art 5.

38 Ibid at art 7.

39 See *Tierra Digna y otros v Presidencia de la República y otros*, Colombian Constitutional Court, ruling T-622 of 10 November 2016, Expediente T-5.016.242 (full text in Spanish at <www.corteconstitucional.gov.co/relatoria/2016/t-622-16.htm> last accessed 15 December 2021). Since this decision, various Colombian courts and tribunals have also recognised other natural entities – such as rivers and the Amazon rainforest – as subjects of rights along the same lines as those given to the Atrato River. See, for instance, on the Amazon, Paola Villavicencio Calzadilla, 'A Paradigm Shift in Courts' View on Nature: The Atrato River and Amazon Basin Cases in Colombia' (2019) 15 LEAD Journal 49.

being infringed by intensified illegal mining activities in the vicinity of the river and its tributaries that they alleged affected its ecological integrity and the well-being of the populations that depend on the river.

Following unsuccessful first instance and appeal rulings, the plaintiffs took the case to the Constitutional Court for review. Acknowledging the vulnerability of the river and its destruction because of pollution, the Constitutional Court ruled in favour of the plaintiffs to guarantee the effective enjoyment of their rights. By adopting an ecocentric and biocultural legal interpretation approach, it recognised the Atrato River not as an object to be used for the benefit of humans, but as a legal subject with concrete rights. In this way, considering the river as a living entity that sustains other forms of life (and indigenous cultures more generally), the Court initiated a paradigm shift by granting the Atrato River specific rights, including the right to protection, conservation, maintenance and restoration. Moreover, with the view to ensuring that the river's rights are actually guaranteed in practice, the Court formulated a number of orders to enforce its decision, including the elaboration of action plans for the restoration and conservation of the river.[40] At the time of writing, some progress had been made in complying with the Court's orders; however, they have not yet been fully implemented.[41]

Collectively considered, these ground-breaking developments demonstrate the increasing relevance of the rights of nature paradigm to enhance protection of an increasingly vulnerable non-human world. At least on paper, they provide an opportunity to move away from structurally deeply embedded neoliberal and anthropocentric paradigms and, ultimately, to provide a different legal and governance context that can transform the human-nature relationship on the basis of non-anthropocentric world views. Importantly though, these innovative legal developments neither ensure the immediate and effective protection of nature and people, nor do they guarantee ongoing and unimpaired well-being, or prompt comprehensive restoration. This is clear in the light of the "Latin American paradox", in terms of which unabated mining, hydrocarbon activities, and monoculture exports continue to fund social spending and public works despite rights of nature provisions being recognised by some Latin

40 Ibid.

41 See, for instance, Comité de Seguimiento, 'Quinto informe de seguimiento Sentencia T-622 de 2016' (March 2020), <uploads-ssl.webflow.com/5f330f48105fd08d006005e0/5f6acb5346e543414fc9e93a_QUINTO%20INFORME%20DE%20SEGUIMIENTO%20CC%20-TAC%2003-2020.pdf> last accessed 28 March 2022; and Ambiente y Ciencia, 'Ríos, sujetos de derecho: lento avance' (25 January 2020), <elnuevosiglo.com.co/articulos/01-2020-rios-sujetos-de-derecho-lento-avance> last accessed 15 December 2021.

American legal systems.[42] So, while optimistic about the potential of rights of nature, we are also aware that their implementation in Latin America has been contradictory and uneven and that one must guard against romanticising indigenous onto-epistemologies.[43] We must instead be aware that "the expression of the principles and rights of Buen Vivir [living well] should not be confused with their implementation and attainment, for the latter requires much more time".[44] In essence this means that when rights of nature are recognized, it is important that such rights are also deliberately enforced. Below we reflect on how the operationalisation of laws and court decisions recognising rights of nature, including pathways to ensure the representation and 'participation' of nature, still face multiple challenges, but also opportunities.

4 Letting Nature Participate: Who Speaks for Nature?

Although subject to criticism, as we have shown above, granting rights to nature is generally considered to be an innovative way than can help humans to reenvision our relationship with non-human living entities based on the understanding that non-humans are legal subjects with inherent rights that have to be protected for the sake of protection because it is the right thing to do; *not* because of nature's economic or instrumental value for humans. To this end, the rights of nature paradigm might also present a viable opportunity to extend participation opportunities to the non-human world through a range of innovative legal and related political mechanisms. Under traditional environmental and other legal arrangements, humans – individually and collectively – are able to participate in governance processes and institutions, and can only make *indirect* arguments in support of protecting nature. As principle 10 of the Rio Declaration states: "[E]nvironmental issues are best handled with participation of all concerned *citizens*, at the relevant level."[45] Clearly, the

42 Miriam Lang, 'Prologue: Crisis of Civilisation and Challenges for the Left' in Miriam Lang and Dunia Mokrani (eds), *Beyond Development: Alternative Visions from Latin America* (Transnational Institute/Rosa Luxemburg Foundation 2013).

43 Eija Ranta, '*Buen Vivir* as Transformative Alternative to Capitalist Coloniality' in SA Hamed Hosseini *et al* (eds), *The Routledge Handbook of Transformative Global Studies* (Routledge 2020).

44 Unai Villalba, '*Buen Vivir* vs Development: A Paradigm Shift in the Andes?' (2013) 34 TWQ 1427.

45 United Nations, 'Report of the United Nations Conference on Environment and Development' (Rio de Janeiro 3–14 June 1992), General Assembly, United Nations publications (Vol. I), U.N. Doc. A/CONF.151/26, 31 ILM (1992) 874 (Rio Declaration) (own emphasis).

extant legal provisions embrace a people-centred orientation and, therefore, the potential interests of nature are seen primarily through the lens of competing interests, values, needs and rights (between humans *inter se* to gain as much access to limited 'natural resources' as possible, and between humans and nature). Thus, we participate in decision-making processes to protect and conserve the environment "*for us* – for the greatest good of the greatest number of human beings".[46] However, non-human living entities have intrinsic value that is much greater than the value humans assign to them; this is a core insight from the rights of nature paradigm as we have argued above.

The rights of nature paradigm opens up the traditional anthropocentric approach of participation by providing the opportunity to include the rights, needs and interests of nature, so that nature can 'participate' in the governance processes and institutions that affect her in a way that recognises that humans and non-humans "are all part of Mother Earth, an indivisible, living community of interrelated and interdependent beings with a common destiny".[47] In terms of this view, it would be beneficial for the living order if nature also had a voice and a place of her own in governance, judicial and legislative processes that relate to activities that threaten or affect her. This would certainly also enable the full enjoyment of the entire range of legal protection benefits that are created by rights generally. Obviously, however, non-human entities cannot physically appear in a courtroom, nor can they 'speak' in governance processes and institutions. Our anthropocentric laws, and legal and political institutions, have not been designed to accommodate nature's participation, despite rights of nature's attempts to militate against these parochial closures and exclusions of modernist 'Western' law. This conundrum raises several questions including, at a general level: who belongs to communities of justice in the Anthropocene; and how can law address the living order's shared but differentially distributed vulnerability in the face of accelerating earth system decay and diminishing planetary integrity?[48] At a more practical level, the question is: who can speak on nature's behalf to uphold her rights, needs and interests in decision-making spaces and governance processes that affect her?

46 Christopher Stone, 'Should Trees Have Standing? Towards Legal Rights for Natural Objects' (1972) 45 S Cal L Rev 450.

47 World People's Conference on Climate Change and the Rights of Mother Earth, 'Proposal Universal Declaration of the Rights of Mother Earth', Cochabamba (Bolivia), April 2010 (PWCC, date unknown), <pwccc.wordpress.com/programa/> last accessed 30 March 2022.

48 See, generally, Joshua Gellers, 'Earth System Law and the Legal Status of Non-humans in the Anthropocene' (2021) 7 Earth System Governance 100083, <https://doi.org/10.1016/j.esg.2020.100083> last accessed 30 April 2022.

We would argue that the rights of nature paradigm potentially offers an answer to these questions by reframing the issue of participation as one of *representation* and/or *guardianship*.[49] We agree in principle that "[n]ature does not need human beings to exercise her rights to exist and to regenerate"; however, because rights of nature are still exercised within the larger domain of traditional anthropocentric 'Western' law, "if human beings destroy her, pollute her, depredate her, she will need human beings, as representatives, to demand the prohibition of entering into a contract or agreement by which a protected primary forest is to be cut down or to sue for her reparation or restoration".[50] The need for pragmatism that is responsive to the larger anthropocentric reality that 'we' (humans and non-humans) find ourselves in, is already evident in some jurisdictions. For example, in 1972 Justice William O Douglas of the Supreme Court of the United States suggested, in his dissenting opinion in *Sierra Club v Morton*, that the legitimate guardians and representatives of the non-human world are those who have an intimate relationship with it:

> The river as plaintiff speaks for the ecological unit of life that is part of it. Those people who have a meaningful relation to that body of water –whether it be a fisherman, a canoeist, a zoologist, or a logger – must be able to speak for the values which the river represents, and which are threatened with destruction.[51]

In the case of Latin American countries, such as in Ecuador, Bolivia and Colombia, a variety of practical measures are being adopted under the rights of nature approach to determine who can act and speak on behalf of nature, and take action to protect and enforce her rights, as well as what the respective roles and responsibilities of these guardians are. Although these approaches vary from one jurisdiction to another, one does observe the promising emergence of representation and guardianship processes. In particular, in terms of the understanding that the state is not, or should not be, the only entity

---

49 For the cases of Australia, New Zealand and India where legal rights were also recognized for rivers, see Erin O'Donnell and Julia Talbot-Jones, 'Creating Legal Rights for Rivers: Lessons from Australia, New Zealand, and India' (2018) 23 Ecology and Society 7, <https://doi.org/10.5751/ES-09854-230107> last accessed 30 April 2022.

50 Ramiro Ávila Santamaría, 'El Derecho de La Naturaleza: Fundamentos' in Alberto Acosta and Esperanza Martinez (eds), *La Naturaleza Con Derechos. De La Filosofía a La Política* (Ediciones Abya Yala 2011), 201 (translation by the authors).

51 Supreme Court of the United States of America, *Sierra Club v Morton*, 405 US 727 (1972) at <www.oyez.org/cases/1971/70-34> last accessed 30 April 2022.

that speaks for nature, the laws and jurisprudence on rights of nature in these countries provide for the appointment of guardians or representatives to care for, and act on behalf of, nature. We briefly reflect on some of these below.

In Ecuador, the Constitution incorporates provisions specifying who can speak for nature and participate on her behalf in decision-making processes. While providing that the State has a guardianship role in respect of the environment,[52] the Constitution allows any person – individually or collectively – to act on behalf of nature and to take action against public authorities to enforce her rights.[53] In this sense, a wide *locus standi* is recognised by the supreme law to enable anyone to represent and enforce the rights of nature, regardless of whether a direct interest exists.[54] This approach has been confirmed by the *Código Orgánico General de Procesos*,[55] which includes an entire chapter on the "representation of nature" in which it provides that any natural or legal person, group or collective, or the Ombudsman, can represent nature and call upon public authorities to enforce her rights.[56] In the case of the Ombudsman, it must carry out the protection of nature's rights *ex officio*.[57] Those representing and acting on behalf of nature can then directly revert to the Constitution to invoke protection of her rights through legal actions, notably through the constitutional protection proceeding (*Acción de Protección*).[58] It is precisely on this basis that civil society and indigenous and environmental organizations have filed several cases (admittedly with diverse results) against the government and private project developers to challenge activities; for instance, to suspend large-scale extractive projects that affect and violate nature's rights.[59]

---

52 Constitution of Ecuador, n 29, at art 399.

53 Ibid, at art 71. The same art provides that "The State shall give incentives to natural persons and legal entities and to communities to protect nature and to promote respect for all the elements comprising an ecosystem."

54 See, also Constitution of Ecuador, n 29, at arts 10, 11, and 396–97.

55 General Organic Code of Processes of the Republic of Ecuador (Código Orgánico General de Procesos (COGEP)), 22 May 2015, Official Registry No 506.

56 Ibid, at Cap II, art 38.

57 Ibid. See also Organic Law of the Ombudsman's Office (Ley Orgánica de la Defensoria del Pueblo), 6 May 2019, Official Registry No 481, at arts 2–6, 9, 22.

58 Constitution of Ecuador, n 29, at art 88. The *Acción de Protección* is a form of constitutional action which aims to ensure direct and efficient protection of the rights enshrined in the Constitution.

59 Some of these cases involved specific natural entities in the country, such as the Vilcabamba River, the Blanco and Piatúa Rivers, Paramo Tangabana, and a protected forest area Los Cedros. See Observatorio Jurídico de Derechos de la Naturaleza, 'Casos de Ecuador' (2018) <www.derechosdelanaturaleza.org.ec/casos/> last accessed 30 April 2022.

In the case of Bolivia, the Constitution establishes that it is the duty of "all Bolivians" to "protect and defend an environment suitable for the development of living beings".[60] By enshrining such a right, the Constitution recognises that "[A]ny person, in his own right or on behalf of a collective, is authorized to take legal action in defense of environmental rights, without prejudice to the obligation of public institutions to act on their own in the face of attacks on the environment."[61] Moreover, recognising that an infringement of the rights of Mother Earth constitutes an infringement of the collective and individual rights of people,[62] the relevant legislation on the rights of Mother Earth states that the exercise of the rights of nature is entrusted to "all Bolivians" who are part of "the community of beings that form Mother Earth" and establishes State responsibilities and societal duties to guarantee respect for these rights.[63] In this sense (and this was recently confirmed by the national courts),[64] the Constitution and laws on rights of nature provide for a wide *locus standi* in favour of public authorities, the Public Prosecutor's Office, the Agro-environmental Court, individuals, and groups of people directly affected by an alleged violation of nature's rights, as well as any person who has knowledge of such violations, to enforce the rights of nature.[65] These legal guardians acting on behalf of nature can, for instance, instate an *actio popularis* procedure as established by the Constitution to defend and protect the rights, needs and interests of nature.[66] Importantly, the legal framework on the rights of Mother Earth provides for the creation of a Mother Earth Ombudsman Office (*Defensoría de la Madre Tierra*), a counterpart to the Human Rights Ombudsman office. The Mother Earth Ombudsman has been granted powers of enforcement to enable it to bring proceedings before administrative and/or judicial authorities on behalf of nature to ensure her protection and the fulfilment of her rights.[67] Yet, at the time of writing, this office has not yet been created, and its structure, duties and tasks remain undefined under the relevant laws.

60 Constitution of the Plurinational State of Bolivia, n 33, at art 108.16.

61 Ibid at art 34.

62 Framework Law 300, n 35, at art 38.

63 Law 071 of the Rights of Mother Earth, n 34, at arts 6 and 8–9.

64 See, for instance, *Tribunal Agroambiental de Bolivia*, Auto Agroambiental S1ª Nº 40/2021, 5 May 2021.

65 Framework Law 300, n 35, at art 39.

66 Constitution of the Plurinational State of Bolivia, n 33, at art 34. This constitutional remedy, termed 'popular action' (*acción popular*) was created as a mechanism to protect and defend collective rights and interests, including those embraced by the environmental right and the rights of nature (see also arts 135–36).

67 Law 071 of the Rights of Mother Earth, n 34, at art 10; Framework Law 300, n 35, at arts 39.I and 52.VI.

The approach adopted by Colombia differs from Ecuador and Bolivia. The Constitutional Court, in the Atrato River decision, also issued several orders in the judgment's operative part, notably with the purpose of ensuring that the river's rights are respected and guaranteed in practice. The Court ordered that the national government, in conjunction with the indigenous communities living along the river, exercises a joint guardianship and legal representation role for the river.[68] As a consequence, the Atrato River should be legally represented by two guardians: one representative of the national government, and one representative of the river's communities.[69] In order to ensure the protection, recovery and conservation of the river, the Court also ordered the guardians to establish a Guardianship Commission (*Comisión de Guardianes del Río Atrato*)[70] that can be supported by an advisory team consisting of public, private, scientific and technical entities with knowledge of the river and its ecological processes. This Commission must develop different action plans to address threats to the integrity of the Atrato River, its tributaries and its communities.[71] In addition, the Court stated that the panel of experts that is responsible for ensuring compliance with its orders must also supervise and advise on the work of the river's guardians.[72] By appointing legal guardians who have the duty to act on behalf the river, and by facilitating institutional

68 See *Tierra Digna y otros v Presidencia de la República y otros*, n 39.

69 In 2017, the Colombian government designated the Ministry of Environment and Sustainable Development as the River's legal representative. In addition, the local communities chose fourteen representatives coming from seven community organisations to act as "community guardians" of the river. See Presidencia de la República de Colombia, 'Supreme Decree 1148' (5 July 2017) on the "community guardians" of the Atrato River, <www.guardianesatrato.co/quienes-somos> last accessed 10 December 2021.

70 The Commission of the Guardians of the Atrato River was stablished in May 2018. See Ministerio de Ambiente y Desarrollo Sostenible, 'Resolución 907 de 22 de mayo de 2018' Diario Oficial No 50.602 de 23 de mayo de 2018.

71 These plans include: (i) a decontamination plan of the Atrato River basin (Operative part pt 5); (ii) a coordinated action plan to neutralise and eliminate illegal mining in the Atrato River and its tributaries, as well as in all of the Chocó department (Operative part pt 6); (iii) an integrated action plan for traditional livelihood and food retrieval (Operative part pt 7); and, (iv) conducting toxicological and epidemiological studies in the Atrato River, its tributaries and neighbouring communities to determine the degree of contamination and the possible impact on human health (Operative part pt 8). In 2018, the Atrato River Guardianship Commission was created as a coordination space for the fulfilment of the Court's orders. It has the competency to define its own rules of procedure. See Resolución 907, n 70, at art 3.

72 The Compliance Committee, which is headed by the *Procuraduría General de la Nación* and the *Defensoría del Pueblo,* was also set up in 2017.

support and coordination to ensure the protection of its rights, needs and interest, the Court sought to address the challenges posed by the practical enforcement of rights of nature.

Several important steps have been taken to date to comply with the Court's orders. However, there is still a lack of clarity regarding the scope of the river's recognition as a subject of rights and the responsibilities (for example, in case of non-compliance) of the actors involved, especially of the legal representatives of the river. Despite attempts to provide a voice to the river through its legal guardians and attempts to promote intra and interinstitutional cooperation between these and other public and private actors, the necessary means and details to meaningfully operationalize guardianship tasks have not been provided. For instance, funding and organisational support are key to uphold the rights of nature,[73] but in this case neither the expected level of coordination between the guardians and other actors has been fully achieved, nor has additional funding to support the guardians' new duties been provided (especially in relation to indigenous communities).[74] Moreover, there has been criticism that guardians from indigenous communities were excluded from protection initiatives led by various government bodies, even though they are the people who best know the territory and the state of the river.[75] The guardians also complained about threats against them, and lack of government protection when they are threatened by armed groups and promoters of illegal agricultural and other activities in the area.[76] Environmental defenders are increasingly oppressed and criminalized, and they face stigmatisation from the government and media as they are branded "anti-development" and even "terrorists".[77] The killing of environmental defenders in Colombia (65 in 2020) remains a major and deepening concern.[78]

73 O'Donnell and Talbot-Jones, n 49, at 6–7.

74 Comité de Seguimiento, n 41.

75 Ibid at 99–100.

76 Carolina Ávila, 'Guardianes del río Atrato: amenazados e ignorados' *El Espectador* (22 April 2018), <www.elespectador.com/colombia-20/conflicto/guardianes-del-rio-atrato-amenazados-e-ignorados-article> last accessed 28 March 2022.

77 Global Witness, 'Defending Tomorrow' (*Global Witness*, 29 July 2020), <www.globalwitness.org/en/campaigns/environmental-activists/defending-tomorrow/> last accessed 15 February 2022.

78 Global Witness, 'Last Line of Defence' (*Global Witness*, 13 September 2021), <www.globalwitness.org/en/campaigns/environmental-activists/last-line-defence/> last accessed 15 February 2022.

5 Conclusion

The rights of nature paradigm that has been adopted in countries such as Ecuador, Bolivia and Colombia represents a paradigm shift in the way that we perceive and interact with the non-human world, helping us, as it does, to (re)visualize, (re)conceptualize and ultimately, to *reimagine* nature/society relations. Perhaps even more importantly, it also helps us to better appreciate how human-made laws can better protect the non-human world, not for human benefits, but *because it is the right thing to do*. One of the additional advantages of the rights of nature paradigm, is that it opens up the notions of participation and associated representation and guardianship possibilities in this respect, by extending law's protective embrace to non-human living entities so they can 'participate' in decision-making processes, mostly through innovative representation and guardianship measures provided by legal and quasi-legal arrangements.

But this approach also has its challenges. It remains unclear, for example, what the full scope of implications of recognising nature as a rights-bearing subject will be, and if these legal and jurisprudential developments will actually be able to effectively enhance participation practices for the benefit of nature. Will such recognition only be limited to a symbolic step, or will it generate the necessary thoroughgoing transformations that we need to see? Our analysis tentatively suggests that rights of nature and several practical measures such as the appointment of guardians, is only a first, but necessary, step in what will probably be a much longer process of realising a more comprehensive and effective approach to protect non-human beings.[79]

Our analysis also suggests that, while laudable, in order to be more effective, efforts to represent nature in law and governance through guardianship functions will have to address several concerns. For example, and in addition to those mentioned above, representation and guardianship duties have been entrusted to the state and other public agencies at regional or local levels, alongside indigenous communities. However, designating the state as the central guardianship authority raises doubts over its true commitment to speak on behalf of nature and to protect her rights given the extractivist policies enacted by the very same state. In these countries, as in other countries throughout Latin America, the unsustainable anthropocentric and neoliberal logic of development based on the exploitation of nature continues to be promoted,

79 In fact, despite advances in environmental legislation and institutions in Latin America, their effectiveness and efficiency are still limited. N Gligo *et al*, *La tragedia ambiental de América Latina y el Caribe* (CEPAL 2020).

and this is causing major environmental destruction and socio-ecological conflicts.[80] Deforestation also continues, with Ecuador having the highest annual deforestation rate in the region, and extractive activities and projects such as agro-industry, mega-mining, and mega-dams due to expand.[81]

Ensuring independency and impartiality of guardians, clearly defining their duties and tasks, and developing supervision and monitoring mechanisms, are key elements for nature guardianship procedures to respond to the particular needs and vulnerabilities of non-human living entities, and to continuously ensure the quality of guardianship practices. In many instances, these support mechanisms still seem to be largely absent. Governments' lack of political will also remains a concern, as the case of Bolivia suggests. More than ten years after the law created the legislative foundations for the establishment of an independent and impartial office entrusted with guardianship functions, this has not yet been achieved. Colombia for its part shows the risks that some guardians of nature, especially those from indigenous and Afro-descendant communities, face when defending nature and their territories and culture, and when they resist development projects that impact their rights and the rights of nature.

Despite these challenges, we agree with Gellers that the rights of nature paradigm holds out considerable promise to "force humanity to reconsider the range of ideas eligible for inclusion in legal systems and the kinds of entities deserving of legal personhood and rights. The prospects for achieving socioecological justice may depend upon this kind of ontologically broad and epistemologically diverse alteration of the status quo."[82] In our view, rights of nature remains one of the most viable, and certainly *exciting*, prospects to extend law's care to the non-human world, and to draw non-humans within the protective embrace of the law through innovative ways to facilitate meaningful 'participation' through representation and guardianship roles.

---

80 Ibid.

81 El Universo, 'Cuáles son los 5 desafíos de Ecuador para el medioambiente en 2020' (17 January 2020) <www.eluniverso.com/noticias/2020/01/17/nota/7694943/cuales-son-desafios-ecuador-medioambiente-2020/> last accessed 15 February 2022; Santiago Valenzuela and Pamela Sanabria Cuervo, 'Una Selva que arde' (*El Tiempo*, date unknown), <www.eltiempo.com/vida/amazonia-deforestacion-mineria-agricultura-y-cultivos-ilicitos-577536> last accessed 15 February 2022; Fernando Chávez Virreira, 'Día Mundial del Medio Ambiente: Bolivia y América Latina necesitan repensar los modelos de desarrollo' (*Página Siete*, 6 June 2021) <www.paginasiete.bo/ideas/2021/6/6/dia-mundial-del-medio-ambiente-bolivia-america-latina-necesitan-repensar-los-modelos-de-desarrollo-297066.html> last accessed 15 February 2022.

82 Gellers, n 48.

Bibliography

Adelman S, 'Epistemologies of Mastery' in Grear A and Kotzé L (eds), *Research Handbook on Human Rights and the Environment* (Edward Elgar 2015).

Adelman S, 'The Sustainable Development Goals, Anthropocentrism and Neoliberalism' in Kotzé L and French D (eds), *Sustainable Development Global Goals: Law, Theory and Implementation* (Edward Elgar 2018).

Alam S and others (eds), *International Environmental Law and the Global South* (CUP 2015).

Ambiente y Ciencia, 'Ríos, sujetos de derecho: lento avance' (25 January 2020) <www.elnuevosiglo.com.co/articulos/01-2020-rios-sujetos-de-derecho-lento-avance> accessed 15 December 2021.

Ávila C, 'Guardianes del río Atrato: amenazados e ignorados' *El Espectador* (Bogotá, 22 April 2018) <www.elespectador.com/colombia-20/conflicto/guardianes-del-rio-atrato-amenazados-e-ignorados-article> accessed 28 March 2022.

Ávila Santamaría R, 'El derecho de la naturaleza: fundamentos' in Acosta A and Martinez E (eds), *La Naturaleza Con Derechos. De La Filosofía a La Política* (Ediciones Abya Yala 2011).

Bawaka Country and others, 'Co-becoming Bawaka: Towards a Relational Understanding of Place/Space' (2016) 40(4) Progress in Human Geography 455.

Beierle T, *Democracy in Practice: Public Participation in Environmental Decisions* (Routledge 2002).

Biermann F, '"Earth System Governance" as a Crosscutting Theme of Global Change Research' (2007) 17 Global Environmental Change 326.

Burdon P, 'Rethinking Global Ethics in the Anthropocene' in Burdon P, Bosselmann K and Engel K (eds), *The Crisis in Global Ethics and the Future of Global Governance: Fulfilling the Promise of the Earth Charter* (Edward Elgar 2019) 92.

'Casos de Ecuador', Observatorio Jurídico de Derechos de la Naturaleza (2018) <www.derechosdelanaturaleza.org.ec/casos/> accessed 30 April 2022.

Chávez Virreira F, 'Día Mundial del Medio Ambiente: Bolivia y América Latina necesitan repensar los modelos de desarrollo' *Página Siete* (La Paz, 6 June 2021) <www.paginasiete.bo/ideas/2021/6/6/dia-mundial-del-medio-ambiente-bolivia-america-latina-necesitan-repensar-los-modelos-de-desarrollo-297066.html> accessed 15 February 2022.

Clark W, Crutzen P and Schellnhuber H, 'Science for Global Sustainability: Towards a New Paradigm' in Schellnhuber H and others (eds), *Earth System Analysis for Sustainability* (MIT Press 2004).

'Defending Tomorrow' (*Global Witness*, 29 July 2020) <www.globalwitness.org/en/campaigns/environmental-activists/defending-tomorrow/> accessed 15 February 2022.

Delanty G and Mota A, 'Governing the Anthropocene: Agency, Governance, Knowledge' (2017) 20(1) European Journal of Social Theory 9.
Dryzek J, 'Institutions for the Anthropocene: Governance in a Changing Earth System' (2016) 46(4) British Journal of Political Science 937.
'Cuáles son los 5 desafíos de Ecuador para el medioambiente en 2020' *El Universo*, (Guayaquil, 17 January 2020) <www.eluniverso.com/noticias/2020/01/17/nota/7694943/cuales-son-desafios-ecuador-medioambiente-2020/> accessed 15 February 2022.
Fineman M, 'The Vulnerable Subject: Anchoring Equality in the Human Condition' (2008) 20(1) Yale JL & Feminism 1.
Gellers J, 'Earth System Law and the Legal Status of Non-humans in the Anthropocene' (2021) 7 Earth System Governance <https://doi.org/10.1016/j.esg.2020.100083> accessed 30 April 2022.
Gligo N and others, *La tragedia ambiental de América Latina y el Caribe* (CEPAL 2020).
Grear A, 'The Vulnerable Living Order: Human Rights and the Environment in a Critical and Philosophical Perspective' (2011) 2(1) Journal of Human Rights and the Environment 23.
Grear A, 'Legal Imaginaries and the Anthropocene: "Of" and "For"' (2020) 31 Law & Critique 351.
Hamilton C, 'The Anthropocene as Rupture' (2016) 3(2) The Anthropocene Review 93.
Harris A, 'Vulnerability and Power in the Age of the Anthropocene' (2014) 6 Washington and Lee Journal of Energy, Climate, and the Environment 98.
Houston D, 'Crisis is Where we Live: Environmental Justice for the Anthropocene' (2013) 10(3) Globalizations 439.
Kotzé L, 'International Environmental Law and the Anthropocene's Energy Dilemma' (2019) 36 Environmental and Planning Law Journal 437.
Kotzé L, 'The Anthropocene, Earth System Vulnerability and Socio-ecological Injustice in an Age of Human Rights' (2019) 10(1) Journal of Human Rights and the Environment 62.
Kotzé L and Adelman S, 'Environmental Law and the Unsustainability of Sustainable Development: A Tale of Disenchantment and of Hope' (2022) Law & Critique, <https://doi.org/10.1007/s10978-022-09323-4> accessed 12 September 2022.
Kotzé L and Villavicencio Calzadilla P, 'Somewhere between Rhetoric and Reality: Environmental Constitutionalism and the Rights of Nature in Ecuador' (2017) 6(3) Transnational Environmental Law 401.
Lang M, 'Prologue: Crisis of Civilisation and Challenges for the Left' in Lang M and Mokrani D (eds), *Beyond Development: Alternative Visions from Latin America* (Transnational Institute/Rosa Luxemburg Foundation 2013).
'Last Line of Defence' (*Global Witness*, 13 September 2021) <www.globalwitness.org/en/campaigns/environmental-activists/last-line-defence/> accessed 15 February 2022.

Li H, 'Rethinking Vulnerability in the Age of Anthropocene: Toward Ecologizing Education' (2017) 67(4) Educational Theory 435.

Nash R, *The Rights of Nature: A History of Environmental Ethics* (University of Wisconsin Press 1989).

O'Donnell E and Talbot-Jones J, 'Creating Legal Rights for Rivers: Lessons from Australia, New Zealand, and India' (2018) 23(1) Ecology and Society <https://doi.org/10.5751/ES-09854-230107> accessed 30 April 2022.

Ranta E, '*Buen Vivir* as Transformative Alternative to Capitalist Coloniality' in Hosseini H and others (eds), *The Routledge Handbook of Transformative Global Studies* (Routledge 2020).

Steffen W, Crutzen P J and McNeill J R, 'The Anthropocene: Are Humans Now Overwhelming the Great Forces of Nature?' (2007) 36 Ambio 614.

Stone C, 'Should Trees Have Standing? Towards Legal Rights for Natural Objects' (1972) 45 Southern California Law Review 450.

Valenzuela S and Sanabria Cuervo P, 'Una Selva que arde' (*El Tiempo*, date unknown) <www.eltiempo.com/vida/amazonia-deforestacion-mineria-agricultura-y-cultivos-ilicitos-577536> accessed 15 February 2022.

Villalba U, '*Buen Vivir* vs Development: A Paradigm Shift in the Andes?' (2013) 34(8) Third World Quarterly 1427.

Villavicencio Calzadilla P and Kotzé L, 'Living in Harmony with Nature? A Critical Appraisal of the Rights of Mother Earth in Bolivia' (2018) 7(3) Transnational Environmental Law 397.

Villavicencio Calzadilla P, 'A Paradigm Shift in Courts' View on Nature: The Atrato River and Amazon Basin Cases in Colombia' (2019) 15(1) Law, Environment and Development Journal 49.

PART 2

National Perspectives

CHAPTER 3

Comparative Administrative Law Perspectives – Europe, Latin-America, Africa

Eva Julia Lohse

1 Introduction

Questions of 'sustainability' are mostly approached from the level of international or regional law (like EU law) – disregarding the fact that domestic legal orders have used comparable concepts in their nature protection laws or administrative practice even before the Brundtland Report or the Rio Declaration existed. The idea of sustainability as a way of safeguarding natural resources for future use or of seeing nature as a holistic concept,[1] albeit not necessarily under this name, has been a reason to promote causal and medial environmental protection.[2] Although my research found no clear evidence that international instruments are based on pre-existing national concepts of sustainability, there is some indication that the German concept of *Nachhaltigkeit*[3] was transferred to early 20th century US-American forestry management, and from there – under German influence –into 'The Limits of Growth' by the Club of Rome (1972) and back into § 1 Bundeswaldgesetz,[4] prior to publication of the Brundtland Report.[5] International law has subsequently informed transformation processes within domestic legal orders and has led

1 Like 'Pacha Mama' (now protected by the Constitution of Ecuador from 2008, which also gives constitutional rights to 'nature' in Art. 71 et seq.), see Tristan Lefort-Martine, *Des droits pour la nature? L'expérience équatorienne* (Editions L'Harmattan 2018) at 9ff.

2 Birgit Peters, 'The Historical Perspective' in this book, chapter b.(1).

3 Which was mostly restricted to economically informed aspects of forestry, see ibid, section II Nr.1.

4 Gesetz zur Erhaltung des Waldes und zur Förderung der Forstwirtschaft (BWaldG), 2.5.1975, BGBL. I p 1037, last amended by Artikel 112 des Gesetzes vom 10. August 2021 (BGBL. I S. 3436) – Federal Forestry Act.

5 Diethelm Klippel and Martin Otto, ‚Nachhaltigkeit und Begriffsgeschichte', in Wolfgang Kahl (ed), *Nachhaltigkeit als Verbundbegriff* (Mohr Siebeck 2008) at 53–56. This can also be read into Karen Morrow, 'Sustainability, environmental citizenship rights and the ongoing challenges of reshaping supranational environmental governance', in Anna Grear and Louis J Kotzé (eds), *Research Handbook on Human Rights and the Environment* (Edward Elgar 2015) at 203, who claims that the 'wealth of nuanced and conceptually rich material that had been

DOI:10.1163/9789004509382_005

to an implementation of sustainability concepts.[6] Finally, a horizontal cross-fertilisation between legal orders can be observed.[7]

The same applies to participatory instruments meant to enable neighbours, specific societal groups, the public concerned or the general public to raise concerns and make their voices heard in administrative or legislative decision-making or in judicial control of decisions. Although the original concepts of participation have most likely been modified through the influence of inter- or supranational instruments, like Directive 2003/35/EC[8] or the Rio Declaration[9], it seems important to look at pre-existing and persisting models[10] on how to integrate the goal of 'sustainable development' or of 'participation' into a legal order and on how to make it work in daily administrative business.

Therefore, this comparative study not only seeks to explore the variety of regulation on sustainability and participation, but also to search for a common core underlying environmental laws in various legal orders. It is vital to show how different interpretations develop under different constitutional settings and to explore various models of linking participation to sustainability in order to promote environmental protection and to control adherence to environmental regulation. Different from international treaties and supranational law, domestic law is directly applicable and thus able to govern the behaviour of governments, administrative bodies and individuals. Its use in various legal orders, only connected by the weak bond of international, or the slightly stronger bond of supranational law, bears the danger of fraction and misinterpretation, as domestic administrative bodies and courts will be more acquainted with the respective understanding of 'their' system. Thus, a

produced (...) was, perhaps inevitably, reduced to the pervasive and still prevalent media-friendly sound-bite of the "Brundtland definition"'.

6 This is e.g. reported for the legal order of South Africa (Jan Glazewski, *Environmental Law in South Africa* (2nd edn, LexisNexis Butterworth 2005) at 12ff) as well as for New Zealand, cf. Klaus Bosselmann, 'Sustainability and the Law', in Peter Salmon and David Grinlinton (eds), *Environmental Law in New Zealand* (2nd edn, Thomson Reuters, 2018) at 75–6.

7 On this Ivano Alogna, 'The Circulation of the Model of Sustainable Development: Tracing the Path in a Comparative Law Perspective', in Volker Mauerhofer (ed), *Legal Aspects of Sustainable Development* (Springer 2016) at 24–25.

8 Directive 2003/35/EC of the European Parliament and of the Council of 26 May 2003 providing for public participation in respect of the drawing up of certain plans and programmes relating to the environment and amending with regard to public participation and access to justice Council Directives 85/337/EEC and 96/61/EC, OJ L 156, 25.6.2003, p 17–25.

9 Rio Declaration on Environment and Development, A/CONF.151/26 (Vol I).

10 For the history of these concepts see Peters, Sustainability through Participation? The Historical Perspective, this volume, section II Nr. 1.

comparative analysis might contribute to a better understanding of the differences and communalities of the concepts. This analysis should ideally enable us to find an encompassing and comparative definition for regulatory contexts in environmental law[11] and beyond. It tries to approximate the meaning and connection of sustainability and participation from the perspective of national legal orders.

2 Course of the Comparative Analysis

2.1 *Choice of Legal Orders*

The analysed legal orders were chosen by applying the following (alternating) criteria:

- legal orders from all around the globe (except Asia),[12] therefore with different legal and constitutional traditions,
- signatories of the Aarhus Convention (1998) or the Escazú Agreement (2018) as well as non-signatories (African states),
- legal orders with a tradition of or a need for participatory elements due to history, indigenous population, strong cultural identification with participation of the people or dialogic elements and transparent decision-making of the state,
- countries with rich natural resources or are especially affected by climate change,
- countries with different approaches to nature due to their spiritual or cultural heritage.

The comparison concentrates on laws and regulations as well as case-law from South Africa, Namibia, Kenya, Brazil, Ecuador, Costa Rica, New Zealand and Germany. It mentions some other legal orders, when suited.

2.2 *Comparative Method*

A functional comparative analysis was used in order to explore the use of the legal concepts. For this purpose, the general questions underlying all chapters have been turned into a kind of questionnaire to render various approaches

11 The aim of this book is to abandon the perception that sustainability (and participation) are inextricably interlinked with environmental law. However, domestic legal orders often connect the concepts and therefore, for reasons of space and time, this comparative analysis is focussed on environmental law.

12 For China see Daniele Brombal, 'Comparative Administrative Law Perspectives – China', in this book, chapter c.(2).

comparable. This chapter is not an indepth analysis of the connection between sustainability and participation in specific legal orders, as it is mostly lacking the socio-legal perspective on implementation, effectiveness and enforcement. A black-letter approach is surely not sufficient for a true understanding of the working mechanisms in the respective legal orders, even if it is enriched by a look at case-law and scholarly works, articles and textbooks.[13] The aim is rather a macro-comparison showing possible connections between the two concepts, the implementation of international and supranational goals in domestic legal orders and ways to regulate the concepts. It should thus be seen as a first, incomplete approach: an incentive for lawmakers to test their own legal settings against these suggestions and for academics to further study the connection between sustainability and participation.[14]

2.3 *Examples for the Regulation of Sustainability and Participation*

In this part, some regulatory models are introduced in an overview. The legal orders are used as examples for specific models that are reflected further down.

2.3.1 Brazil – Sustainable Development as a 'Diffuse' Environmental Right for Everyone

Brazil is known for its early adoption of a constitutional right to a healthy environment including the Intergenerational Responsibility Principle[15] in 1988 (Art 225 BrazC).[16] Art 225 is inextricably linked to Art 170 (economic order). It obliges the public powers in a very detailed manner to protect the environment, to prevent detrimental action and to strive for sustainable mining.[17] These obligations are to be taken into account when the administrative authorities

---

13 This aspect is highlighted by Mark van Hoecke and Mark Warrington, 'Legal Cultures, Legal Paradigms and Legal Doctrine: Towards a New Model for Comparative Law' [1998] ICLQ 495 at 496–97; see also Mark Van Hoecke, 'Deep Level Comparative Law', in Mark Van Hoecke (ed), *Epistomology and Methodology of Comparative Law* (Hart Publishing 2004) at 166–72.

14 On this function of comparative law see also Francois Venter and Louis J Kotzé, 'The methodology of environmental constitutional comparison', in Andreas Philippopoulos-Mihalopoulos and Victoria Brooks (eds), *Research Methods in Environmental Law* (Edward Elgar 2017) at 248.

15 Reis Friede, 'The Protection of the Environment in the Brazilian Supreme Federal Court: Analysis of Real Cases' [2016] Revista Semioses 78 at 79.

16 Constituição da República Federativa do Brasil de 1988 (BrazC), 5 October 1988.

17 Andreas Krell, ‚Die normative Ausgestaltung des brasilianischen Umweltrechts und die Hauptprobleme seiner methodisch abgesicherten Anwendung' [2014] 62 JöR 693 at 696.

exercise discretionary powers; their use can be controlled by the courts.[18] Art 225 is perceived as a third generation right and constitutes a 'direito difuso', i.e. a diffuse right.[19] Diffuse rights are defined as 'indivisible trans-individual rights held by unidentifiable persons linked by factual circumstances' (Art 81 (1) Consumer Protection Code);[20] the same provision allows for 'collective' and 'homogenous individual rights' to be possibly claimed.

Thereby, firstly, access to justice[21] for everyone is guaranteed in a kind of class action both on the constitutional level (ação popular ambiental)[22] for all natural persons and on the level of civil law remedies (ação civil pública) for associations, communities, and the Ministério Público,[23] a special authority vested with the power to control the implementation of environmental rights.[24] The claimants are not required to argue a violation of an own individual right. Rather claiming a violation of environmental goods suffices, as the safeguard of the environment is perceived to be in the diffuse interest of everyone.[25] The civil law remedy can be used to claim damages for environmental pollution, but also for prohibitory actions.[26]

Secondly, Art 225 § 1 IV BrazC guarantees an environmental impact assessment, which is, however, not directly linked to public participation in the text. The statutory law, foremost the Forestry Code, as well as the provisions on Environmental Impact Assessment (which have existed since 1981) include rights of indigenous people. However, the implementation of environmental impact assessment is deemed to be imprecise and has overlooked inter alia

18 Erasmo Marcos Ramos, *Brasilianisches Umweltrecht als Biosphärenschutzrecht* (Shaker Verlag 2005) at 38; Friede, n 15, at 86.

19 Ramos, ibid at 49; Steffen Kommer, 'Diffuse Umweltrechte in Brasilien am Beispiel von Kollektivklagen gegen ökologische Schäden durch queimadas' [2012] ZUR 459 at 461.

20 Diàro Oficial, 1990-09-12, núm. 176, pags.1–8, Ley Nr. 8.078, 11 September 1990.

21 One of the legs of participation according to both Art 8 Escazú Agreement (Regional Agreement on Access to Information, Public Participation and Justice in Environmental Matters in Latin America and the Caribbean, 4.3.2018) and Art 9 Arhus Convention (Convention on access to information, public participation in decision-making and access to justice in environmental matters, 25.6.1998, ECE/CEP/43).

22 Art. 5 LXXIII BrazC.

23 Ley Nr. 7.347, 24 July 1985 (Art. 1, 5).

24 See also Tito de Andrade, Gláucia Coelho and Gisela Mation, *Class/collective actions in Brazil: overview*, available at: <https://uk.practicallaw.thomsonreuters.com/9-617-6649?contextData=(sc.Default)&transitionType=Default&firstPage=true (last visited 12/09/2022)>; Sérgio Pinhero Marcal and Lucas Pinto Simao, 'Brazil', in Camilla Sanger (ed), *The Class Actions Review* (3rd edn, Law Business Research 2019) at 14–16.

25 Ramos, n 18, at 49–50; Krell, n 17, at 698; Kommer, n 19, at 461–62.

26 Marcal and Simao, n 24, at 16.

indigenous land and connected interests in recent administrative decisions.[27] One reason might be the actual lack of effective participation by large parts of the population due to socio-economic and cultural reasons.[28]

Thirdly, the constitution contains substantial obligations for private persons to protect and restore natural resources, combined with a close connection between property and sustainable use.[29] As in other Latin American legal orders,[30] many natural resources are publicly owned, therefore the (constitutional) responsibility for sustainable use falls (also) upon the state. This 'ecological function of property' is seen as a key concept as it demands activities that are consistent with sustainable development both from private land owners (via a 'green' reading of the social responsibility clause in Art 186 BrazC) and the state.[31] This duty is reinforced by the 2012 Forest Code,[32] which demands rural landowners to set aside a so-called legal reserve. It can only be sustainably managed in order to preserve the environment for future generations.[33]

2.3.2 New Zealand – A Long History of Sustainable Resource Management Under (Indigenous) Participation

Neither sustainability nor participation or comparable concepts are mentioned in constitutional law.[34] Thus, the central legal document is the Resource Management Act (RMA)[35] from 1991, amended in 2017, which covers both sustainable resource management and participation. This has established an

27 Camila D. Ritter et al., 'Environmental Impact Assessment in Brazilian Amazonia: Challenges and prospects to assess biodiversity' [2017] Biological Conservation 161 at 164 and 166, especially stressing the technical problems of analysis and the lack of un-biased experts.

28 This is, at least, claimed by Krell, n 17, at 695–96.

29 Krell, n 17, at 696–97; Antonio Herman Benjamin and Nicholas Bryner, 'Brazil', in Jorge E. Viñuales and Emma Lees (eds), *Oxford Handbook of Comparative Environmental Law* (OUP 2019) at 87ff.

30 For example, Constitución de la Republica del Ecuador (Const.), Articulo 10, Art. 71, Art. 83 de octubre de 2008.

31 Benjamin and Bryner, n 29, at 87–88.

32 Publicacao Original [Diário Oficial da Uniao de 28/05/2021], p1, col. 1, Lei no 12.651, 25 May 2012.

33 Supreme Court of Brazil, Resp 1.276.114/MG, 2nd panel, DJe 11 October 2016; see also Benjamin and Bryner, n 29, at 95.

34 Martin Kment, *Die Neujustierung des Nachhaltigkeitsprinzips im Verwaltungsrecht* (Mohr Siebeck 2019) at 53.

35 Resource Management Act 1991 (1991 No 69), Date of assent: 22 July 1991 (<www.legislation.govt.nz/act/public/1991/0069/latest/whole.html#DLM7236258> last accessed 18.10.2022).

eco-centric view by enshrining the concept of sustainability for all environmentally relevant actions of humans.[36]

New Zealand was the first state to develop a comprising legal instrument to prioritise sustainable development in reaction to the Brundtland report of 1987. The RMA has acted as a blueprint for similar legislation, e.g. in Canada and Ecuador.[37] It is complemented by statutory instruments like the Forest Act (FA) and the Fisheries Act 1996, which contain specific definitions of sustainable management (e.g. s 2 Forest Amendment Act (1993)).[38] S 5 (2) RMA defines the sole purpose of the act, i.e. sustainable development, as:

> managing the use, development, and protection of natural and physical resources in a way, or at a rate, which enables people and communities to provide for their social, economic, and cultural well-being and for their health and safety while (a) sustaining the potential of natural and physical resources (excluding minerals) to meet the reasonably foreseeable needs of future generations; and (b) safeguarding the life-supporting capacity of air, water, soil, and ecosystems; and (c) avoiding, remedying, or mitigating any adverse effects of activities on the environment.

S 6 and 7 go on to list measures to be taken and principles to be observed in order to sustainably manage resources, like protection of specific areas and habitats, recognition of the benefits of renewable energies or respect for the intrinsic value of ecosystems. A striking feature, which can only be explained by the legislative history, is the focus on management as the link to a centralistic planning of infrastructure and allocation of natural resources by the government. This therefore speaks of the need for management criteria[39] to attain a twofold goal: avoiding detriment to nature without impeding development.

The RMA follows an eco-centric understanding of 'sustainable development' rather than the 'three-legged-stool' model supported by international

36 Nicola Wheen, 'A history of New Zealand environmental law', in Eric Pawson (ed), *Environmental histories of New Zealand* (OUP 2002), 261–74 at 271: 'golden thread'.

37 Grant Hewison, 'The Resource Management Act 1991', in Peter Salmon and David Grinlinton (eds), *Environmental Law in New Zealand* (Thomson Reuters 2018) at 581–82.

38 Public Act 1993, (1993 No 7), Date of assent: 24/3/1993 (<www.legislation.govt.nz/act/public/1993/0007/latest/whole.html> last accessed 18.10.2022). Len N. Gillman, 'Assessment of sustainable forest management in New Zealand indigenous forest' [2008] New Zealand Geographer 57 at 58–59.

39 Similar ibid at 58; Kment, n 34, at 55; Wheen, n 36, at 269–71.

law,[40] although other considerations should be taken into account in the overall balancing process in an administrative planning decision.[41] Key instrument of the RMA is a hierarchy of policy statements and plans for sustainable management and development directed at the implementing local authorities.[42] This yields a procedural approach that necessitates public participation in a structured notification process in order to evaluate the impact on the environment.[43] In general, participation is seen to be crucial for good environmental decision-making as it supports 'robust evaluation processes'.[44] At the same time, it is linked to environmental justice and the requirement of equality of arms that needs to be provided by law. This approach, albeit through the differing mechanism of controlling the private processing of timber,[45] is also reflected by s 2 FA: the use of products and amenities of indigenous forests requires the user to maintain the ability of the forest to provide those products in the future and to keep its natural values. Indigenous timber needs to be harvested sustainably in order it can be milled and sold.[46] Overall, participation under the RMA is strongly institutionalised and proceduralised by laying the focus on local councils.

The legal order – like many of the Latin American legal orders – shows a strong link to the recognition of indigenous rights as well as to rights of nature[47] which have been developed over recent decades and nowadays form the core of legislation connected to sustainability and participation. This is especially reflected by the explicit reference to the Treaty of Waitangi in s 8 RMA, which

40 Sumudu A. Atapattu et al., 'Intersections of Environmental Justice and Sustainable Development: Framing the Issues', in Sumudu A. Atapattu, Carmen G. Gonzalez and Sara L. Seck (eds), *Environmental Justice and Sustainable Development* (CUP 2021) at 4–5. This opinion is also held by the NZ Government, see <www.environmentguide.org.nz/rma/> (last accessed 12/09/2022); see also Kment, n 34, at 63.

41 *North Shore City Council v Auckland Regional Council* [1997] NZRMA at 59, 93–94.

42 Hewison, n 37, at 611ff. These can be found under https://environment.govt.nz/acts-and-regulations/national-policy-statements/ (last visited 12/09/2022).

43 See Kate Mitcalfe, 'Valuing our Environment – The costs of the RMA' [2002] Forest and Bird; Hewison, n 37, at 632ff.

44 Stephen Kós, 'Public Participation in Environmental Adjudication: Some Further Reflections' [2017] *Opening Address at the Environment Adjucation Symposium.*

45 Gillman, n 38, at 58.

46 Wheen, n 36, at 271.

47 See below 3.1.7. Whanganui River (Te Awa Tupua Act 2017) and Te Urewera (Te Urewera Act 2014). Both Acts are rooted in previous conflicts and negotiations between indigenous peoples and the Crown of New Zealand (Boyd 2017, 134–135).

lays down rights and principles about the (indigenous) ownership of areas, natural resources and ancestral lands and sites.[48]

The landscape of New Zealand is marked by significant geothermal activity. Its simultaneous exploitation as an energy source and touristic attraction despite the fragility of geothermal features risks its destruction. This fact coupled with the significance as a cultural site for the Maori can be seen as formative for today's understanding both of sustainable resource management and participation of Iwi authorities and Maori communities.[49] This is reflected by s 58N ff of the RMA Amendment Act (2017) introducing *Mana Whakahona a Rohe* as a specific binding statutory agreement entered during the planning process by the councils and Iwi that allows for participation in resource management and decision-making processes.

2.3.3 South Africa and Namibia – Social, Economic and Environmentally Sustainable Development as an Enforceable Human Right

The principle of sustainable development features as part of the fundamental right to 'an environment that is not harmful to human health and wellbeing' and to protection of the environment in s 24 SAConst.[50] It includes a clear reference to all three pillars of sustainable development: the promotion of economic and social development, the benefit of present and future generations, and an ecologically sound use of natural resources. The strong connection between environment and economic and social development establishes a sphere model.[51] S 24 is interpreted in the light of the three main international documents, the Stockholm Declaration, the Brundtland Report and the Johannesburg Declaration on Sustainable Development,[52] mirroring the approach to sustainability contained within.[53] The constitutional provision

---

48 Nigel Jollands and Garth Harmsworth, 'Participation of indigenous groups in sustainable development monitoring: Rationale and examples from New Zealand' [2007] Ecological Economis 716 at 716–17.

49 Katherine Luketina and Phoebe Parson, 'New Zealand's Public Participation in Geothermal Resource Development', in Adele Manzella, Agnes Allansdottir and Anna Pellizzone (eds), *Geothermal Energy and Society* (Springer 2019) at 209.

50 Constitution of the Republic of South Africa No. 108 of 1996.

51 Anél Du Plessis, *Environmental Law and Local Government in South Africa* (Juta 2015) at 5 and 9.

52 Anél Du Plessis, *Fulfilment of South Africa's Constitutional Environmental Right in the Local Government Sphere* (Wolf Legal Publishers 2008) at 47.

53 This becomes clear from the interpretation of s 24 SAConst by the Constitutional Court in *Fuel Retailers Association of Southern Africa v Director-General*, 2007 (6) SA 4 (CC) para 45 and *BP Southern Africa (Pty) Ltd v MEC for Agriculture, Conservation and Land Affairs* 2004 (5) SA 124 (W) para 144A-C.

is understood as an individual and justiciable fundamental right with a wide scope of application and has thus initiated the development and informed the implementation of several environmental laws.[54] Sustainable development puts considerations of balancing between environmental and socio-economic interests to the centre, ideally to reconcile them.[55]

Similar to New Zealand, South Africa has introduced a National Environmental Management Act (NEMA),[56] which serves as framework legislation with the primary goal to reconcile all three pillars of sustainable development (s 2 (3)).[57] The goal is that development serves present and future generations.[58] However, although the equal balance between all elements of sustainable development is also stressed by non-binding policy instruments like the *National Framework for Sustainable Development in South Africa*, the legislation on sustainability seems fragmented, leaning towards an understanding of sustainable development as 'protection of natural resources and a green environment'.[59] This reading is supported by s 4 (a) NEMA that defines sustainable development more precisely by listing general principles of environmental law, like the precautionary principle or waste avoidance.[60] A definition of sustainable, which is solely directed at the protection of natural resources for the needs of present and future generations, can be found in s 1 Biodiversity Act[61] – sustainable use involves impeding the long term decline and the disruption of ecological integrity. A look at several other sectoral laws as well as the White Paper on an Environmental Management Policy for South Africa, shows that the greening of governmental management practices is the key aspect, although – given the apartheid past of South Africa – aspects of non-discrimination, equality and social as well as economic development might play a more important role than in other legal orders.[62]

A forerunner and possible blueprint for the South African regulation is the Constitution of Namibia (1990), which includes in Art 95 (1) a state obligation

54 Du Plessis, n 51 at 5–6.
55 See Jan Glazewski, 'South Africa', in Emma Lees and Jorge E. Viñuales (eds), *The Oxford Handbook on Comparative Environmental Law* (OUP 2019) at 317ff.
56 National Environmental Management Act 107 of 1998, Gazette 19703 of 29 January 1999.
57 Du Plessis, n 51, at 18.
58 S 1 (1) (XXIX) NEMA.
59 Ibid at 18ff.
60 Glazewski, n 55, at 323.
61 The National Environmental Management: Biodiversity Act 10 of 2004, Gazette 27161 of 6 January 2005.
62 This can be gathered from commenting literature, see Glazewski, n 6, at 14ff; Du Plessis, n 51, at 5 and also from the key case, *Fuel Retailers Association of Southern Africa v Director-General*, 2007 (6) SA 4 (CC).

(not a fundamental right) to actively promote 'the welfare of the people' by 'maintenance of ecosystems, essential ecological processes and biological diversity (…) and utilisation of living natural resources on a sustainable basis for the benefit of all Namibians, both present and future'.[63] Again, the anthropocentric take and the connection to (economic) use of natural resources is obvious. It demonstrates an understanding of sustainability reduced to intergenerational justice.[64] The main document is the Environmental Management Act (EMA),[65] which is complemented by various other acts and statutes. S 26 ff EMA include an environmental impact assessment procedure to ensure sustainable use, demanding consultations with any affected or interested person by the Environmental Commissioner, if deemed necessary (s 44 EMA). A further participatory instrument is the Sustainable Development Advisory Council (s 6 EMA), whose task is to promote cooperation between state actors and, inter alia, non-governmental organisations, and to advise the government in questions of sustainability.[66]

Provisions on public participation in environmental decision-making stem likewise from s 24 SAConst and further constitutional provisions and have been fleshed out by non-binding instruments on the sustainable management of resources as well as the above-mentioned statutory instruments.[67] This is meant to avoid vague obligations and an enforcement gap – the stated principles include procedural rules like inclusivity, diversity and transparency.[68] S 2 (4) (f) NEMA lays down that 'participation of all interested and affected parties in environmental governance must be promoted' and also demands capacity-building measures for 'equitable and effective participation'. Participation may be partly linked to local government, where local authorities need to take decisions that contribute locally to the implementation of environmental rights and sustainable development.[69] By encouraging dialogue between the local government authority and the community, participation is said to have

63 Further constitutions on the African continent that contain similar obligations are Art 13 Constitution of the Republic of Malawi 1994; Art 39 Constitution of the Republic of Angola 2010; Art 117 Constitution of the Republic of Mozambique 2004.

64 Oliver C Ruppel and Katharina Ruppel-Schlichting, *Environmental Law and Policy in Namibia* (2nd edn, Welwitschia Verlag 2013) at 106.

65 Environmental Management Act 7 of 2007, Government Gazette no. 3966 on 27 December 2007.

66 Its activities can be found at <https://sdacnamibia.org/> last accessed 18.10.2022.

67 Anél Du Plessis, 'Public Participation, Good Environmental Governance and Fulfilment of Environmental Rights' [2008] PELJ 170 at 183.

68 Ibid at 185–86.

69 Du Plessis, n 51, at 6; Du Plessis, n 67, at 185.

become 'a "sub-right" of the substantive right to a qualified environment'.[70] *Du Plessis* sees the high potential for the domestic implementation of international concepts, if participation is not limited to the (interested) public partaking in decisionsmaking processes, but encompasses evaluation of environmental processes, estimation of environmental impacts, and the analysis of needs.[71] Also, the focus on communitybased natural resource management is seen as an effective means especially for (African) impoverished rural areas, as it strengthens responsibility by participation and therefore helps to close the implementation gap in environmental protection.[72] The South African framework for participation in environmental decision-making is seen as an example of how a fundamental right, broadly understood, can further legislatory development on the side of 'law in the books'[73] and even progressive judicial lawmaking (especially in a mixed legal system with common law elements), whilst neglecting socio-economic challenges that might impede effective participation for sustainable development on the side of 'law in action'.[74]

2.3.4 Germany – in the Search of Effective Individual Rights and an Encompassing Definition

Being a European Union (EU) member state, German environmental law is influenced by an additional layer of law. The EU has competence for the harmonisation of environmental law under Art 191 ff TFEU[75] which has been used not only for directives on medial and causal environmental protection, but also to implement the participatory regime introduced by the Aarhus Convention.[76] Via Art 11 TFEU (so-called environmental horizontal integration clause) the EU and member states alike are obliged to include considerations of sustainable development in their implementation of EU politics.[77] The European

70 Du Plessis, n 51, at 85.

71 Ibid at 85.

72 Glazewski, n 6, at 19.

73 The distinction between law in the books and law in action stems back to Roscoe Pound, Law in the books and Law in action, in ALRev 1910, 12, describing the fact that black letter law must not correspond with the law that is implemented by courts and administrative bodies.

74 In this direction Du Plessis, n 67, at 190–91.

75 Treaty on the Functioning of the European Union of 13 December 2007—consolidated version (OJ C 202, 7.6.2016, pp 47–360)

76 See ECJ, *Altrip*, Decision, 7 November 2013, C-72/12, EU:C:2013:712, para 28; ECJ, *Lünen*, Decision, 12 May 2011, C-115/09, EU:C:2011:289, paras 41, 44; ECJ, *Slovak Brown Bear*, Decision, 8 March 2011, C-240/09, EU:C:2011:125, paras 28ff.

77 See Fraenkle-Haeberle, Impact of Supranational Conceptions of Participation and Sustainability on National Administrative Law, this volume, section III Nr. 3.

benchmark is mostly informed by UN-principles on sustainable development and directed towards maintaining ecological resources for future generations.[78] Sustainability has additionally been a reason to safeguard causal and medial environmental protection.

Sustainability and participation in German law are used as examples for the implementation of supranational law in domestic administrative law. They demonstrate a process of norm-creation that is strongly influenced by the specific compliance and enforcement mechanism of a supranational legal order. Simultaneously, on local and state level, Germany has a long tradition of direct democracy not restricted to questions of sustainability, environmental protection or planning law.[79] There is, however, a significant overlap, especially at local or municipal level both in the choice of topics for local referenda, which often address aspects of all three legs of sustainability.[80]

On the other hand, the Grundgesetz (Federal Constitution, hereafter: GG)[81] neither explicitly mentions sustainability nor participation – Art 20a GG is a non-justiciable obligation of all state power to safeguard the means of livelihood (also) for future generations. Thus, it only addresses one strand of sustainability (intergenerational justice)[82,83]. This is commonly interpreted as containing a principle of economical use of resources,[84] while social aspects rather form part of the principle of the welfare state in Art 20 GG.

Starting with s 1 BWaldG, German administrative laws have continuously codified both the principles of sustainability (*Nachhaltigkeit*) and of public participation in planning processes (*Öffentlichkeitsbeteiligung*) especially medial and causal environmental protections acts and regulations. For

---

78 See Christian Calliess, 'Art 11 EUV' in Christian Calliess and Matthias Ruffert (eds), *EUV/AEUV* (6th edn, C.H.Beck 2022), para 13.

79 E.g. Art 74 Bavarian Constitution dates back to 1947 and there had been plebiscitary elements in the Weimar Constitution of 1919.

80 See Christoph Popp, *Nachhaltigkeit und direkte Demokratie* (Mohr Siebeck 2021) at 191ff.

81 Grundgesetz für die Bundesrepublik Deutschland, (BGBL. 1949, p 1), last modified through Art 1 of the law from 28/06/2022 (BGBL. I, p 968). English translation: <www.gesetze-im-internet.de/englisch_gg/> (last accessed 12/09/22).

82 Guy Beaucamp, *Das Konzept der zukunftsfähigen Entwicklung im Recht* (Tübingen 2002) at 168ff; Jörg Tremmel et al., 'Die Verankerung von Generationengerechtigkeit im Grundgesetz' [1999] ZRP 432 at 432; Wilfried Berg, 'Nachhaltigkeit und Umweltstaat', in Wolfgang Kahl (ed), *Nachhaltigkeit als Verbundbegriff* (Mohr Siebeck, 2008) at 432; Johanna Monien, *Prinzipien als Wegbereiter eines globalen Umweltrechts* (Baden-Baden 2014) at 163; Joachim Wieland, 'Verfassungsrang für Nachhaltigkeit' [2016] ZUR, 473 at 476.

83 Cf Eva Julia Lohse in Helge Sodan, Markus Möstl and Klaus Stern (eds), *Das Staatsrecht der Bundesrepublik Deutschland*, (2nd edn, C.H. Beck 2022), § 26 paras 22–23.

84 See already Tobias Brönneke, *Umweltverfassungsrecht* (Nomos 1999) at 204–05.

instance the Federal Immission Control Act (BImSchG), the Water Resources Act (WHG), the Closed Substance Cycle Act (KrWG), the Soil Protection Act (BBodSchG) or the Act for the Protection of Nature (BNatSchG).[85] As there exists no encompassing act on environmental law, sustainability is mentioned in some, but not all of the specialised laws on environmental protection. There is no general definition included in the Administrative Procedural Act[86] that could inform all action by the administration but only definitions specific to the respective areas of environmental law mainly with a focus on planning law or resource management. Looking at the scholarship, it remains unclear, at least on first sight, what the legal nature of those provisions is and whether they are regarded to mean the same and hold the same function in the various acts, and sometimes even, whether it is a legal principle at all. Within statutory law it is used as a balancing criterion or optimising principle.

It is claimed that the understanding is patchy with some of the statutes following an ample understanding reflecting the three-pronged-approach of international law (such as s 1 (5) Town Planning Act,[87] which explicitly mentions the social, economic and ecological aspects of town planning, also with respect for future generations),[88] while others rest on a clear green notion.[89] In all acts, the position of the principle is rather weak as a mere 'purpose' of the law, which is not justiciable, but might be used to guide the interpretation and application of the laws. However, the use in environmental impact assessments clearly favours the ecological leg of sustainable development. It is also partly seen as a tool to move away from the traditional anthropocentric approach in German environmental law towards a more eco-centric approach.[90] The main gateway for all three aspects of sustainable development is seen in the

85 A full list can be found at Kment, n 34, at footnote 16.

86 Verwaltungsverfahrensgesetz in der Fassung der Bekanntmachung vom 23. Januar 2003 (BGBL I p 102).

87 Baugesetzbuch in der Fassung der Bekanntmachung vom 3. November 2017 (BGBL I p 3634).

88 Ulrich Battis, '§1 BauGB', in Ulrich Battis, Michael, Krautzberger and Rolf-Peter Löhr (eds), *Baugesetzbuch* (15th edn, Beck 2022), para 45; Michael Ronellenfitsch, ‚Umwelt und Verkehr unter dem Einfluss des Nachhaltigkeitsprinzips' [2006] NVwZ, at 387; Kment, n 34, at 21–22. This seems to be the overarching interpretation by Popp, n 79, at 23.

89 Also reflected by the use of *Nachhaltigkeit* instead of *nachhaltige Entwicklung*. See Kment, n 34, at 34–35.

90 Dietrich Murswiek, 'Art. 20a GG', in Michael Sachs (ed), *Grundgesetz* (9th edn, C.H.Beck 2021), para 22; mediating: Astrid Epiney,'Art. 20a GG', in Hermann von Mangoldt, Friedrich Klein and Christian Starck, *Das Bonner Grundgesetz* (7th edn, Verlag Franz Vahlen 2018), para 28.

administrative balancing process – where all interests and aspects, guided by substantive constitutional principles and proportionality, need to be brought into a balance. However, this needs an active administrative that seriously takes into account Art. 20a GG, the sustainability clauses of the respective state constitution and also constitutional aspects of the social welfare state, as well as the demands of the respective sectoral laws.

On the other hand, public participation in all administrative decisions that involve planning decisions is well established and has been around even before international and EU law demanded so. Whether there is a link to the concepts of sustainability or whether they are seen as mere objective guiding principles for state action remains to be seen. A procedural link between the substantive principle of sustainability (or rarely sustainable development) and participation can be established in the rules of public participation in planning law – participation is used to enforce aspects of sustainability, for example in environmental impact assessments or plan approval procedures.[91]

2.3.5 Costa Rica and other Latin American Legal Orders Rights of Indigenous People and Rights of Nature

The combination of principles of sustainable development (mostly with a focus on the green leg) and participation through access to justice, rights of nature and rights of indigenous communities features in many Latin American legal orders, most prominently in Costa Rica, Ecuador, Argentina and Colombia. The Environmental Protection Act of Costa Rica (EPA CR) not only sets 'sustainability' (*utilization sostenible*), responsibility for future generations and the right to a healthy environment as a goal for state policies, it also establishes a (non-enforceable) duty for every inhabitant and obliges the state to support active participation of the public in environmental decision-making.[92] Costa Rica has, as early as 1997, based on its Forestry Law 7575, introduced a marketbased solution in order to promote sustainable ecosystem management by paying private landowners for environmental services – and therefore catching all three prongs of sustainable development by a new instrument, mostly aimed at forest protection.[93] This can also be seen as a form of actual

91 Kment, n 34, at 26ff.

92 Ley número 7554 del 04 de octubre de 1995, publicada en el Diario Oficial La Gaceta número 215 del 13 de noviembre de 1995. ‚Participación de los habitantes – El Estado y las municipalidades, fomentarán la participación activa y organizada de los habitantes de la República, en la toma de decisiones y acciones tendientes a proteger y mejorar el ambiente.

93 See analysis by Melissa Bollman and Scott D. Hardy, 'A multi-level analysis of Costa Rica's payments for environmental services programme', in Thoko Kaime (ed), *International Climate Change Law and Policy* (Routledge 2014) at 183ff.

participation in sustainable management of forests, as the landowners, since 2003, can apply to partake in the programme.

3 Sustainability and Participation Compared

The comparative analysis will first explore where the principles occur and how they manifest before comparing the approaches of the different legal orders.

3.1 *Manifestation of the Principles and Legal Approaches to the Concepts*

3.1.1 Multi-level Approaches and Foundation of the Principles in Constitutional Law

Both concepts can be found at various levels of a legal order. Administrative legislation (or case-law) is widely used to put constitutional provisions into effect. Several legal orders have regulated sustainability (or related concepts) on a constitutional level, some of them also contain participatory instruments such as referenda or rights to information (e.g. s 112 Constitution of Norway).[94] Despite differences in the understanding of constitutionalism,[95] the rule of law obliges state powers to legislate in conformity with the constitution, to adhere to legal provisions and often also to actively implement constitutional goals and human rights on the level of laws and regulations.[96] Support by the government is seen as vital for the implementation of sustainability goals.[97] An obligation of state authorities can regularly be found in constitutions, alternatively social fundamental rights to a healthy environment, which directly oblige the administrative bodies to further sustainable development in their

94 See also, e.g. – restricted to sustainability – Art 6 French Constitution (développement durable); mention of participatory rights (in the context of environmental law) Art 29 Constitution of Georgia, or Art 128 Constitution of Croatia via the right to municipal self-administration; right to participation in decision-making (not restricted to environmental issues) § 14 Constitution of Finland.

95 Which has been pointed out by Venter and Kotzé, n 14, at 243.

96 Ruppel and Ruppel-Schlichting, n 64, at 106, concerning the relation between Article 95 (1) of the Namibian Constitution and the Environmental Management Act, No. 7 of 2007, Government Gazette No. 4878, Notices 28–30 on becoming operational. See also David Boyd, 'Constitutions, human rights, and the environment: national approaches', in Anna Grear and Louis J Kotzé (eds), *Research Handbook on Human Rights and the Environment* (Edward Elgar 2015), at 187–88; Albrecht Weber, *Europäische Verfassungsvergleichung* (C.H.Beck 2010) at 92–93 and 153: 'adherence to the constitution as central element of western-style liberal constitutionalism'.

97 Du Plessis, n 51, at 9.

decision-making. Constitutions usually also influence the interpretation of laws, inform the actions of administrative bodies in a specific way and have a strong symbolic value. Sometimes, they additionally contain altruistic obligations of private parties. Therefore, in order to understand different administrative models one has to start at the constitutional level.

As of 2015 about 100 constitutions embodied some kind of substantive environmental right, today there are about 150.[98] Yet, one must be careful to equate a 'right to a healthy environment' or a constitutional imperative to protect the environment or the natural foundations of life with concepts of sustainability, sustainable development or a state obligation to guarantee participation (even in environmental matters). There is an overlap of sustainability with the right to live in a healthy environment in substantive elements of 'intergenerational equity', 'preservation of natural systems' and 'sustainable exploitation of natural resources'.[99] Still, not all constitutional rights to a healthy environment also convey an individual right to sustainable development, and if so, they mostly do not include its social, economic or cultural aspect.[100]

Sustainability is explicitly mentioned more often in provisions that formulate state obligations, i.e. Art 7bis Belgian Constitution.[101] This applies also to some aspects like intergenerational equity or respect for future generations, like Art 20a GG.[102] Some states make reference to frugality in the use of natural resources or energy,[103] which highlights the aspect of conserving parts of non-renewable resources for future generations.[104] All these aspects can be part of balancing processes by administrative bodies and need to be included in proportionate decision-making, if the constitution requires this.

---

98 Boyd, n 96, at 177. For a recent overview see <www.iucn.org/news/world-commission-environmental-law/202110/right-a-healthy-environment> (last accessed 12/9/22).

99 For those aspects see Glazewski, n 6, at 13.

100 Like Art 24 of the African Charter on Human and Peoples Rights (27 June 1986, UNTS 1520 (p. 217) No 26363), see Lilian Chenwi, 'The Right to a Satisfactory, Healthy, and Sustainable Environment in the African Regional Human Rights System', in John H. Knox and Ramin Pejan (eds), *The Human Right to a Healthy Environment* (CUP 2018), at 66–67.

101 It reads: 'in the exercise of their respective competences, the Federal State, the Communities and the Regions pursue the objectives of sustainable development in its social, economic and environmental aspects, taking into account the solidarity between the generations.', available at: </www.dekamer.be/kvvcr/pdf_sections/publications/constitution/GrondwetUK.pdf> last accessed 18.10.2022.

102 For example, German Federal Constitutional Court (BVerfG), Beschl. v. 24.3.2021 – 1 BvR 2656/18 u.a., BVerfGE 157, 30, paras 183 and 192–93 on Art 20a GG.

103 Like Art 39 (4) Constitution of the Land Brandenburg (Verfassung des Landes Brandenburg, 20 August 1992, GVBL I/92, 298, available at: <www.landtag.brandenburg.de/media_fast/6/Landesverfassung-BB-Sept2019-englisch.pdf.> (last accessed 12/09/22)).

104 See Brönneke, n 84, at 202–04.

However, objective state obligations rarely contain an explicit link to participation. Sometimes they constitute a legislatory duty to create statutory participatory rights in administrative procedures with an impact on nature or natural foundations of life.[105] Rarely, a direct and individual constitutional right to participate (mostly in the form of access to justice, like Art 42, 70 of the Constitution of Kenya)[106] exists. Another approach is taken by Art 66 of the Portuguese Constitution, which connects a state obligation 'to ensure enjoyment of the right to the environment within an overall framework of sustainable development' with the 'involvement and participation of citizens' – thereby not only framing the governmental duty to support environmental initiatives by the public, but also demanding citizens to act. A justiciable and fundamental right to a healthy environment that explicitly mentions sustainable development is s 24 SAConst – a so-called 'social right' interpreted by the Constitutional Court as an enforceable obligation of the state to promote sustainable development. In consequence, the courts play a very active role in implementing sustainable development by using s 24 SAConst and other constitutional procedural guarantees to grant standing, which relates to the third pillar of participation, access to justice.[107] Further constitutions that contain some sort of a link between the two concepts are: Argentina (environmental protection linked to the possibility of a people's initiative on administrative environmental law), Bulgaria (right to a healthy environment as a justiciable individual right), Finland (strong connection to participative/procedural rights), Georgia (right to environmental protection and information in environmental affairs), Croatia (responsibility for the environment lies with parliament and the people as well as local selfgoverning entities), Moldavia (right to a healthy environment and right to information), same in Montenegro, Poland, Serbia and Slovakia.

In all legal orders, even in those where quite detailed constitutional provisions existed, sustainable development as well as participation were further specified in statutory law or extensive judicial interpretation of constitutional provisions. Administrative laws provide various means to effectuate constitutional, but also international requirements mostly in environmental protection laws. Some legal orders, like New Zealand or South Africa, have enacted general, comprehensive legislation for the concepts of sustainability and

105 E.g. Art 39 (8) Constitution of the Land Brandenburg, n 102.

106 David Boyd, *The Environmental Rights Revolution* (UBC Press 2012), at 155, assuming that only the insertion of these provisions has changed governmental action in environmental matters.

107 Ibid at 151–53.

participation. It can be demonstrated that they are thereby applied in the same way in different statutes. On the other hand, in German law, as there is no encompassing environmental protection act, sustainability is mentioned in some, but not all of the relevant statutes and applied in different ways within the same legal order. However, as can be seen from Brazilian law, neither a constitutional guarantee nor statutory law providing for class actions, (indigenous) participation and environmental impact assessment is sufficient, if those requirements are imprecise and participation or indigenous rights are neglected for economic reasons.[108]

Finally, the comparative analysis has taken into account influences from inter- or supranational law, especially if its implementation is binding like under Art 288 TFEU for EU directives. They might function like 'legal transplants' and thus eventually modify the domestic legal order, if certain requirements for a successful transplant are fulfilled.[109] One example is how 'standing' in German administrative court procedure has been continuously modified by EU law in environmental matters and the implementation of the Aarhus Conventions.[110] Sometimes, the legislation was also influenced or even determined by international law (e.g. in South Africa) or regional human rights law (like the IACHR, the ECHR or the ACHR).[111] International and regional instruments, advisory opinions or judgements have sparked the development of environmental law and participatory instruments. They can even lead to cross-fertilisation between legal orders, as has best been demonstrated by the right to a healthy environment.[112]

108 See the analysis by Ritter et al., n 27, at 166; also, more generally, Krell, n 17, at 693.

109 On this Roberto Caranta, Anna Gerbrandy and Bilun Müller, 'Introduction', in Roberto Caranta, Anna Gerbrandy and Bilun Müller (eds), *The Making of a New European Legal Culture: The Aarhus Convention* (European Law Publishing 2018) at 9–10 and more general Eva Julia Lohse, *Rechtsangleichungsprozesse in der Europäischen Union* (Mohr Siebeck 2017) at 93ff and 246ff.

110 Prominently ECJ, *Altrip*, Decision, 7 November 2013, C-72/12, EU:C:2013:712, para 28; ECJ, *Lünen*, Decision, 12 May 2011, C-115/09, EU:C:2011:289, paras 41, 44; ECJ, *Slovak Brown Bear*, Decision, 8 March 2011, C-240/09, EU:C:2011:125, paras 28ff, which have led to several modifications of the Environmental Appeals Act (Gesetz über ergänzende Vorschriften zu Rechtsbehelfen in Umweltangelegenheiten nach der EG-Richtlinie 2003/35/EG, Umwelt-Rechtsbehelfsgesetz in der Fassung der Bekanntmachung vom 23. August 2017 (BGBL. I S. 3290)).

111 Boyd, n 106, at 96–111.

112 Ibid, at 96–107.

3.1.2 Role of the Courts

In general, there are three ways for a legal concept to enter a legal order: (1) even in common-law countries nowadays the regular way, by legislatory intervention answering a regulatory need, is either by a modification of the constitution or by statutory law, (2) both in civil law and common law countries, by judicial activism creating new norms and standards and (3) increasingly, as an answer to obligations in international or supranational law, either in order to implement legal obligations into domestic law or to value a decision by an international or regional court or commission.

Based on constitutional provisions, constitutional or supreme courts might play a central role in developing both principles out of a right to a healthy environment.[113] This seems to be true in Brazil as well as in South Africa – this stresses that for sustainable development environmental, social and economic interest must be reconciled and that this balance can only be struck on a case-by-case-basis.

Yet, also in those legal orders, like New Zealand and, to a lesser extent also Germany, where the introduction of the principles was instituted by statutory law, courts are seen as central for the implementation and development of the rather vague principle of sustainability and for the effective implementation of participation provisions in administrative proceedings. In New Zealand, even a specific Environmental Court exists, based on the idea of ensuring 'good environmental decision-making and appropriate case management' by the administration.[114] However, it has been doubted whether the court has used its powers to put life into the principle of sustainable management.[115] In most legal orders, environmental adjudication is also not limited to administrative courts, but takes place in criminal law cases, tort litigation/litigation for damages, or property-related cases.[116]

3.1.3 Rights-based Approaches

Both concepts can be established as substantive rights of the individual – either at a constitutional or statutory level. Substantive rights give the individual power to demand – at least – protection, sometimes also to gain access

113 See Krell, n 17, at 699–700; similar Emma Lees, 'Adjudication Systems', in Emma Lees and Jorge E. Viñuales (eds), *Oxford Handbook on Comparative Environmental Law* (OUP 2019), at 807–08.

114 Ibid at 805.

115 Kment, n 34 at 93.

116 Examples can be found at Lees, n 112, at 769; Ricardo Luis Lorenzetti, 'Complex Judicial Remedies in Environmental Litigation: The Argentine Experience' [2017] JEnvL 1 at 1–2; Kommer, n 19, at 463–67.

to courts in environmental matters, or to claim positive action from state institutions. In some legal orders, constitutional fundamental rights to a healthy environment exist, which are combined with a procedural right to information and/or participation or access to courts.[117] In other constitutions, the right to live in a healthy environment is combined with a duty of the state to guarantee the natural foundations of life and ecosystems.[118] S 24 SAConst is understood in a way that an enforceable environmental right can only be guaranteed, if statutory law enables public participation in decision-making processes. This is supported by further constitutional provisions which guarantee the rights to access to information and to just administrative action (s 32 and 33) as well as principles on involvement of communities in local government and public participation and transparency (s 152 (1) and s 195 (e)).[119] It shows that the constitutional framework can foster the development of strong participatory instruments. It can also oblige the state to enhance access to justice.

This type of regulation can also be found in Kenya, where Art 3 EMCA[120] combines the right to a healthy environment with an individual procedural right in case the state obligations for the protection of the environment or the principle of sustainable development are violated. Also, the idea of the 'amparo environmental/ação', which can be found in a number of Latin American states (e.g. Argentina, Brazil, Ecuador, Chile), gives the individual, sometimes also communities or NGO's the right to seek judicial redress against violations of environmental provisions.[121] The peculiarity is that – although it is a rights-based approach – a violation of an individual right of the claimant is not necessary (transindividual or collective right). At the same time, this rights-based approach is regularly linked to either rights of nature and/or indigenous rights. The public trust doctrine established in the NEMA SA as well as several sectoral laws in South Africa can also be seen as a way to fortify the fundamental right to a healthy environment, as it obliges the state to act in a manner that sustainably develops various natural resources.[122]

117 Boyd, n 96, at 190–91. One clear example is Art 29 Constitution of Georgia, which follows the three elements of participation laid down in the AC (information, administrative decision-making, access to courts) and links it both to a right to live in a healthy environment and 'sustainable ecological development'.

118 Like Art 225 BrazilC or s 24 SAConst.

119 Du Plessis, n 52, at 183–84.

120 Environmental Management and Co-ordination Act, No 8 of 1999 (Cap 387).

121 More examples are given at Thomas Gross, 'Climate change and duties to protect with regard to fundamental rights', in Wolfgang Kahl and Marc-Philippe Weller (eds), *Climate Change Litigation* (C.H.Beck 2021) at 91, para 39; Boyd, n 95, at 190–91.

122 See eg MPDRA or s 2 (4) NEMA, see also Glazewski, n 55, at 323–24.

Rather than substantive rights, the procedural perspective of human rights is addressed by either including a constitutional state obligation to introduce participatory rights (information, administrative decision-making, access to justice) or by giving the individual a right to participate in sustainable management.

3.1.4 Altruistic Obligation of the Individual

A way to support sustainable development, mainly as regards protection of the environment and wise use of natural resources, might be an obligation of private parties – either as an individual duty to act in an altruistic way or as a non-justiciable appeal on constitutional level. Often, this obligation correlates to a duty of the state to protect the environment or to respect sustainable development and to a right to a healthy environment, as can be seen in Art 66 (2) Portuguese Constitution and less explicitly in Art. 39 (1) Landesverfassung Brandenburg. In some cases, the right is linked to constitutional provisions on property or the economic order (Art. 170 BrazilC), demanding a socially compatible use of property also by private actors and an economy which respects the environment.[123]

However, in legal orders that follow the liberal Western-style concept of fundamental rights as state duties to protect, binding individual environmental duties are difficult to reconcile with the doctrine of horizontal effect and the idea that individual freedom can only be restricted by other legal interests of the individual.[124] At the core lies the debatable relation between society or even humankind and individual freedom: if a person uses a fundamental right altruistically for ecological purposes, it is questionable under classical social contract theory whether this could justify the restriction of another person's freedom. As all humans are perceived equal and free, restrictions can only be justified by the legitimate aim of colliding fundamental rights or human common welfare.[125] An exception is s 8 (2) SAConst,[126] which enables horizontal

123 Krell, n 17, at 696–97; Benjamin and Bryner, n 29, at 87ff. Another example is Art 41 (6) Constitution of Romania (obligation to respect the environment for the proprietor).

124 On this debate, whether there is a legal duty of the individual to serve the common good or a duty of solidarity towards the community (as was claimed by Rousseau), or whether such an understanding contravenes social contract theory, because the individual cannot be free in this case, see e.g. Peter Saladin, *Verantwortung als Staatsprinzip* (UTB 1984) at 68–69.

125 On this see Eva Julia Lohse and Valeria Berros, 'You cannot have the cake and eat it', in Vienna Journal of International Constitutional Law Special Issue 'Climate Change and Social Contract Theory' (forthcoming 2023).

126 'A provision of the Bill of Rights binds a natural or a juristic person if, and to the extent that, it is applicable, taking into account the nature of the right and the nature of any duty imposed by the right.'

application in general, however, it has not been used in this way for an environmental duty, not even via intergenerational justice as an aspect of s 24 SAConst.[127] Therefore, they are commonly assumed to hold only symbolic value and not to be an enforceable duty to participate.[128]

3.1.5 The Special Role of Indigenous Peoples and Local Communities

A striking aspect of linking the two concepts is that the legal recognition of (fundamental, sometimes procedural) rights for indigenous peoples and/or local communities is often mentioned in tandem with participatory rights, and even more so with sustainability and the protection of the environment. Indigenous peoples therefore seem to play a special role. They are seen as the best promoters of earth law or so-called ecocentric approaches to sustainability.[129]

However, this connection needs to be clarified: although the recognition of specific rights for indigenous or local communities is often a requirement of international[130] or – as in New Zealand[131] – constitutional law and has been the focus of civil rights movements especially in Latin America,[132] this does not per se yield a sustainable management or a guardianship for nature. Primarily, it is a human right aimed at the wellbeing of these communities and people living within (sometimes linked to the right to health and life or, like in Art 24 of the Banjul Charter, to collective rights to development, growth and a sound environment).[133] Indigenous rights include an (often) actionable

---

127 It is disputed whether s 24 SAConst is an obligation of individuals, as sustainable development is a social right and a typical state task, see Thomas Heinicke, *Umweltschutz im Grundgesetz und in der Verfassung der Republik Südafrika* (WiKu-Verlag 2007) at 141 and 368.

128 See also Boyd, n 96, at 180–81.

129 See Yann Aguila and Shehana Gomez, 'United Nations Sustainable Development Initiatives', in Anthony R. Zelle et al. (eds), *Earth Law* (Wolters Kluwer 2021) at 426ff; similar Lena Heinämäki, 'Protecting the rights of indigenous people – promoting sustainability of the global environment?' [2009] ICLR 3 at 4–5.

130 Emma Mittrota and Federica Cittadino, 'The Case of Biodiversity Protection', in this book, chapter d.(1); Violeta S Radovich, 'The Law of the High Seas', in this book, chapter e.(4).

131 The constitutional recognition of the Treaty of Waitangi lead to many public sector statutes to reference Maori rights or to give them special procedural rights in order to claim their interests, see Philip A. Joseph, *Constitutional and Administrative Law in New Zealand* (2nd edn, Brookers 2001) at 74–75, many of them with a relation to environmental law or sustainable management. See also Chris R. de Freitas and Martin Perry, *New Environmentalism – Managing New Zealand's Environmental Diversity* (Springer 2012) at 80.

132 On the development see Rodolfo Stavenhagen, 'Indigenous Peoples and the State in Latin America: An Ongoing Debate', in Rachel Sieder (ed), *Multiculturalism in Latin America* (Palgrave Macmillan 2002) at 27ff.

133 Chenwi, n 99, at 65–67.

duty of the state to safeguard their cultural heritage as well as the right to self-determination and indigenous property rights.[134] Therefore, participatory rights might foremost stem from the need to guarantee these rights in administrative procedure[135] and not from the political will to utilize them for more sustainable development.

Yet, those societies where nowadays indigenous rights are valued account for a certain interlink, drawing from the respect for different concepts of law, property and nature as well as a (perceived) better guardianship for nature and natural resources. Partly, this must be seen from the perspective of decolonising the concept of sustainability.[136] Partly, indigenous environmental justice, a concept reflecting the differing conception of a more than human world and another position of humankind than the Western understanding of human beings being the 'crown of creation', is used as an antagonistic concept to sustainable development.[137] Legal systems in Latin America,[138] Africa (e.g. Kenya) and New Zealand resort to indigenous participation or management schemes in the context of environmental law and protection of natural resources. Thereby, they also aim to resolve environmental and land use conflicts that originate in the exploitation of land and resources through forestry or mining by the state or non-indigenous investors.[139] It can also be seen as one aspect of environmental justice trying to create an inclusive access to political deliberation, especially by those who have been marginalised in the past and might still not be represented equally in the conventional political system.[140] This approach still has many deficits – e.g. it is claimed that the Escazú Agreement omits indigenous rights in the context of participation in environmental

134 Stavenhagen, n 132, at 31–32.

135 See, e.g. ConstEcuador, which ensures collective ownership of land as well as participation in decision-making in questions affecting the indigenous community.

136 Deborah McGregor, 'Indigenous Environmental Justice and Sustainability', in Sumudu A. Atapattu, Carmen G. Gonzalez and Sara L. Seck (eds), *Environmental Justice and Sustainable Development* (CUP 2021) at 59–60 for the international perspective. From a regional, Latin American, perspective Patrícia G. Ferreira and Mario Mancilla, 'Indigenous Environmental Rights and Sustainable Development', ibid at 165.

137 McGregor, n 136, at 63.

138 On this see also the contribution by Louis Kotzé and Paola Villavincencia-Calzadilla, 'Re-imagining Participation in the Anthropocene: The Potential of the Rights of Nature Paradigm' in this book, chapter b.(2).

139 For examples see Gillman, n 38, at 58; Luketina and Parson, n 49, at 203; Ferreira and Mancilla, n 136, at 166; Elizabeth Jane MacPherson, *Indigenous Water Rights in Law and Regulation* (CUP 2021) at 55ff, 168ff; Stavenhagen, n 131, at 33; Donna Lee Van Cott, 'Constitutional Reform in the Andes: Redefining Indigenous-State Relations', ibid, at 47.

140 On this aspect more generally and recurring to the theories of Nancy Fraser, Eva-Maria Isabell Ehemann, *Umweltgerechtigkeit* (Mohr Siebeck 2020) at 84ff.

decision making despite it being one of the most prominent legal topics in most Latin American countries[141] – but the obvious inclusion in some national legal frameworks on participation and sustainable development cannot go unnoticed.

Another approach has been taken in Costa Rica by allowing indigenous communities, who collectively own land, to partake in the 'payment for ecological services' programme and therefore 'sell' their sustainable management of land.[142] Art 3 EMCA includes cultural and social principles traditionally applied by any community in Kenya for the management of the environment into the principles for sustainable development – this is not a participatory approach, but another way of including traditional knowledge into administrative decision-making and of valuing different approaches to maintain a sound environment.[143] It can be seen as a step towards co-production of knowledge, which might be a further stepping stone in participatory approaches.

The German perspective adds another idea of local responsibility for sustainable development; that of municipal referenda, which exist in all German states with slight modifications, and where the local community gains the possibility to influence decision making within municipal self-government. They often, albeit not always seem to enhance sustainable decision-making in all three dimensions (ecological, economic and social).[144] As main reasons for non-sustainable decision-making in singular cases *Popp* identifies nimbyism and procedural deficits of specific referendum provisions, but he also finds that all three aspects of sustainability are equally addressed in those local referenda, even if the singular voter has a preferred reason for their vote.[145]

3.1.6 Perspectives from Administrative Procedural Law

Participation has a long tradition in the administrative law of several states in the form of public participation in the planning process. Historically, there might also be roots of sustainable development, e.g. in nature protection laws. Through formation by EU law and public international law, the two concepts might have been incorporated into the regulations of special environmental law and are being applied and interpreted by the authorities and courts.

141 Ferreira and Mancilla, n 136, at 171–72.

142 Bollman and Hardy, n 93, at 191.

143 Heinämäki, n 129, at 10.

144 See Popp, n 80, at 375–76, also referring to further empirical studies in Switzerland by Andreas Glaser and in Austria by Wolfgang Kahl.

145 Ibid at 376–77.

In several legal orders,[146] statutory law focuses on sustainable management and thereby tries to implement the principle of sustainability via guiding principles for the government or ministries planning infrastructural projects or the exploitation and allocation of natural resources.[147] In the sector specific resource protection laws of South Africa, the idea of sustainable management is combined with the public trust doctrine, which establishes the environment and natural resources as common heritage of all the people and the state as the custodian responsible for the public trustee thereof.[148] Therefore, management of these resources must be for the benefit of all persons, referring back to the general idea of sustainable development.

Participation of, at least, 'affected and interested parties',[149] is established as a means to reach sustainable use of a natural resource in administrative procedure. This is mostly effectuated by participation in environmental impact assessments, in the making of decisions that might affect the environment and/or in the administrative process of issuing a resource (or management) consent by the environmental authority.[150] Even where environmental impact assessment is not directly linked to participatory elements, it can be seen as a means to foster at least the green aspect of sustainable development. In the case where environment is conceived more broadly and depending on the criteria to be taken into consideration, the social-cultural aspects might also be addressed.[151] The RMA NZ includes significant participatory rights in the process of developing sustainable management plans, demanding resource consent – comparable to participatory rights that exist in some of the German environmental acts.

Another procedural link between sustainability and participation is established wherever the administration needs to balance various interest – partly at the constitutional level, partly at the statutory level, like in German town planning or water law. Here, public participation might also provide facts and interests that administrative bodies need to consider in the balancing process. Yet, if sustainability is only one of the aspects to be considered, it has a rather weak position for the outcome of the balancing process.[152]

---

146 E.g. s 5 RMA NZ, s 23 NEMA SA or s 2 EMA NA.

147 For New Zealand see Kment, n 34, at 55ff.

148 S 3 (1) National Water Act 36 of 1998, 1 October 1998 (Gazette 19269 of 25 September 1998). See also The Mineral and Petroleum Resources Development Act 28 of 2002 (MPRDA), 1 May 2004 (Gazette 26264 of 23 April 2004).

149 S 2 (c) EMA NA.

150 Examples are the RMA NZ, or s 23 NEMA SA (integrated environmental management).

151 See Ritter et al, n 27, at 161.

152 For German law see Beaucamp, n 82, at 265–66.

Finally, even if not linked to participatory requirements, sustainable management can include the establishment of specific administrative bodies, like in South Africa, Brazil or New Zealand, and the obligation for the government or sub-entities to draw up implementation or management plans. The idea is to give effect to substantive demands of sustainable development via procedure and institutions[153] – and in some legal orders this is again linked to participatory elements. Another way was explored in New Zealand with the institution of a specialised environmental court – however, it did not take off right away with both sides in a litigation being hesitant to bring the matter before a court. This has led to a rather scattered interpretation of the guiding principles of the RMA.[154]

3.1.7 Rights of Nature as a Special case of Participation?

A more eco-centric understanding of the relationship between humankind and nature – which might be demanded by sustainable development – is attempted by legal orders, like in many Latin American countries[155] or New Zealand,[156] through introducing rights of nature. This can be seen as a special case of participation, allowing nature itself to partake in environmental decision-making or others to altruistically enforce the rights of nature.[157] In most cases, the guardians come from indigenous communities. The link to sustainability is furthermore drawn in those constitutions that obligate individuals to respect the rights of nature and therefore, to use natural resources sustainably.[158]

3.2 *Comparative Analysis of the Concepts*

The central aim of this paragraph is to establish whether there is a common understanding of sustainable development and if not, what the differences are. It is analysed whether there have been legal transplants, imports of legal concept or communication between legal orders, especially in the same region. In order to establish best practices, ways and goals of participatory instruments and their possible connection to sustainable development are explored.

---

153 For South Africa see Glazewski, n 6, at 142ff.

154 See Kment, n 34, at 93–94.

155 Kotzé and Villavincencia-Calzadilla, n 139. 'Examples are Chapter 7 of the Constitution of Ecuador (2008), further examples can be found at Boyd, n 96, at 182–83.

156 New Zealand: Whanganui River (Te Awa Tupua Act 2017) and Te Urewera (Te Urewera Act 2014).

157 See eg Art 71 ConstEcuador: 'All persons, communities, peoples, and nations can call upon public authorities to enforce rights of nature'.

158 On this see David Boyd, *The rights of nature* (EWC Press 2019) at 172ff.

3.2.1 Use of the Legal Notion 'Sustainability'

It has been claimed that the international conception of sustainable development requires 'nothing less than the radical refashioning of the relationship between humanity and the environment.'[159] However, implementing legislation is still, nearly 35 years after the Brundtland report, strongly anthropocentric with a focus on future generations, intra-generational justice and an understanding of nature and natural resources as an asset for the wellbeing of humankind. As *Aguila* and *Gomez* put it: 'Sustainable development is currently the predominant global model for protecting the environment while ensuring quality of life for humans',[160] thereby stressing (and criticising) the mostly anthropocentric approaches.

Legal orders either include the three-pronged approach of international law (Brundtland Commission)[161] or focus on resource management and intergenerational justice and therefore environmental law from a human perspective: The environmental pillar of sustainable development in most legal orders is linked to different areas of law that reflect natural resources and ecosystems, demanding their protection and 'sustainable management', most importantly agriculture, fisheries, mining, energy (including geothermal features) and forestry as well as water (from ground water to oceans) and biodiversity (or more general nature protection/conservation). Most legal orders in this analysis have passed acts that link the use, management and enjoyment of these natural features to a sustainability goal. Sometimes, this link is already established by constitutional law, by mentioning areas or resources of increased protection (cf Art 225 (4) BrazC). Some legal orders also include pollution control, waste management[162] and land use planning – all of which are activities of the present generation capable of affecting the choices and planning of future generations. Sometimes, sustainability is not explicitly mentioned. Management of environmental resources is rather structured by alternative criteria. One example is 'best practise' (*gute fachliche Praxis*) in German agricultural law, which is perceived as including sustainable agricultural use,[163] allowing an 'optimising process' with other concepts that pertain to this area of law.

---

159 Morrow, n 5, at 203–04.

160 Aguila and Gomez, n 129, at 403.

161 See e.g. Part I Art 2, Part III Art 37 (2) (d); Part V Art 47 (1) (2) (e), EMCA 1999 Kenya.

162 Especially nuclear waste, see EMA NA, but also Art 39 (9) Constitution of the Land Brandenburg (Verfassung des Landes Brandenburg of 20 August 1992, GVBl.I/92, p 2989.)

163 Silke Klinck, *Agrarumweltrecht im Wandel vom Subventionsrecht zum Recht der Umweltdienstleistung* (Duncker & Humblot 2012) at 150ff.

All legal orders have to deal with the fact that sustainable development often remains a rather vague and open 'container term',[164] that requires concretisation by the competent authorities and can cause problems in its implementation and interpretation.[165] They have tried to solve this problem by procedural requirements – ideally including participatory elements –, by a list of substantive requirements at statutory level, that need to be followed for sustainable decisions, or by relying on court decisions. Many legal orders, following the example of the RMA NZ, have established an 'integrated environmental management' that lays down an encompassing definition of sustainable as well as principles for decision-making in order to attain the specified sustainability goals in all areas.[166] In German law, however, an overreaching or all-encompassing definition does not exist. On the contrary, in some statutes it is reduced to (specific aspects of) ecological sustainability, meaning the management of resources, whereas in other areas of administrative law it includes economic and social aspects to be balanced and reconciled with each other.[167] An integrated approach seems to be the better solution in order to avoid friction between sector-specific laws and to guarantee consistent standards.[168]

A balancing process is part of the principle of sustainable development in all analysed legal orders, apart from the RMA NZ, which from its outset demands priority of ecological considerations.[169] By not referring to sustainable development in general, the RMA NZ deliberately uses a notion that is different from the Brundtland Report – which would include social aspects and global equality. It has a narrower focus on the management of resources and the protection of the environment.[170] S 5 RMA[171] includes care for future

164 Edmund A. Spindler, 'The History of Sustainability – The Origins and Effects of a Popular Concept', in Ian Jenkins and Roland Schröder (eds), *Sustainability in Tourism* (Springer 2013) at 9.

165 Wheen, n 36, at 271; De Freitas and Perry, n 130, at 66.

166 Wheen, n 36, at 272–73.

167 Ronellenfitsch, n 88, at 387.

168 See also Glazewski, n 6, at 231ff.

169 See however the mellowing in decisions like *Environmental Defence Society Inc v The New Zealand King Salmon Co Ldt* [2014] 1 NZLRev 593 para 153.

170 About the legislative history see Kment, n 34, at 60. On the necessity of the three-pillar-model see Popp, n 80, at 23. For the international trend to align sustainability and development and to address rather general questions of social equity and economic prosperity see Ehemann, n 140, at 117ff. However, stressing the inextricable link between 'economic development, social development and environmental protection' in later documents Atapattu et al., n 40, at 3.

171 '(1) The purpose of this Act is to promote the sustainable management of natural and physical resources. (2) In this Act, sustainable management means managing the use, development, and protection of natural and physical resources in a way, or at a rate,

generations as an important aspect of sustainability – however, the law of New Zealand also aims at realising the special requirements of Maori law and society and understands this as part of resource management.[172] Uncertainty concerning the interpretation of s 5 as a priority rule for ecological sustainability standards that would trump other considerations of economic or cultural wellbeing in planning decisions ('bottom-line approach') was addressed by the Supreme Court in 2014 in a way that those ecological principles establish a core interest that still needs to be balanced with other interests.[173] Therefore, ecological aspects are most likely not treated with more priority than in other legal orders and the three-pronged approach used in international law is also implicitly applied in New Zealand.[174]

On the other hand, s 24 SAConst contains an explicit obligation 'to secure sustainable development and use of natural resources while promoting justifiable economic and social development', which requires a complicated balancing process between those three aspects. Additionally, all action needs to be 'for the benefit of present and future generations'. This can be read as highlighting one aspect of sustainability, i.e. intergenerational and intragenerational justice, or as a statement that those aspects of justice are a (maybe even prioritised) goal in the balancing process, not part of sustainable development, meant as a compensation for not including an altruistic obligation of the individuals living today to protect the environment.[175] In the African context, Art 24 of the Banjul Charter also plays a role in the interpretation and balancing process, as it guarantees a collective right to a healthy and sustainable environment as well as a right to development, highlighting the close connection between environmental degradation and social and economic development

---

which enables people and communities to provide for their social, economic, and cultural well-being and for their health and safety while (a) sustaining the potential of natural and physical resources (excluding minerals) to meet the reasonably foreseeable needs of future generations; and (b) safeguarding the life-supporting capacity of air, water, soil, and ecosystems; and (c) avoiding, remedying, or mitigating any adverse effects of activities on the environment.'

172 On the importance of this aspect see De Freitas and Perry, n 131, at 68 and 79–80; Luketina and Parson, n 49, at 203–04.

173 *Environmental Defence Society Inc v The New Zealand King Salmon Co Ldt* [2014] 1 N.Z.L.Rev. 593 para 24, 153.

174 This result is also reached by Kment, n 34, at 64–65.

175 This is raised and – as concerns priority – denied by Heinicke, n 126, at 368–69; see also Loretta A Feris and Dire Tladi, 'Environmental Rights', in Daniel Brand and Christof Heyns (eds), *Socio-Economic Rights in South Africa* (PULP 2005) at 260.

processes and at the same time the need to reconcile them in the balancing process.[176]

In most cases, the constitutional and statutory obligations are directed towards state actors rather than private actors and demand foresighted planning and setting of frameworks for sustainable management and development.[177] This becomes clear for example by the anthropocentric definition given in S 1 EMA NA:

> "sustainable development" means human use of a natural resource, whether renewable or non-renewable, or the environment, in such a manner that it may equitably yield the greatest benefit to present generations while maintaining its potential to meet the needs and aspirations of future generations including the maintenance and improvement of the capacity of the environment to produce renewable resources and the natural capacity for regeneration of such resources.

3.2.2 Ways and Goals of Participation

Common ground in all legal orders in this comparison is the underlying idea (also reflected in international and regional law and the principle of co-operation)[178] that decision-making should rest on the three pillars of information, participation in administrative procedures and access to courts.[179] The aim is to enable individuals to (altruistically) claim (often) collective or diffuse ecological and social interests, sometimes also in the name of those who cannot participate, like future generations or nature itself. These criteria are understood as an expression of the ideal of deliberative democracy.[180] No matter which of these goals are intended to be reached by participation, the basic question for the legislator is: How is participation possible and for whom? A

---

176 Chenwi, n 100, at 66.

177 See e.g. Glazewski, n 6, at 137.

178 Thomas Bunge, 'Information der Öffentlichkeit, Mitwirkung an behördlichen Verfahren und Rechtsschutz in Umweltangelegenheiten', in Sabine Schlacke, Christian Schrader and Thomas Bunge (eds), *Aarhus-Handbuch* (2nd edn, Erich Schmidt Verlag 2019), para 1.

179 Cf Maria Adebowale et al., *Environment and Human Rights: A New Approach to Sustainable Development* (2001) at 3; Alan Boyle, 'Human Rights and the Environment – Where Next?', in Ben Boer (ed), *Environmental Law Dimensions of Human Rights* (OUP 2015) at 216–17.

180 Tim O'Riordan and Susanne Stoll-Kleemann, 'Deliberative democracy and participatory biodiversity', in Tim O'Riordan and Susanne Stoll-Kleemann (eds), *Biodiversity, Sustainability and Human Communities* (CUP 2002) at 88.

state needs to decide on a political basis whether participation of the following actors is intended:

- the general public
- the public concerned/individuals (like neighbours)
- experts[181]
- groups (like indigenous people, local communities,...)
- associations (like NGOs) with specific goals like the protections of the environment
- other, especially specific institutions vested with the power to control state action in the area of sustainability.

The analysis is mostly based on the previously mentioned three ways to guarantee participation in environmental matters as established by the Aarhus Convention and the Escazú Agreement.

Participation in administrative procedures (e.g. planning procedures, environmental impact assessment) forms part of statutory law, and is often seen as the way to include different interests and rights in the balancing process. Modelled after US law, the EU Directive on Environmental Impact Assessment,[182] and implementing German legislation, define 'public' very broadly and try to involve various stakeholders at all levels of the decision-making process.[183] Participation as such follows formalised procedures – the legal orders mostly defer on a) who has a right to participate, b) on what stage the participation takes place and c) what impact does the participation have on the result.[184] It is stressed that rights are worthless without formalised processes to claim them.

Indigenous and local communities are attributed specific importance to raise awareness and guarantee participation. For example, s 2 (4) (f) NEMA SA contains provisions for public participation in environmental matters, providing guidance for local governance and encouraging local communities and municipalities to get involved in the decision-making process.[185] This might

181 For example s 10 (3a) German Federal Immission Control Act (Bundes-Immissionsschutzgesetz in der Fassung der Bekanntmachung vom 17. Mai 2013 (BGBL I p 1274; 2021 I p 123)).

182 Directive 2011/92/EU of the European Parliament and the Council of 13 December 2011 on the assessment of the effects of certain public and private projects on the environment Text with EEA relevance, OJ L 26, 28.1.2012, p 1.

183 See e.g. Neil Craik, 'The Assessment of Environmental Impact', in Emma Lees and Jorge E. Viñuales (eds), *Oxford Handbook on Comparative Environmental Law* (OUP 2019) at 890–91.

184 Federica Cittadino, 'Public Participation in the Water Framework Directive: A Contribution to Deliberative Democracy?', in Eva Julia Lohse and Margherita Poto (eds), *Best Practices for the Protection of Water by Law* (BWV 2017) at 50.

185 Du Plessis, n 52, at 112.

help to promote environmental protection and sustainable development by participation.[186] The RMA NZ follows a similar approach by establishing participatory rights of indigenous communities.[187] Another way of (indirect) participation, established in several countries, is an advisory committee (e.g. in Namibia, Germany[188] or Canada), which includes at least representatives from NGO's, environmental associations or civil society, and usually publishes reports and non-binding opinions.

As far as access to justice is concerned, the main obstacle to standing in sustainability cases are legal requirements of either a violation of individual rights[189] or of a personal interest. Many legal orders have found ways to address the conundrum that the promotion of sustainable development or sustainability is a collective, diffuse or altruistic interest, often framed under public welfare, common goods or even socio-economic rights and yet, compliance to those provisions needs to be claimed by individuals before courts.[190] There are several options on the procedural level: altruistic claims (actio popularis) of individuals, for example in the Netherlands,[191] Portugal,[192] Pakistan,[193] Kenya[194] or Brazil (and most other Latin American legal orders),[195] a further modification of standing requirements like s 38 SAConst,[196] class action or even the possibility for a constitutional actio popularis. The latter can be found in about 30 constitutions,[197] however, mostly the fundamental right to a healthy environment as well as constitutional imperatives for sustainable

186 Glazewski, n 6, at 19 and 332.

187 For example, Jollands and Harmsworth, n 48, at 722.

188 Sachverständigenrat in Umweltfragen.

189 See e.g. s 42 (2) German Administrative Procedure Code (Verwaltungsgerichtsordnung in der Fassung der Bekanntmachung vom 19. März 1991 (BGBL I p 686)).

190 Ramos, n 18, at 129–30, 137; Kommer, n 19, at 461.

191 Section 305a of the Dutch Civil Code (class actions of public interest groups), which can also be used for human rights matters (see Gerichtshof Den Haag, decision of 9/10/2018, ECLI:NL:GHDHA:2018:2591, para 45), however so far restricted to living (and not future) generations.

192 Art 52 Constitution of Portugal (guarantee of an actio popularis as well as a right to address administrative appeals).

193 Public interest litigation to enable individuals to enforce public interest through court action.

194 Art 70 Kenyan Constitution.

195 Ação Civil Pública, see Kommer, n 19, at 461.

196 It reads: '... (c) anyone acting as a member of, or in the interest of, a group or class of persons, (d) anyone acting in the public interest (e) an association acting in the interest of its members', on this see Glazewski, n 6, at 73–74.

197 Boyd, n 111, at 71ff.

development are non-justiciable,[198] so even if those legal remedies exist they cannot be used in order to claim the infringement of sustainability provisions. The idea of granting standing to individuals acting in the public or collective interest can also be found in regional human rights treaties, like the Banjul Charter or the Inter-American Convention on Human Rights,[199] creating the ground for an interconnection between participation and – at least – the environmental leg of sustainable development before the courts.

Finally, a weak constitutional imperative can be found in some of the German state constitutions: Art 39 (8) Constitution of Brandenburg seems to contain a direct right for environmental associations to participate and to gain access to justice, however, this provision is seen as a mere obligation to institute a form of class action on statutory level.[200] It shows another trend, namely to attribute access to justice in environmental or sustainability matters to groups or communities, associations (NGOs) or specific institutions (like an ombudsperson or a specific governmental agency, like in Brazil). This can be found in the RMA NZ, where specific rights are granted to the Iwi/Maori, and in the various versions of group action, for example in the German Environmental Appeals Act,[201] which implements Art 9 (3) AC. Supranational and international law also incited a change in administrative court procedure by moving towards access to justice for all persons interested, allowing for transindividual

198 James R. May, 'Constituting Fundamental Environmental Rights Worldwide' [2006] Pace EnvtlLRev., 113 at 134ff; Ramos, n 18, at 128ff.

199 See the famous Ogoni-Case (AfrCHR, *The Social and Economic Rights Action Center and the Center for Economic and Social Rights v. Nigeria, African Commission on Human and Peoples' Rights* (2001), Comm. No. 155/96): 'which is wisely allowed under the African Charter'. Similar Art 44 ACHR, see Riccardo Pavoni, 'Environmental Jurisprudence of the ECtHR and IACtHR', in Ben Boer (ed), Environmental Law Dimensions of Human Rights (OUP 2015) at 93.

200 See Brönneke, n 84 at 98, 380ff; Steffen J Iwers, 'Art. 39', in Hasso Lieber, Steffen J Iwers and Martina Ernst (eds), *Verfassung des Landes Brandenburg* (Kommunal- und Schulverlag 2012), paras 3, 9; OVG Frankfurt (Oder), decision of 27 August 1997 – 3 A 37/96, LKV 1998, 490 at 492. In contrast, Art 10 (2) Constitution of Saxony is clearly formulated as a mandate for the legislative to create a group action for environmental associations, SächsVerfGH, decision of 20 April 1995 – Vf. 18-II-93, LKV 1995, 399 at 400; Christoph Degenhart, 'Die Staatszielbestimmungen der Sächsischen Verfassung', in Christoph Degenhart and Claus Meissner (eds), *Handbuch der Verfassung des Freistaates Sachsen* (Boorberg 1997) at 174–75.

201 Umweltrechtsbehelfsgesetz, Gesetz über ergänzende Vorschriften zu Rechtsbehelfen in Umweltangelegenheiten nach der EG-Richtlinie 2003/35/EG vom 7. Dezember 2006 (BGBL I p 2816).

protection of rights.[202] Another option are substantive individual rights to a healthy environment or to sustainable management or development, either at constitutional or statutory level, which are combined with provisions on standing.[203] All of this is aimed at abolishing the gap between objective imperatives for the state and individual power to enforce compliance with individual as well as collective and altruistic interests. This seems to be a global movement, mostly incited by sustainability provisions.

The largest implementation problem seems to be ensuring equality of arms, especially in court decisions due to lack of expertise, insufficient evidence (leading to wrong decisions) and a high cost risk, which might yield a preference for governmental participants by legislators.[204] These factors might impede participation, especially by certain groups in society. An implementation deficit of participative democracy, mostly if the political system excludes large parts of the population from efficient participation and if awareness for the importance of sustainable development is low, affects the link to sustainable management by the state and thus the government duty to sustainably manage resources.[205]

3.2.3. Established Connections and Interdependencies

The last question to be answered is whether there is an intended connection between the two concepts and how this is construed. One example is the Finnish Environmental Protection Act,[206] which in s 1 states as its purpose both sustainable development and enhancing public participation in decision-making.[207] In a similar way, s 3 EMCA Kenya ties environmental litigation to

---

202 On this see Christoph Enders, 'Subjektiv-rechtliche Fundierung des Umweltschutzes: Das Bundesverwaltungsgericht als Motor der Rechtsaktualisierung im Zeichen des Europarechts' [2016] ZUR, 387 at 387.

203 Martin Kind, *Umweltschutz durch Verfassungsrecht* (Springer-Verlag 1994) at 284; Wieland, n 81, at 480; Felix Ekhardt, 'Umweltverfassung und "Schutzpflichten"' [2013] NVwZ, 1105 at 1107; Michael Kotulla, 'Verfassungsrechtliche Aspekte im Zusammenhang mit der Einführung eines Umweltgrundrechts in das Grundgesetz' [2000] 33 KJ, 22 at 23ff.

204 Kós, n 44.

205 Krell, n 17, at 696.

206 Environmental Protection Act (No. 527 of 2014) Consolidated version of Act No. 527 of 2014 as last amended by Act No. 119 of 18 December 2020.

207 'The purpose of this Act is to:
1) prevent the pollution of the environment and any risk of this, prevent and reduce emissions, eliminate adverse impacts caused by pollution and prevent environmental damage;
2) safeguard a healthy, pleasant, ecologically sustainable and biologically diverse environment, support sustainable development and combat climate change;

the principle of sustainable development and defines public participation in the decision-making process as one aspect of sustainability.[208] Participatory instruments might therefore be purposefully established in order to promote sustainable development, environmental protection, wise use of resources or safeguard future generations' rights as well as other aspects of sustainability. It might, however, also be a foremost separate (maybe older) development, informed by human rights' thinking, protection of indigenous communities or more deliberative understandings of democracy and justice, like referenda and plebiscites as well as the actio popularis.

Also, procedural approaches like environmental impact assessment, public participation by submissions in planning processes for sustainable management[209] or involvement of certain groups, who might hold a substantial right in the decision-making process, are used to establish a link between participation and sustainable development, with a certain emphasis on the environmental leg. This procedural approach, which allows a variety of persons and groups the possibility to participate in decision-making, is important in order to concretise the vague concept and to add various interests to the balancing process. Ideally, as a result better informed decisions are reached.[210]

However, it is doubtful whether public participation leads to an effective promotion of sustainability. This must be attributed to the way the statutes and provisions are constructed, especially if the final balancing of interests is left to the authorities, if public participation is only required in a small amount of proceedings, or if there is no encompassing control by the courts.[211] Mostly, individuals participate not out of altruistic sustainability reasons, but motivated by their very personal interests – thus, the outcome depends on whether these interests are aligned with sustainable development or not. Participation often favours rather the protection of individual rights of those involved and not public interests, which do not need to be congruent. This reflects the problems encountered with anthropocentric rather than

---

3) promote sustainable use of natural resources, reduce the amount and harmfulness of waste, and prevent adverse impacts caused by waste;

4) make the assessment of activities causing pollution and the consideration of the impacts as a whole more effective;

5) improve the opportunities of citizens to affect decision-making concerning the environment.'

208 EMCA Kenya s 3 para 5 (a).

209 Like in Germany or New Zealand, see Hewison, n 37, at 640ff.

210 For the importance of this connection see Jollands and Harmsworth, n 48, at 724.

211 See the account by Kment, n 34, at 82–83 for New Zealand and at 28ff for Germany and similar Luketina and Parson, n 49, at 206.

eco-centric environmental protection clauses. This seems to be different with collective mechanisms of participation, where egoistic motivations are mellowed by the quorum.[212]

4 Conclusions: Best Practises and Communalities

To summarise, in all legal orders in this analysis both concepts had a strong focus on the green leg of sustainable development and mostly materialised in connection with environmental protection laws or the right to a healthy environment. However, mostly in the Global South, the importance of balancing ecological with social and economic interests is emphasised and included in the pertinent legislation. Participation for sustainable development should rather be attributed to collectives like local communities as this might enhance acceptance of decisions taken and likewise lead to more sustainable decisions as individual egoistic interests are watered down. Rights-based approaches that enable trans-individual action and participation seem to have a positive effect on sustainable development, especially if the right gives standing to groups or even individuals.

Finally, the analysis has shown that there is a strong need to concretise vague notions in the constitutions or statutory law – either by governmental plans on a more general basis or on a case-to-case basis by courts. However, general plans seem to be the better solution for sustainable development as they have the potential to guide administrative decision making and individual balancing processes and lead to a more consolidated use of the principle of sustainable development.

Bibliography

Aguila Y and Gomez S, 'United Nations Sustainable Development Initiatives' in Anthony R. Zelle, et al. (eds), *Earth Law* (New York: Wolters Kluwer, 403, 2021).

Alogna I, 'The Circulation of the Model of Sustainable Development: Tracing the Path in a Comparative Law Perspective' in Volker Mauerhofer (ed), *Legal Aspects of Sustainable Development* (Springer, 13, 2016).

Atapattu SA, Gonzalez CG and Seck SL, 'Intersections of Environmental Justice and Sustainable Development: Framing the Issues' in Sumudu A. Atapattu, Carmen

212 Popp, n 80, at 375ff.

G. Gonzalez, and Sara L. Seck (eds), *Environmental Justice and Sustainable Development*(Cambridge: CUP, 2021, 1).

Benjamin AH and Bryner N, 'Brazil' in Jorge E. Vinuales and Emma Lees (eds.), *Oxford Handbook of Comparative Environmental Law* (Oxford, 82, 2019).

Berg W, ‚Nachhaltigkeit und Umweltstaat' in Wolfgang Kahl (ed), *Nachhaltigkeit als Verbundbegriff* (Tübingen: Mohr Siebeck, 425, 2008).

Bollman M and Hardy SD, 'A multi-level analyisis of Costa Rica's payments for environmental services programme' in Thoko Kaime (ed), *International Climate Change Law and Policy* (London, New York: Routledge, 183, 2014).

Bosselmann K, 'Sustainability and the Law', in Peter Salmon and David Grinlinton (eds), *Environmental Law in New Zealand* (2nd edn., 2018, 75–106).

Boyd D, *The Environmental Rights Revolution* (Vancouver: UBC Press, 2012).

Boyd D, 'Constitutions, human rights, and the environment: national approaches', in Anna Grear and Louis J Kotzé (eds), *Research Handbook on Human Rights and the Environment* (Cheltenham: Edward Elgar, 170, 2015).

Louis J Kotzé, *The rights of nature* (EWC Press, 2019).

Boyle A, 'Human Rights and the Environment - Where Next?' in Ben Boer (ed), *Environmental Law Dimensions of Human Rights* (Oxford: OUP, 201, 2015).

Brönneke T, *Umweltverfassungsrecht* (Baden-Baden: Nomos, 1999).

Chenwi L, 'The Right to a Satisfactory, Healthy, and Sustainable Environment in the African Regional Human Rights System' in John H. Knox and Ramin Pejan (eds), *The Human Right to a Healthy Environment* (Cambridge: CUP, 59, 2018).

Cittadino F, 'Public Participation in the Water Framework Directive: A Contribution to Deliberative Democracy?' in Eva Julia Lohse and Margherita Poto (eds), *Best Practices for the Protection of Water by Law* (Berlin: BWV, 45–62, 2017).

Craik N, 'The Assessment of Environmental Impact' in Emma Lees and Jorge E. Vinuales (eds), *Oxford Handbook on Comparative Environmental Law* (Oxford: OUP, 876, 2019).

du Plessis A, 'Public Participation, Good Environmental Governance and Fulfilment of Environmental Rights' (2008) 11 *PELJ*, 170–200.

du Plessis A, *Fulfilment of South Africa's Constitutional Environmental Right in the Local Government Sphere* (Nijmegen: Wolf Legal Publishers, 2008).

du Plessis A, *Environmental Law and Local Government in South Africa* (Cape Town: Juta, 2015).

Ehemann E, *Umweltgerechtigkeit* (Tübingen: Mohr-Siebeck, 2020).

Feris LA and Tladi D, 'Environmental Rights' in Danie Brand and Christof Heyns (eds), *Socio-Economic Rights in South Africa* (Pretoria: PULP, 249–64, 2005).

Ferreira PG and Mancilla M, 'Indigenous Environmental Rights and Sustainable Development' in Sumudu A. Atapattu, Carmen G. Gonzalez and Sara L. Seck (eds), *Environmental Justice and Sustainable Development* (Cambridge: CUP, 164, 2021).

Friede R, 'The Protection of the Environment in the Brazilian Supreme Federal Court: Analysis of Real Cases' (2016)*Revista Semioses,* 10 (3).

Gillman LN, 'Assessment of sustainable forest management in New Zealand indigenous forest' (2008) 64 *New Zealand Geographer,* 57.

Glazewski J, *Environmental Law in South Africa* (2nd edn.; Durban: LexisNexis Butterworth, 2005).

Glazewski J, 'South Africa', in Emma Lees and Jorge E. Vinuales (eds), *The Oxford Handbook on Comparative Environmental Law* (Oxford: OUP, 315, 2019).

Gross T, 'Climate change and duties to protect with regard to fundamental rights' in Wolfgang Kahl and Marc-Philippe Weller (eds), *Climate Change Litigation* (München: C.H.Beck, 81–96, 2021).

Heinämäki L, 'Protecting the rights of indigenous people - promoting sustainability of the global environment?' (2009) *ICLR,* (11), 3.

Heinicke T, *Umweltschutz im Grundgesetz und in der Verfassung der Republik Südafrika* (Düsseldorf: WiKu-Verlag, 2007).

Hewison G, 'The Resource Management Act 1991' in Peter Salmon and David Grinlinton (eds), *Environmental Law in New Zealand* (Wellington, 579, 2018).

Jollands N and Harmsworth G, 'Participation of indigenous groups in sustainable development monitoring: Rationale and examples from New Zealand' (2007) 62 *Ecological Economis,* 716.

Joseph PA, *Constitutional and Administrative Law in New Zealand* (2nd edn.; Wellington: Brookers, 2001).

Klinck S, *Agrarumweltrecht im Wandel vom Subventionsrecht zum Recht der Umweltdienstleistung* (Berlin: Duncker & Humblot, 2012).

Klippel D and Otto M, ‚Nachhaltigkeit und Begriffsgeschichte' in Wolfgang Kahl (ed), *Nachhaltigkeit als Verbundbegriff* (Tübingen: Mohr Siebeck, 39, 2008).

Kment M, *Die Neujustierung des Nachhaltigkeitsprinzips im Verwaltungsrecht* (Tübingen: Mohr Siebeck, 2019).

Kommer S, 'Diffuse Umweltrechte in Brasilien am Beispiel von Kollektivklagen gegen ökologische Schäden durch queimadas' (2012) *ZUR,* 459.

Kotulla M, 'Verfassungsrechtliche Aspekte im Zusammenhang mit der Einführung eines Umweltgrundrechts in das Grundgesetz' (2000) 33 *KJ,* 22.

Krell A, 'Die normative Ausgestaltung des brasilianischen Umweltrechts und die Hauptprobleme seiner methodisch abgesicherten Anwendung' (2014) 62 *JöR,* 62.

Lees E, 'Adjudication Systems' in Emma Lees and Jorge E. Vinuales (eds), *Oxford Handbook on Comparative Environmental Law* (Oxford: OUP, 790–810, 2019).

Lefort-Martine T, *Des droits pour la nature? L'expérience équatorienne* (Paris: ed. L'Harmattan, 2018).

Lorenzetti RL, 'Complex Judicial Remedies in Environmental Litigation: The Argentine Experience' (2017) 29 *Journal of Environmental Law,* 1.

Luketina K and Parson P, 'New Zealand's Public Participation in Geothermal Resource Development' in Adele Manzella, Agnes Allansdottir, and Anna Pellizzone (eds), *Geothermal Energy and Society*, (Springer, 193, 2019).

MacPherson EJ, *Indigenous Water Rights in Law and Regulation* (Cambridge: CUP, 2021).

Marcal SP and Simao LP, 'Brazil' in Camilla Sanger (ed), *The Class Actions Review* (3rd edn., 14, 2019).

May, JR, 'Constituting Fundamental Environmental Rights Worldwide' (2006) 23 *Pace Envtl. L. Rev.*, 113.

McGregor D, 'Indigenous Environmental Justice and Sustainability' in Sumudu A. Atapattu, Carmen G. Gonzalez, and Sara L. Seck (eds), *Environmental Justice and Sustainable Development* (Cambridge: CUP, 58, 2021).

Monien, J, *Prinzipien als Wegbereiter eines globalen Umweltrechts* (Baden-Baden: Nomos, 2014).

Morrow K, 'Sustainability, environmental citizenship rights and the ongoing challenges of reshaping supranational environmental governance' in Anna Grear and Louis J Kotzé (eds), *Research Handbook on Human Rights and the Environment* (Cheltenham: Edward Elgar, 200–18, 2015).

O'Riordan T and Stoll-Kleemann S, 'Deliberative democracy and participatory biodiversity' in Tim O'Riordan and Susanne Stoll-Kleemann (eds), *Biodiversity, Sustainability and Human Communities* (Cambridge: CUP, 87–112, 2002).

Pavoni R, 'Environmental Jurisprudence of the ECtHR and IACtHR' in Ben Boer (ed), *Environmental Law Dimensions of Human Rights* (Oxford: OUP, 69, 2015).

Popp C, *Nachhaltigkeit und direkte Demokratie* (Tübingen: Mohr Siebeck, 2021).

Ramos EM, *Brasilianisches Umweltrecht als Biosphärenschutzrecht* (Aachen: Shaker Verlag, 2005).

Ritter CD, et al., 'Environmental Impact Assessment in Brazilian Amazonia: Challenges and prospects to assess biodiversity' (2017) 206 *Biological Conservation,* 161–68.

Ronellenfitsch M, 'Umwelt und Verkehr unter dem Einfluss des Nachhaltigkeitsprinzips' (2006) *NVwZ,* 385.

Ruppel OC and Ruppel-Schlichting, *Environmental Law and Policy in Namibia* (Welwitschia Verlag, 2013).

Spindler, EA, 'The History of Sustainability - The Origins and Effects of a Popular Concept' in Ian Jenkins and Roland Schröder (eds), *Sustainability in Tourism* (Springer, 9, 2013).

Stavenhagen R, 'Indigenous Peoples and the State in Latin America: An Ongoing Debate' in Rachel Sieder (ed), *Multiculturalism in Latin America* (Chippenham: Palgrave Macmillan, 24, 2002).

Tremmel J, Laukemann M, and Lux C, 'Die Verankerung von Generationengerechtigkeit im Grundgesetz' (1999) *ZRP*, 423.

Van Cott DL, 'Constitutional Reform in the Andes: Redefining Indigenous-State Relations' in Rachel Sieder (ed), *Multiculturalism in Latin America* (Chippenham: Palgrave Macmillan, 45, 2002).

Venter F and Kotzé LJ, 'The methodology of environmental constitutional comparison' in Andreas Philippopoulos-Mihalopoulos and Victoria Brooks (eds), *Research Methods in Environmental Law* (Cheltenham: Edward Elgar, 237, 2017).

Wheen N, 'A history of New Zealand environmental law' in Eric Pawson (ed), *Environmental histories of New Zealand* (Auckland: OUP, 261, 2002).

Wieland J, 'Verfassungsrang für Nachhaltigkeit', (2016) *ZUR 473*.

CHAPTER 4

Comparative Administrative Law Perspectives: China

Daniele Brombal

1 Introduction

Public participation in environmental decision-making is widely considered positive for sustainability. There are a number of good reasons for this: allowing citizens to participate strengthens the legitimacy, efficacy and inclusiveness of decisional processes, as well as the accountability of legislative and government authorities. It can also empower communities and individuals who would otherwise be marginalized. It can promote environmental awareness and harness traditional knowledge of great value for sustainability. This positive outlook on participation is supported by a wealth of evidence,[1] yet its rationale and application vary widely, depending on the cultural, social and political situation in which participation is embedded.[2] The actual design of participation is much influenced by normative stances concerning the role citizens are allowed to play in political life and the desirability of different trade-offs between human welfare and ecological integrity.

This chapter outlines the role of these factors in shaping public participation in environmental issues in China and shares new evidence on their potential to enable or constraint citizens' contribution to sustainability. I focus on what is arguably China's most carefully designed platform of citizen consultation in environmental matters, i.e. public participation in Environmental Impact Assessment (henceforth EIA PP). Section 2 illustrates the broader context and significance of public participation in Communist China's political life. Section 3 introduces the process of institutionalisation of EIA PP since the late twentieth century, touching on its main achievements and shortcomings. Section 4 introduces implications for public participation of the EIA reform launched

1 Anne. N Glucker, Peter PJ Driessen, Arend Kolhoff and Hens AC Runhaar, 'Public participation in environmental impact assessment: why, who and how?' (2013) 43 Environmental Impact Assessment Review 104.

2 Dang Wenqi, 'How culture shapes environmental public participation: case studies of China, the Netherlands and Italy' (2020) 5:3 Journal of Chinese Governance 390.

© DANIELE BROMBAL, 2023 | DOI:10.1163/9789004509382_006

in 2016. Finally, I discuss recent developments in China's EIA legislation in the light of the participation-sustainability nexus, summarizing the insights of this study and their implications for research and practice.

2 Roots and Emergence of Public Participation in Communist China's Political Life

China is not a place one would readily associate with impactful participation of citizens in political life. It is a country under authoritarian rule, and such has been for a very long time. Yet even in the darkest hours of Maoism, there were pathways that allowed a certain degree of interaction between citizens and decisionmakers. Twentieth-century China saw significant waves of political activism, which erupted at critical moments in the country's social, economic and political life. Such was the case in the second half of the 1970s and the 1980s, until the bloody Tiananmen showdown on 4 June 1989 terminated prospects for regime change. In the two decades that followed, bottom-up attempts to influence the political fabric of the country became less systemic in their goals, but by no means less common. On the contrary, civil society played a fundamental role in promoting transparency and accountability of party and state authorities. Protests triggered by state failures and cadre corruption became the norm in the late 1990s.[3] Most sprang from the sideeffects of China's economic growth on people's livelihoods and the environment: the increase in the prices of daily necessities, forced relocations to make way for infrastructure, lack of healthcare and welfare, strained labour relations, destruction of cultural heritage and natural habitats, environmental pollution – to name just the most common. When we look at individual manifestations of popular unrest, it appears that in most cases their impact was at best temporary or partial: e.g. delaying construction of a dam or a polluting factory, or managing to achieve some degree of impact mitigation, often by project relocation.[4] Yet when taken as a whole, citizen participation and protests promoted a reconsideration of the role that public opinion and sustainability should have in the country's governance.

---

3 Christian Göbel, Lynette H Ong, 'Social Unrest In China' (2013) Europe China Research and Advise Network (ECRAN) <www.chathamhouse.org/sites/default/files/public/Research/Asia/1012ecran_gobelong.pdf> accessed 6 December 2021.

4 See e.g. Andrew Mertha, '"Fragmented Authoritarianism 2.0": Political Pluralization in the Chinese Policy Process' (2009) 200 The China Quarterly 995.

Since the 1990s, a number of mechanisms have been put in place to allow people's participation in government affairs. Their roots and ideological legitimacy can be traced back to the early days of Chinese Communism, when the Party's rhetoric propagated forms of mobilization designed to catalyse the will of the masses and serve the people.[5] However, the legal foundations of today's public participation in China rest on political developments that occurred after the end of the Cultural Revolution. In the late 1970s, the second generation of leaders – epitomized by Deng Xiaoping – inherited a country torn by social conflict and widespread poverty, where the legitimacy of the Party State had been undermined by years of political violence and appalling sufferings across vast sectors of society. As part of the broader effort to rebuild the social fabric and trust in the Party, the 1982 Constitution established that state organs should "rely on the support of the people [...] heed their opinions and suggestions, accept their supervision."[6] These provisions found their first nationwide application in the establishment of village elections in the 1980s, where rural communities were in principle granted the possibility of freely choosing their leaders.[7]

The turbulent years of students' protests and State repression culminating in the Tiananmen massacre of 4 June 1989 did not halt the expansion of public participation mechanisms, which in fact gained momentum in the 1990s. Local authorities experimented with new forms of involvement in areas of pressing public concern. In 1997, Guangdong province adopted a regulation on public hearings (*tingzhenghui* 听证会) about pricesetting. A year later, national authorities took the same path, establishing hearing requirements in the Price Law.[8] The year 2000 was a watershed in establishing the political legitimacy and legal basis for the right of the people to take part in decision-making. The National People's Congress – China's highest legislative body – passed the Law on Legislation, requiring that Chinese citizens be given the possibility to participate through various channels in the legislative process.[9] The early 2000s witnessed the nationwide institutionalization of public participation. The term itself was standardized in

5 Wen-hui Tsai, 'Mass Mobilization Campaigns in Mao's China' (1999) 6 1 American Journal of Chinese Studies 21.

6 Constitution of the People's Republic of China 1982, art 27.

7 In fact, most village elections remained controlled or heavily influenced by the Party.

8 Jamie P. Horsley, 'Public Participation in the People's Republic: Developing a More Participatory Governance Model in China' (2009) Yale Law <https://law.yale.edu/sites/default/files/documents/pdf/Intellectual_Life/CL-PP-PP_in_the__PRC_FINAL_91609.pdf>, accessed 14 December 2021.

9 Legislation Law of the People's Republic of China 2000.

Chinese legal language in 2003, when important official documents began to use the expression *gongzhong canyu* 公众参与.[10] Forms of participation became standardized too, including public hearings (*tingzhenghui* 听证会), auditing (*panting* 旁听), expert meetings (*lunzhenghui* 论证会), workshops (*zuotanhui* 座谈会) and seeking public opinion on draft regulations (zhengqiu yijian 征求意见).[11,12] The latter form expanded rapidly thanks to the internet and was eventually favoured by the authorities, because it gave them the possibility to manage interactions with the public in an "orderly" fashion. In the first decade of the 2000s, authorities solicited public opinion on a number of draft laws and regulations addressing issues of pressing social concern, including Property Law, Labour Contract Law and the Healthcare Reform Plan.[13,14,15] These developments would not have been possible without the gradual introduction of mechanisms of government information disclosure (*xinxi gongkai* 信息公开) that culminated in 2008 in adoption of the Open Government Information (OGI) Regulations.[16] The OGI Regulations paved the way to a huge increase in information available to the public, relevant to government decision-making and policy implementation.

Until recently, these innovations generated widespread optimism about the prospects for public participation and its role in addressing sustainability challenges. This optimism was damped in recent years by concerns over changes in the country's political climate. Indeed, the leadership has embraced a more controlling attitude towards civil and political rights. The very same technologies that enabled more transparent and participatory politics are now being employed to monitor individual and collective behaviour of Chinese citizens, targeting dissent and activism. Recent evidence also shows that the technocratic rationale underlying much Chinese decision-making may be gaining ground, impacting on processes once designed to allow wider participation of the public.[17] Overall, the emergence of institutionalised public participation

---

10 Horsley (no. 8).

11 Ibid.

12 Daniele Brombal, Angela Moriggi and Antonio Marcomini, 'Evaluating Public Participation in Chinese EIA. An Integrated Public Participation Index and its Application to the Case of the New Beijing Airport' (2017) 62 Environmental Impact Assessment Review 49.

13 Jasper Becker, 'Public Consultations in China' (2012) Short Term Policy Brief 56, Europe China Research and Advice Network (ECRAN).

14 Daniele Brombal, 'Private Interests in Chinese Politics. A Case Study on Health Care Sector Reforms', In Kjeld Erik Brødsgaard (ed), *Chinese Politics as Fragmented Authoritarianism*: Earthquakes, Energy and Environment (Routledge 2017) 98–119.

15 Horsley (no. 8).

16 Regulations of the People's Republic of China on Open Government Information 2008.

17 Xiangbai He, 'In the Name of Legitimacy and Efficiency: Evaluating China's Legal Reform on EIA' (2020) Journal of Environmental Law 1. Similar evidence can be found

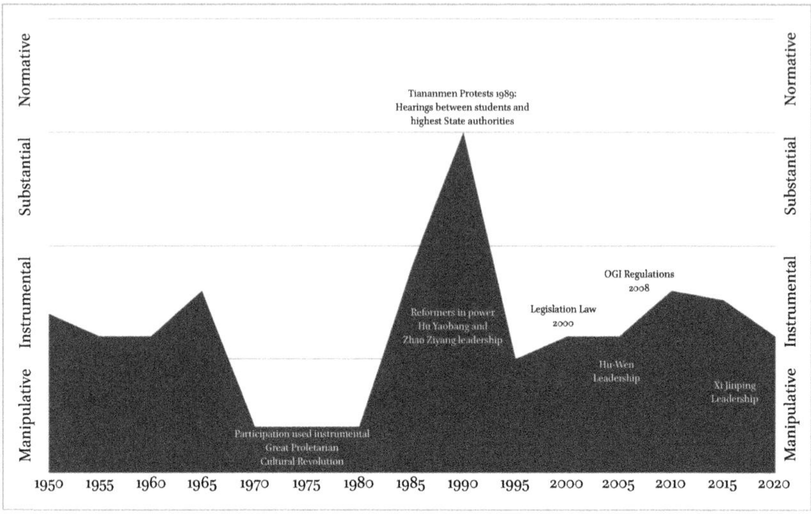

FIGURE 4.1 Timeline and overarching rationales of institutionalised public participation in Communist China[18]

in the last 30 years offers a mixed picture. While regulations appear to have a normative rationale – empowering citizens through their full participation in political life – real life application of participation is pretty much about enhancing the legitimacy of decision-making processes and ensuring stability of China's political system.

3 Institutionalization of Public Participation in China's Environmental Planning

China's environmental governance has long epitomized the sustainability challenges faced by the country and the political motifs behind the adoption of participatory pathways. Already at the outset of the reform era – initiated in

in unpublished research notes shared on the *Researchgate* portal by Dr. Ceren Ergenc (Xi'An Jiaotong-Liverpool University), indicating that participatory urban planning has been shifting towards wider use of expert meetings (*lunzhenghui* 论证会), rather than allowing wider citizen participation. See <https://www.researchgate.net/publication/353793328_From_representation_to_expertise_in_participatory_policymaking_in_urban_China> accessed 15 December 2021.

18 Original figure, sketched by the author on the basis of various sources, for his course in Chinese politics and society. For an updated list of references used to draw this figure, see: <https://www.unive.it/data/course/348546/programma> accessed 15 December 2021.

1978–79 – part of the Chinese leadership was aware that in the long run, the environmental devastation and social disruption caused by modernization could jeopardize the very goals of socioeconomic progress the reforms were designed to sustain, eventually undermining the legitimacy of the PartyState. The 1970s saw the establishment of the legal foundations of China's environmental governance apparatus, with the inclusion of environmental protection as a State function in the 1978 Constitution,[19] and the adoption of the first Environmental Protection Law in 1979 (EPL, amended in 1989 and 2014).[20] These developments were also made possible by China's opening to the West. China's (proto)sustainability concerns sprang from the report "The Limits to Growth" (1972) commissioned by the Club of Rome, and from the neo-Malthusian argument, which eventually resulted in adoption of the contentious One-Child Policy (1980).[21] China's participation at the 1972 UN Stockholm Conference on the Human Environment laid the ground for the first national conference for environmental protection (1973) and the establishment of a first administrative body for environmental protection under the State Council (1974), the embryo of what later became the State Administration of Environmental Protection (SEPA).[22] Another milestone was the Chinese participation at the UN Rio Earth Summit (1992) and the endorsement of sustainable, just and inclusive development principles outlined in Agenda 21.

The establishment of China's environmental governance apparatus was thus favoured by endogenous and exogenous factors: increasing awareness of the negative sideeffects of industrial development, also sustained by emergent activism; preoccupations about PartyState legitimacy and social stability; exposure to the theory and practice of environmental governance developed in industrialized countries. It was against this background that in the 1980s, the Chinese government piloted its first Environmental Impact Assessment (EIA) procedures, translating into practice the provisions contained in the 1978 EPL. Despite the early introduction of impact assessment, the first regulation containing detailed provisions for EIA was not adopted until 1998, when the Regulations on Environmental Management of Construction Projects

19 Constitution of the People's Republic of China 1978, art. 11.

20 Environmental Protection Law of the People's Republic of China (for Trial Implementation) 1979.

21 Susan Greenhalgh, *Just One Child: Science and Policy in Deng's China* (University of California Press, 2008).

22 Richard Sanders, 'The Political Economy of Chinese Environmental Protection: Lessons for the Mao and Deng Years' (1999) 20, 6 Third World Quarterly 1201.

streamlined EIA architecture and core responsibilities.[23] By that time, though not mandated by law, public participation had already become part of EIA. First introduced by an Asian Development Bank (ADB) training program in 1991, EIA PP was recommended by the State Council in 1996 and later made mandatory in the first EIA dedicated legislation, the Environmental Impact Assessment (EIA) Law, adopted in 2002 (revised in 2016 and 2018).

The early 2000s were a fundamental time in the establishment of the practice of EIA in China. The process was not unchallenged: ensuring compliance by project proponents and local governments proved quite arduous. This was due to a number of factors, including the predominance attributed to economic over environmental goals, bureaucratic incentive systems skewed towards the attainment of short-term growth, widespread local protectionism tying developers to local leaders, and the weakness of environmental authorities, which did not attain full ministerial status until 2008.[24] Such were the difficulties, that in 2005 SEPA launched a nationwide campaign for the enforcement of the EIA Law, which would later become known as the "EIA Storm".[25] Meanwhile, the legal basis of EIA PP was strengthened by adoption of the Provisional Measures for Public Participation in EIA in 2006.[26] The measures were of great importance for the institutionalization of EIA PP, in that they clarified both its guiding principles (openness, equality, inclusiveness and convenience) and its mechanisms (timing, information provision, and consultation arrangements). More specifics were provided in the Technical Guidelines for Environmental Impact Assessment Public Participation (EIA PP) (2011),[27] which became a benchmark for EIA practitioners. The Guidelines further specified the goals of PP as: a) protecting the people's environmental rights as guaranteed by law; b) providing a more thorough understanding of the environmental problems that may arise from projects; and c) improving the effectiveness of environmental protection and

---

23 Regulations on Environmental Management of Construction Projects of the People's Republic of China 1998.

24 That year SEPA was transformed into the Ministry of Environmental Protection (MEP), which would become the Ministry of Ecology and Environment (MEE) in 2018.

25 He (no. 17).

26 Provisional Measures for Public Participation in Environmental Impact Assessment, State Environmental Protection Administration of the People's Republic of China 2006.

27 Technical Guideline for Environmental Impact Assessment Public Consultation - Solicit Opinions Draft, Ministry of Environmental Protection of the People's Republic of China 2011.

mitigation measures.[28] More broadly, the Technical Guidelines appeared to signal a willingness to infuse EIA PP with a substantive rationale, i.e. enabling the public to provide meaningful and actionable input to improve decision-making.

Sustainability scholars and advocates placed much faith in the potential of these developments to empower communities and activists in their fight against environmental destruction. However, results were at best mixed and to some extent counterintuitive from a political standpoint. Mandatory EIA PP proved virtually unable to make a positive, sustainabilitydriven impact on decision-making. This was due to the technical features of the PP process itself and to the wider cultural and political context. In the 2010s, a number of procedural shortcomings in China's EIA PP became evident, including the following:[29,30]

- the timing of PP was too narrow and too late with respect to project approval procedures;
- the information was incomplete and/or unintelligible to the average citizen due to the use of technical jargon;
- the scope of consultation was narrow and essentially concerned with mitigation measures and economic compensation;
- consultation arrangements and methods were unsuited to promoting collaborative decision-making, let alone empowering individuals and communities;
- inclusiveness was limited and certain categories of stakeholders, such as technical experts, were given priority over others;
- incorporation of results in documents informing decision-making (i.e. the EIA Report) was partial, and no feedback regarding people's demands was provided.

These problems affected even those cases considered to be exemplary of best "practices": in a detailed analysis of the EIA for the new Beijing Airport, the author of this chapter, with colleagues Moriggi and Marcomini, identified major issues across all criteria mentioned above,[31] indicating an instrumental

28 Ibid.

29 Yang Yang, 'Reformed Environmental Impact Assessment in China: An Evaluation of its Effectiveness' (2020) 11 Journal of Environmental Protection 889.

30 Brombal, Moriggi and Marcomini (no. 12).

31 Brombal, Moriggi and Marcomini (no. 12). Results were based on the application of an original multicriteria Public Participation Index (PPI), which we developed in 2016. Criteria include timing, information provision, consultation arrangements, consulted public, and incorporation of consultation results in documents informing decision making.

use of participation. Procedural obstacles to meaningful participation were – and still are – heightened by a political and professional culture that overlooks the potential of social collaboration and dialogue in designing sustainable projects, instead favouring technological solutions and technocratic approaches.[32] This tendency is more acute when the public is composed of individuals and communities who have been sidelined by industrialization and urbanization (for example rural communities and minorities).[33] These people are sometimes referred to by experts as "low quality" (*suzhi di* 素质低) and therefore unlikely to bring any positive input to the decision-making process.[34] Overall, poor procedures and the sociocultural context created a huge gap between the spirit of the law and its concrete application. While EIA PP enacted in the 2000s and early 2010s called for a substantive rationale and proactive collaboration, the common practice was that of instrumental use of participation, which became a tickbox exercise. Paradoxically, this gap has had a remarkable effect in empowering Chinese citizens and civil society in their pursuit of sustainable and just futures.[35] In a number of instances, local communities and civil society have appealed to environmental authorities after EIA PP processes had been conducted, to denounce their inconsistency with goals and procedures outlined in national laws. This has given the leverage needed to ask for project adjustments and broader processes of consultation. In some cases, it has also resulted in ex-novo assessment of project impacts.[36]

32 Greenhalgh (no. 21). For another take on this matter issue, cf. Yongmu Liu, 'The Benefits of Technocracy in China' (2016) XXXIII 1 Issues in Science and Technology <https://issues.org/perspective-the-benefits-of-technocracy-in-china/> accessed 20 December 2021.

33 Tamara Jacka, 'Cultivating citizens: suzhi (quality) discourse in the PRC' (2009) 17, 3 Positions 523.

34 Interviews #141001, 141211, 151015a, in Brombal, Moriggi and Marcomini (12).

35 Thomas Johnson, 'Public Participation in China's EIA Process and the Regulation of Environmental Disputes' (2020) 81 Environmental Impact Assessment Review 106359.

36 This has been a common trend in China for the most part of the last two decades, in some cases yielding victories and impacting for good on decision-making. In one notorious case – the 2008 Xiamen anti-paraxylene (PX) plant protests – these processes resulted in project relocations, rather contentious from an environmental justice standpoint. On the PX case, see: Environmental Justice Atlas, 'Controversy over planned paraxylene (PX) plant in Xiamen, Fujian, China' 2017 <https://ejatlas.org/conflict/controversy-over-planned-paraxylene-px-plant-in-xiamen-fujian-china> accessed 20 December 2021.

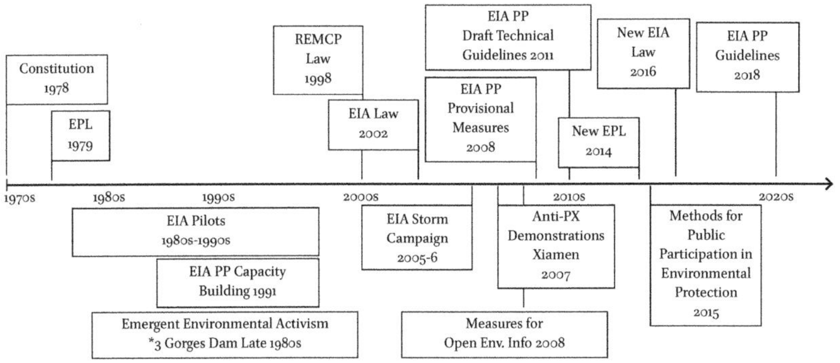

FIGURE 4.2 Milestones in the institutionalization of PP in China's EIA (1978–2020)[37]

4 Recent Developments in EIA PP and Likely Implications for Sustainability

4.1 *Changes in EIA Regulation*

The mixed picture we have just outlined also applies to EIA impacts on promoting environmental sustainability. While the introduction of impact assessment was a positive development in advancing the country's environmental agenda, in practice its enforcement has been piecemeal. The very mild penalties for noncompliance have certainly played a role in this respect.[38] But there have been other causes as well. First, the potential for sustainability has been jeopardized by the conflict of interest inherent in the EIA system, whereby the assessment is conducted by licensed entities hired by the developer. While this issue is common to many EIA regimes, in China it has been exacerbated by the fact that many entities licenced to produce EIA REPORTS frequently employed staff from government agencies responsible for EIA authorization. This generated a situation where the controller and the controlled were often identical, or at least shared an affiliation with the same organisation.[39] In this context, decisions were unlikely to be based solely on bonafide professional judgement, creating an ideal habitat for corruption. Against this background, EIA has long

37 Daniele Brombal, 'Public Participation in China's EIA. Potential and Limits in Fostering Sustainability' (2020). Presentation delivered during the SUSTAINET conference *Sustainability Through Participation? Legal Perspectives*, University of Trier, 04 December.

38 Yang (no. 29).

39 Daniele Brombal, 'Accuracy of Environmental Monitoring in China: Exploring the Influence of Institutional, Political and Ideological Factors' (2017) 9 3 Sustainability 324.

been considered a mere tickbox exercise for developers, a process to complete before getting down to real business.

After approval of the new EPL in 2014, the Chinese government embarked on a thorough reform of EIA regulations, revising the EIA Law (2016, 2018), the Regulations on Environmental Management of Construction Projects (REMCP) in 2017 and the EIA PP Guidelines (2019).[40,41,42] Another fundamental change was the revision of the Catalogue for the Administration of EIA for Construction Projects (henceforth *the Catalogue*, 2018).[43] The declared goals of the reform were to promote better environmental outcomes and improve the efficiency of the EIA process. Five interrelated areas of reform are of particular interest:

- a change in screening criteria, to define which projects should be subject to EIA;
- a broader range of EIA-related responsibilities and liabilities entrusted to the project proponent;
- decentralisation of EIA approval;
- revised provisions regulating consultation arrangements in EIA PP;
- higher penalties for violations of EIA requirements.[44,45]

With reference to the first of these reform areas, the revision of the Catalogue led to the downgrading of 30 categories of projects, which now no longer need to undergo a full EIA, but are subject to a simpler procedure, i.e. submitting an Environmental Impact Form (EIF) or filing an Environmental Impact Registration Form, neither of which requires PP.[46] Data from the Ministry of Ecology and Environment (MEE) indicates that 80% of all projects can now undergo a simplified EIA process, a result praised by the MEE as a significant reduction of workload for environmental bureaucracies.[47] The same logic appears to apply to recent modifications in EIA timing and approval responsibilities. Under the

40 Environmental Impact Assessment Law of the People's Republic of China 2002, 2016, 2018.

41 Regulations on Environmental Management of Construction Projects of the People's Republic of China 2017.

42 Measures for Public Participation in Environmental Impact Assessment, Ministry of Ecology and Environment of the People's Republic of China 2019.

43 He (no. 17).

44 Ibid.

45 Yang (no. 29).

46 As a matter of fact, the Environmental Impact Registration Form does not even require approval by the environmental authorities.

47 Xinhua News, 'Ministry of Ecology and Environment: Out of 10 projects, 8 Do Not Need Approval. A Further Enhancement of Approval Efficiency' (生态环境部：八成项目

previous regulation, EIA statements were prepared and submitted for approval at feasibility study stage,[48] whereas the new EIA Law allows project proponents to submit them just before the commencement of construction. To further simplify the procedure, approval has been decentralized, entrusting it to municipal and county authorities. Responsibilities for the actual process of conducting the EIA and drafting the report have also been amended. Project proponents can now take direct responsibility for undertaking the EIA and preparing the report for submission. Higher penalties are set for misconduct, whether for fake or incomplete data in the EIA, or for commencing construction before EIA approval.

Overall, these measures make the process easier for proponents, while lowering the workload for environmental authorities, especially those at central level. However, at the same time, their environmental rationale is unclear. Indeed, many of these measures undermine the preventive nature of EIA, transforming it from an environmental planning instrument to a management tool of much narrower scope and time horizon. The decentralization of approval may heighten local protectionism, with local authorities and powerful economic actors complying selectively with regulations, in order to preserve economic interests. Finally, lifting the requirement of hiring a licensed entity to prepare an EIA looks pretty much as if the legislator threw out the baby with the bathwater: in order to curb corruption, it created an incentive to get rid of what could potentially have been if not a third party oversight – EIA entities are paid by proponents anyway – at least a collaborative process engaging practitioners trained to design sustainable solutions. All of this has clear implications for EIA PP. Under the new regulatory scenario, the capacity of the public to scrutinize harmful projects and contribute to environmental sustainability is curtailed, since fewer projects now have to undergo a full EIA process, the only case in which PP is mandatory. Moreover, the fact that EIA can now take place after the feasibility study stage makes the cost of stopping project implementation even higher than in the past, encouraging proponents to design EIA PP in ways instrumental to the smooth implementation of projects, which was precisely the main problem with the previous regulatory environment.

环评无需审批将进一步提高审批效率) 23 September 2018 <http://www.xinhuanet.com/2018-09/02/c_1123368507.htm> accessed 20 December 2021.

48 He (no.17).

TABLE 4.1 Recent developments in EIA regulation and implications for PP[49]

Regulatory Source	Change	Implications for EIA PP
EIA Project Catalogue	Fewer projects now subject to full EIA process	Limited scope and capacity to influence decision-making
EIA Law 2018	EIA report can now be submitted before start of construction instead of at feasibility study stage	Participation loses its capacity to influence project alternatives. Incentive to instrumental participation
EIA Law 2018	EIA process can now be entirely conducted by project proponents	Lack of a third party – the EIA-licensed entity – who can mediate collaboration between the public and project proponents.
EIA Law 2018	Higher penalties for misconduct in carrying out the EIA process and in reporting	This may prompt the developer and/or the EIA entity to be more careful in incorporating consultation results in EIA reporting
EIA Law 2018	Decentralization of approval procedures	Ambivalent: it may make it easier for the public to reach out to authorities when things go wrong; on the other hand, it may strengthen local protectionism

4.2 *New EIA PP Guidelines*

4.2.1 Overall Principles

The rationale guiding the revision of the EIA PP guidelines was to streamline procedures. The outcome is more clarity in legal provisions, along with a higher degree of rigidity that could actually constrain participation, rather than enabling it. The overall tenor of the regulation is skewed towards a more restrictive interpretation of what the goals and boundaries of participation should be. In the following subsections, changes in the EIA PP regulation are analysed, based on five criteria: a) timing; b) information provision; c) consultation arrangements;

49 Sources: He (no. 17), Yang (no. 29), Brombal Moriggi and Marcomini (no. 12), Environmental Impact Assessment Law 2002, 2018 (no. 40).

d) public targeted; e) incorporation of PP results in documents informing decision-making. The capacity of participation processes to actually make an impact is also assessed.

4.2.2 Timing

The time-window allowed for public consultation remains limited, although more space is now provided for ex-post participation. The Guidelines envisage the possibility of additional consultation after acceptance of the EIA report (art. 24–25) should the authorities find any evidence or be informed of insufficient public participation. The Guidelines specifically provide that members of the public may report violations of the EIA regulation.

4.2.3 Provision of Information to the Public

With reference to completeness of information, the Guidelines foresee disclosure of the entire EIA Report, whereas previously only the abridged version was to be disclosed during the PP process (art. 20). The developer and/or the entity conducting the EIA are now required to disclose more thorough information about the contents, results, and outcomes of public consultations, including the reasons why suggestions made by the public were not accepted (art. 19). Finally, the project proponent is invited to conduct awarenessraising campaigns among affected communities, publicizing scientific knowledge (*xuanchuan… kexue zhishi* 宣传科学知识) about project impacts (art. 12).[50]

4.2.4 Consultation Arrangements

The Guidelines now foresee in-person forms of consultation only when the public provides many "doubting opinions" (*zhiyixing yijian duo* 质疑性意见多) about project impacts (art. 14). While this is not substantially different from the previous guidelines, which gave EIA entities discretionary power to decide whether or not to hold these consultations, it is nonetheless highly problematic, especially when it comes to defining a tolerable level of doubt or criticism. Another problematic aspect concerns the way the Guidelines discriminate between cases where criticism is directed at "environmental predictions" (*huanjing yuce jielun* 环境预测结论) contained in the EIA – in which case the general public is allowed to take part in additional in-person consultations – and cases regarding professional and technical methods (*zhuanye jishu fangfa*

50 In the Chinese context, where phenomena of politicization of science are widely documented, this may result in political propaganda campaigns.

专业技术方法) (art. 14). In this second instance, consultation is restricted to experts, in the form of argumentation meetings. This is again a highly problematic mechanism, since issues that are eminently social and political may be framed in technical terms, so as to remove them from the arena of public debate.

4.2.5 Public Targeted

The public is now defined in a narrower way than in the old guidelines. Art. 5 of the new measures specifies that the public to be consulted only includes citizens, legal persons and organizations falling within the scope of the area of the EIA assessment (*pingjia fanwei nei* 评价范围内), while inclusion of a broader audience is discretionary. This is likely to limit the inclusion of organizations such as NGOs and research institutions that are not located in the geographical area directly impacted by the project, but which could nonetheless provide meaningful input to enhance project sustainability. This is of great importance in the Chinese context, where successful cases of public participation, i.e. cases in which the public managed to influence the outcomes of decision-making, were often based on coalitions of actors at different scales, local and national.[51] The Guidelines introduce principles that are hardly inspired by broad and inclusive participation. In the guiding principles, reference to equality (*pingdeng* 平等) and extensiveness (*guangfan* 广泛) has been removed, while principles of legality (*yifa* 依法) and orderliness (*youxu* 有序) are now made explicit. (art. 4; art. 3). This tone is echoed by the reference to social stability (*shehui wending* 社会稳定) as an important objective to consider when designing participation and implementing information disclosure (art. 8).

4.2.6 Incorporation of Participation Results in Decision-making

The new Guidelines mandate inclusion of a higher level of detail of information on participation results in the EIA report. This information now also has to include an explanation of the reasons for non-acceptance of suggestions made by the consulted public (art. 19)

51 Mertha (no. 4).

TABLE 4.2 New Guidelines for EIA PP and likely impacts on participation[52]

Criterion	Change	Impacts
Timing	Additional window for ex-post consultation	Enabling
Information provision	More complete information on project impacts and participation	Enabling
	Outreach 'scientific' information campaigns for the wider public	Ambivalent
Consultation arrangements	Discretionary power to decide whether to carry out in-person consultation with the general public, based on the level of 'doubt' and the issues to be discussed	Constraining
Public targeted	Narrower and more rigid definition of public	Constraining
Incorporation of PP results in EIA	Review of consultation results	Enabling

5 Discussion: Implications for Sustainability

Since the 1980s, public participation has played an important role in pushing forward China's sustainability agenda, fostering state accountability and transparency, and broadening environmental awareness. The role of the public became particularly important in the early 2000s, also thanks to an increasing commitment to public participation by parts of the country's leadership.[53] Mechanisms of formal participation in environmental planning have played an important role in this respect, establishing pathways of consultation and enabling citizens to make their voice heard in a system lacking other formal representation mechanisms, and where the judiciary is hardly independent. To quite a few observers – mostly foreign – the establishment of such pathways

52 Sources consulted: Measures for Public Participation in Environmental Impact Assessment, Ministry of Ecology and Environment of the People's Republic of China 2002, 2019.

53 Pan Yue, 'The Environment Needs Public Participation' (2006) China Dialogue <https://chinadialogue.net/en/pollution/604-the-environment-needs-public-participation/> accessed 20 December 2021.

may be interpreted as a sign of a gradual shift of the country's polity towards democratic mechanisms. In fact, as we have seen in this chapter, it has targeted specific areas of decision-making and its rationale has been largely instrumental: enhancing legitimacy of decision-making and thus the stability of China's political system, harmonizing the pluralisation of interests brought about by economic development since the 1990s.

When interpreting developments in EIA PP and their impacts on wider issues of participation and sustainability, we must be mindful that these phenomena unfold over a long period of time, and implications for the political and environmental situation of the country may therefore be hard to ascertain over a short period. Nevertheless, we can venture a few hypotheses about the likely impacts of recent legislation. Overall, EIA reforms appear to be shaped by the need to provide a clear blueprint to companies and state organs for conducting the EIA process in a cost-effective way. Many recent changes point in this direction, most notably the decision to limit the categories of projects that have to undergo a full EIA. The same applies to the new EIA PP Guidelines: while easier to implement, they introduce elements of rigidity that are likely to constrain meaningful and creative participation, of the kind needed to trigger lasting change for sustainability. The approach taken by Chinese authorities is not enabling the public in finding sustainable alternatives to proposed projects. Quite to the contrary, it appears oriented towards streamlining the procedure in such a way as to favour smooth project implementation, reinforcing instrumental trends that have long beset PP architecture in EIA.

Clearly, the way the new regulatory framework will impact sustainability outcomes will also depend on its interaction with the broader political and socioeconomic environment. In this respect, small but significant changes in the terminology used in the EIA PP Guidelines seem influenced by the dominant ideological imprint of today's China, with citizens' democratic empowerment pretty low on the Party agenda. In fact, the legal goal of 'orderly' (*youxu* 有序) participation procedures resonates with the overarching goal of 'social stability' (*shehui wending* 社会稳定), often used instrumentally to curtail possibilities for meaningful public participation. Implementation of the new regulatory framework may also be influenced by the need to sustain economic recovery after the COVID pandemic.[54] While China has not suffered as much as other industrialized countries, its growth rate has slackened considerably and recovery has been slower than expected.[55] Seen in this light, decentralising

54 As this chapter was being finalized (November 2021), a new outbreak of COVID has prompted severe restrictions in Beijing.

55 The World Bank, GDP growth (annual%) - China <https://data.worldbank.org/indicator/NY.GDP.MKTP.KD.ZG?locations=CN> accessed 20 December 2021.

EIA approval and entrusting more responsibilities to project proponents give companies and local governments greater leeway to pursue economic growth, possibly at the expense of the environment.

What is happening in China resonates with wider trends unfolding globally. Activists, civil servants and common citizens in Europe are increasingly concerned by ongoing and proposed procedural simplifications of environmental planning, which are often justified by lawmakers on the pretext of economic growth.[56] The apparently schizophrenic swing between environmental commitments and the inertia of social and economic policies – testified at the COP 26 of Glasgow – is simply the real-life application of weak sustainability, whereby infinite growth is pursued on a finite planet. Against this background, technology – not participation – is seen as the ultimate saviour. Due to the political culture and power structure of the Party-State, China today reflects and magnifies the global appreciation of technology and technocratic modes of dealing with human-nature relations, with active participation in decision-making relegated to a marginal role.

6 Conclusion: Notes for Future Studies

To conclude, let me briefly mention three possible pathways for future research on participation and sustainability in the Chinese context. The first is strictly legal and relates to what happens when 'things go wrong.' While the role of the Chinese judiciary is often downplayed,[57] an accurate analysis of court pronouncements on cases of public interest linked to EIA procedures would be useful to understand whether the judiciary is playing a part in promoting sustainable decision-making outcomes. It could also provide a basis to understand more about how court pronouncements could impact EIA practice beyond the single case. The second possibility for research relates to the impact of social, political and economic factors on the capacity of EIA PP to promote sustainability goals. A study of these aspects would be of great societal relevance for the times ahead, with governments in China and elsewhere at work to offset the economic damage caused by the COVID pandemic, quite possibly at the expense of the environment. The third area for research would be to develop new metrics to benchmark EIA and related PP procedures against goals of harm avoidance and regeneration, going beyond reductionist approaches that consider mitigation as the only possible outcome of environmental planning.

56 Personal communication #21080 Environmental Activist a,b; #211115. Civil Servant.

57 He (no. 17).

Acknowledgments

This study was supported by the fellowship program of the European Institute for Chinese Studies (EURICS) in Paris. I wish to thank Dr. Jing Bian (University of Greenwich, EURICS fellow 2021) for meaningful comments and discussion. I would also like to share my appreciation for the volume editors Dr. Eva Julia Lohse and Dr. Birgit Peters who have done an amazing job in pulling this volume project through at a very difficult time for collaborative projects in academia.

Bibliography

Becker J, 'Public Consultations in China' (2012) Short Term Policy Brief 56, Europe China Research and Advice Network (ECRAN).

Brombal D, 'Accuracy of Environmental Monitoring in China: Exploring the Influence of Institutional, Political and Ideological Factors' (2017) 9(3) Sustainability 324.

Brombal D, Moriggi A and Marcomini A, 'Evaluating Public Participation in Chinese EIA. An Integrated Public Participation Index and its Application to the Case of the New Beijing Airport'(2017) 62 Environmental Impact Assessment Review 49.

Brombal D, 'Private Interests in Chinese Politics. A Case Study on Health Care Sector Reforms' in Brødsgaard K E (ed), *Chinese Politics as Fragmented Authoritarianism: Earthquakes, Energy and Environment* (Routledge 2017) 98–119.

Brombal D, 'Public Participation in China's EIA. Potential and Limits in Fostering Sustainability', Sustainability Through Participation? Legal Perspectives, Trier University, 04 December 2020.

Dang W, 'How Culture Shapes Environmental Public Participation: Case Studies of China, the Netherlands and Italy' (2020) 5(3) Journal of Chinese Governance 390.

Environmental Justice Atlas, 'Controversy over Planned Paraxylene (PX) Plant in Xiamen, Fujian, China' (2017) <https://ejatlas.org/conflict/controversy-over-planned-paraxylene-px-plant-in-xiamen-fujian-china> accessed 20 December 2021.

Glucker A N and others, 'Public Participation in Environmental Impact Assessment: Why, Who and How?' (2013) 43 Environmental Impact Assessment Review 104.

Göbel C and Ong L H, 'Social Unrest in China' (2013) Europe China Research and Advice Network (ECRAN) <www.chathamhouse.org/sites/default/files/public/Research/Asia/1012ecran_gobelong.pdf> accessed 6 December 2021.

Greenhalgh S, *Just One Child: Science and Policy in Deng's China* (University of California Press, 2008).

He XB, 'In the Name of Legitimacy and Efficiency: Evaluating China's Legal Reform on EIA' (2020) 32(3) Journal of Environmental Law 441.

Horsley J P, 'Public Participation in the People's Republic: Developing a More Participatory Governance Model in China' (2009) Yale China Law Center <https://law.yale.edu/sites/default/files/documents/pdf/Intellectual_Life/CL-PP-PP_in_the__PRC_FINAL_91609.pdf> accessed 14 December 2021.

Jacka T, 'Cultivating Citizens: Suzhi (quality) Discourse in the PRC (2009) 17(3) Positions 523.

Johnson T, 'Public Participation in China's EIA Process and the Regulation of Environmental Disputes' (2020) 81 Environmental Impact Assessment Review 106359, 1.

Liu YM, 'The Benefits of Technocracy in China' (2016) 33(1) Issues in Science and Technology <https://issues.org/perspective-the-benefits-of-technocracy-in-china/> accessed 20 December 2021.

Mertha A, '"Fragmented Authoritarianism 2.0": Political Pluralization in the Chinese Policy Process' (2009) 200 The China Quarterly 995.

Pan Y, 'The Environment Needs Public Participation' (*China Dialogue*, 5 December 2006) China Dialogue <https://chinadialogue.net/en/pollution/604-the-environment-needs-public-participation/> accessed 20 December 2021.

Sanders R, 'The Political Economy of Chinese Environmental Protection: Lessons for the Mao and Deng Years' (1999) 20(6) Third World Quarterly 1201.

The World Bank, GDP growth (annual%) - China <https://data.worldbank.org/indicator/NY.GDP.MKTP.KD.ZG?locations=CN> accessed 20 December 2021.

Tsai WH, 'Mass Mobilization Campaigns in Mao's China' (1999) 6 1 American Journal of Chinese Studies 21.

Xinhua News, 'Ministry of Ecology and Environment: Out of 10 projects, 8 Do Not Need Approval. A Further Enhancement of Approval Efficiency (生态环境部：八成项目环评无需审批将进一步提高审批效率) 23 September 2018 <http://www.xinhuanet.com/2018-09/02/c_1123368507.htm> accessed 20 December 2021.

Yang Y, 'Reformed Environmental Impact Assessment in China: An Evaluation of its Effectiveness' (2020) 11 Journal of Environmental Protection 889.

PART 3

The European Union Perspective

CHAPTER 5

The Scope and Requirements of Public Participation in EU Environmental Law

Giacomo Gattinara and Magnus Noll-Ehlers

1 Introduction*

Art 191 (1) first indent TFEU sets out that EU environmental law seeks to preserve, protect and improve the quality of the environment. Secondary law adopted to achieve this objective applies in many situations where there are conflicting interests. Such conflict can occur between different persons concerned with the same activity. For example, on the one hand, the project[1] applicant has an interest in obtaining the entitlement to proceed with the project. On the other hand, the neighbours of the site of that project, and more generally "the public concerned"[2] will regularly have other interests, in particular to minimise any adverse environmental effects of the project.

Notably, a single person can also have conflicting interests. For example, car emissions can be a main contributor to exceedances of air quality limit-values protecting human health.[3] Appropriate measures to keep "the exceedance

* Views and comments contained in this Chapter are exclusively of the Authors and do not reflect the position of the European Commission nor of its Legal Service.

1 Directive 2011/92/EU of the European Parliament and of the Council of 13 December 2011 on the assessment of the effects of certain public and private projects on the environment [2012] OJ L 026/1(EIA Directive) defines a project as the "the execution of construction works or of other installations or schemes, or other interventions in the natural surroundings and landscape including those involving the extraction of mineral resources", see art 1(2) lit a.

2 Art 1(2) lit d and e of the EIA Directive define the public as "one or more natural or legal persons and, in accordance with national legislation or practice, their associations, organisations or groups", and as a sub-set thereof "the public affected or likely to be affected by, or having an interest in … environmental decision-making procedures … For the purposes of this definition, non-governmental organisations promoting environmental protection and meeting any requirements under national law shall be deemed to have an interest". This definition corresponds to the notion of "public concerned" contained in art 2(5) of the Aarhus Convention (see below footnote 6).

3 Directive 2008/50/EC of the European Parliament and of the Council of 21 May 2008 on ambient air quality and cleaner air for Europe [2008] OJ L 152/1, requires Member States to respect certain limit values for the most important pollutants, see art 13(1) in conjunction with Annex XI and art 16(2) in conjunction with Annex XIV.

DOI:10.1163/9789004509382_007

period … as short as possible"[4] may therefore require the limitation of vehicle use, and residents in a given area would benefit from cleaner ambient air. However, such limitations conflict with their interest to use their vehicle freely, eg without being banned from city centres.

In both cases, public participation can be helpful to allow competent authorities to balance the conflicting interests in decisions having environmental impacts, and thus to contribute to sustainability in the sense of preserving the environment.[5] In this regard, the Aarhus Convention on Access to Information, Public Participation in Decision-Making and Access to Justice in Environmental Matters, which the EU is a contracting party of since 2005,[6] has become the most important legal source of the obligation to ensure public participation in environmental matters. In particular, according to one of the main purposes of the convention, public participation is the legal instrument that citizens have in order to assert their right to live in an environment adequate to their health and well-being and to ensure transparency of decision-making and accountability of public authorities as well as the quality of administrative decisions.[7]

As regards sustainability, the Aarhus Convention refers to it only in two paragraphs of its preamble but always within the definition of 'sustainable development',[8] a wording that recalls the definition and practice of the United Nations, where the reference to 'sustainable development' mainly considers environmental concerns as a possible reason to constrain economic development.[9] In EU law (see art 11 TFEU) the definition of sustainability "includes" environmental aspects,[10] but it is sufficiently broad to cover other policy-related aspects.

A thorough look into how the Aarhus Convention operates in practice shows however an important evolution. The different Declarations of the Meeting of the Parties to the Aarhus Convention reveal not only a progressive autonomy of the word 'sustainable' as referring to the protection of the environment in

4 Art 23(1) second subparagraph, Ambient Air Quality-Directive 2008/50.

5 "Sustainable development is development that meets the needs of the present without compromising the ability of future generations to meet their own needs", Report of the World Commission on Environment and Development, GAOR, 42nd Session Supplement No. 427 U.N. Doc. A/42/427 (1987), Annex "Our Common Future" p 54, para 1.

6 Council Decision 2005/370/EC of 17 February 2005 on the conclusion, on behalf of the European Community, of the Convention on access to information, public participation in decision-making and access to justice in environmental matters [2005] OJ L 124/1.

7 See seventh, eighth and ninth paragraphs of the Preamble to the convention.

8 See the fifth and fourteenth paragraphs of the Preamble to the convention.

9 Following the definition of the Brundtland Commission Report (see n 6), according to which sustainable development is "development that meets the needs of the present without compromising the ability of future generations to meet their own needs".

10 Case C-377/12 Commission v Council [2014] EU:C:2014:1903, para 42.

general, but also a tighter link with public participation. This is acutely illustrated by para 7 of the Chisinau Declaration, adopted at the fourth Meeting of the Parties in 2011:

> [s]imilarly to the greening of the economy, public participation in decision-making is not a self-standing objective, but rather an instrument for achieving the sustainability and well-being of society. We consider that, [...], citizens should be invited to participate in defining and implementing green economy programmes and in choosing the most appropriate road maps to sustainability.[11]

This chapter outlines the different sources in EU law that provide for the obligation to hold public participation and how this can contribute to ensuring sustainability.[12] It shows what public participation in EU environmental law consists of and in which fields it is applied. In particular, it considers the scope of the obligation under the provisions of the Aarhus Convention and the requirements of that obligation particularly for Member States. Further, this chapter then turns to the remedies for breach of public participation. A particular place is occupied in this study by the case law of the Court of Justice of the European Union. Indeed, the Court has the task to clarify the content and effects of EU environmental law and of the Aarhus Convention as part of the EU legal order, which is binding not only for the EU institutions and bodies, but also for the Member States of the European Union when acting in the scope of EU law.

2 The Origins of Public Participation in EU Law and the Legal Relevance of these origins

2.1 *Chronological overview*

The first European Directive providing for a clear requirement on public participation and for a tight link with environmental protection was Directive

---

11 Economic Commission for Europe Meeting of the Parties to the Convention on access to information, public participation in decision-making and access to justice in environmental matters Rio plus Aarhus – 20 years on: Bearing fruit and looking forward Chisinau Declaration, U.N. Doc. ECE/MP.PP/2011/CRP.4/rev.1 (2011).

12 Due to the limits within which this study had to remain, we did not consider all EU environmental directives containing provisions on public participation. Rather, we focused on those that generated more case law than others on the topic of this book.

85/337/EEC.[13] This piece of legislation then introduced – 20 years before the ratification of the Aarhus Convention by the European Union – the principle that certain projects can be realised only when the competent administration has ensured that all people concerned have been informed and heard.

The nuclear accident of Chernobyl on 26 April 1986 clarified the need to have rules at the European level aimed at ensuring transparency in environmental decision-making procedures. Thus, Directive 90/313/EC on access to environmental information was approved a couple of years later,[14] setting forth for the first time the principle of access to environmental information as a public right.

The Convention on Environmental Impact Assessment in a Transboundary Context was adopted in Espoo, Finland on the 26 February 1991 (the 'Espoo Convention').[15] Where an activity listed in that convention is likely to cause a significant adverse transboundary impact, the Party of origin (where the activity is going to take place) is required to notify the Party which is likely to be affected by the activity (the affected Party). In addition, the Party of origin has to make available the information from an environmental impact assessment to the affected party. This is not only to prepare consultations between the Parties, but also to allow for public participation concerning the activity in the territory of the affected Party.

Moreover, in 1996 the then European Community (EC) approved the Integrated Pollution Prevention and Control Directive (the 'IPPC Directive').[16] Art 15 of the IPCC Directive provided for the first time a right of "the public" to participate in administrative procedures for the grant of permits to installations used to perform certain polluting activities (listed in Annex I to the Directive) before the adoption of any final decisions.

Following the conclusion of the Aarhus Convention in 1998, the then EC decided first to modify Directive 90/313/EC in order to align it completely

---

13 Council Directive 85/337/EEC of 27 June 1985 on the assessment of the effects of certain public and private projects on the environment [1985], OJ L 175/40.

14 Council Directive 90/313/EEC of 7 June 1990 on the freedom of access to information on the environment [1990], OJ L 158/56.

15 Convention on environmental impact assessment in a transboundary context [1992], OJ 1992 C 104/7. The Espoo Convention was concluded for the then European Community as a mixed agreement together with the Member States. The European Community ratified it on 24 June 1997, see recital 15 of the EIA Directive.

16 Council Directive 96/61/EC of 24 September 1996 concerning integrated pollution prevention and control [1996], OJ L 257/26.

with the convention. This was done with Directive 2003/4/EC.[17] The EC also adopted a general Directive on public participation (Directive 2003/35/EC, the 'Public participation Directive') aimed at better ensuring that existing provisions in the relevant Directives ensured this fundamental requirement of the Aarhus Convention.[18]

2.2 *Directive 85/337/EEC: A sectoral approach with a promising general application*

Directive 85/337/EEC was the first piece of European legislation mentioning the requirement of an environmental impact assessment ('EIA') to grant a permit for a project having significant effects on the environment. EIA is a different rule from public participation. It requires that the competent authorities assess the potential consequences for the environment of a certain project, and to take that assessment into account when granting the permit to carry it out. In this regard, by introducing the obligation of an EIA in EU law, the first EIA Directive also introduced the concept of public participation. In particular, the first recital of the Directive mentioned the need highlighted in the first general action programmes on environment "to take effects on the environment into account at the earliest possible stage in all the technical planning and decision-making processes". The 'earliest possible stage' was referred to in order to ensure the effectiveness of any public participation according to art 6(1) of the Aarhus Convention. More importantly, the sixth recital of directive 85/337/EEC stated that the EIA had to be "conducted on the basis of the appropriate information supplied by the developer, which may be supplemented by the authorities and by the people who may be concerned by the project in question". This was mirrored in art 6(2) second indent of the Directive, according to which Member States had to ensure that "the public concerned is given the opportunity to express an opinion before the project is initiated". This provision was in the initial text of Directive 85/337/EEC. In 2003 however, that Directive was modified by the Public Participation Directive, which *inter alia*

17 Directive 2003/4/EC of the European Parliament and of the Council of 28 February 2003 on public access to environmental information and repealing Council Directive 90/313/EEC [2003], OJ 2003 L 41/26.

18 Directive 2003/35/EC of the European Parliament and of the Council of 26 May 2003 providing for public participation in respect of the drawing up of certain plans and programmes relating to the environment and amending with regard to public participation and access to justice Council Directives 85/337/EEC and 96/61/EC - Statement by the Commission [2003], OJ L 156/17.

added to the notion of 'public concerned' the notion of 'public' in general, along the lines of art 2 of the Aarhus Convention.[19]

2.3 *The Public Participation Directive (2003/35/EC) and the Transparency Directive (2003/4/EC)*

In 2003 the EU legislator adopted measures having the purpose to ensure consistency of the existing EU legal framework with the Aarhus Convention, which had already been concluded in 1998, and to which the then EC would have become a Contracting Party in 2005. The so called Public Participation Directive modified the EIA Directive and the IPPC Directive in order to further streamline the requirements of public participation.

2.4 *EU Directives and the International negotiations having led to the Aarhus and Espoo Conventions*

While the Aarhus Convention is the most important source of obligations for the EU and its Member States as regards public participation today, EU law played a meaningful role in the drafting of the convention. In particular, the notion of EIA was introduced by Directive 85/337/EEC and appears still today in art 6 of the Aarhus Convention. In particular, art 6(2) of the convention recalls that public participation must be ensured in cases where the law of the Contracting Party provides for environmental impact assessment. In the same vein, Annex I, point 20 of the convention considers as proposed activities within the meaning of art 6(2)(b) of the convention those activities for which the corresponding law provides for such environmental impact assessment. In turn, Directive 90/313/EC on access to environmental information has had a bearing in the drafting of art 4 of the Aarhus Convention, which, in turn, is relevant for the interpretation of art 6(6) of the convention. Indeed, that Directive showed that Member States had already accepted the obligation to disclose environmental information to the public. Moreover, both Directives 85/337/EEC and 96/61/EC already contained the notion of "public concerned"[20] and public "likely to be affected", respectively.[21] This fundamental notion would have then been used by the drafters of the Aarhus Convention to shape the notion of "public concerned" contained today in art 2(5) of the convention.

On the other hand, when concluding the Aarhus Convention, the then EC issued a Declaration stating that "the Community institutions will apply the Convention within the framework of their existing and future rules on

---

19 Directive 85/337/EEC, n 14, art 1(2), as modified by the Public participation Directive.
20 Directive 85/337/EEC, n 14, art 6(2), second indent.
21 Directive 96/61/EEC, n 17, recital 27.

access to documents and other relevant rules of Community law in the field covered by the Convention".[22] As the Court clarified,[23] the legal effect of that Declaration today – and of the reference to the acquis existing at the time of the conclusion as well as to its further adaptations – is that of recalling that the convention itself was conceived and drafted by having national states in mind. Subsequently, when coming to the interpretation and application of the Aarhus Convention, the specific features – namely its legal and institutional setup – of the EU should not be ignored.[24] This should also be considered as regards public participation in the sense that, on the one hand, the EU has a rather limited role in issuing decisions on proposed activities or in adopting plans and programmes. This administrative function is linked to the management of national territory and falls normally with the remit of Member States. This also explains why in the Regulation adopted to contribute to the implementation of the Aarhus Convention in the EU legal order, ie Regulation (EC) 2006/1367 (the 'Aarhus Regulation'), public participation is provided for the adoption of plans and programmes and not for decisions on proposed activities, since the EU institutions do not adopt such decisions. On the other hand, the relevance of the Aarhus Convention as regards the EU on public participation is mainly linked with its legislative role, ie with its function of setting forth obligations for its Member States, as the Aarhus Compliance Committee (ACCC) also recently pointed out.[25]

3 The requirements of Public Participation in the Aarhus Convention

3.1 *How 'Aarhus Law' Applies*

3.1.1 The Convention

The Aarhus Convention provides for the obligation to ensure public participation when a public authority takes a decision to permit certain proposed activities, ie those listed in Annex I to the convention and those not listed therein having a "significant effect on the environment". The provision sets

---

22 Quoted in CaseC-612/13 P *ClientEarth* [2015] EU:C:2015:486, para 41.

23 *Ibidem*, para 40.

24 The EU is the only regional economic organisation that is Party to the convention according to the definition contained in art 11 of the Aarhus Convention. Also, Directives 85/337/EEC and 90/313/EC set forth obligations only for Member States, which are their addressees according to what is today art 288 TFEU.

25 ACCC/C/2010/54, European Union, ECE/MP.PP/C.1/2012/12, para 75–76.

out four main obligations, indicated as follows. First, the competent authority has to ensure that the "public concerned" is informed at an early stage in the "environmental decision making", meaning when all options are still open.[26] Moreover, the administrative procedure has to be organised in such a way that the participation is effective.[27] This has to be ensured by setting reasonable deadlines, timeframes and adequate access to relevant information to the "public concerned".[28] It is also necessary to take into account the outcome of public participation.[29] Finally, "the public" has to be informed of the decision of the public authority, once it has been taken. With the exception of this last obligation, the same obligations exist as regards public participation concerning plans and programmes, as provided in art 7, first three sentences of the convention. Obligations concerning public participation do exist as regards the deliberate release of genetically modified organisms (GMO) into the environment and are provided for in the new art 6(11) and in art 6a of the Aarhus Convention as introduced in 2005.[30] Given their quite specific nature, they will not be considered in this chapter.

The convention also provides for public participation during the preparation of executive regulations or generally applicable legally binding instruments in art 8 as well as in the preparation of policies relating to the environment according to art 7, last sentence of the convention. Still, in the words of one of the drafters of the convention,[31] these provisions set forth more political recommendations and general procedural requirements than strict obligations. The Aarhus Implementation Guide (the 'Guide'; see section '3.1.2', below) and the ACCC have further clarified the content of those provisions.[32] In particular, the Guide recalls that art 8 sets forth minimum procedural requirements that Contracting Parties have to follow when granting public participation in the preparation of executive regulations or generally applicable legally binding instruments. As for the ACCC, it put particular emphasis on the final sentence

26 Art 6(2) and (4) of the convention.
27 Art 6(3) of the convention.
28 *Ibidem.*
29 Art 6(8) of the convention.
30 Economic Commission for Europe Report of the second Meeting of the Parties Addendum Decision II/1 Genetically Modified Organisms, U.N. Doc. ECE/MP.PP/2005/2/Add.2 (2005).
31 Jerzy Jendrośka, 'Public Participation in Environmental Decision-Making. Interactions Between the Convention and EU Law and Other Key Legal Issues in its Implementation in the Light of the Opinions of the Aarhus Convention Compliance', in M Pallemaerts (ed), *The Aarhus Convention at Ten* (Groningen, 2011) p 91 ff, at p 97.
32 See ACCC/I/2014/1, Belarus, ECE/MP.PP/C.1/2017/11, para 50 and ff p185 of the Guide quoted therein; ACCC/C/2010/53, United Kingdom, ECE/MP.PP/C.1/2013/3, para 84.

of art 8 of the convention, according to which "the final version of a normative instrument [has to] be in practice accompanied by an explanation of the public participation process and how the results of the public participation were taken into account".[33]

3.1.2 The Implementation Guide to the Aarhus Convention

The Guide contains very helpful clarifications on the meaning of the public participation provisions and on the delimitation of the scope of the obligations relating thereto. It is an instrument elaborated by a group of experts of the convention and is structured as a commentary to the convention. The indications presented in the text were drafted following (good) examples and practices contained in the national law of some of the Contracting Parties and in European Directives as well as the practices developed on the basis of the Espoo Convention. The Guide also contains a collection of Declarations of the Meeting of the Parties and is periodically updated.[34]

Concerning the legal effects of the Guide in the EU legal order, according to the Court of Justice this instrument has only persuasive (and not binding) authority to interpret the Aarhus Convention.[35] The Court of Justice and national courts of law can then consider it but they are not obliged to.

3.1.3 The Findings of the Aarhus Compliance Committee ('ACCC')

The ACCC was established under Decision I/7 of the first Meeting of the Parties held in Lucca, Italy, on the 21–23 October 2002, adopted on the basis of art 15 of the Aarhus Convention. According to this provision of the convention, Contracting Parties may have "on a consensual basis… optional arrangements of a non-confrontational, non-judicial and consultative nature" to review compliance with the provisions of the Convention. While the ACCC is not a court of law and its procedural rules are rather flexible,[36] it examines all instances

---

33 ACCC/I/2014/1, Belarus, ECE/MP.PP/C.1/2017/11, para 59.

34 United Nations Economic Commission for Europe, 'The Aarhus Convention: An Implementation Guide' (2014) https://unece.org/DAM/env/pp/Publications/Aarhus_Implementation_Guide_interactive_eng.pdf last accessed 20 September 2022.

35 Case C-619/19, *Land Baden-Württemberg* [2021] EU:C:2021:35 para 51 and case law quoted therein.

36 For instance, the rule on the previous exhaustion of domestic remedies – well known in international law and according to which it is not possible to ask for the intervention of an international court or body if the concerned party has not exhausted all means of redress existing at national level – does not apply strictly. Thus, according to Rule 21 of the Annex to the decision I/7, "[t]he Committee [the 'ACCC'] should at all relevant stages take into account any available domestic remedy unless the application of the remedy is

of non-compliance that may be brought to it also by individuals.[37] Indeed, according to art 15 of the Aarhus Convention, the rules on review of compliance can include the option of "considering communications from members of the public on matters related to the Convention". In particular, both individuals and non-governmental organisations ('NGOs') for the protection of the environment, can submit information and factual elements on which the concerned Party is then called to make its views known; they can also appoint experts.[38] This has the merit of enriching the quality and the level of detail of the analysis contained in the findings.

Once final, the ACCC's findings need to be endorsed by the Meeting of the Parties in order to produce legal effects.[39] Even though the Court of Justice of the EU did not yet have the chance to make its views known as regards the legal effects of the ACCC's findings in the EU legal order, it can be considered that those findings once adopted by the Meeting of the Parties contain an authoritative interpretation of the provisions of the Aarhus Convention. They are then relevant to carve out the correct interpretation of the provisions concerning public participation.

Besides the Maastricht recommendations on public participation in multi-stage proceedings[40] and the works of the Task force set up under the Convention on public participation in decision-making,[41] the work of the ACCC is by and large the richest source of clarification as regards the interpretation of the convention.

In this regard, the cases concerning compliance are particularly helpful to have a clear understanding of public participation under the Aarhus

---

unreasonably prolonged or obviously does not provide an effective and sufficient means of redress".

37 See recently Gor Samvel, 'Non-Judicial, Advisory, Yet Impactful? The Aarhus Convention Compliance Committee as a Gateway to Environmental Justice', in *Transnational Environmental Law*, [2020] 9:2 p 211. See also Jerzy Jendrośka, 'Aarhus Convention Compliance Committee: Origins, Status and Activities' [2011] 8 *Journal for European Environmental Planning Law* 301.

38 Margherita Poto, 'Strenghts and Weaknesses of Environmental Participation', in Eva Julia Lohse, Giulia Parola, Margherita Poto (eds), *Participatory Rights in the Environmental Decision-Making Process and the Implementation of the Aarhus Convention: a Comparative Perspective* (Berlin 2015), p 93 ff, 95.

39 See Rule 35 and ff of the Annex to Decision I/7.

40 United Nations Economic Commission for Europe, 'Maastricht Recommendations on Promoting Effective Public Participation in Decision-making in Environmental Matters prepared under the Aarhus Convention' (2015) https://unece.org/sites/default/files/2022-03/1514364_E_web.pdf last accessed 20 September 2022.

41 United Nations Economic Commission for Europe, 'Task Force on Public Participation in Decision-making' Task Force on Public Participation in Decision-making | UNECE.

Convention. This is because the ACCC assesses the level of consistency with the convention concerning concrete instances of public participation. Its case law, then, contains a useful set of examples of how decision-making procedures concerning the environment can be shaped in such a way as to ensure public participation.

Therefore, understanding the relevance of public participation for sustainability is not possible without considering the findings of the ACCC, which has interpreted and clarified the meaning of the provisions and principles of the convention, both as regards the procedure and the substance of public participation. For instance, on procedural aspects, the ACCC has provided a fundamental clarification concerning the fourteenth paragraph of the Preamble to the convention on public participation and sustainable development.[42] In a case in which the competent authority of the Contracting Party had differentiated in regulating the modalities to exert the right to public participation between private operators on the one hand, and NGOs promoting environmental protection on the other, the ACCC considered that this difference of treatment was inconsistent with the purpose of the convention. The ACCC considered that

> there was a considerable span of time for participation of private stakeholders compared to that granted to other members of the public, to the extent that the authority exercised its discretion in a way that ran counter to the objectives of the Convention; in particular "to encourage widespread public awareness of, and participation in, decisions affecting the environment and sustainable development" by involving, among others, NGOs promoting environmental protection. While the closer inclusion of the private stakeholders in the process may have been justified, there was still an obligation on the public authority to act in accordance with the objectives of the Convention and not to abuse this provision to effectively bar or significantly reduce the effective public participation of other members of the public.[43]

Turning now to some selected clarifications on substantial aspects of public participation contained in the findings of the ACCC, it is useful to examine four different sets of findings. Respectively, they concern the scope of public participation, the obligations stemming from public participation, the organisation of the decision-making procedure where public participation has to be

42 See Council Decision, n 7.

43 ACCC/C/2012/70, Czech Republic, ECE/MP.PP/C.1/2014/9, para 59.

ensured, and the effect of public participation. These four aspects will now be examined.

A first set of findings concerns the general aspects of public participation, including the delimitation of the scope of the provisions on public participation contained in the convention. Thus, if it appears problematic to draw a clear dividing line between the decisions falling within the scope of art 6 and those caught by art 7 of the convention, attention has to be paid to the issue whether the decision paves the way "for specific activities to take place".[44] In that case, the decision will fall within the scope of the first provision. This approach focusses on the function and legal effects of the decision at stake.[45] Accordingly, the decision of a financial institution "to provide a loan or other financial support" does not fall within the scope of art 6 of the convention.[46] Conversely, "any change to the permitted duration of an activity", be it a reduction or an extension, falls within the scope of this provision under art 6(10) of the convention.[47] Interpretation of Annex I to the convention is also relevant: should a proposed activity fall out of that list and not have significant effects on the environment, the convention would then not apply.[48]

A second set of findings concerns the content of the obligations on public participation. Regarding art 6(4) of the convention, allowing for public participation in a multi-stage procedure only after the decision on the location of the proposed activity has been taken without public participation is not compliant with that provision.[49] Similarly, a change in the technical features of the project cannot in principle be included in the final decision without public participation.[50] Moreover, the need to keep options "open" as required by this provision means that at each stage of the decision making, certain options are discussed and selected with the participation of the public "and each consecutive stage of decision-making addresses only the issues within the option already selected at the preceding stage".[51]

A third group of findings concerns organisation of the decision-making procedure. As to art 6(7) of the convention, the ACCC held that the Parties retain

44 ACCC/C/2004/08, ECE/MP.PP/C.1/2006/2/Add.1, para 28.
45 ACCC/C/2006/16, Lithuania, ECE/MP.PP/2008/5/Add.6, para 58.
46 ACCC/C/2007/21, European Community, ECE/MP.PP/C.1/2009/2/Add. 1, para 36. The financial institution was the European Investment Bank.
47 ACCC/C/2014/104, The Netherlands, ECE/MP.PP/C.1/2019/3, paras 65–66.
48 ACCC/C/2008/27, United Kingdom, ECE/MP/C.1/2010/6/Add.2, paras 38–40.
49 ACCC/C/2005/12, Lithuania, ECE/MP.PP/C.1/2007/4/Add.1, paras 79–82.
50 ACCC/C/2009/38, United Kingdom, ECE/MP.PP/C.1/2011/2/Add.2, paras 83–85.
51 ACCC/2006/16, Lithuania, quoted, para 71.

discretion in organising public participation, provided that the arrangements are appropriate in light of the proposed activity. In this regard, a hearing is not necessary to ensure public participation but, if it is held,[52] the Party shall prove that the outcome of the procedure takes account of those views under art 6(8) of the convention.[53] As to the effectiveness of participation, the possibility to consult thousands of documents only on two computers without any opportunity to take copies (eg on a CD-ROM) and the imposition of tight deadlines to file comments is not in compliance with art 6(3) and (6) of the convention.[54] Clearly, the width of the obligations to ensure appropriate and effective information does vary according to the dimensions of the proposed activity. However, should this take place in a transboundary context, then the extent of the public concerned will be much larger than those of the population living on the territory of the Party concerned.[55] In such a situation the obligation of notification under art 6(2) of the convention applies to "all those who potentially could be concerned, including the public concerned outside its [of the Party] territory".[56] As regards the content of the public notice when notifying (ie giving the first information) the public of a decision making procedure concerning a proposed activity, a deviation from the minimum content set out in art 6(2)(a-e) is considered a breach of the convention.[57] Still, what information has to be made available is a different aspect and is regulated in art 6(6) of the convention.[58]

Finally, concerning art 6(8) of the convention, the obligation to take into account the views of the public expressed during public participation should be read in conjunction with art 6(9) in the sense that that the written decision should include "a discussion on how the public participation was taken into account".[59]

3.2 *The Environmental 'Effects' Requirement under the New Aarhus Regulation and its meaning for Public Participation*

The Aarhus Regulation contributes to the implementation of the Aarhus Convention in the EU legal order, since it contains provisions implementing the

52 ACCC/C/2015/45, United Kingdom, ECE/MP.PP/C.1/2013/12, para 78.
53 ACCC/A/2014/1, Belarus, quoted, paras 45 and, as regards art 8 of the convention, para 53.
54 ACCC/C/2009/36, Spain, ECE/MP/PP/C.1/2010/4/Add.2, para 62.
55 ACCC/C/2012/71, Czechia, ECE/MP.PP/C.1/2017/3, paras 71–77.
56 ACCC/C/2013/91, United Kingdom, ECE/MP.PP/C.1/2017/14, para 82.
57 ACCC/C/2013/88, Kazakhstan, ECE/MP.PP/C.1/2017/12, para 100.
58 ACCC/C/2013/89, Slovakia, ECE/MP.PP/C.1/2017/13, paras 77 and 79.
59 ACCC/C/2008/24, Spain, ECE/MP.PP/C.1/2009/8/Add.1, para 100.

three pillars of the Aarhus Convention as regards the EU institutions and bodies. In other words, access to environmental information, public participation and access to justice. The text was amended in 2021,[60] in order to widen the scope of the mechanism for internal review provided for in art 10 of the Aarhus Regulation, which can now be triggered against all administrative acts that may contravene environmental law.[61] Conversely, prior to this amendment a request for internal review could be filed only against acts "of individual scope". This previous definition made it impossible for certain applicants, such as NGOs, to seek review of general administrative measures having effects on the environment.

As to this recently adopted amendment, while adopted in the different field of access to justice in environmental matters, it is also relevant for public participation. Indeed, the amending Regulation has placed significant emphasis on the possible detrimental effects a measure has to have in order to be qualified as an administrative act within the meaning of art 2 of the Aarhus Regulation. More generally, the amended Aarhus Regulation insisted on the need to ensure a review of only those acts that can contravene environmental law.[62] This reference confirms the need to have a clear understanding of the material scope of the convention and of the measures concerning its implementation such as the Aarhus Regulation or the EU environmental directives. This need is also expressed in the words "environmental decision-making process", albeit that it was unfortunately not further defined, which the draft documents of the Aarhus Convention often mention and that appear in particular in art 6 of the convention.[63] Accordingly, the scope of public participation under the Aarhus Convention should be strictly limited to the adoption of measures clearly concerning the environment and not, for instance, to that of acts having only *indirect* effects on it.[64]

---

60 Regulation (EU) 2021/1767 of the European Parliament and of the Council of 6 October 2021 amending Regulation (EC) No 1367/2006 on the application of the provisions of the Aarhus Convention on Access to Information, Public Participation in Decision-making and Access to Justice in Environmental Matters to Community institutions and bodies [2021] OJ L 356/1.

61 See art 2(1)(g) of the Aarhus Regulation.

62 See in particular recitals 3, 7, 9 and 10 of Regulation 2021/1767.

63 J Jendrośka, n 32, at 94.

64 See on this Eva Julia Lohse, 'Access to Justice – Main Challenge for Implementing the Aarhus Convention', in Eva Julia Lohse, Giulia Parola, Margherita Poto (eds), *Participatory Rights*, (Duncker&Humblot 2015).

4 The scope of Public Participation in the provisions of the Aarhus Regulation

4.1 *Defining Plans and Programmes at EU Level*

According to art 9(1) of the Aarhus Regulation, EU institutions and bodies

> shall provide, through appropriate practical and/or other provisions, early and effective opportunities for the public to participate during the preparation, modification or review of plans or programmes relating to the environment when all options are still open. In particular, where the Commission prepares a proposal for such a plan or programme which is submitted to other Community institutions or bodies for decision, it shall provide for public participation at that preparatory stage.

The definition of "plans and programmes relating to the environment" follows very much that contained in art 7 of the Aarhus Convention. Indeed, under art 2(1)(e) of the Aarhus Regulation, this definition refers to

> plans and programmes, which are subject to preparation and, as appropriate, adoption by a Union institution or body which are required under legislative, regulatory or administrative provisions; and which contribute to, or are likely to have significant effects on, the achievement of the objectives of Union environmental policy, such as laid down in the Sixth Community Environment Action Programme, or in any subsequent general environmental action programme.[65]

In turn, and always in keeping with the convention,[66] "[g]eneral environmental action programmes shall also be considered as plans and programmes relating to the environment".

However, the definition of plans and programmes relating to the environment contains an exclusion. That definition does not indeed apply – always according to the same provision of the Regulation – to

---

65 The change of 'Community' into 'Union' follows from art 1, number 7, of Regulation 2021/1767.

66 Even though it is not clear with which provision, since plans and programmes are in art 7 whilst generally binding normative instruments are in art 8 of the convention.

> financial or budget plans and programmes, namely those laying down how particular projects or activities should be financed or those related to the proposed annual budgets, internal work programmes of a Community institution or body, or emergency plans and programmes designed for the sole purpose of civil protection.

This limitation concerns a financial or budget plan or programme, ie an act that, as such, cannot be considered yet as relating to the environment. Indeed, its consequences on the environment would seem to stem from a further measure, whether a plan, programme or other, to be adopted following a decision on the use of the financial resources. Conversely, as the Guide clarifies, the notion of plans and programmes would actually concern strategies to manage land or natural resources or measures setting out certain requirements and conditions to develop concretely certain activities on the territory of the authorities concerned, such as transport or touristic services.[67] Notably, it is also in this meaning that the same notion is used in EU legislation.[68] The need for such specification is unavoidable, given the wide area of competencies of the EU institutions and bodies and the need to then distinguish when the plan or programmes actually concern the environment.

4.2 *Public Participation and limits to Access to Environmental Information under the exception of the Decision-making Process*

Before examining how public participation is ensured in EU law as regards Member States in the provisions of several EU directives, it is necessary to mention a last issue concerning public participation at EU level. This concerns the interplay with the exception regarding access to documents under Regulation (EC) 1049/2001 due to a pending decision-making procedure. This exception is provided for in art 4(3) first subparagraph of the said Regulation and is particularly relevant in environmental matters since that Regulation is applicable to all requests of access to environmental information addressed to the EU institutions and bodies, pursuant to art 3 of the Aarhus Regulation. Hence, Regulation (EC) 1049/2001 is also supposed to be the *lex generalis* as regards the implementation in the EU legal order of the first pillar of the

---

67 See in this vein The Aarhus Convention: An Implementation Guide, n 35, p 176.

68 See in this regard recital 10 and art 3 of Directive 2001/42/EC of the European Parliament and of the Council of 27 June 2001 on the assessment of the effects of certain plans and programmes on the environment [2001] OJ L 197/30, *which provides that plans and programmes setting the framework in a number of given sectors are subject to an environmental assessment.*

Aarhus Convention, ie the right of access to environmental information, whilst the Aarhus Regulation completes the provisions of EU secondary law that are required to implement the convention.[69]

According to art 6(1), second sentence of the Aarhus Regulation, the exception allowing for refusal of granting access to documents because of a pending decision-making process, set forth in art 4(3) first subparagraph of Regulation (EC) 1049/2001,[70] must be interpreted in a restrictive way. When applied to the latter provision, according to which a request for access can be temporarily refused until the decision is taken if disclosure brings prejudice to the decision-making process, art 6(1), second sentence of the Aarhus Regulation seems to significantly reduce even further the already narrow application of that exception to access to public documents, laid down in Regulation (EC) 1049/2001.[71] In fact, where the adoption of plans or programmes concerning the environment is envisaged, while that adoption could be considered as a decision-making procedure according to art 4(3) first subparagraph of Regulation (EC) 1049/2001, the obligation to ensure public participation would inevitably apply. Thus, when those plans and programmes have to be adopted by an EU institution, art 4(3) first subparagraph of Regulation (EC) 1049/2001 would not seem to provide a strong ground to refuse access to documents linked to the decision-making procedure aimed at the adoption of those plans and programmes; this is, of course, without prejudice for the applicability of other exceptions provided for in that Regulation (1049/2001).

In practice, the right of seeking access to environmental information is a complementary tool to public participation, should the information released be inadequate, incomplete or should the definition of 'plans and programmes' laid down in the Aarhus Regulation not be fulfilled.[72] This approach is confirmed in the practice of the ACCC, which, as regards obligations to provide the

69 See in this vein recital 13 of the Aarhus Regulation.

70 According to which "[a]ccess to a document, drawn up by an institution for internal use or received by an institution, which relates to a matter where the decision has not been taken by the institution, shall be refused if disclosure of the document would seriously undermine the institution's decision-making process, unless there is an overriding public interest in disclosure".

71 According to the case-law on Art 4(3) first subparagraph, of Regulation (EC) 1049/2001 in general the possibility to apply the exception in case of ongoing decision-making processes is already severely limited only to situation in which the EU institutions can demonstrate a serious and concrete risk to the interest protected (See for instance Case C-60/15 P, *Saint Gobain* [2017] EU:C:2017:540, para 82). Moreover, Regulation (EC) 1049/2001 uses for the risk to that interest the term "seriously undermine the decision-making" whilst for other exceptions the term "undermine" is used.

72 For example in case of budgetary or financial plans and programmes.

public with adequate information when handling public participation, relies on both art 4(4) and 6(6) of the convention.[73]

5 Defining the scope of Public Participation in the EU Environmental Directives

5.1 Examples of Public Participation as express legislative requirement

5.1.1 EIA Directive 2011/92

Art 1 of the EIA Directive sets out that the Directive applies to the assessment of the environmental effects of projects which are likely to have significant effects on the environment. That assessment is to contribute to sustainability considerations, eg to increase resource efficiency and to reduce the unsustainable increase of settlement areas over time.[74] At the same time, the EIA Directive also transposes the relevant provisions on public participation in the Aarhus Convention and, as far as transboundary environmental effects are concerned, the Espoo Convention into EU law.[75] The Directive summarises the importance of public participation as follows:

> Effective public participation in the taking of decisions enables the public to express, and the decision-maker to take account of, opinions and concerns which may be relevant to those decisions, thereby increasing the accountability and transparency of the decision-making process and contributing to public awareness of environmental issues and support for the decisions taken... Participation, including participation by associations, organisations and groups, in particular non-governmental organisations promoting environmental protection, should accordingly be fostered ... .[76]

73 ACCC/C/2005/15, Romania, ECE/MP.PP/2008/5/Add.7, para 30; ACCC/C/2009/37, Belarus, ECE/MP.PP/2011/11/Add.2, para 72; ACCC/C/2009/44, Belarus, ECE/MP.PP/C.1/2011/6/Add.1, para 69.

74 See recitals 8 and 9 of Directive 2014/52/EU of the European Parliament and of the Council of 16 April 2014 amending Directive 2011/92/EU on the assessment of the effects of certain public and private projects on the environment Text with EEA relevance [2014] OJ L 124/1.

75 Ibid at 15 and 18.

76 Ibid at 16 and 17.

The Court of Justice of the EU has consistently held that public participation is a procedural right included in the Directive.[77] It constitutes one of the objectives of the Directive to put in place procedural guarantees to ensure that the public is more able to participate in EIA.[78] Accordingly, art 6 of the EIA Directive requires Member States to inform the public of the details of the EIA procedure early in the decision making process (para 2), make the related environmental assessments and information available to the public (para 3), and to provide early and effective opportunities to participate in the environmental decision-making process (para 4).

The importance of those rules is reflected in the case law of the Court. It has held that when the public concerned is informed of the project's existence and the consultation that is going to take place, the principle of effectiveness under EU law has to be observed. The information channels used, including electronic media, must be appropriate to reach the members of the public concerned.[79]

If the documentation made available to the public is insufficient to allow for a proper assessment of the project, then there is no effective public participation. Incomplete files or data that are scattered, incoherently, across a multitude of documents do not make it possible for the public concerned to participate effectively in the decision-making process and, therefore, do not satisfy the requirements stemming from art 6 of the EIA Directive.[80]

In addition, for the public concerned to exercise its rights effectively, accessibility to the file on which there is public participation has to be granted under easy conditions.[81] Although the EIA Directive does not as such preclude fees for the participation, such fees cannot, however, be fixed at a level which would prevent the directive from being fully effective, in accordance with the objective pursued by it. This would be the case if, due to its amount, a fee were liable to constitute an obstacle to the exercise of the rights of participation.[82]

On the other hand, the public participation is not an end in itself. For example, in Member States that split the environmental decision-making procedure up into (1) an environmental decision and then (2) a development consent, it

77 Case C-72/12, *Gemeinde Altrip* [2013] EU:C:2013:712, paras 48, 52.

78 Case C137/14, *Commission v Germany* [2015] EU:C:2015:683, para 55: case C-535/18, Land *Nordrhein-Westfalen*, EU:C:2020:391, para 49.

79 Case C-280/18, *Flausch* [2019] EU:C:2019:928, paras 30–35, 52.

80 CaseC-535/18 *Land Nordrhein-Westfalen*, n 79, paras 62, 87.

81 CaseC-280/18, *Flausch*, n 80, paras 37–40.

82 Case C-216/05, *Commission v Ireland* [2006] EU:C:2006:706, paras. 43–44

would be formalistic to require carrying out the public participation twice.[83] This sheds light on the serving function of the public participation, which allows the competent authorities to include the issues raised into the development consent taken.

Sustainability, even though not expressly mentioned in the EIA Directive, is ensured by taking the results of the consultations duly into account in the development consent procedure, as set out in art 8. The results of the assessment of the environmental effects, including the results from the public participation, are to be integrated into the decision to hand out a development consent, as set out in art 1(2)(g). Thus, the EIA Directive contributes to the sustainability of the projects that receive a development consent. However, that provision as such does not give the right to verify how the results are taken into account.[84] In consequence, public participation in the EIA process informs the competent authority, but it also binds the authority in the sense that it would necessarily lead to a specific outcome in the development consent procedure.

Once a decision to grant or refuse the development consent is taken, art 9(1) lit b. of the EIA Directive requires Member States to make available any information about the public participation process, including how the results of the consultations have been incorporated or otherwise addressed. The information provided under that provision has to be complete, because it must allow the public to assess the decision taken and to effectively use the judicial review procedure provided in art 11(1) of the EIA Directive.[85] In order to protect the right to public participation, Member States have to give access to a judicial review procedure under the specific conditions set out in art 11(1) of the EIA Directive. While initially not limiting the scope of that provision, but concluding that this provision is applied within the "scope of the Directive",[86] the Court later clarified that the requirement for access to judicial review only extends to aspects of a dispute which concern the public's right to participate in decision making.[87] In any case, the fact that art 11 protects at the least public participation, underlines the fundamental importance of the process of public participation in the EIA Directive.

83 Case C-121/21 *Czech Republic v Poland* [2022] EU:C:2022:74, Opinion of AG Pikamäe, paras 96–102.

84 Ibidem, para 151. Conversely, art 11 of the Directive gives a right of judicial review, see below.

85 Ibidem, para 171.

86 Case C-570/13, *Gruber* [2015] EU:C:2015:231, para 30.

87 Case C 470/16, *North East Pylon Pressure Campaing and Sheehy* [2018] EU:C:2018:185, paras 36–44.

Within the scope of art 11 of the EIA Directive, in accordance with the aim of giving the public concerned wide access to justice, the public concerned must be able to invoke any procedural defect in support of an action challenging the legality of decisions covered by that directive.[88] In that context, prior participation in the decision-making procedure under art 6(4) of the Directive has no effect on the conditions of the review procedure, because public participation is separate and has a different purpose from a legal review.[89]

Member States may however provide that, when a procedural defect vitiating the decision approving a project does not alter the meaning of that decision, an application for annulment of that decision is admissible only if the irregularity at issue has denied the claimant his or her right, guaranteed by art 6 of that directive, to participate in the environmental decision-making process.[90]

Public participation under the EIA Directive thus allows the public to increase its knowledge and influence on decisions, as well as challenge decisions for procedural flaws in the public participation. It is therefore not surprising that the public concerned shows vivid interest in establishing whether and how early in the procedure an environmental authorisation is subject to public participation.[91]

5.1.2 Directive 2001/42 on the Assessment of the effects of certain Plans and Programmes on the Environment ("SEA Directive")

In addition to the EIA Directive, the SEA Directive[92] provides for a similar assessment including public participation, albeit on a different level of decision-making processes. The authorities competent for handing out development consents in the sense of the EIA Directive do not act in the void, but on the basis of the applicable rules. To the extent that the rules on granting development consent already establish the framework[93] for handing out such

---

88 Case C137/14, *Commission v Germany*, n 79, para 55.

89 Case C-263/08, *Djurgården* [2009] EU:C:2009:631, para 38.

90 Case C-535/18, *Land Nordrhein-Westfalen*, n 79, para 63.

91 See for example Case C-463/20, *Namur Est Environement* [2022] EU:C:2022:121, paras 27, 29, 31.

92 Directive 2001/42/EC of the European Parliament and of the Council of 27 June 2001 on the assessment of the effects of certain plans and programmes on the environment [2001] OJ L 197/30.

93 In the context of the SEA Directive, the Court has defined the notion as a "measure which establishes, by defining rules and procedures for scrutiny applicable to the sector concerned, a significant body of criteria and detailed rules for the grant and implementation of one or more projects likely to have significant effects on the environment", see Case C-300/20, *Bund Naturschutz in Bayern* [2022]EU:C:2022:102, para 60 and case-law cited.

a consent, certain decisions that impact on the environment have already been taken. It follows that they are then excluded from the margin of decision of the competent authority when deciding on concrete projects, and can at that stage no longer usefully be made subject to public participation. SEA Directive 2001/42 thus extends the concept of assessing the environmental impact of individual development consents, including the requirement to provide for public participation, further upstream to so-called "plans and programmes" that set the framework for handing out those consents.[94]

The Directive aims to increase the sustainability of the decisions taken. It integrates environmental protection requirements into the definition of policies and activities in the EU, in particular with a view to promoting sustainable development (art 1). By doing so, it also contributes to the conservation and sustainable use of biological diversity, in line with the Convention on Biological Diversity.[95] More generally, the public participation provided for in the SEA Directive contributes to more sustainable and effective solutions.[96]

Similar to the EIA Directive, sustainability in the sense of the SEA Directive can therefore be understood as integrating environmental considerations into public policies. This reduces adverse environmental effects from the outset. Sustainability is also a factor when determining which plans and programmes are to be made subject to a SEA. The relevance of the plan or programme for the integration of environmental considerations particularly with a view to promoting sustainable development is one of the criteria for the likely significance of effects.[97] This needs to be taken into account by Member States when determining which plans or programmes (in addition to those in specific sectors that are in any case made subject to a SEA due to their environmental sensibility)[98] require an assessment and thus public participation.[99] As a consequence, the more a plan or programme is relevant for sustainable

94 Case C-671/16 Inter Environnement Bruxelles and Others [2019] EU:C:2019:56, Opinion of AG Kokott, para 36.

95 In that regard, the Court has held in C43/18, CFE, EU:C:2019:483, para 52, that it does not follow from the fact that the EU legislature did not consider it necessary, in the context of the Habitats Directive, to lay down rules on environmental assessment and public participation in connection with the management of Natura 2000 sites that it wished to exclude, when it subsequently adopted general rules on environmental assessment. The assessments which are made pursuant to other environmental protection instruments coexist with and complement the rules of the Habitats Directive, as regards the assessment of potential effects on the environment and public participation.

96 See recitals 1–5.

97 Annex II 1, third indent.

98 Art 3(2) lit b, recital 10.

99 Art 3(5), recital 11.

development, the more likely it is that the SEA Directive and its public participation element applies to it.

As to the process of public participation itself, the SEA Directive provides that the public is consulted during the assessment of such a framework within appropriate time frames (art 6(2)). This contributes to more transparent decision making with the aim of ensuring that the information supplied for the assessment is comprehensive and reliable. The integration of the opinions expressed by the public into the plan or programme is done by taking them into account during the preparation of and before its adoption or submission to the legislative procedure (art 8). Finally, ex-post transparency on the process and the outcome of public participation is fostered by making a summary available to the public (art 9).[100]

5.1.3 Noise Directive 2002/49

The Noise Directive[101] aims to avoid, prevent or reduce the harmful effects due to exposure to environmental noise. Amongst others, it provides for the adoption of action plans by the Member States which are designed to manage noise issues and effects, including noise reduction if necessary. At the same time the aim is to prevent and reduce environmental noise where necessary (particularly where exposure levels can induce harmful effects on human health) and preserve environmental noise quality where it is good (art 1(1) lit c.).

In that way, the Noise Directive aims to increase the sustainability of human activities that cause harmful noise. The Directive focuses specifically on noise from major roads, railways and airports (art 8). While the Directive does not impose a ban on such activities, it does require Member States to look into reducing noise from those activities. Hence, the sustainability of roads, railways and airports is to be increased by considering measures that serve the protection of human health against noise.

In that context, art 8(7) sets the requirement for the provision of public participation of those action plans which gives early and effective opportunities to participate in the preparation and review of the action plans. Logically it follows that the public consultation needs to precede the adoption of action plans. The action plans can only be regarded as final after the public

100 On the process of public participation, also see recitals 15ff of the SEA Directive.

101 Directive 2002/49/EC of the European Parliament and of the Council of 25 June 2002 relating to the assessment and management of environmental noise - Declaration by the Commission in the Conciliation Committee on the Directive relating to the assessment and management of environmental noise [2002] OJ L 189/12.

consultation has taken place,[102] otherwise it would not be possible to take the result of the public participation into account and improve the sustainability of those policies affecting the noise situation.

5.1.4 What is left of Directive 2003/35/EC?

Directive 2003/35 integrated certain aspects of public participation into the EIA Directive and the IPPC Directive. It also expressed the future intention to incorporate public participation requirements in line with the Aarhus Convention into the relevant legislation from the outset.[103] The Directive also included a self-standing set of rules applying the principles of public participation into plans or programmes already provided for in Union law.[104] They are listed in Annex I to that Directive and relate to the area of waste, water protection, and air quality. As a result, for example, the air quality plans as a core obligation of the current air quality directive 2008/50 are still subject to those rules.[105]

Given the overlap between the public participation provided for in Directive 2003/35 and the broader requirement for an environmental assessment in the SEA Directive, art 2(5) of Directive 2003/35 excludes from its scope those plans or programmes in respect of which public participation is carried out under Directive 2001/42. The Court clarified that it would be inconsistent to accept that action programmes fall within the scope of art 2 of Directive 2001/42 in relation to provisions concerning public participation regarding the adoption of the plan or programme. The exception is when the same action programmes no longer fall within the scope of that provision where they touch upon EIA.[106] While Directive 2003/35 aimed to include public participation into existing

102 Case C-683/20, *Commission v Slovakia* [2022] EU:C:2022:22, paras 19–28.

103 See second sentence of recital 10.

104 The first sentence of Recital 10 reads: "Provision should be made in respect of certain Directives in the environmental area which require Member States to produce plans and programmes relating to the environment but which do not contain sufficient provisions on public participation, so as to ensure public participation consistent with the provisions of the Aarhus Convention…".

105 Annex I(f) of Directive 2003/35 refers to plans or programmes under art 8(3) of Council Directive 96/62/EC of 27 September 1996 on ambient air quality assessment and management on "the plan or programme … prepared or implemented for attaining the limit value [of 13 different pollutants set out in its Annex I] within the specific time limit". That provision of Directives 96/62/EC was repealed as from 11 June 2010 by Directive 2008/50 and replaced by art 23 of the latter Directive [see art 31(3) and correlation table in Annex XVII to 2008/50].

106 Case C-105/09, *Terre wallonne and Inter-Environnement Wallonie* [2010] EU:C:2010:355, para 40.

categories of plans or programmes, it did not however intend to do away with the existing environmental assessments of those plans or programmes.

5.2 *Public Participation without an express legislative requirement*

5.2.1 Right to Information under the Aarhus Convention

In its landmark judgment *Varkens in Nood*, the Court provided an important clarification concerning public participation under the Aarhus Convention. In this judgment, which exclusively consists of an interpretation of the convention, the Court clearly acknowledged that art 6(2) of the convention enshrines a "right to information".[107] That right, however, is not granted to the public in general but only to the "public concerned".[108] The reason for this is that "the different stages of the public participation procedure are applicable to the public concerned only" and the right to information is considered by the Court as being instrumental to exercise the other right of that public, which is indeed the right to public participation.[109]

5.2.2 Direct effect of Article 6 of the Aarhus Convention

If in *Varkens in Nood* the Court acknowledged without doubt that the public concerned also has a right to public participation, it had already taken the view that art 6 of the convention had direct effect. Accordingly, the breach of those provisions could be put forward before a national court, as the Court held in the *Protect Natuur* case.[110] However, in that judgment there still remained an ambiguity, the Court having considered that the public, and not the public concerned, was the beneficiary of that right.[111] That ambiguity has now been clarified in the sense that it is only the public concerned that can benefit from a right to public participation stemming from the convention. The words 'public concerned' mean for the Court the circle of persons affected or likely to be affected by the "envisaged act or transaction".[112]

107 Case C-826/18, *Varkens in Nood* [2021] EU:C:2021:7, para 40.

108 *Ibidem.*

109 *Ibidem* at 41 and 43.

110 Case C-664/15, *Protect-Natuur* [2017] EU:C:2017:987.

111 See in particular ibidem at 63: "[…] Article 6 thereof confers on the public, in particular, the right to participate 'effectively during the environmental decision-making' by submitting 'in writing or, as appropriate, at a public hearing or inquiry with the applicant, any comments, information, analyses or opinions that it considers relevant to the proposed activity'".

112 *Ibidem* at 37.

In *Varkens in Nood*, the preliminary ruling originated from a challenge of a permit to build a new pen for 855 dry and pregnant sows, exchanging 484 breeding sows for 125 farrowing sows in the existing pens and constructing a covered run for sows. The action had been lodged by an NGO active in animal welfare and by a veterinarian, the latter living 20 km from the place of the project. Both applicants sought annulment of the permit but for different reasons. The NGO challenged the lack of a previous environmental assessment and the veterinarian the breach of her right to public participation. Subsequently, as the veterinarian had not been considered as a member of the public concerned by the administration, the national judge asked the Court to clarify whether the limitation of access to justice to 'interested parties' only, within the meaning of national law, was compatible with the Aarhus Convention.

The Court concluded that the members of the public concerned are those "who may participate in the decision-making procedure",[113] and then not only those who actually participate in it. The decision-making procedure in this case concerned implementation of an EU environmental provision, such as the obligation to carry out an EIA concerning a permit to construct a pig farm building. According to the Court, who is part of the public concerned has to be indicated by Member States "reasonably and in accordance with the objective of giving the public concerned wide access to justice",[114] meaning access to justice under art 9(2) of the convention. The Court concluded that only the first applicant (the NGO) could be considered as being a member of the public concerned.

The *Varkens in Nood* judgment is a landmark decision not only as to the definition of 'public concerned', but also regarding access to justice as further explained in the following section. In this regard, the judgment finally clarifies the consequences for an applicant of the articulation between the administrative procedure having led to the grant of a permit and the further access to court against the decision concerning that permit. The Court has eventually acknowledged that previous participation in the administrative procedure cannot prejudge the admissibility of the further judicial application. This is clearly due to art 9(2) of the Aarhus Convention, which grants members of the public the right to "challenge the substantive and procedural legality of any decision, act or omission subject to the provisions of article 6". In other words, those decisions, acts or omissions that have to undergo public participation. However, art 9(2) of the convention does not confine the grounds of review to those concerning public participation; neither does it provide for participation

113 *Ibidem* at 38; see also paragraph 43.

114 *Ibidem*.

in the previous administrative procedure as a condition of admissibility of the action in court.

It may be useful to recall that, as regards the objective to grant wide access to justice under art 9(2) of the Aarhus Convention, and according to the ACCC, the Parties have admittedly a certain room for manoeuvre in setting requirements. However, such requirements have to be "clearly defined", they do not have to cause "excessive burden" on environmental NGOs and they have not to be applied "in a manner that significantly restricts access to justice to such NGOs".[115]

6 The Remedies for breach of Public Participation: Public Participation and Access to Justice

6.1 The Possible Applicants

6.1.1 The Dividing Line between the Public and the Public Concerned

Under art 2(4) of the Aarhus Convention the public is "one or more natural or legal persons, and in accordance with national legislation or practice, their associations, organisations or groups". Under art 2(5) of the convention the public concerned is

> '[...] the public affected or likely to be affected by, or having an interest in, the environmental decision-making'. Article 2(5) specifies that, 'for the purposes of this definition, non-governmental organisations promoting environmental protection and meeting any requirements under national law shall be deemed to have an interest.

Whether an applicant falls in one or the other of these two categories, different obligations under the convention – and different rights – apply. Indeed, art 6 of the Aarhus Convention on public participation as well as art 9(2) on access to justice refer to the notion of 'public concerned'; that notion is however distinct from the general notion of 'member of the public', which is used in art 9(3) of the convention (the more general provision on access to justice).

Both notions of 'public' and 'public concerned' are defined in the convention, as recalled above. This is why the ACCC has recalled that in the definition of these categories the discretion of the Contracting Parties is limited.[116] In this

---

115 ACCC/C/2008/31, Germany, ECE/MP.PP/C.1/2014/8, para 71.

116 ACCC/C/2010/50, Czechia, ECE/MP.PP/C.1/2012/11, paras 65 to 67 and 70; ACCC/C/2010/51, Romania, ECE/MP.PP/C.1/2014/12, para 109.

regard, the Court has provided for some clarifications as to the applicability of these definitions in the EU legal order. Thus, in *Burgenland Wasserbetriebe*,[117] the Court held that even individuals who could be harmed by the use of a polluted natural resource, such as the user of a well who then cannot use any clean water anymore, is a member of the public concerned. Similarly, in the *Folk* case,[118] a person using river waters to fish and who was no longer able to take any healthy fish was considered as a member of the public concerned. Indeed, as noted the Court in *Burgenland Wasserbetriebe*, being a member of the 'public concerned' under the Aarhus Convention depends from the fact of being "directly concerned" by the breach of the relevant EU environmental law provisions. Another important clarification has been provided in the *Varkens in Nood* judgment, quoted above.

6.1.2 Access to Justice in the Judgment in *Varkens in Nood*, C-826/18

In *Varkens in Nood*, the Court considered that only members of the public concerned can benefit from the right to public participation. Thus, in that judgment, the Court held that the absence of a right of judicial review against a decision falling within the scope of art 6 for a member of the public (and not for a member of the public concerned), like the veterinarian in that case, was not contrary to the Aarhus Convention.[119] A different reading would blur the distinction between art 9(2) and (3) of the convention.[120] In this regard, the Court was keen to recall the "more limited regime" laid down in art 9(3) of the convention.[121]

Still, the Court also added that the conclusion for a member of the public would be different should a Member State provide in its environmental law for more extensive rights of public participation for members of the public. Should such a more extensive right be established, not allowing a member of the public to have "any access to justice" for the purposes of relying on those more extensive right would then be contrary to art 9(3) of the Aarhus Convention.[122]

The Court then concluded that art 9(2) of the Aarhus Convention must be interpreted as not precluding members of the 'public' referred to in art 2(4) of that convention from having no access, as such, to justice for the purposes of challenging a decision which falls within the scope of art 6 of that convention.

---

117 Case C-197/18, *Wasserleitungsverband Nördliches Burgenland* [2019] EU:C:2019:824, paras 33–34.

118 Case C-529/15, *Folk* [2017], EU:C:2017:419, paras 43–46.

119 Case C-826/18, n 108, para 46.

120 *Ibidem*, para 44.

121 *Ibidem*, para 37.

122 *Ibidem*, paras 47–51.

However, art 9(3) of the convention precludes such persons from not being able to have access to justice for the purposes of relying on more extensive rights to participate in the decision-making procedure, which may be conferred on them solely by the national environmental law of a Member State.

6.2 *Administrative or Judicial Review?*

In all the provisions concerning access to review mechanisms, the Aarhus Convention allows the Contracting Parties to provide for a previous filter of administrative review. In principle, both art 9(2) and 9(3) of the convention would be consistent with only an instance of administrative review, should that instance of review be so crafted that the reviewing body could be considered impartial.[123] Nonetheless, as a matter of EU law, since all measures having legal effects in the EU legal order are as such subject to the constitutional requirement of judicial review, even decisions of bodies performing a task of administrative review should be challengeable in court.

According to the convention, however, the issue is not whether administrative or judicial review is provided for, since the convention puts emphasis on the need to have an effective review and, more importantly, on the need to widely interpret access to justice under art 9(2) for the public concerned and art 9(3) for all members of the public. Rather, when administrative review is foreseen, the main problem of compatibility with the Aarhus Convention stems from the articulation between administrative and judicial review. Once more, in *Varkens in Nood* the Court has provided further important clarifications.

In particular, the referring court in that case asked the Court to clarify at which conditions the previous participation in the decision-making procedure "preparatory to the contested decision" of both the public concerned under art 6 of the Aarhus Convention and of a member of the public under national environmental law can influence admissibility of the judicial application. This clarification was sought regarding actions under art 9(2) and (3), respectively, unless the applicant cannot be reasonably criticised for not having intervened. The latter was a specification under Dutch law referring to cases where the lack of participation can be justified by – for instance – the flawed notifications of the draft decisions or other procedural mistakes.[124] Regarding the public concerned, the Court recalled its case law, according to which this category of applicants must be able to bring legal actions whatever role may

123 This could not be the case should that body be structurally linked with the public authority.

124 See Case C-826/18 *Varkens in Nood* [2020] EU:C:2020:514, Opinion of the AG Bobek, paras 16–18

have played in the decision-making procedure.[125] The Court thus confirmed its previous case law,[126] according to which "participation in the decision-making procedure has no effect on the conditions for access to that review procedure".[127] The Court also recalled, first, the fact that admissibility requirements concerning the interest to act are deemed to be met as regards NGOs, which also constitute the public concerned within the meaning of art 2(5) of the convention. Second, the Court recalled the objective of a wide access to justice under art 9(2) of the Aarhus Convention, which does not allow for an admissibility requirement whereby an application of an NGO can be admissible or not depending on the role an NGO may or may not have played in the decision-making procedure.[128] The Court then concluded that under art 9(2) of the Aarhus Convention the admissibility of actions of NGOs, considered then as public concerned, cannot be contingent upon their participation in the decision-making procedure which led to the adoption of the contested decision.[129] As to the relevance of the condition of not being able to be reasonably "criticised for not having participated in that procedure", it does not modify the conclusion of the Court on the inconsistency with art 9(2) of the convention of the previous participation in the administrative procedure as an admissibility requirement for a further judicial application.[130]

However, unless the member of the public seeks the protection of the more extensive public participation rights granted by national environmental law, as recalled above,[131] in case of an application lodged by a member of the public, the issue of access to justice should be assessed under art 9(3) of the convention. In this case, the "more flexible framework" laid down in art 9(3) of the convention allows for a procedural condition according to which "the applicant has submitted his or her objections in good time following the opening of the administrative procedure".[132] Such a limitation of the right to judicial protection under art 47 of the Charter of Fundamental Rights of the European Union (the 'Charter') is considered as justified by the Court according to the criteria laid down in art 52 of the Charter. In particular, the justification corresponds to the objective of general interest of ensuring a quick and effective

125 Case C-826/18, n 108, para 55.
126 Case C–263/08, *Djurgården* [2009], EU:C:2009:631, paras 38 and 39.
127 Case C-826/18, n 108, para 56.
128 *Ibidem*, paras 57 and 58.
129 *Ibidem*, para 59.
130 *Ibidem*, para 60.
131 *Ibidem*, paras 61 and 62.
132 *Ibidem*, para 63.

dispute-settlement, without having to go to court, which is deemed as being the purpose of the participation in the previous administrative procedure.[133]

As to the condition of not being reasonably criticised for not having participated in the decision-making procedure, this is proportionate according to the Court if it is assessed in light of the circumstances of the case.[134] Thus, the previous participation "in the procedure preparatory to the contested decision" is an illegal admissibility requirement for applications lodged by the members of the public concerned under art 9(2), even though that condition does not apply (where such NGOs cannot be reasonably criticised for not having participated in that procedure). Nevertheless, the condition of the previous participation in the administrative procedure is consistent with art 9(3) of the Aarhus Convention when judicial review is sought by members of the public, unless the applicant cannot be reasonably criticised in light of the circumstances of the case for not having participated in that procedure.[135]

6.3 *The Judicial Review*

6.3.1 The Subject Matter and the Scope of the Review

Judicial review in the EU constitutes the instrument to ensure that the rights stemming from the EU legal order are respected. This holds true as regards actions both before the EU Courts and national courts, which are essential in interpreting and applying EU law and that are linked to the Court via the preliminary ruling procedure laid down in art 267 TFEU.[136] For this reason they are considered as 'ordinary courts of EU law'.[137]

When applied to the rights that can originate from the Aarhus Convention, this guarantee further interacts with the provisions of the convention concerning 'access to justice' and contained in art 9 of the convention. The latter constitutes the third pillar of the procedural rights enshrined in the convention (after the first pillar, concerning the right of access to environmental information, and the second pillar, concerning the right to public participation, recalled above) and it has the purpose of making the first two rights effective.[138]

Against this backdrop, as the right to public participation has to be perceived as an instrument to ensure sustainability (as recalled at paragraph 7 of the Chisinau Declaration), according to which "public participation in

---

133 *Ibidem*, paras 63 to 66.

134 *Ibidem*, para 67.

135 *Ibidem*, para 69.

136 Case C-911/19, *FBF v ACPR* [2021] EU:C:2021:599, para 60 and the case law quoted therein.

137 Opinion 1/09 of the Court (Full Court), *Creation of a Unified Patent Litigation System* [2011] EU:C:2011:123, ground 80.

138 See in particular art 9(4) of the convention.

decision-making is [...] an instrument for achieving the sustainability and well-being of society",[139] that instrument is effective if judicial review relating thereto is effective.

Regarding the right to public participation under the Aarhus Convention, art 9(2) of the convention in particular provides for a "right" of the public concerned of bringing an action against decisions and other acts, which fall within the scope of art 6 of the convention. This right is acknowledged as such by the Court and constitutes a guarantee that the right to public participation stemming from art 6 of the Aarhus Convention is safeguarded.[140]

As to the concrete application of art 9(2) of the convention, the main concern is to not restrict the category of applicants in a way that is incompatible with the convention. In this regard, Member States have to define the categories of potential applicants by ensuring that the objective of giving them wide access to justice is safeguarded. Such a wide objective is satisfied if, as regards NGOs, their role is limited to asking a court of law to verify compliance with environmental law.[141]

6.3.2 The Remedies between Effectiveness and Procedural Autonomy

According to art 47 of the Charter of Fundamental Rights, the EU and the Member States acting within the scope of EU law must ensure effective judicial protection. Failing any rule adopted at the EU level, the competence to regulate the procedural aspects belongs to the Contracting Parties. In the EU, failing the adoption of a horizontal legislative instrument on access to justice in environmental matters, the competence to adopt procedural rules (and then to set out admissibility requirements) lies with the Member States, since it is in their competence that this issue "primarily" falls, as recalled by the Court.[142] This means that for cases concerning the Aarhus Convention, but relating to public participation in procedures handled by national authorities, it will be necessary to determine whether the domestic procedural rules do not either create a discrimination between situations treated under national law and EU law, or make the judicial protection extremely difficult or impossible. Indeed, according to the principle of equivalence Member States cannot treat rights stemming from EU law (such as the Aarhus Convention, which is a part of the EU legal order under art 216 TFEU) worse than those rights stemming from

139 See Chisinau Declaration, n 12.
140 Case C-826/18, n 108, para 36.
141 Case C-535/18, *IL aos*, [2020] EU:C:2020:391, para 45.
142 Joined Cases C-401/12 P to C-403/12 P, *Council aos* v *Vereniging Milieudefensie aos*, [2015] EU:C:2015:4, para 60.

domestic provisions. According to the principle of effectiveness, they cannot make the protection of the rights stemming from EU law excessively difficult or impossible.[143]

It should be noted that the principles of equivalence and of effectiveness also apply regarding administrative procedures organised by Member States in order to give effect to public participation according to the EU environmental directives. Accordingly, the procedural arrangements adopted by the Member States to ensure public participation cannot be less favourable than those governing similar domestic situations and cannot render impossible in practice or excessively difficult the exercise of rights conferred by the EU legal order.[144]

6.3.3 Is 'Invokability of Exclusion' still possible?

According to the case law an applicant could invoke the provisions of Directive 85/337 to set aside inconsistent provisions (or administrative measures) adopted in breach of those provisions. The judgments in *Linster* and *Grosskrotzenburg* are two cases in point. In *Linster*,[145] the applicants in the main proceedings relied upon the provisions of Directive 85/337/EEC in order to argue the unlawfulness of the expropriation of their own land parcels to allow for the construction of a motorway. The Court followed its previous case law, in particular the *Kraijeveld* judgment,[146] and without assessing whether the provisions invoked had direct effect held that the discretion left to the legislator in the transposition of the directive did not "preclude judicial review of the question whether it has been exceeded by the national authorities".[147] Those provisions could then be considered by the national court to set aside provisions of domestic or even administrative measures that were contrary to the Directive. This approach, constantly followed by the Court and based on an analysis of the existence of an obligation in the Directive more than on its precise content,[148] allowed national courts to ensure the effectiveness of environmental directives.

---

143 Case C-201/02, *Wells*, [2004] EU:C:2004:12, para 67 and Case C-420/11, *Leth*, [2013] EU:C:2013:166, para 38.

144 Case C-280/18, n 80, para 27.

145 Case C-287/98, *State of the Grand-Duchy of Luxembourg v Linster*, [2000] EU:C:2000:468.

146 Case C-72/95, *Kraaijeveld aos*, [1996] EU:C:1996:404, para 59 and case-law quoted therein.

147 C-287/98, n 146, para 37.

148 Case C-431/92, *Commission v Germany (Grosskrotzenburg)*, [1995] EU:C:1995:260, para 40: "[r]egardless of their details, those provisions therefore unequivocally impose on the national authorities responsible for granting consent an obligation to carry out an assessment of the effects of certain projects on the environment".

This assumption has now been put into question following the *Poplawski* (*II*) judgment,[149] and recently confirmed as being of general application in *Thelen Park*.[150] According to these judgments,

> even a clear, precise and unconditional provision of a directive does not allow a national court to disapply a provision of its national law which conflicts with it if, were that court to do so, an additional obligation would be imposed on an individual".[151] Accordingly, "a national court is not required, solely on the basis of EU law, to disapply a provision of its national law which is contrary to a provision of EU law if the latter provision does not have direct effect.[152]

Such a conclusion could be highly problematic in terms of ensuring the necessary effectiveness to EU environmental directives, in particular to those, such as the EIAD, which contribute to the implementation of public participation.

However, it could still be argued that, on the one hand, in so far as the provisions of EU environmental law are sufficiently precise, even though they are not such as conferring a right upon an individual, they would still meet the requirement of being directly enforceable in court if they do not impose any obligation on an individual.[153] Their breach would then trigger the effect of allowing the court to set aside the inconsistent national provision. On the other hand, a court of law of a Member State can always argue that a provision of the Charter or a general principle of EU law relevant for the interpretation of an EU environmental provision has direct effect, possibly after making a preliminary reference to the Court under art 267 TFEU. It could then conclude in the sense of giving precedence to the EU environmental provision.

6.3.4 The issue of Damages

The breach of the obligation to carry out an environmental impact assessment is also normally a breach of the obligation to ensure public participation. In

149 Case C573/17, *Popławski*, [2019]EU:C:2019:530, paras 65–67 and the case-law cited. See L.S. Rossi, Effetti diretti delle norme dell'Unione europea ed invocabilità di esclusione: i problemi aperti dalla seconda sentenza Popławski, in giustiziainsieme.it, www.giustiziainsieme.it/it/news/123-main/diritto-ue/1517-effetti-diretti-delle-norme-dell-unione-europea-ed-invocabilita-di-esclusione-i-problemi-aperti-dalla-seconda-sentenza-poplawski, at section 4

150 Case C-261/20, *Thelen Technopark Berlin GmbH*, [2022] EU:C:2022:33.

151 *Ibidem*, at 32.

152 *Ibidem*, at 33.

153 See in this vein Case C-205/20, *NE*, [2022] EU:C:2022:168, paras 28 (where the *Kraijveld* is mentioned) and 29 (where there is no reference to a 'right' to be conferred on the individual).

cases where this breach occurred and were brought to the Court, the latter recalled the possibility to regularise the breach and to apply the principle of State liability for breach of EU law.[154] Still, as the Court has finally acknowledged in *Varkens in Nood* the right to information and the right to public participation to the members of the public concerned, a member of the public concerned should be able to claim damages for breach of such rights. Indeed, these are clearly 'rights' within the meaning of the *Francovich* principle, according to which

> individuals who have been harmed have a right to reparation for damage caused by breaches of EU law attributable to a Member State when three conditions are met, namely, the rule of EU law infringed must be intended to confer rights on individuals, the breach of that rule must be sufficiently serious, and there must be a direct causal link between the breach and the loss or damage sustained by those individuals.[155]

Needless to say, members of the public concerned, including NGOs, should be assimilated to individuals for the sake of applying this principle, something on which, however, the Court has not had a word yet. In this regard, Member States are "required to make good any harm caused by the failure to carry out an environmental impact assessment";[156] this obligation might well also include damages stemming from the breach of the right to public participation. Indeed, these damages could further be considered as "resulting" from the breach of the applicable provisions.[157]

6.4 *Access to Justice at EU Level*

While the requirements concerning access to justice as regards public participation under the Aarhus Convention are clearly spelled out in the case-law of the Court, the main principles of which have been recalled above, it is worthwhile recalling the implications of the convention as to the EU institutions and bodies. The Aarhus Regulation has been modified to consider the findings

154 See Judgments in Joined Cases C-196 and 197/16, *Comune di Corridonia*, [2017] EU:C:2017:589 and in Case C-117/17, *Comune di Castelbellino*, [2018] EU:C:2018:129, where the issue was precisely how to ensure respect of the obligations stemming from the EIAD once the planned works had been entirely completed without the operator having ever held a permit. On State liability see Case C-41/11, *Inter-Environnement Wallonie ASBL e. a.*, [2012] EU:C:2012:103, para 43.

155 Case C-129/19, *Presidenza del Consiglio dei Ministri*, [2020] EU:C:2020:566, para 34 and case law quoted therein.

156 Case C-201/02, *Wells*, [2004] EU:C:2004:12, para 66.

157 Case C-261/18, *Commission v Ireland*, [2019] EU:C:2019:955, para 96.

of the ACCC on the consistency of the system of EU judicial review with the convention in case ACCC/2008/32.[158] The mechanism of internal review has subsequently been modified accordingly with Regulation 2021/1767, recalled above. However, regarding public participation, a member of the public concerned is without any doubt the addressee of possible measures adopted by an EU institution or body in, say, the procedure to adopt a plan or a programme under art 9(1) of the Aarhus Regulation. That member of the public concerned could then be able to challenge this act in the General Court under art 263(4) TFEU and, if necessary, raise a plea of illegality of a possible general measure under art 277 TFEU. Should further acts not be challengeable by such an applicant, that applicant could yet still have recourse to the recently amended mechanism of internal review laid down in art 10 of the Aarhus Regulation.

7 Final remarks

In a wide range of areas of EU environmental law, public participation is an essential part of decision-making procedures to increase the sustainability of decisions. Public participation typically consists of several steps. These include making the information of the relevant facts available to the public early in the process, the possibility to provide views on the decision to be taken when they can still feed into the process, the requirement for the competent authority to take the results into account and to inform the public about how this was done and what decision it resulted in.

Sustainability in that sense is twofold. First, public participation can contribute to including environmental considerations into public policies and individual projects, thereby preventing adverse environmental effects that would eventually prohibit the carrying out of those activities in the future.

158 United Nations Economic Commission for Europe, ACCC/C/2008/32 European Union www.unece.org/env/pp/compliance/Compliancecommittee/32TableEC.html last accessed 27 September 2022. The Meeting of the Parties eventually considered that "in accordance with the Committee's report on the implementation of request ACCC/M/2017/3, upon its entry into force the Party concerned will have fully met the requirements of paragraph 123 of the Committee's findings on communication ACCC/C/2008/32 (part II)": Decision VII/8f of the Meeting of the Parties, point 5, Economic Commission for Europe Meeting of the Parties to the Convention on Access to Information, Public Participation in Decision-making and Access to Justice in Environmental Matters, Excerpt from the addendum to the report of the seventh session of the Meeting of the Parties Decision VII/8f concerning compliance by the European Union with its obligations under the Convention, U.N. Doc. ECE/MP.PP/2021/2/Add.1.

Second, public participation can increase the acceptance of the opposing interests on both sides, and in that manner contribute to adopting policies and permitting projects that have broader support. EU rules set out when and how to provide for public participation and provide the possibility to challenge any shortcomings of that procedure.

Bibliography

Jendrośka J, 'Aarhus Convention Compliance Committee: Origins, Status and Activities' (2011) 8 Journal for European Environmental Planning Law 301.

Jendrośka J, 'Public Participation in Environmental Decision-Making. Interactions Between the Convention and EU Law and Other Key Legal Issues in its Implementation in the Light of the Opinions of the Aarhus Convention Compliance', in Marc Pallemaerts (ed.), *The Aarhus Convention at Ten* (Europa Law Publishing 2011).

Lohse EJ, 'Access to Justice – Main Challenge for Implementing the Aarhus Convention', in Eva Julia Lohse, Giulia Parola, Margherita Poto (eds.), *Participatory Rights* (Duncker&Humblot 2015).

Poto M, 'Strenghts and Weaknesses of Environmental Participation', in Eva Julia Lohse, Giulia Parola, Margherita Poto (eds.), *Participatory Rights in the Environmental Decision-Making Process and the Implementation of the Aarhus Convention: a Comparative Perspective* (Duncker&Humblot 2015).

Rossi, L S, *Effetti diretti delle norme dell'Unione europea ed invocabilità di esclusione: i problemi aperti dalla seconda sentenza Popławski*, in giustiziainsieme.it, www.giustiziainsieme.it/it/news/123-main/diritto-ue/1517-effetti-diretti-delle-norme-dell-unione-europea-ed-invocabilita-di-esclusione-i problemi-aperti-dalla-seconda-sentenza-poplawski.

Samvel G, 'Non-Judicial, Advisory, Yet Impactful? The Aarhus Convention Compliance Committee as a Gateway to Environmental Justice' (2020) 9 Transnational Environmental Law 211.

CHAPTER 6

Supranational Concepts of Participation and Sustainability Impacting on Administrative Legal Systems

Cristina Fraenkel-Haeberle

1 Introduction: Normative Sources of Ecological Sustainability in the Multilevel System

Due to the short life of democratic legislatures, political decisions tend to focus on the present and ignore the future. This postpones the burden of today's decisions to tomorrow, limiting the scope for future political action. Investment in the future tends to be delayed in favour of consumer spending, while natural resources are used without considering future availability.[1]

At international level, the desire to counteract this short-sighted attitude led to a report of the World Commission on Environment and Development entitled *Our Common Future* (Brundtland Report)[2] in 1987 and to the Rio Declaration of the United Nations in 1992.[3] Preserving a viable environment was described in these documents according to the constitutional theory of *intergenerational equity*.[4] The concept of intergenerational equity, originally associated with providing effective social security systems, has thus become part of a broader sustainability concept.

The principle of sustainability is widely upheld by European Union primary law. Art 11 of the Treaty on the Functioning of the European Union (TFEU) contains the so-called "cross-cutting clause", extending to all areas of EU and member state policies, which incorporates environmental protection requirements to promote sustainable development. Art 37 of the European Charter of Fundamental Rights (CFR) reiterates the aim of a qualitatively and quantitatively

---

1 Wolfgang Kahl, 'Staatsziel Nachhaltigkeit und Generationengerechtigkeit' (2009) 1 DÖV 2.

2 Mostafa Kamal Tolba and Asit K Biswas, *Earth and Us: Population, Resources, Environment, Development* (Butterworth-Heinemann 1991).

3 Report of the United Nations Conference on Environment and Development, General Assembly, United Nations publications (Vol. I), U.N. Doc. A/CONF.151/26 (1992) (Rio Declaration).

4 Kahl, n 1, at 3 ff; Wolfgang Kahl, '"Soziale Gerechtigkeit" oder Generationengerechtigkeit? Zur Notwendigkeit der Wiederbelebung einer verfassungspolitischen Debatte aus aktuellem Anlass' (2014) 1 ZRP 1.

high level of environmental protection and improvement of environmental quality, associated with sustainable development.

In the Section specifically dedicated to environmental policies, art 191 (2) TFEU does not explicitly mention the sustainability principle, but it does break down the EU's environmental policy into the four principles of precaution, prevention, priority action to address pollution at its source, and the polluter-pays principle, which are the premises for sustainable development. Thus, an *ex-ante* and pro-active approach (precaution, prevention) is combined with an *ex-post* response based on consequence elimination and compensation (source elimination, polluter-pays principle). All these principles are designed to reduce the likelihood and extent of environmental damage, in harmony with the sustainability principle, which is also mentioned by legal sources not directly connected to environmental law.[5]

In particular, the principle of preventive action introduced by the Maastricht Treaty (1992) can be seen as a first step towards sustainable development.[6] Its (partial) overlap with the precautionary principle is probably due to the fact that originally the German word '*Vorsorge*' covered both concepts semantically. The principle of prevention becomes relevant when damage is certain, while the purely precautionary principle applies to cases in which a harmful event is possible.[7] The difference therefore depends on how certain the likelihood of harm

---

5 For example in the context of public procurement, Parliament and Council Directive 2014/24/EU (second recital) of 26 February 2014, [2014] Official Journal of the EU (OJ) L 94/65, Parliament and Council Directive 2014/23/EU (third recital), [2014] OJ L 94/1 and Parliament and Council Directive 2014/25/EU (fourth recital), [2014] OJ EU L 94/243 combine the concept of sustainability with the policy of public procurement, stressing that: "*Public procurement plays a key role in the Europe 2020 strategy, set out in the Commission Communication of 3 March 2010 entitled 'Europe 2020, a strategy for smart, sustainable and inclusive growth', as one of the market-based instruments to be used to achieve smart, sustainable and inclusive growth while ensuring the most efficient use of public funds*".

6 Treaty of 1 January 1958 establishing the European Economic Community (TEEC)[1957] EUR-Lex 11957E, art 130 r (2) TEEC; Treaty of 1 November 1993 on European Union (TEC or Treaty of Maastricht) [1992] OJ C 191/1, art 174 (2) TEC.

7 In international law, the precautionary principle was initially mentioned in relation to damage to the marine environment, and the precautionary measures were based on the best available information (Francesco de Leonardis, 'Tra precauzione, prevenzione e programmazione', in Loredana Giani, Marina D'Orsogna and Aristide Police (eds.), *Dal diritto dell'emergenza al diritto del rischio* (Editoriale Scientifica Napoli 2018)49. Another area is air pollution control, eg the "precautionary measures" mentioned in the preamble of the Vienna Convention to protect the ozone layer, entered into force 22 September 1988, 1513 UNTS 293; see Paolo Giargiulo, 'Brevi riflessioni sulla natura giuridica e il contenuto dei principi di precauzione e di prevenzione nel diritto internazionale', in Loredana Giani, Marina D'Orsogna and Aristide Police (eds.), *Dal diritto dell'emergenza al diritto del rischio* (Editoriale Scientifica Napoli 2018)31.

is. Precaution plays a role in risk situations and risk management.[8] In the case of prevention, one speaks of a threat; in the case of precaution, one speaks of risk, under which the probability of danger may sometimes be uncertain.[9]

In addition, constitutional comparisons show that the sustainability principle is now a structural element of European constitutional law (*Ius Commune Europaeum*) and is thus part of the common constitutional tradition of the member states,[10] where it covers economic, social and environmental sustainability.[11]

In some legal systems, like that of Germany, only the principle of ecological sustainability has been explicitly constitutionalized. It became a "state goal" (*Staatszielbestimmung*) in 1994.[12] According to this provision, the *contrat*

---

8 See de Leonardis F, 'Tra precauzione, prevenzione e programmazione', in Loredana Giani, Marina D'Orsogna and Aristide Police (eds.), Dal diritto dell'emergenza al diritto del rischio (Editoriale Scientifica Napoli 2018), at 52 f.

9 The concept of danger is drawn from German police law and concerns a sequence of events, objectively foreseeable unless measures are taken and sufficiently likely to damage legally protected property. On the other hand, risk falls in the category of danger that has not yet materialized (*Noch-nicht-Gefahr*). Although the parameters are again the extent and probability of damage (ie the greater the asset threatened, the lower the probability threshold for intervention), the harmful event is less plausible than in the case of danger, and the danger threshold has not yet been crossed, as the situations at stake are only potentially critical; see Wolf-Rüdiger Schenke, *Polizei- und Ordnungsrecht* (10th ed, C.F. Müller 2018), para 261; Fritz Ossenbühl, 'Vorsorge als Rechtsprinzip im Gesundheits- Arbeits- und Umweltschutz' (1986) 2 NVwZ 161 ff; Rüdiger Breuer, 'Immissionsschutzrechtliche Vorsorge und Stand der Technik' (2016) 12 NVwZ 822. Furthermore, from a chronological point of view, there is no situation of danger when the damage is likely to occur in the distant future (Elena Buoso, 'I principi di precauzione e prevenzione nel diritto ambientale', in Simone Budelli (ed.), *Società del rischio, Governo dell'emergenza*, (Ambientediritto Editore 2020).

10 Kahl, n 1, at 3 ff. The author mentions various comparative law references. Thus, art 6 of the Charte de l'Environnement, part of the French Constitution, envisages reconciling "développement durable" with economic development and social progress. This shows that the French Constitution clearly recognizes the 'three-pillar' concept of sustainability. The principle of sustainability is also contained in the Preamble to the Swiss Federal Constitution (2000). According to art 24 (1) of the Greek Constitution, protection of the natural and cultural environment is a public duty. The Swedish Constitution also defines the principle of ecological sustainability with regard to future generations in § 2 (3). Finally, the Polish Constitution (art 5) explicitly mentions the principle of environmental sustainability, as does the Constitution of Portugal (art 66 (2)).

11 Gerd Winter, 'Ökologische Verhältnismäßigkeit' (2013) 7–8 ZUR 387.

12 See art 20a of the German Basic Law (Grundgesetz – GG). 'State goals' are less than fundamental rights and do not grant individuals any legally enforceable right. They are more than program norms, since they oblige the state to work to achieve them, which is why they are primarily a legislative mandate. See more extensively Karl-Peter Sommermann, *Staatsziele und Staatszielbestimmungen* (Mohr Siebeck 1997).

naturel between nature and human beings complements the interpersonal *contrat social* and ensures more "intergenerational justice".[13] On the other hand, social sustainability is implicitly guaranteed by the welfare state principle,[14] as well as in connection with the grant of a minimum wage, according to the case law of the Federal Constitutional Court (*BVerfG*) on the principle of human dignity.[15] The principle of economic sustainability is also implicitly taken into account by the "debt brake" (*Schuldenbremse*) introduced in 2009.[16]

In other countries, like Italy, the principle of ecological sustainability was, till recent times,[17] only promoted by ordinary law. For example art 3-*ter* of the Italian Environmental Code (*Codice dell'ambiente*), considering responsibility for future generations, invokes the sustainability principle, together with the precautionary principle and the principle of preventive action to monitor the long-term consequences of human action.[18] These principles also establish the principle of environmental action (*principio di azione ambientale*) in Italian law, with preserving as well as proactive functions.[19]

In recent times, the principle of sustainability, in the sense of *responsibility for future generations,* has gained momentum, particularly under the pressure of the 2015 Paris Agreement, which set out a global framework to avoid dangerous climate change.[20] In tune with this commitment, the German Federal

---

13 "Mindful also of its responsibility towards future generations, the state shall protect the natural foundations of life and animals by legislation, executive and legal action, according to law and justice, all in the framework of constitutional law." See Winter, n 11, at 387.

14 Art 20 and 28 German Basic Law.

15 BVerfGE 82, 60, 80.

16 See in particular art 109 and 115 of the German Basic Law, amended by the law of 29 July 2009 (BGBL. I p. 2248).

17 The recent constitutional reform, implemented with the constitutional law no. 1 of 11 February 2022 (Official Gazette no. 44 of 22 February 2022) has, however, amended art 9 of the Italian Constitution (in the section dedicated to the "fundamental principles") with the introduction of a provision, according to which "The Republic [...] protects the environment, biodiversity and ecosystems, also in the interest of future generations. State law regulates the methods and forms of animal protection". In art. 41 (in the section dedicated to the "rights and duties of citizens") has been further introduced among the limitations to private economic initiative a prohibition to cause damage to health and the environment.

18 Ruggiero Dipace, 'Sviluppo sostenibile, prevenzione e precauzione nella disciplina dei lavori pubblici', in Loredana Giani, Marina D'Orsogna and Aristide Police (eds.), *Dal diritto dell'emergenza al diritto del rischio* (Editoriale Scientifico Napoli 2018).

19 Pierluca Maceroni, 'L'organizzazione amministrativa del diritto ambientale', in Paolo Dell'Anno and Eugenio Picozza (eds.), *Trattato di diritto dell'ambiente* (Vol. 2, CEDAM 2013) 861.

20 Paris Agreement, entered into force 4 November 2015, 3156 UNTS 54113, unfccc.int/process/conferences/pastconferences/paris-climate-change-conference-november-2015/paris-agreement last accessed 17 September 2021. The Paris Agreement, which was signed

Constitutional Court (Bundesverfassungsgericht - *BVerfG*) showed to be well aware of the problem of sustainable political decision-making, also in view of the time dimension of adoption of decisions and the "right to future" of young generations.[21] In March 2021, it issued an order in which it held that the provisions of the Federal Climate Change Act of 2019 (*Bundes-Klimaschutzgesetz* – KSG),[22] governing national climate targets[23] and the annual emission quotas allowed until 2030, were incompatible with fundamental rights insofar as they lacked sufficient specifications for further emission reductions after 2030.[24] Although the *BVerfG* found that the legislator had not violated the obligation of climate action arising from art 20a Grundgesetz (GG), the provisions infringed the fundamental rights of the (very young) complainants, because they postponed major emission reduction burdens to periods after 2030. The *BVerfG* invited the legislator to enact detailed provisions by 31 December 2022, regulating in more detail how the reduction targets for greenhouse gas emissions should be established after 2030.[25] This decision of the *BVerfG* put pressure on

---

by the EU and member states (a so-called 'mixed agreement'), is well known for being the first ever, universal, legally binding document. The general goal is to reduce greenhouse gas emissions and limit global average temperature increase to well below 2 C° and preferably 1.5 C° above pre-industrial levels. Another goal is to strengthen and support the efforts of the signatory states in dealing with the impacts of climate change, by 'mitigation and adaptation'. The Paris Agreement was adopted at the Paris climate conference in December 2015. The EU and its member states are among the almost 190 parties to the Paris Agreement. The EU formally ratified the agreement on 5 October 2016, enabling it to come into force on 4 November 2016. See European Commission, 'Climate Action – Paris Agreement' (European Commission) https://ec.europa.eu/clima/eu-action/international-action-climate-change/climate-negotiations/paris-agreement_de (last accessed 28 September 2021).

21 See Constanze Janda, 'Sozialstaat for Future – Der Klima-Beschluss des BVerfG und seine Bedeutung für die Sozialgesetzgebung' (2021) 5 ZRP 149.

22 *Bundes-Klimaschutzgesetz* of 12 December 2019 (BGBL. I p. 2513).

23 The Federal Climate Change Act makes it compulsory to reduce greenhouse gas emissions by at least 55% by 2030 compared to 1990 levels and defines reduction pathways with sectoral annual emission quotas (§ 3(1) and § 4(1)).

24 First Senate of the Federal Constitutional Court, Order of 24 March 2021, BVerfGE 157, 30–177.

25 For a comparison with other judgements on climate protection, see Andrea de Petris, 'Protezione del clima e dimensione intertemporale delle libertà fondamentali: Karlsruhe for Future?' (2021) 4 Ceridap 127. See also: Jörg Berkemann, '"Freiheitschancen über die Generationen" (Art. 20a GG) Intertemporaler Klimaschutz im Paradigmenwechsel' (2021) 16 DÖV 701; Walter Frenz, 'Klimaschutzpflichten als Grundrechtsvoraussetzungsschutz nach Klimabeschluss und Jahrhunderthochwasser' (2021) 16 DÖV 715. For a comparison with the previous self-restraint of the German Constitutional Court see Rainer Wolf, 'Das Bundesverfassungsgericht – Hüter der Umwelt?' (1984) 3 Kritische Justiz 239; Andreas Voßkuhle, 'Umweltschutz und Grundgesetz' (2013) 1 NVwZ 1.

the federal government, which in the midst of the campaign for the September 2021 parliamentary elections, rapidly presented a new bill to the Parliament (*Bundestag*) acknowledging the complaints of the Constitutional Court.[26]

2 Impact of Supranational Concepts through Transposition of Directives in EU Member States

The European Union is not only a legal community but also an implementation community.[27] It is based on the idea of integration through law, which implies European harmonization through common rules.[28] There are countless studies and publications on the interaction between the law of the European Union and that of member states, and in particular on the Europeanisation of national administrative law. Little attention has been paid to the *different transposition* of European law by member states, despite its fundamental impact on national implementation practices.[29] This particularly applies to the implementation of directives, which are binding according to

26 Die Bundesregierung, 'Klimaschutzgesetz 2021 Generationenvertrag für das Klima', bundesregierung.de/breg-de/themen/klimaschutz/klimaschutzgesetz-2021-1913672 last accessed 17 September 2021. On the social dimension of climate protection, see Janda, n 21, at 149 ff.

27 See more extensively on this point, Karl-Peter Sommermann and Cristina Fraenkel-Haeberle, 'L'Unione Europea come comunità di implementazione - Strategie nazionali di recepimento delle direttive europee' (2021) 2 Ceridap 111.

28 Mauro Cappelletti, Monica Seccombe and Joseph H. H. Weiler, 'Integration Through Law: Europe and the American Federal Experience', in Mauro Cappelletti, Monica Seccombe and Joseph H. H. Weiler (eds.), *Integration through* Law (Vol. 1, DeGruyter 1986) 3–68. For an evaluation of the investigation perspective 'integration through law' see Antoine Vauchez, '"Integration-through-law". Contribution to a socio-history of EU political commonsense'(2008) EUI Working Papers RSCAS 2008/10.

29 An international research project, conducted at the German Research Institute for Public Administration (Speyer) from 2015 to 2019, was dedicated to implementation of EU directives and the adaptation strategies of selected EU member states in the environmental field. The results of this project were published in Cristina Fraenkel-Haeberle, Johannes Socher and Karl-Peter Sommermann (eds.), *Praxis der Richtlinienumsetzung im Europäischen Verwaltungsverbund: die Reichweite der Umgestaltung der nationalen Umwelt- und Energieverwaltung* (Duncker&Humblot 2020); Cristina Fraenkel-Haeberle, Diana-Urania Galetta and Karl-Peter Sommermann (eds.), *Europäisierung und Internationalisierung im Vergleich: deutsch-italienische Analysen zur Denationalisierung der Öffentlichen Verwaltung* (Duncker&Humblot 2017). A previous comparative study on the implementation of environmental directives can be found in Heinrich Siedentopf and Jacques Ziller, *Making European policies work. The implementation of Community legislation in the member states, Volume 2: National Reports* (SAGE Publications Ltd 1988).

art 288 (3) TFEU with regard to the result to be achieved, but "leave the choice of form and methods to the national authorities", and therefore raise the need to ensure equivalent standards in national legal systems, despite the margin of appreciation granted to member states by European law.

EU law also requires effective enforcement, which according to art 291 (1) TFEU is fundamentally the responsibility of member states. Implementation (in the French language version *mise en oeuvre*) encompasses both legislative and administrative enforcement. Thus the implementation study not only involves interpretation and implementation of EU law by national authorities, but also and above all how the directives are transposed. Factors that strongly influence the implementation of EU law are administrative procedure, administrative organization and the judicial review system, as well as the legal and administrative culture of the respective administrative bodies.[30]

In analysing the methods of implementation of directives in member states, three variants are of particular interest, since they are often linked to strategic considerations: first, minimal implementation, aimed at interfering as little as possible with the legal system of the member state; secondly, *gold-plating*, which involves adding conditions not envisaged by European law (it is disapproved of by Brussels, as it can lead to distortions or hybridization and can threaten achievement of European goals);[31] thirdly, *spillover*, which extends the scope of implementation beyond what is specified by a directive and may even lead to structural reform of national law. The latter, in particular, highlights an innovative potential of EU law, which goes far beyond its scope.

2.1 *Do Member States Tend to Prefer Minimal (One-to-One) Implementation?*

Implementation allows various interpretations by member states: on one hand, the directives are to be implemented "without omissions" and in line with the objectives of European law; on the other hand, the requirements of European law are not to be "over-fulfilled".[32] At first glance, almost all member states seem to prefer minimal implementation. In this sense, the (now abolished) Transposition Guidance of the UK Department for Business,

30 Karl-Peter Sommermann, 'Die Umsetzung von Richtlinien im Umwelt- und Energiebereich durch die EU-Mitgliedstaaten: vergleichende Schlussfolgerungen', in Fraenkel-Haeberle, Socher, Sommermann n 29, at 321 ff.

31 Ulrich Stelkens and Melanie Payrhuber, '*Gold-Plating* bei der Umsetzung der Dienstleistungsrichtlinie durch extensive Auslegung des § 42a VwVfG? Vom Rechtsvergleich als Instrument zur Bestimmung des Ziels einer Richtlinie' (2018) 4 NVwZ, 195.

32 Jürgen Schwarze, 'Richtlinienumsetzung "eins zu eins"', in Rainer Pitschas *et al.* (eds.), *Festschrift für Rupert Scholz zum 70. Geburtstag* (Duncker & Humblot 2007).

Enterprise & Regulatory Reform set out the following fundamental principle for the implementation of directives "Save in exceptional circumstances, ensure that the UK does not go beyond the minimum requirements of the measure to be transposed".[33] Early implementation is also to be avoided.[34] In Germany, too, the declared goal of 'one-to-one implementation' of the European law requirements was clearly expressed in the coalition agreement of 7 February 2018 (as well as in the agreements of previous legislatures), where "1:1 implementation of EU directives" is stated as a guiding principle for government policy and mentioned several times in the text itself.[35] Similar guidelines exist in other member states (such as Austria).[36] In Italy, "no gold-plating" is subject to "prospective and verificatory regulatory impact assessment".[37] At EU level, the Agenda for Better Regulation of the European Commission (2015)[38] recommends that member states avoid unwarranted gold-plating when implementing EU legislation, since among other things it can be costly for companies and public administrations (so-called "regulatory burden").[39]

---

33 Department for Business, Innovation and Skills, 'Transposition Guidance: How to implement European Directives effectively' (London, 2011) para 2.2: "When transposing EU legislation the aim should be to avoid going beyond the minimum requirements of the measure being transposed. Taking such an approach will ensure that the UK does not create unnecessary legislative burdens and place UK business at a competitive disadvantage."

34 Department for Business, Innovation and Skills n 33, at 8.

35 CDU, CSU und SPD, 'Ein neuer Aufbruch für Europa – Eine neue Dynamik für Deutschland – Ein neuer Zusammenhalt für unser Land - Koalitionsvertrag zwischen CDU, CSU und SPD' (19th legislature, Berlin, 7 February 2018), pp 13, 57, 64, 137, www.cdu.de/system/tdf/media/dokumente/koalitionsvertrag_2018.pdf, last accessed 17 September 2018; similar wording was already contained in the coalition agreement between CDU, CSU and SPD, of 18th legislature at p 15 and in the coalition agreement between CDU, CSU and FDP of 17th legislature at p 115. The newly elected Chancellor Merkel had already affirmed this principle in her first government declaration of 30 November 2005.

36 Since 2000, with its commitments against excessive implementation in government programs, Austria has also been strong in minimalist implementation of European law. The elimination of gold-plating was even defined as a priority in the current government program 2017–22; see Franz Leidenmühler, 'Die freiwillige "Übererfüllung" unionsrechtlicher Vorgaben durch die Mitgliedstaaten. Ein Beitrag zur rechtsdogmatischen und rechtspolitischen Diskussion um das sog. "Gold Plating"' (2019) 4 EuR 383.

37 Elena Buoso, 'Prospektive und verifizierende Regelungsfolgenabschätzung sowie "Gold-Plating"-Verbot als allgemeine Strategie der Umsetzung des Unionsrechts in Italien', Fraenkel-Haeberle, Socher, Sommermann, n 29, at 119.

38 Communication of the European Commission COM/2015/0215 final 'Better regulation for better results - An EU agenda'(2015).

39 Communication from the Commission COM/2014/0368 final, 'Regulatory Fitness and Performance Programme (REFIT): State of Play and Outlook' (2014) 6 f.

This raises the question of how such policies affect the transposition of EU directives.[40] The minimalist solution, which in many cases leads to "copy-out" (literal adoption of directive provisions), aims to reduce the need to adapt legislation and administration.[41] Thus in 2006, the French *Conseil d'État* recommended such an implementation strategy to the French government, and wherever possible, word-for-word transposition (*transposition par recopie*), which is less susceptible to violating primary and secondary law. Nothing should be added, nothing should be reworded or omitted.[42]

However, the shortcomings of this strategy should be borne in mind: on one hand, implementation has to consider the idea of subsidiarity (pursuant to art 5 [3] TEU), which also means self-determination and responsibility of the member states. On the other hand, it should enable member states to fit the requirements, which are sometimes effectively legal transplants,[43] harmoniously into their legal system.[44] The free choice of form, which is inherent to transposition of a directive into national law, enables member states to do what is referred to in political science literature as "customization", namely adapting the standard program of the directive to national traditions.[45] The European Commission also states that

> member states have the important responsibility of the timely implementation and full application of EU Law. In that regard, it is up to member state authorities to use simplification options offered by EU legislation and ensure that EU laws are applied at national, regional and local level as effectively and efficiently as possible.[46]

---

40 On this question, see more broadly Johannes Socher, 'Annäherung nationaler Verwaltungssysteme trotz "no gold-plating"-*Politiken?*', in Fraenkel-Haeberle, Galetta and Sommermann n 29, at 67.

41 See Melanie Payrhuber and Ulrich Stelkens, '1:1-Umsetzung von EU-Richtlinien: Rechtspflicht, rationales Politikkonzept oder (wirtschafts)politischer Populismus? – zugleich zu Unterschieden zwischen Rechtsangleichungs- und Deregulierungsrichtlien' (2019) 2 EuR, 190.

42 Ibid at 190.

43 For a definition see Eva Julia Lohse, *Rechtsangleichungsprozesse in der Europäischen Union* (Mohr Siebeck2017) 109: "A legal transplant is any expression of a legal idea existing in a state that is adopted into another legal system voluntarily or due to actual or normative pressure from a legal system in which it previously and independently existed and also (mostly) continues to exist."

44 Sommermann, n 29, at 325.

45 Payrhuber and Stelkens, n 41, at 201.

46 REFIT, n 39, at 7.

2.2 *Gold-plating or Introducing Conditions beyond Those Set Out in the Directive*

Based on this quick overview, the widespread preference for 'no gold-plating', under which any non-minimalist transposition of European law has a negative connotation, would mostly seem to discourage gold-plating implementation practices. Gold-plating means that the scope or legal consequences of implementation go further than the directive provisions themselves.[47] One example, concerning over-fulfilment of the scope of a certain European regulation, is extension of the obligation to conduct environmental impact assessment (EIA) to projects not covered by the directive in question.[48] The same is also conceivable for the legal consequences. In this case, stricter sanctions or enforcement mechanisms than required by Union law are introduced.[49]

Certain situations may justify gold-plating: eg if national law was already compliant with the requirements of Union law and included areas that went beyond the European requirements before transposition of the directive. Conversely, when the Environmental Information Directive was implemented in Poland, the exact opposite occurred: national rules were restricted as a result of implementation of the directive on environmental information.[50] Gold-plating can also make sense if the legislator perceives inconsistency between regulations determined by Union law and other sectors not determined by Union law.[51] Political questions may also be at stake. In terms of legal policy, a solution found at EU level may be deemed particularly convincing and promising if for instance it is more advanced than the provisions of national law.[52] For example, Directive 2003/35/EC,[53] which implements the second pillar of

---

47 See on this point Lohse, n 43, at 360 ff.

48 Council Directive 96/61/EC of 24 September 1996 concerning integrated pollution prevention and control (1996) OJ L257/26 contained six system categories subject to the integrated pollution prevention and control (IPPC). Italy added many other annexes with Legislative Decree no 128/2010 (Annex VIII).

49 A German example of exorbitant implementation of s 11 (1) of the EIA Directive is § 4 (1) *Umweltrechtsbehelfsgesetz* (UmwRG), according to which certain violations of the EIA regulations are classified as "absolute procedural errors" and are therefore not subject to the irrelevance regulation according to § 46 VwVfG. See Payrhuber and Stelkens, and also differences between legal approximation and deregulation directives, n 41, at 218.

50 Claus Dieter Classen, 'Überschießende Effekte der Umsetzung von Richtlinien in den EU-Mitgliedsstaaten aus rechtlicher Perspektive', in Fraenkel-Haeberle, Socher, Sommermann (eds.), n 29, at 293.

51 Anne-Christin Mittwoch, 'Richtlinienkonforme Auslegung bei überschießender Umsetzung' (2017) 4 JuS 296.

52 Classen, n 50, at 295.

53 Directive 2003/35/EC of the European Parliament and of the Council of 26 May 2003 providing for public participation in respect of the drawing up for certain plans and

the Aarhus Convention[54] and allows the participation of individuals and non-government organizations in projects of environmental importance, has been considered particularly suitable for promoting environmental democracy, and extensions of it have been viewed with approval.

Another goal could be to avoid discrimination against nationals. Particularly in the area of internal market law (primary and secondary), EU rules concern matters of a cross-border character, whereas purely domestic questions are left to national law. In this case, gold-plating may only be a matter of avoiding unequal treatment in the national legal system,[55] although it should be borne in mind that any non-minimalist implementation of European law leads to national differences and fragmentation of the internal market, the opposite of legal harmonization.[56]

Gold-plating possibilities also depend on the degree of harmonization that European law requires of the national legislator. If it aims for complete harmonization, national regulations are completely replaced with a common standard. Conversely, if a directive envisages minimum harmonization, member state laws will only partially converge, even if greater protection measures are adopted. In the latter case, the leeway available to member states remains outside the sphere of EU law.[57] The choice between complete or minimum harmonization must be established on a case-by-case basis. The EU Treaty only specifies this in certain instances. For example, pursuant to art 114 (4) and (5) TFEU, in the framework of establishment and functioning of the internal market, member states may derogate from the requirements of art 114 (1) TFEU, *inter alia* for the sake of environmental protection.[58]

Gold-plating can also be implemented in the case of directives that stipulate complete harmonization, as long as primary law includes a protection enhancement clause that allows member states to maintain higher national standards.[59] For example, art 193 TFEU provides that measures in the field of

programmes relating to the environment and amending with regard to public participation and access to justice in Council Directives 85/337/EEC and 96/61/EC (2003) OJ L156/17.

54 United Nations Economic Commission for Europe (UNECE) Convention on Access to Information, Public Participation in Decision-Making and Access to Justice in Environmental Matters (Aarhus Convention), entered into force 30 October 2001, 2161 UNTS 447.

55 Classen, n 50, at 295.

56 Leidenmühler, n 36, at 393.

57 Lohse, *n 43, at 566ff.*

58 Classen, n 50, at 300.

59 Leidenmühler, n 36, at 394.

environmental protection, adopted under art 192, do not prevent individual member states from introducing stricter standards of protection. In this sector, gold-plating is encouraged by an explicit provision of the Treaties, as in the context of consumer protection, where the right to introduce higher protection standards is envisaged by art 169 (4) TFEU.[60]

2.3 *Indirect Europeanisation (Spillover) as an Opportunity to Promote Wide-ranging Reforms in Areas Not Concerned by European Union Law*

Besides modifications resulting directly from provisions of Union law (direct Europeanisation), there may be indirect transformations in administrative law (indirect Europeanisation or spillover) which cannot be directly traced to explicit requirements outlined in EU directives, but are somehow linked to them.[61] Spillover may be when standards, procedures and organisational structures established by EU law are extended to neighbouring areas.[62] Unlike gold-plating, spillover is not problematic in the case of legal changes that cannot be directly traced back to explicit requirements outlined in EU directives, as its goal is not to increase the scope of directives, but rather to adopt the requirements of a directive outside its scope. As in the case of gold-plating, the reasons for spillover may depend on how consistent and homogeneous the national legal system is, as well as on avoidance of unwarranted distinctions.[63]

At first glance, 'no gold-plating' policies seem to exclude such over-implementation. However, the freedom of information principle is an example of how a hesitant direct transposition of EU laws in the field of access to environmental information may nevertheless *nudge*[64] national legislators to implement similar principles in other areas of the law. If we examine the German example, there is a broad consensus among scholars that the legislation on access to environmental information (first pillar of the Aarhus Convention,

60 Ibid at 398.

61 Karl-Peter Sommermann, 'Veränderungen des nationalen Verwaltungsrechts unter europäischem Einfluss – Analyse aus deutscher Sicht', in Jürgen Schwarze (ed.), *Bestand und Perspektiven des Europäischen Verwaltungsrechts* (Nomos 2008), 195.

62 Karl-Peter Sommermann, 'Gemeineuropäische Verwaltungskultur als Gelingensbedingung Europäischer Integration?' (2015) 11 DÖV, 449.

63 Leidenmühler, n 36, at 387

64 Margit Seckelmann, Wolfram Lamping, 'Verhaltensökonomischer Experimentalismus im Politik-Labor – Rechtliche Rahmenbedingungen und Folgerungen für die Evaluationsforschung' (2016) 5 DÖV 189.

AC 1998)[65] triggered a broadening of transparency legislation in Germany.[66] In particular, Freedom of Information Laws (*Informationsfreiheitsgesetze*) at federal[67] and *Land* level[68] now envisage transparency rights beyond environmental issues, granting a general right of access to public information. Some German *Land* (federate state) laws go even further. The Transparency Law of Hamburg imposes an active obligation to publish information (proactive disclosure).[69] The same applies to the Transparency Law of Rhineland-Palatinate,[70] which links the right of access to environmental information based on EU law to the right of access to "public information", ie "all records made for public purposes".[71] In doing so, this innovative law overcomes the different regulation of environmental information and freedom of information in general.[72]

In the United Kingdom, contextually with the Environmental Information Regulations (EIR), the Freedom of Information Act (FOIA) came into force in 2004, establishing the office of Information Commissioner to enforce a general right of access to administrative information.[73] Independent information

65 unece.org/DAM/env/pp/documents/cep43e.pdf> last accessed 19 September 2021.

66 See eg Hartmut Maurer and Christian Waldhoff, *Allgemeines Verwaltungsrecht* (C.H. Beck 2017) para 31; Bernhard Wegener, 'Aktuelle Fragen der Umweltinformationsfreiheit' (2015) 10 NVwZ 609.

67 Law regulating access to information (Gesetz zur Regelung des Zugangs zu Informationen des Bundes: Informationsfreieheitsgesetze – IFG) of 5 September 2005, Federal Law Journal I (BGBL I 2005), 2722.

68 With the exception of Bavaria and Lower Saxony, all German *Länder* enacted corresponding laws. Even local government statutes dealing with access to information were recently passed, for example the 'Satzung zur Regelung des Zugangs zu Informationen in weisungsfreien Angelegenheiten der Stadt Leipzig – Informationsfreitssatzung – (IFS)' of the city of Leipzig (Leipzig, 26 January 2013)2 Official Journal of the City of Leipzig 9; Roman Götze, 'Aktuelle Entwicklungen im Umweltinformationsrecht, Landes- und Kommunalverwaltung' (2013) 6 LKV 241 f.

69 Transparency Act of Hamburg (Hamburgisches Transparenzgesetz – HmbTG) of the city of Hamburg (Hamburg, 19 Juny 2012) 29 Official Journal for law and regulation of thy city Hamburg I 271.

70 Official Journal of Rhineland-Palatinate, 2015, p. 383.

71 Ibid, para 5, s 2.

72 Cristina Fraenkel-Haeberle and Johannes Socher, 'Direct and indirect Europeanisation of national administrative systems. Implementation and spillover effects of the environmental information directives in a comparative perspective' (2018) 56 Revista Catalana de Dret Public 125.

73 Freedom of Information Act 2000 c. 36, legislation.gov.uk/ukpga/2000/36/contents last accessed 19 September 2021.

tribunals were created outside the scope of the EIR.[74] They are a completely new control body in the English administrative system and have fostered a true cultural shift from *secrecy* to the *legal right to know*.[75]

A particularly good example of spillover in member states on implementation of the Environmental Information Directives occurred in Italy. The most recent regulation dealing with transparency is the Transparency Decree (Legislative Decree no 97/2016), which aims for a *complete right* to access public information, irrespective of legal position (protected or otherwise) (art 7), and uses the same wording as Directive 2003/4/EC on environmental information. Art 2(1) of the Transparency Decree envisages "free access for all to data and documents held by the public administration", which in addition to the objective of transparency, also aims at combatting corruption among civil servants.[76]

Regarding public participation, spillover can also be seen in the new Italian Code on public procurement,[77] which envisages the possibility of public debate (*débat public*) with a view to conducting feasibility studies on major infrastructure projects. This form of participation was based on the French *Commission Nationale du Débat Public*, which has a role in testing the environmental compatibility of major construction projects.[78] As a legal institution, public debate is not mentioned in the three new public procurement

74 On the genesis of the Freedom of Information Act 2000, see Sebastian Roll, '*Zugang zu Umweltinformationen und Freedom of Information*' (Duncker&Humblot 2003), in particular 62–75 and 172–196.

75 Johannes Socher, 'Die Umsetzung organisations- und verfahrensrechtlicher Vorgaben des Umweltrechts in Großbritannien' (2017) in Fraenkel-Haeberle, Galetta, Sommermann (eds.), n 31, at 99; Karl-Peter Sommermann, 'La exigencia de una Administración transparente en la perspectiva de los principios de democracia y del Estado de Derecho' in Ricardo García Macho (ed.), *Derecho administrativo de la información y administración transparente* (Marcial Pons 2010).

76 See more extensively Diana-Urania Galetta, 'Accesso civico e trasparenza della Pubblica Amministrazione alla luce delle (previste) modifiche alle disposizioni del Decreto Legislativo 33/2013' (federalism.it, n 5, 2 March 2016) https://air.unimi.it/bitstream/2434/446537/2/SaggioTrasparenzaMadiaPubblSuFederalismi.pdf last accessed 22 August 2022; Diana-Uriana Galetta, 'La trasparenza per un nuovo rapporto tra cittadino e la P.A.: un'analisi storico-evolutiva nella prospettiva di diritto comparato europeo' (2016) 5 Rivista di diritto pubblico comparato 1019; Diana-Uriana Galetta, 'The Italian Freedom of Information Act 2016. Why transparency-on-request is a better solution?' (2016) 2 IJPL 268.

77 Legislative Decree no. 50/2016, art 22.

78 Nicola Posteraro, 'Grandi opere e partecipazione democratica: alcune riflessioni sul dibattito pubblico italiano *à la française*' (2020) 3 Istituzioni del Federalismo 607: regione.emilia-romagna.it/affari_ist/rivista_3_2020/Posteraro.pdf last accessed 21 September 2021.

directives[79] or in the previous regulation, but rather ensues from the participation rights granted by the Aarhus Convention.[80]

3 A Paradigmatic Shift towards Public Participation under the Pressure of European Environmental Law

The European Union is committed to protecting and preserving the environment and improving its quality. To do so and to implement its obligation under the second pillar of the Aarhus Convention, the Public Participation Directive 2003/35/EC reviewed the EIA Directive[81] and the IPPC Directive.[82] The two procedures had already become important instruments for integrative and preventive environmental protection.[83] With the EIA Directive, European law

79 Directives of the European Parliament and of the Council 2014/23/EU of 26 February 2014 on the award of concession contracts Text with EEA relevance (2014) OJ L94/1, 2014/24/EU of 26 February 2014 on public procurement and repealing Directive 2004/18/EC (2014) OJ L94/65 and 2014/25/EU of 26 February 2014 on procurement by entities operating in the water, energy, transport and postal services sectors and repealing Directive 2004/17/EC (2014) OJ L 94/243.

80 Ruggiero Dipace, 'Sviluppo sostenibile, prevenzione e precauzione nella disciplina dei lavori pubblici' (2018) 18 IRIS Catalogo Istituzionale della Ricerca dell'Università degli Studi del Molise 278. The public debate regulation was implemented by Prime Ministerial Decree (D.P.C.M.) of 10 May 2018, which laid down the implementation rules, categories and quantitative thresholds. The National Commission for Public Debate will be established at the Ministry for Infrastructure and Transport; see Giacinto della Cananea, 'Exit or voice? Débat public goes to Italy' (2019) 2 European Public Law 157.

81 The initial Directive of the European Parliament 1985/335/EEC of 13 June 1985 granting a discharge to the Commission in respect of the financial management of the fifth European Development Fund during the 1983 financial year (1985) OJ L174/51 and its amendments were consolidated by Directive of the European Parliament and the Council 2011/92/EU of 13 December 2011 on the assessment of the effects of certain public and private projects on the environment Text with EEA relevance (2011) OJ L26/1. Directive 2011/92/EU was amended by Directive of the European Parliament and the Council 2014/52/EU of 16 April 2014 amending Directive 2011/92/EU on the assessment of the effects of certain public and private projects on the environment Text with EEA relevance (2014) OJ L124/1.

82 Council Directive 96/61/EC of 24 September 1996 concerning integrated pollution prevention and control (1996) OJ L257/26, as amended by Directive of the European Parliament and the Council 2010/75/EU of 24 November 2010 on industrial emissions (integrated pollution prevention and control) Text with EEA relevance (2010) OJ L334/17.

83 See art 3 and 4 of Directive of the European Parliament and of the Council 2003/35/EC of 26 May 2003 providing for public participation in respect of the drawing up of certain plans and programmes relating to the environment and amending with regard to public participation and access to justice Council Directives 85/337/EEC and 96/61/EC - Statement by the Commission (2003) OJ L156/17.

introduced a multi-phase procedure for early identification of the impact of a project on certain environmental factors, thus enabling a shift from media to over-media, integrative protection.

A preferred area for application of the precautionary and preventive principles is regional planning, where sustainability is a top priority under European law. In this context, risk assessment has to be conducted in a general framework and case-by-case solutions are considered an option of last resort. This approach led the European Union to adopt the SEA (strategic impact assessment) Directive[84] with a view to preventive environmental protection. SEA is an independent part of the administrative procedure for drawing up and amending plans and programmes and for avoiding multiple audits.[85] Unlike the EIA, it does not concern specific projects but examines plans and programmes, such as urban planning laws, expected to have significant environmental impacts. The purpose of the SEA is to identify likely significant environmental impacts and "reasonable alternatives" and to document them in an environmental report.[86] The report is the result of extensive public participation. The decision-making process must consider the comments submitted when adopting the plan.[87] In addition, subsequent monitoring is contemplated in art 10.[88]

Concerning administrative procedure, two trends have emerged in connection with the new provisions on public participation: a deviation from the general rules of procedure when environmental concerns come into play, combined with the choice of a special procedure with a focus on the crucial role of public participation.[89] Under art 2 (2) of the Public Participation Directive 2003/35/EC, the public should be given an "early and effective" opportunity to participate in the preparation or revision of plans and programs. In this context

---

84 Directive of the European Parliament and of the Council 2001/42/EC of 27 June 2001 on assessment of the effects of certain plans and programmes on the environment, OJ L197/30 (SEA Directive).

85 Ibid, art 4 (3).

86 Ibid, art 5 (1).

87 Ibid, art 8.

88 Both are procedural norms. As with the EIA Directive, a distinction is made between mandatory SEA (§§ 14b (1), 14c UVPG) and conditional SEA (§ 14b (2), 14d (1) UVPG). Conditional SEA depends on a preliminary screening in individual cases. Like EIA, the SEA process is divided into the following steps: 1) definition of the scope of the investigation (scoping); 2) preparation of the environmental report with a view to the alternative assessment; 3) involvement of other authorities; 4) involvement of the public; 5) cross-border public and public participation; 6) announcement of the decision to accept or reject the plan or program; 7) monitoring (see Wilfried Erbguth and Sabine Schlacke, *Umweltrecht* (Nomos 2014), § 5, para 74.

89 Nicola Lugaresi, *Diritto dell'ambiente* (CEDAM 2015) 75.

both natural and legal persons are referred to as "the public", and according to the Aarhus Convention definition, the public includes "one or more natural or legal persons" and their "associations, organizations and groups", ie also environmental associations representing supra-individual interests.[90]

As a result of these Directives, the German legal doctrine emphasizes a transition from a "serving function of the procedure" (*dienende Funktion des Verfahrens*) to the "own value of the procedure" (*Eigenwert des Verfahrens*)[91] or rather to the "procedure as a mode of implementation of administrative law" (*Verfahren als Verwirklichungsmodus des Verwaltungsrechts*),[92] which means that the specification and enforcement of substantive law requires an adaptation of procedural law.[93] Thus, the EIA and the SEA Directives both implement three essential environmental law principles, consisting of environmental precaution through early determination of the effects of plans and projects, integrative examination of all environmental media and their interactions, as well as cooperation between state and society, in particular through public participation initiatives aimed at sharing information with private and public stakeholders.

According to the above-mentioned Public Participation Directive, the results of the deliberation process must be adequately considered in regulatory decision-making. The Directive covers projects subject to EIA or approval under the IPPC directive (now the Industrial Emissions Directive, IE).[94] Plans and programs under the SEA[95] and Water Framework Directives (WFD) have their own rules on public participation.[96]

90 Aarhus Convention, n 54, art 2 (4).

91 Ulrich Stelkens, 'Der Eigenwert des Verfahrens im Verwaltungsrecht' (2010) 17 DVBL 1078.

92 Rainer Wahl, 'Verfahrensrecht zwischen Verwaltungseffizienz und Rechtsschutzauftrag', (1983) 41 VVDStRL 151.

93 See more extensively Chien-Liang Lee, 'Verfahrensrecht und Rechtsschutz im Wandel – dargestellt anhand der UVP im Rechtsvergleich' (2019) 3 VerwArch 370

94 Directive 2010/75/EU, n 82.

95 Directive 2001/42/EG recital no 15, n 84.

96 Prevention (avoidance) of environmental damage is also addressed by Directive of the European Parliament and of the Council 2004/35/EC of 21 April 2004 on environmental liability for the prevention and remedying of environmental damage, which prescribes the precautionary principle (avoidance activity) in art 5 (1), and in the event of immediate risk of such damage, commits the operator to taking the necessary mitigation measures. With regard to public participation, art 12 (1) of this directive provides that those who will be affected or are likely to be affected by the environmental damage, as well as those who claim 'sufficient interest' in environmental proceedings for fear of harm or infringement, may make observations to the competent authorities and may invite them to act in accordance with the Directive. Non-government organizations recognized under national law

The Public Participation Directive amends the EIA and IPPC directives by requiring that the public concerned, having either a "sufficient interest" or "maintaining impairment of a right" under national law, "have access to a review procedure before a court or other independent and impartial body established by law" if the law of a member state so requires.[97]

In this way, art 9 (2) of the Aarhus Convention is implemented by European law. Thus the public participation system, *alias* the second pillar of the Aarhus Convention, also strengthens procedural rights in judicial procedures.[98] The German literature repeatedly emphasizes the aim of "mobilizing the citizen to enforce the law",[99] which expresses "functional subjectification" (*funktionale Subjektivierung*) in European environmental protection, since environmental organizations act as trustees of the public, adopting a *status procuratoris* on behalf of the people concerned.

4 Obstacles to Implementation Linked to Public Participation and Sustainability According to the Water Framework Directive

The case law of the European Court of Justice (ECJ) on the role of national administrative courts in the enforcement of European environmental law poses a challenge for administrative judges of various member states, where the task of administrative jurisdiction is subjective legal protection, completed in environmental matters by association rights. The case law of the ECJ, based on the provisions of art 9 of the Aarhus Convention, seems to call for a switch to objective administrative control concerning participatory rights

are considered to have sufficient interest. The procedural element and democratic participation in the risk management process are thus clearly visible; see on this point A. Barone, 'The "Reflexive" Public Administration', in Loredana Giani, Marina D'Orsogna and Aristide Police, *Dal diritto dell'emergenza al diritto del rischio* (Editoriale Scientifica 2018) 83.

97 See the EIA Directive 2014/52/EU, n 81, at art 10a and the IPPC Directive 2010/75/EU, n 82, at art 15a.

98 The concern is not defined individually but implemented by German legislation with introduction of the action of legally recognized associations (representatives of the *public concerned*) in the Environmental Action Act (*Umweltrechtsbehelfsgesetz - UmwRG*).

99 Johannes Masing, *Die Mobilisierung des Bürgers zur Durchsetzung des Rechts* (Duncker&Humblot 1997), quoted by MatthiasRuffert, 'Umweltrechtsschutz ohne methodische Grundlage? Zur neueren Rechtsprechung des EuGHs und ihren Folgen für Deutschland' (2019) 16 DVBL 1033.

of environmental organizations and their access to justice, thus promoting a structural change in the scope of administrative justice.[100]

The protection of water resources is an example of the important role of public participation. With adoption of the Water Framework Directive (WFD) 2000/60/EC,[101] member states of the European Union committed themselves to ambitious water quality targets, in particular in the context of aquatic ecology. The environmental objectives are defined in art 4 WFD for surface waters, groundwater and protected areas. A water deterioration ban must be observed in any approval procedure as an immediate requirement, whereas the water improvement requirement must be reconciled with the other aims of the WFD and must be specified by planning measures.[102]

As a key implementation tool, the WFD prescribes the drawing up of river basin management plans[103] and programs of measures,[104] based on which member states determine their waterbody management. These were first to be compiled in December 2009 and updated every six years.[105]

Concerning the WFD, the *Protect* decision of 20 December 2007 is worth mentioning with reference to the link between participatory rights and the right of action of environmental associations.[106] In this dispute, based on art 4 of the WFD, the Austrian environmental organization *Protect* put forward objections in court against approval of a snowmaking system, because exploitation of the water had significantly worsened the condition of the creek in question (*Einsiedlbach*). On request of the Austrian Administrative Court, the ECJ was called to make a preliminary ruling on whether a breach of the obligations under art 4 of the WFD authorized a legally recognized water protection association to challenge decisions made within the framework of water law permit procedures, even when an EIA-compliant project, for which art 9 para 2 of the Aarhus Convention awarded a right to sue, was not concerned. The ECJ stated that where participation as a party to the administrative procedure was

100 Klaus Rennert, 'Verwaltungsrechtsschutz auf dem Prüfstand' (2017) 1 DVBL 69; Klaus Rennert, 'Funktionswandel der Verwaltungsgerichtsbarkeit' (2015) 13 DVBL 793.

101 Directive of the European Parliament and of the Council 2000/60/EC of 23 October 2000 establishing a framework for Community action in the field of water policy, OJ L 327/1.

102 Björn Tänzer, 'Aktuelle Entwicklungen bei der Umsetzung der Wasserrahmenrichtlinie' (2017) 20 DÖV 868.

103 WFD, n 101, at art 11.

104 WFD, n 101, at art 13.

105 See more extensively Moritz Reese, 'Die Wasserrahmenrichtlinie in der Umsetzungskrise' (2018) 21 NVwZ 1592.

106 Case C-664/15 *Protect Natur-, Arten- und Landschaftsschutz Umweltorganisation v Bezirkshauptmannschaft Gmünd* (2017) ECLI:EU:C:2017:987 (hereinafter ECJ Protect).

required for judicial review, such participatory rights had to be recognised to environmental NGOs.[107] National procedural rules, such as § 42 (1) of the AVG (*Austrian General Administrative Procedure Act*), which would result in loss of party status (and therefore concomitant rights to judicial review) for failure to intervene in a timely manner, were not allowed where they appeared to constitute unfair or impossible standards.[108] This legal situation was declared incompatible with art 9 (3) AC and art 47 CFR, since right of action cannot be denied to an environmental organization duly established under national law.

Thus, the ECJ promoted an extension of the procedural participation rights of environmental associations by pleading that *Protect* should be involved as a party in proceedings concerning implementation of the WFD. Here, the ECJ explicitly mentioned art 14 of the WFD (public information and consultation), which states that member states should "encourage active involvement of all interested parties (…), in particular in the production, review and updating of river basin management plans".[109] The ECJ emphasized that the phrase "in particular" implies that public participation cannot be limited to management plans, even though the verb "encourage", with its programmatic meaning, might limit the binding nature of the provision.[110] With this judgement, the ECJ updated jurisdiction in the first *Slovak Brown Bear Case* of 2011, which paved the way for broader rights of action for environmental organizations.[111]

Already in a previous judgement the ECJ also stated that Germany had failed to fulfil its obligations under art 11 of EIA Directive 2011/92/EU, because

---

107 Ibid, at para 68.

108 Regarding the ban on material preclusion, see also Case C-137/14, *European Commission v Federal Republic of Germany* (2015), ECLI:EU:C:2015:683 and the comment of Birgit Peters, 'Konvergenz der nationalen Verwaltungsverfahrensrechte durch europäische Einflüsse?', in Fraenkel-Haeberle, Galetta and Sommermann, n 29, at 41 f; Claudio Franzius, 'Genügt die Novelle des Umwelt-Rechtsbehelfsgesetzes den unionsrechtlichen Vorgaben?' (2018) 4 NVwZ 219

109 ECJ (Protect), n 106, at para 71.

110 ECJ (Protect), n 106, at para 72 and 73.

111 Case C-240/09 *Lesoochranárske zoskupenie VLK v* Ministerstvo životného prostredia Slovenskej republiky (2011), ECR 2011 I-01255 (hereinafter Slovak Brown Bear); in the second *Slovak Brown Bear Case* (Case C-243/15 *Lesoochranárske zoskupenie VLK v Obvodný úrad Trenčín*, OJ C 6/16), the ECJ linked art 47 CFR with art 9(2) and (4) of the Aarhus Convention to ensure wide access to justice for an environmental organization recognized under the Habitat Directive 92/43/EEC. Thus the ECJ meant to preclude an interpretation of national procedural law rules, according to which an action against a decision refusing such an organisation the status of party to an administrative procedure for the authorisation of a project to be carried out on a site protected pursuant to art 6(3) of the Habitat Directive, does not necessarily have to be examined in the course of that procedure, which may be fully concluded before a definitive decision on the status of party.

under para 2(3) of the Law on supplementary provisions governing actions in environmental matters under Directive 2003/35/EC (*Umwelt-Rechtsbehelfsgesetz*) of 7 December 2006, as amended by the Law of 21 January 2013,[112] an environmental organization's standing to bring proceedings and the scope of review by the courts were limited to the objections already raised during the administrative procedure that led to adoption of the decision, within the deadlines set by law.[113]

Other limitations to access to justice by an environmental organization, pursuant to art 10a of the EIA directive, as amended by Directive 2003/35/EC on public participation, had also previously been brought before the ECJ, and had consequently lead to a modification of the above-mentioned *Umwelt-Rechtsbehelfsgesetz*.[114]

Finally on 14 January 2021, the ECJ clarified the meaning of access to justice of the "public" and the "public concerned", according to the Aarhus Convention.[115] In the underlying legal dispute before a Dutch court, a natural person, who had not made a statement in the public participation procedure, took action against approval of a pig farm that was subject to environmental impact assessment. According to the Dutch court, the plaintiff (a veterinarian) was not a "party" in the sense intended by Dutch administrative law, since she did not live near the project concerned. Seeking a preliminary ruling, the court asked the ECJ whether restriction of access to justice to "parties" as intended by the national law was compatible with the Aarhus Convention (AC). The ECJ clarified that Art 9 (2) AC only bestows legal standing on "public concerned" but that exclusion of legal standing due to absence of prior participation in an administrative procedure infringed EU law. This would be assessed differently if a member state granted 'the public' a further right of participation according to art 9 (3) AC. In this case, such persons must have access to justice based on the more extensive rights to participate in the decision-making procedure,

112 *Umwelt-Rechtsbehelfsgesetz*, republished on 23 August 2017 (BGBL. I p. 3290), which was last amended by art 8 of the law of 25 February 2021 (BGBL. I p. 306); Claudio Franzius, 'Verbandsklage im Umweltrecht' (2019) 41 Natur und Recht 649; Annette Guckelberger, 'Aarhus-Konvention und Unionsrecht als prägende Faktoren für die Verbandsklage im UmwRG' (2020) 42 Natur und Recht 149.

113 Case C-137/14, n 111.

114 Case C-115/09 Bund für Umwelt und Naturschutz Deutschland, Landesverband Nordrhein-Westfalen eV v Bezirksregierung Arnsberg (2011), ECLI:EU:C:2011:289; see Angela Schwerdtfeger, 'Erweiterte Klagerechte für Umweltverbände – Anmerkung zum Urteil des EuGH v. 12.5.2011 in der Rechtssache Trianel' (2012) 1 EuR80.

115 Case C–826/18 *LB and Others v College van burgemeester en wethouders van de gemeente Echt-Susteren* (2021) ECLI:EU:C:2021:7 (hereinafter Rechtbank Limburg); Dominik Römling, 'EuGH, Urteil vom 14. Januar 2021 – Rs. C-826/18' (2021) 4 ZUR 229.

conferred by the national environmental law of the member state. Conversely, the admissibility of legal proceedings brought by non-governmental organisations, belonging to "public concerned", cannot be made conditional on their participation in the decision-making procedure which led to adoption of the contested decision.[116]

5 Conclusions

Since correct functioning of the Union legal system depends on effective enforcement of primary and secondary law, correct transposition and implementation of directives by member states play a key role. Directives are a compromise between preserving national characteristics and the requirements of a uniform EU-wide legal system.[117] Implementation must take place in such a way that the leeway granted in addition to binding requirements (art 288 (3) TFEU: "the choice of form and means") ensure the practical effectiveness of Union law in the national context. Without effective implementation of Union law, the legal community loses its integrative power and its compliance with the "rule of law".[118] The present analysis of the relationship between sustainability and public participation in environmental law leads to the following conclusions.

The implementation of EU law is now changing not only the substantive but also the procedural and organisational law of member states. The focus on public participation is a clear example of this development. On the other hand, a tendency to standardize regulatory areas can be observed at European level. The rules on public participation – apart from those of EIA and SEA – are now included in various directives, such as the WFD, the IE Directive and the directive on environmental liability.[119] Various procedures that originally identified SEA (detailed preliminary report, environmental report, monitoring scheme) have also been transferred to EIA, so as to promote uniform procedural standards.[120] The concept of integrative, multimedia environmental protection, as embodied in the SEA, EIA and IE directives, is also becoming increasingly widespread.

---

116 Ibid Rechtbank Limburg, para 59.

117 Leidenmühler, n 36, at 396.

118 Sommermann, n 30, at 322.

119 Directive of the European Parliament and of the Council 2004/35/CE of 21 April 2004 on environmental liability with regard to the prevention and remedying of environmental damage, OJ L 143/56.

120 See the last EIA amendment Directive 2014/52/EU, n 81.

Difficulties of EU member states in implementing the directive on public participation have induced the ECJ to intervene repeatedly in order to clarify the meaning and extension of the concept of '(affected) public participation' and access to justice. This induced a dynamic process in various stages that increasingly precisely and incisively underpins the extent of obligations under European Union law. However, in the field of public participation and the right of action of environmental organizations, a gap remains between projects subject to EIA, where the position of environmental organizations and public participation is ensured by binding provisions, due to the "significant impact on the environment" of these projects, and other (possibly smaller) projects, which violate other environmental protection legislation, where public participation and the subsequent right of action under national law is not mandatory.

Under the pressure of European law, a redefinition of the time dimension of sustainability has taken place, due to the emphasis given to precautionary and preventive action. As far as environmental protection is concerned, there are two well-known conceptual possibilities: either an *anthropocentric* approach, meaning that environmental protection is for the benefit of man, or an *ecocentric* approach, in which environmental protection is focused on the protection of nature (soil, water and air).[121] The concept of sustainability tends to focus attention on people, namely future generations, following the anthropocentric approach. Under the Aarhus Convention, environmental protection, in the sense of healthcare and human well-being, has therefore given environmental organizations the role of "nature advocates" taking "altruistic collective action" (*altruistische Verbandsklagen*)[122] to protect the human future.

Bibliography

Barone A, 'The "Reflexive" Public Administration', in Loredana Giani, Marina D'Orsogna and Aristide Police (eds.), *Dal diritto dell'emergenza al diritto del rischio* (Editoriale Scientifica 2018).

Berkemann J, '"Freiheitschancen über die Generationen" (Art. 20a GG) – Intertemporaler Klimaschutz im Paradigmenwechsel' (2021) 16 Die Öffentliche Verwaltung 701.

Breuer R, 'Immissionsschutzrechtliche Vorsorge und Stand der Technik' (2016) 2 Neue Zeitschrift für Verwaltungsrecht 822.

121 Burkhard Schöbener and Matthias Knauff, *Allgemeine Staatslehre* (5th edition, C. H. Beck 2023), § 5, para 219.

122 BVerwGE 147, 312 (318 ff).

Buoso E, 'I principi di precauzione e prevenzione nel diritto ambientale', in Simone Budelli (ed.), *Società del rischio, Governo dell'emergenza* (Vol. 1, Ambientediritto Editore 2020).

Cappelletti M, Seccombe M and Weiler JH, 'Integration through law: Europe and the American federal experience', in Mauro Cappelletti, Monica Seccombe and Joseph H Weiler (eds.), *Integration through* Law (Vol. 1, De Gruyter 1986).

Della Cananea G, 'Exit or voice? Débat public goes to Italy' (2019) 2 European Public Law 157.

De Leonardis F, 'Tra precauzione, prevenzione e programmazione', in Loredana Giani, Marina D'Orsogna and Aristide Police (eds.), *Dal diritto dell'emergenza al diritto del rischio* (Editoriale Scientifica Napoli 2018).

De Petris A, 'Protezione del clima e dimensione intertemporale delle libertà fondamentali: Karlsruhe for Future?' (2021) 4 Ceridap 127.

Dipace R, 'Sviluppo sostenibile, prevenzione e precauzione nella disciplina dei lavori pubblici', in Loredana Giani, Marina D'Orsogna and Aristide Police (eds.), *Dal diritto dell'emergenza al diritto del rischio* (Editoriale Scientifica Napoli 2018).

Erbguth W and Schlacke S, *Umweltrecht* (Nomos 2014).

Fraenkel-Haeberle C, Galetta DU and Sommermann KP (eds.), *Europäisierung und Internationalisierung im Vergleich: deutsch-italienische Analysen zur Denationalisierung der Öffentlichen Verwaltung* (Duncker&Humblot 2017).

Fraenkel-Haeberle C, and Socher J, 'Direct and indirect Europeanisation of national administrative systems. Implementation and spillover effects of the environmental information directives in a comparative perspective' (2018) 56 Revista Catalana de Dret Public 125.

Fraenkel-Haeberle C, and Socher J and Sommermann KP (eds.), *Praxis der Richtlinienumsetzung im Europäischen Verwaltungsverbund: die Reichweite der Umgestaltung der nationalen Umwelt- und Energieverwaltung* (Duncker&Humblot 2020).

Franzius C, 'Genügt die Novelle des Umwelt-Rechtsbehelfsgesetzes den unionsrechtlichen Vorgaben?' (2018) 4 Neue Zeitschrift für Verwaltungsrecht 219.

Franzius C, 'Verbandsklage im Umweltrecht' (2019) 41 Natur und Recht 649.

Frenz W, 'Klimaschutzpflichten als Grundrechtsvoraussetzungsschutz nach Klimabeschluss und Jahrhunderthochwasser' (2021) 16 Die Öffentliche Verwaltung 715.

Galetta DU, 'Accesso civico e trasparenza della Pubblica Amministrazione alla luce delle (previste) modifiche alle disposizioni del D. Lgs. N. 33/2013' (federalism.it, n5, 2 March 2016) https://air.unimi.it/bitstream/2434/446537/2/SaggioTrasparenzaMadiaPubblSuFederalismi.pdf last accessed 22 August 2022.

Galetta DU, 'La trasparenza per un nuovo rapporto tra cittadino e la P.A.: un'analisi storico-evolutiva nella prospettiva di diritto comparato europeo' (2016) 5 Rivista di diritto pubblico comparato 1019.

Galetta DU, 'The Italian Freedom of Information Act 2016. Why transparency-on-request is a better solution?' (2016) 2 Italian Journal of Public Law 268.

Giargiulo P, 'Brevi riflessioni sulla natura giuridica e il contenuto dei principi di precauzione e di prevenzione nel diritto internazionale', in Loredana Giani, Marina D'Orsogna and Aristide Police (eds.), *Dal diritto dell'emergenza al diritto del rischio* (Editoriale Scientifica Napoli 2018).

Götze R, 'Aktuelle Entwicklungen im Umweltinformationsrecht, Landes- und Kommunalverwaltung' (2013) 6 Landes- und Kommunalverwaltung 241.

Guckelberger A, 'Aarhus-Konvention und Unionsrecht als prägende Faktoren für die Verbandsklage im UmwRG' (2020) 42 Natur und Recht 149.

Janda C, 'Sozialstaat for Future – Der Klima-Beschluss des BVerfG und seine Bedeutung für die Sozialgesetzgebung' (2021) 5 Zeitschrift für Rechtspolitik 149.

Kahl W, 'Staatsziel Nachhaltigkeit und Generationengerechtigkeit' (2009) 1 Die Öffentliche Verwaltung 2.

Kahl W, '"Soziale Gerechtigkeit" oder Generationengerechtigkeit? Zur Notwendigkeit der Wiederbelebung einer verfassungspolitischen Debatte aus aktuellem Anlass' (2014) 1 Zeitschrift für Rechtspolitik 1.

Leidenmühler F, 'Die freiwillige "Übererfüllung" unionsrechtlicher Vorgaben durch die Mitgliedstaaten. Ein Beitrag zur rechtsdogmatischen und rechtspolitischen Diskussion um das sog. "Gold Plating"' (2019) 4 Zeitschrift Europarecht 383.

Lohse EJ, *Rechtsangleichungsprozesse in der Europäischen Union* (Mohr Siebeck 2017).

Lugaresi N, *Diritto dell'ambiente* (CEDAM 2015).

Maceroni P, 'L'organizzazione amministrativa del diritto ambientale', in Paolo Dell'Anno and Eugenio Picozza (eds.), *Trattato di diritto dell'ambiente* (Vol. 2, CEDAM 2013).

Masing J, *Die Mobilisierung des Bürgers zur Durchsetzung des Rechts* (Duncker&Humblot 1997)..

Maurer H and Waldhoff C, *Allgemeines Verwaltungsrecht* (C.H. Beck 2017).

Mittwoch AC, 'Richtlinienkonforme Auslegung bei überschießender Umsetzung' (2017) 10 JuristenZeitung 296.

Ossenbühl F, 'Vorsorge als Rechtsprinzip im Gesundheits- Arbeits- und Umweltschutz' (1986) 2 Neue Zeitschrift für Verwaltungsrecht 161.

Payrhuber M and Stelkens U, '1:1-Umsetzung von EU-Richtlinien: Rechtspflicht, rationales Politikkonzept oder (wirtschafts)politischer Populismus? – zugleich zu Unterschieden zwischen Rechtsangleichungs- und Deregulierungsrichtlien' (2019) 2 Zeitschrift Europarecht 190.

Posteraro, 'Grandi opere e partecipazione democratica: alcune riflessioni sul dibattito pubblico italiano à la française' (2020) 3 Istituzioni del Federalismo 607.

Reese M, 'Die Wasserrahmenrichtlinie in der Umsetzungskrise' (2018) 21 Neue Zeitschrift für Verwaltungsrecht 1592.

Rennert K, 'Funktionswandel der Verwaltungsgerichtsbarkeit' (2015) 13 Deutsches Verwaltungsblatt 793.

Rennert K, 'Verwaltungsrechtsschutz auf dem Prüfstand' (2017) 1 Deutsches Verwaltungsblatt 69.

Roll S, *Zugang zu Umweltinformationen und Freedom of Information* (Duncker& Humblot 2003).

Ruffert M, 'Umweltrechtsschutz ohne methodische Grundlage? Zur neueren Rechtsprechung des EuGHs und ihren Folgen für Deutschland' (2019) 16 Deutsches Verwaltungsblatt 1033.

Schenke WR, *Polizei- und Ordnungsrecht* (10th ed., C.F. Müller 2018).

Schöbener B and Knauff M, *Allgemeine Staatslehre* (5th edition, C.H. Beck 2023).

Schwarze J, 'Richtlinienumsetzung ‚eins zu eins', in Rainer Pitschas et al. (eds.), *Festschrift für Rupert Scholz zum 70. Geburtstag* (Duncker&Humblot 2007).

Seckelmann M and Lamping W, 'Verhaltensökonomischer Experimentalismus im Politik-Labor – Rechtliche Rahmenbedingungen und Folgerungen für die Evaluationsforschung' (2016) 5 Die Öffentliche Verwaltung 189.

Siedentopf H and Ziller J, *Making European policies work. The implementation of Community legislation in the member states, Volume 2: National Reports* (SAGE Publications Ltd 1988).

Sommermann KP, *Staatsziele und Staatszielbestimmungen* (Mohr Siebeck 1997).

Sommermann KP, 'Veränderungen des nationalen Verwaltungsrechts unter europäischem Einfluss – Analyse aus deutscher Sicht', in Jürgen Schwarze (ed.), *Bestand und Perspektiven des Europäischen Verwaltungsrechts* (Nomos 2008).

Sommermann KP, 'La exigencia de una Administración transparente en la perspectiva de los principios de democracia y del Estado de Derecho', in Ricardo García Macho (ed.), *Derecho administrativo de la información y administración transparente* (Marcial Pons 2010).

Sommermann KP, 'Gemeineuropäische Verwaltungskultur als Gelingensbedingung Europäischer Integration' (2015) 11 Die Öffentliche Verwaltung 449.

Sommermann KP, and Fraenkel-Haeberle C, 'L'Unione Europea come comunità di implementazione - Strategie nazionali di recepimento delle direttive europee' (2021) 2 Ceridap 111.

Stelkens U, 'Der Eigenwert des Verfahrens im Verwaltungsrecht' (2010) 17 Deutsches Verwaltungsblatt 1078.

Stelkens U, and Payrhuber M, '*Gold-Plating* bei der Umsetzung der Dienstleistungsrichtlinie durch extensive Auslegung des § 42a VwVfG? Vom Rechtsvergleich als Instrument zur Bestimmung des Ziels einer Richtlinie' (2018) 4 Neue Zeitschrift für Verwaltungsrecht 195.

Tänzer B, 'Aktuelle Entwicklungen bei der Umsetzung der Wasserrahmenrichtlinie' (2017) 20 Die Öffentliche Verwaltung 867.

Vauchez A, 'Integration-through-law. Contribution to a socio-history of EU political commonsense' (2008) EUI Working Papers RSCAS 2008/10.

Voßkuhle A, 'Umweltschutz und Grundgesetz' (2013) 1 Neue Zeitschrift für Verwaltungsrecht 1.

Wahl R, 'Verfahrensrecht zwischen Verwaltungseffizienz und Rechtsschutzauftrag' (1983) 41 VVDStRL 151.

Wegener B, 'Aktuelle Fragen der Umweltinformationsfreiheit' (2015) 10 Neue Zeitschrift für Verwaltungsrecht 609.

Winter G, 'Ökologische Verhältnismäßigkeit' (2013) 7–8 Zeitschrift für Umweltrecht 387.

Wolf R, 'Das Bundesverfassungsgericht – Hüter der Umwelt?' (1984) 3 Kritische Justiz 239.

CHAPTER 7

The Law of Public Finance

Matthias Valta

1 Introduction

The modern democratic welfare state is a key institution to secure human rights and the capabilities[1] of their enjoyment. Yet, it is prone to an unsustainable overreach that can be attributed to a lack of participation. The anonymous burden of taxpayers and further future obligations from debt financing pale in comparison to spending decisions whose beneficiaries can be easily identified. Parliamentary budgetary powers are seen as a remedy, but already *Wicksell* has argued that the parliamentary political process is biased in favour of the short-term advantages of spending against the medium- to long-term detrimental effects of high taxes and interest obligations of public debt.[2]

Graphs on the historic development of government debt show that the expansion of modern infrastructure and the welfare state as well as the expansion of state indebtedness occurred more or less in parallel. The sustainability of debt financing was put to the test in the aftermath of the 2008 financial crisis and many states failed to secure debt capital on the financial market. Constitutional limitations on debt were employed, but their effectiveness and their adverse effects on both investments and vulnerable groups are disputed, especially in a time of low interest and urgent challenges like climate change. Nevertheless, government debt poses the provocative question of whether sustainable financing of the state can only be achieved if the power of the democratic legislator is curtailed. Does less participation really lead to more sustainability?

To answer this question, this contribution takes account of selected constitutional or factual limitations on debt and analyses their effectiveness and consequences (see supra 2.). While the European legal framework paints the big picture in the context of the Economic and Monetary Union, the examples of

1 Amartya Sen, *Development as Freedom* (OUP 1999); Martha Nussbaum, *Frontiers of Justice* (HUP 2006); Martha Nussbaum, *Creating Capabilities* (HUP 2011).

2 Knut Wicksell, *Finanztheoretische Untersuchungen nebst Darstellung und Kritik des Steuerwesens Schwedens* (Gustav Fischer 1896); concurring: Geoffrey Brennan and James M Buchanan, *The Power to Tax: Analytical Foundations of a Fiscal Constitution* (CUP 1980).

DOI:10.1163/9789004509382_009

Germany and Portugal provide different experiences. Based thereon, different notions of sustainability will be identified (see supra 3.). It will be established that sustainability in public finance is multidimensional. The sustainability of the financing policy (choice of tax, debt, size of government) must be discerned from the financed policy. The following part explorers the different modes of participation, from the traditional parliamentary budgetary process over special sustainability funds to direct participation through referenda and participatory budgets to the role of expert bodies (see supra 4.). The conclusion will connect the issues, identify the need for imperfect second-best solutions and sketch proposals for reform (see supra 5.).

2 Overview: Constitutional and Similar Legal Limitations on Debt

2.1 *The European Legal Framework*

Within the Eurozone, constitutional or para-constitutional limitations of debt financing are imposed by European and public international law. Accordingly, the legal framework restricts borrowing to a small share of GDP with exceptions for natural disasters and "breathing limitations" that allow additional spending in times of recession in return for additional amortisation in the following years.

The Maastricht Treaty of 1992 and the respective protocol included in the wake of the Economic and Monetary Union prescribed two main limits for government debt: a 3 per cent of the GDP annual cap on incurring new debt and an overall 60 per cent of the GDP for the whole public sector.[3] Originally only an entrance threshold to the common currency, the criteria have been made permanent in the Stability and Growth Pact.[4] The preambles do not mention sustainability as such, but focus on "sound government finances as a means of strengthening the conditions for price stability and for strong sustainable growth conducive to employment creation".[5] The 3 per cent threshold was seen as a sufficient reserve to allow for deficit spending in the case of a

3 Treaty on European Union [1992] OJ C191/1, art 104c; Protocol on the excessive deficit procedure to the Treaty on European Union [1992] OJ C191/81, art 1.

4 Council Regulation (EC) 1466/97 of 7 July 1997 on the strengthening of the surveillance of budgetary positions and the surveillance and coordination of economic policies [1997] OJ L209/1; Council Regulation (EC) 1467/97 of 7 July 1997 on speeding up and clarifying the implementation of the excessive deficit procedure [1997] OJ L209/6; Council Resolution 97/C 236/01 of 7 July 1997 on the Stability and Growth Pact [1997] OJ C236/1.

5 Council Regulation (EC) 1466/97, n 4, at preamble (1); Council Regulation 1467/97, n 4, at preamble (2).

recession, while the 60 per cent ceiling was just the average indebtedness at that time.[6]

In 2005, political pressure prevented sanction proceedings against Germany and France thus crippling the functionality of the Stability and Growth Pact.[7] The debt crisis from 2009 on led to a reform of the Stability and Growth Pact through the so called 'sixpack', six regulations and directives.[8] The annual thresholds has been reduced from 3 per cent to 1 per cent and member states exceeding the overall 60 per cent threshold are now obliged to reduce the excess amount by one twentieth a year. Sanctions have been partially automatised with now a qualified majority necessary to stop proceedings under article 6(2) Regulation 1173/2011. Furthermore, preventive measures like monitoring[9] and mandatory deposits[10] have been introduced. The directive urges the member states to introduce effective national rules that constrain the incurring of new debt.[11] The preambles do not include references to sustainability but focus on the functioning of the Economic and Monetary Union.

Only a year later in 2012, the Stability and Growth Pact was complemented by a public international law treaty, the Treaty on Stability, Coordination and Governance in the Economic and Monetary Union, or in short: the European

6 Critically on the perpetuation of this arbitrary number: Achim Truger, 'EU Governments Must not Return to Their Dysfunctional Fiscal Rules' (2021) 1 The Economists' Voice 2.

7 Commission, 'The situation of Germany and France in relation to their obligations under the excessive deficit procedure following the judgement of the Court of Justice' (Communication) COM (2004) 813 final, p 9; Roel MWJ Beetsma and Xavier Debrun, 'Implementing the Stability and Growth Pact: Enforcement and Procedural Flexibility' (2005) IMF Working Paper 05/59, 3 <www.imf.org/en/Publications/WP/Issues/2016/12/31/Implementing-the-Stability-and-Growth-Pact-Enforcement-and-Procedural-Flexibility-18017> last accessed 30 April 2022.

8 Parliament and Council Regulation (EC) 1173/2011 of 16 November 2011 on the effective enforcement of budgetary surveillance in the euro area [2011] OJ L306/1; Parliament and Council Regulation (EC) 1174/2011 of 16 November 2011 on enforcement measures to correct excessive macroeconomic imbalances in the euro area [2011] OJ L306/8; Parliament and Council Regulation (EC) 1175/2011 of 16 November 2011 amending Council Regulation (EC) 1466/97 on the strengthening of the surveillance of budgetary positions and the surveillance and coordination of economic policies [2011] OJ L306/12; Parliament and Council Regulation (EC) 1176/2011 of 16 November 2011 amending Council Regulation (EC) 1466/97 on the prevention and correction of macroeconomic imbalances [2011] OJ L306/25; Council Regulation (EC) 1177/2011 of 8 November 2011 amending Regulation (EC) No 1467/97 on speeding up and clarifying the implementation of the excessive deficit procedure [2011] OJ L306/33; Council Directive 2011/85/EU of 8 November 2011 on requirements for budgetary frameworks of the Member States [2011] OJ L306/41.

9 Parliament and Council Regulation 1175/2011, n 8, arts 1, 2a, 6, 10, 11.

10 Parliament and Council Regulation 1173/2011, n 8, arts 4ff.

11 Council Directive 2011/85/EU, n 8, art 5.

fiscal compact. It further lowers the annual threshold of incurring new debt to 0.5 per cent of GDP. The 1 per cent threshold still applies for countries under the 60 per cent threshold and with a low individual sustainability risk. The term sustainability is used in this context to describe the capacity of a country to incur and pay back debt. Exemptions are granted in exceptional circumstances (art 3(3)) including force majeure and severe recession. These rules on a balanced budget must be transformed in national law, preferably on a constitutional level.

A report of the European Commission on the transformation of the balanced budget rule from 2017 observed that out of 22 members states only 11 had transformed the balanced budget rule in their national constitutional law or other laws of higher hierarchical status like the ordinary budget law.[12] Four states made other arrangements or indirect use of constitutional norms to give the budget rule a comparable level of binding force. Five states used special independent institutions to supervise non-constitutional balanced budget rules.

Furthermore, bail out programmes lead to de facto limitations on the incurring of debt. Several states faced downgrades of their credit ratings resulting in their inability to incur further debt on the market or with interest rates that were perceived as affordable.[13] To prevent state bankruptcy within the Eurozone, financial aid, so called bail-outs, were granted not only by the International Monetary Fund (IMF) but also by special newly founded vehicles, the European Financial Stabilisation Mechanism[14] and the European Financial Stability Facility[15] and their replacement European Stability Mechanism.[16]

12 Commission, "Report from The Commission presented under article 8 of the Treaty on Stability, Coordination and Governance in the Economic and Monetary Union" COM (2017) 1201 final.

13 Bartholomew Paudyn, 'Credit rating agencies and the sovereign debt crisis: Performing the politics of creditworthiness through risk and uncertainty' (2013) 20 Review of International Political Economy 788; Kathleen McNamara, 'Banking on Legitimacy: The ECB and the Euro Zone Crisis' (2012) 13 Georgetown Journal of International Affairs 143; Silvia Ardagna and Francesco Caselli, 'The Political Economy of the Greek Debt Crisis: A Tale of Two Bailouts' (2014) 6 American Economic Journal: Macroeconomics 291; Ian Traynor and Phillip Inman, 'Eurozone bank bailout deal throws lifeline to Spain and Italy' *The Guardian* (Brussels and London, 29 June 2012) <www.theguardian.com/business/2012/jun/29/eurozone-bank-bailout-spain-italy> last accessed 30 April 2022.

14 Council Regulation (EC) 407/2010 of 11 May 2010 establishing a European financial stabilisation mechanism [2010] OJ L118/1.

15 Council, 'Extraordinary Council meeting Economic and Financial Affairs' (Press Release) 9596/10 of 9/10 May 2010.

16 Commission, 'Treaty Establishing the European Stability Mechanism (ESM)' (Press Release) D/12/3 of 1 February 2012; For a detailed analysis see Mauro Megliani, 'From the

Both entities were created under an international law treaty, but are supervised by the European Commission. For the administration of bailouts, the so called 'troika' was formed comprised out of the European Commission, the European Central Bank (ECB) and the IMF. Prerequisite for payments was the commitment to and subsequent fulfilment of deficit reduction and structural reform policies.[17] Also, the signing of the European Fiscal Compact and the transposition of its limitations on debt in national law was a prerequisite of further payments.[18]

This led to a problem well known from the practice of the IMF with regard to developing and emerging countries: the national democratic process is 'short-circuited', as the states are dependent on the payments and thus need to commit and fulfil the commitments. While the intentions of the conditionalities are good, their effectiveness and suitability are put into doubt by the lack of local participation.[19] Moreover, it is disputed whether a state bankruptcy or an exit from the Eurozone would have been better alternatives, even if they would also have had adverse effects.[20]

An overall assessment of the European framework shows a tension between the imposition of hard limits on debt and the political character of the enforcement mechanisms. While reforms on the one hand have tightened the rules and placed them on a constitutional level, they have grown more complex and opened up space for the flexibility and discretion needed in addressing the multiple crises Europe faces.[21] Thus, the European framework can be described as a principled framework for budgetary dialogue for the purpose of ensuring sustainable fiscal policies.[22] The interlocutors are commission and

European Stability Mechanism to the European Monetary Fund: There and Back Again' (2020) 21 German Law Journal 674.

17 For an analysis of deficit reductions in Ireland see Robert Hick, 'Enter the Troika: The Politics of Social Security during Ireland's Bailout' (2018) 47 Journal of Social Policy 1.

18 Treaty on Stability, Coordination and Governance in the Economic and Monetary Union [2012] T/SCG/en 1, 8.

19 Tony Killick, *IMF Programmes in Developing Countries: Design and Impact* (Routledge 1995); Shantayanan Devarajan *et al*, *Aid and Reform in Africa: Lessons from 10 Case Studies* (World Bank 2001).

20 Antonio Estella, 'Potential Exit from the Eurozone: The Case of Spain' (2015) 22 Indiana Journal of Global Legal Studies 335; Ruby Devine, 'Emerging Issues: Is a Grexit - A Greek Exit from the Eurozone - the Solution?' (2016) 4 University of Baltimore Journal of International Law 157; Lee C Buchheit *et al*, 'Revisiting Sovereign Bankruptcy' (2013) <www.ssrn.com/abstract=2354998> last accessed 30 April 2022.

21 Matthias Goldmann, 'art 126 TFEU', in Helmut Siekmann (ed), *The European Monetary Union: A Commentary on the Legal Foundations* (Hart Publishing 2022).

22 Ibid at 145.

governmental officials and experts. Therefore, this dialogue is not participatory and the democratic link to national parliaments is weak. Its legitimation is technocratic and thus frail.[23]

2.2 *Germany – The Much-disputed Constitutional Limitation on Debt*

2.2.1 Historical Development

Historically, the German constitution limited the incurring of new debt at the federal level to cover only extraordinary circumstances (1848,[24] 1871[25]) with the later addition of fiscal space for investments (1919,[26] 1949[27]). These rules had their background in 19th century economic thinking, according to which a state should in principle finance all its needs through taxation and debt should be used only to create or acquire businesses that will create profits to offset the debt.[28]

In 1969, the restriction on extraordinary circumstances was abolished while the limitation on investments was maintained. The vagueness of the exception rendered the limit on investments widely ineffective. The parliament was more or less free to assign the label 'investment' for specific expenditures. The German Federal Constitutional Court abstained from defining 'investments' out of respect for the budgetary prerogative of the legislator and only urged the legislator to do so – but to no avail.[29] The legislator informally followed a wide macroeconomic understanding covering any investment that maintains, expands or enhances the means of production for the whole economy.[30]

Yet, a further exemption was introduced that allowed for non-investment to intercept a disturbance in the economy's equilibrium ("gesamtwirtschaftliches Gleichgewicht"). This exemption allowed for Keynesian deficit spending in an attempt to globally control the economic cycles.[31] There was no exhaustive constitutional definition of economic equilibrium and it was also deliberately left open to be adapted to new economic findings. Systematic reference was

23 Ibid at 148.

24 Sec 51 Frankfurt German Imperial Constitution (Verfassung des deutschen Reiches ("Paulskirchenverfassung") of 28 March 1849, RGBL 1849, 101.

25 Sec 73 German Imperial Constitution (Verfassung des Deutschen Kaiserreichs ("Bismarcksche Reichsverfassung")) of 16 April 1871, RGBL 1871, 6.

26 Art 87 German Imperial Constitution (Verfassung des Deutschen Reichs ("Weimarer Reichsverfassung")) of 11 August 1919, RGBL 1919, 1383.

27 Art 115 German Basic Law (Grundgesetz), BGBL I 1949, 1.

28 Lorenz v Stein, *Lehrbuch der Finanzwissenschaft* (5th edn, Nabu Press 1885); Adolph Wagner, *Finanzwissenschaft* (3rd edn, C.F. Winter 1883).

29 BVerfGE 79, 311,352; BVerfGE 119, 96,160.

30 BVerfGE 79, 311, 354; BVerfGE 119, 96, 179.

31 Cf. BVerfGE 119, 96, 157.

applied to the so-called magic rectangle that tried to convene stability of prices, high employment, balance of payments and steady growth.[32] While the federal constitutional court interpreted the exemption as a concretisation of the extraordinary circumstances rule, and thus retained a narrow interpretation,[33] the legislator made wide use of it.[34] A disturbance of the economic equilibrium was claimed in eight years each between 1991 and 2009. Public debt increased between 1969 to 2009 from 23 billion Euros to 940 billion Euros.

In 2006, there was an attempt for a holistic constitutional reform that explicitly included the principle of sustainability.[35] The already existing art 20a Basic Law that protects the environment with an implicit regard to sustainability should have been complemented by an art 20b Basic Law that would have explicitly obliged the state on the principle of sustainability and the protection of future generations. With regard to public debt, the 'disturbance of the equilibrium of the economy'-clause in art 109(2) Basic Law was to be complemented by an additional specific reference to the principle of sustainability and the protection of future generations. Even though the bill was supported by 105 members of the parliament from all caucuses except the far left, it did not reach the required majority. One reason might be that the proposal called at the same time for the reduction of government debt as well as for more investment into education and research without resolving the conflict of goals.[36]

2.2.2 The Current Constitutional Limitation on Debt and its Exemptions

In 2009, a constitutional limitation was introduced, the so called *Schuldenbremse*, literally 'debt brake'. It has been modelled after examples from the Swiss practice, where debt brakes known on the cantonal level since 1929 are widespread.[37] Art 109(3) of the Basic Law in principle forbids the incurring of debt for the federal as well as the state level with the relevant exemptions of social security as well as the municipalities. The interdiction of debt financing in principle has several exemptions.

---

32 Sec (1)(2) Act to Promote Economic Stability and Growth (Gesetz zur Förderung der Stabilität und des Wachstums der Wirtschaft) of 8 June 1967, BGBL I, 1967, 582.

33 BVerfGE 119, 96, 163.

34 Critical Ekkehart Reimer, 'Nachhaltigkeit durch Begrenzung der Staatsverschuldung', in Wolfgang Kahl (ed), *Nachhaltige Finanzstrukturen im Bundesstaat* (Mohr Siebeck 2011).

35 Bill of 9 November 2006, BT.-Drucks 16/3399.

36 Joachim Wieland, 'Soziale Nachhaltigkeit und Finanzverfassung', in Wolfgang Kahl (ed), *Nachhaltige Finanzstrukturen im Bundesstaat* (Mohr Siebeck 2011).

37 Gebhard Kirchgässner, 'Fiscal Institutions at the Cantonal Level in Switzerland' (2013) 149 Swiss Journal of Economics and Statistics 139.

The limitations first allow for Keynesian deficit spending policy with its economic cycle clause. Both the federal level as well as state level can incur debt during an economic downturn to foster a quick recovery. In that case, the debt has to be paid back in a symmetrical manner. Thus, for example three years of deficit spending must be paid back in the following three years of boom. This obligation is meant to fix the common implementation problem of Keynesian economic policy: while deficit spending often finds political majorities, stopping it and transitioning to paying the debt back seldom does. Yet, the question remains: when does the economic cycle allow the transition without curbing the growth and so where to draw the symmetry axis under limited knowledge?

A second exemption applies to natural disasters or extraordinary emergency situations that go beyond the control of the state and have relevant effects on the budgets. Unfortunately, the past two years provided us with an example: the Covid-19 pandemic. The federation and the states incurred high amounts of debt under this exemption for direct measures against the pandemic as well as economic measures to stabilise the economy like lump-sum payments for entrepreneurs or short-time work / furlough schemes. Affected states also invoked the clause with regard to catastrophic floods in the Ahr and Erft valleys of Summer 2021.

This leads us to the question of whether ongoing climate change as such allows for a general exemption. The German government has not yet tried to directly invoke the emergency exemption with regard to climate change but wants to retroactively reassign unused emergency debt authorisations from the pandemic response to climate change. This reassignment is constitutionally doubtful and pending before the Federal Constitutional court. If the government could directly and fully invoke the emergency exemption, this would on the one hand render the debt limitation ineffective over the next decades and thus seems excessive. On the other hand, damage resulting from events like floods or extreme droughts constitute natural disasters. Why should the prevention and mitigation of damages be excluded when the compensation for damages can be paid out of debt? Where to draw the line between 'controlled' preventive measures and 'reacting' mitigation measures? At this point, one has to be reminded that the limitation on debt does not hinder action on climate change but only debt-financing in cases where the deficit could have been avoided through planned alternative financing sources like tax increases or budgetary shifts. While natural disasters can make any financial planning obsolete and thus need the flexibility of raising debt, medium to long-term preventions and mitigation programmes can be systematically financed by taxation and budget policy, eg the proposed introduction of wealth taxes to combat climate change.

Even if the scope of this exception clause can be delimited with this respect, one weakness still remains. The exception clause does not oblige for 'symmetrical' repayment, as this is not feasible with regard to natural disasters. It only obliges the state to have a repayment plan. A comparison of the different repayment plans of the federal level and the state level with regard to Covid-19 show huge differences between three and fifty years.[38] The repayment can thus be dragged along over decades.

A third 'de minimis'-exemption only applies on the federal level. art 109 (3) (4) Basic Law allows for the incurring of new debt if it does not exceed 0.35 per cent of the GDP. This amount of new debt is seen as unproblematic, as its interest burden is offset by inflation. Yet, the questions remain, why this exemption does not apply to the states.

2.2.3 A Loophole by Design?

Besides the three exemptions, the German debt limitation is additionally prone to circumvention. While it applies to the regular budgets of the federal level and the states, it does not apply to social security authorities and legally independent special estates, even if they are fully owned by the state.[39] Thus, it is possible to establish private law companies, provide them with a small amount of equity from the budget and then let the company incur debt unconstrained by the debt limitations. While this extra budgetary debt will be subject to review under the European debt limitation, it will not be considered under German constitutional law. The legislative materials justify this exemption with unrealisable information requirements in the case of legally independent companies and estates, which is rather unconvincing. Being the owner, the federation would have the possibility to account for all its special estates and it does so according to the European Union rules. More likely, the legislator wanted to preserve a loophole for incurring debt for special purposes.

Limitations to this approach are discussed with regard to the general disallowance of an abuse of law, especially if the private company or estate only serve as a shell to formally incur the debt while the instalments are directly paid by the state.[40] The use of these loopholes is currently under discussion within the new German government, consisting of Social Democrats, Greens

---

38 Tobias Hentze, 'Anhörung des Haushalts- und Finanzausschusses: Stellungnahme zum Entwurf des Haushaltsgesetzes 2022 des Landes Nordrhein-Westfalen' (2021) 37 IWReport 6.

39 Hanno Kube, 'Art 109 GG', in Günter Dürig, Roman Herzog and Rupert Scholz (eds), *Grundgesetz-Kommentar* (C.H. Beck supp 95 July 2021).

40 Ibid.

and Liberals. There are plans to form a federal investment company that allows for debt-financed investments in infrastructure and measures to mitigate climate change.[41] The fully federal owned German railway company could incur more debt for infrastructure investments and the privately organised motorway planning and administration company could be provided with some toll income and then incur debt for motorway repairs.

2.2.4 Summary

Constitutional limitations on debt have a long history in the German constitution. While the current absolute limitation on debt is relatively rigid, it contains many exemptions and possibilities of circumvention. It has a de-minimis threshold, allows for Keynesian deficit spending, yet with a rigid symmetry of debt repayment, and contains a natural disaster and extraordinary exemption clause. The latter is open to generous interpretation and might be employed to – at least temporarily – finance urgent measures against climate change. Finally, state-owned special estates and companies are not covered by the limitations. This seems to be a loophole that has been deliberately left open and will most probably also be used to finance measures against climate change.

2.3 *Portugal – The Power of the Financial Market vs. Fundamental Rights*

2.3.1 Introduction

The sustainability of debt limitations has been litigated before the Portuguese constitutional court following so called austerity measures during the first half of the last decade. Portugal was affected by the financial crisis beginning in 2008. It had already seen the need for fiscal consolidation in the years before and the economic crisis exacerbated the fiscal situation.[42] In 2011, after several rating downgrades and difficulties in incurring debt at the financial market, Portugal applied for a bail out with the 'troika' of the ECB, the Commission and the IMF: the Financial and Economic Adjustment Programme. In return for loans with a submarket interest rate, Portugal undertook international commitments for yearly fiscal objectives as well as public policy reforms.[43] These reforms included pay cuts and additional working hours for public service

---

41 Coalition Agreement between SPD (Social Democrats), den Grünen (Greens) and FDP (Liberals), 'Mehr Fortschritt wagen' (2021) 159.

42 Mariana Canotilho, Teresa Violante and Rui Lanceiro, 'Austerity measures under judicial scrutiny: the Portuguese constitutional case-law' (2015) 11 European Constitutional Law Review 155.

43 Ibid at 155, 157.

workers, cuts for retired persons and pensioners as well as tax measures, that raised the rates and reduces deductions.

2.3.2 Civil Service

The cases on public workers cover a steady flow of impairments of their status.[44] While public servants have special obligations to the public good and thus have to endure some pay cuts, the limits of sacrifice have been seen as violated following the 2013 pay cuts, especially as the abolished 13th and 14th salary was also common in the private economy.[45] The constitutional court stressed the importance of the deficit reduction, the international and European law commitments and the prerogative of parliament to decide between expenditure cuts and revenue increases.[46] It gave less weight to economic fundamental rights or specific legitimate expectations as to the general principle of equality, deeming the burden placed on public sector workers was far greater than that of private sector workers.

Furthermore, the reduction of overtime payments and benefits as well as the increasing of the weekly working hours from 35 to 40 and beyond in 2012 and 2013 were approved by the constitutional court with the argument that public sector workers would then be treated in a way more similar to private sector workers. As an increase of working time equals a factual pay cut, this differentiation seems to be inconsistent. Yet, some coherence can be detected: after public sector workers had been subjected to similar working conditions as private sector workers in 2013, specific pay cuts to public sector workers could not be justified anymore. Notably, one difference remained: the protection against dismissal except for subjective due reason was upheld in 2013, but also in regard to the 2012 pay cut that had been justified with the special status of public workers.

This leads to a coherent picture, where some pay cuts were allowed with regard to the role of public servants and their job security, while working times could be equalised to those of private sector workers. Further cuts to payments or dismissals were interdicted by the constitutional court. In result, the public servant workforce was maintained and thus the potential production of public goods and services upheld, while achieving some deficit reduction.

---

44 Ibid at 155, 160 ff.

45 Portuguese Constitutional Court 5 April 2013 187/13 summary <www.tribunalconstitucional.pt/tc/en/acordaos/20130187e.html> last accessed 30 April 2022.

46 Canotilho, Violante and Lanceiro, n 42, at 155, 160.

2.3.3 Social Security

With regard to social security expenditures, Portugal applied measures to retired people.[47] As part of their benefits, they have also been eligible for a 13th and 14th payment at holiday and Christmas time. The cut was declared unconstitutional as a violation of equality.[48] Similar to the reasoning in case of public sector workers, the court found no justification to burden this group of people. Furthermore, retired persons have been seen as more in need of protection, as they had legitimate expectations with regard the economic security in old age.

Another measure was the special solidarity contribution commencing in 2011 for high payments, a special due that was applied to public and private pension payments. Effectively this reduced the payments. Rates increased in 2012 with the result of a further reduction. In 2013, a new system was founded starting with pensions from 1,800 to 3,600 Euros facing a 16 per cent contribution, higher pension a schedular system with rates from 10 per cent from the first Euro up to 50 per cent beyond 7,545 Euros. The court qualified this measure as a temporary special security contribution that was justified and proportional with regard the international law obligations of the state to reduce its deficit.[49] The additional cut to the more generous benefits of public servants was declared as unconstitutional, as its lump-sum cuts would violate legitimate interest of the beneficiaries. While some rules of the special pension system were favourable to the general system, some were less so. Thus, a thorough reform and recalculation was permissible only if the systems should be made more equal.

The temporal special solidary contribution was to be replaced by a permanent special sustainability contribution from 2014 onward. It applied a contribution to all public pension payments starting at 2 per cent for people earning less than 2,000 Euros, 5.5 per cent for people earning between 2,000 Euros and 3,500 Euros, and 3.5 per cent for people earning over 3,500 Euros, in all cases applying to the whole amount. Private pensions were not burdened. The court ruled that by excluding private pensions and being made permanent, the contribution equalled a cut to the public pension system.[50] It was declared unconstitutional, as its lump-sum approach violated equality, proportionality and the protection of legitimate expectations. Austerity measures could not

---

47 Canotilho, Violante and Lanceiro, n 42, at 155, 172 ff.

48 Portuguese Constitutional Court 5 April 2013 187/13 summary <www.tribunalconstitucional.pt/tc/en/acordaos/20130187e.html> last accessed 30 April 2022.

49 Ibid.

50 Portuguese Constitutional Court 14 August 2014 575/14, summary <www.tribunalconstitucional.pt/tc/en/acordaos/20140575s.html> last accessed 30 April 2022.

simply be relabelled to being made permanent. Structural reforms of social security could be justified by sustainability concerns, but not lump sum reductions that also privileged higher pensions.

A similar reasoning was applied with regard to sick and unemployment contributions, which also resulted in a cut of the respective benefits. The court ruled in 2013 this cut to be unconstitutional, as its lump-sum approach also applied to cases where the benefits only reached the minimum amount for subsistence.[51] A reformed version of 2014 was again declared unconstitutional, this time under a more fundamental reasoning. The court ruled that even in the time of financial crisis, further burdens on people affected by disease or unemployment were not reasonable.[52]

2.3.4 Tax Law

Portugal introduced a special 45.88 per cent personal income tax rate bracket for high income earners starting from 150,000 Euros in 2010 before the bailout.[53] In 2013, a 3.5 per cent surtax was introduced that applied to the tax base above the minimum wage and certain special income items (ie so called 'unjustified wealth increases'). The tax raised specific questions under the Portuguese constitutional provision of income taxation, especially as it decreased the progressiveness of the personal income taxation system but was deemed to be within the legislator's margin of appreciation.[54] The temporal nature as well as the 'extraordinary' needs of public finances were also taken note of.[55]

The 2013 tax reform reduced the number of tax rate brackets from eight to five and generally increased tax rates, while again reducing the level of progressivity – the rate difference between small incomes and high incomes further decreased, even though the top rate had been raised. Again, the constitutional court accepted the reform with regard to the margin of appreciation. Furthermore, the 2013 tax reform reduced the number and scope of itemised deductions for inter alia health, education, housing or senior care expenses. This affects the ability to pay principle, that calls for some expense deductions in order achieve an equal tax burden. Yet, the court ruled that the legislator again has some margin to define ability to pay and thus can also broaden the tax base in line with the revenue needs.[56]

---

51 Portuguese Constitutional Court 5 April 2013 187/13, n 49, at 20.

52 Portuguese Constitutional Court 5 April 2013 187/13, n 49.

53 Canotilho, Violante and Lanceiro, n 42, at 155, 176.

54 Portuguese Constitutional Court 5 April 2013 187/13, n 49.

55 Canotilho, Violante and Lanceiro, n 42, at 155, 178.

56 Portuguese Constitutional Court 5 April 2013 187/13, n 49; Canotilho, Violante and Lanceiro, n 42, at 155, 180.

2.3.5 Summary

The Portuguese legislator resorted to very rough measures of deficit reduction, trying to generally cut expenses and raise additional revenue in a lump-sum manner. While some of the first reforms tried to spare vulnerable groups and burden people with higher income, further measures also burdened vulnerable groups. The exclusion from the financial market and the troika's conditionalities therefore led not only to structural reforms, but also to rigid measures resulting in hardships.

The constitutional court acknowledged the severe financial situation and the urgency of deficit reduction as well as commitments at the international and European level. While it mainly allowed for the first wave of deficit reduction measures, arguing also with their temporal measures, additional and permanent measures led to a verdict of unconstitutionality. The constitutional court took account of the cumulation of burdens in the payment of workers, social security and taxation and paid special attention to unequal burdens and the protection of vulnerable groups. Financial sustainability must thus be achieved through an even distribution of burden. Cutting expenditures, especially benefits and wages, is therefore more problematic than general increases of personal income tax, which is the best instrument for equally distributing burden. Cutting expenditures can threaten social responsibility, as vulnerable groups might not be able to maintain the capabilities needed for exercising their fundamental rights. Disallowing tax deductions can have the same effect. To prevent the protection of problematic privileges, the constitutional court wisely chose the equality principle. However, one can argue that the courts' guidelines on public service interfered with the role of the legislator and thus also aimed for sustainability by curbing participation.

Overall, the Portuguese experience shows the importance of a sustainable fiscal policy that limits dependence on the financial markets and maintains a good credit rating. Otherwise, the need for emergency debt reductions arises and can cause severe hardships. Notably the parliamentary democratic process was neither capable of avoiding the excess debt nor balancing the debt reduction in a proportionate manner. The alternative of exiting the Eurozone and paying the debt by devaluation and inflation has not been seriously pursued by any affected European government regardless of their political direction and would have entailed adverse consequences.

3 The Notion of Sustainability

3.1 From Fiscal Policy to Monetary Policy

The limitations on debt financing point at first glance to a rather limited understanding of sustainability. Sustainability is seen an as the capacity to incur and pay back debt on the capital market. At first glance, this seems to be a rather technical and abstract concept. The exemptions suggest that there might be other important principles or alternative notions of sustainability.

Nevertheless, the consequences of debt financing are more profound and thus also the notion of sustainability has to be extended. The limitations on debt financing within the EU are a foremost part of its monetary policy; art 126 Treaty on the Functioning of the European Union (TFEU) has to be seen in the context of art 127 ff. TFEU. It is part of the goal of price stability and thus the control and limitation of inflation. Inflation reduces the burden of government debt but poses a hidden burden on citizens diminishing their wages and savings. The use of inflation to reduce government debt can be seen as functional equivalent of a hidden tax on workers and small savers that do not possess the economic capabilities to invest in more inflation-safe assets like real estates or shares.[57] Outside monetary unions, government debt can also affect exchange rates leading to a burden on cross border activities.[58]

Finally, interest rates may be affected by debt financing. While the ECB is independent, there is the argument that its interest rate policy is also made with consideration of the consequences to indebted states. Even if the central bank directors try to ignore the repercussions on debt financing of the states, there is the danger of a subliminal bias. Furthermore, states will probably nominate experts whose views are favourable to their policy goals. A recent empirical study showed that there is a correlation between the monetary policy views of ECB directors and their home state indebtedness. The higher the level of indebtedness of the home state the more likely the ECB director endorses expansive monetary policies with their inherent danger of increases in inflation.[59]

The example of Portugal illustrates further consequences. Due to the Monetary Union and the fear of its collapse, there was no room to use inflation or exchange rates to reduce the debt burden. Severe tax increases and spending cuts were the consequence and, especially the cuts, provided hardships

57 James Tobin, 'Taxes, Saving, and Inflation' (1949) 39 The American Economic Review 1223; The Yale Law Journal Company, Inc., 'Inflation and the Federal Income Tax' (1973) 82 The Yale Law Journal 716; Martin Feldstein, 'Inflation, Tax Rules, and the Prices of Land and Gold' (1980) 14 Journal of Public Economics 309.

58 Jan Toporowski, 'International credit, financial integration and the euro' (2013) 37 Cambridge Journal of Economics 571; Philip R Lane, 'The Real Effects of European Monetary Union' (2006) 20 The Journal of Economic Perspectives 47.

59 Friedrich Heinemann and Jan Kemper 'The ECB Under the Threat of Fiscal Dominance – The Individual Central Banker Dimension' (2021) 18 The Economists' Voice 5, <www.doi.org/10.1515/ev-2021-0014> last accessed 30 April 2022.

to groups that led to interventions and then basically to adjustments by the constitutional court.

In times of long-ranging low or sometimes even negative interest rates, the aforementioned dangers are greatly relativised. It is seen as a missed opportunity that low interest rates are not used to debt finance a green transformation of the economy with regard to climate change.[60] This suggests that a limitation on debt should not be absolute but dependent on the general interest rate level. However, such a relationship would intensify the influence of state indebtedness on monetary policy.

3.1.1 Cultural Aspects

Cultural aspects may provide additional legitimacy. The German Chancellor Angela Merkel used the metaphor of the 'Swabian housemaker',[61] who is associated with being very frugal and avoiding debt. Thinking further, these cultural differences may be ascribed to the protestant work ethic,[62] which roughly correlates with the faction building between the northern and southern European states. Yet, these cultural aspects are not universal and cannot substitute the search for an underlying rationality.

3.1.2 Trade-offs and Multidimensionality

The European as well as the constitutional limitations on debt financing are not absolute and provide for exceptions. Thus, not every debt seems to be unsustainable. Exemptions for unforeseeable circumstances like disasters date back to the 19th century.[63] There is also some tradition in exempting investments or literally expenditures that help to raise new income ("Ausgaben für

---

60 Deirdre Cooper, 'Low rates provide a historic opportunity to tackle climate change' *Financial Times* (London 26 December 2019) <www.ft.com/content/c752698c-200c-11ea-92da-f0c92e957a96> last accessed 15 December 2021; regarding green bonds see Sarah La Monaca, Katherine Spector and James Kobus, 'Financing the Green Transition: Addressing Barriers to Capital Deployment' (2019) 73 Journal of International Affairs 17.

61 Anton Hunger, 'Die schwäbische Hausfrau' *FAZ* (Frankfurt, 14 July 2016) <www.faz.net/aktuell/wirtschaft/wirtschaftspolitik/sparpolitik-merkel-und-die-schwaebische-hausfrau-14333164-p2.html> last accessed 30 April 2022; Julia Kollewe, 'Angela Merkel's austerity postergirl, the thrifty Swabian housewife' *The Guardian* (London, 17 September 2012) <www.theguardian.com/world/2012/sep/17/angela-merkel-austerity-swabian-housewives> last accessed 30 April 2022; Raymond Guess, 'Economies: Good, Bad, Indifferent' (2012) 55 Inquiry 331.

62 Max Weber, *Die protestantische Ethik und der Geist des Kapitalismus* (4th edn, C.H. Beck 2013).

63 Matthias Valta, 'The Law of Public Finance', in this book, part 3 chapter 7, sec 2.2.

werbende Zwecke").[64] A "golden rule of public investment" calls for debt financing of net investments, as it would realise a pay-per-use principle that increases inter-generational equity.[65] Net public investment increases the public and/or social capital stock and thus also generates benefits for future generations. This leads to the argument that future generations should contribute to the financing of these investments. If debt rules disallow burden distributions, the burden of the present generation would be too high, as it would lead to high tax burdens or low spending. This would result in incentives for the under-provision of public investment to the detriment of future generations.

The idea of 'good debt', that offsets itself by generating additional income, can also be found in Keynes-inspired deficit spending. Under this perspective, the question of incurring debt is a technocratic one. The optimal debt financing ratio would be determined by economists with regards to the need of the economy and capacity provided by the financial market, especially interest and exchange rates. The exemption for Keynesian deficit spending is seen as to narrow.[66]

For the sake of analytical clarity, the financing policy and the financed policy must be distinguished. Debt can finance very sustainable policies, eg with regard to education or conservation of natural resources. Yet, these policies could also be financed by taxation and especially by higher taxation on corporate and capital income. In consequence, a distinction should be made between the financing of state expenditures and the policies financed.

Nevertheless, political and legal practice also takes account of the policy financed. Exemptions to limitations on government debt for emergencies or recessions show that trade-offs exist between the sustainability of financing policy and the policy financed. Sustainability in this regard is multidimensional. Limitations of debt might ensure the sustainability of state financing, but in certain contexts the sustainability effects of the policy financed might be more important (eg climate change). This analytical differentiation is important to make the trade-off transparent and the decision on the preference accountable. In consequence, an overall assessment is needed: the prima facie unsustainability of debt financing can be compensated and outweighed by the sustainability of the policy financed.

---

64 Art 87 German Imperial Constitution (Verfassung des Deutschen Reichs ("Weimarer Rechtsverfassung")) of 11 August 1919, RGBL 1919, 1383.

65 Truger, n 6, at 3.

66 Dwight R Lee, 'The Keynesian Path to Fiscal Irresponsibility' (2012) 32 Cato Journal 473.

3.1.3 Negative Impact on Investment

Furthermore, it is argued that constitutional limitations disproportionately affect long-term investments[67] and thus contribute to the decay of public infrastructure and the underfunding of public schools. The original critique of *Wicksell* emphasised that the parliamentary process has a bias for short term consumptive spending over long-term investments. This bias is not resolved but the underlying distribution conflict exacerbated, as the potential amount of spending is reduced. Under constrained budgetary options, long-term investment expenditures more often fall victim to short-term consumptive spending, at least in the absence of an exception for investments. Even then, the question remains how to define investment in a way that provides guidance and boundaries.

3.2 *Sustainability as a Problem of Lacking Inter-generational Democracy?*

Sustainability is a matter of inter-generational equity. To all appearances, incurring debt for today's investments seems not to be equitable with regard to the following generations and their parliaments which will still have to pay interest as well as repay the principal for past investments. Nevertheless, it is often argued that some level of debt or debt-financed investments are sustainable.

With regard to investments, the argument is made that the debt-financed investment also benefits future generations.[68] The debt-financed school built today will be of benefit tomorrow. Measures against climate change today will help to contain its consequences tomorrow.

Yet, there are several limitations to this argument. Most investments lose value over time due to wear and tear or changing technologies and needs. A school build today as well as a bridge must be renovated after thirty years or maybe even replaced. This concern is relativised by data analysis, which suggests that there is a public capital-growth-nexus and that it yields high marginal returns of 10 to 30 per cent of public capital.[69] This would likely outweigh the costs of depreciation and interest in the long run.[70] Yet, problems

---

67 Truger, n 6, at 3.

68 Hermann Pünder,'§ 123 Staatskredit', in Josef Isensee and Paul Kirchof (eds), *Handbuch des Staatsrechts der Bundesrepublik Deutschland: Band V Rechtsquellen, Organisation, Finanzen* (3rd edn, C.F. Müller 2007); Truger, n 5, at 3; Richard Abel Musgrave and Peggy B Musgrave, *Public Finance in Theory and Practice* (5th edn, MC Graw-Hill Inc. 1989).

69 Pedro R D Bom and Jenny E Ligthart, 'What Have We Learned from Three Decades of Research on the Productivity of Public Capital?' (2014) 28 Journal of Economic Surveys 889.

70 Truger, n 6, at 3.

remain if the infrastructure built today becomes superfluous because of technical changes or is under- or oversized due to changing demands. Furthermore, it seems paternalistic and also undemocratic in an intertemporal sense to predetermine the investments and relevant parts of the budget of future generations.[71]

A looser connection is drawn by concepts of supply side economics that advocate deficit spending to overcome recessions. However, already in the original concept by Keynes, the repayment of excessive spending in boom times was an essential part of the concept. Economic history shows that the repayment part was often skipped or fell off in quantity. Nevertheless, European law allows for a 'breathing' limitation of debt with some deficit spending on the condition that its repayment is legally secured.

Climate change is also a good example for a trade-off that should qualify as a 'natural disaster' under the exemptions from the debt limitation. Yet, there are already tendencies to include a wide range of policies under programmes to tackle climate change. While measures against climate change should not be limited to damage response and should include prevention and long-term adaption, permanent measures as well as general social or economic policies have to be excluded for the purpose of debt limitations otherwise they could be effectively undermined.

As the 'breathing' limitation on debt and the disaster exemption shows, the law leaves space for different concepts of sustainability that can still be concretised by participation of the public. As the concept of sustainability is remarkably blurred in the context of debt financing, this seems to be a good design, albeit one hardly acknowledged in the current debate.

4 Role and Perspectives of Participation

4.1 Introduction

The provocative research question of this contribution is whether the law of public finance is an exemption, where participation does not aid, but harms sustainability. Constitutional limitations on debt after all curtail the parliamentary budgetary process and thus impair the participation through representative democracy. But we have already seen in the previous section, that the limitations on debt often contain exemptions that have to be concretised by the legislator. Furthermore, we have seen that while the sustainability of

71 Christian Calliess, 'Innovationsföderalismus und nachhaltige Finanzverfassung', in Wolfgang Kahl (ed), *Nachhaltige Finanzstrukturen im Bundesstaat* (Mohr Siebeck 2011).

the financing policy is increased, the sustainability of financed policies might be harmed, as long-term spending is said to suffer under the consolidation pressure.

This all suggests that there is still room and also a need for participation. Even if there is a problem with the parliamentary budgetary process, it might be reformed (see infra 4.2.) and also complemented by means of direct participation (see infra 4.3.). Finally, also institutionalised expert knowledge plays a role in the limitations on debt and provides further input (see infra 4.4.).

4.2 *Prevalence, Pitfalls and Perspectives of Representation*

Public participation is limited to voting decisions, as other instruments of participation like referenda often explicitly exclude funding decisions.

The limitation of direct participation can be explained by the budgetary prerogative of the parliament. The budget not only allows for control of the government by parliament, but its spending decisions are also of tantamount importance in the modern welfare state. The parliament shall not only have the power to appropriate funds but also bears the responsibility for the budget and its balancing.

In theory, representative democracy seems to be suited for this process, as there are always winners and losers of the spending decisions. Yet, as already seen in the introduction, the political economy of this process is flawed because of a tendency to make the current electorate the winner at the expense of future electorates. And this tendency has not been taken care of by constitutional limitations on debt; on the contrary, it has been exacerbated. The smaller the cake, the relatively bigger are the short-term expenditures.

A modification of the budgetary process would provide an alternative. The basic idea is to remove infrastructure expenditures from the general budget and finance them through special separate budgets or infrastructure funds. While different technical constructions are possible, they all would enable long-term spending commitments on infrastructure. For example, an infrastructure funds could be created with a long-term political commitment to fund such projects according to an objective estimate of the needs. This would keep infrastructure out of day-to-day politics. A new government might change the commitment, but any change would be rather transparent and subject to relatively high political costs.

This model has proven to be quite effective in the Netherlands. In 2020, the Dutch government funded a National Growth Fund that was administered by the Ministry of Finance and the Ministry of Economics and Climate protection. The sum of 20 billion Euros was earmarked for the period of five years for projects including: knowledge development, research, development and innovation as well as infrastructure.[72] While the fund is administered by both ministries, all projects undergo an application procedure, where they are assessed by an independent advisory commission. The commission consists of scientists, entrepreneurs and top civil servants. The first application round was concluded in April 2021, when the government adopted the recommendations by the commission.[73] The funding goes to research programmes in the areas of AI, quantum computing, hydrogen economy and medicine as well as public transport infrastructure and projects for digitalised lifelong learning. The funding is partly granted at once, partly subject to conditionalities and partly only reserved within the fund for the following years.

Such funds or separate budgets pose problems with regard to budgetary law and democratic control. Two common main principles of budgetary law are that all expenditures must go into the general budget and that there must be a new general budget every year. These principles secure the parliamentary democratic control of the budget. The exclusion of any parts via earmarking will over several years severely reduce democratic parliamentary control and thus needs to be justified. It is questionable whether the cause and the advisory committee provide sufficient legitimacy as compensation. While technical micromanagement can be delegated, the principal distribution decision usually is not. The idea that a small group of talented experts can make an objective and to a certain extent de facto binding recommendation, is technocratic. It adds some input legitimacy but cannot substitute participation.

4.3 *Direct Participation*

4.3.1 Financial Referenda

While budgetary sensitive decisions are barred from referenda in Germany,[74] Switzerland regularly has referenda on specific parts of a budget at the cantonal and communal level.[75] The applicable rules might provide for facultative

72 De Rijksoverheid voor Nederland, 'The National Growth Fund', <www.nationaalgroeifonds.nl/english/the-national-growth-fund> last accessed 30 April 2022.

73 De Rijksoverheid voor Nederland, 'Government allocates €646 million to projects to boost economic growth', <www.nationaalgroeifonds.nl/english/government-allocates/government-allocates-%E2%82%AC646-million-to-projects-designed-to-boost-economic-growth> last accessed 30 April 2022.

74 See for example art 60 sec 6 Constitution of Baden-Württemberg and sec 21 Cl. 2 Gemeindeordnung (Law on communal self-government); art 73 Constitution of Bayern; art 68 sec 1 p 3 Constitution of North Rhine-Westphalia.

75 Gebhard Kirchgässner and Lars Feld, 'On the effectiveness of debt brakes', in Reinhard Neck and Jan-Egbert Sturm (eds), *Sustainability of Public debt* (MIT Press 2008).

as well as obligatory referenda. Facultative referenda are subject to prior signature collection. Obligatory referenda may be triggered by the amount or duration of certain expenditures. A financial referendum is not admissible, if the spending is prescribed by law.

It is argued that financial referenda lead to more sustainable budgets, as expenditures are subject to closer scrutiny and need greater legitimisation.[76] Empirical research shows that financial referenda curb government spending.[77] Yet, even if one assumes a high effectiveness of these financial referenda, many Swiss cantons saw the need to additionally introduce constitutional limitations on debt.[78] While a reduction of government spending might reduce the amount of indebtedness, there is no evidence that the spending choices as such are sustainable. There is the danger of a similar bias like in the case of constitutional debt brakes; when the amount of spending is limited, short term spending will most probably displace long-term spending. Voters generally can only accept or reject the budget. Thus, the effectiveness of control differs between the general amount of spending and the distributive spending decisions.

4.3.2 Participatory Budgets

While referenda are an exception, low-level forms of participation are more widespread. At the municipal level, there is a practice of participatory budgets. These budgets are mostly only advisory in nature but ensure greater transparency in the allocation of funds. Citizens become aware of the financial possibilities and can voice their needs and prevalence, for example, whether to build a public library or swimming pool. Therefore, this early mode of participation can also complement financial referenda.

A model project in the German state of North Rhine-Westphalia conducted and analysed participatory budgets in six cities with different sizes (between 21,000 and 181,000 inhabitants), partly with balanced budgets and partly with financial problems. The participation consisted of three steps.[79] The first step included the provision of information concerning the draft budget via leaflets, information books, presentations and an internet portal. The second step is the consultation of the citizens on the whole draft or certain parts of it.

---

76 Ibid.

77 Patricia Funk and Christina Gathman, 'Does direct democracy reduce the size of government? New Evidence from historical data 1890–2000' (2011) 121 The Economic Journal 1252.

78 Kirchgässner and Feld, n 76, at 228.

79 Bertelsmann-Stiftung, *Kommunaler Bürgerhaushalt: Ein Leitfaden für die Praxis* (Innenministerium Nordrhein-Westfalen) 9.

A specific question asks the citizen to prioritise items on a list of planned investments or possible expenditure cuts. After the second step, the city council will take note of the proposals and prioritisations and decide on the budget. The third step informs citizens about the decision and ensures its transparency. The acceptance and feedback on the model project were positive both from the citizens and the members of the city council. While citizens lauded the transparency and the sheer informative value, the members of the city council found the proposals useful in their decision-making.[80] Yet, not all of the participating cities have continued the practice of a participatory budget as of today. A 2018 report from Germany counts 102 active cities, 13 on pause and 153 cities where the participatory budget has been discontinued.[81]

Generally, the quality of participatory budgets is heterogeneous, as there are no norms or standards. Sometimes only the draft budget is downloadable and accompanied by an email-address. Sometimes the participatory budget is part of a bigger participation portal with visualised data. Sometimes leaflets[82] and invitations to workshops are sent by post.

Overall, the experience with participatory budgets is mixed. While it is in principle seen as a useful tool, it is often only a part of the general information and participation offer. Though, without tailored presentations and data visualisations, the barrier for participation is high. The German experience of many discontinued participatory budgets suggests that there is room for improvement.

4.4 *Participation through Experts?*

Under European and German law, participatory elements of debt limitations are left to scientific councils that search for an economically 'optimal level' of indebtedness. Yet the optimal level of indebtedness is highly disputed in economic science with senior researchers changing their positions under limited knowledge and changing trade-offs. Due to the lack of agreed objective standards, decisions are prone to be influenced by political preferences and, the experts are most probably selected with regard to political preferences. A pluralistic composition of membership can reduce these biases. Overall, the inclusion of expert advice is an important element of good governance and

80 Ibid, at 32 ff.

81 Statusbericht Bürgerhaushalt (2018) 21, 22 <www.buergerhaushalt.org/sites/default/files/downloads/9._Statusbericht_Buergerhaushalt.pdf> last accessed 30 April 2022.

82 For example, in the German City of Stuttgart <www.buergerhaushalt-stuttgart.de/d/faltblatt_buergerhaushalt_2021_0.pdf> last accessed 30 April 2022.

provides some participation in the wider sense but cannot substitute other modes of participation and legitimation.

5 Conclusion: Securing Participation by All Generations in a Second-best World

Is the issue of state indebtedness the big exception, where less participation leads to more sustainability? In an ideal world: no. In the real world of second-best solutions: yes, but ...

The question whether to incur debt is a question of inter-generational equity and distributive justice. It is the question of how much of the resources should be consumed and how much should be invested for the benefit not only of the current electorate but also future generations. A certain amount of debt financing of such investments can be justified, as it equally distributes benefits and burdens between the generations.

The problem lies in the incentives for the current electorate to pass on the burden to future generations, as it allows for lower taxes or more short-term spending. The history of rising debt levels and their socially regressive reduction through inflation or exchange rate shifts shows that there is a strong tendency to shift burdens into the future. A tendency that is abetted by the lack of participation of future generations.

An optimal solution would thus be to increase the participation of younger and future generations. While unborn generations cannot participate, it is important that the voices of young people and also the parents and guardians of young people get the opportunity to be heard. Unfortunately, the changing demographic relegates the young generation to the permanent minority. And unlike earlier generations, the promise that every further generation will be better off than the preceding, sounds doubtful in the terms of changing demographics and climate change. Thus, we need more participation with regard to the budget and its financing. Participatory budgets should be mandatory on a communal as well as state level and its accessibility secured and improved through digitalisation. Special attention should be drawn to the participation of the younger generations, eg through youth councils or youth parliaments, as they are more affected by and thus tendentially more aware of the negative effects of the shifting burden.

While there are some ways to increase the participation of the younger generation, it will most probably only have a small impact on the majority decisions of the electorate. Furthermore, neither the whole electorate nor the younger generations can see into the future and so we still have the problem of limited knowledge with regard to inter-generation equity. In cases where there is enough knowledge, for example, in climate change or demographic change, and where it is clear that actions have to be implemented as soon as possible for the benefit of younger generations and vulnerable groups, the constitutional courts can and should intervene for their protection. The German constitutional court's decision on climate protection is a good example, where there is scientific knowledge that further burden shifting does not lead to a deus ex machina, a miraculous future solution, but to tragedy.[83] But in contrast to climate change, adjudication of the solution of budgetary problems is not as clear-cut. An intervention by constitutional courts can only urge the legislator to do something effective without being able to rewrite the budget or introduce new taxes.

As participation and constitutional courts are insufficient to overcome the short-term bias of the parliamentary democratic process, second-best solutions have to be employed. While they reduce the participation of the current electorate, they preserve the participation of future electorates. The participation of one generation has to find its limitations, particularly when the resulting dispositions generally reduces the effectiveness of participation by younger and future generations.

Constitutional limitations on debt are second-best solutions, not perfect ones, in some instances harmful in the short term, but poised to avoid harm in the long term. The current absolute limitations on incurring new debt in the fiscal compact are better than their reputation. They allow for Keynesian deficit spending and their natural disaster exemption is open for a wide interpretation covering also climate change. On the downside, there is no need to curb new debt to just 0.5 per cent of the GDP, especially in times of low interest. Long-term spending is even more likely to lose out against short-term spending. Also, they are prone to circumvention through special entities and budgets. However, they have a strong symbolic value and thus influence the political process and the stability perceptions of financial markets.

An alternative or cumulative measure would be the return to investment exceptions that allow for an unlimited debt financing of investments. The big advantage of this clause is its multidimensionality, combining sustainability in both the financing policy as well as in the financed policy. Its biggest disadvantage is the need to define investments that securely provide benefits for younger and future generations. While too narrow a definition can give wrong incentives ('concrete instead of people'), history shows that the legislator is prone to giving itself a free pass if he defines it by himself. Thus, a constitutional investment clause should include an enumerative specific list of investments that can

83 BVerfG, 'Verfassungsbeschwerden gegen das Klimaschutzgesetz teilweise erfolgreich' (2021) 24 NJW 1723.

be debt-financed. Along with tangible infrastructure projects like roads, rails, energy or water grids, selected infrastructure improvements for the benefit of the younger generation for the formation of immaterial property in the wider sense, such as: kindergartens, schools, youth centres, youth welfare offices, universities and the undertaking of research, should also be allowed. Such an investment clause should be limited to a certain amount of investments (eg 75 per cent), so that the current electorate has to finance part of the investment out of current revenues. This ensures that the burden is really shared and not only shifted and is a further prevention against the abuse of the investment clause.

A combination of a symbolic, but nevertheless politically and not irrelevant commitment against new debt, a binding reasonable high allowance to incur new debt and a limited enumerative investment exemption should provide a comprehensive second-best solution. This, however, has to be complemented with more participation in the budgetary process on all levels of government. This combination might have the chance to influence the political process, so that the future (financial) freedom of the young and future generations is preserved to a greater extent.

Bibliography

Ardagna S and Caselli F, 'The Political Economy of the Greek Debt Crisis: A Tale of Two Bailouts' (2014) 6 American Economic Journal: Macroeconomics 291.

Beetsma RMWJ and Debrun X, 'Implementing the Stability and Growth Pact: Enforcement and Procedural Flexibility' (2005) IMF Working Paper 05/59, 3 www.imf.org/en/Publications/WP/Issues/2016/12/31/Implementing-the-Stability-and-Growth-Pact-Enforcement-and-Procedural-Flexibility-18017 last accessed 30 April 2022.

Bom PRD and Ligthart JE, 'What Have We Learned from Three Decades of Research on the Productivity of Public Capital?' (2014) 28 Journal of Economic Surveys 889.

Brennan G and Buchanan JM, *The Power to Tax: Analytical Foundations of a Fiscal Constitution* (CUP 1980).

Buchheit Lv *et al*, 'Revisiting Sovereign Bankruptcy' (2013) www.ssrn.com/abstract=2354998 last accessed 30 April 2022.

Calliess C, 'Innovationsföderalismus und nachhaltige Finanzverfassung', in Wolfgang Kahl (ed), *Nachhaltige Finanzstrukturen im Bundesstaat* (Mohr Siebeck 2011).

Canotilho M, Violante T and Lanceiro R, 'Austerity measures under judicial scrutiny: the Portuguese constitutional case-law' (2015) 11 European Constitutional Law Review 155.

Cooper D, 'Low rates provide a historic opportunity to tackle climate change' *Financial Times* (London 26 December 2019) www.ft.com/content/c752698c-200c-11ea-92da-f0c92e957a96 last accessed 15 December 2021.

De Rijksoverheid voor Nederland, 'The National Growth Fund', www.nationaalgroeifonds.nl/english/the-national-growth-fund, last accessed 30 April 2022.

De Rijksoverheid voor Nederland, 'Government allocates €646 million to projects to boost economic growth', www.nationaalgroeifonds.nl/english/government-allocates/government-allocates-%E2%82%AC646-million-to-projects-designed-to-boost-economic-growth last accessed 30 April 2022.

Devarajan S *et al*, *Aid and Reform in Africa: Lessons from 10 Case Studies* (World Bank 2001).

Devine R, 'Emerging Issues: Is a Grexit - A Greek Exit from the Eurozone - the Solution?' (2016) 4 University of Baltimore Journal of International Law 157.

Estella A, 'Potential Exit from the Eurozone: The Case of Spain' (2015) 22 Indiana Journal of Global Legal Studies 335.

Feldstein M, 'Inflation, Tax Rules, and the Prices of Land and Gold' (1980) 14 Journal of Public Economics 309.

Funk P and Gathman C, 'Does direct democracy reduce the size of government? New Evidence from historical data 1890–2000' (2011) 121 The Economic Journal 1252.

Goldmann M, 'art 126 TFEU', in Helmut Siekmann (ed.), *The European Monetary Union: A Commentary on the Legal Foundations* (Hart Publishing 2022).

Guess R, 'Economies: Good, Bad, Indifferent' (2012) 55 Inquiry 331.

Heinemann F and Kemper J 'The ECB Under the Threat of Fiscal Dominance – The Individual Central Banker Dimension' (2021) 18 The Economists' Voice 5, https://doi.org/10.1515/ev-2021-0014 last accessed 30 April 2022.

Hentze T, 'Anhörung des Haushalts- und Finanzausschusses: Stellungnahme zum Entwurf des Haushaltsgesetzes 2022 des Landes Nordrhein-Westfalen' (2021) 37 IW-Report 6.

Hick R, 'Enter the Troika: The Politics of Social Security during Ireland's Bailout' (2018) 47 Journal of Social Policy 1.

Hunger A, 'Die schwäbische Hausfrau' *FAZ* (Frankfurt, 14 July 2016) www.faz.net/aktuell/wirtschaft/wirtschaftspolitik/sparpolitik-merkel-und-die-schwaebische-hausfrau-14333164-p2.html last accessed 30 April 2022.

'Inflation and the Federal Income Tax' (1973) 82 The Yale Law Journal 716.

Killick T, *IMF Programmes in Developing Countries: Design and Impact* (Routledge 1995).

Kirchgässner G, 'Fiscal Institutions at the Cantonal Level in Switzerland' (2013) 149 Swiss Journal of Economics and Statistics 139.

Kirchgässner G, and Feld L, 'On the effectiveness of debt brakes', in Reinhard Neck and Jan-Egbert Sturm (eds.), *Sustainability of Public debt* (MIT Press 2008).

Kollewe J, 'Angela Merkel's austerity postergirl, the thrifty Swabian housewife' *The Guardian* (London, 17 September 2012) www.theguardian.com/world/2012/sep/17/angela-merkel-austerity-swabian-housewives last accessed 30 April 2022.

Kube H, 'Art 109 GG', in Günter Dürig, Roman Herzog and Rupert Scholz (eds.), *Grundgesetz-Kommentar* (C.H. Beck supp 95 July 2021).

La Monaca S, Spector K and Kobus J, 'Financing the Green Transition: Addressing Barriers to Capital Deployment' (2019) 73 Journal of International Affairs 17.

Lane PR, 'The Real Effects of European Monetary Union' (2006) 20 The Journal of Economic Perspectives 47.

Lee DR, 'The Keynesian Path to Fiscal Irresponsibility' (2012) 32 Cato Journal 473.

McNamara K, 'Banking on Legitimacy: The ECB and the Euro Zone Crisis' (2012) 13 Georgetown Journal of International Affairs 143.

Megliani M, 'From the European Stability Mechanism to the European Monetary Fund: There and Back Again' (2020) 21 German Law Journal 674.

Musgrave RA and Musgrave PB, *Public Finance in Theory and Practice* (5th edn., MC Graw-Hill Inc. 1989).

Nussbaum M, *Frontiers of Justice* (HUP 2006).

Nussbaum M, *Creating Capabilities* (HUP 2011).

Paudyn B, 'Credit rating agencies and the sovereign debt crisis: Performing the politics of creditworthiness through risk and uncertainty' (2013) 20 Review of International Political Economy 788.

Pünder H, '§ 123 Staatskredit', in Josef Isensee and Paul Kirchof (eds.), *Handbuch des Staatsrechts der Bundesrepublik Deutschland: Band V Rechtsquellen, Organisation, Finanzen* (3rd edn., C.F. Müller 2007).

Reimer E, 'Nachhaltigkeit durch Begrenzung der Staatsverschuldung', in Wolfgang Kahl (ed.), *Nachhaltige Finanzstrukturen im Bundesstaat* (Mohr Siebeck 2011).

Sen A, *Development as Freedom* (OUP 1999).

Stein Lv, *Lehrbuch der Finanzwissenschaft* (5th edn., Nabu Press 1885).

Tobin J, 'Taxes, Saving, and Inflation' (1949) 39 The American Economic Review 1223.

Toporowski J, 'International credit, financial integration and the euro' (2013) 37 Cambridge Journal of Economics 571.

Traynor I and Inman P, 'Eurozone bank bailout deal throws lifeline to Spain and Italy' *The Guardian* (Brussels and London, 29 June 2012) www.theguardian.com/business/2012/jun/29/eurozone-bank-bailout-spain-italy last accessed 30 April 2022.

Truger A, 'EU Governments Must not Return to Their Dysfunctional Fiscal Rules' (2021) 1 The Economists.

Valta M, 'Sustainability and Participation in the Law of Public Finance', in Eva Julia Lohse and Birgit Peters (eds), *Sustainability Through Participation? International, Supranational and National Perspectives* (Brill – Nijhoff 2023).

Wagner A, *Finanzwissenschaft* (3rd edn., C.F. Winter 1883).

Weber M, *Die protestantische Ethik und der Geist des Kapitalismus* (4th edn., C.H. Beck 2013).

Wicksell K, *Finanztheoretische Untersuchungen nebst Darstellung und Kritik des Steuerwesens Schwedens* (Gustav Fischer 1896).

Wieland J, 'Soziale Nachhaltigkeit und Finanzverfassung', in Wolfgang Kahl (ed.), *Nachhaltige Finanzstrukturen im Bundesstaat* (Mohr Siebeck 2011)

CHAPTER 8

State Aid Law

Julius Buckler

1 Introduction

While EU law initially and almost exclusively focused on economic integration, it has since evolved into a comprehensive legal order. Even though this focus on economic integration has not shifted, EU law must now also take into account environmental issues. In fact, art 11 Treaty on the functioning of the European Union (TFEU) obliges the EU to "[integrate environmental protection requirements] into the definition and implementation of the Union's policies and activities, in particular with a view to promoting sustainable development." Likewise, art 37 Charter of Fundamental Rights of the European Union (CFR) states: "A high level of environmental protection and the improvement of the quality of the environment must be integrated into the policies of the Union and ensured in accordance with the principle of sustainable development." Whereas the exact meaning and nature of art 37 CFR remains under debate,[1] European Court of Justice (ECJ) case law is clear when it comes to the relevance of art 11 TFEU. For example, even where a decision taken by the EU and its bodies is outside the field of environmental protection, the impact of said decision on the environment and/or sustainability have at least to be taken into account.[2]

Notwithstanding this general obligation to consider the environmental impact of every decision taken by EU authorities, at least at first glance, EU state aid law[3] does not seem to be a reference area for sustainability and

1 Whereas the EU General Court, Case T-600/15 *PAN Europe and others* [2016], para 48 characterised art 37 CFR as a mere "principle", the ECJ may appear to lean into a different direction, see ECJ, Case C-444/15 *Associazione Italia Nostra Onlus* [2016], para 62; ECJ, Case C-594/18 P *Austria/Commission* [2020], para 42.

2 See ECJ, Case C-594/18 P *Austria/Commission* [2020]; further on this below at 2.2 and 4.

3 When referring to state aid law, this chapter primarily refers to primary state aid law and state aid procedures conducted by the Commission, thereby mostly setting aside legislative procedures concerning state aid regulations and state aid procedures conducted by member states. This focus is not only dictated by considerations of space, but mostly by the fact that – as will be shown below – sustainability and participation and their interplay are of particular importance when it comes to individual state aid procedures.

participation; state aid law is primarily a means to contain subsidies by member states. Whereas the aim of EU competition law is to prevent *companies* from achieving and/or exploiting a dominant position on the single market by illicit means and thus distort competition,[4] state aid law aims at preventing *member states* from conferring unfair financial advantages to *their* companies through subsidies. State aid law thus complements EU competition law and, beyond that, EU law concerning freedom of movement rules in general. In short, and even based on this very general overview, it becomes clear that while not its sole objective, the primary purpose of EU state aid law is to protect the functioning of the single market.[5]

Considering its primary focus and the fact that it may appear as a rather technical matter, it might be surprising when one takes a closer look, even EU state aid law relates to both sustainability and participation. In fact, considering that the undistorted functioning of the market usually yields the most efficient and thus durable results,[6] even though this would necessitate a departure from art 11 TFEU[7] and may seem a rather unusual approach to the concept of sustainability, it might even be said that EU state aid law is in fact closely linked to sustainability. However, even when one focusses on a more common definition of sustainability as spelt out in art 11 TFEU and participation, state aid law touches upon both these concepts, at least in their specific meaning for state aid law. Whereas sustainability is primarily, but not exclusively, touched upon by state aid law as an objective that may justify the granting of state aid (see 2.), participation in state aid law is most prominently concerned when it comes to the procedural rights of third parties in individual state aid procedures (see 3.).

The importance of both concepts and their interplay in EU state aid law, which is of particular relevance for, but not limited to, legal proceedings, has increased in recent times (see 4.), illustrating that both sustainability and participation have made their way into the seemingly rather technical domain of EU state aid law.

---

4 See Matthias Uffer, 'Competition Law', in this book, infra chapter 9.

5 For an extensive study of the relationship between State aid law and environmmental protection see Olivier Peiffert, *L'application du droit des aides d'État aux mesures de protection de l'environnement* (Bruylant 2015).

6 Vincent Verouden and Philipp Werner, 'Introduction – The Law and Economics of EU State aid Control' in Philipp Werner and Vincent Verouden (eds), *EU State aid Control* (Kluwer 2017), 9, 11 ff.

7 Cf, however, art 3 (1) Treaty on European Union (TEU) whereby "[the internal market] shall work for the sustainable development of Europe based on [...] a high level of protection and improvement of the quality of the environment."

2 Sustainability in EU State Aid Law

2.1 *Sustainability as Sustainability of the Market?*

As pointed out above, state aid law does not primarily, and at least not specifically, address the concept of sustainability as widely understood. The rationale behind the general prohibition of state aid as enshrined in art 107 (1) TFEU is of course that all financial advantages granted by member states, except those falling under the *Altmark Trans* criteria[8] which are rarely fulfilled, are generally subject to the Commission's (albeit sometimes predetermined, art 107 (2) TFEU) explicit approval.[9] The requirement of prior explicit approval by the Commission is thus key in preventing member states from interfering in the internal market by means of subsidies for *their* companies. At the outset, the primary objective of state aid law is thus the protection of the functioning of the internal market from even the slightest of distortions caused

8 ECJ, Case C-280/00 *Altmark Trans* [2003], ECR I-7747. According to this judgment, subsidies are not caught by art 107 (1) TFEU if they are to be regarded as compensation for the services provided by the recipient undertakings in order to discharge public service obligations. This requires four conditions to be fulfilled simultaneously:
(1) the recipient undertaking is actually required to discharge public service obligations and those obligations have been clearly defined.
(2) the parameters on the basis of which the compensation is calculated have been established beforehand in an objective and transparent manner.
(3) the compensation does not exceed what is necessary to cover all or part of the costs incurred in discharging the public service obligations, taking into account the relevant receipts and a reasonable profit for discharging those obligations.
(4) fourth, where the undertaking which is to discharge public service obligations is not chosen in a public procurement procedure, the level of compensation needed has been determined on the basis of an analysis of the costs which a typical undertaking, well run and adequately provided with means of transport so as to be able to meet the necessary public service requirements, would have incurred in discharging those obligations, taking into account the relevant receipts and a reasonable profit for discharging the obligations.

9 However, measures falling within the scope of state aid regulations based on art 108 (4) TFEU are exempt from prior approval if they meet the *exact* criteria set out in the respective regulation, see art 3 ff. of the General Block Exemption Regulation (GBER), Commission Regulation (EU) 651/2014 of 17 June 2014 declaring certain categories of aid compatible with the internal market in application of Articles 107 and 108 of the Treaty [2014], OJ L 187/1, art 3 Commission Regulation (EU) 1407/2013 of 18 December 2013 on the application of Articles 107 and 108 of the Treaty on the Functioning of the European Union to de minimis aid [2013], OJ L 352/1. The GBER has been modified several times (last amendment by Commission Regulation (EU) 2021/1237 of 23 July 2021 amending Regulation (EU) No 651/2014 [2021], OJ L 270/39), however the provisions cited in this chapter have remained (largely) unchanged.

by subsidies.[10] This prohibition is to be interpreted rather widely, as member states are prone to endow *their* companies with financial advantages to boost their competitiveness, often out of considerations strange to the logic of the (internal) market.[11]

Considering this and starting from the assumption that the free and unhindered interplay of market forces usually yields the most efficient and accepted and permanent results,[12] one might say that sustainability is not only touched upon by state aid law, but that sustainability could even be considered as being at the centre of state aid law. State aid law could thus be seen as being connected with sustainability insofar as it serves to ensure that the internal market continues to function unhindered by financial infractions, permanently, and thus sustainably, ensuring that the most efficient and therefore sustainable solutions are achieved at any given moment for all goods. State aid law is thus a means to secure the functioning of the internal market as a sustainable system for the coordination of supply and demand.

While the internal market and its functioning certainly touches upon aspects of sustainability, it is also obvious that this approach to sustainability and its connection to state aid law would necessitate an understanding of 'sustainability' that would at the very least be rather 'creative'. Furthermore, even if understood in the sense pointed out above, sustainability could only be seen as the primary object of state aid law or closely linked to it insofar as the general ban on state aid as spelled out in art 107 (1) TFEU is concerned. However, such an understanding could not explain the exemptions to the prohibition of state aid as set out in EU primary law. Subsidies falling within the scope of art 107 (1) TFEU may be authorised by the Commission. Regardless of whether they must be authorised following art 107 (2) TFEU or if their authorisation is at the discretion of the Commission in the cases covered by art 107 (3) TFEU, the Commission authorises an impairment of the otherwise unhindered

10 Vincent Verouden and Philipp Werner, 'Introduction – The Law and Economics of EU state aid Control' in Philipp Werner and Vincent Verouden (eds), *EU state aid Control* (Kluwer 2017) 7, 9 ff.

11 Therefore, subsidies granted by a member state to companies regardless of their company seat, but limited to EU companies, generally do not pose problems from a state aid point of view. Subsidies granted exclusively to EU companies may however raise questions regarding WTO law.

12 Cf Vincent Verouden and Philipp Werner, 'Introduction – The Law and Economics of EU State aid Control' in Philipp Werner and Vincent Verouden (eds), *EU State aid Control* (Kluwer 2017) 7, 41 ff.

functioning of the internal market by the subsidy in question.[13] Given the fact that a subsidy is usually paid to sustain an operation that by itself is not viable under market conditions, the authorisation of state aid would thus be contrary to the concept of sustainability as pointed out above.

On the contrary, however, the Commission may only approve state aid for the reasons spelled out in art 107 (2) and art 107 (3) TFEU. On one hand, and roughly speaking, article 107 (2) TFEU concerns cases where the granting of subsidies has to be authorised *qua legem* because these subsidies either profit individuals or because the granting of subsidies is necessary to overcome particular difficulties.[14] Art 107 (2) TFEU thus addresses situations in which the treaty makers assumed the (internal) market would not provide the desired results and therefore deemed subsidies to be an appropriate remedy for this anticipated failure of the (internal) market.

On the other hand, 107 (3) TFEU authorises the Commission to approve state aid whenever it considers that the positive effects of state aid outweigh its negative impacts on the (internal) market. Put briefly, the grounds for approval of state aid as spelled out in art 107 (3) TFEU mostly concerns cases in which the market does not by itself provide results that are deemed desirable from political, social, environmental or cultural considerations.[15]

Accordingly, state aid may be authorised if its aim is to promote objectives whose importance outweighs negative impacts caused by interference to the functionality of the internal market through the granting of state aid.[16] This applies, but is not limited to, state aid granted to ensure that otherwise unprofitable ferry routes are served[17] or to certain cultural institutions so that they may continue to operate even if they are not profitable.[18]

---

13 Cf Vincent Verouden and Philipp Werner, 'Introduction – The Law and Economics of EU State aid Control' in Philipp Werner and Vincent Verouden (eds), *EU State aid Control* (Kluwer 2017) 7, 29, 51–53.

14 This assumption is of course not any more correct when it comes to art 107 (2) (c) TFEU, as the economic problems of German reunification can probably be considered as largely solved and at least may not be assimilated to a "special event" anymore.

15 Cf Vincent Verouden and Philipp Werner, 'Introduction – The Law and Economics of EU State aid Control' in Philipp Werner and Vincent Verouden (eds), *EU State aid Control* (Kluwer 2017) 7, 29–53.

16 Cf Vincent Verouden and Philipp Werner, 'Introduction – The Law and Economics of EU State aid Control' in Philipp Werner and Vincent Verouden (eds), *EU State aid Control* (Kluwer 2017) 7, 52 ff.

17 See, e.g, art 51 GBER and for an example of recent Commission practice Commission decision (EU) 2022/756 of 30 September 2021 on the measures SA.32014 […] [2022], OJ L 138/19.

18 See art 107 (3) (d) TFEU and further art 53 GBER.

This is also true for the promotion of electricity production from renewable energies, which at least for a long time was unable to compete against conventional energy production.[19] At the same time, the authorisation of state aid for the production of renewable energy is a perfect example of the rationale behind art 107 (3) TFEU. Even though the promotion of renewable energies is desirable for numerous reasons (including the reduction of carbon dioxide emissions),[20] they could not compete against conventional energy production because the market, among others reasons, insufficiently takes into account the negative externalities of conventional energy production; thus, the market failed.[21]

Against this background, it may be considered that state aid can contribute to the restoration of the functioning of the market as a 'sustainable' system by granting a currently incompetitive good or company an advantage it would have if the market also took into account externalities and thus functioned properly. It must of course be stressed that there is always a risk that such interferences into the market miss the set goal, making their strict limitation – as is practice of the Commission[22] – even more important.[23]

Beyond that, and on a more general level, state aid may contribute to the achievement of a 'sustainable' result insofar as it may help to secure the permanent availability of goods or services which are politically considered desirable or necessary by a member state, but which the market does not provide for. As has been touched upon above, this is for example the case when it comes

19 Cf Kai Struckmann and Geza Sapi, 'Energy and Environmental Aid', in Philipp Werner and Vincent Verouden (eds), *EU State aid Control* (Kluwer 2017) 663, 666 ff.

20 On the measures taken by the EU to promote sustainability in the energy sector see eg Farah Jerrari, 'La durabilité énergétique en droit de l'Union européenne', [2021] Revue Trimestrielle de Droit Européen 87.

21 See recitals 55 ff. of the GBER: "The area of environmental protection is confronted with market failures so that, under normal market conditions, undertakings may not necessarily have an incentive to reduce the pollution caused by them since any such reduction may increase their costs without corresponding benefits. When undertakings are not obliged to internalize the costs of pollution, society as a whole bears these costs."

22 For a relatively recent overview on Commission practice in the area of state aid for renewables see Julia Schimpfhuber, 'Beihilfen für Grüne Energie: Neue Fälle' in Thomas Jaeger and Birgit Haslinger (eds), *Beihilferecht Jahrbuch 2019* (NWV 2019), 339. Cf recital 3 and art 3 GBER.

23 Cf Vincent Verouden and Philipp Werner, 'Introduction – The Law and Economics of EU State aid Control' in Philipp Werner and Vincent Verouden (eds), *EU State aid Control* (Kluwer 2017) 7, 29–53 and see below n 32 for the case of the Environmental and Energy aid Guidelines.

to cultural services such as small cinemas displaying movies in minority languages[24] or in the case of ferry routes to remote islands.[25]

2.2 *The Classical Notion of Sustainability: Promoting Sustainability as Grounds for Approval of State Aid*

The aforementioned examples of state aid are of course not what usually springs to mind when thinking about state aid and its relation to sustainability, with support for ferry routes even being possibly regarded as the exact opposite of sustainability.

Rather, state aid and sustainability are usually associated and, in fact, primarily concerned with those cases already referred to above where state aid is granted for the promotion of technologies or products that are themselves regarded as being sustainable or more sustainable than others. Further, at least at the time the subsidy is granted, such technologies or products cannot compete against conventional (less sustainable) alternatives for reasons mentioned above. From this perspective, while state aid itself does not become sustainable, the relationship between state aid and sustainability as commonly understood becomes clear. As pointed out above, state aid may on the one hand help to overcome a punctual market failure and thus restore the functioning of the internal market, while on the other hand the market often fails where it does not take into account externalities, which is especially true whenever economical decisions have a notable environmental impact.[26]

In fact, it is exactly in this respect that both conceptions of sustainability are most closely intertwined with state aid, the numerous shades of sustainability being an objective whose pursuit may generally justify the grant of state aid under EU law. While this is not immediately apparent when looking at the relevant *specific* provisions of primary law,[27] it becomes obvious when looking, for example, at the General Block Exemption Regulation (GBER),[28] which exempts certain forms of state aid from prior approval by the Commission if they do meet conditions spelled out for different sectors. In fact, the conditions that must be met for an exemption tend to be slightly less restrictive for subsidies granted to projects aimed at bolstering sustainability than for other

---

24 Communication from the Commission on state aid for films and other audiovisual works [2013], OJ C 332/1, para 16.

25 See n 17.

26 See n 21.

27 This goes especially for art 107 (3) (c) TFEU which is usually the basis for these authorisations and which does not contain the slightest reference to environmental aspects.

28 Art 36 ff. GBER.

subsidies equally covered by the GBER such as subsidies for broadband.[29] This is completely in line with the importance accorded to environmental protection and thus the essence of sustainability as enshrined in art 11 TFEU and set out above.

With regard to art 11 TFEU, it is obvious that state aid aimed at contributing to environmental protection and therefore sustainability may not only be approved by the Commission and, consequently, granted by members when it fulfils the conditions set out in the GBER. The reason for this is that while the GBER renders the formal state aid authorisation procedure oblivious in cases it covers,[30] environmental aid may of course by no means only be authorised in these cases, the GBER only being a means to simplify state aid procedures.[31]

The same goes for the area of state aid law probably most closely linked to sustainability: state aid granted for the production of notably electricity from renewable energy sources aimed at reducing carbon dioxide emissions. While partly falling under the scope of the GBER, state aid in this area is often authorised on the basis of art 107 (3) (c) TFEU and the Climate, Energy and Environmental Aid Guidelines (CEEAG).[32] While art 107 (3) (c) TFEU is the basis for the Commission's discretionary approval of "aid to facilitate the development of certain economic activities or of certain economic areas" including renewable energy production, the CEEAG outline the conditions for discretionary approval of state aid covered by them in great detail. Even though power generation from renewable energy sources has long been addressed by EU internal market regulations,[33] the answer to the question of how to

29 For the "generous" treatment of subsidies granted to nature preservatives and national parks see, eg, Thomas Müller and Daniel Wächter, 'Schwerpunkt Infrastruktur III: Natur- und Nationalparks im Fokus des Beihilferechts' in Thomas Jaeger and Birgit Haslinger (eds), *Beihilferecht Jahrbuch 2019* (NWV 2019), 411.

30 Cf recital 3 and art 3 GBER.

31 See for the possibility to approve state aid *directly* on grounds of art 107 (3) (c) TFEU below n 48.

32 For the current guidelines, see Communication from the Commission – Guidelines on state aid for climate, environmental protection and energy 2022 [2022] OJ C 80/1. For the previous guidelines of the Commission see Communication from the Commission – Guidelines on state aid for environmental protection and energy 2014–2020 [2014] OJ C 200/1. See in more detail Kai Struckmann and Geza Sapi, 'Energy and Environmental Aid', in Philipp Werner and Vincent Verouden (eds), *EU State aid Control* (Kluwer 2017), 663, 695 ff.; Rike U. Krämer, 'Die neuen Leitlinien für Umweltbehilfen', in Thomas Jaeger and Birgit Haslinger (eds), *Beihilferecht Jahrbuch 2015* (NWV 2015), 327.

33 See European Parliament and Council Directive 2001/77/EC of 27 September 2001 on the promotion of electricity produced from renewable energy sources in the internal electricity market [2001] OJ L 283/33; European Parliament and Council Directive 2009/28/EC of 23 April 2009 on the promotion of the use of energy from renewable sources and

increase and bolster the part of renewable energies in a market still largely dominated by conventional and/or nuclear power[34] has mostly been left to the member states.[35] They have accordingly invented different support schemes for renewable energies that often do amount to state aid.[36] While these support schemes may also fall under the GBER, they are usually examined by the Commission under art 107 para 3 lit. c) TFEU. In fact, it is this provision of EU primary law, and which gives the Commission discretionary powers in state aid procedures,[37] that usually is the grounds for the approval of environmental/energy state aid by the Commission.[38] When approving subsidies or other support schemes/mechanisms for renewable energy production amounting to state aid, the Commission usually makes its decisions based on art 107 para 3 c) TFEU in conjunction with the CEEAG mentioned above. It is in this specific context that the connection between state aid law and sustainability as commonly understood is closest and does, at the same time, play an important role in EU state aid law.

However, even where the relationship between State aid law and sustainability may seem particularly close as is the Case when it comes to Support for renewable energy, this must be put into perspective: the application of state aid law always necessitates that a member state grants aid which falls under the scope of art 107 (1) TFEU, as only then the Commission's approval is generally necessary. The controlling or mitigating effect of state aid law is unfolded primarily through the design and interpretation of the exception rules and in particular art 107 (3) TFEU by the Commission,[39] which spells out the cases in which the Commission may approve state aid at its discretion. Therefore, EU state aid law is not a means to achieve or promote sustainability by itself, but

---

amending and subsequently repealing Directives 2001/77/EC and 2003/30/EC [2009] OJ L 140/16; European Parliament and Council Directive 2018/2001 of 11 December 2018 on the promotion of the use of energy from renewable sources (recast) [2018] OJ L 328/82.

34 While electricity generated from nuclear power is carbon-neutral, its sustainability may be questionable considering the impact of nuclear waste.

35 While internal market legislation has addressed the necessity to promote renewables relatively early on, more precise rules for promotion schemes have only been introduced into the corresponding directives recently, see art 4 ff. Directive 2018/2001 (n 33). The ECJ did not oppose member states limitation of promotion schemes to electricity generated on their territory, see ECJ, Case C-573/12 *Ålands Vindkraft AB* [2014].

36 See for the example of the French support system ECJ, Case C-262/12 *Vent de Colère* [2013].

37 See, e.g., ECJ, Case C-372/97 *Italy v Commission* [2004], ECR I-3679, para 83.

38 See, for example, the Commission's most recent approval of the German support scheme (EEG), C (2021) 2960 of 29 april 2021 [2021], p. 104: "compatible with the internal market pursuant to Article 107(3) (c) of the (TFEU)".

39 Cf CEEAG (n 32), para 22 ff.

primarily a reactive mechanism designed to contain financial intervention by the member states. The role of the Commission in EU state aid procedures is, however, not strictly limited to the mere approval or denial of aid granted by the member states. In the course of state aid procedures, the Commission may ask member states to modify the conditions under which they grant state aid or ask them to make concessions in other areas not covered by state aid law or the procedure at hand as a precondition for approval of state aid and thereby play a proactive role during state aid procedures.[40]

Accordingly, it is through its practice of state aid control that the Commission may exercise considerable influence on the policies of the member states including those aimed at improving sustainability. Beyond this, when exercising its powers under art 108 TFEU, which is the main provision for state aid procedures, and even when the aid in question is *not* specifically targeted at improving sustainability notably by promoting environmental-friendly projects,[41] the Commission also has to take into account the compatibility of the subsidy at hand with other relevant provisions of EU law. While the Commission's powers in state aid procedures are limited by the scope of art 107 ff. TFEU, meaning its decision is only valid insofar as the relevant provisions of state aid law are concerned, it has long been established that the Commission may, on the contrary, not approve state aid that runs counter to other provisions of EU law such as the rules on the free movement of goods.[42]

More recently, the ECJ has ruled and thereby confirmed[43] that in state aid Procedures, the Commission must also pay due regard to environmental

40 See for an example Commission Decision on state aid SA.21918 (C17/07) (ex NN 17/07) implemented by France of 12 June 2021 – Regulated electricity tariffs in France [2012], OJ C 398/10, whereby France conceded to open up access to parts of its nuclear power capacities for new market entrants.

41 The answer to the question of whether a project is sustainable or not is facilitated by the provisions of EP and Council Regulation (EU) 2020/852 of 18 June 2020 on the establishment of a framework to facilitate sustainable investment, and amending Regulation (EU) 2019/2088 [2020] OJ L198/13.

42 This has long been established, see ECJ, Case 73/79 *Commission/Italy* (*"sovraprezzo"*) [1980] ECR 1534, para 11.

43 See ECJ, Case C-594/18 P *Austria/Commission* [2020]. It is however a question of one's point of view whether the ECJ confirmed or invented this position. Further on this Merit Olthoff and Andreas von Bonin, 'Das "Hinkley Point"-Urteil des EuGH: Berücksichtigung von Nachhaltigkeitsaspekten in der beihilferechtlichen Prüfung sowie allgemein im EU-Kartell und Fusionskontrollrecht'[2021] EuZW, 181; Birgit Peters [2021] EuZW 83 (note); Jean-Noël Caubet-Hilloutou, 'L'affaire de la centrale nucléaire Hinkley Point, un bouquet d'énergie où économie et environnement tenten de fusionner' (2020) 12 Energie-Environnement-Infrastructures 30; Julius Ecker, 'Das Endurteil Hinkley Point C' in Thomas Jaeger and Birgit Haslinger (eds), *Beihilferecht Jahrbuch 2021* (NWV 2021), 341.

protection and the concept of sustainability as enshrined in art 11 TFEU and art 37 CFR. The obligation to take into consideration environmental aspects exists regardless of whether the aid under scrutiny is targeted at improving sustainability or not.[44]

Yet, as the relevant provisions of EU primary law are of a rather vague and general nature, it is doubtful whether this obligation results in any concrete consequences as far as EU primary law is concerned. It may however result in an obligation of the Commission to deny the approval of state aid in cases where either the principles enshrined art 11 TFEU are clearly violated or, more importantly, where the approval of state aid runs contrary to relevant provisions of secondary EU law aimed at protecting the environment or at fostering sustainability.[45]

At the same time, conversely, the Commission may not approve the grant of state aid by a member state *solely* because it aims to improve or achieve sustainability. This would run against the essence of EU state aid law, whose aim is to protect free market forces from distortions caused by subsidies granted by the member states. Deviations from this guiding principle may only be accepted if the advantages and importance of the goal pursued by the subsidy outweighs the negative impact on the market.[46] There is no exception to this when it comes to state aid granted for environmental protection or the promotion of renewables. The GBER as well as CEEAG do in fact spell out the specific conditions for granting state aid out and thereby try to strike a predetermined balance between environmental protection/sustainability as legitimate object of state aid and the negative impacts this aid has on the internal market.[47] Of course, the Commission may also approve aid solely on grounds of art 107 para 3 (c) TFEU,[48] which gives the Commission discretionary powers to approve aid for certain economic activities including the promotion of renewables. It gives the Commission substantial discretion and thereby also the possibility to deviate from its guidelines, but it may only do so when this is justified by the

---

44 ECJ, Case C-594/18 P *Austria/Commission* [2020], para 44 ff., 100.

45 Cf Christian Wagner, 'Über Århus nach Luxemburg – Neue Rechtsbehelfsmöglichkeiten im Beihilferecht?' [2021] EuZW 817, 818.

46 Cf Vincent Verouden and Philipp Werner, 'Introduction – The Law and Economics of EU State aid Control' in Philipp Werner and Vincent Verouden (eds), *EU State aid Control* (Kluwer 2017), 7, 29, 51–53.

47 Cf CEEAG (n 32), para 23 ff., 77 ff. and, inter alia, art 4 (1) (s) GBER.

48 See Kai Struckmann and Geza Sapi, 'Energy and Environmental Aid' in Philipp Werner and Vincent Verouden (eds), *EU State aid Control* (Kluwer 2017), 663, 691 ff., 715, who also correctly note that the Commission may also approve state aid based on art 106 (2) TFEU (693).

circumstances of the case, for example because the situation at hand is not *exactly* covered by the guidelines. Even then, it will have to pay due regard to the impact of the state aid in question on the internal market.

Summing up, just as sustainability as commonly understood touches upon almost every aspect of daily life, it is needless to say that EU state aid law, which in turn covers almost every aspect of the EU internal economy, is also connected with sustainability. Accordingly, and in line with the overarching provisions of EU primary law concerning environmental protection and sustainability, the Commission has to take into consideration the effects of state aid granted by the member states on these aspects even when the aid in question is unrelated to sustainability. As the primary aim of EU state aid law is the protection of the internal market from distortions caused by subsidies and the like, it is by itself not a means to foster sustainability. Yet, sustainability, being closely linked with environmental considerations, is an objective that may justify the approval of otherwise prohibited state aid, and it is exactly in this regard that sustainability and state aid law are most closely connected. However, and this is of particular importance, sustainability alone and by itself may not justify the granting of state aid.[49]

3 Participation

While the connection between EU state aid law and sustainability might seem hard to identify initially, the opposite is true when it comes to the relationship between EU state aid law and participation. Participation in this context may briefly, and on a very general level be defined as the democratic process of involving stakeholders concerned by a legislative or administrative procedure into the decision-making process by, for example, giving them the opportunity to voice concerns or lay out their position. Depending on the procedure at hand and the stakeholder, participation may also present an opportunity to point to issues of environmental protection and sustainability, notably in the framework of the Aarhus Convention.[50]

Given this, the first and most natural approach to the relationship of participation and state aid law would be to look at the mechanisms of participation intended for provisions of EU derived law relevant for state aid practice. From

49 This is regardless of the provisions of EP and Council Regulation (EU) 2020/852 of 18 June 2020 on the establishment of a framework to facilitate sustainable investment, and amending Regulation (EU) 2019/2088 [2020] OJ L198/13.

50 See further that below 4.

a participatory perspective, state aid regulations may appear to be no different from any other EU secondary law and thus share their fate. However, a closer look at participatory rights as regards state aid regulations reveals that, in fact, the opposite is true.

State aid regulations such as the GBER are quite naturally of major importance not only to member states but also to individual companies. Therefore, the right to be heard for entities concerned by the corresponding regulations would therefore seem close at hand. However, EU law chooses a very different path for state aid regulations: unlike the majority of EU secondary law, state aid regulations are passed in special procedures either by the Council or by the Commission. The Council legislates state aid regulations based on art 109 TFEU and thus in a procedure where even the EP only has a right to be heard. On the other hand, the Commission is conferred legislative powers for state aid in art 108 para 4 TFEU insofar as it has been authorised to do so by Council regulations. These regulations establish an Advisory Committee for state aid that must be heard by the Commission whenever implementing decisions.[51] The Advisory Committee itself does not appear to be a body that could compensate for the lack of a broader participation in the drafting of state aid regulations as it is composed of representatives of the member states and not of members of the general public.[52] Its purpose thus primarily appears to be the facilitation of state aid procedures and their coordination with member states and not so much the establishment of broad participation. At least, "interested parties" are also given the chance to be heard in the drafting of tertiary state aid regulations by the Commission, but they are not accorded any specific rights beyond that which could make up for the generally limited participation of the public insofar as sustainability is concerned.[53]

This limitation of participatory rights also applies when it comes to the Commission's state aid guidelines, which, as set out above, play a very important role in guiding the Commission's state aid practice even though they are not formally binding:[54] it is true that when these guidelines are drafted or revised, the respective stakeholders are regularly consulted. Accordingly, during the

51 Art 7 ff. Council Regulation (EU) 2015/1588 of 13 July 2015 on the application of Articles 107 and 108 of the Treaty on the Functioning of the European Union to certain categories of horizontal State aid (codification) [2015] OJ L248/1.

52 Art 7 Council Regulation (EU) 2015/1588 (n 52).

53 Cf art 6 Council Regulation (EU) 2015/1588 (n 52).

54 ECJ, Case C-288/96 *Germany/Commission* [2000] ECR I-8237, para 62 and more recently ECJ, Case C-439/11 P *Ziegler SA/Commission* [2013], para 59. Further on the relevance of Commission guidelines particularly in state aid procedures Jörg Gundel, 'Der prozessuale Status der Beihilfenleitlinien der EU-Kommission' [2016] EuZW 606.

consultation for the evaluation of the EEAG 2014–2020, the Commission also sought and collected the opinion of NGOs concerned with environmental questions and questions of sustainability.[55] However, the consultation of third parties at this level is not mandated by higher ranking EU law but rather an informal procedure that the Commission might abandon just as well. While third parties nevertheless have the opportunity to participate during the drafting of state aid *regulations*, it seems difficult to characterise this mere possibility as a satisfactory form of participation from a legal point of view, as this position is not enforceable.

The situation is, however, different when one turns to individual state aid procedures. This difference results from the fact that regardless of the object of a subsidy, whenever the Commission investigates the compatibility of state aid, the investigation *may* amount to a formal administrative procedure.[56] This aspect is of crucial importance for the existence and extent of participatory rights granted in state aid procedures: just as in every other branch of EU law, this entails the applicability of EU law's provisions on administrative procedures, whose core is now enshrined in 41 CFR.[57] The procedural rights set out in art 41 CFR include, *inter alia*, the right to be heard when one's rights are impeded by the procedure at hand; being rooted in art 41 CFR or general principles, the right to be heard in formal administrative procedures is not particular to state aid law.

What is particular to EU state aid law, however, is that while state aid procedures formally only concern the Commission and the member state granting the aid, there is in fact usually at least a triangular relationship between the member state granting the aid, the company/entity receiving the aid and the competitors of the latter. As selectivity is inherent to the notion of state aid, this implies that there are individuals or companies who are not recipients of state aid and accordingly may be disadvantaged by the granting of aid to its recipient. Because of this, the participatory rights mentioned above – especially the right to be heard – not only regularly concern the

---

55 Cf https://ec.europa.eu/competition-policy/public-consultations/2021-ceeag_en.

56 Even when a measure duly notified by a member state to the Commission amounts to state aid, this is not necessarily followed by the initiation of formal state aid procedure, cf. art 108 (3) TFEU, art 4 (3) Council Regulation (EU) 2015/1589 of 13 July 2015 laying down detailed rules for the application of Article 108 of the Treaty on the Functioning of the European Union (codification) [2015] OJ L 248/9.

57 Unlike in most other areas of the CFR, the corresponding preexisting general principles are still of particular importance for the member states and procedures conducted by the member states, cf. ECJ, Case C-419/14 *WebMindLicenses* [2015], para 83 ff.; ECJ, Case C-521/15 *Spain/Council* [2017], paras 61, 88 ff.

recipient of state aid and the member state granting the state aid, but also extend to third parties. Accordingly, art 6 (1), art 1 (h), art 24 (1) of the regulation on state aid procedures[58] expressly grants so-called "interested parties" the right to be heard, yet they do not – for example – have a right to access the files of the state aid procedure;[59] in this context, interested parties are all those whose interests may be affected by the state aid in question, the interest thus necessarily being of an economic nature.[60]

However, although the aforementioned right to be heard is limited to the *formal* investigation procedure,[61] during the preliminary and informal examination procedure, the granting of these participatory rights is not mandatory.[62] To compensate for this lack of participation in the preliminary procedure, third parties may initiate proceedings against the Commission's decision not to initiate a formal procedure before the EU courts claiming a violation of their right to be heard: otherwise, they would not be able to enforce their right to be heard. This point cannot be stressed enough, as it illustrates that actual participation, or the right hereto are closely linked with the possibility of initiating legal proceedings.[63]

To conclude, it seems fair to say that while the possibilities for formal participation at the level of rule-making in EU state aid law seem quite limited, they are somewhat broader at the level of individual state aid procedures. This is, however, not due to the fact that EU state aid law would be particular generous when it comes to participatory rights, but rather a result of the multitude of actors usually concerned by state aid procedures. Even where third parties are accorded participatory rights in state aid law, these are usually limited to the right to be heard.

4 Sustainability, Participation and EU State Aid Law: Triangulation (Im)possible?

As set out above, state aid law does not contain specific participatory rights for stakeholders or what one may also call 'advocates of sustainability': just as with

58 See n 56.

59 See for example EU General Court, Case T-168/17 CBA *Spielapparate- und Restaurantbetriebs GmbH* [2019]; further on the position of recipients of State aid Ludger Giesberts and Michael Gayger, 'Kein Akteneinsichtsrecht des Beihilfenempfängers?' [2019] EuZW 669.

60 See below n 65.

61 See Art 6 (1) of the regulation on state aid procedures [n 56].

62 See for example ECJ, Case C-198/91 *Cook/Commission* [1993] ECR I-2487, para 22 ff.

63 See for example ECJ, Case C-367/95 P *Commission/Sytravel* [1998] ECR I-1719, para 40.

other stakeholders, the relevant stakeholders in the field of sustainability are only accorded very limited means of participation in regard of general state aid regulations. It may, therefore, be assumed that, at least based on EU primary law, the link between sustainability and participation in state aid law is generally rather weak. Even though participation of advocates of sustainability may have an impact on state aid rules and their application, their influence is necessarily limited to "soft power", which may be of great political relevance, but is mostly irrelevant from a legal point of view. Moreover, even when considering the fact that the Commission must pay due regard to art 11 TFEU,[64] the influence of advocates of sustainability does not – again from a legal point of view – appear to be a determining factor in the Commission's decision practice.

Based on general EU law and notwithstanding the provisions of the Aarhus Convention, the link between sustainability and participation seems to be slightly stronger where EU Law grants third parties specific participatory rights in EU state aid law procedures. As the Commission has to pay due regard to art 11 TFEU regardless of whether the aid at hand is targeted at bolstering environmental protection, one might assume that third parties may generally challenge Commission decisions authorising state aid on grounds of incompatibility with art 11 TFEU. However, regardless of whether the Commission decides to initiate a formal investigation procedure or not, because of the rationale of state aid law, the status of interested party presupposes that the economic interests of the party in question are affected.[65]

Therefore, a third party only has to be consulted and therefore only is an interested party in state aid procedures when its economic interests are affected by the Commission's decision. Conversely, this implies that by itself, the fact that a third *party's* non-economic interests are adversely affected by a decision authorising state aid, is not sufficient to establish its role as participant in state aid procedures.[66] Accordingly, mere advocates of sustainability such as NGOs are not considered third parties in state aid procedures and are, therefore, currently in all likelihood barred from challenging state aid authorisations based

64 See above n 43 ff.

65 Cf art 1 (h) of the regulation on state aid procedures [n 56], whereby "interested party means (...) *in particular* the beneficiary of the aid, *competing undertakings and trade associations*." (My italics). See also, and with an emphasis on the requirements imposed by art 263 (4) TFEU, ECJ, Case C-640/16 P *Greenpeace Energy and others/Commission* [2017], para 38. This has recently also been pointed out by the EU General Court, Case T-777/19 *CAPA* [2021], paras 88 ff.

66 Cf recital 37 of the regulation on state aid procedures [n 56]: Commission as "defender" of public interest before *national* courts, whereas there is no mention of public interest in this regulation in other places.

on their alleged incompatibility with substantive EU law in court. They *may,* however, become interested third parties and thus have participatory rights to the extent that they are also active in the market and the aid at hand may have an impact on their market position, as highlighted in the *Green Peace Energy* case, where the EU courts made it clear that the requirements for challenging state aid *could* generally be met by *Green Peace Energy,* but were not met by the applicants in the respective cases.[67]

However, and this is important to stress, even when an entity and more precisely a third party is considered an interested party and is thus accorded procedural rights, this does *not necessarily* imply that it might challenge state aid authorisations on grounds of substantive law and thus art 11 TFEU. While every interested party may challenge Commission decisions on grounds of violation of their procedural rights as set out before, challenging the state aid decisions on substantial grounds and, therefore, violation of EU environmental law requires the interested party to be "individually concerned" in the sense of art 263 (4) TFEU as well, and the CJEUs definition of individual concern traditionally is rather narrow.[68] While it may be safe to say that everyone who is individually concerned by a state aid decision is at the same time an interested party, the opposite is not true.[69] Therefore, even when the Commission would authorize state aid in flagrant contempt of art 11 TFEU and even pertinent secondary law, an interested party other than a member state, who may challenge the Commission decision without having to meet special procedural requirements, would not be able to successfully challenge this decision *solely* based on an alleged violation of environmental protection regulations unless it could somehow establish that it is individually concerned. This seems hard to imagine unless its procedural rights in the specific state aid procedure have been violated.[70] Accordingly, general procedural law further narrows the group of possible applicants who might substantially challenge state aid decisions.

---

67 EU General Court, Case T-382/15 *Greenpeace Energy and others/Commission* [2016], where of course the standing of the applicants was denied by the General court, whose decision was however upheld by the ECJ, see ECJ, Case C-640/16 P (n 65).

68 See for example in the specific context of state aid and sustainability EU General Court, Case T-382/15 (n 67) and ECJ, Case 640/16 P (n 65). This is also true for the rules Intervention of third parties in pending proceedings, see Juliette Delarue and Sebastian D. Bechtel, "Access to justice in state aid: how recent legal developments are opening ways to challenge Commission state aid decisions that may breach EU environmental law" (2021) 22 ERA Forum, 253, 259 ff.

69 EU General Court, Case T-382/15 (n 67), para 39.

70 Cf. EU General Court, Case T-777/19 (n 65), para 96, whereby an association of fishermen is not considered to be immediately affected by a Commission decision authorizing state aid for renewable energy production solely because the establishment of offshore wind

At first, the picture may appear to be completely different if one takes into account the provisions of the Aarhus Convention[71] that have been implemented into EU law by the according Aarhus regulation.[72] Put briefly, the Aarhus Convention requires its members, including the EU, to fulfill requests by the public for information in administrative proceedings dealing with environmental matters.[73] Additionally, according to art 9 (3) of the Aarhus Convention, members of the public including NGOs as prime stakeholders of sustainability may challenge administrative acts on grounds that they were made in breach of the relevant national environmental law. Therefore, the Aarhus rules may appear to override the procedural limitations imposed to the challenging of EU state aid decisions pointed out above, establishing a strong link between sustainability and participation in EU state aid law as well.

On the one hand, it has to be noted that firstly, the Aarhus Convention does not apply to *legislative* and *judicial* procedures even where they are explicitly relating to environmental law,[74] meaning that, inter alia state aid *regulations,* as opposed to individual state aid procedures and so on, may not be challenged on grounds of the Aarhus Convention.[75]

On the other hand, however, one could assume that third parties and especially NGOs might be able to challenge state aid decisions concerned with environmental aspects based on art 9 (3) of the Aarhus Convention, which stipulates that "members of the public have access to administrative or judicial procedures to challenge [by] public authorities which contravene provisions of its national law relating to the environment.". Even though this provision may appear to override the restrictions imposed by art 263 (4) TFEU,[76] EU

power might have an impact on fishing grounds because the impact depends on numerous factors not covered by the Commission's decision.

71 Convention on Access to Information, Public participation in Decision-Making and Access to Justice in Environmental Matters, entered into force 30 October 2001, 2161 UNTS 447.

72 EP and Council Regulation (EC) 1367/2006 of 6 September 2006 on the application of the provisions of the Aarhus Convention on Access to Information, Public participation in Decision-making and Access to Justice in Environmental Matters to Community institutions and bodies [2006] OJ L264/13.

73 See art 4 of the Aarhus Convention (n 71).

74 Cf art 2 of the Aarhus Convention (n 71).

75 However, art 2 (1) c) of the Aarhus regulation (n 72) gives the public a right to access environmental information even where this information is produced in legislative procedures.

76 See Juliette Delarue and Sebastian D. Bechtel, 'Access to justice in state aid: how recent legal developments are opening ways to challenge Commission state aid decisions that may breach EU environmental law' (2021) 22 ERA Forum 253, 262 ff.

law explicitly exempts state aid decisions[77] from the application of Aarhus rules.[78] This exemption is based on the assumption that in state aid procedures, the Commission acts as a review body whose decisions are similar to that of the judiciary[79] and therefore fall outside the scope of the Aarhus Convention.[80] Even though this has been criticised by the Aarhus Compliance Committee,[81] the recent amendment of the Aarhus regulation has not profoundly changed this. While the rights of, for example, NGOs have been somewhat extended, the provisions of the Aarhus regulation exempting state aid procedures from *public* scrutiny have not been affected by this amendment.[82]

Regardless of whether the exception of state aid procedures from the Aarhus regulation is in line with the commitments undertaken within the framework of the Aarhus Convention and if its specific provisions on judicial review (i.e. art 9 (3) of the Aarhus Convention) produce direct effect, even the inclusion of state aid procedures into the Aarhus-based procedures would most likely not be a game changer. While this would also enable third parties to challenge state aid even when they are not economically affected by the decision at hand, they could only do so successfully if they meet the criteria set out in EU legislation and especially when the Commission's decision is actually in breach of pertinent provisions, and not only the spirit of EU environmental rules, which should rarely be the case.[83]

---

77 For a recent example of the relevance of the Aarhus Convention in proceedings before the EU courts see EU General Court, Case T-9/19 *ClientEarth/EIB* [2021], para 126.

78 Cf art 2 (2) EP and Council Regulation (EC) 1367/2006 of 6 September 2006 (n 72).

79 See the position of the Commission in Aarhus Compliance Committee, Findings and recommendations with regard to communication ACCC/2015/128 concerning compliance by the European Union of 17 march 2021, ECE/MP.PP/C.1/2021/21, <https://unece.org/sites/default/files/2021-10/ECE_MP.PP_C.1_2021_21_E.pdf> last accessed 09 August 2022, para 52.

80 Cf art 2 of the Aarhus Convention (n 71).

81 See Aarhus Compliance Committee, Findings and recommendations with regard to communication ACCC/2015/128 (...) of 17 March 2021 (n 79).

82 See EP and Council Regulation (EU) 2021/1767 of 6 October 2021 amending Regulation (EC) No 1367/2006 on the application of the provisions of the Aarhus Convention on Access to Information, Public participation in Decision-making and Access to Justice in Environmental Matters to Community institutions and bodies [2021] OJ L356/1 and Christian Wagner, 'Über Århus nach Luxemburg – Neue Rechtsbehelfsmöglichkeiten im Beihilferecht?' [2021]EuZW 817 ff.

83 This has already been highlighted by Christian Wagner, 'Über Århus nach Luxemburg – Neue Rechtsbehelfsmöglichkeiten im Beihilferecht?' [2021]EuZW 817, 818; Birgit Peters [2021] EuZW 83 (note); see also Julius Ecker, 'Das Endurteil Hinkley Point C' in Thomas Jaeger and Birgit Haslinger (eds), *Beihilferecht Jahrbuch 2021* (NWV 2021), 341, 359.

5 Conclusion

While it is hard to perceive sustainability as the primary object of state aid law, it certainly is an important objective that may justify the granting of state aid. Accordingly, state aid aimed at promoting sustainability such as state aid granted for renewable energy production, may be authorised by the Commission. While this possibility is not limited to state aid granted for projects aimed at promoting sustainability, given the importance of sustainability in the EUs general policy, such aid tends to be authorised easier.

However, there currently are no specific mechanisms in EU state aid law allowing for participation in state aid procedures in ways that promote sustainability by, for example, giving NGOs a specific right to be heard. Even though, while in state aid procedures, third parties will probably be affected more often than in other branches of EU Law, and thus will have to be accorded participatory rights. The status of interested third party is dependent on the third party being affected economically by the state aid procedure at hand, usually meaning that the third party has to be a competitor of the company receiving the aid. And even where this is the case, given the state of EU law and ECJ jurisdiction, and notwithstanding the fact that this might be in contravention of the Aarhus Convention, it seems hard to imagine that a third party may challenge a Commission decision authorising state aid solely based on the fact that the decision in question is in disregard of EU environmental law, as there would have to be a clear breach of the corresponding rules.

While the link between sustainability and participation therefore currently seems to be rather weak in the context of EU state aid procedures, the increasing focus on sustainability in EU politics[84] may also lead to an extension of corresponding participatory rights for the general public. This may in turn also lead to an extension of the possibilities of challenging state aid decisions before EU courts. On the one hand, this appears to be the most promising avenue for the enforcement of sustainability rules, but on the other hand, risks placing a, maybe unduly, heavy burden on state aid procedures since both worlds have long been separated.[85] Thus, given the current state of the relevant provisions, they might in the end collide in a way that neither would profit from. Therefore, notwithstanding the question whether such an extension seems

84 See Communication from the Commission "The European Green Deal", COM(2019) 640 final [2019] of 11 December 2019 and more on that Rainer Luktis, 'Der europäische Grüne Deal' in Thomas Jaeger and Birgit Haslinger (eds), *Beihilferecht Jahrbuch 2021* (NWV 2021), 317.

85 Cf Julius Ecker, 'Das Endurteil Hinkley Point C' in Thomas Jaeger and Birgit Haslinger (eds), *Beihilferecht Jahrbuch 2021* (NWV 2021), 341, 358 ff.

desirable, specific attention should be paid to the risk that an uncoordinated 'collision' of these spheres might pose, making a timely intervention by the EU legislator desirable.

Bibliography

Delarue J, and Bechtel SD, "Access to justice in State aid: how recent legal developments are opening ways to challenge Commission State aid decisions that may breach EU environmental law" (2021) 22 ERA Forum, 253.

Ecker J, "Das Endurteil Hinkley Point C" in Jaeger T, and Haslinger B, (eds), *Beihilferecht Jahrbuch 2021* (NWV 2021), 341.

EU General court, Case T-382/15 Greenpeace Energy and others/Commission [2016].

EU General Court, Case T-777/19 CAPA [2021].

ECJ, Case C-594/18 P Austria/Commission [2020].

Peiffert O, *L'application du droit des aides d'État aux mesures de protection de l'environnement* (Bruylant 2015).

Struckmann K, and Sapi G, "Energy and Environmental Aid", in Werner P, and Verouden V, (eds), *EU State aid Control* (Kluwer 2017), 663.

CHAPTER 9

Competition Law

Sustainability Through Competition and Participation

Matthias Uffer

1 Introduction

The prohibitions of cartels in art 101 of the Treaty on the Functioning of the European Union (TFEU) and of abusive behaviour by dominant firms in art 102 TFEU provide, along with the EU Merger Control and State Aid Regulation, the core of EU competition law. The primary aim of EU competition law is to preserve and promote economic efficiency and thereby foster consumer welfare by fighting conduct that is harmful to competition, whether static or dynamic (innovation driven).[1] Moreover, competition is seen as necessary to fully implement the EU Internal Market (cf art 3(3) of the Treaty on European Union (TEU)). In spite of a focus over the last 25 years on economics, sustainability concerns are increasingly entering the equation of competition law.[2]

1 Cf Svend Albæk, 'Consumer Welfare in EU Competition policy' in Caroline Heide-Jørgensen *et al* (eds), *Aims and Values in Competition Law* (DJØF Publishing 2013); Joaquín Almunia, 'Competition and consumers: the future of EU competition policy' (SPEECH/10/233,European Competition Day, Madrid, 12 May 2010) <https://ec.europa.eu/commission/presscorner/api/files/document/print/en/speech_10_233/SPEECH_10_233_EN.pdf> last accessed 26 September 2022; Marino Baldi and Felix Schraner, '20 Jahre – und kein bisschen weiter? Zum wettbewerbspolitischen Verständnis von Art. 5 Kartellgesetz' (2015) 11 AJP 1529.

2 Giorgio Monti, 'Four options for a greener competition law' (2020) 11 Journal of European Competition Law & Practice 124; Murco Mijnlieff, 'Draft Guidelines on Sustainability Agreements – Opportunities within competition law', (Autoriteit Consument & Markt (ACM), 26 January 2021) <www.acm.nl/en/publications/guidelines-sustainability-agreements-are-ready-further-european-coordination> last accessed 20 August 2022), regarding proposals by the Dutch competition authority; cf Studienvereinigung Kartellrecht, 'Stellungnahme der Studienvereinigung Kartellrecht e.V. im Rahmen der Öffentlichen Konsultation der Europäischen Kommission über "Wettbewerbspolitik des Grünen Deals" (20 November 2020) <www.studienvereinigung.de/publikationen/stellungnahmen> last accessed 20 August 2022; Suzanne Kingston, 'Integrating environmental protection and EU competition law: Why competition isn't special' (2010) 16 ELJ 780; Andreas Heinemann, 'Nachhaltigkeitsvereinbarungen' (2021) 5 sic! Zeitschrift für Immaterialgüter-, Informations- und Wettbewerbsrecht 213; Mathias Kyrklund, 'EU Competition Policy and the Environment: The Role of Environmental considerations under Article 101 TFEU' (Thesis in Competition Law, Uppsala Universitet 2020) <www.diva-portal.org/smash/get/diva2:1387072/FULLTEXT01.pdf> last accessed 1 August

DOI:10.1163/9789004509382_011

The form in which they are taken into account still awaits further clarification by competition authorities and case law. Participation is important here for two principal reasons. First, in the sense of private actors' abilities to freely engage in professional activities and thus contribute to market efficiency by competing on the merits of the products or services they provide. Second, it is also important as a provider of legitimacy.

2 Definitions and Preliminary Considerations

2.1 *Cartel Prohibition and Abuse of Dominance*

The cartel prohibition of art 101 TFEU bans agreements and concerted practices among undertakings which restrict competition.[3] In cases of *by object* restrictions such as horizontal price-fixing, a harm to competition is considered obvious based on the very nature and purpose of the agreement, so no detailed examination of anti-competitive effects is required. Restrictions *by effect*, in turn, require a full analysis of the likely consequences and proof by the competition authority that the agreement appreciably restricts competition for the cartel-prohibition of art 101(1) TFEU to be applied. In by object cases, harm to competition is presumed.[4] A restrictive agreement might be granted an exemption on efficiency grounds pursuant to art 101(3) TFEU if it does not harm competition on balance due to its contribution to improving the production or distribution of products or to technical progress, provided that the affected consumers get a fair share of the benefits.[5]

The abuse of a dominant position[6] prohibited by art 102 TFEU consists in particular in the conduct of a firm (or firms) with significant market power which restricts the capability of efficient rivals to compete.[7]

2022; Andrea Pezza, 'The European Green Deal: shaping environmentally friendly policies under Article 101 TFEU' (2020) 4 M & CLR 139; cf also OECD Roundtable, 'Sustainability and Competition' (OECD December 2020), documents available under: <www.oecd.org/daf/competition/sustainability-and-competition.htm> last accessed 20 August 2022; Maarten Pieter Schinkel and Lukas Toth, 'Balancing the Public Interest-Defense in Cartel Offenses' (2017) Amsterdam Law School Legal Studies Research Paper No. 2016-05.

3 Art 101 (1) TFEU also requires that the agreement is capable of appreciably affecting trade within the EEA, a criterion delimiting its application from otherwise equivalent national provisions; moreover, the provision also explicitly bans "*decisions by associations of undertakings*" with such effects.

4 Cf Case C-226/11 *Expedia Inc. v Autorité de la concurrence and Others* (2012) OJ C 38/6.

5 Matthias Uffer, 'Competition law', in this book, chapter d.(5) sec 4.

6 Ibid, sec 5.

7 Cf Case 27/76 *United Brands Co and United Brands Continental BV v Commission* (1978) 1 CMLR 429: a "*dominant position*" according to Article 102 TFEU is a "*position of economic strength*

2.2 *Environmental Sustainability*

The idea of sustainability and the concept of sustainable development are typically considered to encompass an environmental, an economic and a social dimension. By promoting economic efficiency and consumer welfare (eg quality, lower prices, variety, and innovation), competition law favours economic sustainability. Insofar as competition law enforcement benefits consumers and safeguards the economic freedom of smaller market actors in the face of abusive conduct of powerful rivals, it also benefits social sustainability.[8] Further, competition law naturally benefits environmental sustainability in several ways, in particular via technological developments or resource-efficiency, both of which are typical features of a well-functioning, undistorted competitive market. Some types of sustainability benefits of products or services can furthermore be something that firms directly compete about, provided that a sufficient number of customers values the characteristics in question.[9] That said, until recently environmental sustainability has hardly ever been an explicit antitrust concern. That is likely to change, as discussed below:[10]

A typical feature of contemporary competition law is its quest for purity, which leaves it mostly unresponsive to expectations emanating from public interests unrelated to market efficiency.[11] That is not unreasonable. It helps prevent a politicisation of antitrust law and mitigates the risk of over- and under-enforcement based on ideological grounds. There are several examples of noble-aimed restrictions of competition law which resulted in great damage

---

8 *enjoyed by an undertaking which enables it to prevent effective competition being maintained on the relevant market by affording it the power to behave to an appreciable extent independently of its competitors, customers and ultimately of its consumers".*
Cf Kyrklund, n 2, at 59; Heinemann, n 2, at 215, pointing out that there can only be a presumption of a nexus between the price-damping function of competition and harm to the environment if no price is paid for the consumption of environmental goods; Lars Lundgren, 'A competitive environment? Articles 101 and 102 TFEU and the European Green Deal' (Uppsala Universitet 2021) Master's Thesis; Cento Veljanovski, 'The Case against Green Antitrust'(2022) European Competition Journal, <https://doi.org/10.1080/17441056.2022.2056346> last accessed 26 September 2022; Katharina Biely and Steven van Passel, 'Market power and sustainability: a new research agenda' (2022) 3 Discover Sustainability, <https://link.springer.com/article/10.1007/s43621-022-00073-y> last accessed 26 September 2022.

9 Heinemann, n 2, at 215; Jeffrey G York, 'Pragmatic Sustainability: Translating Environmental Ethics into Competitive Advantage' (2009) 85 Journal of Business Ethics 97.

10 Uffer, n 5, sec 2, 4 and 5.

11 Cf for instance Rupprecht Podszun, 'Ausserwettbewerbliche Interessen im Kartellrecht und ihre Grenzen' in Juliane Kokott, Petra Pohlmann, Romina Polley (eds), *Europäisches, deutsches und internationales Kartellrecht - Festschrift Dirk Schroeder* (Otto Schmidt 2018); Schinkel and Toth, n 2.

to economic efficiency, but also to society and the noble aims supposedly pursued in the first place. For example, the National Industrial Recovery Act 1933 exempted several industry sectors from US antitrust law, provided that the undertakings raised wages and accepted collective bargaining with independent labour unions. The ensuing legalised collusion over prices and quantities led to increased steel and wholesale prices, stifled product innovation and finally resulted in more unemployment, the exact opposite of what the Act sought to achieve.[12] Another example of expensive failure are the policies which led to the current structure of the European gas- and energy-market (ie excessive tolerance of increased concentration particularly by one behemoth (Gazprom) with a history of abuses and an origin in an illiberal autocracy which doesn't value economic liberty and participation. In several European states, governments tolerated growing concentrations on their domestic markets resulting in the creation of vertically integrated national 'champions'). By virtue of their increased bargaining power vis-à-vis global suppliers, at times it was hoped that the big dominant firms would be able to get better conditions.[13] However, on the gas market, the result was increasing dependence from Gazprom, the dominant supplier controlled by the Russian government, which has frequently used its position to engage in various instances of abuses of dominance and other anti-competitive behaviour (not to speak of its involvement in hybrid wars).[14] In spite of the hard evidence of the unreliability of both Gazprom and its owner, certain European politicians nevertheless tirelessly argued that even closer gas ties with Russia, through Nordstream 2 in particular, would benefit not just the economy and consumers but also contribute to peace, encourage Russia to become a less oppressive state and benefit the environment.[15] This evolution of the European gas- and energy-market was in part rushed through via political decisions and against the concerns

12 John D Harkrider, 'Lessons from the Great Depression' (2009) 23 Antitrust 6; cf Veljanovski, n 8 with further reference.

13 The opposite is true: Competition would have increased incentives to diversify suppliers, which would have kept prices lower and Europe safer.

14 C 128/15 *Polskie Górnictwo Naftowe i Gazownictwo v Commission* (*Commitments by Gazprom*) (2022) OJ C 128/15, The EU General Court dismisses the action brought against the Commission's decision to make a gas company's commitments binding in order to address competition concerns in relation to the national markets for the upstream wholesale supply of gas in eastern and central Europe (Gazprom), (a years-long investigation ended in 2018 with a commitment decision)

15 The latter because of the theory that gas could become a driver of the transition towards a climate-neutral economy through its possible role in the scaling up of hydrogen.

of competition authorities (eg the merger of Ruhrgas and E.ON, allowed via a ministerial decision).[16]

Such experiences illustrate why competition law's quest for (economic) purity should not just be substituted by a balancing of all conceivable public benefits and detriments in the assessment of restrictions of competition or efficiency-based justifications thereof.[17] However, even though sustainability as such is too broad and abstract a concept[18] by itself to build the basis of a practicable exception to that rule, there are some environmental effects which should be taken into account.[19] Those include reducing greenhouse gases (GHG) emissions and the prevention and removal of environmentally toxic waste (eg plastic in the oceans), tasks that deserve special consideration for three reasons. First, their impact can be measured objectively and ascribed an economic value.[20] Second, they affect the conditions and the quality of (human) life more significantly than most other specific economic or non-economic outcomes of antitrust enforcement, due to the wide, sometimes global reach of environmental damages and in part their irreversibility.[21] Third, the Treaty demands environmental considerations within competition law.[22] Taking non-speculative and not merely symbolic sustainability benefits into account under art 101 or 102 TFEU[23] therefore does not imply that all types of public interests should be balanced against economic effects and efficiencies,[24] something most experts rightly and firmly oppose.[25]

---

16 Der Spiegel, 4.7.2002, Herbe Kritik an der Ministererlaubnis; cf. FAZ, 1.5.2022, Gazprom: Fusion von Eon und Ruhrgas und die Folgen, <www.faz.net/aktuell/wirtschaft/gazprom-fusion-von-eon-und-ruhrgas-und-die-folgen-17990639.html> last accessed 1 August 2022.

17 Cf Podszun, n 11, at 628.

18 Schinkel and Toth, n 2, at 5.

19 Cf Kyrklund,n 2, at 69–101; Suzanne Kingston, *Greening EU Competition Law and Policy* (CUP 2011); Pezza, n 2, at 140.

20 That is, they can be (Pezza, n 2, at 157) "*translated into economic efficiencies*" which makes them usable in determining consumer welfare, i.e. through an "*economisation of environmental benefits*" (Hans Vedder, Competition Law and Environmental Protection in Europe: Towards Sustainability? The Netherlands, Europa Law Publishing, 2003, 321).

21 Cf Kingston, n 19.

22 Cf Uffer, n 5, sec 4.3.1.

23 Uffer, n 5, sec 2–5.

24 Cf Heinemann, n 2, at 218; Ernst-Joachim Mestmäcker und Heike Schweitzer, *Europäisches Wettbewerbsrecht* (C.H. Beck 2014).

25 Legal uncertainty and political discretion are the main concerns, cf Okeoghene Odudu, 'The Boundaries of EC Competition Law: The Scope of Article 81' (OUP 2006); Schinkel and Toth, n 2, at 26 (also arguing in p5 that a broad public interest-defence would impose an excessive burden on competition authorities, which would have to engage in a "*complex*

2.3 *Participation*

Competition law protects efficient competition and the freedom to pursue professional activities (economic liberty), and thereby also promotes the participation of a plurality of market actors in economic life. In that sense, functioning, competitive markets are democratic institutions.[26] Conversely, high concentrations of market power typically entail significant risks of restrictions of competition and thus of harm to consumer and social welfare.[27] Competition authorities can mitigate such risks by obliging firms which control key infrastructure (including pipelines, electricity grids, and telecommunication networks) or widely indispensable platforms (eg Google's Android)[28] to grant smaller rivals access to fair and reasonable conditions. Moreover, citizen and consumer involvement in shaping market values can create incentives for sustainability efforts and thus increase the likelihood that a functioning, competitive market contributes to environmental sustainability.[29]

Political participation in its broad sense is also important as a legitimising basis of competition law.[30] The need for legitimacy through public discourse

---

monitoring and balancing task"); Podszun n 11, at 622; Baldi and Schraner, n 1, at 1535; Heinemann, n 2, at 222, 225.

26 Podszun, n 11, at 632, stating that the markets themselves are democratic institutions, and competition law protects their functioning. Cf, regarding the importance of market access and market power in antitrust assessments, Carles Esteva Mosso, 'The Contribution of Merger Control to the Definition of Harm to Competition' (March 2016) <https://ec.europa.eu/competition/speeches/text/sp2016_03_en.pdf> last accessed 1 August 2022).

27 That assumption is largely consistent with the competition law theory of the Harvard School, which unlike its more intervention-sceptic rival (Chicago School) argues that there is a necessity to preserve certain market structures which it sees as per se pro-competitive, and thus to limit tendencies of increased market concentration cf Carl Baudenbacher, 'Markt und Wettbewerb in der Rechtsprechung des EFTA-Gerichtshofs', in Juliane Kokott, Petra Pohlmann and Romina Polley (eds), *Europäisches, deutsches und internationals Kartellrecht – Festschrift für Dirk Schroeder* (Otto Schmidt 2018).

28 Cf Bundeskartellamt, 'Google: Feststellung der überragenden marktübergreifenden Bedeutung für den Wettbewerb' (Fallbericht, 5 January 2022) <www.bundeskartellamt.de/SharedDocs/Entscheidung/DE/Fallberichte/Missbrauchsaufsicht/2022/B7-61-21.pdf?__blob=publicationFile&v=7> last accessed 10 October 2022, declares Android […], as "Infrastrukturcharakter".

29 Alex Bruce and Thomas Faunce, 'Sustainable fuel, food, fertilizer and ecosystems through a global artificial photosynthetic system: overcoming anticompetitive barriers' (2015) 5 Interface Focus, http://dx.doi.org/10.1098/rsfs.2015.0011 last accessed 1 August 2022.

30 Cf Bruno S Frey and Gebhard Kirchgässner, *Demokratische Wirtschaftspolitik* (Vahlen 2002); Sarah Beeston, 'Competition Law and Sustainability Initiatives', in Juliane Kokott, Petra Pohlmann and Romina Polley (eds), *Europäisches, deutsches und internationals Kartellrecht – Festschrift für Dirk Schroeder* (Otto Schmidt 2018), referring to the evolution of

and public support has repeatedly been emphasised in the debate about the need for sustainability objectives to be taken into account by antitrust authorities.[31] In that regard, most experts apparently agree that there is no need for new legislative acts (let alone a Treaty amendment) in order for a more sustainability-oriented enforcement-approach to be possible.[32] Public consultation procedures, which help gather the views of stakeholders and the wider public, or consumer surveys regarding the willingness to pay higher prices for certain environmental measures can also serve legitimacy. However, amendments to antitrust regulations might nevertheless be the chosen strategy of some Member States in imposing a more sustainability-oriented antitrust enforcement.[33] The possibility for environmental objectives to be achieved by new (public) climate regulations is of some importance in assessing the justifications of private initiatives which restrict competition, due to the requirement that an otherwise prohibited agreement (art 101 TFEU) or exclusionary conduct (art 102 TFEU) be indispensable (cf art 101(3) lit a TFEU) to reach the objectives pursued. For instance, if a new climate regulation is better because it does not create opportunities for collusion or greenwashing, then antitrust exemptions are not warranted.[34] That said, the slow pace of legislation or the unlikeliness of a theoretically better regulation can render sustainability initiatives temporarily indispensable and thus lawful.[35]

---

the Dutch competition law, which is much committed to the "*ideal of social participation and social responsibility*" (ibid, at 125); Aandreas Glaser, *Nachhaltige Entwicklung und Demokratie*, (Mohr Siebeck 2006).

31 Cf Podszun, n 11, at 622–623; Baudenbacher, n 27, at 78.

32 Pezza, n 2, at 139–141; Kyrklund, n 2, at 54, 57, 61; cf Podszun, n 11, at 624.

33 A case in point is Austria's recent (2021) amendment to its cartel act, which widened the possibilities of justifications for sustainability agreements by introducing a presumption of consumer compensation by agreements which "*contribute substantially to an ecologically sustainable or climate-neutral economy*" (cf Uffer, n 5, sec 4.2.3), see: Federal Law amending the Cartel Act 2005 and the Competition Act, BGBL. I No. 176/2021 (KaWeRÄG); cf also Austria's written note on 'Environmental Considerations in Competition Enforcement' submitted on behalf of the 136th OECD Competition Committee meeting on 1–3 December 2021, available on www.oecd.org/daf/competition/environmental-considerations-in-competition-enforcement.htm last accessed 10 October 2022. Cf Austrian Federal Competition Authority (FCA), 'Draft Sustainability Guidelines', 1 June 2022, <www.bwb.gv.at/en/news/news-2022/detail/afca-publishes-draft-guidelines-on-the-application-sustainability-agreements-asking-for-comments> last accessed 10 October 2022.

34 Cf Schinkel and Toth, n 2, at 27.

35 Christopher Townley, *Article 81 EC and Public Policy* (Hart Publishing 2010); Pezza, n 2, at 146.

3 Sustainability through a Limitation of Article 101(1) TFEU?

3.1 Exemptions of Sustainability Agreements from Competition Law?

A radical proposal to boost the importance of environmental concerns in the context of antitrust enforcement consists in declaring art 101(1) TFEU (inherently) inapplicable to agreements that benefit environmental sustainability.[36] The rationale of such an inherent limitation of art 101 (1) TFEU is often seen in a resolution of a conflict of Treaty objectives in favour of "*a high level of protection and improvement of the quality of the environment*" (art 3(3) TEU). Given the equal primary law basis[37] and the potential weight of environmental damages, the idea of an inherent limitation of art 101 TFEU which could apply whenever[38] competition law clashes with environmental objectives[39] is no doubt tempting. The case law invoked in support of such a limitation-approach goes back to the *Albany* or *Wouters* decisions.[40] In *Albany*, the Court admitted a limitation to antitrust law based on the indispensability of collective agreements for the pursuit of the Treaty's social policy objectives. It found that an effective and consistent interpretation of the Treaty required that collective agreements between management and labour fell outside the scope of the Treaty's prohibition of cartels.[41] In *Wouters*, the Court excluded measures by legal professional bodies which restricted competition among lawyers from the EU cartel-prohibition on the grounds that such restrictions were inherent in or necessary for the pursuit of legitimate objectives, which in that case were related to the lawyers' role in promoting the rule of law and facilitating the administration of justice. A core assumption of the Wouters doctrine is that some economic actors ought to be freed from the shackles of antitrust law for legitimate objectives to be satisfied.[42] The Wouters doctrine was later referred

---

36 Kingston, n 21, at 236–237; discussed with further references in Pezza, n 2, at 147–152, in support of a cautious exclusion of some sustainability agreements from the scope of competition law, based on a balancing of the objectives involved; cf Christopher Townley, 'Is anything more important than consumer welfare (in Article 81 EC)? Reflections of a Community lawyer' (2008) 10 Cambridge Yearbook of European Legal Studies 345.

37 That same art 3 (3) TEU considers "*a highly competitive social market economy*" to be one of the other fundamental objectives.

38 Kingston, n 19, at 113–114; cf Lundgren, n 8.

39 Pezza, n 2, at 151.

40 Cf references in Kyrklund, n 2, at 62–68.

41 Cf Kyrklund, n 2, at 40.

42 Cf Podszun, n 11, at 627 f; Alexander Merkulov, 'European Union Competition Law and Environmental Policy' (2021) Maastricht Center for European Law, Master Working Paper 2021/2 <www.maastrichtuniversity.nl/sites/default/files/mcel_mwp_2021-2.pdf> last accessed 10 October 2022.

to in cases involving the rules of other professional bodies, such as the rules of chartered accountants for training their members,[43] fees set by an association of geologists[44] or minimum prices for road haulage services fixed by a body composed of the operators which deliver such services.[45] All of those cases concerned professional activities which are closely related to the fulfilment of important public interests. In the end, however, the Court did not limit the scope of the cartel prohibition in those cases, as it found that the restrictions to competition in question went beyond what was necessary to pursue the legitimate objectives. In other words, the Wouters doctrine appears to require a balancing of interests and Treaty objectives rather than the mere identification of inherent limitations to art 101 (1) TFEU.[46]

Limiting the scope of art 101 TFEU does have practical advantages for the promotion of environmental objectives within competition law. It removes the need to show that environmental benefits qualify as efficiencies which outweigh restrictive effects and that consumers affected by the agreement are compensated with a fair share of the resulting benefits, as art 101(3) TFEU requires. That is also the weakness of such an approach, one which is rejected by most experts:[47] A transparent balancing of competing interests and objectives under art 101(3) TFEU provides more legitimacy to a possibly resulting prioritisation of sustainability concerns. If limiting the scope of art 101 TFEU does what art 101(3) TFEU could (at least *praeter verba legis*) do, then it is obsolete. If it does more, it lacks legitimacy and risks harming economic efficiency and environmental progress.[48] In brief, such limitations to the scope of art 101 TFEU should only be admitted with the greatest of caution, for instance if an efficient sustainability initiative of great environmental benefit could not be

43 Case C-1/12 *Ordem dos Téchnicos Oficiais de Contas* (OTOC) *v Autoridade da Concorrencia* [2013] EU:C:2013:127; [2013] 4 C.M.L.R. 20.

44 Case C-136/12 *Consiglio Nazionale dei Geologi* (CNG) *v Autorita Garante della Concorrenza e del Mercato* [2013] EU:C:2013:489; [2013] 5 C.M.L.R. 40.

45 C-184/13 *API - Anonima Petroli Italiana SpA v Ministero delle Infrastrutture e dei Trasporti* [2014] EU:C:2014:2147; [2014] 5 C.M.L.R. 21.

46 Cf Kyrklund, n 2, at 40; Merkulov, n 44, at 31; Pezza, n 2, at 147.

47 Cf Podszun, n 11, at 625; Baldi and Schraner, n 1, at 1529–1537, referring to analogous Swiss cartel law and not specifically to sustainability-based limitations; cf Heinemann, n 2, at 222.

48 The Commission, 'Guidelines on the applicability of Article 101 of the Treaty on the Functioning of the European Union to Horizontal Co-Operation Agreements' (2011) OJ C 11/1 (para 548) (the Commission's horizontal Guideline) itself seems to reject the reasoning from *Albany* or *Wouters*: "*agreements that restrict competition cannot escape the prohibition of Article 101(1) for the sole reason that they are necessary for the pursuit of a sustainability objective*".

granted an exemption under art 101(3) TFEU due to a classical understanding of the consumer-sharing requirement.

3.2 *Lawful Sustainability Agreements and Enforcement Restraint*

3.2.1 Existing Room for Lawful Sustainability Agreements (Block Exemptions)

Art 101(1) TFEU only applies if an agreement has appreciable anti-competitive effects. Some agreements will not raise competition concerns at all, including agreements to phase out single-use plastics in business premises or supermarkets, not to exceed certain temperature levels in buildings, establishing joint databases about sustainable suppliers, distributors or production processes, and coordinated industry-wide awareness campaigns.[49] Other agreements are lawful under certain conditions based on the European Commission's (the Commission) block exemption regulation under art 101(3) TFEU, including in areas relevant for sustainability-initiatives such as joint research and development efforts, standardisation agreements or some vertical agreements.[50] There are also sector specific exemptions, notably a new derogation for sustainability agreements along the "farm to fork" supply-chain.[51] Furthermore, agreements among smaller firms beneath certain market share thresholds, which are assumed to not restrict competition and which often enable competition (against stronger rivals) typically benefit from exemptions, provided that there is no hardcore restriction (eg price-fixing, limitation of output or market sharing).[52]

49 Ibid, at para 551.

50 Cf the Commission, 'Antitrust: Commission adopts new Vertical Block Exemption Regulation (VBER) and vertical guidelines (VGL)', published on 10 May 2022 in Brussels, which entered into force on 1 June 2022.

51 The derogation was adopted through art 210a of Regulation 2021/2117, amending the CMO Regulation 1308/2013 by the European Parliament and Council of the EU. After current consultations of stakeholders, the Commission is set to issue draft guidelines on the application of that derogation.

52 Cf C 291/1 Communication from the Commission, 'Notice on agreements of minor importance which do not appreciably restrict competition under Article 101(1) of the Treaty on the Functioning of the European Union (De Minimis Notice) [2014] OJ C 291/1, which clarifies that the safe harbour will not apply to any restrictions of competition by "object" or restrictions listed as "hardcore" in any current or future block exemption; cf Baldi and Schraner, n 1, at 1535. For hardcore restrictions in vertical agreements, cf art 4 of Commission Regulation (EU) No 330/2010 of 20 April 2010 [2010] OJ L 102/1 (imposing of minimum sales price, customer or territory restriction clauses). For horizontal agreements, art 5 Commission Regulation (EU) No 1217/2010 of 14 December 2010 on research and development agreements [2010] OJ L 335/36, and art 4 Commission Regulation (EU) No 1218/2010 of 14 December 2010 on specialization agreements[2010] OJ L 335/43.

It thus appears that considerable room for lawful joint initiatives on sustainability issues already exists. Does this demonstrate that competition law is already permissive enough, or that there's hardly any sustainability agreement which firms would enter into if it were not for the (chilling) threat of competition law enforcement?[53] That must not be the case. Even if there has never been much of a chilling effect there is still value in the explicit encouragement of sustainability agreements in order to reach market actors which so far were neither chilled from nor tempted to look into such possibilities.[54]

3.2.2 Enforcement Restraint within the Discretion of Competition Authorities

In 2011, the Dutch Authority for Consumers and Markets (ACM) decided not to investigate an arrangement by a fishing association which set out fishing quotas, as it found the arrangement necessary to prevent overfishing.[55] In the beginning of 2022, the German competition authority greenlighted an initiative of major retailers for a gradual implementation of common standards on wages in the banana sector. It argued that the initiative did not raise competition concerns, due to the absence of hardcore restrictions and the fact that the retailers' joint working group would not fix minimum prices or price mark-ups (the agreement was thus lucky to escape a difficult test of consumer-compensation).[56]

---

53 In that sense, Veljanovski, n 8, at 3; Schinkel and Toth, n 2, at 15, which describe how incentives for firms to engage in sustainability initiatives require that each firm's costs of contributing to sustainability progress cannot exceed the extra profits it yields by the higher price charged on consumers.

54 Cf Heinemann, n 2, at 216.

55 Or Brook, 'Struggling with Article 101(3) TFEU: Diverging Approaches of the Commission, EU Courts, and five Competition Authorities' (2019) 56 Common Market Law Review 121; cf Authority for Consumers and Markets, 'NMa [Netherlands Competition Authority] is positive towards Dutch shrimp-fishing industry's plans to make shrimp-fishing sustainable', <www.acm.nl/en/publications/publication/6535/NMa-is-positive-towardsDutch-shrimp-fishing-industrys-plans-to-make-shrimp-fishing-sustainable>, last accessed 19 July 2022; critical Schinkel and Toth, at 2 and 5.

56 Cf BananaLink, 'Living wages initiative given anti-trust green light' (21 January 2022) www.bananalink.org.uk/news/living-wages-initiative-given-anti-trust-green-light/ last acces-sed 1 August 2022); in an earlier case regarding a fairtrade-system the Bundeskartellamt refrained from undertaking an antitrust investigation even though it involved fixed minimum prices (that initiative however involved small overall market shares, cf Bundeskartellamt, 'Tätigkeitsbericht 2017/2018' (19 June 2019) Bundestags-Drucksache 19/10900, at 52; cf Felix Engelsing and Moritz Jakobs, 'Nachhaltigkeit und Wettbewerb' (2019) 69 WuW 16; Heinemann, n 2, at 220).

Competition authorities enjoy a certain discretion in deciding whether to take up a case.[57] They are free to rely not just on considerations of market efficiency and narrow consumer welfare, but on a broader range of prioritisation criteria in applying such discretion. These include considerations of substantive public interests[58] such as environmental sustainability. Within their discretion, competition authorities can 'turn a blind eye' on certain restrictions related to sustainability initiatives.[59] It appears unlikely that any European competition authority would prosecute a restrictive agreement if they thought that its harm to competition is considerably less significant than any resultant sustainability benefits.[60] In such cases, it is reasonable to understand 'appreciable' in a partly relative way, which is not indifferent to such a sharp contrast of effects.

If the overall risks and benefits of an initiative are not obvious, a more participative approach to enforcement can yield reasonable results. Competition authorities can demand more information in the course of a preliminary investigation, and possibly seek to engage in an informal exchange and quest for solutions with the firms involved. This allows them to provide guidance on how to minimise harm to competition and possibly suggest minor modifications,[61] or in some cases to make their restraint (informally) dependent on conditions such as an improvement of compliance efforts and periodical reports about the outcomes (which reduces the authority's monitoring burden).[62] The flexibility of what is a more participative approach allows for some "trial and error"

---

57 Heinemann, n 2, at 220.

58 Cf ECN (European Competition Network), 'ECN Recommendation on the Power to set Priorities', at para 3, <https://ec.europa.eu/competition/ecn/recommendation_priority_09122013_en.pdf> last accessed 10 October 2022: "*Prioritisation criteria used by the Authorities may include, among others, public interest […], or other substantive, institutional or procedural considerations. […] Although in different degrees, most [national] Authorities already have the ability to set priorities in their enforcement activities*".

59 Sarah Beeston, n 30, at 115–125, with detailed discussion of the Dutch competition authority's "turn a blind eye"-commitment.

60 Cf Veljanovski, n 8, at 3.

61 Cf The Netherlands Authority for Consumers and Markets (ACM), 'Draft guidelines on sustainability agreements' (9 July 2020) (ACM, Draft guidelines 7/2020), at para 61: "*If undertakings are unsure about the reliability of their self-assessments, they are invited to contact ACM and to discuss their agreements, preferably at an early stage. ACM will then indicate what concerns it may have, and it will help find possible solutions.*"; for an example of non-investigation following a minor change to the agreement the German case about an animal welfare initiative is relevant, where the firms agreed to add a label to the products concerned, thus increasing consumer choice: Bundeskartellamt, n 60.

62 Transparency and strong compliance efforts are recommended by experts as a strategy to reduce antitrust-risks: cf Heinemann, n 2, at218; egarding the fear of such a burden,

with sustainability agreements, something that would otherwise require a formal authorisation procedure with conditions and time-limitations. Due to the lack of a formal decision, it is important that competition authorities report at least annually about their decisions not to take up cases or to discontinue certain investigations, in order to allow for a critical public debate regarding such non-enforcement policies.[63]

Enforcement restraint for green cartels which lack basic social support, such as a sudden tripling of fuel prices,[64] is not advisable, as it could be seen as a means to circumvent the democratic process, which in turn would harm important institutional interests such as public trust and political support.[65]

4 Sustainability through Enforcement of Article 101 TFEU

The least controversial way for competition authorities to promote environmental sustainability is to fight cartels which are likely to harm both competition *and* environmental progress.[66] In contrast to private agreements imposing sustainability standards in an industry, which often appear unnecessary (and thus disproportional) due to better regulatory alternatives, a vigorous enforcement against such cartels is indispensable.[67]

In its 8 July 2021 decision on the *car emissions cleaning cartel* the Commission found that five carmakers had agreed not to compete on cleaning better than to the minimum extent required by EU emission standards. It considered

---

see: Schinkel and Toth, n 2, at 5 and 7: "*The information requirements for a competition agency* [...] *seem prohibitively large*".

63 Podszun, n 11, at 620.

64 Cf Heinemann, n 2, at 216.

65 Cf ACM, 'Draft guidelines on sustainability agreements' (26 January 2021' (ACM, Draft guidelines 1/2021), at para 75–76, <www.acm.nl/en/publications/second-draft-version-guidelines-sustainability-agreements-opportunities-within-competition-law> last accessed 30 August 2022; ACM, n 65, at para 65, regarding the requirement of showing support for the initiative among those affected by its rules. Cf Beeston, n 30, at 115–116 and 124, referring to the ACM's policy of requiring the sustainability agreement to enjoy broad social support for it to refrain from performing any enforcement actions.

66 Cf Lundgren, n 8, at 84, 85: "*The fact that the Commission indeed does consider limiting environmental protection as an issue under Article 101 TFEU is hopeful from the European Green Deal perspective, as it also indicates that an agreement creates efficiencies if it leads to increased environmental protection under Article 101 TFEU. Thus, the application of Article 101 TFEU as a sword may clarify the state of the law even as regards the Article's application as a shield, and be beneficial to the development of the law as regards antitrust as a whole*"; Schinkel and Toth, n 2, at25.

67 Schinkel and Toth, n 2, at 27; cf Heinemann, n 2, at 223–225.

that they had engaged in unlawful cooperation on the limitation of technical development in the sense of art 101(1) TFEU. The Commission thus fined the cartel based on a coordinated limitation of technical development, even if other issues such as price fixing, market sharing or output limitation were absent. Besides arguing that the cartel caused harm to economic welfare and consumers interests, the Commission also stated in its press release that competition and innovation regarding emission cleaning were "*essential for Europe to meet its ambitious Green Deal objectives*".[68] The case also illustrates how an initially legal horizontal cooperation (on developing the AdBlue-technology) carries risks of collusion, which have to be accounted for before granting sustainability exemptions.[69]

For an agreement to harm competition and the environment, it must not necessarily be related to efforts at reducing such emissions. Other areas of interest for the fight against cartels which harm the environment might include markets for: energy, recycling and waste; plant protection products; electronic goods, where market leaders have incentives not to improve product longevity or repairability; and technologies of great potential for environmental sustainability (eg new gene-editing tools for agricultural uses)[70] if limited access to foundational patents risks blocking technological advances.

5 Environmental "Efficiencies" under Article 101(3) TFEU?

5.1 Legal Limitations, Cases and Challenges

Cases involving environmental efficiencies under art 101(3) TFEU are rare. Nevertheless, national competition authorities, the Commission and the courts have sometimes had the opportunity to deal with different types of environmental efficiencies.

---

68 Cf European Commission, 'Statement by Executive Vice-President Vestager on the Commission decision to fine car manufacturers €875 million for restricting competition in emission cleaning for new diesel passenger cars' (8 July 2021, Brussels) STATEMENT /21/3583.

69 Cf Schinkel and Toth, n 2, at 4.

70 Cf regarding the rising levels of concentration in the agrochemical markets and challenges related to new gene-editing technologies, Ioannis Lianos, 'Agro-chemical Mega-mergers and Innovation, Between Competition Law, Regulation and IP Rights', in Gabriella Muscolo and Marina Tavassi (eds.), *The interplay between competition law and intellectual property: an international perspective* (Alphen aan den Rijn 2019), CLES Research Paper Series 7/2018 <www.ucl.ac.uk/cles/research-papers> last accessed 30 August 2022.

In its *Webtaxi*-decision, the Luxembourg Competition Council (the Council) examined a cooperation by several taxi companies involving an application with an algorithm used to assign drivers and calculate prices based on pre-determined variables such as the length of the trip, coverage and traffic conditions. The algorithm-based price was non-negotiable, which is why the agreement involved price-fixing, typically a 'by object' restriction for which efficiency-defences are rarely examined at all. In that case, the Council cleared the cooperation, noting that it allowed for a multitude of efficiency gains, including fewer empty taxi rides and less air pollution, and that consumers would get a fair share of those gains. Moreover, consumers were likely to pay *less* per ride on average.[71] Agreements leading to both (economic) cost efficiencies, sustainability gains and also to better conditions for consumers might be rather rare and their appeal as precedents limited, but the case nevertheless shows the willingness of a national competition authority to take environmental benefits into account in assessing efficiency-exemptions.

In its older case law, the Court had repeatedly taken a wider view of the required 'efficiencies' under (now) art 101(3) TFEU. In *CECED* (1999)[72] it approved an agreement among manufacturers of washing machines (covering 95 % of the market) to discontinue the production of less energy-efficient older machines, as it found that consumers would benefit from energy savings and that the agreement could result in an increased competition on prices. It also found that lower electricity usage and decrease in GHG emissions constituted relevant efficiencies. It is unclear whether the reduction in negative emissions was decisive or whether it merely reinforced the Court's conclusion that the efficiencies outweighed the anti-competitive effects.

Other decisions admit environmental benefits as 'efficiencies' under art 101(3) TFEU even if the competition authority finally deems the grounds for an exemption to be insufficient. In a case concerning a sustainability initiative of three major consumer detergent manufacturers, the Commission found that the firms had restricted competition in the sense of art 101 TFEU by aiming at ensuring that none of them would try to use the environmental initiative to gain a competitive advantage over the others.[73] They had agreed to keep the price of washing powder packages unchanged in spite of cost-savings due to

71 *Webtaxi S.à.r.l.* Decision of Conseil de la Concurrence No. 2018-FO-01 of 7 June 2018.

72 European Commission 2000/475/EC Decision of 24 January 1999 relating to a proceeding under Article 81 of the EC Treaty and Article 53 of the EEA Agreement relating to a proceeding under Article 81 of the EC Treaty and Article 53 of the EEA Agreement (Case IV.F.1/36.718.CECED)[1999] OJ L 187/47.

73 *Consumer Detergents* (Case COMP/39579) Commission Decision of 13 April 2011 [2011] OJ C 193/13.

reducing the weight and volume of the products' packaging and the number of wash loads per package, and to increase those prices at a later stage. While the Commission found that conduct to be prohibited, it did not outlaw the voluntary code on producing and packaging more sustainable detergent.[74]

The *Chicken of Tomorrow* (2015) decision[75] by the Dutch ACM regarded an industry-wide agreement among supermarkets, poultry farmers and broiler meat processors to promote the selling of chicken meat produced under more sustainable and animal welfare-friendly conditions. Under that agreement, regular chicken meat would have been removed from the shelves of the main Dutch supermarkets. The ACM found that the additional costs for consumers due to the agreement outweighed any resulting sustainability benefits. In order to compare economic and sustainability benefits, the ACM resorted to a consumer survey establishing the willingness to pay for sustainability improvements. This naturally had the effect of limiting the value of sustainability benefits to a subjective appreciation by present consumers.[76] Consumers were prepared to pay more, the ACM found, but not enough to outweigh the costs of the agreement.

5.2 *Necessity of Comparable (Measurable) Values*

As illustrated by the *Chicken of Tomorrow* case, one of the difficulties in taking environmental benefits into account is that many of the benefits are not as simple to measure as most economic efficiencies for which the market sets a price. The environmental benefits of agreements can only be balanced with other effects and efficiencies if the different types of outcomes and objectives are essentially comparable.[77] There are different plausible methods for

---

74 Veljanovski, n 8, at 5; cf Jurgita Malinauskaite, 'Competition Law and Sustainability: EU and National Perspectives' (2022) 13 Journal of European Competition Law & Practice 336 <https://doi.org/10.1093/jeclap/lpac003> last accessed 1 August 2022; Heinemann, n 2, at 218.

75 ACM, 'Industry-wide arrangements for the so-called Chicken of Tomorrow restrict competition' (26.1.2015) case number 13.0195.66, <www.acm.nl/en/publications/publication/13761/Industrywide-arrangements-for-the-so-called-Chicken-of-Tomorrow-restrict-competition> last accessed 20 August 2022; cf Beeston, n 30, at 114.

76 As pointed out by Schinkel and Toth, n 2, 25, another problem of the ACM's "willingness to pay"-test is that it is vegetarians who are most likely to have the highest willingness to pay, not consumers of cheap chicken meat, which are most affected by anti-competitive effects on prices and choice and for which the improvements in animal-welfare and meat quality are not of any significant compensating value.

77 ACM,Draft guidelines 1/2021, n 65, at 53: "*the pros and cons of an agreement can only be compared if the same measurement unit is used, which is done by expressing them in monetary terms*"; cf. Podszun, n 11, at 629.

assessing the value of environmental benefits in an objective way, for instance through "shadow prices" which are not market based.[78] For the purpose of this chapter, it suffices to say that the objective valuation of important sustainability benefits (eg reducing carbon dioxide (CO_2) and other GHG emissions) in economic terms is possible, even if it is more complex than classical valuation.[79] Moreover, a quantitative examination should not always be required; a qualitative assessment should suffice at least for agreements involving limited market shares or obvious cases.[80]

5.3 *Steps towards a More Sustainability-Sensitive Approach*

5.3.1 The Arguments in Favour of (more) "Sustainability Exemptions"

While it is not controversial that economically measurable environmental benefits such as energy-savings constitute efficiencies which can justify exemptions under art 101(3) TFEU,[81] there exists increased support for other, more complex environmental costs and benefits to be taken into account as well.[82] Support for such a broader approach is found in art 3 TEU ("*high level of protection and improvement of the quality of the environment*" as a fundamental objective of the Union), along with the integration principle of art 11 TFEU. According to art 11, the Treaty's environmental protection requirements "*must be*"[83] taken into account in the definition and implementation – of the Union's

78 Cf Roman Inderst, Eftichios Sartzetakis, Anastasios Xepapadeas, 'Technical Report on Sustainability and Competition' (Athens University of Economics and Business 2021) DEOS Working Papers 2103 jointly commissioned by the Hellenic Competition Commission (HCC) and the Netherlands Authority for Consumers and Markets (ACM) on the methods to quantify the efficiency gains of environmental sustainability initiatives. Cf Eva van der Zee, 'Quantifying Benefits of Sustainability Agreements under Article 101 TFEU in terms of Human Well-Being' (University Hamburg 2020) Working Paper 2020 No. 31, at 12–15 (capability approach).

79 Cf. Pezza, n 2, at 157–158, with further references.

80 Heinemann, n 2, at 225; Theon van Dijk, 'A New Approach to Assess Certain Sustainability Agreements under Competition Law', in Simon Holmes, Dirk Middelschulte and Martijn Snoep (eds) *Competition Law, Climate Change and Environmental Stability* (Concurrences 2021); ACM, Draft guidelines 1/2021, n 65, at para 53–56.

81 A position shared by sceptics of a greener competition law, cf. Podszun, n 11, at 627–628.

82 Simon Holmes, 'Climate change, sustainability and competition law' (2020) 8 Journal of Antitrust Enforcement 354; Pezza, n 2, at 139.

83 As pointed out by Ludwig Krämer, 'Giving a voice to the environment by challenging the practice of integrating environmental requirements into other EU policies', in Suzanne Kingston (ed), *European Perspectives on Environmental Law and Governance* (Routledge 2012) and Pezza, n 2, at 145, that is a stronger wording than the usual "shall be" of the Treaty's other policy linking clauses.

"*policies and activities*".[84] The European Court of Justice (ECJ) has in its rulings repeatedly interpreted various Treaty provisions based on the integration principle, including in areas related to competition law like public procurement, state aid or the prohibition of import restrictions.[85] The wording of art 101(3) TFEU creates sufficient room for an assessment of exemptions which takes a broader range of (environmental) efficiencies into account, in conformity with the integration principle (art 11 TFEU).[86] While integration as such cannot signify an automatic prioritisation of environmental sustainability over competition concerns[87] (that would be *contra verba legis*), it does provide a clear basis for a more environmentally sensitive and less reductionist assessment of efficiencies under art 101(3) TFEU.[88]

5.3.2 Current Evolution: Revised Block Exemptions and Horizontal Guidelines

The Commission's 2004 Guidelines on art 101(3) TFEU and the 2011 Horizontal Cooperation Guidelines focused (restrictively) on "*objective economic efficiencies*" and required an agreement to result in gains in consumer welfare.[89] This narrowed the room for justifications of sustainability agreements.[90] On 1 March 2022, the Commission published its draft revised Horizontal Block Exemption Regulations (HBER) on research & development (R&D) and specialisation agreements for consultation, as well as its draft new Horizontal Cooperation Guidelines, which (like those from 2001) contain a chapter on the assessment

84 Suzanne Kingston, n 2; Julian Nowag, *Environmental Integration in Competition and Free Movement Laws* (OUP 2016); Pezza, n 2, at 144–146; Maurits Dolmans, 'Sustainable Competition Policy' (2020) 5 and 6 Competition Law and Policy Debate 4; cf Kingston, n 21, at 108; Giorgio Monti, 'Article 81 EC and public policy'(2002) 39 Common Market Law Review 1057; Heinemann, n 2, at 218.

85 Case C-487/06P *British Aggregates* v Commission [2008] ECR *2008 I-10515*, para 73 (State Aid); Case C-513/99 *Concordia Bus v. Helsingin kaupunki* [2002] ECR *2002 I-07213*, para 57 (public procurement); Case C-2/90 *Walloon Waste, Commission of the European Communities v. Kingdom of Belgium* [1992] ECR 1992 I-04431 (free movement of goods); cf Pezza, n 2, at 144–149 with further references.

86 Julian Nowag, *Environmental Integration in Competition and Free Movement Laws* (OUP 2016); Pezza, n 2, at 144–145, 153; cf Odudu, n 27, at 160.

87 Pezza, n 2, at 151 (cf at 146 note 29); in favour of systematically giving more weight to environmental concerns in turn Kingston, n 21, at 113–114.

88 Kyrklund, n 2, at 78–95.

89 See Commission's Guidelines, n 51; unlike the preceding 2001 Horizontal Guidelines, they no longer specifically dealt with sustainability agreements.

90 Cf Akman, p 115; Heinemann, n 2, at 217.

of sustainability cooperation.[91] The Commission moreover encourages sustainability efforts by granting a new (*soft*) *safe harbour* for agreements that harmonise behaviour through sets of standard practices (eg replacing non-sustainable products with sustainable ones or harmonising packaging materials).[92]

The revised block exemptions and draft revised Horizontal Cooperation Guidelines are expected to enter into force on 1 January 2023. They conclude a substantial effort by the Commission to gather and evaluate information, and to seek inputs from stakeholders and the interested public in order to ensure the legitimacy and effectiveness of its evolving regulations, guidelines and institutional practice. The evaluation of the R&D block exemption regulation published on 6 May 2021 had already led to the key finding that sustainability objectives needed to be better accommodated and that the scope of permissible 'sustainability' cooperation between competitors under art 101 TFEU should be further clarified.[93] Likewise, in its 10 September 2021 Competition Policy Brief (the Policy Brief) published following public consultations on the Green New Deal, the Commission found that more guidance was necessary on the assessment of sustainability benefits and on how sustainability objectives could be pursued via different types of cooperation without restricting competition.[94] Regarding efficiencies under art 101(3) TFEU, the Policy Brief notes that sustainability benefits could be assessed as *qualitative efficiencies* resulting in an increased quality or longevity of products (eg replacement of plastic with wood in toys or the use of recycled materials for clothing) or *cost efficiencies* (eg reduction of costs for materials, transport and storage). According to the Policy Brief, the assessment of such benefits should be limited to the same relevant market, an interpretation which limits the types of reductions

91 EC Communication Guidelines on the applicability of Article 101 of the Treaty on the Functioning of the European Union to horizontal cooperation agreements, Case C 164/1 Commission Decision C/2022/1159 [2022] OJ C 164/1, draft 1 March 2022 (Commission, Draft revised Horizontal Guidelines 3/2022), EC draft revised Horizontal Block Exemption Regulations on Research & Development (R&D BER) and on Specialisation agreements (Specialisation BER; together HBERS); both draft revised regulations and the draft guidelines are available under <https://competition-policy.ec.europa.eu/public-consultations/2022-hbers_en> last accessed 30 August 2022.

92 Cf Heinemann, n 2, at 223.

93 Inception Impact Assessment and Staff Working Document (SWD), discussed in Malinauskaite, n 74.

94 Directorate- General for Competition (European Commission), 'Competition Policy in Support of Europe's Green Ambition'(2021), Competition policy brief Issue 2021-01, <https://competition-policy.ec.europa.eu/publications/competition-policy-briefs_en> last accessed 30 August 2022, (Policy Brief Issue 2021-01).

of emissions which can qualify as efficiencies under art 101(3) TFEU.[95] However, the Policy Brief acknowledges that out-of-market efficiencies (benefits on other markets) could be taken into account *if* the group of consumers affected by the restriction of competition substantially correlates with the group of consumers which benefit from the efficiencies, provided that the benefits fully compensate the consumers for the harm. The draft revised Horizontal Cooperation Guidelines confirm the Policy Brief's approach. They acknowledge three types of consumer benefits resulting from sustainability agreements which might be taken into account as efficiencies: lower prices or product improvements (eg healthier food, longer product-lifespan); benefits determined based on the value which consumers ascribe to the improved environmental quality of a product; and certain "collective benefits" to wider society, albeit under the condition mentioned before of a substantial overlap between the affected consumers and those that benefit from the agreement.

While the Commission has not gone as far as some of the Member States' competition authorities have suggested, it does support taking a wider range of environmental benefits into account and to grant efficiency exemptions for certain sustainability agreements, provided that the requirements of art 101(3) TFEU are satisfied (ie efficiencies outweighing the harm to competition, a fair share of the gains passed over to the affected consumers, indispensability of the agreement to reap such efficiency-benefits, not affording undertakings the possibility of eliminating competition).[96] It sees room for efficiency justifications *inter alia* in cases where a cooperation is necessary in order to "*avoid free-riding on the investments required to promote a sustainable product and to educate consumers*", and thereby to overcome first mover disadvantages.[97] The new sustainability-approach of the Commission will thus in particular depend on its interpretation of the (tricky) fair-share-requirement.

5.3.3 Consumer-compensation as the Main Challenge

Under art 101(3) TFEU, an individual exemption for a restrictive cooperation among competitors requires consumers to get a fair share of the benefits resulting from that cooperation. This criterion has been one of a number of focal points of the debate regarding environmental sustainability and competition law. Notably, it has been debated whether out of market efficiencies such as benefits that accrue to the environment and society at large can be taken into account. According to the traditional view based on the narrow

95 Ibid, at 5; cf Malinauskaite, n 74.

96 Cf. Heinemann, n 2, at 218.

97 Commission, Draft revised Horizontal Guidelines 3/2022, n 51, at para 584.

consumer-welfare-approach, art 101(3) TFEU required full compensation in terms of 'in-market benefits' of those consumers that suffered from the anti-competitive effect (eg price increases). However, such a restrictive interpretation of art 101(3) TFEU renders justifications on efficiency grounds for sustainability agreements all but impossible, except where environmental benefits correlate with economic efficiencies. Therefore, it has rightly and frequently been suggested that the definition of 'consumers' ought to be somewhat broadened, be it, for instance, by including indirect consumers such as users lower in the production chain,[98] by taking the interests of future consumers (or "delayed benefits")[99] into account,[100] or more radically by seeing all citizens which benefit from an agreement as "consumers" (eg of cleaner air).[101]

An approach which *de facto* amounts to the latter has recently been implemented by the Austrian legislator, through an amendment of the "fair share to consumer"-criterion under the exemption equivalent to art 101(3) TFEU in its antitrust law. The amendment sets an irrefutable legal presumption that the fair-share-criterion is met as soon as the efficiency benefits resulting from an agreement or cooperation "*contribute substantially to an ecologically sustainable or climate-neutral economy*".[102] Such a provision allows for justifications of agreements even when consumers affected by the restrictive effects such as higher prices do not directly benefit in any way from the environmental progress pursued.[103]

According to its January 2021 (revised) draft guidelines on sustainability initiatives, the Dutch ACM intends to relax the requirement of full compensation of the affected users for the harm caused by restricted competition by "environmental-damage agreements" if three criteria are met. First, the agreement must aim at preventing or limiting any "obvious environmental damage".[104] Second, it must help in an efficient way to comply with international or national standards to prevent environmental damage to which the

98 ACM, Draft guidelines 1/2021, n 65, at 36.

99 Pezza, n 2, at161, with further references.

100 ACM, Draft guidelines 1/2021, n 65, at 36, 43 and 61; Schinkel and Toth, n 2, 26; future consumers are already to be taken into account according to Communication from the Commission Notice 2004/C 101/08 of 27 April 2004, Guidelines on the application of Article 81 (3) of the Treaty [2004] OJ C 101/97 (hereafter: Guidelines on the Application of 101 (3) TFEU), marginals 43 and 85), but their interests are typically discounted to an important extent due to future uncertainties.

101 Cf Pezza, n 2, at 158–162.

102 KaWeRäG, n 33.

103 In its result, the Austrian law now resembles its Swiss counterpart, which never explicitly required consumer-compensation; cf Heinemann, n 2, at 222–224.

104 ACM, Draft guidelines 1/2021, n 65, at point 38–39.

government is bound (such as policy objectives of reducing CO_2 emissions).[105] Third, the sustainability measures must be cost-efficient, ie not more costly (for consumers) than a government measure with the same sustainability benefits. The second requirement is based on the idea that any relaxation *praeter verba legis* of the "fair share"-requirement must be justified by some degree of democratic participation. For other sustainability agreements, such as those aiming at improving labour conditions or animal welfare, the ACM does not relax the requirement of full compensation of consumers. As a consequentialist, the author supports that differentiation: reducing negative externalities is the most urgent task, given its importance for the prevention of major damages to the whole of society[106] and the conditions of life. The pursuit of distributional justice and improvements of individual conditions through other sustainability agreements, in turn, are (comparatively) less urgent, and more difficult to assess.

In contrast, the Commission's sustainability chapter of the draft revised Horizontal Cooperation Guidelines sticks to the traditional framework in requiring compensation of consumers negatively affected by the agreement. The "fair share"-criterion of art 101(3) TFEU thus remains restrictive, due to the requirement of a substantial overlap between the group of affected consumers and those that benefit from the agreement for any "collective benefits" to be taken into account. Such an overlap might for instance be admitted in assessing drivers' compensation for higher fuel prices by the benefit of cleaner air, given that most citizens are at least occasionally either drivers or car users affected by fuel prices.

In the author's view, while the Commission's draft revised Horizontal Cooperation Guidelines somewhat broaden the scope for sustainability agreements, its interpretation of the "fair share"-requirement of art 101(3) TFEU still fails to integrate environmental concerns to the extent warranted by art 11 TFEU.[107] Two wider reaching, non-legislature dependent approaches which the Commission could consider will be discussed next.

---

105 Ibid.

106 Cf ibid, at 40; cf also Economist, 'ESG should be boiled down to one simple measure: emissions' (21 July 2022) <www.economist.com/leaders/2022/07/21/esg-should-be-boiled-down-to-one-simple-measure-emissions> last accessed 17 October 2022.

107 Cf Holmes, 'Preface: How Sustainability Can Be Taken Into Account in Every Area of Competition Law' in Simon Holmes, Dirk Middelschulte and Martijn Snoep (eds) *Competition Law, Climate Change and Environmental Stability* (Concurrences 2021), p 9: "*There is no basis for the adoption of a narrow 'consumer welfare' test anywhere in the Treaties – and therefore in EU law (or the analogous national competition regimes in Europe)*".

5.3.4 Solutions (Taking Fairness Seriously)

One approach consists in taking into account the likelihood that the willingness-to-pay for sustainability improvements may be higher for future consumers than it is for current consumers.[108] The more future consumers would be willing to pay for sustainability improvements related to certain products, the likelier it is that any environmental benefits contribute to a fair compensation of consumers as required under art 101(3) TFEU. Regarding the consumption of non-renewable natural resources in particular, the threat of scarcity and its impact on prices justifies the assumption that future consumers would be willing to pay significantly more for sustainability initiatives. Giving more weight to the expected perspective of future consumers would also correct the problem of "hyperbolic discounting" of future damages.[109] That said, while the willingness to pay for efforts to protect the environment will likely increase over the years, this is not always the case, as it might also happen that technical improvements render earlier solutions obsolete (or much cheaper).

Another way would be to take into account whether the former prices paid by consumers were artificially low in the sense of being the result not only of supply and demand in a free market, but also the consequence of negative externalities not hitherto internalised, and thus of market failures.[110] In the author's view, the requirement to pass over a "fair share" of an agreement's gains cannot imply that compensation for consumers is due even where an agreement's restrictive effects (eg price increases) and its benefits both result from an effort to internalise costs of negative externalities such as plastic waste or GHG emissions which were not reflected in the original prices.[111] In other

---

108 Stefan Thomas and Roman Inderst, 'Integrating Benefits from Sustainability into the Competitive Assessment - How Can We Measure Them?' (2021) 12 Journal of European Competition Law & Practice 705.

109 Regarding hyperbolic discounting, cf Nick Wilkinson and Matthias Klaes (eds), *An Introduction to Behavioral Economics*, (Palgrave 2012).

110 Cf Kingston, n 2, at para 801; extensively on the problematic of market failures and their internalisation, see: Michael Fritsch, *Marktversagen und Wirtschaftspolitik*, (Vahlen 2018); cf Heinemann, n 2, at 215–216.

111 Cf Martijn Snoep, 'Keynote speech for IBA 2020 - 24th Annual Competition Virtual Conference' (9 September 2020) <www.acm.nl/nl/publicaties/keynote-speech-martijn-snoep-voor-iba-annual-competition-conference> last accessed 17 October 2022: "*The counterfactual of this situation is that non-users carry the burden of the externalities that users create, without having the advantages of lower prices that are the result of competition. That is neither fair nor efficient.*"; ACM, Draft guidelines 1/2021, n 69,at para 39–42, in particular 41: "*it can be fair not to compensate users fully for the harm that the agreement causes because their demand for the products in question essentially creates the problem for which society needs to find solutions*".

words, the internalisation of such externalities does not distort competitive market prices: it removes a distortion.[112] Moreover, as long as the sustainability initiative is not used as a camouflage for collusive rent-seeking, the undertakings' gains (reputational or strategic benefits aside) from joint sustainability efforts will often amount to zero.[113] In that case even the most generous 'share' of (zero) cartel gains to be passed over to consumers cannot be superior to zero either.[114] Thus, provided that the undertakings involved respect the necessity-criterion and that they do not use the environmental initiative in order to reap profits at the expense of consumers or the environment, an individual exemption under art 101(3) TFEU should not be denied.

If the notion of zero gains being passed over to consumers appears counter-intuitive, one might consider a fictive case: Some firms have for years engaged in an ecologically destructive trade with wood from primary forests. They sold greater quantities of wood at low prices, in order to defend market shares against producers of less precious but more sustainably produced wood. The firms' new directors intend to change the strategy in order to also protect their resources. In the absence of state measures to protect the forests, the major undertakings which engaged in the sale of precious wood agree to massively limit the quantities of wood sold and to increase prices to make their product unaffordable to most consumers, while maximising benefits from the limited remaining sales in order to ensure their economic survival along with the best possible protection of the forests concerned. Is there any doubt that consumers' "fair share" of the benefits in that fictive case is zero (apart from general sustainability benefits), given that the former prices did not account for massive negative externalities?

6 Sustainability in the Context of Abuse Control (Article 102 TFEU)

The issue of abuses of a dominant position (art 102 TFEU) has so far received less attention than the cartel-prohibition (art 101 TFE) in the rich debate regarding sustainability and competition law. Hereafter, some selected issues shall briefly be discussed.

112 Cf Dolmans, n 84, at para 20.

113 Cf Schinkel and Toth, n 2, at 6–8.

114 That is, aside from environmental benefits, which are "*by their (open and diffusive) nature – always passed onto consumers in significant quantities*" (Pezza, n 2, at 159).

6.1 *Abusive Restrictions of Economic Freedom and Participation*

Art 102 TFEU *inter alia* entrusts competition authorities with the task of preventing dominant firms from (abusively) foreclosing reasonably efficient rivals and solidifying a position of dominance without having to compete on the merits. In protecting competition, including innovation-driven (dynamic) competition, abuse control also tends to benefit the environment.

The abusive (exclusionary or exploitative) conduct by dominant undertakings banned by art 102 TFEU evokes related abuses in the political sphere. If competition is a democratic institution,[115] then abuses of a dominant (market) position are analogous to the manoeuvring of dominant political parties who use their might to restrict rivals' access to public discourse and ability to participate in elections on an equal footing, in order to keep power without having to compete on the merits. There is a risk of self-perpetuation of abuses of a dominant position in the sense of art 102 TFEU, due to incentives to hide past abuses in order to prevent financial damage or political backlash (eg severe regulation) and due to the increased power-based ability to succeed in doing so. That, too, is reminiscent of abuses in the political sphere, where the fear by dominant political forces of getting caught for some initial acts of corruption encourages more corruption, deception and further abuses including attempts at clinging to power by all means.

It is therefore important that antitrust enforcement is not content with merely intervening against abuses of dominance, but that it also prevents firms from acquiring or strengthening a dominant position. It does so by prohibiting (abusive) exclusionary conduct which forecloses rivals and thus results in more dominance (art 102 TFEU), and through merger control.[116]

Antitrust efforts against abuses of dominant positions also serve environmental sustainability, due to the higher risk (compared with weaker rivals) that a dominant firm restricts competition in a way that also harms the environment.[117] That risk is particularly significant if the dominant firm is not incentivised to increase its efficiency by fierce countervailing buyer power, challenges from substitute products or international market leaders.

115 Podszun, n 11, at 632 Competition democratic institution, cf above.

116 See Council Regulation No 139/2004 of 20 January 2004 on the control of concentrations between undertakings (EC Merger Regulation) [2004] OJ L 024/1; Uffer, n 5, sec 6.

117 Lundgren, n 8, at para85: "*there appears to be a connection between market power and unsustainable conduct insofar as it is easier for a dominant undertaking to act unsustainably.*"; cf Heinemann, n 2, at 215: "die Verfolgung von Sozial- und Nachhaltigkeitszielen [ist] für eine Vielzahl von Unternehmen eine Voraussetzung für wirtschaftlichen Erfolg geworden".

6.2 *Preventing Foreclosure of Reasonably Efficient Competitors*

A more permissive enforcement of art 102 TFEU than the cartel-prohibition of art 101 TFEU would risk incentivising mergers.[118] Competition authorities should seek to implement a severe enforcement against abuses of dominant positions generally, and in particular against abuses consisting in defending a dominant position by causing substantial negative externalities (pollution), thereby excluding rivals which want to (or must) account for their own negative externalities.[119]

One controversial question is whether and how to apply the 'as efficient competitor'-test (the AEC-test) in the assessment of foreclosure effects, for instance in the analysis of rebate schemes where customers are granted significant rebates if they commit to only or mostly buying products from the dominant company. Such exclusionary conduct likely forecloses rivals and can thus constitute abusive conduct.[120] In the ECJ's 2017 *Intel* decision, concerning rebate schemes by the market leader for computer chips, the ECJ dismissed the lower court's idea that rebate schemes were *per se* abusive. It held that efficiency defences by the dominant undertakings would have to be examined through a full market analysis if a defendant puts forward reasons as to why its rebate scheme would have no exclusionary effects. For the ECJ, rebate schemes are not abusive if they do not exclude (foreclose) competitors which are "as efficient as" the dominant company.[121] The foreclosure of less efficient rivals is merely seen as a normal expression of the competitive process.[122]

Such a severe AEC-test risks rendering antitrust enforcement against dominant behaviour unreasonably burdensome. Neither the wording of art 102 TFEU nor its historical or teleological interpretation require a restriction of the definition of abuses to conduct which hurts equally efficient competitors. As under art 101 TFEU, the decisive question is whether the conduct in question harms competition. Rebate schemes, pricing below costs and other exclusionary conducts can significantly harm competition even when an "as efficient" competitor would have managed to resist foreclosure. This is due to the fact that a less efficient competitor can benefit competition by pressuring the market leader to maintain a minimum of efficiency. In particular, the foreclosure of a less efficient competitor in markets with limited remaining competition

118 Cf Michael Funk, Christian Jaag and Samuel Rutz, 'Gefährdete Kohärenz im Kartellrecht' (2018) Swiss Economics Working Paper 0061 <www.swiss-economics.ch/RePEc/files/0061FunkJaagRutz.pdf> last accessed 17 October 2022.

119 Cf Lundgren, n 8, at para 86.

120 Case C-413/13 P *Intel Corp. v European Commission* [2017], ECLI:EU:C:2017:632, para 137.

121 Ibid, paras 138–140.

122 Ibid, paras 133–134.

can also result in less choice of products and services, thereby depriving buyers of alternatives to the dominant firm's products. This in turn weakens the bargaining power of buyers and results in reduced pressure for the dominant firm to improve the quality of its products or services (including on aspects such as energy-efficient production or product lifespan). Therefore, such foreclosure of less efficient (not inefficient) competitors clearly cause the "*prejudice to consumers*" which art 102 lit b TFEU aims at preventing. Exclusionary conduct also risks causing prejudice to consumers and to the environment (less innovation and competition on sustainability merits), independently of whether the foreclosed rival is as efficient or not.

For that reason, abuse control should focus on ensuring opportunities for all reasonably efficient undertakings to compete on the merits and to potentially *become* as or more efficient than the dominant firm. To require strictly equal efficiency would be unreasonable in view of the effects discussed and in the author's view also contrary to the right to equal treatment and economic liberty. Given that dominant undertakings typically benefit from incumbency-related advantages, antitrust authorities ought to examine to what extent the dominant firm's superior efficiency is power-based (eg economies of scale and scope, differences in fixed costs, name recognition, strong bargaining power, consumer apathy) and to what extent it is merit-based. The more efficiency is unrelated to the dominant firm's productivity or innovation capacity, the harder it is for efficient rivals to be 'as efficient'. Hence, dominant conduct with exclusionary effects in the sense of art 102 TFEU ought to be *presumed* to be unfair (lit a) or to cause prejudice to consumers (lit b) whenever it might result in the foreclosure of competitors which would arguably be as efficient *if* they enjoyed the incumbency-related advantages themselves.[123] Such an approach to abuse control prevents a strengthening of dominant positions which would harm economic efficiency and (indirectly) environmental sustainability.

6.3 *Environmental Benefits through Dominant Behaviour?*

Notwithstanding the above, a dominant firm might pursue sustainability objectives through exclusionary conduct which would typically fall under the scope of art 102 TFEU, such as the imposition of environment-sensitive trading conditions, or by limiting production to the prejudice of consumers.

123 Cf comments under Alfonso Lamadrid and Pablo Ibàñez Colomo, 'Why Article 102 TFEU is about equally efficiant rivals: legal certainty, causality and competition on the merits' (Chillin'Competition, May 2021) <https://chillingcompetition.com/2021/05/10/why-article-102-tfeu-is-about-equally-efficient-rivals-legal-certainty-causality-and-competition-on-the-merits/> last accessed 1 August 2022).

An example is Walmart's decision in 2006 to only sell wild-caught and frozen fish from MSC-certified suppliers in its US stores.[124] In such a case, a defence based on environmental efficiencies could succeed,[125] particularly if the dominant firm's sustainability initiative was openly communicated early on. The (environmental) benefits could therefore justify conducts resulting in the foreclosure of environmentally irresponsible suppliers. Reductions of negative externalities appear particularly well suited to justify exclusionary conduct. This is because it is plausible to argue that imposed trading conditions are not 'unfair' in the sense of art 102 lit a TFEU if the externalities are partly a result of consumer demand[126] and if rather than strengthening the dominant position such imposed trading conditions result in reduced negative externalities which outweigh the detriments to competition. Note that this is provided that any restriction does not surpass what is necessary to account for the internalisation of negative externalities. As to limitations of production or markets "*to the prejudice of consumers*" (art 102 lit b TFEU), it can be argued that there is no "prejudice" in an internalisation of externalities which corrects market failures by allocating the costs to consumers and thereby returning the burden to (one of) its origins.[127] An application of the "principle of practical concordance", as proposed by some experts,[128] would in the author's view lead to the

124 See 'Wal-Mart Takes Lead On Supporting Sustainable Fisheries' (Wal-Mart, 5 February 2006) <https://corporate.walmart.com/newsroom/2006/02/05/wal-mart-takes-lead-on-supporting-sustainable-fisheries> last accessed 1 August 2022.

125 While art 102 TFEU does not have an explicit exemption clause, cases of alleged abuse of dominance are regularly assessed based on an *effects based approach* similar to that under art 101/3 TFEU, rather than through the figure of *per se illegal* behaviour. A successful defence requires that it be shown that exclusionary conduct described in art 102 TFEU is either objectively necessary for legitimate objectives or that it creates efficiencies which outweigh any anti-competitive effects; Communication from the Commission 2009/C 45/02 of 24 February 2009 Guidance on the Commission's enforcement priorities in applying Article 82 of the EC Treaty to abusive exclusionary conduct by dominant undertakings [2009] OJ C 45/7.

126 Cf Schinkel and Toth, n 2, at 26.

127 Cf Dolmans, n 84, at 20, rightly stressing that this is consistent with the polluter pays principle.

128 Cf Boris p Paal, 'Gutachten zu Rechtsfragen im Zusammenhang mit der Berücksichtigung(sfähigkeit) von außer-ökonomischen Zielen auf der Grundlage und am Massstab der europäischen Fusionskontrollverordnung in dem Kartellverfahren betreffend das Zusammenschlussvorhaben von Bayer AG und Monsanto Co' (23 April 2017); cf also Heinemann, n 2, at 221; Marco Fetz and Marc Steiner, 'Öffentliches Beschaffungsrecht des Bundes', in Thomas Cottier, Matthias Oesch, Remo Arpagaus *et al* (eds) *Schweizerisches Aussenwirtschafts- und Binnenmarktrecht* (Helbing and Lichtenhahn 2020); Marc Steiner, 'Ein interdisziplinärer Blick auf Wettbewerb und Nachhaltigkeit' (22 October 2021) Speech at the work session of the Studienvereinigung Kartellrecht in Bern/Center

same result: That principle requires the ponderation of simultaneously applicable and partly conflicting economic and environmental (treaty) objectives in an attempt to seek for both an optimum (or least harmful) solution to the conflict, as opposed to the realisation of one objective at the full detriment of the other.[129] An interpretation of art 102 TFEU which does not consider price-increases merely resulting from the abolition of environmental dumping prices as a consumer-prejudice is consistent with the principle of practical concordance, as it serves both competition (economic efficiency, including through market failure corrections) and sustainability objectives.

That said, even in the case of a well-intentioned sustainability initiative by a dominant undertaking, a severe assessment of anti-competitive effects remains warranted, given that the foreclosure of any direct competitors would accentuate the risks related to a concentration of market power and likely eventually harm innovation and other parameters of competition which are important for environmental progress.[130] Therefore, modest or short term sustainability benefits are unlikely to justify exclusionary conduct under art 102 TFEU.[131] Exemptions should thus be handled more cautiously than under art 101 TFEU.

7 Sustainability and Merger Control Regulation

Unlike the prohibitions of cartels (art 101 TFEU) and dominant abuses (art 102 TFEU), which deal with present or past conduct, merger control under EU Merger Regulation (Council Regulation N°139/2004 of 20 January 2004 on the control of concentrations between undertakings) is concerned with assessing future changes in market structures. The relevant criteria in assessing restrictions of competition through agreements or other coordinated conduct under art 101 TFEU are similar to those applied under the EU Merger Regulation.[132] Moreover, merger control also allows for a balancing of anti-competitive effects with efficiencies similar to the examination of exemptions under art 101(3) TFEU.

for the Law of Innovation and Competition <www.studienvereinigung-kartellrecht.de> last accessed 5 May 2022.

129 On the limits of that principle, cf Matthias Uffer, *Die Grundrechtskollision* (Nomos 2021).

130 Cf Schinkel and Toth, n 2, at 25.

131 Cf Kyrklund, n 2.

132 Mosso, n 26,at 8.

For a merger to be blocked, it needs to result in a "*significant impediment of effective competition*" (SIEC) in the common market or in a substantial part of it, "in particular" through the "*creation or strengthening of a dominant position*" (art 2 EU Merger Regulation). Dominance is thus assumed to significantly impede competition.[133] Conversely, no competition concerns arise if a joint venture (be it a merger or just a cooperation) widens the capabilities of the firms involved to compete in more markets and against bigger rivals.[134] However, dominance is neither necessary nor always sufficient to determine the SIEC. A merger which leads to more concentrated oligopolistic market power and reduces incentives to compete might well amount to SIEC even if it falls short of creating dominance. Conversely, mergers can create dominance and yet not cause SIEC, for example if the dominant firm faces strong countervailing buyer power or pressure from global leaders.[135] The ultimate question of merger control is not dominance as such, but whether the concentration of market power increases to such a degree that competition and consumer welfare deteriorate significantly.[136]

This brings us back to the issue of participation: There is little risk of competition being significantly impeded if the number of market actors which efficiently compete in the affected markets does not decrease post-merger.

In helping to prevent changes in market structures which would significantly harm static and in particular dynamic competition, merger control also benefits sustainability. When it cleared the Dow/DuPont-merger in March 2017, the Commission explained that pesticides were products that "*matter* [...] *to the environment*", and that effective competition was necessary to develop products ever safer for people and better for the environment. The Commission sought to ensure that the merger would not reduce "*innovation for safer and better products in the future*" by conditioning its approval in particular to the divestiture by DuPont of important parts of its global pesticide business.[137] In August 2017, in the context of the Commission's assessment of the Bayer

133 Cf Lars-Hedrik Röller and Miguel de la Mano, 'The Impact of the new substantive test in European merger control' (2006) 2 European Competition Journal 9–28.

134 Cf Baldi and Schraner, n 1, at 1535; a merger which leads to better and a broader range of products and services might for instance enable the new firm to submit tenders in public procurement procedures.

135 Mosso, n 26, at 4–5, 7.

136 Röller and de la Mano, n 141, at 10.

137 Case M.7932 *Dow/DuPont* [2017] Commission Decision declaring a concentration to be compatible with the internal market and the EEA Agreement press release; Podszun, n 11, at623 f.

and Monsanto merger which it conditionally approved in March 2018,[138] Commissioner Vestager acknowledged in her response to (more than a million) petitioners that their repeatedly expressed concerns for human health or the environment were "*of great importance*", but also stressed that such concerns did not "*form a basis for a merger assessment*".[139] In other words, the Commission believes that preserving competition through merger control serves the environment, but it is unlikely to ever prohibit a merger which does not significantly impede competition due to concerns for the environment or clear a significantly competition-impeding merger based on environmental grounds. Not only would such decisions likely lack a legal basis, but such disparities of detriments and benefits are highly improbable in the former case, as a merger is unlikely to raise new environmental concerns but through an impediment of competition. In the latter case, clearing an anti-competitive merger on sustainability grounds is hardly necessary given that cooperation on sustainability issues is also possible under the threshold of a merger.[140]

Typically, as said, a merger will raise environmental concerns if it also impedes efficient competition. The evidence indeed suggests that a reduction in the number of direct competitors is likely to restrict competition on quality, product choice and innovation, thereby harming not just economic efficiency, but indirectly also the environment.[141] Conversely, a merger is unlikely to raise

138 Case M.8084 *Bayer/Monsanto* [2018] Commission Decision declaring a concentration to be compatible with the internal market and the EEA Agreement, OJ C 459/10.

139 Cf Statement by Commissioner Vestager on Commission decision to give conditional approval to the merger (European Commission, 21 March 2018) <https://ec.europa.eu/commission/presscorner/detail/en/IP_18_2322> last accessed 1 July 2022; cf Podszun, n 11, at 613.

140 Uffer, n 5, sec 2–4.

141 Cf Daniel Simon and Jeffrey Prince, 'The Effect of Competition on Toxic Pollution Releases'(2016) 79 J. Environ. Econ. & Management 40; Andreas Heinemann, 'Business Enterprises in Public International Law', in Ulrich Fastenrath, Rudolf Geiger, Daniel-Erasmus Khan *et al* (eds), *From Bilateralism to Community Interest – Essays in Honour of Judge Bruno Simma* (OUP 2011); Maarten Pieter Schinkel and Leonard Treuren, *Corporate Social Responsibility by Joint Agreement*(2021) Tinbergen Institute Discussion Paper No. TI 2021-063/VII <https://ssrn.com/abstract=3878784> last accessed 17 October 2022; Daniel Fernández-Kranz and Juan Santaló, 'When Necessity Becomes a Virtue: The Effect of Product Market Competition on Corporate Social Responsibility' (2010)19 J. Econ. & Management Strategy 453; cf Veljanovski, n 8, at 8 with further references; European Commission, European Competitiveness Report 2008, SEC (2008) 2853, 118: "*for an increasing number of enterprises in a growing number of industries,* CSR [corporate social responsibility] *is becoming a competitive necessity – it is something that they cannot afford not to do*"; Philippe Aghion, Roland Bénabou, Ralf Martin and Alexandra Roulet, 'Environmental Preferences and Technological Choices: Is Market Competition Clean or Dirty?'

environmental concerns if it benefits competition, due to a variety of economic efficiencies which also have an environmental value, such as improved innovation, better product quality (product longevity, packaging, use of safer and cleaner materials) or efficiency of production, storage and transportation.

8 Concluding Thoughts

There are several paths through which competition law enforcement can contribute to environmental sustainability. One path is by doing what it already does: enforce competition law against cartels (art 101 TFEU) and exclusionary or exploitative conduct of dominant undertakings (art 102 TFEU). This should be done vigorously, particularly in cases where anti-competitive conduct causes a significant harm to the environment (eg a cartel which hampers important technical progress, or a dominant undertaking which forecloses less polluting (indirect) competitors).

A second path consists in declaring art 101 (or art 102) TFEU inapplicable to conduct which serves sustainability objectives. That is a high-risk strategy, not just because of the anti-competitive behaviour it certainly invites, but also because of a likely encouragement of greenwashing and indirect harm to the environment resulting from reduced competition and increased concentrations of market power. Moreover, the second path does not appear necessary (proportional) at all, provided that the third path is taken seriously.

The third path consists in defining a broader range of environmental benefits as "efficiencies" under art 101(3) TFEU, and for defences against charges of abusive conduct under art 102 TFEU. That path, some details of which still need to be sorted out, enjoys wide support by scholars, competition lawyers and antitrust authorities. The author supports a bold departure from a narrow consumer-compensation requirement in cases where consumers have caused or significantly contributed to the negative externalities which a sustainability agreement aims at internalising.

A fourth path consists in resolving the challenge of sustainability and competition through decisions not to take up certain cases or to discontinue certain investigations. This is reasonable for instance if a competition authority is convinced that objective and measurable sustainability benefits (eg reductions of emissions, imposition of cleaner production standards) outweigh any

(2021) Harvard University <https://scholar.harvard.edu/aghion/publications/environmental-preferences-and-technological-choices-market-competition-clean-or> last accessed 20 August 2021.

harm to competition to an extent that makes the restriction to competition appear (in contrast) not "appreciable".

Participation is important to the well-functioning of all of those solutions. Participation as economic freedom is the very foundation of competition. In the absence of a possibility for all able undertakings to compete on the merits and to challenge market leaders, there is only distorted competition. Economic participation aside, democratic participation in its broadest sense is of similar importance: participation helps reaffirm the legitimacy of an (evolving) competition law enforcement, not just through democratic legislation (which is the exception), but for instance also through public discourse, reports by competition authorities, detailed consultation procedures, informal exchanges of authorities with undertakings (rather than a command-approach), assessment of social support for certain measures.

Bibliography

Aghion P, Bénabou R, Martin R and Roulet A, 'Environmental Preferences and Technological Choices: Is Market Competition Clean or Dirty?' (2021) Harvard University, https://scholar.harvard.edu/aghion/publications/environmental-preferences-and-technological-choices-market-competition-clean-or (accessed 20 August 2022).

Albæk S, 'Consumer Welfare in EU Competition policy' in Caroline Heide-Jørgensen et al (eds), *Aims and Values in Competition Law* (DJØF Publishing 2013).

Almunia J, 'Competition and consumers: the future of EU competition policy' (SPEECH/10/233,European Competition Day, Madrid, 12 May 2010, https://ec.europa.eu/commission/presscorner/api/files/document/print/en/speech_10_233/SPEECH_10_233_EN.pdf) (accessed 26 September 2022).

Baldi M and Schraner F, '20 Jahre – und kein bisschen weiter? Zum wettbewerbspolitischen Verständnis von Art. 5 Kartellgesetz' (2015) 11 AJP 1529.

Baudenbacher C, 'Markt und Wettbewerb in der Rechtsprechung des EFTA-Gerichtshofs' in Juliane Kokott, Petra Pohlmann and Romina Polley (eds), *Europäisches, deutsches und internationals Kartellrecht – Festschrift für Dirk Schroeder* (Otto Schmidt 2018).

Beeston S, 'Competition Law and Sustainability Initiatives' in Juliane Kokott, Petra Pohlmann and Romina Polley (eds), *Europäisches, deutsches und internationals Kartellrecht – Festschrift für Dirk Schroeder* (Otto Schmidt 2018).

Biely K and van Passel S, 'Market power and sustainability: a new research agenda' (2022) 3 Discover Sustainability, https://link.springer.com/article/10.1007/s43621-022-00073-y (accessed 26 September 2022).

Brook O, 'Struggling with Article 101(3) TFEU: Diverging Approaches of the Commission, EU Courts, and five Competition Authorities' (2019) 56 Common Market Law Review 121.

Bruce A and Faunce T, 'Sustainable fuel, food, fertilizer and ecosystems through a global artificial photosynthetic system: overcoming anticompetitive barriers' (2015) 5 Interface Focus, http://dx.doi.org/10.1098/rsfs.2015.0011 (accessed 1 August 2022).

Directorate-General for Competition (European Commission), 'Competition Policy in Support of Europe's Green Ambition'(2021), Competition policy brief Issue 2021-01, https://competition-policy.ec.europa.eu/publications/competition-policy-briefs_en (Policy Brief Issue 2021-01).

Dolmans M, 'Sustainable Competition Policy' (2020) 5 and 6 Competition Law and Policy Debate 4.

Engelsing F and Jakobs M, 'Nachhaltigkeit und Wettbewerb' (2019) 69 WuW 16.

Fernández-Kranz D and Santaló J, 'When Necessity Becomes a Virtue: The Effect of Product Market Competition on Corporate Social Responsibility' (2010) 19 J. Econ. & Management Strategy, 453.

Fetz M and Steiner M, 'Öffentliches Beschaffungsrecht des Bundes' in Thomas Cottier, Matthias Oesch, Remo Arpagaus et al (eds), *Schweizerisches Aussenwirtschafts- und Binnenmarktrecht* (Helbing and Lichtenhahn, 2020).

Frey BS and Gebhard Kirchgässner G, *Demokratische Wirtschaftspolitik* (Vahlen 2002).

Fritsch M, *Marktversagen und Wirtschaftspolitik*, (Vahlen, 2018).

Funk M, Jaag C and Rutz S, 'Gefährdete Kohärenz im Kartellrecht' (2018) Swiss Economics Working Paper 0061, www.swiss-economics.ch/RePEc/files/0061FunkJaag Rutz.pdf. (accessed 17 October 2022).

Glaser A, *Nachhaltige Entwicklung und Demokratie* (Mohr Siebeck, 2006).

Harkrider JD, 'Lessons from the Great Depression' (2009) 23 Antitrust 6.

Heinemann A, 'Nachhaltigkeitsvereinbarungen' (2021) 5 sic! Zeitschrift für Immaterialgüter-, Informations- und Wettbewerbsrecht 213.

Heinemann A, 'Business Enterprises in Public International Law', in Ulrich Fastenrath, Rudolf Geiger, Daniel-Erasmus Khan et al (eds), *From Bilateralism to Community Interest – Essays in Honour of Judge Bruno Simma* (OUP 2011).

Holmes S, 'Preface: How Sustainability Can Be Taken Into Account in Every Area of Competition Law' in Simon Holmes, Dirk Middelschulte and Martijn Snoep (eds), *Competition Law, Climate Change and Environmental Stability* (Concurrences, 2021).

Holmes S, 'Climate change, sustainability and competition law' (2020) 8 Journal of Antitrust Enforcement 354.

Inderst R, Sartzetakis E, Xepapadeas A, 'Technical Report on Sustainability and Competition' (Athens University of Economics and Business 2021) DEOS Working Papers 2103 jointly commissioned by the Hellenic Competition Commission (HCC) and

the Netherlands Authority for Consumers and Markets (ACM) on the methods to quantify the efficiency gains of environmental sustainability initiatives.
Kingston S, 'Integrating environmental protection and EU competition law: Why competition isn't special' (2010) 16 ELJ 780.
Krämer L, 'Giving a voice to the environment by challenging the practice of integrating environmental requirements into other EU policies' in Suzanne Kingston (ed), *European Perspectives on Environmental Law and Governance* (Routledge 2012).
Kyrklund M, 'EU Competition Policy and the Environment: The Role of Environmental considerations under Article 101 TFEU' (2020) Thesis in Competition Law, Uppsala Universitet.
Lamadrid A and Ibàñez Colomo P, 'Why Article 102 TFEU is about equally efficiant rivals: legal certainty, causality and competition on the merits' (Chillin' Competition, May 2021) https://chillingcompetition.com/2021/05/10/why-article-102-tfeu-is-about-equally-efficient-rivals-legal-certainty-causality-and-competition-on-the-merits/ (accessed 30 July 2022).
Lianos I, 'Agro-chemical Mega-mergers and Innovation, Between Competition Law, Regulation and IP Rights' in Gabriella Muscolo and Marina Tavassi (eds), *The interplay between competition law and intellectual property: an international perspective* (Alphen aan den Rijn 2019, CLES Research Paper Series 7/2018 www.ucl.ac.uk/cles/research-papers) (accessed 30 August 2022).
Lundgren L, 'A competitive environment? Articles 101 and 102 TFEU and the European Green Deal' (Uppsala Universitet 2021, Master's Thesis).
Malinauskaite J, 'Competition Law and Sustainability: EU and National Perspectives' (2022) 13 Journal of European Competition Law & Practice 336, https://doi.org/10.1093/jeclap/lpac003 (accessed 1 August 2022).
Merkulov A, 'European Union Competition Law and Environmental Policy' (2021) Maastricht Center for European Law, Master Working Paper 2021/2 www.maastrichtuniversity.nl/sites/default/files/mcel_mwp_2021-2.pdf (accessed 20 August 2022).
Mestmäcker EJ und Schweitzer H, *Europäisches Wettbewerbsrecht* (C.H. Beck, 2014).
Mijnlieff M, 'Draft Guidelines on Sustainability Agreements – Opportunities within competition law' Autoriteit Consument & Markt (ACM), 26 January 2021, www.acm.nl/en/publications/guidelines-sustainability-agreements-are-ready-further-european-coordination (accessed 20 August 2022).
Monti G, 'Four options for a greener competition law' (2020) 11 Journal of European Competition Law & Practice 124.
Monti G, 'Article 81 EC and public policy' (2002) 39 Common Market Law Review 1057.
Mosso CE, 'The Contribution of Merger Control to the Definition of Harm to Competition' (March 2016) https://ec.europa.eu/competition/speeches/text/sp2016_03_en.pdf (accessed 1 August 2022).

Nowag J, *Environmental Integration in Competition and Free Movement Laws* (OUP 2016).

Odudu O, *The Boundaries of EC Competition Law: The Scope of Article 81* (OUP 2006).

Pezza A, 'The European Green Deal: shaping environmentally friendly policies under Article 101 TFEU' (2020) 4 M & CLR 139; cf also OECD Roundtable, 'Sustainability and Competition' (OECD December 2020) www.oecd.org/daf/competition/sustainability-and-competition.htm (accessed 20 August 2022).

Podszun R, 'Ausserwettbewerbliche Interessen im Kartellrecht und ihre Grenzen' in Juliane Kokott, Petra Pohlmann, Romina Polley (eds), *Europäisches, deutsches und internationales Kartellrecht - Festschrift Dirk Schroeder* (Otto Schmidt 2018).

Röller LH and de la Mano M, 'The Impact of the new substantive test in European merger control' (2006) 2 European Competition Journal.

Schinkel MP and Treuren L, 'Corporate Social Responsibility by Joint Agreement' (2021) Tinbergen Institute Discussion Paper No. TI 2021-063/VII https://ssrn.com/abstract=3878784 (accessed 17 October 2022).

Schinkel MP and Toth L, 'Balancing the Public Interest-Defense in Cartel Offenses' (2017) Amsterdam Law School Legal Studies Research Paper No. 2016-05.

Simon D and Prince J, 'The Effect of Competition on Toxic Pollution Releases' (2016) 79 J. Environ. Econ. & Management, 40.

Snoep M, 'Keynote speech for IBA 2020 - 24th Annual Competition Virtual Conference' (9 September 2020) www.acm.nl/nl/publicaties/keynote-speech-martijn-snoep-voor-iba-annual-competition-conference (accessed 17 October 2022).

Steiner M, 'Ein interdisziplinärer Blick auf Wettbewerb und Nachhaltigkeit' (22 October 2021) Speech at the work session of the Studienvereinigung Kartellrecht in Bern/Center for the Law of Innovation and Competition www.studienvereinigung-kartellrecht.de.

Thomas S and Inderst R, 'Integrating Benefits from Sustainability into the Competitive Assessment - How Can We Measure Them?' (2021) 12 J.E.C.L. & Pract. 705.

Townley C, *Article 81 EC and Public Policy* (Hart Publishing 2010).

Townley C, 'Is anything more important than consumer welfare (in Article 81 EC)? Reflections of a Community lawyer' (2008) 10 Cambridge Yearbook of European Legal Studies, 345.

Uffer M, 'Competition Law. Sustainability Through Competition and Participation' in Eva Julia Lohse and Birgit Peters (eds), *Sustainability Through Participation?* (Brill Academic Publishers 2022).

Uffer M, *Die Grundrechtskollision* (Nomos, 2021).

van der Zee E, 'Quantifying Benefits of Sustainability Agreements under Article 101 TFEU in terms of Human Well-Being' (University Hamburg 2020, Working Paper 2020 No. 31).

van Dijk T, 'A New Approach to Assess Certain Sustainability Agreements under Competition Law' in Simon Holmes, Dirk Middelschulte and Martijn Snoep (eds), *Competition Law, Climate Change and Environmental Stability* (Concurrences 2021).

Vedder H, 'Competition Law and Environmental Protection in Europe: Towards Sustainability?' (2003) The Netherlands, Europa Law Publishing 321.

Veljanovski C, 'The Case against Green Antitrust' (2022) European Competition Journal, https://doi.org/10.1080/17441056.2022.2056346 (accessed 26 September 2022).

Wilkinson N and Klaes M (eds), *An Introduction to Behavioral Economics* (Palgrave 2012).

York JG, 'Pragmatic Sustainability: Translating Environmental Ethics into Competitive Advantage' (2009) 85 Journal of Business Ethics 97.

PART 4

International Legal Perspectives

CHAPTER 10

The Human Rights Dimension

The Impact of the Right to a Healthy Environment

Angela Schwerdtfeger

1 Introduction

Public participation in environmental matters is closely linked to human rights. Based on the rapid evolution of environmental human rights over the last three decades, three paths lead to an internationally recognised right to a healthy environment, as noted by the former Special Rapporteur (2012–2015: Independent Expert) on human rights and the environment *John H Knox*.[1] First, many states incorporated autonomous environmental rights into regional treaties[2] and their national constitutions.[3] Second, basic human rights such as the right to life and health have been applied in the environmental context (the so-called "greening" of human rights).[4] Third, rights to information, public

1 John H Knox, 'Constructing the Human Right to a Healthy Environment' (2020) 16 Annu. Rev. Law Soc. Sci. 79 ff.

2 See art 24 African Charter on Human and Peoples' Rights (1981); art 11 Protocol of San Salvador (1988); art 38 Arab Charter on Human Rights (2004); Principles 28–29 ASEAN Human Rights Declaration (2012). See also Report of the Special Rapporteur on the issue of human rights obligations relating to the enjoyment of a safe, clean, healthy and sustainable environment, UN Doc A/73/188 (19 July 2018), para 33.

3 Lists provided by David R Boyd, 'Catalyst for change: evaluating forty years of experience in implementing the right to a healthy environment' in John H Knox/Ramin Pejan (eds), *The Human Right to a Healthy Environment* (CUP 2018), 19–23; James R May and Erin Daly, *Global Environmental Constitutionalism* (CUP 2015) appendix A. See Report of the Special Rapporteur on the issue of human rights obligations relating to the enjoyment of a safe, clean, healthy and sustainable environment, UN Doc A/73/188 (19 July 2018), paras 30ff for examples; Angela Schwerdtfeger, 'Artikel 37 Umweltschutz' in Jürgen Meyer/Sven Hölscheidt (eds), *Charta der Grundrechte der Europäischen Union* (5th ed, Nomos 2019) paras 5ff on EU member states. According to UN HRC, Res. 48/13 The human right to a clean, healthy and sustainable environment, 8 October 2021 recital 17, more than 155 states have recognized some form of a right to a healthy environment.

4 See eg ECtHR, application no 16798/90 – *López Ostra v Spain* (1994) with regard to Art 8 ECHR – Right to respect for private and family life; African Commission on Human and Peoples' Rights, communication no. 155/96 – *Social and Economic Rights Action Centre v. Nigeria* (2001), para 52. For further examples see Birgit Peters, 'Zur Anwendbarkeit der Europäischen

participation and access to justice were included in multilateral environmental instruments.[5]

The three paths illustrate that the relationship between human rights and the environment can be examined from different perspectives and that human rights and environmental protection are thus interdependent.[6] On the one hand, a clean, healthy and sustainable environment is a prerequisite for the full enjoyment of human rights.[7] Environmental damage and degradation have negative implications for human rights.[8] This is where the greening of human rights comes in.[9] On the other hand, the exercise of human rights is vital to the

Menschenrechtskonvention in Umwelt- und Klimaschutzfragen' (2021) 59 Archiv des Völkerrechts 164, 171ff.

5 See Convention on Access to Information, Public Participation in Decision-Making and Access to Justice in Environmental Matters, 2161 UNTS 447, drafted within the framework of the United Nations Economic Commission for Europe, signed in **Aarhus**, Denmark on 25 June 1998, entered into force on 30 October 2001; Regional Agreement on Access to Information, Public Participation and Justice in Environmental Matters in Latin America and the Caribbean, C.N.195.2018.TREATIES-XXVII.18 (9 April 2018) (Opening for signature) and C.N.196.2018. TREATIES-XXVII.18 (9 April 2018) (Issuance of Certified True Copies), initiated at the United Nations Conference on Sustainable Development (Rio+20) in 2012 (Adoption of the Declaration on the application of Principle 10 of the Rio Declaration on Environment and Development in Latin America and the Caribbean, UN Doc A/CONF.216/13), drafted within the framework of the United Nations Economic Commission for Latin America and the Caribbean, signed in **Escazú**, Costa Rica, on 4 March 2018, entered into force on 22 April 2021. See also the (voluntary) Guidelines for the Development of National Legislation on Access to Information, Public Participation and Access to Justice in Environmental Matters, adopted in Bali, Indonesia, by UNEP Governing Council, decision SS.XI/5 (26 February 2010) part A.

6 Report of the Special Rapporteur on the issue of human rights obligations relating to the enjoyment of a safe, clean, healthy and sustainable environment, UN Doc A/HRC/37/59 (24 January 2018), Annex: Framework principles on human rights and the environment, para 4.

7 Reports of the Special Rapporteur on the issue of human rights obligations relating to the enjoyment of a safe, clean, healthy and sustainable environment, UN Doc A/73/188 (19 July 2018), paras 2, 12–13, 37, 39; UN Doc A/HRC/37/59 (24 January 2018), Annex: Framework principles on human rights and the environment, principle 1, para 4; HRC, The human right to a clean, healthy and sustainable environment, UN Res. 48/ 13 (8 October 2021) recital 15.

8 For example, for the right to life, personal integrity, health, or property. See Report of the Special Rapporteur on the issue of human rights obligations relating to the enjoyment of a safe, clean, healthy and sustainable environment, UN Doc A/HRC/37/59 (24 January 2018), Annex: Framework principles on human rights and the environment, para 1; HRC, The human right to a clean, healthy and sustainable environment, UN Res. 48/13 (8 October 2021) recital 9; UNGA, The human right to a clean, healthy and sustainable environment, Res 76/300 (28 July 2022) recitals 9, 13; IACtHR, *The Environment and Human Rights*, Advisory Opinion (15 November 2017) OC-23/17 paras 47ff.

9 Cf Report of the Special Rapporteur on the issue of human rights obligations relating to the enjoyment of a safe, clean, healthy and sustainable environment, UN Doc A/73/188 (19 July 2018), para 13.

protection of the environment[10] as they allow for informed, transparent, and responsive policymaking.[11] This applies in particular to the procedural rights to information, public participation in decision-making and access to justice (as distinct from substantive rights such as the rights to life and health),[12] which therefore have an instrumental character. Both perspectives can be adopted through the inclusion of autonomous environmental rights in regional treaties and national constitutions.

Two regional treaties are particularly relevant for an analysis of procedural environmental human rights including the right to public participation. The Convention on Access to Information, Public Participation in Decision-Making and Access to Justice in Environmental Matters (1998/2001) (the "Aarhus Convention" (AC))[13] was the first legally binding international instrument specifically dedicated to the procedural environmental rights set out in principle 10 of the *Rio Declaration on Environment and Development*.[14] It was also the first international treaty to stipulate comprehensively – without restriction to a specific environmental medium or particular circumstances – the rights of individuals (and associations) to access to information, public participation in decision-making and access to justice in environmental matters.[15] The example of the AC was followed by the Regional Agreement on

10 Reports of the Special Rapporteur on the issue of human rights obligations relating to the enjoyment of a safe, clean, healthy and sustainable environment, UN Doc A/73/188 (19 July 2018), para 39; UN Doc A/HRC/37/59 (24 January 2018), Annex: Framework principles on human rights and the environment, para 1 principle 2.

11 Preliminary report of the Independent Expert on the issue of human rights obligations relating to the enjoyment of a safe, clean, healthy and sustainable environment, UN Doc A/HRC/22/43 (24 December 2012), para 10.

12 Reports of the Special Rapporteur on the issue of human rights obligations relating to the enjoyment of a safe, clean, healthy and sustainable environment, UN Doc A/73/188 (19 July 2018), para 2; UN Doc A/HRC/37/59 (24 January 2018), Annex: Framework principles on human rights and the environment, paras 4, 6; HRC, The human right to a clean, healthy and sustainable environment, UN Res. 48/13 (8 October 2021) recital 12. Other rights are those of freedom of expression, association and peaceful assembly (in relation to environmental matters); see Report of the Special Rapporteur, UN Doc A/73/188 para 14; IACtHR, *The Environment and Human Rights*, Advisory Opinion, OC-23/17 (15 November 2017) paras 64, 211.

13 Convention on Access to Information, Public Participation in Decision-Making and Access to Justice in Environmental Matters, 2161 UNTS 447.

14 Rio Declaration on Environment and Development of June 1992, UN Doc A/CONF.151/26 (Vol. I) (12 August 1992).

15 Jerzy Jendrośka, 'Aarhus Convention and Community Law: the Interplay' (2005) 2 JEEPL 12; Jerzy Jendroska/Stephen Stec, 'The Aarhus Convention: Towards a New Era in Environmental Democracy' (2001) 9 Env. Liability 140, 148.

Access to Information, Public Participation and Justice in Environmental Matters in Latin America and the Caribbean (2018/2021) (the "Escazú Agreement" (EA)).[16] The provisions of both regional international treaties are designed as binding international minimum standards.[17] Both treaties explicitly aim to contribute to the protection of the right to a healthy environment and provide the procedural rights for this objective.[18]

The two regional international treaties highlight the remarkable implications of the right to a healthy environment for sustainability and public participation. On the one hand, the traditional concept of sustainable development is partially superseded by the orientation of international environmental law towards a right to a healthy environment. On the other hand, the human rights perspective pushes for the elaboration of procedural environmental human rights, including the crucial right to public participation. To substantiate these claims via a comparative analysis of the AC and the EA, this chapter proceeds in four consecutive steps. It starts with a brief overview of the roots of the concepts of sustainability and public participation as well as the right to a healthy environment in international environmental law (section 2). Based on this, the respective relevance of sustainability, public participation and the right to a healthy environment under the AC and the EA will be analysed (section 3), as well as their interconnections (section 4). Finally, key aspects of the procedural environmental human right to public participation will be considered (section 5).

2 The Roots of Sustainability, Public Participation and the Right to a Healthy Environment in International Environmental Law

2.1 *Sustainability in International Environmental Law*

In international environmental law, the concept of sustainability has evolved from the tension between the objectives of economic development and environmental protection.[19] This tension was clearly formulated by the *Club of Rome's* report *The Limits to Growth* in 1972,[20] which argued that the environment

16 Regional Agreement on Access to Information, Public Participation and Justice in Environmental Matters in Latin America and the Caribbean, C.N.195.2018.TREATIES-XXVII.18 (9 April 2018) (Opening for signature) and C.N.196.2018.TREATIES-XXVII.18 (9 April 2018) (Issuance of Certified True Copies).

17 Cf art 3 para 5 AC, art 4 para 7 EA.

18 Art 1 AC, art 1 EA.

19 Benjamin J Richardson, *Time and Environmental Law* (CUP 2017) 125.

20 Donella H Meadows and others, *The Limits to Growth* (Universe Books 1972).

could not sustain continued economic growth.[21] In 1983, the UN General Assembly (UNGA)[22] approved the establishment of the World Commission on Environment and Development to "propose long-term environmental strategies for achieving sustainable development to the year 2000 and beyond".[23] In its landmark report *Our Common Future*[24] (the "Brundtland Report"),[25] the Commission advanced the concept of sustainable development[26] as "development that meets the needs of the present without compromising the ability of future generations to meet their own needs". According to the report, "at a minimum, sustainable development must not endanger the natural systems that support life on Earth: the atmosphere, the waters, the soils, and the living beings".

Sustainable development can therefore be seen as a symbiosis between economic and environmental policy and – at the level of rights – between the right to development and the right to an adequate environment.[27] Conflicting aims seemingly dissolve in this term.[28] In any case, the relative weight given to economic and ecological values in documents committed to sustainable development can vary considerably. Ecologically oriented definitions of sustainable development rely on the natural sciences; they emphasise the need for an absolute reduction of pollution and consumption to levels within the

---

21 Michael Bothe, 'Die Entwicklung des Umweltvölkerrechts 1972/2002' in K-P Dolde (ed), *Umweltrecht im Wandel* (Erich Schmidt Verlag 2011) 51, 56, points out that sustainability is an old principle of economically sensible resource management and that international law has been familiar with it since the Geneva Conventions on the Law of the Sea of 1958, at least regarding marine environmental protection.

22 On earlier steps in the United Nations framework, see Ulrich Beyerlin, 'Sustainable Development', *Max Planck Encyclopedia of Public International Law* (October 2013) paras 2 ff.

23 UNGA, Process of preparation of the Environmental Perspective to the Year 2000 and Beyond, Res 38/161 (19 December 1983), see in particular paras 8(a), 10.

24 World Commission on Environment and Development, Report 'Our Common Future', UN Doc A/42/427 (4 August 1987), endorsed by the General Assembly with UN-Res. 42/187 (11 December 1987); printed version by OUP 1987; German translation: V Hauff (ed), *Unsere gemeinsame Zukunft* (Eggenkamp Verlag 1987).

25 The Commission was chaired by the former Prime Minister of Norway Gro Harlem Brundtland.

26 Cf also Principles 2, 3, 4 of the Rio Declaration on Environment and Development of June 1992, UN Doc A/CONF.151/26 (Vol. I) (12 August 1992). For reference to sustainable development in international case law see ICJ, Gabčíkovo-Nagymaros Project (Hungary v Slovakia), Judgment, I.C.J. Reports 1997, 7, para 140; Pulp Mills on the River Uruguay (Argentina v Uruguay), Judgment, I.C.J. Reports 2010, 14, para. 177.

27 H Hohmann, 'Ergebnisse des Erdgipfels von Rio' (1993) Neue Zeitschrift für Verwaltungsrecht 311, 313–314: law of ecodevelopment.

28 Michael Bothe, 'Die Entwicklung des Umweltvölkerrechts 1972/2002' in K-P Dolde (ed), *Umweltrecht im Wandel* (Erich Schmidt Verlag 2011) 51, 56.

carrying capacity of ecosystems.[29] Against this background, environmental legislation essentially serves to reduce or avoid the most serious impacts on the environment,[30] as it is committed – with a defensive approach – to the concept of sustainability from the perspective of the environmental media under threat. Legal instruments in this field of law set limits to activities that may interfere with the environment. This perspective also explains why, in environmental law, the term "sustainability" is increasingly used in isolation from the term "development". This redefinition emphasises the ecological considerations and implies prioritisation of nature conservation over its economic use.[31]

2.2 *Public Participation in International Environmental Law*

Initial steps towards public participation in environmental matters can be traced back to the *World Charter for Nature* adopted by UNGA in 1982.[32] Its principle 16 clarified the need for the timely disclosure of environmentally relevant information for effective public consultation and participation in planning. Principle 23 went one step further, stating that all persons shall have the opportunity to participate in the formulation of decisions of direct concern to their environment.[33] The *Brundtland Report* also proposed a right to participation in chapter 12 and enumerated it alongside the rights of access to information and access to justice.[34] Subsequently, the documents of the 1992 Earth Summit in Rio de Janeiro, the *Rio Declaration on Environment and Development* (principle 10)[35] and the "Agenda 21" Action Plan[36] linked the rights to access to information, public participation and access to justice. These rights were further differentiated and elaborated in 1995 in the *Sofia Guidelines,* which resulted from the third UNECE Ministerial Conference of the "Environment for Europe" process in Sofia (Bulgaria).[37] The guidelines already established

29 Benjamin J Richardson, *Time and Environmental Law* (CUP 2017) 126.
30 Benjamin J Richardson, *Time and Environmental Law* (CUP 2017) 127, with further classifications.
31 Benjamin J Richardson, *Time and Environmental Law* (CUP 2017) 126.
32 World Charter for Nature, UN Doc A/RES/37/7 (28 October 1982).
33 Cf also principle 24.
34 World Commission on Environment and Development, Report 'Our Common Future', para 82.
35 Rio Declaration on Environment and Development of June 1992, UN Doc A/CONF.151/26 (Vol. I) (12 August 1992).
36 UN Doc A/CONF.151/4 (28 September 1992) section I chapter 8, section III, in particular 8.4.f.
37 Draft Guidelines on Access to Environmental Information and Public Participation in Environmental Decision-Making, submitted by the ECE Working Group of Senior Governmental Officials 'Environment for Europe', UN Doc ECE/CEP/24.

the subsequent three-pillar structure of the AC, which was drafted from 1996 onwards.

The historical development reveals the close connection amongst the procedural environmental rights. Nowadays, the rights to information, public participation in decision-making and access to justice in environmental matters are generally provided for alongside one another. Beyond this, the historical step-by-step process reflects a multi-level model in the relationship between these rights.[38] International documents initially only dealt with aspects of access to information, subsequently with those of public participation, and only finally with access to justice. This development can be explained by the increasing intensity with which citizens can participate in environmental protection. Only gradually were states willing to share responsibility with the public. The historical development also corresponds to a logical sequence in the sense of a multi-level model to realise environmental protection: Access to environmental information can be understood as the first level. It necessarily precedes public participation as the next level at which it is possible to influence decisions with an environmental impact. Finally, access to justice serves to effectively enforce the rights of the lower levels. Conversely, deficiencies at one level may also compromise the effective exercise of rights at the next level.[39]

2.3 *The Right to a Healthy Environment in International Environmental Law*

The history of the right to a healthy environment, which the AC and the EA seek to protect, dates back to 1972.[40] This was the year of the first UN Conference on the Environment which formulated in principle 1 of the *Stockholm Declaration*:[41] "Man has the fundamental right to freedom, equality and adequate conditions of life, in an environment of a quality that permits a life of dignity and well-being, and he bears a solemn responsibility to protect and

---

38 Angela Schwerdtfeger, *Der deutsche Verwaltungsrechtsschutz unter dem Einfluss der Aarhus-Konvention* (Mohr Siebeck 2010) 20–21.

39 Shortcomings in the application of public participation procedures may preclude the exercise of the right of access to justice under art 9(2) AC; cf ACCC, Findings and recommendations with regard to communication ACCC/C/2004/08 (Armenia), ECE/MP.PP/C.1/2006/2/Add.1 (10 May 2006) para 38.

40 The link between human rights and environmental protection had already been established in 1968 by an UNGA resolution including the decision to convene a UN Conference on the Human Environment in 1972 that resulted in the Stockholm Declaration; see UNGA Res 2398 (XXIII) (3 December 1968) on problems of the human environment.

41 Declaration of the United Nations Conference on the Human Environment, see Report of the Conference A/CONF.48/14/Rev.1 (16 June 1972).

improve the environment for present and future generations". Nevertheless, the right to a healthy environment is still not guaranteed in any global human rights treaty. More recently, however, the UN Human Rights Council in October 2021 recognised "the right to a clean, healthy and sustainable environment as a human right that is important for the enjoyment of human rights" and noted that this right is related to other rights and existing international law.[42] UNGA followed this example on 28 July 2022.[43] The right of every person to live in an ecologically sound environment adequate for their health, well-being, dignity, culture and fulfilment is also enshrined in the *Global Pact for the Environment* which the French government presented to UNGA for consideration in 2017.[44] Often, the right to an environment specified by different adjectives is equated with the shorter designation as "right to a healthy environment".[45] Reversely, the right to a healthy environment should also not be understood too narrowly, but rather broadly. The focus on the adjective "healthy" can be justified by its direct connection to individuals.

The realisation of the right to a healthy environment depends to a large extent on procedural rights, as states have some discretion to adopt substantive environmental standards. In contrast, procedural rights are particularly clear and widely recognised: The obligation of states to protect individuals against environmental harm requires them, regardless of the right under threat, to take steps to inform those who may be affected, to facilitate their participation in decision-making and to provide effective remedies for harm.[46] These procedural rights enhance compliance with environmental law and thus contribute to the protection of the environment. By protecting the environment, procedural human rights also protect the substantive human rights – of their rights holders but also of other persons.[47] This is reflected in both the AC and the EA and their respective focus on protecting the right to a healthy environment.

42 HRC, The human right to a clean, healthy and sustainable environment, Res 48/13 (8 October 2021), paras 1, 2.

43 GA, The human right to a clean, healthy and sustainable environment, Res 76/300 (28 July 2022), paras 1, 2.

44 See UNGA, Towards a Global Pact for the Environment, Res 72/277 (10 May 2018).

45 Reports of the Special Rapporteur on the issue of human rights obligations relating to the enjoyment of a safe, clean, healthy and sustainable environment, UN Doc A/73/188 (19 July 2018), para 28; UN Doc A/HRC/37/59 (24 January 2018), para 16.

46 John H Knox, 'Constructing the Human Right to a Healthy Environment' (2020) 16 Annu. Rev. Law Soc. Sci. 79, 87, 90.

47 Cf Report of the Special Rapporteur on the issue of human rights obligations relating to the enjoyment of a safe, clean, healthy and sustainable environment, UN Doc A/HRC/37/59 (24 January 2018), Annex: Framework principles on human rights and the environment, para 6.

3 Sustainability, Public Participation and the Right to a Healthy Environment in the Aarhus Convention and the Escazú Agreement

3.1 Sustainability in the Regional International Treaties

A comparison suggests that the AC and the EA attribute different weight both to the concept of sustainability itself and to the different dimensions of sustainability, i.e. the economic and environmental values.

In the AC, only the preamble refers to the term "sustainability".[48] The Parties to the convention affirm the need to ensure sustainable and environmentally sound development (recital 5), thereby acknowledging that the procedural rights guaranteed in the convention play an important role in achieving sustainable development.[49] State Parties also share the desire to promote environmental education to further understanding of the environment and sustainable development and to encourage widespread public awareness of, and participation in, decisions affecting the environment and sustainable development (recital 14).

The importance of the concept of sustainability is illustrated more clearly in the Implementation Guide to the AC. This is an explanatory document drawn up by international experts.[50] The Court of Justice of the European Union has decided that, although the observations in the Guide have "no binding force" and do not have the "normative effect" of the provisions of the AC, they can be taken into consideration if appropriate among other relevant material for the purpose of interpreting the convention.[51] According to the Implementation Guide, then, the AC provides an effective model for ensuring public participation in, *inter alia*, the definition and implementation of green economy programmes and in the choice of the most appropriate road maps to

---

48 See also UNECE, *The Aarhus Convention, An Implementation Guide* (2nd ed, United Nations Publication 2014) 18.

49 UNECE, *The Aarhus Convention, An Implementation Guide* (2nd ed, United Nations Publication 2014) 28.

50 See also UNECE, *Maastricht Recommendations on Promoting Effective Public Participation in Decision-making in Environmental Matters* (United Nations Publication 2015), prepared under the AC to assist policymakers, legislators and public authorities in their daily work of engaging the public in decision-making processes.

51 Case C-182/10 *Solvay and Others*, [16 February 2012] ECLI:EU:C:2012:82, paras 27–28. Critically, Felix Ekardt/Katharina Pöhlmann, 'Europäische Klagebefugnis: Öffentlichkeitsrichtlinie, Klagerechtsrichtline und ihre Folgen' (2005) Neue Zeitschrift für Verwaltungsrecht 532, 533.

sustainability.[52] The AC, as plausibly interpreted in the Implementation Guide, establishes that sustainable development can only be achieved through the involvement of all stakeholders.[53]

Beyond the explicit reference to the concept of sustainability, the AC emphasises the future perspective that is inherent in sustainability, as it aims at development that does not compromise the ability of future generations to meet their own needs. The Parties to the convention in its preamble recognise "the duty, both individually and in association with others, to protect and improve the environment for the benefit of present and future generations" (recital 7). Moreover, the right of every person to live in an environment adequate to his or her health and well-being, whose protection is the objective of the convention, is explicitly attributed to present and future generations in art 1.

Remarkably, art 1 of the EA establishes sustainable development as an objective of the agreement, placing it on an equal footing with the right to a healthy environment. The provision can even be understood to protect sustainable development as a right.[54] The preamble is replete with references to the concept of sustainable development. The Parties consider the *2030 Agenda for Sustainable Development*[55] as reaffirming UNGA's "commitment to achieving sustainable development in its three dimensions – economic, social and environmental – in a balanced and integrated manner" (recital 9). Furthermore, the principle of non-regression and the principle of progressive realisation (lit c), as well as the principle of permanent sovereignty of states over their natural resources (lit i) are among the principles that shall guide the Parties to the agreement in its implementation (art 3).

In the preface to the EA, *Alicia Bárcena*, the Executive Secretary of the Economic Commission for Latin America and the Caribbean (ECLAC) emphasised that the agreement balances the three dimensions of sustainable development (economic, social and environmental) and refutes "the false dichotomy between environmental protection and economic development". The Executive Secretary underlined that "growth cannot take place at the expense of the environment and the environment cannot be managed if our economies and peoples are ignored".

---

52 UNECE, *The Aarhus Convention, An Implementation Guide* (2nd ed, United Nations Publication 2014) 9, 42.

53 UNECE, *The Aarhus Convention, An Implementation Guide* (2nd ed, United Nations Publication 2014) 15.

54 Stephen Stec/Jerzy Jendroska, 'The Escazú Agreement and the Regional Approach to Rio Principle 10' (2019) 31 J. Environ. Law 533, 537–538.

55 Transforming our World: The 2030 Agenda for Sustainable Development, UN Doc A/RES/70/1 (25 September 2015).

While the AC, with its focus on the right to a healthy environment clearly aims for environmental protection, the EA strives more for a balance between environmental protection and economic growth that should not be at the expense of the other.[56] This different nuance likely results from the different stages of development of the signatory states in Europe representing the Global North on the one hand and the signatory states in Latin America and the Caribbean representing the Global South on the other. It may be regarded as an expression of the principle of common but differentiated responsibility. This principle belongs to the inter-related principles of international law that are instrumental in pursuing sustainable development in an effective way. Among these are also the duty of states to ensure sustainable use of natural resources, the principle of equity which refers to both inter- and intragenerational equity, the principle of the precautionary approach to human health, natural resources and ecosystems, and – of particular importance in the present context – the principle of public participation and access to information and justice.[57] The precautionary principle (lit f) and the principle of intergenerational equity (lit g) are also enumerated in art 3 of the EA and shall guide the parties in its implementation.

3.2 *Public Participation in the Regional International Treaties*

The AC guarantees the right to public participation as one of the three procedural rights that contribute to the protection of the right to a healthy environment (art 1) and can thus also be regarded as instrumental rights. Differing from the right to a healthy environment, the AC defines the right to public participation as an enforceable right and obliges the Parties to the convention to take the necessary legislative, regulatory and other measures as well as proper enforcement measures to implement the relevant provisions of the convention (art 3(1)). This is also illustrated by art 9(2) AC, which provides that members of the public concerned shall have access to a review procedure to challenge the legality of decisions, acts or omissions concerning specific activities for which public participation is provided for under art 6 AC. On the whole, the convention contains extensive provisions on public participation in decisions on specific activities (art 6), in relation to plans, programs and policies relating to the environment (art 7), and during the preparation of executive regulations and/

56 Cf on the "ulterior projects" of the treaties Emily Barritt 'Global Values, Transnational Expression: From Aarhus to Escazú' (2019) 11 TLI Think! Paper 1, 16.

57 Res 3/2002 Sustainable Development of the 70th ILA Conference: New Delhi Declaration of Principles of International Law Relating to Sustainable Development (6 April 2002) 3ff, that furthermore lists the principle of good governance, and the principle of integration and interrelationship, particularly in relation to human rights and social, economic and environmental objectives.

or generally applicable legally binding normative instruments (art 8). These form the second pillar of the convention – alongside access to information (first pillar) and access to justice (third pillar) in environmental matters.

According to art 1 EA, the objective of the convention is to guarantee the full and effective implementation in Latin America and the Caribbean of the right to public participation in the environmental decision-making process – as well as the rights of access to environmental information and access to justice in environmental matters. This objective stands alongside the contribution to the protection of the right to a healthy environment and to sustainable development as further objectives of the agreement. The instrumental character of the procedural rights is less clear than in the AC. Simultaneously, their intrinsic value becomes more apparent.[58] According to art 4, the Parties to the agreement shall ensure that the rights recognised in the agreement are freely exercised (para 2) and shall adopt the necessary measures to guarantee the implementation of its provisions (para 3). Access to justice shall also be ensured to challenge any decision, action or omission related to public participation in the decision-making process regarding environmental matters (art 8(2)(b)). The provisions on public participation are concentrated in art 7.

3.3 *The Right to a Healthy Environment in the Regional International Treaties*

For the first time, art 1 of the AC explicitly and bindingly provides for the right of every person, including future generations, to live in an environment adequate to his or her health and well-being.[59] The rights to access to information, public participation in decision-making and access to justice serve the procedural protection of this right, which highlights the link between environmental protection and the individual. However, art 1 AC recognises the right to a healthy environment only as the objective of the three procedural environmental rights, but not as an enforceable right. The provision does not impose any specific legal obligations on the Parties to the convention beyond guaranteeing the procedural rights of access to information, public participation and access to justice.[60]

---

58 For the relevance of participatory concepts in the Caribbean see Nicole Mohammed, 'Sustainable development goal 16 in the Caribbean context' in Alicia Bárcena/Valeria Torres/Lina M Ávila (eds), *El Acuerdo de Escazú sobre democracia ambiental y su relación con la Agenda 2030 para el Desarrollo Sostenible* (CEPAL 2021) 203ff.

59 See also recital 7; UNECE, *The Aarhus Convention, An Implementation Guide* (2nd ed, United Nations Publication 2014) 15.

60 Marc Pallemaerts, 'The human right to a healthy environment as a substantive right' in Maguelonne Déjeant-Pons/Marc Pallemaerts, *Human rights and the environment*

The preamble connects the idea that adequate environmental protection is essential to the enjoyment of basic human rights (recital 6) with the idea that every person has the right to live in a healthy environment (and the obligation to protect the environment) (recital 7).[61] Thus, the right to a healthy environment not only illustrates the link between human rights and environmental protection. The preamble goes one step further, as the right to a healthy environment is deduced from the fact that a healthy environment is a precondition for the enjoyment of well-established basic rights, such as the right to life and the right to health.[62] Moreover, the AC is the first international treaty that extends the right to a healthy environment to future generations, thus pursuing an intergenerational approach.[63] As already mentioned, the concept of intergenerational equity, i.e. that the impact of current actions on future generations must be taken into account, is also one of the fundamental tenets of sustainable development.[64] Previously, human rights law had tended to avoid identifying the rights of those not yet born.[65]

The EA, according to its art 1, also aims to protect the right of every person of present and future generations to live in a healthy environment. The agreement is even classified as a human rights treaty in the preface,[66] and the preamble refers explicitly to international human rights instruments (recital 5). The general provisions in art 4 on the exercise of the rights recognised and the implementation of the provisions of the agreement also do not explicitly differentiate between procedural rights on the one hand and the right to a healthy environment (or sustainable development) on the other, all of which

(Council of Europe Publishing 2002) 18; Angela Schwerdtfeger, *Der deutsche Verwaltungsrechtsschutz unter dem Einfluss der Aarhus-Konvention* (Mohr Siebeck 2011) 32. See also Emily Barritt 'Global Values, Transnational Expression: From Aarhus to Escazú' (2019) 11 TLI Think! Paper 1, 11.

61 UNECE, *The Aarhus Convention, An Implementation Guide* (2nd ed, United Nations Publication 2014) 18, 22.

62 Cf UNECE, *The Aarhus Convention, An Implementation Guide* (2nd ed, United Nations Publication 2014) 28, 42.

63 UNECE, *The Aarhus Convention, An Implementation Guide* (2nd ed, United Nations Publication 2014) 30, referring also to ICJ, Legality of the Threat or Use of Nuclear Weapons, Advisory Opinion, ICJ Reports 1996, 226.

64 UNECE, *The Aarhus Convention, An Implementation Guide* (2nd ed, United Nations Publication 2014) 42.

65 John H Knox, 'Constructing the Human Right to a Healthy Environment' (2020) 16 Annu. Rev. Law Soc. Sci. 79, 92.

66 See also Emily Barritt 'Global Values, Transnational Expression: From Aarhus to Escazú' (2019) 11 TLI Think! Paper 1, 12.

can be considered environmental human rights.[67] This raises the question of whether the right to a healthy environment is also an enforceable right. However, weighty arguments militate against this assumption. First, art 4(1) EA as a specific provision on the right to a healthy environment suggests that this right is to be distinguished from the procedural rights and should not be subsumed under art 4(2) EA.[68] Accordingly, the Parties to the agreement shall guarantee this right as well as any other universally-recognised human right related to the agreement. Second, the right to a healthy environment is not further specified in the agreement. Third, it is only with regard to procedural rights that art 1 states that the aim of the agreement is to guarantee their "full and effective implementation". With regard to the right to a healthy environment, by contrast, only the creation and strengthening of capacities and cooperation, contributing to the protection of this right, is envisaged. Therefore, despite the divergent provisions on the right to a healthy environment in the two regional international treaties, it can be assumed that its meaning does not differ significantly. The greater openness to recognition of an independent right to a healthy environment that can nevertheless be observed may again at least also be linked to the perspective of the Global South. This is further illustrated by the Advisory Opinion of the Inter-American Court of Human Rights (IACtHR) from 2017.[69]

4 Linkages between Sustainability, Public Participation and the Right to a Healthy Environment

4.1 Sustainability and Public Participation

As previously indicated, the procedural right to public participation in decision-making – as well as the rights to information and to access to justice – in environmental matters has an instrumental character in relation to sustainable development. This is reflected in the preamble to the AC (recitals 5, 14)[70] and in the preamble to the EA. The Parties to the agreement are convinced that access rights contribute to the strengthening of, *inter alia*, democracy, sustainable development and human rights (recitals 4, 8), thus expressing the

67 Cf Stephen Stec/Jerzy Jendroska, 'The Escazú Agreement and the Regional Approach to Rio Principle 10' (2019) 31 J. Environ. Law 533, 538.

68 For a different interpretation see Emily Barritt 'Global Values, Transnational Expression: From Aarhus to Escazú' (2019) 11 TLI Think! Paper 1, 11.

69 See below 4.3.

70 See above 3.1.

instrumental character of the right to public participation. In contrast, art 1 EA lists the procedural rights alongside sustainable development (and the right to a healthy environment), without providing any information on their interrelationship. However, according to the same provision, the agreement shall guarantee the full and effective "implementation" of the procedural rights, while it shall only "contribut(e) to (…) sustainable development". This difference in wording, which is inspired by art 1 AC, implicitly confirms the described linkage between public participation and sustainable development. It is also logical in view of the lesser degree of concretisation of sustainable development compared to the right to public participation in the regional international treaties. While the goal of sustainable development sets the direction, the enforceable procedural right serves as a means to achieve it.

This connection applies to international environmental law in general. The instrumental character of the procedural environmental rights in relation to sustainable development is reflected, for example, in the International Law Association's (ILA) *New Delhi Declaration of Principles of International Law Relating to Sustainable Development* (2002).[71] Furthermore, the ILA's *2012 Sofia Guiding Statements on the Judicial Elaboration of the 2002 New Delhi Declaration* refer to the principles of public participation, access to information and justice as foundational to sustainable development.[72] According to these Statements, treaties and rules of customary international law should in general be interpreted in the light of principles of sustainable development.[73]

4.2 *The Right to a Healthy Environment and Public Participation*

Art 1 AC clearly expresses the instrumental character of the rights to information, public participation in decision-making and access to justice in environmental matters (also) in relation to the right to a healthy environment, when the procedural rights are guaranteed to contribute to the protection of the right to a healthy environment. This is again confirmed by the vague substantive content of the right to a healthy environment and its lack of isolated enforceability.[74]

---

71 Res 3/2002 Sustainable Development of the 70th ILA Conference: New Delhi Declaration of Principles of International Law Relating to Sustainable Development (6 April 2002) para 5.

72 Committee on International Law on Sustainable Development of the 75th ILA Conference, Res 7/2012 (30 August 2012), Annex, para 7.

73 Committee on International Law on Sustainable Development of the 75th ILA Conference, Res 7/2012 (30 August 2012), Annex, para 2.

74 See above 3.2 and 3.3

For the EA, it is possible in this respect to refer to observations on sustainable development, since the right to a healthy environment is granted a parallel status, particularly in art 1 EA. In addition, the general provisions of art 4 reiterate at the outset that "(e)ach Party shall guarantee the right of every person to live in a healthy environment and any other universally-recognized human right related to the Agreement".

4.3 *Sustainability and the Right to a Healthy Environment*

If the right to public participation in decision-making and the other procedural rights in environmental matters are instrumental for both sustainable development and the right to a healthy environment[75] (and also for the environment as a collective interest),[76] the question of their interrelationship also arises as a consequence.

Notably, it is not only the convergence of sustainable development and the right to a healthy environment in the AC and the EA that make it clear that these are largely congruent objectives. In principle 1 of the Rio Declaration on Environment and Development,[77] for example, the states recognised that "(h)uman beings are at the centre of concerns for sustainable development" and that "(t)hey are entitled to a healthy and productive life in harmony with nature". Furthermore, the UN Human Rights Council and UNGA have explicitly recognised "the right to a clean, healthy and sustainable environment as a human right".[78]

Nevertheless, obvious differences exist between sustainable development and the right to a healthy environment. These can be illustrated by the two examples provided. In principle 1 of the Rio Declaration, states acknowledged the great importance of sustainable development for individuals, but avoided mentioning rights.[79] Furthermore, both the AC and the EA aim to protect the

---

75 Report of the Special Rapporteur on the issue of human rights obligations relating to the enjoyment of a safe, clean, healthy and sustainable environment, UN Doc A/HRC/37/59 (24 January 2018), Annex: Framework principles on human rights and the environment, paras 1, 23.

76 Report of the Special Rapporteur on the issue of human rights obligations relating to the enjoyment of a safe, clean, healthy and sustainable environment, UN Doc A/73/188 (19 July 2018), para 42.

77 Rio Declaration on Environment and Development of June 1992, UN Doc A/CONF.151/26 (Vol. I) (12 August 1992).

78 HRC, The human right to a clean, healthy and sustainable environment, Res 48/13 (8 October 2021) para 1; UNGA, The human right to a clean, healthy and sustainable environment, Res 76/300 (28 July 2022) para 1.

79 Dinah Shelton, 'What happened in Rio to human rights?' (1992) 3 Yearbook of International Environmental Law 75, 83.

right to a healthy environment, which does not have to qualify as sustainable at the same time – like in the Human Rights Council and the UNGA resolutions. Rather, the EA places sustainable development as an objective alongside the right to a healthy environment. This raises the question: What does this imply?

First, the recognition of a right, i.e. the right to a healthy environment, already has a different quality from an objective legal principle, i.e. the principle of sustainable development. It goes one step further insofar as it presupposes beneficiaries through its subjective orientation as opposed to an objective law principle. This is fundamentally linked to the idea of simplified enforceability, even if the details depend on the substance of the right in question. However, as mentioned above, art 1 EA can also be read as referring to sustainable development as a right. Second, the characterisation of the environment as healthy establishes the most direct connection to the individual.[80] The recognition of an autonomous right to a healthy environment raises the relationship between negative environmental impacts and individuals to a new level. It is detached from other human rights that are not specifically tailored to this relationship. This is precisely the difference to the greening of generally recognised human rights. A healthy environment is no longer merely the prerequisite for individual human rights, rather it sits central to the individual itself and to the full enjoyment of all human rights.[81] According to the Inter-American Court of Human Rights (IACtHR), the autonomous right to a healthy environment, unlike other rights, even protects the components of the environment (e.g. forests, rivers, and seas) as legal interests in themselves, regardless of the certainty or evidence of a risk to individuals.[82] Moreover, in its collective dimension, it forms a universal value owed to present and future generations.[83]

Finally, since the right to a healthy environment focuses on the protection of the environment as a habitat for individuals, it emphasises one of the three dimensions of sustainable development: Environmental protection is placed above economic and social development. At this point, however, the different accentuations of the AC and the EA should be stressed once again. While

80 Cf UNECE, *The Aarhus Convention, An Implementation Guide* (2nd ed, United Nations Publication 2014) 28.

81 Cf Preliminary report of the Independent Expert on the issue of human rights obligations relating to the enjoyment of a safe, clean, healthy and sustainable environment, UN Doc A/HRC/22/43 (24 December 2012) para 19.

82 IACtHR, *The Environment and Human Rights*, Advisory Opinion OC-23/17 (15 November 2017) para 62, further referring in this context to the progressive recognition of rights of nature.

83 IACtHR, *The Environment and Human Rights*, Advisory Opinion OC-23/17 (15 November 2017) para 59.

the AC clearly highlights the right to a healthy environment, the EA underlines the equal importance of this right and sustainable development (art 1), and the commitment to achieving the three dimensions of sustainable development in a balanced and integrated manner (preamble, recital 9).[84] In other words, under the EA environmental protection should not be given priority as a matter of principle.

Against this background, the focus on environmental protection seems to correspond only to the view of the Global North. For example, the Human Rights Council also juxtaposes sustainable development and environmental protection when it states that both contribute to and promote human well-being and the enjoyment of human rights for present and future generations.[85] Moreover, according to the IACtHR, the recognition of the right to a healthy environment as a right in itself is based on the close connection between environmental protection, sustainable development and human rights.[86] Following the African Commission on Human and Peoples' Rights, the right to a healthy environment gives rise to states' obligations to take reasonable measures to secure an ecologically sustainable development and use of natural resources.[87] What can be concluded in any case, however, is that the orientation towards a right to a healthy environment means that sustainable development must not come at the expense of human rights.[88]

5 A Closer Look at Public Participation

5.1 Participation in the Law-making Process

While the principle of sustainable development and the right to a healthy environment form the basis of the AC and the EA, the treaty provisions focus on the procedural rights of the eponymous treaties. Public participation as the central second pillar of the treaties can therefore be examined in more

84 Cf UNGA, The human right to a clean, healthy and sustainable environment, Res 76/300 (28 July 2022), recital 8.

85 HRC, The human right to a clean, healthy and sustainable environment, UN Res 48/13 (8 October 2021) recital 7.

86 IACtHR, *The Environment and Human Rights*, Advisory Opinion OC-23/17 (15 November 2017) para 55.

87 Cf African Commission on Human and Peoples' Rights, Case of the Social and Economic Rights Center (SERAC) and Center for Economic and Social Rights (CESR) v Nigeria. Communication 155/96 (27 October 2001) paras 52–53.

88 Cf Report of the Special Rapporteur on the issue of human rights obligations relating to the enjoyment of a safe, clean, healthy and sustainable environment, UN Doc A/HRC/37/59 (24 January 2018), Annex: Framework principles on human rights and the environment, principle 16, paras 54–55.

detail below. However, the AC and the EA not only address public participation in decision-making as a central issue, but they were also drafted with the active participation of the public. Numerous non-governmental organisations (NGOs) were involved in the negotiations of the AC. Such a strong participation of NGOs had never occurred before.[89] For the first time, NGOs specifically prepared one session in which government representatives and NGOs debated together.[90] Civil society and the wider public also participated significantly in the EA negotiations.[91] At the first Conference of the Parties in April 2022, it became clear that public participation will continue to be important in the future of the EA. According to the Rules of Procedure of the Conference of the Parties, "(t)he public shall participate meaningfully in the Conference of the Parties and the subsidiary bodies established".[92]

Thus, public participation was realised on the two levels of drafting and content of the treaties. This may be due, on the one hand, to the subject matter of the treaties, namely public participation. The public should be involved in the decisions regarding its participation. On the other hand, the legal field of environmental law may also play a role, since the environment is a common good that can only be protected together. UNGA had already suggested that the World Commission on Environment and Development should "(m)aintain an exchange of views with (…) all (…) sections of public opinion, particularly youth, concerned with the environment"[93] when developing environmental strategies for achieving sustainable development.

5.2 *Links to Concepts of Democracy*

In particular, the right to public participation as a procedural environmental human right also has a democratic dimension. In the preamble to the AC, its parties recognise "the importance of the respective roles that individual

---

89 Cf Katy Brady, 'New Convention on Access to Information and Public Participation in Environmental Matters' (1998) 28 EPL 69; Jerzy Jendrośka, 'Aarhus Convention and Community Law: the Interplay' (2005) 2 JEEPL 12, 14; Jerzy Jendroska/Stephen Stec, 'The Aarhus Convention: Towards a New Era in Environmental Democracy' (2001) Env. Liability 140, 147; Jeremy Wates, 'The Aarhus Convention: a Driving Force for Environmental Democracy' (2005) 2 JEEPL 2, 9–10.

90 Katy Brady, 'Aarhus Convention Signed' (1998) 28 EPL 171ff.

91 Foreword to the agreement by Antonio Guterres, UN Secretary-General; preface to the agreement by Alicia Bárcena, Executive Secretary Economic Commission for Latin America and the Caribbean (UNECLAC); Emily Barritt 'Global Values, Transnational Expression: From Aarhus to Escazú' (2019) 11 TLI Think! Paper 1, 7–8.

92 First meeting of the Conference of the Parties, Doc 22-00344 (22 April 2022), Decision I/1, Annex 1, XIV. 1.; with regard to the Committee to Support Implementation and Compliance see Decision I/3, Annex 1, III. 4., VI.

93 UN Doc A/RES/38/161 (19 December 1983), see in particular para 9(a).

citizens, non-governmental organizations and the private sector can play in environmental protection" (recital 13). The convention as a whole follows the approach of environmental protection through public supervision, and thus through decentralised control of law enforcement. This idea had determined European Union (at that time the European Community) law already before.[94] What is more, public participation under the AC means interaction between the public and state authorities, which is an expression of the idea of participatory democracy.[95]

The EA is also assumed to recognise "core democratic" principles and to strengthen environmental democracy.[96] In its preamble, the Parties to the agreement recognise "the important work of the public and of human rights defenders in environmental matters for strengthening democracy, access rights and sustainable development and their fundamental contributions in this regard" (recital 11). According to art 4(6) EA, "(e)ach Party shall guarantee an enabling environment for the work of persons, associations, organizations or groups that promote environmental protection, by recognizing and protecting them". As a specification of this "general provision", the agreement even contains a separate provision on (the protection of) human rights defenders in environmental matters (art 9).[97]

5.3 *Rights Holders*

This idea of participatory democracy is also reflected in the provisions of the regional international treaties on rights holders. Procedural rights are granted to the public. In environmental law, this approach seems logical due to the character of the protected environment as a common good of mankind. However, it is not always easily compatible with the (different) national perspectives,

---

94 Angela Schwerdtfeger, *Der deutsche Verwaltungsrechtsschutz unter dem Einfluss der Aarhus-Konvention* (Mohr Siebeck 2010) 23ff.

95 Cf preamble, recital 21 AC; Case T-111/11 ClientEarth v Commission [13 September 2013] ECLI:EU:T:2013:482 paras 105–106; Jerzy Jendroska/Stephen Stec, 'The Aarhus Convention: Towards a New Era in Environmental Democracy' (2001) Env. Liability 140, 142–143, 151; Christian Walter, 'Internationalisierung des deutschen und Europäischen Verwaltungsverfahrens- und Verwaltungsprozessrechts' (2005) Europarecht 302, 306.

96 Cf preface to the agreement by Alicia Bárcena, Executive Secretary Economic Commission for Latin America and the Caribbean; preamble, recital 4 EA. See also Daniel Barragán Terán, 'Educación, democracia ambiental y desarrollo sostenible' in Alicia Bárcena/Valeria Torres/Lina M Ávila (eds), *El Acuerdo de Escazú sobre democracia ambiental y su relación con la Agenda 2030 para el Desarrollo Sostenible* (CEPAL 2021) 167ff.

97 On its significance see Emily Barritt 'Global Values, Transnational Expression: From Aarhus to Escazú' (2019) 11 TLI Think! Paper 1, 12; Stephen Stec/Jerzy Jendroska, 'The Escazú Agreement and the Regional Approach to Rio Principle 10' (2019) 31 J. Environ. Law 533, 539–540.

some of which are strongly based on the distinction of the individual from the general public.[98]

The AC distinguishes between "the public" and "the public concerned". According to art 2(4) "'(t)he public' means one or more natural or legal persons, and, in accordance with national legislation or practice, their associations, organizations or groups". According to art 2(5), "'(t)he public concerned' means the public affected or likely to be affected by, or having an interest in, the environmental decision-making (...)". Under the convention, the public concerned has more extensive rights than the (general) public, including in public participation.[99] In this context, however, it should be noted that "non-governmental organizations promoting environmental protection and meeting any requirements under national law" fall within the definition of the public concerned, according to art 2(5) AC.

The EA goes even further. It makes no additional distinction with regard to the public.[100] Art 2(d) EA defines the public as "one or more natural or legal persons and the associations, organizations or groups established by those persons, that are nationals or that are subject to the national jurisdiction of the State Party". In addition, the EA contains special provisions with respect to persons or groups in vulnerable situations.[101] According to art 2(e) EA, this refers to "those persons or groups that face particular difficulties in fully exercising the access rights recognized in the present Agreement, because of circumstances or conditions identified within each Party's national context and in accordance with its international obligations". The Parties to the agreement shall ensure that guidance and assistance facilitating the exercise of access rights is provided particularly to those persons or groups in vulnerable situations (art 4(5) EA).[102] Indigenous people are explicitly mentioned (art 5(4), art 7(15)), again reflecting the particular perspective of the Global South.

98 For the German perspective see Angela Schwerdtfeger, *Der deutsche Verwaltungsrechtsschutz unter dem Einfluss der Aarhus-Konvention* (Mohr Siebeck 2010) 58ff, 69ff.

99 For example with regard to information on the proposed decisions on specific activities, art 6(2) AC, access for examination to all information relevant to the decision-making, art 6(6) AC, and access to a review procedure before a court of law and/or another independent and impartial body established by law, art 9(2) AC. According to the ECJ, art 6 AC as a whole is only applicable to the public concerned, see Case C-826/18 *Stichting Varkens in Nood and Others* [14 January 2021] ECLI:EU:C:2021:7 paras 39ff.

100 See also Stephen Stec/Jerzy Jendroska, 'The Escazú Agreement and the Regional Approach to Rio Principle 10' (2019) 31 J. Environ. Law 533, 537.

101 Cf UNGA, The human right to a clean, healthy and sustainable environment, Res 76/300 (28 July 2022), recitals 11, 15.

102 See also Emily Barritt 'Global Values, Transnational Expression: From Aarhus to Escazú' (2019) 11 TLI Think! Paper 1, 10–11, 18; Stephen Stec/Jerzy Jendroska, 'The Escazú Agreement and the Regional Approach to Rio Principle 10' (2019) 31 J. Environ. Law 533, 541–542.

Specifically on public participation, art 7(14) EA requires that persons or groups in vulnerable situations shall be identified and supported "in order to engage them in an active, timely and effective manner in participation mechanisms". In other words, barriers to participation are to be eliminated.

5.4 *Enforceability*

The regional international treaties provide enforcement mechanisms at two levels for the procedural rights they guarantee. The rights under the first pillar (access to information) and the second pillar (public participation) are safeguarded via the third pillar (access to justice). According to art 9(2) AC and art 8(2)(b) EA, the contracting parties must ensure access to a review procedure to challenge the legality of, *inter alia*, any decision, action or omission related to public participation in the decision-making process regarding environmental matters. Since the AC is a so-called mixed agreement, concluded both by the European Union (EU) Member States and the European Union itself, case law of the Court of Justice of the European Union also exists on public participation under the convention.[103]

The situation differs with regard to the EA and the IACtHR, whose European counterpart is the European Court of Human Rights (ECtHR).[104] In view of the previous case law of the IACtHR, however, it is not unreasonable to expect that the court would affirm its jurisdiction in the case of violations of procedural human rights under the EA.[105] Moreover, it should be noted that both the IACtHR[106] and the ECtHR[107] have already derived environmental procedural rights from other human rights guaranteed in the American Convention on

103 See eg Case C-826/18 *Stichting Varkens in Nood and Others* [14 January 2021] ECLI:EU:C:2021:7 paras 39ff.

104 For references to the AC by the ECtHR in its interpretations of the ECHR see Birgit Peters, 'Unpacking the Diversity of Procedural Environmental Rights' (2018) 30 J. Environ. Law 1, 9–10.

105 Cf Victor R Hernández-Mendible, 'El Acuerdo de Escazú y la Competencia de la Corte Interamericana para Tutelar los Derechos en Materia Ambiental' in Henry J Guanipa/ Marisol L Leal/ Florian Huber (eds), *Crisis climática, transición energética y derechos humanos* (Tomo 1, 2020) 323, 350–353; see also IACtHR, *The Environment and Human Rights*, Advisory Opinion OC-23/17 (15 November 2017), para 218.

106 IACtHR, *The Environment and Human Rights*, Advisory Opinion OC-23/17 (15 November 2017) para 241 with regard to "*the rights to life and to personal integrity as well as any other rights affected*".

107 ECtHR, application no 38182/03 – *Grimkovskaya v Ukraine* (2011), para 72 with regard to participation. For further examples see Birgit Peters, 'Unpacking the Diversity of Procedural Environmental Rights' (2018) 30 J. Environ. Law 1, 18ff.

Human Rights and the (European) Convention for the Protection of Human Rights and Fundamental Freedoms (ECHR).[108]

In addition, both regional international treaties provide for their own supervisory bodies, which are established as subsidiary bodies of the Conferences of the Parties. Based on art 15 AC, the first Aarhus Convention Compliance Committee (ACCC) was elected in 2002. Since 2005, it has submitted almost one hundred findings to the Conference of the Parties on reported violations of the convention.[109] The Committee to Support Implementation and Compliance established in art 18 EA does not yet exist. However, the Conference of the Parties already adopted the Rules relating to the structure and functions of the Committee to Support Implementation and Compliance at its first meeting in April 2022.[110]

5.5 *Findings of the Arhus Convention Compliance Committee*

In its numerous findings, the ACCC also made fundamental remarks on the second pillar (public participation) of the AC. These findings can generally be read as being guided by the concept of participatory democracy on which the convention is based. The corresponding broad understanding of public participation influences both the interpretation of the public concerned and the process of public participation.

Art 6(2) AC requires, *inter alia*, that the public concerned shall be informed in an effective manner. The Committee specifies that all those potentially concerned should have a reasonable chance to learn about the decision-making in question and their possibilities to participate.[111] The public concerned, which, as we have seen, includes both NGOs and individual members of the public, must not be based on discretionary power to pick individual representatives of

108 For decisions of other human rights bodies deriving procedural rights from human rights, see Birgit Peters, *Legitimation durch Öffentlichkeitsbeteiligung* (Mohr Siebeck 2020) 234ff.

109 For further information see <https://unece.org/environment-policy/public-participation/aarhus-convention/compliance-committee> last accessed 10 August 2022.

110 First meeting of the Conference Parties, Doc 22-00344 (22 April 2022) Decision I/3.

111 ACCC, Report with regard to communication ACCC/C/2006/16 (Lithuania), ECE/MP.PP/2008/5/Add.6 (4 April 2008) para 67; Findings with regard to communication ACCC/C/2007/22 (France), ECE/MP.PP/C.1/2009/4/Add.1 (8 February 2011) para 41.

certain groups.[112] Participation in closed advisory groups cannot be considered as fulfilling public participation requirements under the AC.[113]

In substance, the ACCC objects to the assumption that the general public cannot override the judgement of experts. The general public includes persons with different expertise, knowledge, opinions or experiences which, according to the objectives of the AC, should be taken into account in decision-making.[114] The Committee points out that according to the preamble to the convention (recital 9), public participation is a fundamental tool for improving the quality of environmental decision-making. The AC aims to ensure that the public has the opportunity to express its concerns and that public authorities give due consideration to those concerns. In doing so it helps to ensure that environmental considerations are integrated into executive decision-making.[115]

According to art 6(4) AC, each party shall provide for early public participation, when all options are open and effective public participation can take place. In the ACCC's findings on this and other provisions, it is evident that the convention is intended to create real opportunities for the public to influence decision-making. If construction starts before hearings are held, this is clearly not in conformity with the requirement for "reasonable time frames" and "early public participation, when all options are open" under art 6(3), (4) AC.[116] It is important that participation includes public debate and the opportunity for the public to participate in this debate at an early stage of the decision-making process, when the outcome of the public participation can still be taken into account.[117] The ACCC refers to the concept of tiered decision-making, where at each stage only the options already selected at the preceding stage

112 ACCC, Findings and recommendations with regard to communication ACCC/C/2010/51 (Romania), ECE/MP.PP/C.1/2014/12 (14 July 2014) para 109; Findings and recommendations with regard to communication ACCC/C/2014/105 (Hungary), ECE/MP.PP/C.1/2021/16 (6 October 2021) paras 140–141, 144.

113 ACCC, Findings and recommendations with regard to communication ACCC/C/2010/51 (Romania), ECE/MP.PP/C.1/2014/12 (14 July 2014) para 109; Findings and recommendations with regard to communication ACCC/C/2014/105 (Hungary), ECE/MP.PP/C.1/2021/16 (6 October 2021) paras 140–141, 144.

114 ACCC, Findings and recommendations with regard to communication ACCC/C/2012/69 (Romania), ECE/MP.PP/C.1/2015/10 (11 December 2015) para 82; cf ACCC, Findings and recommendations with regard to communication ACCC/C/2014/121 (EU), ECE/MP.PP/C.1/2020/8 (14 September 2020) para 112.

115 ACCC, Findings and recommendations with regard to communication ACCC/C/2012/76 (Bulgaria), ECE/MP.PP/C.1/2016/3 (7 March 2016) para 68.

116 ACCC, Findings and recommendations with regard to communication ACCC/C/2004/02 (Kazakhstan), ECE/MP.PP/C.1/2005/2/Add.2 (14 March 2005) para 25.

117 ACCC, Findings with regard to communication ACCC/C/2008/26 (Austria), ECE/MP.PP/C.1/2009/6/Add.1, para 66; cf Findings and recommendations with regard to communication ACCC/C/2009/41 (Slovakia), ECE/MP.PP/2011/11/Add.3 (12 May 2011) para 40.

are addressed.[118] Therefore, if participation comes too late, alternative options may have already effectively been eliminated and decisive decisions may have been pre-determined.[119] A multi-tiered decision-making procedure that provides for public participation on certain options at an early stage but considers other options only at a later stage without public participation is also incompatible with the AC.[120] Art 6(4) precludes foreclosing any options without public participation.[121] It is not sufficient that there is a formal possibility, *de jure*, to turn down an application, if, in practice (e.g. due to political and commercial pressures or notions of legal certainty), this never or hardly ever happens.[122] Furthermore, it must also be apparent to the public concerned that all options are open at the time of the public participation.[123]

According to art 6(8) AC, each party shall ensure that due account is taken of the outcome of the public participation in the decision. This is the logical consequence of effective public participation. The ACCC recognises that the public authority is ultimately responsible for the decision and must take into account a number of (conflicting) factors, including the comments of the public. The requirement in art 6(8) AC to take "due account" of the outcome of the

118 ACCC, Report with regard to communication ACCC/C/2006/16 (Lithuania), ECE/MP.PP/2008/5/Add.6 (4 April 2008) para 71; Findings and recommendations with regard to communication ACCC/C/2009/44 (Belarus), ECE/MP.PP/C.1/2011/6/Add.1 (19 September 2011) para 77; Findings and recommendations with regard to communication ACCC/C/2010/50 (Czechia), ECE/MP.PP/C.1/2012/11 (2 October 2012) para 69; cf Findings and recommendations with regard to communication ACCC/C/2005/12 (Albania), ECE/MP.PP/C.1/2007/4/Add.1 (31 July 2007) para 79; Findings and recommendations with regard to communication ACCC/C/2014/118 (Ukraine), ECE/MP.PP/C.1/2021/18 (10 September 2021) para 120.

119 ACCC, Report with regard to communication ACCC/C/2006/16 (Lithuania), ECE/MP.PP/2008/5/Add.6 (4 April 2008) para 74; cf ACCC, Findings with regard to communication ACCC/C/2007/22 (France), ECE/MP.PP/C.1/2009/4/Add.1 (8 February 2011) paras 36ff.

120 ACCC, Findings and recommendations with regard to communication ACCC/C/2012/71 (Czechia), ECE/MP.PP/C.1/2017/3 (20 December 2016) para 92.

121 ACCC, Findings and recommendations with regard to communication ACCC/C/2014/100 (UK), ECE/MP.PP/C.1/2019/6 (23 April 2019) para 84; cf ACCC, Findings and recommendations with regard to communication ACCC/C/2004/08 (Armenia), ECE/MP.PP/C.1/2006/2/Add.1 (10 May 2006) para 29; Findings and recommendations with regard to communication ACCC/C/2014/104 (Netherlands), ECE/MP.PP/C.1/2019/3 (21 January 2019) para 76.

122 ACCC, Findings with regard to communication ACCC/C/2007/22 (France), ECE/MP.PP/C.1/2009/4/Add.1 (8 February 2011) para 39; Findings with regard to communication ACCC/C/2009/41 (Slovakia), ECE/MP.PP/2011/11/Add.3 (12 May 2011) para 63.

123 ACCC, Findings and recommendations with regard to communication ACCC/C/2013/98 (Lithuania), ECE/MP.PP/C.1/2021/15 (4 October 2021) paras 117, 121.

public participation therefore does not amount to a "veto right" of the public.[124] Even if this may result in a decision that is not necessarily accepted by the public, the public authority should, however, be able to demonstrate how comments were considered and why it did not follow the views expressed by the public.[125] Therefore, art 6(8), read in conjunction with art 6(9) AC, requires the competent authority to provide reasons for not accepting those options suggested by the public.[126]

The ACCC also clarifies that it is not in line with the requirements of art 6 AC if the developers and not the competent authorities are responsible for organising public participation.[127] The obligation in art 6(8) AC necessarily requires that all comments from the public are fully considered by the competent authority itself and not only by the developer.[128] The administrative functions related to the organisation of the public participation procedure can be delegated to bodies or even private person, who are then considered as falling under the definition of a "public authority" in the meaning of art 2(2) (b) or (c) AC.[129] However, in order to ensure proper conduct of the public participation procedure, the bodies or persons shall specialise in public participation or mediation, be impartial and shall not represent any interests related to the activity under review.[130]

---

124 ACCC, Findings and recommendations with regard to communication ACCC/C/2008/24 (Spain), ECE/MP.PP/C.1/2009/8/Add.1 (8 February 2011) paras 98–99; cf ACCC, Findings and recommendations with regard to communication ACCC/C/2012/68 (GB), ECE/MP.PP/C.1/2014/5 (13 January 2014) para 93.

125 ACCC, Findings and Recommendations with regard to communication ACCC/C/2021/70 (Czechia), ECE/MP.PP/C.1/2014/9 (4 June 2014) para 61.

126 ACCC, Findings and recommendations with regard to communication ACCC/C/2014/100 (UK), ECE/MP.PP/C.1/2019/6 (23 April 2019) para 84; cf ACCC, Findings and recommendations with regard to communication ACCC/C/2008/24 (Spain), ECE/MP.PP/C.1/2009/8/Add.1 (8 February 2011) paras 99–100.

127 ACCC, Report with regard to communication ACCC/C/2006/16 (Lithuania), ECE/MP.PP/2008/5/Add.6 (4 April 2008) paras 78, 90; ACCC, Findings and recommendations with regard to communication ACCC/C/2009/37 (Belarus), ECE/MP.PP/2011/11/Add.2 (12 May 2011) paras 66, 70, 76ff, 104; Findings and recommendations with regard to communication ACCC/C/2010/59 (Kazakhstan), ECE/MP.PP/C.1/2013/0 (16 July 2013) para 45.

128 ACCC, Findings and recommendations with regard to communication ACCC/C/2009/44 (Belarus), ECE/MP.PP/C.1/2011/6/Add.1 (19 September 2011) para 64; Findings and recommendations with regard to communication ACCC/C/2013/98 (Lithuania), ECE/MP.PP/C.1/2021/15 (4 October 2021) paras 138–139.

129 ACCC, Findings and recommendations with regard to communication ACCC/C/2009/37 (Belarus), ECE/MP.PP/2011/11/Add.2 (12 May 2011) para 78.

130 ACCC, Findings and recommendations with regard to communication ACCC/C/2009/37 (Belarus), ECE/MP.PP/2011/11/Add.2 (12 May 2011) paras 79–80.

6 Conclusion

The orientation of international environmental law towards a right to a healthy environment partially overrides the traditional concept of sustainable development. This leads to a stronger focus on environmental protection. At the same time, comparing the AC and the EA also reveals differences between the perspectives of the Global North and the Global South.[131] The EA, despite (or perhaps rather because of) the clearer emphasis on the human rights approach, stresses the principle of sustainable development and the intended balance of its three dimensions.[132] From this perspective, the procedural rights of access to information, public participation in decision-making and access to justice acquire a greater intrinsic value as procedural environmental human rights. These rights are also granted more generously to the general public than in the AC. This corresponds to the claim for collective human rights of the so-called third generation focussing on aspects of solidarity (in distinction to human rights dealing with liberty, participation in political life and equality as well as economic, social and cultural rights), which has been raised in the Global South in particular. From the classical perspective of the Global North, which relates human rights to the individual, a human right to public participation can be seen as self-contradictory. Against this background, the question of how the future Committee to Support Implementation and Compliance will interpret the rights of the EA and contribute to a dynamic development of procedural environmental human rights seems all the more intriguing.

Bibliography

Barragán-Terán D, 'Educación, democracia ambiental y desarrollo sostenible' in Bárcena A, Torres V and Ávila L M (eds), *El Acuerdo de Escazú sobre democracia ambiental y su relación con la Agenda 2030 para el Desarrollo Sostenible* (CEPAL 2021) 167–178.

Barritt E, 'Global Values, Transnational Expression: From Aarhus to Escazú' [2019] 11 TLI Think! Paper 1.

Beyerlin U, 'Sustainable Development', *Max Planck Encyclopedia of Public International Law* (October 2013).

131 See also Emily Barritt 'Global Values, Transnational Expression: From Aarhus to Escazú' (2019) 11 TLI Think! Paper 1ff.

132 Cf UNGA, The human right to a clean, healthy and sustainable environment, Res 76/300 (28 July 2022) recital 8.

Bothe M, 'Die Entwicklung des Umweltvölkerrechts 1972/2002' in Dolde K-P (ed), *Umweltrecht im Wandel* (Erich Schmidt Verlag 2011) 51–70.

Boyd D R, 'Catalyst for Change: Evaluating Forty Years of Experience in Implementing the Right to a Healthy Environment' in Knox J H and Pejan R (eds), *The Human Right to a Healthy Environment* (CUP 2018) 17–41.

Brady K, 'Aarhus Convention Signed' (1998) 28 Environmental Policy and Law 171.

Brady K, 'New Convention on Access to Information and Public Participation in Environmental Matters' (1998) 28 Environmental Policy and Law 69.

Ekardt F and Pöhlmann K, 'Europäische Klagebefugnis: Öffentlichkeitsrichtlinie, Klagerechtsrichtline und ihre Folgen' [2005] Neue Zeitschrift für Verwaltungsrecht 532.

Hauff V (ed), *Unsere gemeinsame Zukunft* (Eggenkamp Verlag 1987).

Hernández-Mendible V R, 'El Acuerdo de Escazú y la Competencia de la Corte Interamericana para Tutelar los Derechos en Materia Ambiental' in Guanipa H J, Leal M L and Huber F (eds), *Crisis climática, transición energética y derechos humanos* (Tomo I, 2020) 323–354.

Hohmann H, 'Ergebnisse des Erdgipfels von Rio – Weiterentwicklung des Umweltvölkerrechts durch die UN-Umweltkonferenz von 1992' [1993] Neue Zeitschrift für Verwaltungsrecht 311.

Jendrośka J, 'Aarhus Convention and Community Law: The Interplay' (2005) 2 Journal for European Enviromental & Planning Law 12.

Jendroska J and Stec S, 'The Aarhus Convention: Towards a New Era in Environmental Democracy' (2001) 9 Environmental Liability 140.

Knox J H, 'Constructing the Human Right to a Healthy Environment' (2020) 16 Annual Review of Law and Social Science 79.

May J R and Daly E, *Global Environmental Constitutionalism* (CUP 2015).

Meadows D H, Meadows D L, Randers J and Behrens III W W, *The Limits to Growth* (Universe Books 1972).

Mohammed N, 'Sustainable Development Goal 16 in the Caribbean Context: The Role of the Escazu Agreement in Addressing Implementation Challenges in the Region' in Bárcena A, Torres V and Ávila L M (eds), *El Acuerdo de Escazú sobre democracia ambiental y su relación con la Agenda 2030 para el Desarrollo Sostenible* (CEPAL 2021) 203–223.

Pallemaerts M, 'The Human Right to a Healthy Environment as a Substantive Right' in Déjeant-Pons M and Pallemaerts M, *Human Rights and the Environment* (Council of Europe Publishing 2002) 17–22.

Peters B, *Legitimation durch Öffentlichkeitsbeteiligung* (Mohr Siebeck 2020).

Peters B, 'Unpacking the Diversity of Procedural Environmental Rights: The European Convention on Human Rights and the Aarhus Convention' (2018) 30 Journal of Environmental Law 1.

Peters B, 'Zur Anwendbarkeit der Europäischen Menschenrechtskonvention in Umwelt- und Klimaschutzfragen' (2021) 59 Archiv des Völkerrechts 164.

Richardson B J, *Time and Environmental Law* (CUP 2017).

Schwerdtfeger A, *Der deutsche Verwaltungsrechtsschutz unter dem Einfluss der Aarhus-Konvention* (Mohr Siebeck 2010).

Schwerdtfeger A, 'Artikel 37 Umweltschutz' in Meyer J and Hölscheidt S (eds), *Charta der Grundrechte der Europäischen Union* (5th ed, Nomos 2019).

Shelton D, 'What Happened in Rio to Human Rights?' (1992) 3 Yearbook of International Environmental Law 75.

Stec S and Jendroska J, 'The Escazú Agreement and the Regional Approach to Rio Principle 10: Process, Innovation, and Shortcomings' (2019) 31 Journal of Environmental Law 533.

Walter C, 'Internationalisierung des deutschen und Europäischen Verwaltungsverfahrens- und Verwaltungsprozessrechts – am Beispiel der Århus-Konvention' [2005] Europarecht 302.

Wates J, 'The Aarhus Convention: A Driving Force for Environmental Democracy' (2005) 2 Journal for European Environmental & Planning Law 2.

CHAPTER 11

The Case of Biodiversity Protection

Sustainability and Participation in the Convention on Biological Diversity, the Ramsar Convention, and the World Heritage Convention

Federica Cittadino and Emma Mitrotta

1 Introduction

The concepts of sustainability and participation are enshrined in international environmental law and have strongly influenced the development of international environmental regimes. Indeed, these two concepts acquire different nuances depending on the environmental issue considered. Therefore, this chapter will focus on biodiversity law and explore the meaning and implications of sustainability and participation in the framework of three biodiversity conventions: the CBD;[1] the Ramsar Convention;[2] and the WHC.[3]

These three conventions have been selected for their global character and almost universal acceptance.[4] Moreover, as framework conventions, these regimes have evolved over time thanks to the work of their governing bodies; the so-called Conference of the Parties (COPs). This feature gives us the opportunity to study sustainability and participation not as static concepts, but as they evolve throughout the years and through international practice, in particular in the case of the Ramsar Convention and the WHC that predate their emergence.

The Ramsar Convention is the first treaty to include the concept of wise use, which is incorporated in the CBD as "sustainable use".[5] Regardless of their

1 Convention on Biological Diversity, entered into force 29 December 1993, 1760 UNTS 79 (CBD).

2 Convention on Wetlands of International Importance Especially as Waterfowl Habitat, entered into force 21 December 1975, 11 ILM 1358 (Ramsar Convention).

3 Convention for the Protection of the World Cultural and Natural Heritage, entered into force 17 December 1975, 11 ILM 135 (WHC).

4 Indeed, the CBD has 196 parties, Ramsar has 170 parties and the WHC has 193 parties, according to the data available in the dedicated websites: <https://www.cbd.int/information/parties.shtml>, <https://www.ramsar.org/document/list-of-the-contracting-parties-and-date-of-entry-into-force-of-the-convention-for-each>, <https://whc.unesco.org/en/statesparties/> accessed 18 November 2021. Please note that all URL cited are last accessed on the same date.

5 Sustainable use is regulated in arts 1, 2 and 10(c) of the CBD. Wise use is mentioned in art 2(6), 3 and 6 of the Ramsar Convention. The WHC does not contain a direct reference to sustainable or wise use in its text. Nevertheless, sustainable development is said to find its roots in its arts 4 and 5 (see at <whc.unesco.org/en/sustainabledevelopment/>).

 | DOI:10.1163/9789004509382_013

explicit inclusion in the three Convention texts, sustainability and participation find room in these regimes through COP decisions, which we have primarily relied upon for the following analysis. Especially in the CBD and the Ramsar Convention, COP decisions serve to promote and advance the correct interpretation and implementation of the conventions concerned.[6] Although these decisions are not mandatory on state parties, they are able to influence practice and treaty development.[7] In the WHC, the Operational Guidelines play a similar role and are validated by parties through the World Heritage Committee that adopts and periodically revises them.[8]

Moreover, these three Conventions complement each other, collaborate with one another through partnership agreements, and can be used as terms of reference in the interpretation and implementation of one another.[9]

As we do not wish to propose abstract conceptualisations of sustainability and participation within this chapter, we need to briefly outline the content of both concepts in order to both inform and guide our analysis throughout the following sections of the abovementioned biodiversity conventions.

1.1 *The Meaning of Sustainability in Terms of Sustainable Development*

Sustainability is defined in this chapter through the legal content of the principle of sustainable development (SD).[10] Over time this principle has shown

---

6 See arts 23(4) and 31(1) CBD; arts 6(1) and 7(2) Ramsar Convention.

7 See Thomas Gehring, 'Treaty-Making and Treaty Evolution' in Daniel Bodansky, Jutta Brunnée and Ellen Hey (eds) *The Oxford Handbook of International Environmental Law* (Oxford University Press 2008), 480–482 and 485–495; Jutta Brunnée, 'COPing with Consent: Law-Making under Multilateral Environmental Agreements' (2002) 15 Leiden Journal of International Law 1. Contra see Veit Koester, 'The Convention on Biological Diversity and the Concept of Sustainable Development: The Extent and Manner of the Convention's Application of Components of the Concept' in Michael Bowman, Peter Davies and Edward Goodwin (eds), *Research Handbook on Biodiversity and Law* (Edward Elgar 2016) 276.

8 See art 8 WHC and <whc.unesco.org/en/committee>. The Operational Guidelines, developed by the World Heritage Committee, are recognised as documents that implement and guarantee the evolution of the WHC. The last revision of the Operational Guidelines occurred in 2019. See <whc.unesco.org/en/guidelines/>. On the role of the World Heritage Committee, see Francesco Francioni (ed), *The 1972 World Heritage Convention: A Commentary* (OUP 2008).

9 The CBD COP encourages the connection and cooperation between biodiversity conventions both at global and national levels. The partnership between the CBD and the Ramsar Convention is ensured by periodical memoranda of cooperation (1996, 2005, 2006 and 2011), between the CBD and the WHC with the memoranda of cooperation signed in 1998 and 2011. See also CBD COP Decisions III/21 (1997), VIII/28 (2006), and X/20 (2010).

10 See Rakhyun E. Kim and Klaus Bosselmann, 'Operationalising Sustainable Development: Ecological Integrity as a Grundnorm of International Law' (2015) 24 Review of European,

its mutable nature in relation to its content, its addressees, and its function in the legal system.[11]

Its historical evolution has led to the consolidation of three main dimensions in terms of defining SD, namely economic, environmental and social.[12] Balancing these three components remains at the heart of SD from its initial legal formulation in the Brundtland report[13] and through its later consolidation by both the Rio and Johannesburg UN declarations.[14] The Rio+20 conference reaffirmed the commitment of the international community to these three dimensions.[15] Although only three out of the seventeen Sustainable Development Goals (SDGs) have clearly stated environmental goals (SDGs 13–15), almost all of the objectives include the integration of environmental aspects in their realisation.[16]

Hence, at the core of SD is the integration of economic, environmental and social dimensions.[17] Integration is an autonomous principle prescribing a

---

Comparative and International Environmental Law 194; Jorge E. Viñuales, 'The Rise and Fall of Sustainable Development' (2013) 22 Review of European, Comparative and International Environmental Law 3.

11 Virginie Barral, 'Sustainable Development in International Law: Nature and Operation of an Evolutive Legal Norm' (2012) 23 European Journal of International Law 377, 382–386. See also Vaughan Lowe, 'Sustainable Development and Unsustainable Arguments' in Alan Boyle and David Freestone (eds), *International Law and Sustainable Development: Past Achievements and Future Challenges* (OUP 2001); Rakhyun E. Kim, 'The Nexus between International Law and the Sustainable Development Goals' (2016) 25 Review of European, Comparative and International Environmental Law 15.

12 Barral 2012, n 11.

13 Report of the World Commission on Environment and Development, *Our Common Future* (1987), 51: development that "meets the needs of the present without compromising the ability of future generations to meet their own needs".

14 Barral 2012, n 11, at 379. See Rio Declaration on Environment and Development, 12 August 1992, UN Doc A/CONF.151/26 (vol. I); Johannesburg Declaration on Sustainable Development, 4 September 2002, UN Doc A/CONF.199/20.

15 See The Future We Want, 11 September 2012, UN Doc A/RES/66/288, Annex, paras 1, 4 and 17; Transforming our world: the 2030 Agenda for Sustainable Development, 21 October 2015, UN Doc A/RES/70/1, preamble, paras 2 and 5. See Marcos Orellana, 'Governance and the Sustainable Development Goals: The Increasing Relevance of Access Rights in Principle 10 of the Rio Declaration' (2016) 25 Review of European, Comparative and International Environmental Law 50, 50; Viñuales, n 10, at 3. Contra Elisa Morgera and Annalisa Savaresi, 'A Conceptual and Legal Perspective on the Green Economy' (2013) 22 Review of European, Comparative and International Environmental Law 14.

16 See SDG 2.4, SDG 3.9, SDG 6.3 and 6.6, SDG 7.2 and 7.3, SDG 8.4, SDG 9.4, SDG 11.4, 11.6, 11.7 and 11b, SDG 12.2, 12.3, 12.4, 12.5, 12.8 and 12c, SDG 17.7 and 17.9.

17 Malgosia Fitzmaurice, 'International Protection of the Environment' (2001) 293 Recueil des Cours 9, 52; Federica Cittadino, *Il principio dello sviluppo sostenibile nel diritto internazionale*, Master's thesis (University of Trento, 2009).

given conduct by states, that is both a duty to incorporate environmental considerations into any social and development plans or policies,[18] and to realise the different SD components jointly.[19] SD is articulated through additional specific principles, namely intergenerational equity, intra-generational equity and sustainable use.[20] Intergenerational equity encapsulates entirely the environmental dimension of SD, according to which natural capital must not be dissipated for the benefit of future generations.[21] Intragenerational equity refers to the integration of social considerations in development including: equity in the distribution of development benefits within nations and between developed and developing countries; and the principle of common but differentiated responsibilities.[22] The latter calls for a consideration of the different responsibilities of states for environmental degradation and thus taking into account these development differences when distributing the burden of obligations in environmental treaties.[23] The demand to preserve natural resources for the benefit of future generations while simultaneously meeting the social and developmental needs of the present generation is also closely linked to the principle of sustainable use.[24] Sustainable use, explicitly defined in the CBD, at a minimum involves the duty to consider the impact that the exploitation of natural resources has on their availability and benefit to present and future generations.[25]

In the following sections, the consideration of sustainability in both the text and practice of the CBD, the Ramsar Convention and the WHC is assessed with reference to the four SD components as illustrated above. As we shall see, this division is illustrative of which aspects of SD prevail in each convention. In particular, we will assess the extent to which the environmental dimension is

18 Virginie Barral, 'Sustainable Development and Equity in Biodiversity Conservation' in Elisa Morgera and Jona Razzaque (eds), *Biodiversity and Nature Protection Law* (Edward Elgar 2017) 62–63.

19 Barral 2012, n 11, at 380.

20 Philippe Sands, 'International Law in the Field of Sustainable Development: Emerging Legal Principles' in Winfried Lang (ed), *Sustainable Development and International Law* (Springer 1995) 57. Contra Barral 2012, n 11, at 381.

21 Barral, ibid at 380. See Principle 3 Rio Declaration.

22 Barral, ibid at 380–381.

23 For instance, under the UN Framework Convention on Climate Change and the Kyoto Protocol developing countries do not have obligations to reduce CO_2 in contrast to developed country parties. For more information on that, see Omondi R. Owino, 'Climate Change Law' in this book, chapter 12.

24 Barral 2012, n 11, at 382.

25 For the evolution, its content and scope of application of the principle of sustainable use, see Cittadino 2009, n 17, at 19–43.

predominant in the cited biodiversity conventions. We will also reach some conclusions as to whether SD coincides with the abovementioned four components or whether new elements emerge.

1.2 *The Meaning of Participation*

Participation can be seen as a guiding principle of international environmental law.[26] Demands for public participation in environmental matters started to emerge in the 1970s in both domestic and international contexts.[27] Its most comprehensive formulation is provided by Principle 10 of the Rio Declaration,[28] which articulates the three components of public participation in environmental matters, namely access to information, participation in decision-making and access to administrative and judicial remedies. In addition, despite describing those components within a national context, Principle 10 highlights the importance of enabling the participation of all citizens concerned at any governance level,[29] including in international arenas.[30] Principle 10 has influenced the successive development of international environmental law treaties[31] and prompted an innovative interpretation and development of existing regimes, for example, on the protection of wetlands of international importance and World Heritage sites analysed below.

26 Public participation in environmental matters can be included among the general principles of international environmental law; see Alessandro Fodella, 'I principi generali' in Alessandro Fodella and Laura Pineschi (eds) *La protezione dell'ambiente nel Diritto internazionale* (G. Giappichelli Editore 2009) 126–127.

27 Jonas Ebbesson, 'Principle 10: Public Participation' in Jorge E. Viñuales (ed) *The Rio Declaration on Environment and Development: A Commentary* (University of California 2017) 288.

28 Principle 10 Rio Declaration reads as follows: "Environmental issues are best handled with participation of all concerned citizens, at the relevant level. At the national level, each individual shall have appropriate access to information concerning the environment that is held by public authorities, including information on hazardous materials and activities in their communities, and the opportunity to participate in decision-making processes. States shall facilitate and encourage public awareness and participation by making information widely available. Effective access to judicial and administrative proceedings, including redress and remedy, shall be provided". See Elsa Tsioumani, 'Public participation in environmental decision-making' in Ludwig Krämer and Emanuela Orlando (eds) *Encyclopedia of Environmental Law: Principles of Environmental Law* (Elgar 2018) 366–378.

29 On this latter point see Ellen Hey, *Advanced Introduction to International Environmental Law* (Edward Elgar 2016) 83.

30 Jonas Ebbesson, 'Public Participation' in Daniel Bodansky, Jutta Brunnée, and Ellen Hey (eds.), The Oxford Handbook of International Environmental Law (Oxford University Press 2008) 682–685.

31 Ebbesson 2017, n 27, at 294–298.

Arguably, public participation has found its most accomplished normative development at regional level, in particular with the 1998 Convention on Access to Information, Public Participation in Decision-making and Access to Justice in Environmental Matters (Aarhus Convention) and, more recently, with the 2018 Regional Agreement on Access to Information, Public Participation and Justice in Environmental Matters in Latin America and the Caribbean.[32] The Aarhus Convention distinguishes between the (general) public and the public concerned. The former includes all actors outside the governmental administration,[33] while the latter refers to a more restricted group of subjects that are "affected or likely to be affected by, or have an interest in, environmental decision-making".[34] This distinction is relevant in the context of the treaties we analyse since some provisions and their practice foresee the involvement of specific actors – especially indigenous peoples – to both enhance the protection of biodiversity and achieve decisions in a fair and effective way.

In the context of the CBD, the Ramsar Convention and the WHC, participation has acquired two further meanings. The first refers to the direct participation of specific actors, usually indigenous peoples and local communities,[35] in the conservation, management and sustainable use of biodiversity resources and areas protected under these regimes. The second relates to the direct involvement of specific actors in the Conventions' processes, as with the case of the Working Group on article 8 (j).[36] In both cases, the emphasis on indigenous peoples emerges from the practice of the treaties analysed in this chapter, especially the CBD. Not only is participation of other subjects less frequently cited, but in our opinion these have also less legal significance since these forms of participation are expressed in vaguer terms.

---

32 Convention on Access to Information, Public Participation in Decision-making and Access to Justice in Environmental Matters, entered into force 30 October 2001, 2161 UNTS 447; Regional Agreement on Access to Information, Public Participation and Justice in Environmental Matters in Latin America and the Caribbean, entered into force 22 April 2021, UNTC Chapter XXVII.18. For a more detailed analysis of these Conventions see Angela Schwerdtfeger, 'The Human Rights Dimension', in this book, chapter 10.

33 Art 2(4) Aarhus Convention.

34 See art 2(5) Aarhus Convention.

35 The terminology used in the CBD to refer to these actors is "indigenous and local communities" (eg art 8(j) CBD). In 2014 the CBD COP has decided to embrace the terminology "indigenous peoples and local communities" (COP dec XII/12). See Federica Cittadino, *Incorporating Indigenous Rights in the International Regime on Biodiversity Protection: Access, Benefit-sharing and Conservation in Indigenous Lands* (Brill 2019), 168. In the following sections we will refer to both terminologies, depending on the formula used in the COP decisions cited.

36 See Section 3.2 *infra*.

For these reasons, the consideration of how participation is regulated in the text and practice of the treaties analysed is assessed with reference to both the public and the public concerned, and by focusing on access to information and participation in decision-making as envisaged in the Aarhus Convention.[37]

1.3 *Outline of the Chapter*

In section 2, we explore whether and in which ways the four subprinciples of SD are integrated in the CBD, the Ramsar Convention and the WHC. In section 3, we assess what are the main characteristics of participation in the same conventions. In both cases, conclusions are drawn as to whether the specific conceptions of sustainability and participation somehow differ from the general notions described in the introduction. Finally, in section 4, we illustrate the connections between sustainability and participation that emerge from our analysis.

2 Sustainability in the Global Regimes on Biodiversity Protection

The principle of SD is explicitly mentioned in the text of the CBD only once in article 8(e), which foresees the obligation for states to "[p]romote environmentally sound and SD in areas adjacent to protected areas" in the context of in-situ conservation. Moreover, multiple references to SD, especially in conjunction with poverty eradication, can be found in CBD COP decisions, including the early ones.[38] Most fundamentally, the essence of the principle of SD can be derived from the interrelation of the three CBD objectives, namely conservation, sustainable use, and benefit-sharing,[39] which in turn echo the three connected components of SD, respectively environmental protection,

---

37 The pillar on access and judicial remedies will not be addressed in this chapter for two reasons. First, the three Conventions analysed lack compliance mechanisms, except for the Nagoya Protocol on Access to Genetic Resources and the Fair and Equitable Sharing of Benefits Arising from Their Utilization to the Convention on Biological Diversity, entered into force 12 October 2014, 29 October 2010, UN Doc UNEP/CBD/COP/DEC/X/1 (Nagoya Protocol). Second, we will not deal with participatory rights at the national level.

38 See CBD: COP dec I/8, paras 7 and 14; COP dec III/9; COP dec VI/9; COP dec VII/11, annex 1, para 1; COP dec VII/16, annex, para 28; COP dec VII/28, para 1; COP dec VII/29; COP dec VIII/21, para 1; COP dec IX/18, paras 6(e) and 19; COP dec X/31, para 32(d); COP dec XI/22, paras 1 and 7; COP dec XII/4; COP dec XII/5, para 5; COP dec XII/19, para 1; COP dec XIII/5; COP dec XIV/2; COP dec XIV/7, preamble; and COP dec XIV/14, preamble and para 1.

39 Art 1 CBD. See Lyle Glowka, Françoise Burhenne-Guilmin and Hugh Synge, *A Guide to the Convention on Biological Diversity* (IUCN 1994).

economic development and social justice.[40] Even the notion of common concern of humankind[41] is used to "strike a balance between the sovereign rights of nations to exploit their natural resources and the interests of the international community in global environmental protection".[42]

The principle of SD is not included in the text of the Ramsar Convention and the WHC for mere chronological reasons. Nevertheless, its ground-breaking character has had an impact on their successive development and implementation. While the 1987 definition of wise use hints at the concept of SD through sustainable utilisation,[43] the latest one clearly sets it "within the context of SD".[44] What is more, the Ramsar Convention's mission identifies SD as the final goal of conservation and wise use of wetlands,[45] and the four Ramsar Convention Strategic Plans approved so far embrace this goal and articulate on it.[46]

Regarding the WHC, the efforts to recognise culture, especially through heritage, as a driver and an enabler of SD[47] has led to an exploration of the sustainability dimension within this regime and an integration of SD into the processes of the Convention through a dedicated policy.[48] The aim of this policy is to contribute to SD and the wellbeing of people by aligning the conservation and management strategies of protected heritage sites with SD objectives through environmental, social and economic dimensions. Since 2005, the Operational Guidelines state that "[t]he protection and conservation of the

---

40 Abdulqawi Yussuf, 'International Law and Sustainable Development: The Convention on Biological Diversity' (1995) 1 African Yearbook of International Law 109, 115.

41 Preambular para 3 CBD.

42 Yussuf, n 40, at 117.

43 On this point see Ramsar COP doc C.4.18, para 239 and Ramsar COP Recommendation III.3.

44 Ramsar COP Res IX.1 Annex A, para 22.

45 See the Ramsar Strategic Plan 1997–2002, at 4.

46 Ibid para 1. See also the second Ramsar Strategic Plan 2003–2008, COP Res VIII.25, General Objective 2 and Operational Objective 3; the third Strategic Plan 2009–2015, COP Res X.1 and COP Res XI.3; the fourth Strategic Plan 2015–2024, COP Res XII.2.

47 UNESCO (2012) *Culture: a driver and an enabler of sustainable development*, Thematic Think Piece, available at <www.un.org/millenniumgoals/pdf/Think%20Pieces/2_culture.pdf>. The role of culture as a driver and enabler of sustainable development has been recently reaffirmed by the UN General Assembly in the Resolution on culture and sustainable development adopted at its 74th session, UN Doc A/RES/74/230, paras 2 and 3. See also Report *UNESCO's Work on Culture and Sustainable Development. Evaluation of a Policy Theme*, IOS/EVS/PI/145 REV.2, paras 29, 34 and 61.

48 Policy for the Integration of a Sustainable Development Perspective into the Processes of the World Heritage Convention, adopted in 2015 by the General Assembly of WHC State parties at its 20 Session in Paris, UN Docs WHC-15/20.GA/13 and WHC-15/20.GA/INF.13.

natural and cultural heritage constitute a significant contribution to SD",[49] and now explicitly invite state parties to observe SD principles when implementing the Convention.[50] Environmental sustainability applies primarily to natural heritage properties where places with "exceptional biodiversity, geodiversity and other natural features, which are essential for human well-being" are protected.[51] Inclusive social development is pursued by article 5(a) of the WHC through its demand to "adopt a general policy which aims to give the cultural and natural heritage a function in the life of the community". This dimension is strongly linked to inclusive governance, ensured through the "full inclusion, respect and equity of all stakeholders, including local and indigenous peoples, together with a commitment to gender equality".[52] The protection of properties should entail the enhancement of the quality of life and wellbeing of all stakeholders.[53] Finally, inclusive economic development can be achieved through management and conservation strategies that contribute to alleviating poverty and enhancing sustainable livelihoods of local communities.[54]

2.1 *Sustainable Use*

Sustainable use is one of the three objectives of the CBD and is defined under its article 2 as the "use of components of biological diversity *in a way and at a rate that does not lead to the longterm decline* of biological diversity, thereby maintaining its potential to meet the needs and aspirations of *present and future generations*".[55] In its definition, sustainable use therefore contains the three components of SD: the economic aspect is represented by use; the environmental points to the limits of the resource base in a longterm perspective; and the social facet is contained in the elements of inter- and intragenerational equity.[56] These elements emerge from both the text of article 2 and its contextual interpretation in light of other CBD provisions and COP decisions.[57]

---

49 Operational Guidelines for the Implementation of the World Heritage Convention, para 6, available at <whc.unesco.org/en/guidelines>. This chapter refers to the latest version of the Operational Guidelines adopted in 2019. Hereinafter Operational Guidelines.

50 Operational Guidelines, paras 15 (o), 112 and 132 (5).

51 Ibid para 14.

52 Ibid paras 17–18. See also paras 21–23.

53 Ibid para 19.

54 Ibid paras 24–27.

55 Emphasis added.

56 As recognized already in early COP decisions: COP dec I/2, section III, para 1; COP dec III/19, annex, para 2.

57 CBD: COP dec II/9, annex, para 12; COP dec VII/11, annex 2.

A reference to the natural limits of the resource base is, for instance, apparent in the formulation of the ecosystem approach embraced in the CBD and recurrently framed in many COP decisions. In this sense, "[e]cosystems must be managed within the limits of their functioning"[58] and sustainable management implies the maintenance of the resource base.[59] Moreover, sustainable use is entrenched with both conservation[60] and the longterm viability of consumptive uses.[61] According to article 8(i), parties must ensure the "compatibility between present uses and the conservation of biological diversity and the sustainable use of its components". Furthermore, as emerges from the Addis Ababa Principles and Guidelines for the Sustainable Use of Biodiversity,[62] "[i]t is possible to use biodiversity components in a manner in which ecological processes, species and genetic variability remain above thresholds needed for longterm viability".[63] In addition, in light of article 10(c) of the CBD, sustainable use includes the "customary use of biological resources" based on the traditional knowledge and cultural practices of indigenous peoples and local communities.[64]

Although the content of the principle may appear complex, the CBD text identifies specific obligations for state parties to realise sustainable use.[65] These obligations include three subcategories: general duties to adopt positive measures, duties to protect traditional knowledge, and duties to ensure international cooperation. Concerning positive measures, in order to achieve sustainable use and conservation, states shall adopt or revise national strategies, plans and programmes, and incorporate sustainable use and conservation into other plans.[66] Positive duties also include monitoring obligations, not only in relation to biodiversity components and their status, but also with respect to major threats to biodiversity.[67] In this respect, the precautionary principle is

58 CBD COP dec V/5, principle 6.

59 CBD: COP dec VII/11, annex 2. See also COP dec VIII/28, para 8; COP dec VI/9, annex, part B; COP dec XI/25, para 13(e); COP dec XIV/6; COP dec X/29.

60 CBD: COP dec II/9, annex, para 13; COP dec II/19, annex, para 6; COP dec IV/4, annex I; COP dec V/5, para 5 and principle 10; COP dec V/23, annex 1, para 9; COP dec V/24, preamble; COP dec VI/13; COP dec VII/11, annex 1, rationale to Principle 10; COP dec VII/12, annex 2, para 2; COP dec VII/28, para 12. See Koester, n 7, at 287. See also Christine Willmore, 'Sovereignty, Conservation and Sustainable Use' in Elisa Morgera and Jona Razzaque (eds), *Biodiversity and Nature Protection Law* (Edward Elgar 2017) 31.

61 CBD: COP dec XIV/7, para 12; COP dec X/29, para 54. See Willmore ibid section 2.3.

62 Hereinafter Addis Ababa guidelines.

63 CBD: COP dec VII/12, annex 2, para 8(a). See also practical principle 5.

64 See CBD: COP dec X/17, target 13; COP dec X/32, para 2(e); COP dec XI/24; COP dec XI/25, para 8; COP dec XII/12, para 6 and annex (Plan of action on customary sustainable use of biological diversity), para 6(a) and (c).

65 Preambular para 5 CBD.

66 Arts 6 and 8(c) CBD.

67 Arts 7, 8(g), 9(c), 10(d) and 14(a) CBD. See Yussuf, n 40, at 118.

mentioned in the Addis Ababa guidelines to complement the management practices of states.[68] The Addis Ababa guidelines also suggest a multilevel approach to sustainable use, meaning that all decision-making authorities should act accordingly to achieve this,[69] including the private sector.[70] The obligation to protect traditional knowledge is embodied in article 8(j), which furthermore connects customary sustainable use under article 10(c) to access and utilisation of traditional knowledge and the obligation to encourage benefit-sharing. Cooperation duties are generally stated under article 5 of the CBD and more concretely defined as "technical and scientific cooperation" under article 18(1).

In the Ramsar Convention, sustainable use finds its alter ego in the concept of wise use; the overlapping of these two concepts emerges from several key Ramsar Convention documents.[71] The wise use of wetlands is the cornerstone of this Convention and applies to all the wetlands and water resources located in the territories of contracting parties, regardless of their inclusion in the List of Wetlands of International Importance (Ramsar List).[72] Its definition was revised in 2005 to be aligned with the language of the CBD and the Millennium Ecosystem Assessment, and now reads: "wise use of wetlands is the maintenance of their ecological character, achieved through the implementation of ecosystem approaches, within the context of SD".[73] This change suggests the will to capture not only the expression, but also the essence of both the concepts of SD and ecosystem approach as emerging from the CBD.

---

68 CBD: COP dec VII/12, annex 2, para 8(f). See also COP dec X/29, para 15.

69 CBD COP dec VII/12, annex 2, para 6 and practical principle 1.

70 CBD COP dec X/32, para 3(c).

71 See, for instance, Ramsar Convention Secretariat (2016) *An Introduction to the Ramsar Convention on Wetlands,* 7th ed. Ramsar Convention Secretariat, Gland, Switzerland, at 14, 37 and 62. See also the Ramsar Strategic Plans adopted at COP6 (1996), COP8 (2002), COP10 (2008), as recalled in Ramsar Convention Secretariat (2010) *Managing wetlands: Frameworks for managing Wetlands of International Importance and other wetland sites,* 4th ed, vol 18, para 2. COP Res VII.11, Annex, para 23.

72 Art 3 requires state parties to "formulate and implement their planning so as to promote the conservation of wetland included in the List, and as far as possible *the wise use of wetlands in their territory*" (emphasis added). Wise use is one of the four main commitments of the Ramsar Convention, together with the designation of wetlands in the Ramsar List (art 2) and their conservation, the establishment of natural reserves in wetlands and the promotion of training for research purposes and effective management (art 4), and international cooperation on transboundary wetlands and shared water systems and species (art 5).

73 Ramsar COP Res IX.1 annex A (2005), para 22.

This stance is confirmed in the Fourth Ramsar Strategic Plan 2016–2024, according to which, wise use "has at its heart the conservation and sustainable use of wetlands and their resources, for the benefit of people and nature".[74] Hence, wise use can be seen as a dynamic objective, whose realisation lays at the intersection of environmental – the benefit of nature – and economic and societal needs – the benefit of people. The environmental component is predominant in the wise use principle due to its tight connection to the obligation to maintain the ecological character[75] of (listed) wetlands and the proper functioning of their ecosystems.[76] In this regard, what matters is the "*humaninduced adverse alteration* of any ecosystem component, process, and/or ecosystem benefit/service".[77]

Furthermore, strategic goals 1 and 2 of the Fourth Strategic Plan revolve around maintaining ecological character by "addressing the drivers of wetland loss and degradation" and "effectively conserving and managing the Ramsar Site Network" respectively. The targets corresponding to strategic goal 1 address the potential threats to ecological character deriving from inappropriate water uses (target 2) under the responsibility of either the public or private sectors (targets 2 and 3), other sectorial policies implemented at any governance level (target 1), and those connected to the introduction and expansion of invasive alien species (target 4). Pursuing strategic goal 2 specifically requires the maintenance and restoration of the ecological character of Ramsar sites (target 5) as well as addressing any potential threats that could cause adverse change (target 7). "Wisely using all wetlands" is listed as strategic goal 3 and has six corresponding targets relating to the characterisation of wetlands,[78] their promotion,[79] and the adoption of effective management strategies with the involvement of all relevant stakeholders.[80] In particular, target 10 focuses on the role of indigenous peoples and local communities,

74 Ramsar COP Res XII.2 (2015), para 2.

75 "Ecological character is the combination of the ecosystem components, processes and benefits/services that characterise the wetland at a given point in time", Ramsar COP Res IX.1, annex A, para 15.

76 Art 3.2 Ramsar Convention.

77 Ramsar COP Res IX.1, annex A, paras 19–20. Emphasis added.

78 The compilation and diffusion of national wetland inventories (target 8).

79 The recognition of the functions, services and benefits that wetlands provide (target 11).

80 These strategies benefit from integrated resource management at the appropriate scale (target 9), the restoration of degraded wetlands (target 12) and enhanced sustainability in relevant sectors that can affect wetland conservation such as water, mining, infrastructure, tourism, etc (target 13).

valuing traditional knowledge, innovation and practices which are relevant for the wise and customary use of wetlands, and asks for their participation at all relevant levels.

In the case of the WHC, the main reference to sustainable use is contained in the Operational Guidelines. The latter recognise that "properties may support a variety of ongoing and proposed uses that are ecologically and culturally sustainable and which may enhance the quality of life and wellbeing of communities concerned".[81] The sustainable use of WHC properties is permitted as long as it does not affect their Outstanding Universal Value (OUV)[82] and it has an equitable character.[83]

Arguably, sustainable use contributes to creating the OUV of properties in the case of cultural landscapes. These result from the combined work of nature and man,[84] and are thus essential for OUV maintenance. According to the Operational Guidelines, the recognition of OUV at the inscription of the property in the WHC List[85] represents "the key reference for the future effective protection and management of the property".[86] When a human component in terms of sustainable use is essential to reach the threshold of OUV, the characteristic use has to be sustainably maintained to ensure the persistence of the OUV. For instance, this is the case of the Lapponian area[87] in Sweden and the winegrowing landscape for Prosecco production area in Italy,[88] included in the WHC List based on criteria (v).[89] Sustainable use is also relevant in the case of properties nominated under the natural criterion (VII) to (x). Such use does

81 Operational Guidelines, para 119.

82 The WHC is meant to protect natural and cultural properties having OUV, as to say "cultural and/or natural significance which is so exceptional as to transcend national boundaries and to be of common importance for present and future generations of all humanity. As such, the permanent protection of this heritage is of the highest importance to the international community as a whole". Ibid para 49.

83 Ibid para 199.

84 Ibid para 47. The Operational Guidelines recognise also traditional cultural landscapes when "the continued existence of traditional forms of landuse supports biological diversity", annex 3, para 9.

85 This is "a list of properties forming part of the cultural heritage and natural heritage, as defined in Articles 1 and 2" having OUV in terms of the relevant natural and/or cultural criteria. Art. 11(2) WHC.

86 Operational Guidelines, para 51.

87 Description available at <https://whc.unesco.org/en/list/774>.

88 Description available at <https://whc.unesco.org/en/list/1571>.

89 To "be an outstanding example of a traditional human settlement, *landuse*, or seause which is representative of a culture (or cultures) or *human interaction with the environment* especially when it has become vulnerable under the impact of irreversible change". Operational Guidelines, para 77(v). Emphasis added.

not affect the "integrity" of these properties since "no area is totally pristine [and all] to some extent involve contact with people",[90] but can rather contribute to the uniqueness of natural sites and to their OUV.

2.2 *Intergenerational Equity*

Intergenerational equity is not fully articulated in the CBD, neither as a principle nor as a set of state parties' obligations. Rather, the reference either to the needs of future generations or to the longterm consequences of policies is functional to the definition of other subcomponents of SD, such as sustainable use, as shown above,[91] and integration.[92]

The Ramsar Convention does not refer to intergenerational equity, nor has this principle been addressed as such at COP meetings. An indirect reference was, however, to be found in the 1987 definition of wise use[93] through the concept of "sustainable utilisation".[94] Nevertheless, this Convention has the potential to contribute to intergenerational equity given its aspiration "to stem the progressive encroachment on and loss of wetlands now and in the future",[95] its indefinite validity,[96] and through the principle of wise (sustainable) use.

Instead, intergenerational equity is at the core of the WHC, being both an objective of this Convention and among the main obligations of contracting parties that have "the duty of ensuring the identification, protection, presentation and *transmission to future generations* of the cultural and natural heritage"

---

90 Ibid para 90.

91 Preambular para 24 CBD: "Determined to conserve and sustainably use biological diversity for the benefit of present and future generations"; art 8(i) CBD; COP dec VII/12, annex 1, operational guideline to practical principle 5: reference to "the long-term sustainability" of use; COP dec VIII/28, box 1: future generations as subjects to be involved in environmental impact assessment; COP dec X/29, para 54: "ensure the longterm sustainability of deepsea fish stocks"; COP dec XIV/6, para 11: pollinator-friendly measures to "contribute to the longterm viability and profitability of food production systems"; COP dec XIV/7, para 17: "sustainable wild management involves sustained activities over the medium and long term". See Yussuf, n 40, at 118.

92 This point is discussed in section 2.4.

93 This first definition was adopted at Ramsar COP 3 and superseded in 2005 by the current definition discussed in section 2.1. It reads: "the wise use of wetlands is their sustainable utilization for the benefit of humankind in a way compatible with the maintenance of natural properties of the ecosystem". COP3 Recommendation 3.3.

94 This was defined as "human use of a wetland so that it may yield the greatest continuous benefit to present generations while maintaining its potential to meet the needs and aspirations of future generations". Ibid.

95 Preamble, Ramsar Convention.

96 According to art 11 Ramsar Convention, it "shall continue in force for an indefinite period".

of OUV situated in their territory.[97] The concept of OUV itself explicitly connects to both intra- and inter-generational equity.[98] In this context, intergenerational equity can be seen as a principle that guides the actions of state parties and binds them to ensure the permanent and effective protection of nominated properties.[99]

2.3 *Intragenerational Equity*

As highlighted by Barral, the CBD displays at least three aspects of intra-generational equity: 1) obligations that are subject to national circumstances ("contextual norms"); 2) provisions on capacity building, technology transfer, and financial transfer; and 3) provisions on benefit-sharing.[100] We also explore a fourth aspect that is the recognition of the role of non-state actors, namely indigenous peoples, and local communities, and their knowledge systems.[101]

First, national circumstances are widely referred to both in the text of the CBD, through the formula "as far as possible and as appropriate" that creates flexibility in the implementation of many obligations,[102] and in CBD COP decisions. The reasons underpinning this differentiation and flexibility lay in the distinction between parties in developed and developing countries.[103] COP decisions also refer to the need to reduce poverty as well as to the specific development and capacity needs of developing countries.[104]

These differentiated needs also underpin article 20 of the CBD, which is the clearest manifestation of the principle of common but differentiated responsibilities therein. This provision provides additional justifications for the special treatment reserved for developing country parties by acknowledging both their dependence on biological resources and their specific environmental

97 Art 4 WHC. Emphasis added. See also Operational Guidelines, para 7. Emphasis added.

98 Operational Guidelines, para 49.

99 Ibid para 109.

100 Barral 2017, n 18, at 66; Koester, n 7, at 280.

101 In this regard, COP dec XIV/8, para 9 provides an interesting definition of equity as encompassing three dimensions: "recognition [respect for rights and diversity], procedure [inclusiveness of decision-making] and distribution [of costs and benefits]".

102 Also, the formula "Subject to its national legislation" contained in art 8(j) CBD is interpreted in this sense. See Cittadino 2019, n 35, at 58–62.

103 COP dec I/2; COP dec VII/8.

104 COP dec VI/9, preamble. COP dec V/13, para 2. COP dec VII/28, para 5. COP dec VII/29, annex, para 4(a). COP dec XII/5, annex, Chennai Guidelines for Implementation of the Integration of Biodiversity and Poverty Eradication, para 3. COP dec XIII/8, annex, Mo'otz Kuxtal guidelines, para 1.

situation.[105] Article 20(2) foresees, this being the second aspect of intra-generational equity, the transfer of financial resources from developed countries to developing ones and, on a voluntary basis, to parties with economies in transition in order to enable them implement the CBD. In line with this obligation, under article 20(4) the compliance of developing countries with CBD provisions is conditional upon the effective implementation of financial transfers under the abovementioned article 20(2).[106] Although some authors maintain that this provision subordinates conservation and sustainable use to economic and social development,[107] in our view article 20(4) and, more generally, the financial provisions of the CBD are an attempt to integrate (intra-generational) equity into the implementation of an environmental treaty. To operationalise financial transfers to developing countries, article 21 foresees the creation of a CBD-based multilateral financial mechanism managed by the COP. This mechanism is the Global Environmental Facility (GEF), created in 1992 later becoming the main financial instrument for both the CBD and the United Nations Framework Convention on Climate Change (UNFCCC).[108]

The CBD does not limit itself to creating obligations on financial transfers, but also defines, through COP decisions, the main purposes for which developing countries should receive funds both from the GEF and from other donors.[109] Conservation, the implementation of the CBD Programme of Work on Protected Areas (PoWPA) and other conservation strategies, as well as the identification of Indigenous and Community Protected Areas (ICCAs) constitute admissible purposes.[110] Another legitimate purpose is the improvement of participation through dedicated funds, in particular of indigenous peoples and local communities, in the implementation of the CBD.[111] Most recently, funds should target indigenous peoples and local communities directly, in

105 Art 20(6) and (7) CBD. Art 17(1) CBD further mentions the special needs of developing countries in the context of obligations concerning information sharing.

106 See Yussuf, n 40, at 134.

107 Koester, n 7, at 280.

108 Some CBD COP decisions confirm the centrality of the GEF: COP dec VI/16, para 5; COP dec VI/17; COP dec VIII/12, paras 11 and 12; COP dec IX/31; COP dec XI/5, para 3.

109 Also, the Executive Secretary of the CBD is called to facilitate capacity building, technology transfer and financial support to developing countries (COP dec IX/3, para 6(d)).

110 COP dec I/2, para 4(m); COP dec VI/9, annex; COP dec VII/20; COP dec VII/28, para 4; annex, suggested activity 3.4.3. COP dec VIII/24, paras 4 and 22; COP dec IX/18, part B, para 1; COP dec X/5, para 1; COP dec X/6, para 10; COP dec X/17, para 5; COP dec X/29, para 38; COP dec X/31, para 9; COP XI/4, para 7(a); COP dec XI/5, para 16; COP XI/16, para 3; COP dec XII/3, para 1(a).

111 COP dec I/2, para 4(j); COP dec III/5, para 5; COP dec V/16, para 12; COP dec VII/16, annex, part G, para 7; COP dec XI/14, para 9.

order for them to map ICCAs, ensure conservation, and promote customary sustainable use.[112]

Funds should also be directed into enhancing the capacity of developing countries to implement the CBD.[113] Capacity-building represents an autonomous expression of intragenerational equity in the context of the CBD, included in both article 12, which contains research and training obligations for realising conservation and sustainable use with particular regard to developing countries' needs, and COP decisions.[114] Moreover, capacity-building measures need to be directed towards nongovernmental actors, especially indigenous peoples and local communities. In particular, the latter subjects need, first, to formulate their own plans in order to realise conservation and sustainable use and, second, to be prepared to participate in decision-making at all government levels.[115]

Another manifestation of intragenerational equity within the CBD are in principle the obligations on technology transfer. These require the adoption of both preferential terms for the access to, and transfer of, biotechnologies to developing countries and national measures to ensure that technologies are transferred to those parties, especially developing countries, which provide genetic resources.[116] These provisions in practice, however, are considered too ambiguous and not specific enough to produce concrete results.[117]

The third aspect of intragenerational equity identified by Barral is that of benefitsharing as an expression of the redistributive aspect of equity.

112 COP dec XII/12, para 6: funds to both developing countries and indigenous and local communities to implement programmes and plans that promote customary sustainable use; COP dec XII/19, para 2(f): "provide support and incentives...to indigenous and local communities" for conservation.

113 COP dec VI/10, part 1: provide funds for the enhancement of national capacities to protect traditional knowledge.

114 COP dec II/7, para 6; COP dec V/7, para 3); COP dec V/16, para 12; COP dec VI/9, preamble; COP dec X/6, para 1; COP XI/4, para 15.

115 COP dec III/15, para 3; COP dec V/26, para 14; COP dec VI/10, part 1; COP dec VII/16, annex, para 26; para 28; part F, Akwé-Kon, paras 9(d), 10, 66 and 70; COP dec VII/19, annex of part F, para 5(j); COP dec VII/28, annex, PoWPA, suggested activity 2.2.4; COP dec VIII/24, para 18(g); COP dec XI/5, paras 17 and 19, and appendix, para 1(d); COP dec XII/18, para 11.

116 Arts 16(2) and (3) CBD. See also art 19 CBD on specific measures concerning biotechnologies. Art 2 CBD defines biotechnologies as follows: ""Biotechnology" means any technological application that uses biological systems, living organisms, or derivatives thereof, to make or modify products or processes for specific use."

117 Yusuf 1995, n 45 at 132. COP dec VII/29, annex, Programme of work on technology transfer and technological and scientific cooperation, para 1; COP dec IX/14, para 15 and annex paras 5 and 10: technology transfer should be adapted to the needs of developing countries and to local needs through a participatory approach; COP dec IX/8, para 7.

Benefit-sharing has both an interstate nature, since it needs to be provided under article 15(7) of the CBD to those countries that allow for the utilisation of their genetic resources, and an intrastate component expressed in article 8(j).[118] Notwithstanding the ambiguities of article 8(j),[119] this provision obliges parties to encourage the fair and equitable sharing of benefits which arise from the utilisation of traditional knowledge and practices of indigenous peoples and local communities.[120] Benefitsharing with indigenous peoples and local communities is foreseen not only in the context of the utilisation of traditional knowledge,[121] but also concerning the effects of the creation of protected areas on the territories of indigenous peoples and local communities.[122]

Finally, the fourth aspect of intragenerational equity is that of recognition, which in the CBD is expressed as both equity in the consideration of the value of traditional knowledge with respect to Western knowledge and equity deriving from the recognition of traditional land tenure of indigenous peoples and local communities.[123] The emphasis on the protection of traditional knowledge represents a link with sustainable use since, as emphasised in section 2.1, the retention of traditional knowledge is instrumental for the conservation and sustainable use of biodiversity.[124]

118 The difference between interstate and intrastate benefitsharing has been conceptualised first by Elisa Morgera and Elsa Tsioumani, 'The Evolution of Benefit-Sharing: Linking Biodiversity and Community Livelihoods' (2010) 15 Review of European Community and International Environmental Law 150.

119 Cittadino 2019, n 35, at 58–62. These ambiguities are partially solved in arts 5(2) and 5(4) of the Nagoya Protocol, which anyway applies only to its parties. Ibid. ch. 3.

120 COP dec VII/12, annex 1, practical principle 12; COP dec X/31, para 31(a); COP dec XIII/8, annex, Mo'otz Kuxtal guidelines, paras 1 and 12.

121 The Nagoya Protocol establishes, in its art 5(2), benefitsharing obligations also in the case of utilization of indigenous genetic resources.

122 COP dec VII/28, annex, PoWPA, suggested activity 2.1.1; COP dec IX/18, paras 6(e) and 19; COP dec X/31, para 32(d); COP X/42, Tkarihwaié:ri Code of Ethical Conduct, para 14.

123 COP dec III/14, preamble, para 9; COP V/5: principle 11 of the ecosystem approach; COP dec X/42: Tkarihwaié:ri Code of Ethical Conduct, preamble and paras 17 and 20–21; COP dec XII/12, annex, Plan of action on customary sustainable use of biological diversity, para 3. The recognition of traditional land tenure is expressed as a recognition of indigenous peoples' rights that is more evident in the Nagoya Protocol but can be derived also from a systemic interpretation of the CBD in light of human rights instruments protecting the rights of indigenous peoples. See Cittadino 2019, n 35, ch. 2.

124 COP dec X/42: Tkarihwaié:ri Code of Ethical Conduct, preamble and para 18; art 9 Nagoya Protocol.

In the Ramsar regime the consideration of national circumstances is included in both the Convention text[125] and COP resolutions and allows parties to implement Ramsar Convention provisions flexibly.

As for the financial aspect, article 6(6) foresees a scale of budget contributions decided on the basis of "the need for an *equitable sharing* among the Parties and the *situation in developing countries*".[126] Moreover, parties that have the capacity to provide additional voluntary payments to the budget are requested to do so,[127] by contributing to the Ramsar Small Grant Fund for Wetland Conservation and Wise Use (SGF)[128] as well as to other grant programmes[129] aimed at strengthening wetland management capacities and supporting the implementation of the Convention in developing countries, including through capacity building, training and education. The specific activities eligible for funding are identified in selected COP decisions[130] and, more recently, through the fundraising priorities listed in the Resource Mobilization Work Plan.[131] Non-party states and other external donors are also invited to contribute to wetland conservation and wise use of wetlands, not only by providing funds,[132] but also by integrating conservation and wise management consideration in any funded activity in developing countries that can have an impact on wetlands.[133]

Although the Ramsar Convention text specifically refers to professionals in its article 4(5), training and capacity building aim to address a wider audience

---

125 Arts 3(1) and 4(2) Ramsar Convention.

126 COP Res 5.2 (1993), para 3. Emphasis added.

127 Ibid para 7.

128 This Fund was established in 1990 with Ramsar COP Res 4.3 and is currently the main mechanism to assist developing countries and countries with economies in transition in implementing the Convention and enhancing the conservation and wise use of wetlands through small-scale projects. Non-contracting parties can also apply to finance "preparatory assistance" useful to progress towards accession to the Convention. See the *2019 Guidelines for the Operation of the Small Grants Fund*, p 2. New funding alternatives will cover small-scale projects in the future since the SGF will be phased out upon exhaustion of the available resources. COP Res XIII.2 (2018), para 31.

129 This is the case for Wetland for future, the Nagao Wetland Fund, and the Swiss Grant for Africa, which have different regional focuses.

130 For the SGF see COP Res 4.3, para (e) and (f) and the related 2019 Guidelines, Section III; in relation to the "Wetlands for the future" Initiative, see the Memorandum of Understanding between the Secretariat of the Ramsar Convention and the U.S. Government, para 8.

131 SC57 Doc.19 (2019).

132 See, for instance, COP Annex to DOC C.4.13 (1990), para 8; COP Res 5.2 (1993), para 9.

133 In particular, this request is directed to development agencies and multilateral development banks. See, respectively, COP Recommendation 3.4 (1987) and COP Recommendation 4.13 (1990).

at regional and local levels.[134] Under the Ramsar Convention, the importance of training and capacity building for realisation of intra-generational equity is confirmed by the creation of dedicated mechanisms that promote international cooperation and facilitate the implementation of this treaty.[135] Cooperation is one of the three pillars[136] of this convention and is key to its implementation, especially in the case of shared wetlands or water systems.[137] Intragenerational equity also unfolds through cooperation, when it promotes expertise and information-sharing on wetland management (e.g. knowledge sharing, training, site twinning or networking)[138] as well as international assistance (e.g. technical and financial) to support wetland conservation and wise use in developing countries.[139]

Promoted by the CBD, the recognition aspect has gained prominence over time and laid the foundation for a more effective participation of local communities and indigenous peoples in wetland conservation and management. The Ramsar COP acknowledges that indigenous peoples and local communities have "longstanding rights, ancestral values, and traditional knowledge and institutions associated with their use of wetlands"[140] and promotes the conservation, integration and exchange of traditional knowledge.[141]

---

134 Ramsar Convention Secretariat 2016, n 72, at 57.

135 *Ramsar Regional Initiatives 2019–2021*, COP Res XIII.9 (2018).

136 The other pillars are the conservation of wetlands of international importance and the wise use of all wetlands. Ramsar Convention Secretariat 2016, n 72, at 37.

137 On the interpretation of art 5, Ramsar Convention Secretariat 2010. *International cooperation: Guidelines and other support for international cooperation under the Ramsar Convention on Wetlands*. Ramsar handbooks for the wise use of wetlands, 4th edition, vol 20. Ramsar Convention Secretariat, Gland, Switzerland, at 8.

138 Ibid at 25–27.

139 Ibid at 27–39.

140 COP Res VII.8 (1999), para 4.

141 Requests in this sense are included in several documents, *in primis*, Target 10 of the 4th (current) Ramsar Strategic Plan. See also the Guidelines for establishing and strengthening local communities' and indigenous people's participation in the management of wetlands, COP Res VII.8 (1999), Annex. COP Res VIII.36 (2002) promotes an integrated approach for the sustainable management of wetlands through the tool of "Participatory Environmental Management" (PEM) that incorporates knowledge from many sources: local and regional, traditional and scientific, administrative, etc. See also the Handbook on International cooperation, n 138, at 25, and the Handbook on participatory skills: Ramsar Convention Secretariat 2010. *Participatory skills: Establishing and strengthening local communities' and indigenous people's participation in the management of wetlands* Ramsar handbooks for the wise use of wetlands, 4th edition, vol 7. Ramsar Convention Secretariat, Gland, Switzerland. Ramsar Convention Secretariat 2016, n 72, at 41. COP Res VIII.19 (2002), Appendix I, para 2; COP Res X.28 (2008), para 10(III).

In the WHC, intragenerational equity is articulated both as an objective[142] – together with intergenerational equity – and as a set of state parties' obligations that unfold primarily through international cooperation and assistance in the protection[143] of natural and/or cultural properties.[144] The preamble highlights that often the protection of heritage at a national level is incomplete due to the lack of economic, scientific, and technological resources of the country hosting the property. To overcome these difficulties and in order to preserve irreplaceable heritage, the WHC aims to put in place "an effective system of collective protection of the cultural and natural heritage", where the international community as a whole can participate in the protection efforts and grant "collective assistance" to complement the action of the state hosting the heritage.[145] Arguably, cooperation and international assistance not only ensure intragenerational equity by supporting the protection efforts of states lacking sufficient means but are essential elements of the WHC.

Indeed, article 4 requires each state party to do all it can to ensure the protection of its properties, "to the utmost of its own resources and … with any international assistance and cooperation, in particular, financial, artistic, scientific and technical". As corresponding obligations, all the other parties shall, while respecting the sovereignty of the state where the heritage is situated, recognise their responsibility to cooperate in the protection of such heritage[146] and commit to offering assistance upon request of the host state.[147] This is a big difference compared to the CBD and the Ramsar Convention, where cooperation is a default obligation.

International assistance can be requested "to secure the protection, conservation, presentation or rehabilitation" of properties,[148] including for properties listed as "in danger",[149] for the identification of properties and preliminary investigation[150] as well as for the preparation and update of the Tentative List.[151] Assistance granted under the World Heritage Fund[152] can take the form of

142 Operational Guidelines, paras 49 and 109.

143 Protection is used as an encompassing term, also entailing the identification, conservation, presentation and transmission to future generations of cultural and natural heritage.

144 Art 7 WHC.

145 Ibid.

146 Ibid art 6(1).

147 Ibid art 6(2).

148 Art 13(1) WHC.

149 Ibid art 11(4).

150 Ibid art 13(2).

151 Operational Guidelines, para 75.

152 Art 16 WHC.

knowledge and technological transfer[153] or training of staff and specialists at all levels for the performance of activities useful at the implementation of this Convention.[154] A further reference to intra-generational equity emerges from article 25 that, among the conditions and arrangements for international assistance, requires a substantial contribution of the state benefitting from international assistance, "unless its resources do not permit this".[155]

Finally, similar to the CBD and the Ramsar Convention, article 5 grants state parties room for manoeuver when adopting measures for the implementation of the WHC in line with their national circumstances.[156] This provision lays the basis for inclusive social development, based on a recognition of cultural diversity, inclusivity and equity of all stakeholders.[157] This inclusive dimension is not fully implemented into WHC processes, but progress has been made in this direction.[158]

2.4 *Integration*

Already in its Preamble, the CBD recognises different values of biodiversity, including ecological, social, economic, and cultural factors.[159] As shown in the previous subsections, the CBD embraces the three components of SD and integration is inherent in how these components play out in the architecture of this convention.

Integration also fulfils a more operative function, which aims to guarantee the mainstreaming of biodiversity in national laws and plans that may somehow affect the attainment of CBD objectives. In this sense, under article 6 of the CBD, parties must integrate "the conservation and sustainable use of biological diversity into relevant sectoral and cross-sectoral plans, programmes, and policies"[160] and, under article 10(a) integration must also be realised in "national decision-making".[161]

---

153 Ibid art 22(b) and (d).

154 Ibid art 22(c). On training see also art 23.

155 In this regard, the Operational Guidelines define international assistance as "supplementary to national efforts… when adequate resources cannot be secured at the national level", para 233.

156 Flexibility is also granted by art 11 WHC.

157 See the Policy for integrating sustainable development into the WHC, n 48, paras 17–23.

158 See Sections 3.1 and 3.2 below.

159 Preamble para 1 CBD.

160 See also COP dec III/19, annex, para 3; COP dec IX/18, para 4(a); COP dec VII/28, annex, PoWPA, suggested activities 3.1.1–3.1.8; COP dec IX/28, preamble; COP dec X/29, paras 7 and 67.

161 See also COP dec V/18, para 1(c); COP dec V/23, annex I, para 2(f); COP dec V/24, preamble; COP dec V/26, para 3; COP dec VII/12 adopting Addis Ababa Principles and Guidelines on sustainable use, para 2(a).

In most cases, mainstreaming implies the integration of biodiversity protection into relevant economic plans and policy measures, as well as through marketbased instruments.[162] This need is expressed in the text of the CBD through its article 11, which establishes the obligation to adopt "economically and socially sound measures" providing incentives for conservation and sustainable use. In addition, COP decisions indicate both specific sectors in which integration must be implemented and a pool of actors, beyond states, that must realise mainstreaming. As for the first aspect, COP decisions mention poverty eradication, monetary and budgetary policies, financial strategies, development cooperation, international trade, agriculture, fisheries, mining, energy, tourism, transportation, and all those policies that provide negative economic incentives to conservation and sustainable use.[163] Concerning the actors that must realise integration, although CBD parties are the primary addressees of CBD COP decisions, their recommendations are also directed towards international financial institutions, such as the World Bank and the International Monetary Fund, international development agencies, such as the United Nations Development Programme, as well as other relevant stakeholders involved in biodiversity and development processes.[164]

In addition, integration not only implies the mainstreaming of biodiversity in decision-making but also includes the consideration of other aspects in the context of biodiversity protection. According to article 8(i) of the CBD, parties must ensure the "compatibility between present uses and the conservation of biological diversity and the sustainable use of its components", thus stressing the importance of conservation and sustainable use. However, COP decisions mention different issues that need to be integrated in biodiversity conservation plans and policy instruments, including climate change,[165] gender issues,[166]

---

162 COP dec X/32, para 2(I).

163 COP dec VI/9, preamble; COP dec VI/10, part 1; COP dec VI/16, paras 7(b) and 8; COP dec VII/12, annex 2, Addis Ababa guidelines, Practical principle 3; COP dec VII/16, annex part F, Akwé-Kon guidelines on impact assessment; COP dec VII/21, para 7; COP dec VII/28, annex, PoWPA, suggested activity 3.4.6; COP dec VIII/24, para 26; COP dec IX/25; COP dec IX/11, annex: Strategy to enhance financial resources, Goals 2.3, 2.4, 5.1–5.3; COP dec X/6, para 1; COP dec X/17, target 11; COP dec X/32, paras 2(b) and 2(h); COP dec XII/3, para 1(b); COP dec XII/4, para 1; COP dec XII/5, para 3; COP dec XIII/8, para 2; COP dec XIV/8, para 12.

164 COP dec VI/16, para 8; COP dec X/6, paras 1, 4, 6(a), and 15.

165 COP dec VII/28, annex, PoWPA, suggested activity 1.4.5; COP dec XI/18, para 12.

166 COP dec X/17, para 5; COP dec XI/9.

the rights of indigenous peoples and their traditional knowledge,[167] access and benefit-sharing,[168] and programmes on protected areas.[169]

CBD COP decisions also suggest ways in which to realise integration, *in primis* through the ecosystem approach.[170] This approach consists of two main tenets: first, that conservation is also the product of human presence and the consideration of human needs in the management of nature;[171] and second, that ecosystems are dynamic functional units where different species and habitats coexist and influence each other.[172] Following these premises, the management of the different natural components, such as land, water and living resources, must be integrated, taking into account the interaction among species, the balance between conservation and sustainable use, and the contribution of specific groups, including indigenous peoples and local communities.[173] This vision in turn must be integrated into crosssectoral legislation and planning at all levels of decision-making in order to realise SD.[174] The precautionary principle is also sparely mentioned as a way to ensure integration in the context of scientific uncertainty.[175]

Finally, a concrete instrument for realising integration is the introduction of impact assessments. Article 14(a) of the CBD requires the establishment of environmental impact assessment procedures for projects that "are likely to have significant adverse effects on biological diversity". This includes, for instance, "any plan or project with the potential to have effects on protected areas".[176] Moreover, the COP has adopted specific guidelines for impact assessments to be conducted when developments are planned to take place on, or

---

167 COP dec VI/10, part 1; COP dec X/31, para 1(1); COP dec X/32, para 2(e): COP dec XI/14, para 4. See also UNEP/CBD/SBSTTA/14/7.

168 COP dec X/31, para 30(b).

169 COP dec X/31, para 1(c).

170 Koester, n 7 at 290: "Generally, the Ecosystem Approach may, as the Strategic Plan shows, be perceived as an instrument of integration" although it also reflects elements of sustainable use, intergenerational and intragenerational equity. See also COP dec IV/1, preamble, para 1: ecosystem approach as a "guiding principle".

171 COP dec II/9, annex, para 4; COP dec V/5, para 7.

172 Art. 2 CBD: definition of ecosystem: ""Ecosystem" means a dynamic complex of plant, animal and microorganism communities and their nonliving environment interacting as a functional unit"; COP dec V/5, para 4.

173 COP dec V/5, para 6; COP dec VI/9, annex, part B; COP dec VII/11, annex I, para 1; COP dec X/31, para 1(d); COP dec XI/18; COP dec XII/12, annex, Plan of action on customary sustainable use of biological diversity, para 6(g).

174 COP dec VI/12; COP dec VII/11, annex I, para 19; COP dec IX/7, preamble and para 1(b); COP dec XII/19, para 2(b) and (c); COP dec XIV/8, para 12.

175 COP dec VIII/28, para 42.

176 COP dec VII/28, annex, PoWPA, suggested activity 1.5.1.

are likely to impact, sacred sites on land and water traditionally occupied or used by indigenous and local communities.[177] Specific recommendations on the conduct of impact assessment are also made in the context of marine conservation areas.[178]

Integration also plays a key role in the Ramsar regime. In the context of article 3(1), it acquires an operative dimension by requiring the inclusion of wetland conservation and wise use considerations in national planning in all the sectors that might have an impact on wetlands.[179] Indeed, the wise use of all wetlands at any relevant governance level (from the basin to the transboundary levels) is favoured by "mainstreaming recognition of ecosystem functions, services and benefits into a wide range of sectors and with a broad array of actors",[180] including development agencies and multilateral development banks.[181] Furthermore, integration can be firmly pursued through "integrated resource management at the appropriate scale"[182] and by incorporating "the traditional knowledge, innovation and practices of indigenous peoples and local communities relevant to the wise use of wetlands and their customary use … in the implementation of the Convention".[183]

Arguably, integration emerges also from article 4(2) through the obligation to compensate – as far as possible – "for any loss of wetland resources" in the attempt to find a balance between wetland conservation and "urgent national interest" leading to the deletion or restriction of listed sites. Along the same lines, efforts to effectively address the drivers of wetland loss and degradation should ponder wetland monetary and non-monetary values into planning and

177 COP dec VII/16, annex, Part F, text of Akwé-Kon Voluntary Guidelines. See also COP dec XI/16, para 1(e).

178 COP dec X/29, para 54.

179 Ramsar Convention Secretariat 2016, n 72 at 14. The importance of integrating Ramsar site management plans into the public and development planning, with a focus on spatial and economic aspects is also highlighted by Ramsar Convention Secretariat, 2010, *Managing wetlands: Frameworks for managing Wetlands of International Importance and other wetland sites*. Ramsar handbooks for the wise use of wetlands, 4th edition, vol 18. Ramsar Convention Secretariat, Gland, Switzerland, at 17 and 19.

180 4th Strategic Plan, Strategic goal 3, at 20.

181 COP Recommendations 3.4 (1987) and 4.13 (1990).

182 4th Strategic Plan, Target 9, at 30. Target 9 is primarily pursued through "promoting wise use, integrated water resources management, and integration of wetlands in other sectoral policies, plans or strategies". Effective planning and integrated management is also required to maintain or restore the ecological character of listed sites in Target 5.

183 Ibid Target 10, at 20.

decision-making to enable an assessment of the environmental functions and benefits wetlands provide to society.[184]

The Ramsar COP has extensively highlighted "the vital contribution of wetlands to human wellbeing, livelihoods and human health, as well as to biodiversity".[185] The Convention text recognises "the interdependence of Man and his environment" and acknowledges the "great economic, cultural, scientific, and recreational value" of wetlands.[186] Based on that, integration finds application in linking the conservation and wise use of wetlands to poverty eradication[187] – in the framework of the Millennium Development Goals[188] – and in the contribution that the fourth Ramsar Strategic Plan provides to the achievement of the SDG s.[189]

Integration acquires a transnational character in article 5, which promotes interstate cooperation for the implementation of the Ramsar Convention, especially through the coordination of wetlandrelated policies and regulations. Integration is also realised within other multilateral environmental agreements, like the CBD and the Convention on Migratory Species, through the design of joint working plans that identify issues and areas of activities of common interest and facilitate collaboration to enhance the implementation of the relevant conventions.[190]

The protection of world heritage has the potential to integrate the environmental, social and economic components of SD and recent evolution of the regime has moved in this direction.[191] Indeed, the Operational Guidelines encourage state parties to mainstream, *inter alia,* SD principles, the inclusion of indigenous peoples and human rights international standards into their programmes and policies implementing the WHC.[192] Furthermore, the Guidelines recall the responsibility of state parties to "contribute to and comply

184 Ibid Strategic goal 1, at 19.

185 COP Res X.3 (2008), para 2.

186 Preamble Ramsar Convention.

187 COP Res IX.14 (2005); COP Res X.28 (2008); COP Res XI.13 (2012). For the integration of wetland and health considerations under the ecosystem approach framework see COP Res X.3, X.23 and X.21 (2008), COP Res XI.12 (2012).

188 In particular MDG 1 "eradicate extreme poverty and hunger" and MDG 7 "ensuring environmental sustainability". COP Res X.28 (2008).

189 4th Ramsar Strategic Plan.

190 See, for instance, COP Res XI.6 (2012). For further information on the partnership with other Conventions see <https://www.ramsar.org/about/partnerships-with-other-conventions>.

191 In this regard, refer to the Policy on integrating sustainable development into the WHC, n 48.

192 Operational Guidelines, para 14bis.

with sustainable development objectives, including gender equity, in the World Heritage processes and in their heritage conservation and management systems".[193] In doing so, they stress the importance of intervening at different levels: both in the governance of the regime and on the ground – at the national and local levels – where it is implemented.[194]

A more operational perspective of integration is pursued by article 5(a), which requires states to mainstream heritage protection into "comprehensive planning programmes". In the WHC, integration can also be read in terms of coordination with other relevant biodiversity conventions, such as the CBD and Ramsar Convention.[195]

2.5 *Preliminary Conclusion on Sustainability*

The analysis above demonstrates that all components of SD can be identified with different degrees in the three biodiversity conventions. For instance, in the Ramsar Convention the environmental and social components of sustainability appear predominant in comparison to the economic component with an emphasis on the wise use and the maintenance of the ecological status of wetlands and their contribution to human wellbeing and poverty eradication. The connection between SD and poverty alleviation is stressed also in the CBD, in line with recent evolutions in the definition of SD at international UN summits. The practice of the three conventions evidences the existence of additional elements in the definitions of the four subprinciples of sustainability that are briefly illustrated below.

One peculiar aspect in the CBD and the Ramsar Convention, which is absent in the general narrative of sustainable use, is the emphasis on the role of preserving the traditional knowledge of indigenous peoples and local communities to realise sustainable and wise use.

In contrast with the CBD and the Ramsar Convention, in the WHC, the inter- and intra-generational components of SD emerge distinctively from the convention text; the former through the objective of the convention, and the latter through the obligations to support other states in the protection of properties situated on their territories through international cooperation and assistance.

Intragenerational equity in the CBD cannot be reduced to the principle of common but differentiated responsibilities and to the transfer of financial

---

193 Ibid para 15(o).

194 The latter aspect emerges also from the management requirement for a complete nomination. Ibid para 132(5).

195 Ibid para 41.

resources and technologies. Instead, it also includes the recognition of the special needs and roles of indigenous peoples and local communities. Furthermore, the practice of the CBD indicates that this principle applies both between state parties and in the internal relations of parties with indigenous peoples and local communities.

Finally, integration is mainly displayed through mainstreaming conservation as articulated in the three conventions in other relevant policies and programmes and through the actions of a broad array of actors. In the CBD, integration appears to have some teeth as it foresees specific implementing instruments, including the obligation to conduct impact assessments.

Based on the above, we can conclude that sustainability in these conventions is the product of the interaction of its four main subprinciples. In this sense, even in the environmental treaties analysed in this chapter, the main aim of sustainability is not exclusively to ensure environmental protection, but to combine environmental objectives with economic and social considerations.

3 Participation in the Global Regimes on Biodiversity Protection

Public participation is not a concern that is fully and explicitly embraced in the text of the CBD, which instead refers to it with respect to some specific subject (women in the Preamble and observers in CBD COP under article 23(5)) and to some specific situations (impact assessment under article 14(1)(a)).[196] This is partly due to the lack of a general strategy on public participation in the CBD. Another reason for the apparent absence of the concept of participation is an ambiguous use of language. For instance, when it comes to indigenous peoples and local communities, their participation in the governance of protected areas and in the utilisation of traditional knowledge is often expressed in terms of "approval and involvement" (article 8(j) CBD) rather than participation as such. Moreover,[197] information is an important component of public participation in the CBD.

The Ramsar Convention and the WHC predate the concept of public participation as evolved from principle 10 of the Rio Declaration onwards.

196 The Cartagena Protocol to the CBD contains a reference to participation in its art 23 with respect to decisions concerning living modified organisms. See Cartagena Protocol on Biosafety to the Convention on Biological Diversity, entered into force 11 September 2003, 2226 UNTS 208.

197 According to Koester, "[t]he other dimensions of "environmental rights", i.e. access to environmental information and access to justice, are more or less ignored" in the CBD. Koester, n 7, at 294.

Nonetheless, the two regimes responded to participatory instances and embodied them in their evolution.

The Ramsar Convention arguably includes a participatory component in articles 6(3) and 7(1). The former introduces the right of information, while the latter arguably allows the inclusion of a diversified array of expertise and interests in national delegations. Moreover, the importance of enhancing participation of all relevant stakeholders, especially in decision-making and management at site level, emerges from efforts to adopt a dedicated strategy and management tool, namely the Programme on Communication, Capacity Building, Education, Participation and Awareness (CEPA) and Participatory Environmental Management (PEM). These elements lay the basis for the participation of non-state actors at all relevant governance levels.

As in the CBD, the Ramsar regime places emphasis on the participation of indigenous peoples and local communities and dedicates specific attention to them in several COP decisions and operational documents *in primis* in its Strategic Plans and the Handbook on participatory skills.[198]

Public participation does not find explicit recognition in the text of the WHC, except for the obligation to inform (top-down) the general public of the dangers threatening world heritage and the activities undertaken under the convention.[199] Access to information by the general public can be further strengthened through the educational and information programmes aimed at reinforcing the recognition and respect of protected properties.[200] The main obligations relating to the identification, protection, conservation and maintenance of the OUV of WH sites bind state parties without further reference to other actors. Although often criticised, especially in relation to the involvement of indigenous peoples and local communities,[201] this attitude is slowly changing. This began with the inclusion of "cultural landscape" as a new category of world heritage[202] in 1992 and the acceptance of traditional management

198 Ramsar Convention Secretariat 2010, *Handbook on Participatory skills*, n 142.

199 Art 27(2) WHC.

200 Ibid art 27(1). See also Operational Guidelines, para 15(m). In addition, the fourth strategic objective of the WHC reads: "increase public awareness, involvement, and support for World Heritage through Communication", ibid para 26(4). Access to information for the general public is also ensured by the Secretariat, see ibid Section IX.C.

201 See, for instance, the Report of the Special Rapporteur on the rights of indigenous peoples, UN Doc A/67/310, para 33. For further discussion on the participatory rights of indigenous peoples refer to Cittadino 2019, n 35, at 299 ff.

202 WH Committee Dec CONF 002 XIII.1–3 (1992).

as appropriate for the properties,[203] to the establishment of the International Indigenous People Forum for World Heritage in 2017 and the updated version of the Operational Guidelines (2019). The latter encourages state parties "to adopt a human-rights based approach and ensure a genderbalanced participation of a wide variety of stakeholders and rightsholders, including ... local communities [and] indigenous peoples ... in the identification, nomination, management and protection processes of World Heritage properties".[204] In so doing, the Guidelines create a framework which frames those actors as public concerned, whose participation must be ensured both at global and national levels.

Based on the practice of the three conventions, in the following sections we will discuss two main aspects: (1) participation in the global governance of biological diversity – i.e. the international decision-making fora that steer the evolution of the treaties analysed; and (2) participation in the implementation of the biodiversity regimes.

3.1 *Participation in the Global Governance of Biological Diversity*

Article 23(5) CBD allows for the participation of organised groups upon request to the Secretariat as observers in CBD COP meetings, which are the main mechanism to promote the correct interpretation and evolution of the CBD regime.[205] Observers cannot cast a vote but may participate and intervene in the meetings of the COP, thus having an influence on both the issues discussed and the decisions taken. Although the criteria for obtaining observer status are formulated very broadly in principle in the text of the CBD, its COP decisions point decisively to the involvement of indigenous peoples and local communities,[206] not only as observers but also as members of national delegations.[207]

To confirm this trend, the CBD COP has created two working groups, in which indigenous peoples' representatives have played a strong role that is testified by the evolution of the regimes on traditional knowledge in both the CBD and the Nagoya Protocol.[208] These groups are the Working Group on Article 8(j)[209] and the Ad-Hoc Openended Working Group to elaborate the Nagoya

203 On this point see milestone 1 in the WHC webpage dedicated to indigenous peoples: <https://whc.unesco.org/en/activities/496/>.

204 Operational Guidelines, para 12.

205 See section 1 above.

206 COP dec III/14, para 12; COP dec III/19, annex, para 18; COP dec V/16, para 18; COP dec VI/10, preamble and para 11; COP dec X/40, Part C, para 3; COP dec XIV/17, para 2.

207 COP dec VII/16, annex, part G, para 1, at 29.

208 On this latter point, see Cittadino 2019, n 35, Conclusion.

209 COP dec IV/9, paras 1 and 2.

Protocol.[210] Since their creation, the participation of indigenous peoples and local communities in these groups has been systematically encouraged by the CBD COP.[211] The role of these actors has been both to provide information on access and benefitsharing issues[212] and to specifically influence the outputs of these working groups, by proposing amendments and concrete formulations of the final texts to be adopted by state parties. To this end, these groups have operated either contextually or before any sessions of the COP.[213] Moreover, the presence of indigenous peoples and local communities both in the COP and in the working groups has been facilitated by states through capacitybuilding and training, dedicated funding, and the provision of information with appropriate means of communication and use of local languages.[214]

In the Ramsar Convention, article 7(1) requires state parties to include among their representatives to the COPs "experts on wetlands or waterfowl by reason of knowledge and experience gained in scientific, administrative or other appropriate capacities", and thus opens up to an inclusive constituency, including local communities and indigenous peoples.[215] Furthermore, the Rules of Procedure of the Ramsar COP[216] enable the participation, upon request to the Secretariat, of "any body or agency, national or international, whether governmental or non-governmental, qualified in fields relating to the conservation and sustainable use of wetlands [as observers…] unless at least one third of contracting parties present at the meeting objects".[217] Although there is no Working Group enabling the participation of specific actors, in particular indigenous peoples, the efforts of the COP and the Convention Secretariat in acknowledging their key role in conserving and managing wetlands and ensuring their participation *de facto* has had an impact on the evolution of the Ramsar regime since COP 6 (1996).[218] Indeed, the Ramsar Bureau can gather

---

210 COP dec V/26, para 11. In principle, other actors are admitted to participate as observers in this group, including "nongovernmental organizations, industry, and scientific and academic institutions, as well as intergovernmental organizations". See COP dec VII/19, part C, para 1.

211 COP dec VII/16, annex, part G, para 3; COP dec VIII/5, paras 6(b) and 6(c).

212 See eg COP dec IX/12, para 9.

213 COP dec XII/8, para 2.

214 COP dec V/16, in particular in para 12; COP dec VI/13; COP dec VIII/5, para 7 and annex; COP dec IX/12, para 19; COP dec XI/14, part B, para 14; COP dec X/40, part C, paras 1–2.

215 Ramsar COP Recommendation 6.3 (1996), para 12 and COP Res VII.8 (1999), para 16.

216 The latest version was adopted in 2018 and is available at <https://www.ramsar.org/sites/default/files/documents/library/ramsar_rules_of_procedure_e_0.pdf>.

217 Rule 7.

218 Ramsar COP Recommendation 6.3 (1996) 'Involving Local and Indigenous People in the Management of the Ramsar Wetlands' is indicated as a landmark decision in Gon-

useful input for the development of this regime on aspects that are particularly relevant to these actors from local communities and indigenous peoples.[219] Moreover, local stakeholders do play a role in the implementation of this Convention in terms of "selection, designation, and [especially] management of Ramsar sites".[220]

Inputs from experts or informed actors are deemed important also for the development and implementation of the WHC. Article 8(3) permits representatives of selected intergovernmental or non-governmental organisations promoting the protection, conservation, and restoration of natural and cultural sites,[221] as well as others upon state request, to attend "in an advisory capacity" the meetings of the WHC Committee. In addition, article 10(2) enables the WHC Committee to "invite public or private organisations or individuals to participate in its meetings for consultation on particular problems".

The involvement of indigenous peoples and local communities has been more challenging. The attempt to establish a World Heritage Indigenous Peoples Council of Experts[222] was dismissed by the World Heritage Committee in 2001.[223] In 2007, the adoption of "Communities" as the fifth strategic objective of the Convention[224] renewed the will to recognise the role of local communities – and indigenous peoples in particular – in the framework of this regime. The WHC Committee amended the relevant paragraphs (40 and 123) of the Operational Guidelines[225] in line with the recommendations formulated in the framework of the 2012 International Expert Workshop on the

---

zalo Oviedo and Mariam Kenza Ali (2018), *Indigenous peoples, local communities and wetland conservation,* Ramsar Convention Secretariat, 14–15. Available at <https://www.ramsar.org/news/new-global-report-on-the-participation-of-indigenous-peoples-and-local-communities-in-wetland>. Hereinafter 2018 Report on the involvement of indigenous peoples and local communities in wetland conservation.

219 For instance, this is the case of the framework on the cultural values of wetlands. COP Res VIII.19 (2002), para 17.

220 COP Res VII.11 (1999), Annex, Objective 3. See also COP Res VII.8 (1999), para 17.

221 The three organizations identified by the provision are the International Centre for the Study of the Preservation and Restoration of Cultural Property, the International Council of Monuments and Sites, and The International Union for the Conservation of Nature (IUCN).

222 The proposal to establish such a body originated from the World Heritage Indigenous Peoples Forum held in conjunction with the 24th session of the World Heritage Committee in 2000. For further information, refer to WHC-2001/CONF.205/WEB.3.

223 WHC-01/CONF.208/XV.1–5.

224 The "fifth C" for "Communities" aims "to enhance the role of communities in the implementation of the World Heritage Convention". WHC-2007/31.COM/13B. In 2007 the UN General Assembly adopted the UN Declaration on the Rights of indigenous peoples (UNDRIP).

225 WHC-15/39.COM/11.

World Heritage and Indigenous Peoples.[226] Participants to this workshop included representatives of indigenous organisations and communities;[227] arguably, through this venue, they were able to influence the evolution of the WHC regime.

Furthermore, the establishment of the International Indigenous Peoples' Forum on World Heritage (IIPFWH)[228] in 2017 has systematised the possibility of indigenous peoples' representatives engaging with the WHC Committee during its meetings by designating delegates to participate in working groups and other processes. The IIPFWH has been shaped according to the examples of similar bodies operating in the context of the CBD and the UNFCCC.[229] This Forum works as a platform that promotes the full respect of indigenous rights in the context of the WHC and its processes. To this end, it engages with the WHC Committee, the WHC Centre, Advisory Bodies and state parties as a "consultative and strategizing body". Furthermore, it provides support and advice to indigenous peoples regarding WHC processes.[230] Indeed, participation of indigenous peoples – and other relevant stakeholders and rights-holders – in the context of the WHC unfolds through their involvement in specific processes; namely the identification of properties, including through the preparation of national Tentative Lists,[231] nomination and designation procedures.[232] Moreover, when evaluating the OUV of proposed natural properties, IUCN "may receive comments from local non-governmental organisations (NGOs), communities, *indigenous peoples* and other interested parties in the nomination".[233] Arguably, the establishment of the IIPFWH will certainly strengthen their role at both global and national levels in the context of the WHC.

226 The Report of this workshop and the relevant recommendations are available at <https://whc.unesco.org/en/events/906/>.
227 The list of participants is included in the Report of the workshop, at 66–67.
228 WHC-17/41.COM/7, para 41.
229 These bodies are the International Indigenous Peoples Forum on Biodiversity (IIPFB) and International Indigenous Peoples Forum on Climate Change (IIPFCC) respectively.
230 For further reference on the structure and activities of the IIPFWC refer to the dedicated website: <https://iipfwh.org/>.
231 Operational Guidelines, para 64.
232 Ibid paras 12, 39–40, 123.
233 Ibid annex 6, at 112.

3.2 *Participation in the Management and Conservation of Biological Diversity at the National Level*

Participation in the implementation of the CBD confirms that the subjects involved in participatory processes are a heterogeneous pool of actors that can be framed as public concerned rather than the general public as such. As anticipated, indigenous peoples and local communities[234] are the stakeholders that are both more consistently and more often indicated as the beneficiaries of participatory rights in the context of the CBD compared to other actors or groups. Additional subjects, however, are included in the group of possible beneficiaries, including "all interested parties"[235] and stakeholders,[236] "affected parties" and "endusers",[237] "women"[238] and "indigenous women",[239] "youth" and "indigenous youth",[240] the "private sector" and NGOs or "civil society",[241] "resource users",[242] and governmental actors such as "cities and local authorities" although in a less consistent way and with less clarity as to the prescriptive content of participation than that seen with indigenous peoples and local communities.[243]

The rationale for participation emerging from COP decisions is that the involvement of the actors listed above in decision-making, especially of indigenous peoples and local communities, may be instrumental for the achievement of the three CBD objectives.[244] Furthermore, indigenous peoples and local communities are considered as rightholders and interest bearers[245] and thus participation is implicitly recognised as a way to protect indigenous

234 Including nomadic communities and pastoralists, in light of COP dec VII/28, annex, PoWPA, suggested activity 2.2.4.

235 COP dec II/9, annex, para 13.

236 COP dec II/9, annex, para 13; COP dec V/23, annex I; COP dec VI/7, annex; COP dec VI/13.

237 COP dec IV/4, annex I, para 9(l)(III).

238 Preamble para 13 CBD; COP dec V/16, preamble and Programme of work on Article 8(j); COP dec VI/13.

239 COP dec V/16, Programme of work on Article 8(j); COP dec VII/16, annex, part F, text of Akwé-Kon guidelines, para 8(c); COP X/42, para 29; COP dec XI/14, part B, para 1; COP dec XII/12, para 3; COP dec XIV/16, annex.

240 COP dec XII/8; COP dec XII/12, para 3; COP dec XIV/16, annex.

241 COP dec V/18, para 1(d); COP dec X/V, para 2; COP dec XI/25, annex, para 2; COP dec XIV/7, para 17. According to Koester, n 7, at 294: "the very focus on indigenous and local communities tends to make the COP overlook the fact that participation in decision-making also includes participation by civil society as such, including NGOs".

242 COP dec VII/12, Addis Ababa guidelines, annex 2, rationale for practical principle 2.

243 COP dec IX/28, para 3; COP dec X/17, para 6(a); COP dec XI/8, part A.

244 COP dec IV/4, annex I; COP dec VI/13, preamble.

245 COP dec V/5, para 10, rationale for principle 1.

peoples' rights in the context of the CBD. Participation is also marginally seen as a way to reinforce local accountability[246] and contribute to poverty reduction.[247]

The forms in which participation is to be ensured vary greatly, ranging from the formula of "involvement and approval" of indigenous peoples and local communities under article 8 (j) of the CBD to "full and effective participation"[248] and "prior and informed consent" in CBD COP decisions. While the content of full and effective participation is not fully described,[249] prior and informed consent or approval and involvement are given a more precise meaning in COP decisions and are mainly conceived as prerogatives of indigenous peoples and local communities. In particular, the Mo'otz Kuxtal guidelines provide the following definition: no coercion, engagement sufficiently in advance of any authorisation and with sufficient information on relevant aspects. While consent implies the agreement of the holders of traditional knowledge, which includes "the right not to grant consent or approval",[250] "involvement" is defined as "full and effective participation" in decision-making processes. Furthermore, consent only implies temporary use and if the purpose changes, the terms must be renegotiated.[251] This is in line with the view that (free) prior informed consent and approval and involvement should constitute a legal contract between indigenous peoples and local communities, on the one hand, and those who access traditional knowledge, on the other.

In this sense, one way of operationalising consent is through the drawing up of mutually agreed terms, which are private contracts between the proponents of any plans or decisions and indigenous peoples and local communities.[252] A

246 COP dec VII/12, Addis Ababa guidelines, annex 2, rationale for practical principle 2.

247 COP dec X/29, para 13(b).

248 COP dec VII/11, para 10; COP dec X/5, para 2; COP dec X/32, para 2(e); COP dec XI/14, part F, paras 8 and 10; COP dec XI/16, para 1(g); COP XI/23, para 7; COP dec XI/25, para 8; COP dec XII/5, para 11. COP dec XII/12, annex, Plan of action on customary sustainable use of biological diversity, paras 1 and 6(d); COP dec XIV/8, para 12.

249 An exception to that is COP dec X/42, Takrihwaié:ri Code, paras 27 and 30.

250 COP dec XIII/18, annex, Mo'otz Kuxtal guidelines, para 7. Para 17 of the same decision lists the procedural aspects of providing consent, while para 9 establishes that any requirements must be adapted to national circumstances, because a one size fits all approach is not "practical". The same definition of (free) prior and informed consent can be found in COP dec X/42, para 11 – as to the term free – and COP dec XIV/13 – as for the other terms. See also COP dec VII/16, annex, part F, text of Akwé-Kon guidelines, para 8(e).

251 COP dec XIII/18, annex, Mo'otz Kuxtal guidelines, paras 11 and 23(f).

252 COP dec VII/16, annex, part F, text of Akwé-Kon guidelines, para 8(i): "Conclusion, as appropriate, of agreements, or action plans, on mutually agreed terms, between" developers and indigenous and local communities. COP dec X/42, para 22: mutually agreed

binding reference is also contained in articles 5(2), 5(5) and 7 of the Nagoya Protocol.

Another important recommendation when considering ways of establishing consent is that any participatory process which aims to reach an agreement with indigenous peoples and local communities must be based on respect, trustbuilding and mutual understanding.[253] These elements require a process of long engagement with the indigenous peoples and local communities concerned, as well as the need to take into account the respect of their community protocols, documents elaborated in autonomy by indigenous peoples and local communities that often contain indications as their willingness to engage with external actors and the modalities to allow for such an engagement.[254] Article 12(1) of the Nagoya Protocol creates an obligation for its parties to consider community protocols when implementing the protocol's provisions on traditional knowledge.

The cases in which consent is required can be grouped into three main kinds of activities: first, when there is access to traditional knowledge;[255] and second, when establishing protected areas or recognising ICCAs;[256] and third, in line with human rights law, when indigenous peoples and local communities are removed from their lands or the activities planned are likely to affect their lands and natural resources.[257] Although the variety of formulations can be inconsistent in some instances, it also reflects the range of possible options in

---

terms for restitution and compensation if activities that take place on indigenous lands cause any adverse effects.

253 COP dec XIII/18, annex, Mo'otz Kuxtal guidelines, para 8.

254 For a definition of community protocols, see COP dec XIII/18, annex, Mo'otz Kuxtal guidelines, paras 10 and 19–20. Other decisions containing a reference to community protocols are COP dec XI/14, para 8; COP dec XII/12, annex, para 9; COP dec XI/5, appendix, para 1(d). The latter decision, in particular, calls for the enhancement of the capacity needs of indigenous peoples and local communities, *inter alia* with a view to facilitating the adoption of community protocols.

255 COP dec V/16, Programme of work on Article 8(j), para 5; COP dec VI/9, annex, part B; COP dec X/42, para 11; COP dec XII/12, annex, Plan of action on customary sustainable use of biological diversity, para 5; COP dec XIII/18, annex, Mo'otz Kuxtal guidelines, para 1. See arts 6(2) and 7 Nagoya Protocol.

256 COP dec VII/28, annex, PoWPA, suggested activity 2.2.5; COP dec XII/12, annex, Plan of action on customary sustainable use of biological diversity, para 9; COP dec XIV/8, para 6.

257 COP dec VII/28, annex, PoWPA, suggested activity 2.2.5; COP dec X/42, paras 4 and 19. Prior and informed consent is also mentioned in some residual options and is in some cases conditioned to the existence of national requirements. COP dec III/5, para 5; COP dec VII/16, annex, part F, text of Akwé-Kon guidelines, para 52(a); COP dec XII/5, annex, Chennai Guidelines for Implementation of the Integration of Biodiversity and Poverty Eradication, point 2(c); COP dec XIII/5, para 13(3); COP dec XIV/14, para 1.

realising participation depending on the subjects involved, the rights affected, and the circumstances at stake. Capacity-building is regarded as a facilitator for any form of participation in the context of the CBD.[258]

Participation, in its multifarious forms, is foreseen in a range of different decision-making activities,[259] including the implementation of article 8(j) of the CBD, conservation and the establishment and management of protected areas, impact assessment, and technology transfer. The implementation of article 8(j) somehow constitutes the red thread between participation at an international level[260] and participation at national and local levels, because COP decisions recognise the importance of ensuring the participation of indigenous and local communities at all levels of decision-making.[261] This kind of participation is also deemed instrumental for integrating biodiversity into poverty eradication and development.[262] Although participation in conservation activities is not clear from the text of the CBD,[263] it is thoroughly articulated in COP decisions. One important aspect of the involvement in conservation activities is public participation (especially of indigenous peoples and local communities) in the management and designation of protected areas,[264] including the realisation of the ecosystem approach.[265] One specific aspect in relation to indigenous peoples and local communities is the mapping and recognition of ICCAs as part of the national network of protected areas.[266] Participation in impact assessment is again addressed to the public concerned at

---

258 COP dec V/16, Programme of work on Article 8(j); task 1; COP dec VI/10, part 1; COP dec VII/16, annex, part F, Akwé:Kon Voluntary Guidelines.

259 COP dec VII/16, part G, para 6(a).

260 See section 3.1 *supra*, with reference to the Working Group on Article 8(j).

261 COP dec III/14, para 1; COP dec V/16, Programme of work on the implementation of Article 8(j), task 2; COP dec VI/10, part 1; COP dec VII/12, annex 2, Addis Ababa guidelines, operational guidelines to Practical principle 4; COP dec VII/16, annex, para 1; COP X/42, Tkarihwaié:ri Code of Ethical Conduct, para 18; para 25.

262 COP dec X/6, para 6(a).

263 Yussuf, n 40, at 121.

264 COP dec IV/4, annex I, para 9(l)(i); COP dec VI/10, part 1; COP dec VII/12, annex 1, operational guidelines to Principles 7 and 9; COP dec VII/16, annex, paras 17 and 20; COP dec VII/28, para 22; annex, PoWPA, suggested activities 1.4.1, 2.1.5, 2.2 and 3.3.3; COP dec VIII/24, para 18(j); COP dec IX/18, paras 6(d) and 19; COP dec X/29, para 13(b); COP dec X/31, paras 1(b), 32(c) and (e).

265 COP dec VII/11, annex 1, para 3(c); COP dec IX/7, paras 1(c) and 2(b).

266 COP dec, V/16, Programme of work on the implementation of Article 8(j), task 2; COP dec VII/28, annex, PoWPA, suggested activities 1.1.4 and 2.1.3; COP dec IX/18, para 6(b): recognizing co-management and ICCAs. On the recognition of ICCAs see also COP dec X/31, para 31(b); COP dec XI/24, para 1(e); COP dec XII/5, para 11; COP dec XII/12, para 5; annex, para 9; COP dec XIV/8, annex 2, para 4.

large,[267] but especially to indigenous peoples and local communities, when developments are planned to take place on their lands or are likely to have an effect on both their lands and the perpetuation of their traditional knowledge.[268] Finally, participatory approaches to technology transfer are said to facilitate the transfer of technologies.[269]

The last point to mention is that participatory rights include access to information, which in the context of the CBD presents two main aspects. The first is the requirement for public authorities to provide information to the public. The second refers to the fact that in the practice of the CBD, the public, and in particular indigenous peoples and local communities, are asked to provide information that is relevant for the attainment of the three objectives of the CBD to states or CBD authorities. The top-down information flow is ensured by a number of decisions requiring state parties to provide information to the public concerned, but especially to indigenous peoples and local communities.[270] In addition, there are also some decisions calling for other kinds of authorities or decisionmakers to do the same, such as the executive bodies of the CBD,[271] as well as developers and managers of protected areas.[272] Moreover, access to information is seen as a precondition for participation,[273] as a way to guarantee parity of bargaining power and thus equity,[274] and as a means to guarantee the full implementation of the CBD framework.[275] Moreover, some decisions list the characteristics of information, which must be prompt, provided sufficiently in advance, complete, transparent, and made available in the language of its main recipients.[276] Concerning the bottom-up information flow, it is usually the Secretariat of the CBD who requires indigenous

267 COP dec V/18, para 1(d); COP dec VIII/28, para 5.

268 COP dec VI/7, annex; COP dec VII/16, annex, part F, Akwé: Kon guidelines, paras 9 and 14–16.

269 COP dec VII/29, annex, para 4(c): the "participation, approval and involvement" of indigenous and local communities is essential for a successful technology transfer; COP dec IX/14, annex, paras 5 and 10.

270 COP dec VI/10, part 1; COP dec VII/16, annex, part F, Akwé Kon, paras 9 and 12–13.

271 COP dec VII/11, para 9(d); COP dec IX/13, part D, paras 7(b) and 7(d); COP dec X/6, para 15(c)(v); COP dec XI/14, part B, paras 5 and 11; COP dec XII/7.

272 COP dec VII/12, annex 1, operational guidelines to Principle 6; COP dec VII/16, annex 1, part G, para 6(d).

273 COP dec IV/4, annex I, para 9(i); COP dec X/31, para 1(g): communication plans on the benefits of protected areas to raise awareness among decision-makers and stakeholders (governmental, NGOs and communities).

274 COP dec V/26, para 12; COP dec X/31, para 1(g).

275 COP dec X/1.

276 COP dec VII/16, annex 1, part F, Akwé Kon guidelines' text, paras 9–11 and 13; COP dec VII/28, annex, PoWPA, suggested activity 1.5.1; COP dec X/42, Takrihwaié:ri Code, para 32.

peoples and local communities to submit information on traditional knowledge, benefitsharing, and conservation practices.[277] The same bottom-up information flow is requested from other actors, including state parties, in a view to promoting a cooperative approach to information-sharing under article 17(1)[278] and relevant COP decisions.[279]

As mentioned, in the wetland regime the participatory strategy is set up through CEPA, which is periodically updated and goes hand in hand with the Ramsar Strategic Plan. The over-arching goal of the 2016–2024 CEPA Programme is "*people taking action* for the conservation and wise use of wetlands", while Goal 5 asks to "develop and support mechanisms to ensure *multistakeholder participation in wetland management*".[280] In addition, the PEM tool aims to enhance the participation of all sectors and relevant social actors in the management and wise use of wetlands. PEM is intended to facilitate an integrated approach to addressing problems and identifying priorities "by including knowledge from many sources – traditional, scientific, technical and administrative, among others".[281] It also aims to improve communication and exchange of information among the different actors and, in so doing, reinforces their mutual trust, helps reducing environmental conflicts as well as promoting continuity and sustainability of management activities.[282]

A participatory approach also emerges from the text of the Ramsar Convention. Its article 6(3) requires state parties to inform "those responsible at all levels of wetland management" of COP decisions relating to the conservation, management and wise use of wetlands and their flora and fauna, to enable their contribution to the implementation of this regime. Arguably, the state obligation to provide information is a precondition for the participation of

277 COP dec II/9, para 2(c); COP dec V/16, Programme of work on Article 8(j), task 5; COP dec VI/10, part 1; COP dec VII/12, annex 1, operational guidelines to Principle 6; COP dec VII/28, annex, PoWPA, suggested activity 3.3.3; COP dec VIII/4, para 3; COP dec VIII/5, part C, paras 2 and 4; COP dec XI/25, para 15(d); COP dec XII/2; COP dec XII/12, para 4; COP dec XIII/18, para 4.

278 Article 17(1) CBD reads: "The Contracting Parties shall *facilitate the exchange of information*, from all publicly available sources, *relevant to the conservation and sustainable use* of biological diversity" (emphasis added).

279 COP dec V/5, principle 12 of ecosystem approach; COP dec VI/9, annex, part A; COP dec VI/10, part 1; COP dec VI/12; COP dec VII/12, annex 1, operational guidelines to Principle 6; COP dec VII/16, annex, part F, Akwé-Kon guidelines, paras 3 and 9(c); COP dec VII/28, annex, PoWPA, suggested activity 2.2.3; COP dec VIII/4, para 3; COP dec XII/2; COP dec XII/5, para 12; COP dec XII/12, para 4; COP dec XIII/18, para 4.

280 COP Res XII.9 (2015). Hereinafter 2016–2024 CEPA Programme. Emphasis added.

281 COP Resolution VIII.36 (2002), annex, para 1.

282 Ibid, para 12 and annex, para 2(h).

non-state actors in the Ramsar regime. Since there is no explicit characterisation of the responsible actors this provision widens the scope of the Ramsar Convention in terms of the addressees of its obligations. Indeed, COP Resolution VIII.36 on the PEM tool provides a clarification on who these "many social actors" should be: "the public and private sectors, non-governmental organisations and local communities, among others".[283] The Resolution "promotes active and full participation of local communities and indigenous peoples in the *adoption and application* of decisions related to the use and sustainable management of wetlands".[284] Participation in wetland management can also strengthen the position of other marginalised actors, namely women[285] and the poor,[286] and thus contribute to the achievement of other internationally agreed goals and targets.[287]

This multistakeholder approach is reiterated in the 2016–2024 CEPA Programme, which promotes the development and support of multi-stakeholder participatory mechanisms,[288] exemplifies possible levels of participation,[289] and identifies potential target groups for CEPA planning and actions to be engaged at local and national levels for their contribution to the conservation and wise use of wetlands. In the civil society subgroup, attention is paid to indigenous peoples and local communities for their knowledge of wetland management and their cultural connection with sites, to women for their central role in the family and in the education of children, as well as to children and youth as the next generations of environmental managers and caretakers.[290] While education and awareness raising activities on wetlands values and ecosystem services should be directed at a wider public, effective involvement in decision-making and wetland management concerns specific actors that are directly interested and potentially affected, and can thus be identified as "public concerned". Indigenous peoples and local communities are certainly part of the latter group, they are recognised as "key stakeholder[s] for conservation

283 COP Res VIII.36 (2002), para 7.
284 Ibid para 10, emphasis added.
285 COP Res XIII.18 (2018).
286 COP Res XI.13 (2012).
287 In this case, a clear contribution can be identified to SDGS 5 and 1 respectively.
288 2016–2024 CEPA Programme, goal 5.
289 Ibid Appendix 1, box 1.
290 Ibid Appendix 3. The other groups are governments at all levels, the education sector and learning institutions, the business sector and international and regional organizations.

and integrated wetland management" and their "active participation" should be promoted, recognised and strengthened.[291]

A decisive turning point for ensuring the participation of indigenous peoples and local communities is represented by Ramsar COP Recommendation 6.3. This reports a lack of appropriate consultative mechanisms and the consequent exclusion of these actors from decision-making,[292] acknowledges "their distinct knowledge, experience and aspirations in relation to wetland management"[293] demonstrated by their direct involvement in the field,[294] and promotes the development of benefit-sharing mechanisms for the conservation and wise use of wetlands.[295] Based on these premises, state parties are requested to encourage their "*active and informed participation* [and] their direct involvement" in wetland management[296] as well as to "recognise the value of the knowledge and skills of local and indigenous people" related to wetland management for their inclusion in wetland policies and programmes.[297] To do so, the development of national and local mechanisms that ensure consultation "with a view to reflecting their needs and values, traditional and other knowledge and practices in national wetland policies and programmes, and in the management planning for Ramsar sites and other significant wetlands" is urged.[298] The "Guidelines for establishing and strengthening local communities' and indigenous people's participation in the management of wetlands" provide practical guidance on how to operationalise these requests and design effective participatory approaches based on lessons learned from case studies.[299] The increasing involvement of indigenous peoples and local communities in wetland conservation is thoroughly studied in a dedicated Report,[300] which reviews both the Convention's policy framework and information collected from state parties. The Report highlights the evolution of the Ramsar Convention's approach with respect to these actors: "from a standard of "recognition" to one of "active involvement"", which now encompasses

291 COP Res XII.2 (2015), para 19. Their "effective participation … at all relevant levels" is also pursued by target 10 of the 4th Strategic Action Plan.
292 COP Recommendation 6.3, para 5.
293 Ibid para 3.
294 Ibid para 6.
295 Ibid para 4.
296 Ibid para 9.
297 Ibid para 11.
298 Ibid para 15.
299 Ramsar COP Res VII.8 (1999).
300 2018 Report on the involvement of indigenous peoples and local communities in wetland conservation, n 219.

"communitybased governance as a legitimate option for wetlands".[301] According to the Report, the concept of wise use, the CEPA and the guiding principles on the cultural values of wetlands[302] fostered this evolution in terms of both policy development and practice.[303]

Since Ramsar COP8, participation of indigenous peoples and local communities is also fostered by tracing a connection between cultural values and wetland conservation; this process can be facilitated by referring to a set of twenty seven guiding principles.[304] In this context, the term "indigenous peoples" acquires the plural form and key concepts are introduced: the principle of prior and informed consent; the inclusion of cultural and social criteria into environmental assessment; and the protection of traditional rights. The connection between culture and wetland conservation, especially when linked to heritage protection, enables cooperation between the Ramsar Convention and the WHC.

The interrelation between culture and conservation is paradigmatic in the case of the WHC and, again, offers a privileged path for the involvement of indigenous people as public concerned.[305] In 2018, the United Nations Educational, Scientific and Cultural Organization (UNESCO) adopted a policy for engaging with indigenous peoples in all areas of its mandate that are relevant for or of potential benefit or risk to them.[306] Although designed to support the efforts of the UNESCO Secretariat in mainstreaming the UNDRIP across all UNESCO's relevant programme areas,[307] arguably, this policy has an impact on how state parties to the relevant UNESCO Conventions meet their commitments. A few provisions strengthen the role of indigenous peoples in the development and implementation of the WHC. In particular, "indigenous peoples should be able to take part in the development of policies concerning their culture, cultural expressions and heritage, including through *effective participation in relevant consultative bodies and coordination mechanisms*".[308] They "have the right to be consulted" on activities concerning their heritage; "transparent collaboration,

301 Ibid p. 8. In this regard, see COP Recommendation 6.3 (1996), paras 9 and 14 and COP Res VII.8, annex, para 6.

302 COP Res VIII.19 (2002).

303 2018 Report on the involvement of indigenous peoples and local communities in wetland conservation, n 219, at 14.

304 COP Res VIII.19 (2002), annex.

305 Operational Guidelines, para 119.

306 2018 UNESCO policy on engaging with indigenous peoples (201/EX6). For the policy section relevant to the WHC refer to 22–27.

307 Ibid para 4.

308 Ibid para 77 (d). Emphasis added.

dialogue, negotiation and consultation" should also be ensured for the future development of such activities.[309] Since natural and cultural heritage can be home to or is located within land managed by indigenous peoples, "in such places, [they] have the right to their traditional lands, territories and resources, and *are partners in site conservation and protection activities* that recognise traditional management system as part of new management approaches".[310] Moreover, they should be granted "adequate consultations, the free, prior and informed consent and equitable and effective participation ... where nomination, management and policy measures of international designations affect their territories, lands, resources and ways of life".[311] Where conservation and management refers to their cultural and natural heritage sites, "equitable and *inclusive governance arrangements, collaborative management systems* and ... redress mechanisms" should be ensured.[312]

In so doing, this policy reinforces and complements the duties emerging from the Operational Guidelines.[313] According to the latter, participation in the protection of world heritage properties can be achieved by adopting a "*partnership approach*, underpinned by *inclusive, transparent and accountable decision-making*, to nomination, management and monitoring" of relevant sites.[314] Partners can be individuals or groups, "*especially local communities, indigenous peoples*, governmental, non-governmental and private organisations and owners" interested or involved in the conservation and management of those sites.[315] This participatory approach should be reflected in an appropriate management system[316] tailored to the specificities of each property (type, characteristics, needs, cultural and natural context), based on "a thorough shared understanding of the property, its universal, national and local values and its socio-ecological context by all stakeholders, including local communities and indigenous peoples", and developed through "inclusive and participatory planning and stakeholder consultations processes".[317] Different

---

309 Ibid para 77 (j).
310 Ibid para 77 (n). Emphasis added.
311 Ibid para 77 (p).
312 Ibid. Emphasis added.
313 According to para 15 of WHC-11/35.COM/12E, "Recalling that being a signatory of the World Heritage Convention entails certain responsibilities, including a requirement to follow the Operational Guidelines".
314 Operational Guidelines, para 39. Emphasis added.
315 Ibid para 40.
316 Ibid para 108.
317 Ibid para 111(b). See also para 117 that requires state parties to implement effective management activities in close collaboration with relevant partners, including local

cultural perspectives can also emerge through the incorporation of traditional practices.[318] Despite all that, state parties are not required to gather and/or include information from other stakeholders in the periodic reports on the implementation of the WHC.[319]

3.3 *Preliminary Conclusion on Participation*

As emerged from the analysis above, participation in international biodiversity law is conceived mainly as participation in decision-making and access to information. In addition, participation of the public concerned is encouraged through the involvement of relevant actors in the conservation, sustainable use and management of biodiversity resources and protected sites. This latter participatory dimension is both a call for states, not always enabled in practice, and a result from practice in the field.

Participation in the CBD and Ramsar Convention has similar peculiarities. First, there is a strong emphasis on the public concerned rather than the general public both at the global level and at the implementation level. Nevertheless, in the wetland regime, the general public can also be informed more broadly about the value of wetland ecosystems and the services they provide through the activities of education and awareness raising promoted at national, subnational, and local levels.[320] Second, there is a clear distinction between participation in global[321] and national decisionmaking,[322] which is not fully spelled out in the definition of participation in international environmental and human rights law. Third, participation at both levels is mainly directed to indigenous peoples and local communities, as depositaries of knowledge and practices that are relevant for conservation and sustainable use. Importance is also given to their cultural connection with protected sites. Fourth, especially in the case of the CBD, information is conceived as a doubletrack information flow, meaning that it should not only be provided by governmental authorities to the general public or to the public concerned (top-down), but it should also flow back from the public to the CBD, governmental and management authorities (bottom-up). Therefore, information is much more bilateral than as intended in the general definition of participation given in section 1.2 above. This is in line with one of the rationales of participation, that is to improve

communities and indigenous peoples, through "equitable governance arrangements, collaborative management systems and redress mechanisms".

318 Ibid para 110.

319 Ibid Section v.

320 2016–2024 CEPA Programme, Goals 6 and 8.

321 See section 3.1 above.

322 See section 3.2 above.

public decision-making. In the context of the Ramsar Convention, information is not limited to these top-down and bottom-up flows but acquires an additional dimension in the context of the CEPA Programme, the PEM tool, and the Ramsar Regional Initiatives through an interactive process of sharing information, knowledge and skills on wetland conservation and wise use among all stakeholders.

Recent evolutions in the WHC also aim to reinforce the role of indigenous peoples at all levels; from global negotiations to the management of cultural and natural properties. Time will prove if this recognition actually strengthens their participation both in the convention processes and in the protection of properties on site.

4 Conclusions: The Connections between Sustainability and Participation in International Biodiversity Law

From our analysis of the biodiversity treaties, we can conclude that a clear two-fold link between sustainability and participation emerges. Perhaps the most obvious link is that participation of all concerned stakeholders, especially indigenous peoples, and local communities, is a prerequisite for both realising conservation and sustainable use and integrating biodiversity into development activities. Participation is also seen as a precondition for guaranteeing equity in representation and recognition and is thus instrumental for the realisation of intragenerational equity and the more social aspects of sustainability. Furthermore, the equity aspects of sustainability, such as capacitybuilding or the provision of resources to enable the presence of local actors in international meetings, are instrumental for operationalising participation.

Interestingly, these regimes show that participation has both a procedural and a substantial dimension when referring to the public concerned. In this regard, we focused on indigenous peoples and local communities because they emerged as primary holders of participatory rights from the practice of the treaties analysed. The procedural dimension is revealed by the repeated calls to include relevant stakeholders in decision-making at the different governance levels and to enable their participation at COP meetings through their inclusion in national delegations, working groups, or advisory bodies. Furthermore, the requests to consult, inform, obtain the approval or the free, prior and informed consent (FPIC) point even more decisively in this direction. Arguably, the three regimes can also ensure substantial participatory rights when foreseeing the inclusion of relevant stakeholders in the actual management of protected areas as well as of Ramsar sites and world heritage properties. For instance, this is the case when recognising ICCAs as appropriate governance framework for the conservation and sustainable use of biodiversity. Participatory management is a crucial aspect in the conservation of wetlands, as demonstrated by the PEM tool and the dedicated Handbook on participatory skills. Similarly, a participatory approach, in which local communities and indigenous peoples are partners in site conservation and protection activities, is pursued by the Operational Guidelines and the 2018 UNESCO Policy on engaging with indigenous peoples in the framework of the WHC.

This aspect leads to a further consideration. The participation of local communities and indigenous peoples has a more operative character than that of other actors. For example, although the participation of all other stakeholders, such as business and women, is promoted, this is done vaguely without saying under which circumstances and in which forms their participation is required.

Another general conclusion is that both sustainability and participation impose duties not only on state parties (in the form of obligations and recommendations), but also voluntary duties on non-governmental actors, such as international organisations, international treaty bodies, developers, managers, indigenous and local communities, and even the public at large.[323] This is evident when it comes to the double-track information flow described above, but it is also true when it comes to both the mainstreaming of sustainability and the duties on financial transfers and capacity-building. The presence of non-governmental duty-bearers is therefore an element that further connects sustainability and participation in international biodiversity law.

Therefore, participation and sustainability appear as complementary. While the involvement of relevant stakeholders can accelerate the move towards SD by ensuring equity in decision-making, sustainable use in a short- and long-term perspective and integration of all the relevant interests and needs, sustainability cannot overlook participation if it aims at effective and long-lasting results in terms of biodiversity conservation. This complementarity emerges in all three regimes. Indeed, the CBD can be identified as the forerunner in tackling these two aspects and connecting them. Nevertheless, the Ramsar Convention took up this challenge promptly by building upon the principle of wise use and the request of its article 6(3) to inform "those responsible at all levels of wetland management", which highlights its inherent vocation to integrate these two concepts. The WHC, although slower, especially regarding the improvement of participatory standards of indigenous peoples, is also converging towards the same direction.

323 These actors are often encouraged but not obligated.

Finally, we would like to point out that, although sustainability and participation in principle are in line with one another, the concrete implementation of measures protecting biodiversity may evidence situations where participation is not realised to the fullest.[324] For the complete integration between sustainability and participation to happen, there is the need to fully recognise the substantive rights of all stakeholders that may be affected by the protection of biodiversity. An assessment of the practice would be indicative in this sense and useful to confirm what emerged through the legal analysis of these three biodiversity regimes.

Reference List

Barral V, 'Sustainable Development in International Law: Nature and Operation of an Evolutive Legal Norm' (2012) 23(2) European Journal of International Law 377

Barral V, 'Sustainable Development and Equity in Biodiversity Conservation' in Morgera E and Razzaque J (eds), *Biodiversity and Nature Protection Law* (Edward Elgar 2017) 59

Brunnée J, 'COPing with Consent: Law-Making under Multilateral Environmental Agreements' (2002) 15(1) Leiden Journal of International Law 1

Cittadino F, *Il principio dello sviluppo sostenibile nel diritto internazionale*, Master's thesis (University of Trento, 2009)

Cittadino F, *Incorporating Indigenous Rights in the International Regime on Biodiversity Protection: Access, Benefit-sharing and Conservation in Indigenous Lands* (Brill 2019)

Ebbesson J, 'Public Participation' in Daniel Bodansky, Jutta Brunnée, and Ellen Hey (eds.), *The Oxford Handbook of International Environmental Law* (Oxford University Press 2008) 682

Ebbesson J, 'Principle 10: Public Participation' in Viñuales J E (ed), *The Rio Declaration on Environment and Development: A Commentary* (University of California 2017) 287

Fitzmaurice M, 'International Protection of the Environment' (2001) 293 Recueil des Cours 9

Fodella A, 'I principi generali' in Fodella A and Pineschi L (eds), *La protezione dell'ambiente nel Diritto internazionale* (G. Giappichelli Editore 2009) 95

Francioni F (ed), *The 1972 World Heritage Convention: A Commentary* (OUP 2008)

Gehring T, 'Treaty-Making and Treaty Evolution' in Bodansky D, Brunnée J and Hey E (eds), *The Oxford Handbook of International Environmental Law* (Oxford University Press 2008) 467

324 See Cittadino 2019, n 35, ch. 1.

Glowka L, Burhenne-Guilmin F and Synge H, *A Guide to the Convention on Biological Diversity* (IUCN 1994)
Hey E, *Advanced Introduction to International Environmental Law* (Edward Elgar 2016)
Kim R E and Bosselmann K, 'Operationalizing Sustainable Development: Ecological Integrity as a Grundnorm of International Law' (2015) 24(2) Review of European, Comparative and International Environmental Law 194
Kim R E, 'The Nexus between International Law and the Sustainable Development Goals' (2016) 25(1) Review of European, Comparative and International Environmental Law 15
Koester V, 'The Convention on Biological Diversity and the Concept of Sustainable Development: The Extent and Manner of the Convention's Application of Components of the Concept' in Bowman M, Davies P and Goodwin E (eds), *Research Handbook on Biodiversity and Law* (Edward Elgar 2016) 273–296
Lowe V, 'Sustainable Development and Unsustainable Arguments' in Boyle A and Freestone D (eds), *International Law and Sustainable Development: Past Achievements and Future Challenges* (OUP 2001) 19
Morgera E and Tsioumani E, 'The Evolution of Benefit-Sharing: Linking Biodiversity and Community Livelihoods' (2010) 19(2) Review of European Community and International Environmental Law 150
Morgera E and Savaresi A, 'A Conceptual and Legal Perspective on the Green Economy' (2013) 22(1) Review of European, Comparative and International Environmental Law 14
Orellana M, 'Governance and the Sustainable Development Goals: The Increasing Relevance of Access Rights in Principle 10 of the Rio Declaration' (2016) 25(1) Review of European, Comparative and International Environmental Law 50
Sands P, 'International Law in the Field of Sustainable Development: Emerging Legal Principles' in Winfried Lang (ed), *Sustainable Development and International Law* (Springer 1995) 57
Tsioumani E, 'Public Participation in Environmental Decision-making' in Kramer L and Orlando E (eds), *Encyclopedia of Environmental Law: Principles of Environmental Law* (Edward Elgar 2018) 366
Viñuales J E, 'The Rise and Fall of Sustainable Development' (2013) 22(1) Review of European, Comparative and International Environmental Law 3
Willmore C, 'Sovereignty, Conservation and Sustainable Use' in Morgera E and Razzaque J (eds), *Biodiversity and Nature Protection Law* (Edward Elgar 2017) 31
Yusuf A A, 'International Law and Sustainable Development: The Convention on Biological Diversity' (1995) 2 African Yearbook of International Law 109

CHAPTER 12

Climate Change Law

Omondi R. Owino

1 Introduction

Sustainability and public participation are two sides of the climate change coin. In other words, public participation is a *sine qua non* for sustainability. This chapter interrogates the link between sustainability and public participation in the corpus of climate change law and governance. As such, this inquiry teases out heuristic conclusions' resident in the linkage which, although not obvious, provide critical insights into the continuing quest to address climate change. In this context, the terms sustainability and participation are used interchangeably with the terms sustainable development and public participation, respectively.

In understanding the nexus between sustainability and participation, the discussion untangles terminological knots that relate to both sustainability and participation within the unique context of climate change law and governance. Terminological clarity aids the evaluation of causality in the relationship between sustainability and participation. In so far as this relationship goes, it is argued that sustainability is a corollary of effective participation.

The chapter identifies and underscores 'hybrid multilateralism' as the most visible typology of participation in climate change governance. Hybrid multilateralism, entails leveraging on the massive potential of NSAs as complementors of state Party commitments. NSAs, among others are identifiable as cities, regional governments, businesses, the financial sector, civil society groups. The potency of this form of participation to usher in sustainability through myriad causal mechanisms is examined and discussed in depth.

The author queries several hurdles and challenges that may undermine seamless hybrid multilateralism leading to a zero-sum game for sustainability. This chapter identifies the tangled power cable effect, asymmetry of participation, bottlenecks in tracking progress, and the unpredictable operation of critical junctures as some of the intractable challenges facing participation in the quest for sustainability.

This chapter concludes by addressing the question whether the terms sustainability and public participation possess unique and singular legal meanings in the context of climate change. It explores how the linkage between

DOI:10.1163/9789004509382_014

sustainability and public participation finds empirical reflection in the context of climate change governance and problematises the challenges apparent in the linkage between sustainability and public participation. This culminates in a general reflection on the link between sustainability and participation in climate change governance. Consequently, part 2 of this chapter demystifies the complex and non-linear nexus between sustainability and participation from a causality perspective. This is achieved by isolating and ferreting out terminological strands of both concepts. Part 3 then considers the causal mechanisms of participation on sustainability in the context of hybrid multilateralism. The discussion in part 3 magnifies the unique purchase that hybrid multilateralism possesses in climate change governance. Part 4 of the chapter identifies and elaborates on the challenges resident in the link between sustainability and participation that threaten to undermine causality. A general reflection on the discussions in the chapter is undertaken in part 5 and relevant conclusions on the nexus between sustainability and participation are drawn in part 6.

2 Climate Change Sustainability and Participation Nexus

Within the scope of international climate change law, although an undeniable link between sustainability and public participation exists, this connection is not obvious. In any event, both terms are substantive and independent principles of international environmental law and neither is a subset of the other.[1] Therefore, the causal relationship between sustainability and public participation is not only non-linear but a complex one.

Complexity and nonlinearity in the causal relationship between sustainability and public participation can partly be attributable to the fluid meaning both terms assume. Sustainable development is difficult to define and in this context is deemed to be coterminous with sustainability. It has been characterised as "an article of faith, a shibboleth; often used but little explained".[2]

Public participation, however, has been described as "an infinitely malleable concept, … [which] can be used to evoke – and to signify – almost anything that involves people".[3] Additionally, the diverse contexts of inquiry within

1 Nicholas A Robinson and Lal Kurukulasuriya, *Training Manual on International Environmental Law* (UNEP 2006).

2 Sharachchandra M Lélé, 'Sustainable Development: A Critical Review' (1991) 19 World Development 607, 607, citing Mostafa K Tolba, *The Premises for Building a Sustainable Society – Address to the World Commission on Environment and Development* (UNEP 1984).

3 Andrea Cornwall, '"Unpacking Participation": Models, Meanings and Practices' (2008) 43Community Development Journal 269–283, 269.

which the terms might be applied, may heighten complexity and nonlinearity in the causal relationship. Indeed, certain types of public participation may be deemed more effective than other types.[4]

For this reason, it is necessary to give a concrete definition of the twin concepts of sustainability and participation in climate change law and governance. This is necessary to mitigate fluidity of inquiry and concretise the meaning of the two terminologies in understanding the nexus between them.

2.1 *Sustainability in Climate Change Law*

The assertion has rightly been made that, "sustainable development and climate change mitigation are inseparable issues".[5] This is because Greenhouse Gas Emissions (GHGs) intensify complex global positive feedback loops that undermine sustainable development. In a similar vein, sustained suppression of GHGs emission will trigger negative feedback loops that are likely to enhance sustainable development. Sustainable development and climate change are therefore inextricably entwined in a "circular relationship".[6]

Art 2 of the United Nations Framework Convention on Climate Change (UNFCCC) embodies the pursuit of sustainable development. The Convention aims at the "stabilisation of GHG concentrations in the atmosphere at a level that would prevent dangerous anthropogenic interference with the climate system".[7] Such stabilisation would "enable economic development to proceed in a sustainable manner".[8]

This discussion interprets the foregoing provision of the Convention as the apt definition of sustainability in a climate change law context. Stabilisation of GHGs bespeaks a quest for climate energy balance by ensuring that economic activities do not accelerate the emission of pernicious GHGs. Such balance if achieved, engenders negative feedback loops, and checks negative anthropogenic activities that accelerate climate change.[9]

Sustainability conceived in the foregoing manner, is in consonance with the universal definition of sustainable development adopted by the Brundtland Commission as development that "meets the needs of the present without

---

4 Ibid.

5 Christina Voigt, *Sustainable Development as a Principle of International Law: Resolving Conflicts between Climate Measures and WTO Law* (Martinus Nijhoff Publishers 2009) 113.

6 Mohan Munasinghe, 'Analysing the Nexus of Sustainable Development and Climate Change: An Overview' (OECD 2003) 14.

7 UNFCCC, entered into force 9 May 1992), 31 ILM (1992) 849 (hereinafter the Convention).

8 Ibid.

9 Noreen Beg *et al*, 'Linkages Between Climate Change and Sustainable Development' (2002) 2 Climate Policy 129, 130.

compromising the ability of future generations to meet their own needs".[10] Permitting dangerous anthropogenic activities to put the earth's climate out of balance will most definitely compromise the ability of future generations to meet their own needs as contemplated under the UNFCCC.[11]

Consequently, the term "dangerous anthropogenic activities" in art 2 of the UNFCCC is decipherable as a euphemism for the pursuit of economic development in complete disregard of its effects on the global climate.[12] The proffered conception of sustainability in a climate change context, resonates with the three-pronged conceptualisation of sustainable development as an embodiment of economic; ecological and social components.[13]

To reify the nexus between sustainable development and climate change, art 7(1) of the Paris Agreement underscores the fact that climate action is geared towards the realisation of sustainable development. It provides:

> Parties hereby establish the global goal on adaptation of enhancing adaptive capacity, strengthening resilience and reducing vulnerability to climate change, with a view to *contributing to sustainable development* and ensuring an adequate adaptation response in the context of the temperature goal referred to in art 2.[14]

Art 4(1) of the Paris Agreement amplifies the inseparable nature of sustainable development and climate change. It predicates limiting of the increase in the global temperature to 1.5°C upon achieving:

> a balance between anthropogenic emissions by sources and removals by sinks of greenhouse gases in the second half of this century, on the basis of equity, and in the context of sustainable development.[15]

Sustainable development in a climate change context, simply put, strives to strike a delicate balance between ecological limitations on GHGs and the realisation of economic development. Art 4(1) of the Paris Agreement above emphasises this balance.

---

10 World Commission on Environment and Development, *Our Common Future* (OUP 1987) para 27.

11 UNFCCC, n 9, art 3(1).

12 UNFCCC, n 9.

13 Dan C Duran *et al*, 'The Components of Sustainable Development - A Possible Approach' (2015) 26 Procedia Economics and Finance 806.

14 Paris Agreement, n 1 (emphasis added).

15 Ibid.

This discussion, therefore, conceives the relationship between sustainable development and climate change as a circular and indivisible one. Figuratively speaking, the two concepts are joined at the hip. The above conception of the nexus between sustainable development and climate change is employed as a springboard in evaluating the larger nexus between sustainable development and participation.

The author takes cognisance of studies that treat sustainable development and climate change as two independent concepts with varying incidences of confluence.[16] It is, nevertheless, argued that this differentiation negates a functional and practical approach to addressing climate change. The differentiation elides indispensable causality in the relationship between sustainable development and climate change impacts.

2.2 *Public Participation in Climate Change Context*

Defining public participation in the context of climate change law is perhaps more technical than defining sustainability. This is because there is no universal definition of public participation that can be extrapolated to the climate change context. Further, the concept of public participation is open to multiple interpretations.[17]

Notwithstanding the difficulties involved in providing a definition, most attempts at evaluating public participation focus on its practical attributes.[18] Thus, for instance, is public participation merely invoked to rubberstamp decisions that have already been taken or is there evidence of actual citizen control and exercise of power over decisions that are made?[19] Does public participation refer to the involvement of sovereign states and other actors on the international plane or does it solely relate to actors within a state?

art 10 of the Rio Declaration provides procedural markers of public participation which conform to a practical attributes test. It highlights:

> Environmental issues are best handled with the participation of all concerned citizens, at the relevant level. At the national level, *each individual shall have appropriate access to information* concerning the environment that is held by public authorities, including information on hazardous materials and activities in their communities, and the *opportunity*

---

16 Jonatan Pinkse and Ans Kolk, 'Addressing the Climate Change—Sustainable Development Nexus' (2012) 51 Business & Society 176.

17 Cornwall, n 3.

18 Ibid.

19 Ibid.

> *to participate in decision-making processes.* States *shall facilitate* and encourage public awareness and participation by making information widely available. Effective *access to judicial and administrative proceedings*, including *redress and remedy*, shall be provided.[20]

It is, therefore, presumable that by guaranteeing access to information; actual participation in decision making processes; access to judicial and administrative proceedings; and appropriate remedies, practical as opposed to theoretical or tokenistic public participation will be achieved.

The foregoing markers of practicality are discernible in both the Convention on Access to Information, Public Participation in Decision-making and Access to Justice in Environmental Matters[21] and the Regional Agreement on Access to Information, Public Participation and Justice in Environmental Matters in Latin America and the Caribbean.[22] In another sense, climate change participation could include but would not be limited to actions contemplated under goal 13 of the Sustainable Development Goals: 'climate action'.[23] The question of who participates is germane in decoding 'participation' as a concept in climate change parlance. This is because the typology of participants and the level of their participation is ultimately informed by the unique nature of climate change. This means that the cadre of climate change participants would not necessarily be generalisable to other subject areas into which this book inquires.

The UNFCCC calls for the "widest possible participation by all countries".[24] On the face of it, a textualist interpretation of the Convention would limit participation to state Parties of the UNFCCC. However, the Lima-Paris Action

20 Report of the United Nations Conference on Environment and Development, General Assembl, United Nations publications (Vol. I), U.N. Doc. A/CONF.151/26 (1992) (emphasis added).

21 Convention on Access to Information, Public Participation in Decision-Making and Access to Justice in Environmental Matter, entered into force 30 October 2001, 2161 UNTS 447 (hereinafter Aarhus Convention).

22 Regional Agreement on Access to Information, Public Participation and Justice in Environmental Matters in Latin America and the Caribbean, adopted 4 March 2018, entered into force 22 April 2021, https://treaties.un.org/doc/Treaties/2018/03/20180312%20 03-04%20PM/CTC-XXVII-18.pdf last accessed 4 March 2020 (hereinafter Escazu Agreement).

23 UNGA, 'Transforming our World: the 2030 Agenda for Sustainable Development' (2015), A/RES/70/1, https://sustainabledevelopment.un.org/content/documents/21252030%20 Agenda%20for%20Sustainable%20Development%20web.pdf last accessed 24 March 2020.

24 See n 9, preamble and art 4(1)(i).

Agenda at the Conference of the Parties (COP20) in December 2014, in Lima, Peru, set the stage for global climate change participation by NSAs.[25] This culminated in the launch of the online portal for Non-State Actor Zone for Climate Action (NAZCA) portal (presently the Climate Action Portal) on either an individual or collaborative basis.[26]

Decision -/CP.21 on the adoption of the Paris Agreement, in Part V, explicitly invited non-Party stakeholders "to [among others] address and respond to climate change" by scaling up their efforts and supporting actions necessary for reducing emissions and decreasing vulnerability to adverse climate change effects and to document such efforts through NAZCA.[27]

With a view to mitigating GHGs and to support the realisation of sustainable development, the Paris Agreement explicitly established a voluntary mechanism to among others "incentivise and *facilitate participation* in the mitigation of greenhouse gas emissions *by public and private entities* authorised by a Party".[28] The agreement further sought to "enhance *public and private sector participation* in the implementation of nationally determined contributions".[29]

Consequently, after the Paris Agreement came into force,[30] participation in the global climate change arena by NSAs has proliferated.[31] NSAs identifiable as cities, regional governments, businesses, the financial sector, civil society groups among others has proliferated. Broad based climate action by NSAs not only augments mitigation targets set by states but also possesses real potential to bridge the emissions gap.[32] Such action proceeds on the bases of both individual and cooperative action[33] and is one of the most innovative approaches to 'participation' in climate change governance.[34]

---

25 Savitri Jetoo, 'Stakeholder Engagement for Inclusive Climate Governance: The Case of the City of Turku' (2019) 11 Sustainability 1, 2.

26 NAZCA is an online platform hosted under the auspices of UNFCCC that shows action taken by cities, companies, investors, and regions (non-state actors) to address climate change, www.cdp.net/en/campaigns/nazca last accessed 24 March 2020.

27 Paris Agreement, n 1, at para 134.

28 Paris Agreement, n 1, art 6(4)(b) (emphasis added).

29 Paris Agreement, n 1, art 6(8)(b) (emphasis added).

30 See n 1, at 5.

31 Thomas Hale, 'The Role of Sub-state and Non-state Actors in International Climate Processes' (2018) The Royal Institute of International Affairs Chatham House.

32 A Hsu *et al*, 'Bridging the Emissions Gap: The Role of Non-state and Subnational Actors' (2018), UNEP 6.

33 Ibid at 7.

34 Liliana B Andonova, Thomas N Hale and Charles B Roger, 'National Policy and Transnational Governance of Climate Change: Substitutes or Complements?' (2017) 61 International Studies Quarterly 253, 254.

With the foregoing terminological fixed points of orientation in mind, it is important to interrogate the causal nexus between the twin concepts of sustainability and participation in climate change law and thereafter demonstrate how such a causal link presents itself.

2.3 *Impact of Participation on Sustainability*

Broad based participation if effective,[35] for instance as contemplated on the NAZCA portal, should result in climate change sustainability previously defined in this context as, "stabilisation of greenhouse gas concentrations in the atmosphere at a level that would prevent dangerous anthropogenic interference with the climate system".[36] The global coterie of climate actors at diverse levels of participation all strive for the common and overarching goal of stabilisation of GHGs in the atmosphere to sustain climate balance. These actors, succeed to varying degrees, but in this way, participation secures and advances sustainability. Put differently, effective participation is indispensable for realisation of climate sustainability.[37]

Indeed, historical attempts at drafting effective international climate change law have gravitated around the quest for a stringent framework that would concomitantly stimulate optimum global participation and be ambitious enough to significantly dent global carbon emissions. The Kyoto Protocol for instance established legally binding Quantified Emissions Limitations and Reduction Commitments (QELRCs) for Annex I Countries and exempted participation by developing countries, based on their low total contribution of global GHGs.

The net effect of this top-down regulatory approach was that the United States, being the largest global emitter of $CO_{2,}$ refused to ratify the protocol as long as other significant developing country CO_2 emitters like Brazil, Russia, India, China and South Africa were left off the hook. Participation was, therefore, not only low but even efforts by participating countries were insufficient to secure significant emission reduction gains.[38] Canada for instance

---

35 Vegard H Tørstad, 'Participation, Ambition and Compliance: Can the Paris Agreement Solve the Effectiveness Trilemma?' (2020) 29 Environmental Politics 761.

36 Kirsten Halsnæs and Priyadarshi Shukla, 'Sustainable Development as A Framework for Developing Country Participation in International Climate Change Policies' (2007) 13 Mitigation and Adaptation Strategies for Global Change 105, 106.

37 Scott Barrett, 'Choices in the Climate Commons' (2018) 362 Science 1217.

38 To stimulate meaningful participation, Art 21 of the Paris Agreement set a pre-condition that the Agreement would only enter into force when "at least 55 Parties to the Convention accounting in total for at least an estimated 55 per cent of the total global greenhouse gas emissions have deposited their instruments of ratification, acceptance, approval or accession."

completely withdrew from the Protocol to avoid $14 billion in penalties for failing to meet its obligations[39] and even the zealous European countries that strived to meet their QELRCs missed their targets. The low uptake of binding targets by Annex I countries in the second commitment period proposed under the Doha Amendments was also a major indictment of participation under the Kyoto Protocol.

Participation alone is not a silver bullet for achieving sustainability. It must also be effective.[40] For instance, whereas the 2009 Copenhagen Accord elicited broad based participation, its quest towards stabilisation of GHGs was unsuccessful. Described as a "non-binding political statement",[41] the Copenhagen Accord essentially invited developed countries to submit voluntary quantified economy-wide emissions targets while developing countries were to submit "nationally appropriate" mitigation actions by January 2010.

The number of countries making quantified pledges accounted for over 80 per cent of global emissions;[42] however, the pledges made were effete and insufficient to meet the 2°C objective specified in the accord.[43] The country pledges represented nothing more than prevailing state practice of the parties that were not ambitious enough to tilt the balance in favour of deeper emission cuts.

The Glasgow Pact 2021 concluded at COP 26 bears promise for participation by NSAs. The Pact underscores the commitment by Heads of Government to partner with non-Party Stakeholders to enhance sectoral action for cutting back emissions by 2030.[44] Furthermore, the Pact engenders participation by calling for collaboration among a constellation of climate actors that include non-Party Stakeholders, civil society, indigenous peoples, local communities, youth, children, local and regional governments as well as other stakeholders

---

39 Anonymous, 'Canada Pulls Out of Kyoto Protocol' The Guardian (13 December 2011) www.theguardian.com/environment/2011/dec/13/canada-pulls-out-kyoto-protocol last accessed 25 March 2020; See also Amanda M Rosen, 'The Wrong Solution at the Right Time: The Failure of the Kyoto Protocol on Climate Change' (2015) 43 Politics & Policy 30, 37.

40 Daniel Bodansky, 'The Legal Character of the Paris Agreement' (2016) 25 Review of European, Comparative & International Environmental Law (RECIEL) 142, 149.

41 Lilian Yamamoto and Miguel Esteban, *Atoll Island States and International Law: Climate Change Displacement and Sovereignty* (Springer 2016) 109.

42 Gregory Briner, Takayoshi Kato and Hattori Takashi, 'Built to Last: Designing a Flexible and Durable 2015 Climate Change Agreement' (2014) OECD; IEA 10.

43 UNEP, *The Emissions Gap Report: Are the Copenhagen Accord Pledges Sufficient to Limit Global Warming to 2° C or 1.5° C?* (2010).

44 UNFCCC, 'Decision -/CP.26 on the Adoption of the Glasgow Pact' (3rd session) published 13 November 2021, FCCC/PA/CMA/2021/L.16.

in realising the overarching objective of the UNFCCC and the Paris Agreement 2015.[45]

2.4 *Participation under Paris Agreement*

The architecture and design of the Paris Agreement essentially catalyses broad-based global participation while simultaneously heightening emission reduction commitments of Parties.[46] The "effectiveness of an international agreement is a function not only of the stringency of its commitments but also the levels of participation and compliance by states".[47]

In terms of participation, the historic Paris Agreement managed for the very first time to forge a global consensus on collective climate action among the assembly of more than 195 developed and developing nations that met at Le Bourget Airport in Paris after over two decades of futile attempts. The inherent contentions in global climate change politics and blame shifting between developed and developing nations that undermine participation, had become emblematic of climate negotiations over the years and had seriously hampered meaningful progress.[48]

For instance, the question of compensation for developing nations by developed nations for extreme climate events was a stumbling block in the negotiations at COP19 held in Warsaw in 2013 that saw the mass walkout by G77 and China from the talks. Another illustrative example of this schism was the refusal by the United States to ratify the Kyoto Protocol ostensibly because large developing CO_2 emitters like China, India, Indonesia, South Africa and Brazil were exempted from binding emission commitments.[49]

To achieve effectiveness, the Paris Agreement provides for Nationally Determined Contributions (NDCs) that ratchet up progressively and which are verifiable through stringent and transparent accounting procedures.[50] The NDCs though anodyne at the beginning, are expected to become progressively more stringent with successive state Party commitments. The ratchet-up clause in the Paris Agreement can, for instance, be contrasted to the very

45 Ibid.

46 Zou Ji, 'Enhancing Climate Mitigation Ambition Successively: The Drivers' in Stavins Robert N. and Stowe Robert C. (eds), *The Paris Agreement and Beyond: International Climate Change Policy Post-2020* (Harvard Project on Climate Agreements 2016) 29.

47 Daniel Bodansky and Elliot Diringer, 'Building Flexibility and Ambition into A 2015 Climate Agreement' (2014), Centre for Climate and Energy Solutions 3.

48 Adil Najam, Saleemul Huq and Youba Sokona, 'Climate Negotiations Beyond Kyoto: Developing Countries Concerns and Interests' (2003) 3 Climate Policy 221.

49 Todd Sandler, *Global Collective Action* (CUP 2004) 223.

50 Paris Agreement, n 1, art 4.

insipid "voluntary quantified economy-wide emissions targets" and "nationally appropriate" mitigation actions for developed and developing countries respectively in the Copenhagen Accord.

In summary, the Paris Agreement has catalysed overwhelming global participation and buy-in, as evidenced by its entry into force barely 10 months after its adoption.[51] By combining both top-down features of the Kyoto Protocol and bottom-up elements of the Copenhagen Accord, the agreement catalysed global confidence and shored-up optimism that it will deliver the ambitious goal of climate sustainability in terms of the UNFCCC.

Suffice to say, in the context of this discussion, long-term climate sustainability is predicated upon effective and broad-based participation. More importantly, however, the Paris Agreement embodies 'hybrid multilateralism' by complementing State Party participation with voluntary commitments by non-state and NSAs.[52]

3 Participation as a Causal Mechanism for Sustainability

In this analysis, as opposed to a focus on a diffuse and amorphous group of public participators, participation causal mechanisms focus chiefly on participation by state and NSAs. NSAs constitute a distinct emergent group of global climate actors that consist of cities, regional governments, businesses, the financial sector, and civil society.[53] The architecture of the Paris Agreement embraces 'hybrid multilateralism' which basically entwines states and non-state participation in climate governance.[54]

Analysing causality for all potential cadres of diffuse public participators within states would be a Sisyphean task. Further causality in terms of tangible emission reduction outcomes by participators would be difficult to quantify due to the absence of established reporting platforms for such actors. This discussion focusses on the participation by states as principal climate actors and how their role is complemented by NSAs. This approach not only brings the causal effect of participation on sustainability to the fore but also makes it tangible.

---

51 See Paris Agreement, n 1, at 5.

52 Karin Bäckstrand *et al*, 'Non-State Actors in Global Climate Governance: from Copenhagen to Paris and Beyond' (2017) 26 Environmental Politics 561, 562.

53 See Hale, n, at 8.

54 Jonathan W Kuyper, Björn-Ola Linnér and Heike Schroeder, 'Non-State Actors in Hybrid Global Climate Governance: Justice, Legitimacy, and Effectiveness in a Post-Paris Era' (2018) 9 Wiley Interdisciplinary Reviews: Climate Change 497.

Two or more NSAs that cooperate on a global level constitute International Cooperative Initiatives (ICIs).[55] ICIs are more effective in delivering greater GHG emission reductions than singular action by individual NSAs.[56] This analysis on the participation of NSAs therefore focuses on ICIs as a subset of NSAs.

The role of ICIs as complementors of state participation in climate governance is rapidly gaining currency. ICIs are not only instrumental in bridging emission targets, but they possess unique attributes which position them as critical catalytic agents in the delivery of the broader climate change agenda. Participation by ICIs can, therefore, drive the quest for climate change sustainability in a myriad of ways as discussed below.

3.1 *Direct Emission Reduction Targets*

The full emission reduction potential of ICIs has been estimated at "15-23 $GtCO_2e$ per year by 2030".[57] Therefore, as significant emitters, ICIs can through appropriate practices directly cut their emissions thereby bridging projected emission gaps.

Cities are, for instance, estimated to be responsible for about 70 per cent of global emissions and they possess influence over critical sectors that can increase or reduce emissions such as "planning, energy, transport and infrastructure".[58] In this respect, notable GHG emission reduction initiatives include carbon*n* Cities Climate Registry,[59] the C40 Cities Initiative,[60] and the Covenant of Mayors.[61] Reductions of "0.4 $GtCO_2e$ emissions from a baseline level of 3.5 $GtCO_2e$ by 2020 and 0.5 $GtCO_2e$ emissions from a level of 4.1$GtCO_2e$ by 2030" are projected from the C40 initiative.[62] The Covenant of Mayors is projected

---

55 Fatemeh Bakhtiari, 'International Cooperative Initiatives and the United Nations Framework Convention on Climate Change' (2018) 18 Climate Policy 655, 657.

56 Ibid.

57 Hsu *et al,* n, at 8.

58 Hale, n 31, at 8; see also Karen C Seto *et al*, 'Human Settlements, Infrastructure, and Spatial Planning' in Ottmar Edenhofer *et al* (eds), *Climate Change 2014: Mitigation of Climate Change. Working Group III Contribution to the Fifth Assessment Report of the Intergovernmental Panel on Climate Change* (CUP 2014) 935.

59 Constitutes a platform launched in Mexico City in 2010 for monitoring, reporting and evaluating climate action by local and subnational actors.

60 This is a network of 75 large cities that account for per cent of global greenhouse gas emissions and members are required to pledge and achieve a GHG reduction target that surpasses the EU 20 per cent reduction target for 2020.

61 A group launched by the European Union (EU) in 2008 presently consisting of 5729 signatories. The Covenant of Mayors pledge to voluntary reduce GHG emissions and benchmark their efforts against the EU target of 20 per cent GHG reduction for 2020.

62 Mark Roelfsema *et al*, 'Climate Action Outside the UNFCCC: Assessment of the Impact of International Cooperative Initiatives on Greenhouse Gas Emissions' (2015) PBL Netherlands Environmental Assessment Agency 19.

to "reduce emissions by 0.3 $MtCO_2e$ by 2020 from a baseline level of 1.4 $GtCO_2e$ and by 0.3 $GtCO_2e$ by 2030 from a level of 1.7 $GtCO_2e$".[63]

Companies constitute a significant category of GHG emitters. One study for instance observed that between 1988–2015, just 100 fossil fuel companies were responsible for 71 per cent of global emissions.[64] A 2014 emission reductions survey undertaken by the Carbon Disclosure Project (CDP) of the 500 largest global corporations indicated that 65 per cent of these surveyed had set emission reduction targets.[65] Their estimated GHG emission reductions was projected at "0.7 $GtCO_2e$ by 2020 compared to a baseline of 3.8 $GtCO_2e$; 1.3 $GtCO_2e$ by 2030 compared to a baseline of 4.2 $GtCO_2e$".[66] The RE100 initiative is noteworthy for its quest by influential businesses to transit to 100 per cent renewable energy. Most of member businesses have set a target of 100 per cent renewable energy by 2028 with three quarters aspiring for 2030 at the latest. If this target is met, it is projected that ensuing GHG reductions will halve GHG emissions reductions in the next 10 years in conformity to the objectives of the Paris Agreement.[67]

Regional initiatives also bear great potential for GHG reductions. Ambitious actions taken by the Compact of States and Regions[68] for instance includes 651 adaptation actions, 3821 actions to mitigate climate change across 11 sectors, and an undertaking to reduce emissions by an average 14 per cent.[69] If regions achieve their set target, it is projected that they will cumulatively cut about 21.9 GtCO2e between 2010 and 2050.[70]

Specific sector GHG emission reduction projections for ICIs are also significant.[71] The effectiveness of direct GHG emission reductions and projections

63 Ibid at 20.

64 Paul Griffin, 'The Carbon Majors Database: CDP Carbon Majors Report 2017' (2017) Carbon Disclosure Project 14.

65 Roelfsema *et al*, n 64, at 18.

66 Ibid.

67 The Climate Group, 'RE100 Annual Report: Going 100% Renewable: How Committed Companies are Demanding a Faster Market Response' (2019) The Climate Group 5.

68 This initiative provides a single global account for state and regional governments to tackle climate change by setting clear, transparent and verifiable GHG reduction targets. To track progress, states and regions globally are required to annually disclose GHG reduction action, targets and progress to both The Climate Group and CDP.

69 The Climate Group, 'Global States and Regions Annual Disclosure 2019: How States and Regions are Preparing for the Climate Decade' (2019) CDP and The Climate Group 4.

70 The Climate Group, 'Global States and Regions Annual Disclosure: 2017 Update: How Over 100 States and Regions are Acting on Climate Change.' (2017) The Climate Group 4.

71 Roelfsema *et al*, n 62, at 20; Bakhtiari, n 55, at 658–660.

are, however, vitiated by several factors such as opacity of provided data, inconsistent reporting that hinders implementation tracking, and the absence of a permanent secretariat responsible for tracking ICIs commitments.[72] Measuring the effectiveness of ICIs in emission reduction is however a technical exercise and focus has been placed on the potential of ICIs to reduce emissions as opposed to their actual effectiveness. An assessment of an ICI's potential can for instance evaluate the sector relevance of an ICI and presence of capacity for the ICI to achieve set targets.[73]

When one attempts to measure the direct GHG emission reductions attributable to ICIs, it is instructive that action is being measured by such ICIs against the desired goal of keeping global temperatures "to well below 2°C above pre-industrial levels" and striving to constrain any increase in temperature to 1.5°C above pre-industrial levels.[74] Sustainability is achieved where this goal is realised. Misgivings on accurate computation of GHGs notwithstanding, the crux of this discussion is to demonstrate the massive potential that resides in broad based global participation and how it spurs on the quest for sustainable development in a climate change context.

3.2 *Enhancement of Ambitions under UNFCCC*

The criticality of ICIs participation in heightening ambition of state Parties under the UNFCCC is not in doubt.[75] This essentially means that ICIs should 'pick up the tab' on the 'emission gap' left uncovered by state Party commitments. By making their own commitments, ICIs help to raise cumulative global ambition to a desirable level namely, where all commitments would keep aggregate global temperature significantly below 2°C and constrain an increase in temperature to 1.5°C above pre-industrial levels. In the face of acrimonious pre-Paris Agreement climate negotiations, much hope was vested in the potential of ICIs to enhance pledges by nation states. However, the lack

72 Hsu *et al*, n, at 6.

73 Oscar Widerberg and Philipp Pattberg, 'International Cooperative Initiatives in Global Climate Governance: Raising the Ambition Level or Delegitimizing the UNFCCC?' (2015) 6 Global Policy 45, 47.

74 Paris Agreement, n 1, art 2(1)(a).

75 Hsu *et al*, n, at 6; Thomas Hale, 'How the UNFCCC Can Drive Climate Ambition in Advance of a Treaty: Record, Review, Reinforce, Recruit' (Oxford 2013) University of Oxford; Thomas Hale and Charles Roger, 'Orchestration and Transnational Climate Governance' (2014) 9 The Review of International Organizations 59.

of formal recognition of ICIs under UNFCCC and their conception by some actors as a possible threat to sovereignty created ambivalence.[76]

Explicit recognition of ICIs under the Paris Agreement, therefore, legitimises their participation through their commitments in pursuit of the overarching goal in the Paris Agreement. Furthermore, the requirement under the Paris Agreement that parties ratchet up their successive party NDCs, offers more than a forlorn hope that combined commitments of state parties and ICIs may be enhanced well beyond what would otherwise have been possible without the Paris Agreement.

In 2017, UNEP indicated that party NDCs alone covered only a third of global GHG emission reductions required to meet the goal set in art 2 of the Paris Agreement and are, therefore, largely inadequate.[77] The need to increase ambitions constituted one of the major findings in the successive 2018 Emissions Gap Report.[78] In fact this report projected that a tripling of ambitions would be necessary to make the goal under the Paris Agreement reachable.[79]

The 2019 Emissions Gap Report underscores the fact that "even if all unconditional NDCs under the Paris Agreement are implemented", that still puts the globe "on course for a 3.2°C temperature rise".[80] Consequently, increased but structured participation by ICIs possesses massive yet unexhausted potential to enhance ambition and close the emissions gap highlighted in the three successive reports cited above. The acute inadequacy of NDCs means that the realisation of ICIs potential is indispensable in putting the globe on a course where the overarching goal under the Paris Agreement becomes achievable.

In enhancing collective ambition for climate change by states and ICIs, the UNFCCC process enshrines an inclusive, transparent and participatory framework under the *Talanoa* Dialogue Platform. This is a broad-based participatory forum convened under the UNFCCC that allows participants to enagage in transparent dialogue on the best means of enhancing ambitions to swiftly

---

76 Nicholas Harrison, 'Enhancing Ambition through International Cooperative Initiatives' (TemaNord 2014:518, Nordic Council of Ministers 2014) 14.

77 UNEP, *Emissions Gap Report 2017: A UN Environment Synthesis Report* (UNEP 2017) 1.

78 UNEP, *Emissions Gap Report 2018* (UNEP 2018) XIV underscored the fact that 'current commitments expressed in the NDCs are inadequate to bridge the emissions gap in 2030. Technically, it is still possible to bridge the gap to ensure global warming stays well below 2°C and 1.5°C, but if NDC *ambitions are not increased* before 2030, exceeding the 1.5°C goal can no longer be avoided. Now more than ever, unprecedented and urgent action is required by all nations. The assessment of actions by the G20 countries indicates that this is yet to happen; in fact, global CO2 emissions increased in 2017 after three years of stagnation' (emphasis added).

79 Ibid at XV.

80 UNEP, *Emissions Gap Report 2019* (UNEP 2019) XIII.

achieve the goal under art 2 of the Paris Agreement.[81] Anticipatory of the global stock takes envisaged under the Paris Agreement,[82] the dialogue was intended to discuss the first round of NDCs that were due in 2020. The dialogue is informed by three fundamental questions on ambition to wit, *Where are we? Where do we want to go? How do we get there?* A wide array of states, non-Party stakeholders and individuals participate in the UNFCCC process by considering the foregoing questions and submit their opinions on a portal established by the UN climate change secretariat.

Complementary platforms through which ICIs strive to enhance ambition are rapidly emerging, for instance, the Climate Initiatives Platform and the Global Climate Action Summit.[83] Whereas participation is certainly on the rise, determining progress towards the Paris Agreement goal still remains a challenge.[84] It is, however, enough for this discussion to demonstrate that participation where it is sufficient to raise ambition to address GHG reduction, will contribute to the sustainable goal of keeping aggregate global temperature significantly below 2°C and constraining the increase in temperature to 1.5°C above pre-industrial levels.

3.3 *Channeling Climate Finance*

Climate finance[85] plays a central role in GHG emission reduction and in the overall realisation of "climate-resilient development".[86] The 2016 Climate Change Adaptation Finance Gap Report projects that adaptation costs in the run up to 2030 will amount to US$140-300 annually and that international public finance available will be inadequate to meet the projected costs.[87] Input of private sector finance will therefore be indispensable in realising adaptation targets. To this end, ICIs constitute appropriate vehicles for mobilising and channeling climate finance.[88]

---

81 The platform draws input from Parties, cities, regions, companies, civil societies and NGOs among other actors.

82 Paris Agreement, n 1, art 14.

83 Jørgen Fenhann, 'The Climate Initiatives Platform: Towards Greater Transparency in International Cooperative Climate Initiatives (ICIs)' (TemaNord 2018:552, Nordic Council of Ministers 2018) 11.

84 Ibid at 29.

85 Neil Bird, Charlene Watson and Liane Schalatek, 'The Global Climate Finance Architecture' (2017), ODI; HBS. In the context of discussion, climate finance is understood to mean financial resources that are mobilised to finance climate mitigation and adaptation actions globally as well as 'public climate finance commitments' of developed countries.

86 Ibid at 1; See also Paris Agreement, n 1, art 2(1)(c), art 6(8), art 9(3).

87 Daniel Puig *et al* (eds), *The Adaptation Finance Gap Report* (UNEP 2016) XIV.

88 Harrison, n 8, at 79.

The Green Climate Fund (GCF) established under the UNFCCC, proffers an ideal platform on which non-Party stakeholders with significant financial capabilities can augment state party contributions for climate mitigation and adaptation in developing countries. Non-party stakeholders' contributions to the GCF, for instance, helped plug the deficit of about US$ 2 billion created when the US under the then President Trump repudiated its commitment under the Paris Agreement.[89]

In 2017 for instance, subnational governments of Brussels, Wallonia and Flanders and Quebec together with the cities of Paris pledged US $48.2 million to diverse global climate funds including GCF.[90] On the whole, sizeable funding by non-Party stakeholders would in the long run serve to mitigate the unpredictability of Party capitalisation of the GCF.[91]

The Marrakech Partnership for Global Climate Action is reflective of the proliferation of non-Party stakeholders' participation under the Paris Agreement. It underscores the fact that "the momentum created in the lead up to Paris among public and private entities in *mobilising financial resources* for climate action continues to grow". Consequently, it invites ICIs to inter alia help state parties "scale up investment in infrastructure that delivers a range of benefits, including ones for addressing climate change in cities and communities".[92]

Private climate funding constitutes the bulk of global climate finance. In 2017-18 this funding amounted to US$ 326 billion accounting for 56 per cent of climate finance.[93] ICIs and particularly financial institutions can narrow the climate funding gap by redirecting further capital away from high-carbon intensive sectors towards more climate friendly sectors.[94] Such "climate-aligned capital mobilisation" would be a step closer to realisation of the overarching goal under the Paris Agreement.[95]

3.4 *Technological Transformation to Zero-Carbon Technologies*

A radical technological shift from the utilisation of path dependent fossil fuel intensive technologies to zero-carbon technologies lies at the heart of realising

---

89 Megan Bowman and Stephen Minas, 'Resilience through Interlinkage: The Green Climate Fund and Climate Finance Governance' (2019) 19 Climate Policy 342, 343.

90 Bird, Watson and Schalatek, n 5.

91 Bowman and Minas, n 89, at 347.

92 COP 22, 'Marrakech Partnership for Global Climate Action' (2016) 1 (emphasis added).

93 Climate Policy Initiative, 'Global Landscape of Climate Finance 2019' (2019) Climate Policy Initiative 5.

94 Ibid at 6.

95 Ibid.

the Paris Agreement target of global temperature below 2°C and not more than 1.5°C.

To achieve the goal of the Paris Agreement, a technological shift to a zero-carbon pathway by 2050 is sacrosanct. The most radical technological shift is premised among others on the "carbon law" which presupposes the halving of GHGs every decade until 2050.[96] Participation must, therefore, embrace a two-pronged strategy that encourages increased and widespread uptake and dissemination of renewables and other zero emissions technologies, while contemporaneously scaling down "fossil-based value propositions" to completely eliminate then from the market.[97]

To realise the desired technological shift, there is need for joint action by public and private sector actors. Investment of public funds alone in the desired technological transformation is grossly inadequate. Consequently, a collaboration between state and non-state stakeholders is indispensable in setting the world on a zero-carbon technological trajectory.[98]

To this end, diverse and laudable innovation initiatives and strategies are emerging. For instance, Breakthrough Energy Coalition (BEC) was unveiled by Bill Gates at COP 21 in Paris in 2015. The coalition brings together individual investors, financial institutions and organisations to transform the world from the current annual emission of 51 billion tons of GHGs to a net-zero world by funding cutting-edge research, technological innovations and advocating clean energy policy interventions.

Mission Initiative (MI) was also launched at COP 21 in Paris in 2015 and comprises 24 countries and the European Commission. MI aims to "reinvigorate and accelerate global clean energy innovation with the objective to make clean energy widely affordable".[99] In this quest, MI pursues four key objectives that include bolstering public sector investment; enhancing private sector participation and investment; increasing awareness on the transformative power of energy innovation and accelerating international collaboration.[100] It aims to accelerate innovation in eight key technological areas: smart grids; off-grid access to electricity; carbon capture; converting sunlight; clean energy materials; affordable heating

96 Johan Rockström *et al*, 'A Roadmap for Rapid Decarbonisation' (2017) 355 Science 1269.

97 Ibid at 1269.

98 Philibert Cédric, 'International Energy Technology Collaboration and Climate Change Mitigation' (2004), IEA and OECD, COM/ENV/EPOC/IEA/SLT(2004)1.

99 Mission Innovation, 'Overview' http://mission-innovation.net/about-mi/overview/ last accessed 13 April 2014.

100 Mission Innovation, 'By the Numbers Infographic' http://mission-innovation.net/wp-content/uploads/2019/07/MI-By-the-Numbers-infographic.pdf last accessed 13 April 2020.

and cooling of buildings; and renewable and clean hydrogen.[101] To achieve its goal, MI collaborates with other like-minded organisations such as BEC; Global Covenant of Mayors for Climate and Energy (GCoM); International Energy Agency (IEA); International Renewable Energy Agency (IRENA); World Bank Group (WBG); and World Economic Forum (WEF).[102]

Other noteworthy initiatives include the One Planet Summit which is a joint initiative of France, the World Bank and the United Nations geared towards an accelerated implementation of the Paris Agreement; RE100 which is a collaborative forum of 'influential' businesses spanning North America, Europe, China and India that aspire to 100 per cent renewable electricity in their operations at the latest by 2050; New Energy Nexus an initiative to support clean energy entrepreneurs, etc.

The proliferation of emergent zero-carbon initiatives globally should trigger positive contagion dynamics that will herald an inflection point at which fossil fuel intensive technologies are consigned to the archives. An ingrained zero-carbon culture should in turn spur a rapid realisation of the technological aspirations set out in both the UNFCCC[103] and the Paris Agreement.[104]

In summary, participation in making effective climate policy is one avenue through which fairness and sustainability can be enhanced.[105] Climate policy if effective should advance sustainability as envisaged under art 2 of the UNFCCC and art 2(1)(a) of the Paris Agreement. Participation by ICIs at the four levels discussed: direct emission reduction targets; enhancement of ambition; mobilisation of climate finance; and technological transformation to zero-carbon technologies should drive concomitant policy initiatives globally. Caution has, however, been sounded against over expecting NSAs to result in the successful implementation of the Paris Agreement. This is owing to the fact that the Paris Agreement fails to define their roles with specificity and does not stipulate how roles of NSAs should be implemented.[106]

4 Challenges of Participation that Undermine Sustainability

From the preceding discussion, climate change sustainability is evidently an outcome of effective multi-stakeholder participation. A collective failure by

101 Ibid.
102 Ibid.
103 Convention, n 7, art 4(1)(c), art 4(2)(a), art 9(2)(c) among other provisions.
104 Paris Agreement, n 1, art 10(1), art 10(2), art 10(5), art 10(6), art 11(1).
105 Beg *et al*, n 9, at 131.
106 Jonathan Kuyper, Heike Schroeder and Björn-Ola Linnér, 'The Evolution of the UNFCCC' (2018) 43 Annual Review of Environment and Resources 343, 354.

actors to achieve their emission reduction targets, or to enhance ambitions to match the goal of stabilising global temperature at 1.5°C will have a knock-on effect on sustainability. Similarly, the inability of such actors to mobilise adequate financial resources or intervene with innovative zero-carbon technologies will vitiate the quest for sustainability. However, beyond these broad conclusions, participation in the realm of climate change governance is a black-box fraught with challenges that invite a more nuanced discussion.

4.1 *Tangled Power Cable Effect*

Climate change governance is inherently "characterised by a multitude of institutions and initiatives with overlapping mandates".[107] Participation must therefore be structured, targeted and well-coordinated to preclude what the author terms a tangled power cable effect. The author conceives the tangled power cable effect as a phenomenon where a myriad of overlapping and rapidly emerging participatory initiatives result in confusion and curtail the very goal and rationale of participation. Consequently, a chaotic global scenario of saturation and congestion of participatory initiatives without any concomitant rise in effectiveness. In this case, participation will exist for the sake of participation but with neither quantifiable nor meaningful output. This risk is particularly veritable in the post Paris Agreement era where the Agreement's "all hands-on deck" approach has thrown the doors open to a broad range of stakeholders, both typical and atypical.[108]

Whereas Decision -/CP.21 preempts the tangled power cable effect by institutionalising participatory initiatives of NSAs within NAZCA, it does not cure it.[109] The larger question of how to structure participation of NSAs under UNFCCC remains. For instance, should NSAs initiatives be mainstreamed within UNFCCC or should they be left within the twilight zone of non-stringent regulation? How does the UNFCCC regime account for NSAs initiatives that report action on parallel climate registries? Does the NAZCA platform provide an adequately robust framework to coordinate, track, synthesise and accurately quantify NSAs GHG emission reductions?

One source, for instance, observes that "registries for reporting climate initiatives are proliferating but in a haphazard way. Most have a narrow focus and

107 Naghmeh Nasiritousi and Karin Bäckstrand, 'International Climate Politics in the Post-Paris Era' in Lars Calmfors *et al* (eds), *Nordic Economic Policy Review 2019: Climate Policies in the Nordics* (Nord. Nordic Council of Ministers 2019) 41.

108 Thomas Hale, '"All Hands on Deck": The Paris Agreement and Nonstate Climate Action' (2016) 16 Global Environmental Politics 12.

109 See Paris Agreement, n 1, at para 118.

differ in their criteria for inclusion and reporting".[110] The global labyrinth of climate actors and data lends veracity to the apprehension of a tangled power cable effect.

Gaps in NAZCA, among them a bias of pledges by developed countries, low participation by "heavy-polluting" sectors and non-reflection of efforts by small and medium sized players come to the fore and reify concerns for a better structured NAZCA.[111] If NSAs initiatives proceed uncoordinated globally, the same will result in a highly bureaucratic and labyrinthine network that will impede progress towards the end goal of climate sustainability. This concern has been captured as follows:

> Although several initiatives (eg NAZCA, Carbonn, CID, SD in Action) aim to provide broad overviews of non-state and subnational climate initiatives, questions about their effectiveness and performance remain. The sheer amount and diversity of climate actions also complicates their comparability, and the devising of methodologies that can be applied across different samples.[112]

4.2 *Asymmetry of Participation*

One of the structural 'defects' of the Kyoto Protocol that the Paris Agreement sought to alleviate was the lopsidedness of participation. Allocation of QELRCs to Annex I countries and the absence of corresponding commitments for Non-Annex I countries stirred discontent and has among other factors, been attributed to the Protocol's failure.[113] The Paris Agreement institutionalised parity of participation by stipulating NDCs for all Parties. However, they were subject to "common but differentiated responsibilities" (CBDR) of the Parties and their "respective capabilities, in the light of different national circumstances" (RCNC).[114] The short-handedness of CBDR vis a vis NDCs with regard to developing countries has been explained thus:

> ...in a climate regime that is increasingly nationally determined and (transnationally) complex, questions of equity and responsibility cannot

110 Angel Hsu, 'NAZCA: Track Climate Pledges of Cities and Companies' (2016) 532 Nature 303, 303.

111 Ibid at 304.

112 Sander Chan and Thomas Hale, 'Galvanizing the Groundswell of Climate Actions in the Developing World' (2015) GGCA, Working Paper 11.

113 Christopher Napoli, 'Understanding Kyoto's Failure' (2012) 32 SAIS Review of International Affairs 183, 194.

114 Paris Agreement, n 1, art 4(3).

> be addressed by CBDR, as transnational arrangements are generally voluntary and self-organising. Yet their location, impacts, and investments have considerable impact on global equity. In our opinion, a more comprehensive framework could help international organisations and governments to steer climate actions towards greater equity.[115]

A global survey of participation by developing countries on NAZCA and other platforms reveals an acute underrepresentation of developing country initiatives in a manner reminiscent of the Kyoto Protocol regime.[116] Developed countries and associated NSAs exercise a monopoly of climate action in terms of enhancement of ambition, financial investments, technological interventions and other regulatory initiatives. Comparatively, developing countries are passive recipients of climate solutions who play second fiddle to developed countries. Consequently, though well intentioned, the letter of the Paris Agreement on parity of participation has until now not been matched by a corresponding spirit.

The asymmetry of participation between developing and developed countries is attributable to initiatives which are too small that they barely make a blip on the climate radar.[117] It could also be explained away in terms of financial constraints that prohibit developing countries from participating in global climate action. For instance, cost implications may hamper developing countries from tracking and reporting their GHG reduction efforts on established reporting platforms.[118] Lack of goodwill and feet dragging by developing countries could also be a decisive factor. Opposition to the participation by NSAs in the UNFCCC climate regime emerged among some G77 countries in Lima in 2014 when NAZCA was established and has continued.[119] Lack of awareness in developing countries due to weak research and development capacity could also account for the asymmetry.

As the aphorism goes, whether the rock hits the pitcher, or the pitcher hits the rock it is generally bad for the pitcher. Participation asymmetry is the rock that poses an existential threat to the pitcher of global climate action, and it will undermine the stabilisation of global temperature at 1.5°C if it continues unchecked. Whereas macro interventions by large emitters are 'writ large' on the global climate wall, seemingly innocuous micro-effects from developing

115 Chan and Hale, n 112, at 10.
116 UNEP,n 78, at 30; See also Hsu, n 110, at 304.
117 Hsu, ibid.
118 Ibid.
119 Hale,' n, at 16.

countries if ignored, will over time coalesce to undermine the macro-efforts by industrialised nations.

4.3 *Bottlenecks in Tracking Progress*

The Paris Agreement establishes a flexible Enhanced Transparency Framework (ETF) that helps to track the progress of Parties in achieving their NDCs and their adaptation actions under the agreement.[120] This is achieved by requiring parties to regularly provide information that can enable tracking of their progress in implementing and achieving their NDCs.[121]

The aphorism "if you can't measure it, you probably can't manage it" vindicates the operationalisation of the ETF to track overall progress towards the stabilisation of global temperature at 1.5°C. Progress in reducing GHGs consistent with the overarching goal of 1.5°C validates global climate participation. Essentially, therefore, all efforts aimed at reaching the foregoing goal, rise and fall with how accurately progress is tracked.

Tracking collective progress in the reduction of GHGs *vis a vis* the 1.5°C goal, forms the basis for the global stocktake.[122] The stocktake will seek answers to questions posed within the Talanoa dialogue platform: Where are we? Where do we want to go? How do we get there? Bottlenecks, however, exist that blur answers to these questions and undermine both participation and sustainability.

First, the transparency Modalities, Procedures and Guidelines (MPGs) for the operationalisation of the ETF do not address the absence of standardised reporting indicators. This will complicate and possibly obscure the tracking of progress. The non-standardisation of indicators will affect reporting on mitigation measures where NDCs are presented in terms of diverse, non-standardised, non-GHG indicators.[123] With respect to adaptation, different countries experience diverse and varied climate change impacts. The infeasibility of a one-size-fits-all approach in tracking the implementation of adaptation measures, will therefore precipitate accounting difficulties.

---

120 Paris Agreement, n 1, art 13(5).

121 Paris Agreement, n 1, art 13(7)(b).

122 The periodical 'global stocktake' envisaged under art 14 of the Paris Agreement will 'assess the collective progress towards achieving the purposes of [the] Agreement and its long term goals'.

123 UNFCCC, '18/CMA.1 MPGs for the Transparency Framework for Action and Support Referred to in Article 13 of the Paris Agreement', *Report of the Conference of the Parties serving as the meeting of the Parties to the Paris Agreement on the third part of its first session, held in Katowice from 2 to 15 December 2018. Addendum 2. Part two: Action taken by the Conference of the Parties serving as the Meeting of the Parties to the Paris Agreement* pgh 66.

Second, effective tracking is underpinned by assumptions on the accuracy and reliability of information, the monitoring capabilities of parties and low administrative costs. Where these assumptions fail to hold true, as they will do particularly in the case of many developing countries, tracking will very likely be dogged by serious inexactitude possibly characterised by overly optimistic projections.[124] The capacity of the technical expert review to address the challenges related to the foregoing assumptions will be severely tested.

Third, the significant participation by NSAs in enhancing ambition and stopping emission gaps, means that computation of NDCs will significantly rely on extraneous information beyond that furnished by parties. This might blur the accuracy of party commitments. Similarly, in undertaking the global stocktake, financial information by NSAs such as "multilateral development banks, environmental funds, international organisations" will be indispensable.[125] Aggregating financial information for diverse parties across many NSAs with diverse tracking and reporting approaches will be highly technical and complicated.[126]

4.4 *Critical Junctures*

Parties were required to update their NDCs and communicate their long-term strategies under the Paris Agreement starting 2020 and thereafter every five years. The litmus test for the Paris Agreement going forward, will be the potential of communicated NDCs to narrow the emissions gap and align with the achievement of a 1.5°C pathway.[127] However, certain critical junctures exogenous to the Agreement may intervene to undermine this goal.

For instance, shifting Party commitments influenced by geopolitical events, force majeure and other unforeseen circumstances are a cause for concern. Where Parties are forced to renege on their commitments, it will be difficult to hold them to account in the absence of enforcement mechanisms in the

124 Elinor Ostrom, *Understanding Institutional Diversity* (Princeton University Press 2005) 51, observes 'When joint outcomes depend on multiple actors contributing inputs that are costly and difficult to measure, incentives exist for individuals to behave opportunistically. Opportunism — deceitful behaviour intended to improve one's own welfare at the expense of others — may take many forms, from inconsequential, perhaps unconscious, shirking to a carefully calculated effort to defraud others with whom one is engaged in ongoing relationships. The opportunism of individuals who may say one thing and do something else further compounds the problem of incomplete information'.

125 Gregory Briner and Sara Moarif, 'Unpacking Provisions Related to Transparency of Mitigation and Support In The Paris Agreement' (2016) OECD Climate Change Expert Group Paper No. 2016(2), 34.

126 Ibid.

127 Hale, n, at 11.

Paris Agreement. The Agreement is essentially a facilitative and collaborative framework that precludes punitive enforcement mechanisms.

In the context of this discussion, therefore, critical junctures are understood as a mixed bag of global events synonymous with a 'turning point', 'crisis', and 'unsettled times'.[128] These events, previously unforeseen, might negatively impact climate action by precipitating path dependent choices that might be extremely difficult to alter at later stages.[129]

The United States and China closed ranks under the leadership of President Obama and President Xi to galvanise global participation that saw the signing and subsequent ratification of the Paris Agreement in record time in 2015. Five years later, the set of geopolitical dynamics that coalesced to catapult the historic climate pact into reality have dissipated.

The United States under the administration of President Donald Trump declared its intention to withdraw from the Paris Agreement on 1 June 2017. Pursuant to art 28 of the Paris Agreement, on 4 November 2019, the United States began the formal process of withdrawal by submitting its formal notification of withdrawal to the United Nations.[130]

Effectively, on 5 November 2020 the United States had ceased to be a Party to the Paris Agreement. The domino effect of this withdrawal would have been momentous and far reaching on global climate action had Joe Biden not been elected as President.[131] The capacity of the American private sector to fill the hiatus that was left by the Federal Government particularly in as far as galvanising global action by other players was in doubt. Whereas the private sector could have mitigated some effects of the withdrawal, it could not have supplanted Federal Government action. Concomitantly, a blistering trade war between the United States and China threatened goodwill, trust and the modest gains for the Paris Agreement that were birthed out of the pre-2015 collaboration.[132]

---

128 Giovanni Capoccia and Roger D Kelemen, 'The Study of Critical Junctures: Theory, Narrative, and Counterfactuals in Historical Institutionalism' (2007) 59 World Politics 341, 341.

129 Ibid at 342.

130 Michael R Pompeo, 'On the U.S Withdrawal from the Paris Agreement' (*U.S. Departement of State,* 4 November 2019) https://2017-2021.state.gov/on-the-u-s-withdrawal-from-the-paris-agreement/index.html last accessed 17 October 2021.

131 Yong-Xiang Zhang *et al*, 'The Withdrawal of the U.S. from the Paris Agreement and Its impact on Global Climate Change Governance' (2017) 8 Advances in Climate Change Research 213, 215.

132 James Fernyhough, 'Trade War Threatens Progress on Climate Change, Warns China' (*Financial Review,* 21 November 2019) www.afr.com/companies/energy/trade-war-threatens-progress-on-climate-change-warns-china-20191120-p53c72 last accessed 20 April 2020.

An unfolding economic downturn has seen China waver on its steadfast commitment to the Agreement as one of its leaders.[133] Investments in coal are picking up and the Chinese Government has substantially cut back on its aggressive renewable energy subsidies.[134] Bearing in mind the incentive-laden nature of climate change inaction, flagging commitment from China and the withdrawal by the United States will have a significant knock-on effect on the commitment and participation of other Parties. The feasibility of meaningful global climate action without the critical leadership and support of the United States and China, both as major economic powers and emitters, appears dead in the water.

Previously unforeseeable events such as the coronavirus (COVID-19) pandemic, have already dulled climate change momentum, for instance through the cancellation of important climate talks and initiatives such as COP 26 that was initially set for 2020 in Glasgow but later convened in 2021.[135] The pandemic will fundamentally impact climate change action globally going forward at a scale that will be felt for years to come. The global economic morass resulting from the pandemic will certainly shift priorities of most parties to the Paris Agreement.

The impact of critical junctures on climate agreements is not unprecedented. The failure of the Kyoto Protocol has, among other factors, been attributed to a slew of critical junctures that ensued in the wake of its entry into force in 2005.[136] For instance, the election into the White House of George W. Bush a "Texas oilman" over Al Gore an "environmentalist Democrat" led to the non-ratification of the Kyoto Protocol.[137] In the post Kyoto ratification period Chinese GHG emissions grew three times. Further the 2007-08 global financial crisis did not help climate matters. Considerable thought, therefore, needs to be invested on how to counter the enduring effects of identified critical junctures on participation and sustainability in the Paris Agreement.

133 Leslie Hook, 'Climate Change: How China Moved from Leader to Laggard' *Financial Times* (Baoding, 25 November 2019) www.ft.com/content/be1250c6-0c4d-11ea-b2d6-9bf4d1957a67 last accessed 20 April 2020.

134 Ibid.

135 Leslie Hook and Aleksandra Wisniewska, 'How Coronavirus Stalled Climate Change Momentum: Emissions Have Fallen but the Pandemic Will Hit Policy Commitments as Nations Look to Kick-start Their Economies' *Financial Times* (London,14 April 20204) www.ft.com/content/052923d2-78c2-11ea-af44-daa3def9ae03 last accessed 20 April 2020.

136 Noah M Sachs, 'The Paris Agreement in the 2020s: Breakdown or Breakup?' (2019) 46 Ecology Law Quarterly 865, 886.

137 Malcolm Gladwell, *What the Dog Saw: And Other Adventures* (Penguin 2010) 161.

5 Reflections on Sustainability and Participation

This chapter underscores climate sustainability as a corollary of effective participation. In section 4, it identifies and discusses frustrating barriers in this nexus that threaten to impede sustainability. Consequently, a reflection on how some of the features of participation in the Paris Agreement affect the quest for sustainability is necessary. This reflection is intended to stimulate thinking on the evolving architecture of the Paris Agreement. Additionally, reflection highlights how participation pursues the overarching 'below 2°C but not beyond 1.5°C' temperature goal of the Paris Agreement.

5.1 *If You Aim at Nothing*

The greatest obstacle in the Paris Agreement to stabilising global temperature at below 2°C but not beyond 1.5°C is perhaps its' lack of individual binding targets and a concomitant enforcement mechanism. It has been argued that:

> a top-down allocation of binding individual emission reduction obligations, perhaps even with an enforcement mechanism would have been a more direct and predictable way of staying below that threshold, but that proved impossible to agree on.[138]

Whereas the overarching goal spelt out in art 2 of the Agreement is clear to all, Parties neither bind themselves to nor aim at specific individual targets in delivery of this overall goal. NDCs, in their discretionary and voluntary character, aim at nothing specific by failing to apportion individual party ambition for realisation of the collective goal.

I do not argue here for parity of apportionment of emission reduction targets among parties for obvious reasons. Nevertheless, NDCs presently allow parties to make only lowest common denominator commitments most of which are commensurate to paying climate alms.[139] This approach is reminiscent of the apothegm "if you aim at nothing, you will hit it every time". Therefore, whereas the Paris Agreement has galvanised near global participation, its ability to deliver sustainability in climate change terms largely remains doubtful.

An agreement without binding targets renders stringent enforcement mechanisms superfluous. This logic explains the absence of concrete enforcement mechanisms in the Paris Agreement. The absence of enforcement

138 Report of the Secretary-General, UNGA, 73rd Session, Agenda Item 14, U.N. Doc. A/73/419 (2018).

139 Sachs, n 136, at 878.

mechanisms in the agreement affirms Hobbes' *ipssisma verba*, "covenants, without the sword, are but words and of no strength".[140] Ultimately therefore, whereas the flexible and voluntary nature of NDCs incentivises participation, mere carrots without corresponding sticks are unlikely to lead to sustainability.

The regulatory pathway parties elected in the Paris Agreement due to the "wicked"[141] nature of the climate change problem is one that "begin[s] with an agreement that has broad based participation and is at least moderately legalised (legally binding) but includes only shallow substantive commitments, and deepen the substantive content over time".[142] This architecture has been described as offering "no action, just promises".[143] A disjunction between the collective climate goal and individual Party commitments will persist and continue widening the global emission gap.[144]

Does this pathway offer a future possibility for Parties to adopt ambitious individual binding emission reduction commitments? Would provisions for taxing GHGs across the board find accommodation within the Paris Agreement? How can underlying political will for radical global climate action be stimulated? Answering these questions will ultimately determine the trajectory of climate sustainability.

5.2 *Big Emitters Small Participators*

A defining debacle of the Kyoto Protocol was the weak participation by otherwise large emitting non-Annex I countries which did not have binding targets. The Paris Agreement sought to redress this drawback by institutionalising NDCs across the board for all Parties based on CBDR.

---

140 Thomas Hobbes, *The English Works of Thomas Hobbes of Malmesbury/ / now first collected and edited by Sir William Molesworth* (first published 1839--45, London J. Bohn 1839-45)154.

141 Charles West Churchman, 'Wicked Problems' (1967) 14 Management Science B-141-B-142 B-141 describes a wicked problem as one that refers to a 'class of social system problems which are ill-formulated, where the information is confusing, where there are many clients and decision makers with conflicting values, and where the ramifications in the whole system are thoroughly confusing'; See also Frank P Incropera, *Climate Change: A Wicked Problem: Complexity and Uncertainty at the Intersection of Science, Economics, Politics and Human Behaviour* (CUP2016); HorstW J Rittel and Melvin M Webber, 'Dilemmas in a General Theory of Planning' (1973) 4 Policy Science 155.

142 Kenneth W Abbott and Duncan Snidal, 'Pathways to International Cooperation' in Moshe Hirsch and Eyal. Benvenisti (eds), *The Impact of International Law on International Cooperation: Theoretical Perspectives* (CUP 2004) 55.

143 Oliver Milman, 'James Hansen, Father of Climate Change Awareness, Calls Paris Talks 'A Fraud'' *The Guardian* (12 December 2015) www.theguardian.com/environment/2015 /dec/12/james-hansen-climate-change-paris-talks-fraud last accessed 28 April 2020.

144 Kuyper, Schroeder and Linnér, n 6, 347.

However, stipulating NDCs for all Parties has morphed into a conundrum that allows big emitters to adopt extremely anodyne NDCs. The 2018 Intergovernmental Panel on Climate Change's (IPCC) special report on the impacts of global warming of 1.5°C was instructive that the current NDC pledges are consistent with the realisation of global warming of 3°C.

For instance, notwithstanding that Russia is the fourth biggest GHG emitter, its' NDC "is so weak that Russia is already achieving its 2030 target".[145] Other notable big emitters with insufficient NDCs include United States, Canada, and Japan. The identified countries are not even on track to achieve their initial weak ambitions for 2015.[146]

Among the Group of 77 and China, (Brazil, India, China, South Africa and Mexico) Brazil, Russia, India, China, South Africa and Mexico (BRICSAM countries) have in their ranks NDCs that are acutely insufficient and do not reflect their significant GHG emissions.[147] In this group, it is noteworthy that China is the biggest emitter and India is the third largest emitter. Indeed, the combined emissions of the United States, China and India account for almost half of global emissions.[148]

It is a cruel paradox, however, that some vulnerable and low GHG emitting countries, have committed to more ambitious NDCs in comparison to the big emitters.[149] In this respect the argument may be advanced that smaller countries have less to lose economically by embracing greater ambitions. However, by the same token, it is a fact that Small Island Developing States (SIDS) are also the most vulnerable group of countries.

The robust and meaningful participation by big emitters is indispensable for sustainability. This was possibly the wisdom of requiring "at least 55 Parties to the Convention accounting in total for at least an estimated 55 per cent of the total global GHGs" to ratify the Paris Agreement before it could enter into force.[150]

---

145 Sachs, n 136, 877.

146 Ibid at 893.

147 Taryn Fransen and David Waskow, 'Which Countries Will Strengthen Their National Climate Commitments (NDCs) by 2020?' (*World Resources Institute*, 20 September 2019) www.wri.org/blog/2019/09/which-countries-will-strengthen-their-national-climate-commitments-ndcs-2020 last accessed 30 April 2020.

148 Kuyper, Schroeder and Linnér, n 106, 348.

149 IRENA, 'Small Island Developing States: Renewable Ambition in Pursuit of Climate Change Adaptation' (*International Renewable Energy Agency,* 10 December 2019) www.irena.org/newsroom/articles/2019/Dec/SIDS-Renewable-Ambition-in-Pursuit-of-Climate-Change-Adaptation last accessed 30 April 2020.

150 Art 21.

Cumulatively therefore, present NDCs are a harbinger of successive weak commitments that will not limit warming to 1.5°C. The inability of the Paris Agreement to resolve disputes that relate to the inadequacy of NDCs or even call out laggards and ask them to do more raises concern.[151] This then begs the question, how can big emitters become big participators?

5.3 *Climate Politics and Participation*

Climate change is no doubt the most obstinate political issue of the day on the global stage. This is because participation by states and NSAs is ultimately driven by political will. The observation that UNFCCC decisions "reflect the will of the laggards" certainly rings true.[152] The failure to reach actionable outcomes in previous climate talks such as Bali 2007 and Copenhagen 2009 are largely attributable to the lack of political will.

The optimism of Paris 2015 as a milestone representing a break with a past of elusive political will, was palpable in the exultation "there's never been such political will as we have today".[153] As has already been mentioned, however, this triumph seems to have been short lived. This is evidenced by a deterioration in the geopolitical relations responsible for the consensus in Paris and a dissipation of factors which made that consensus possible. Withdrawal from the Paris Agreement by the United States was emblematic of the nadir of political will in the Paris Agreement.

In climate change governance, the nub of elusive political will lies in pursuit of short-term economic goals, strategic interests and myopia to seemingly remote long-term consequences.[154] The most rabid form of elusive political will goes beyond mere inaction and entails deliberate action to scupper the Paris Agreement and brake its momentum, as the United States attempted to do under former President Donald Trump.[155]

It will, therefore, be critical to see whether buoyant 'political will' can weigh heavier than the floundering goodwill of the United States and other laggards. The European Union and a significant number of States in the United States under the America's Pledge initiative, have remained steadfast and demonstrated goodwill in realising commitments in the Paris Agreement.[156]

---

151 Sachs, n 136, 896.

152 Kuyper, Schroeder and Linnér, n 106, 345.

153 Rodger A Payne, 'The Global Politics of Climate Change' (2018) Sustain 18, 18.

154 Ibid at 20.

155 Sachs, n, 890.

156 Lars Calmfors *et al* (eds), *Nordic Economic Policy Review 2019: Climate Policies in the Nordics* (Nord, Nordic Council of Ministers 2019) 35.

A critical feature of the Paris Agreement is "creative ambiguity" without which a political compromise for its adoption would have been almost impossible.[157] It will be critical to understand how this feature of the Paris Agreement acts as a brake-block or an accelerator. Laggards are likely to continue exploiting creative ambiguity for maximum advantage whereas leaders will be unlikely to generate sufficient lift for enhancement of collective ambition.

As withdrawal by the United States perfectly illustrated, participation under the Paris Agreement will be susceptible to domestic politics and strategic interests of the parties. Domestic political interference it has been observed 'has the potential to uproot and gut any meaningful impact of' the Paris Agreement.[158] This is a veritable challenge not the least because participation in the agreement is founded on voluntary national contributions.

The sum-total of the foregoing political considerations invites further reflection on avenues for engendering goodwill and in turn enhancing participation and sustainability within the climate change regime. The very nature of climate change means laggards cannot be left to poetic justice since everyone is ultimately imperiled and developing states even more so.

5.4 *Non-state Actors under Paris Agreement*

This chapter has underscored the unique and massive potential NSAs possess to complement efforts by state parties in limiting warming to 1.5°C. Indeed the "all hands on deck" approach of the Paris Agreement is the culmination of an idea that has been gradually gaining momentum across many COPs.[159] Yet beyond NAZCA, the "multi-actor, multi-sector, and multilevel" participation by NSAs within the Paris regime remains largely ad hoc and unstructured in the extreme.[160]

NSAs are explicitly recognised in Decision -/CP.21 on the Adoption of the Paris Agreement, however, they are not expressly incorporated in the operative text of the Paris Agreement. This has the effect that NSAs are outside the formal Paris Agreement structures but are at the same time generally recognised under the UNFCCC as being complementary to state commitments under the Paris Agreement.[161]

157 Kuyper, Schroeder and Linnér, n 106, 354.

158 Clark Kayla, 'The Paris Agreement: Its Role in International Law and American Jurisprudence' (2018) 8 Notre Dame Journal of International & Comparative Law 107, 108.

159 Hale, n 110.

160 Kuyper, Schroeder and Linnér, n 106, at 351.

161 Meinhard Doelle, 'The Paris Agreement: Historic Breakthrough or High Stakes Experiment?' (2016) 6 Climate Law 1, 5.

One source pertinently underscores the "surprisingly little attention paid in the Paris Agreement to the role of NSAs and subnational governments",[162] notwithstanding their potential role in enhancing the mitigation ambition of parties. Several challenges of participation by NSAs within this so called 'hybrid multilateralism'[163] architecture of the Paris regime present themselves, summed up variously under the UNFCCC.[164]

First, most NSAs initiatives are largely uncoordinated. Second, structures for disclosure of conflicts of interest are not apparent. Third, a dearth of funds afflicts the ability of NSAs to participate, particularly those from vulnerable developing countries. Finally, there is lack of a permanent forum within which activities of NSAs are housed The foregoing challenges in turn undermine "the quality, practicality" of NSAs initiatives under the UNFCCC thereby attenuating their potency.[165]

Consequently, there is a general need to retool the participation of NSAs under the Paris Agreement for the realisation of sustainability benefits that can emerge from broad based participation. In this sense, it is necessary to alleviate hurdles that stymie effective participation.[166]

To this end, recommendations are to:[167] establish appropriate coordination mechanisms of NSAs initiatives; enhance transparency among NSAs by creating avenues for disclosure of conflicts of interest; craft-out means of funding participation by NSAs from vulnerable developing and small island States; and initiate a permanent forum for NSAs through which they can engage in dialogue and exchange views tailored along the lines of the UNEA model which hosts a two day multi-stakeholder forum prior to the Assembly. The Marrakech Platform for Global Climate Action has been identified as a potential permanent forum.[168]

6 Conclusion

Causality underpins the nexus between sustainability and participation. This means that effective participation accompanied by compliance with stringent

162 Ibid at 17.
163 Kuyper, Linnér and Schroeder, n 54, at 1.
164 Freedom-Kai Phillips, 'Participation of Non-party Stakeholders under the UNFCCC: Options for Future Engagement' (2018) Centre for International Governance Innovation, CIGI Papers No. 205 7.
165 Ibid.
166 Kuyper, Linnér and Schroeder, n 54, at 11.
167 Phillips, n.
168 Ibid at 14.

commitments should result in the sustainable quest under the Paris Agreement to limit global temperature rise to 1.5°C. The success of the Montreal Protocol on Substances that Deplete the Ozone Layer,[169] for instance, has been attributed to the coincidence between participation and stringency accompanied by compliance.[170] Whereas the Paris Agreement to date has achieved remarkable participation and possibly compliance, stringent commitments for the realisation of zero emissions or net negative emissions remain elusive.[171]

The situation is, however, not all together lost. This chapter has underscored the massive potential that resides with participators within the framework of hybrid multilateralism to catalyse sustainability through direct emission reductions, enhancement of state party ambitions, provision of climate finance and technological transformation among other avenues. The causal pathway between participation and sustainability is, nevertheless, littered with many complex and vexing challenges. Notable challenges include the unstructured proliferation of NSAs; bias of participation by developed countries; difficulties and inefficiencies in tracking progress towards GHG emission reduction; and the negative impact of unforeseeable critical junctures, among others. The realisation of climate sustainability will, therefore, be dependent upon successful alleviation of these hurdles by participating entities.

Several architectural gaps or 'flaws' at the core of the Paris Agreement that might render participation fruitless need to be addressed. Consequently, consideration should be given on how to tweak NDCs to reflect stringent individual binding targets. This may negate the current *laissez-faire* approach that favours lowest common denominator commitments. It will be necessary to reconcile the asymmetry between weak NDCs and significant GHG emissions by big emitters such as the United States, Canada, Japan and BRICSAM countries. The current trajectory of the Paris Agreement reflects the will of laggards and it will be critical for leaders to emerge to change this self-destructive course. Since the success of the Paris Agreement is heavily dependent on participation of NSAs, it will be necessary to properly structure these entities within the UNFCCC.

The Paris Agreement embraces a flexible and evolutionary architecture which allows participators, especially state parties, to ratchet up ambition. It is also possible to tweak other aspects of the Paris Agreement evidenced, for instance, by the adoption of MPG for the transparency framework for action

169 Protocol on Substances that Deplete the Ozone Layer (Montreal) 16 September 1987, entered into force 1 January 1989, 26 ILM (1987) 1541 (hereinafter Montreal Protocol).

170 Barrett, n, 1217.

171 Ibid.

and support contemplated under aartrt 13 of the agreement.[172] Sustainability, equitable to the achievement of zero emissions or net negative emissions, is heavily predicated on the growing stringency of party commitments. The evolutionary nature of the Paris Agreement provides a window of opportunity for parties to adjust stringency provided they can marshal elusive political goodwill. Sustainability will, therefore, ultimately rise and fall with the will of participators. Progress will, however, depend on the will of the laggards given the nature of climate change as a wicked problem.[173]

Acknowledgements

“Funded by the Deutsche Forschungsgemeinschaft (DFG, German Research Foundation) under Germany's Excellence Strategy – EXC 2052/1 – 390713894“

Bibliography

Abbott KW and Snidal D, ‘Pathways to International Cooperation’ in Hirsch M and Benvenisti E (eds), *The Impact of International Law on International Cooperation: Theoretical Perspectives* (Cambridge University Press 2004).

Andonova L B, Hale T N and Roger C B, ‘National Policy and Transnational Governance of Climate Change: Substitutes or Complements?’ (2017) 61(2) International Studies Quarterly 253.

Anonymous, ‘Canada Pulls Out of Kyoto Protocol’ *The Guardian* (London, 13 December 2011) <http://www.theguardian.com/environment/2011/dec/13/canada-pulls-out-kyoto-protocol> last accessed 25 March 2020.

Bäckstrand K and others, ‘Non-State Actors in Global Climate Governance: from Copenhagen to Paris and Beyond’ (2017) 26(4) Environmental Politics 561.

Bakhtiari F, ‘International Cooperative Initiatives and the United Nations Framework Convention on Climate Change’ (2018) 18(5) Climate Policy 655.

Barrett S, ‘Choices in the Climate Commons’ (2018) 362(6420) Science 1217.

Beg N and others, ‘Linkages Between Climate Change and Sustainable Development’ (2002) 2(2-3) Climate Policy 129.

Bird N, Watson C and Schalatek L, ‘The Global Climate Finance Architecture’ (2017) ODI; HBS.

---

172 UNFCCC, n 122.

173 See n 140 for a definition of a “wicked problem”.

Bodansky D, 'The Legal Character of the Paris Agreement' (2016) 25(2) Review of European, Comparative & International Environmental Law 142.

Bodansky D and Diringer E, 'Building Flexibility and Ambition into a 2015 Climate Agreement' (Centre for Climate and Energy Solutions 2014).

Bowman M and Minas S, 'Resilience through Interlinkage: The Green Climate Fund and Climate Finance Governance' (2019) 19(3) Climate Policy 342.

Briner G, Kato T and Hattori Takashi, 'Built to Last: Designing a Flexible and Durable 2015 Climate Change Agreement' (2014) OECD; IEA.

Briner G and Moarif S, 'Unpacking Provisions Related to Transparency of Mitigation and Support in The Paris Agreement' (2016) OECD, Climate Change Expert Group Paper No. 2016 (2).

Calmfors L and others (eds), *Nordic Economic Policy Review 2019: Climate Policies in the Nordics* (Nordic Council of Ministers 2019).

Capoccia G and Kelemen R D, 'The Study of Critical Junctures: Theory, Narrative, and Counterfactuals in Historical Institutionalism' (2007) 59(3) World Politics 341.

Chan S and Hale T, 'Galvanizing the Groundswell of Climate Actions in the Developing World' (2015) Working paper, GGCA.

Churchman C W, 'Wicked Problems' (1967) 14(4) Management Science B141–B142.

Climate Policy Initiative, 'Global Landscape of Climate Finance 2019' (2019) Climate Policy Initiative.

Cornwall A, '"Unpacking Participation": Models, Meanings and Practices' (2008) 43(3) Community Development Journal 269.

Doelle M, 'The Paris Agreement: Historic Breakthrough or High Stakes Experiment?' (2016) 6(1-2) Climate Law 1.

Duran DC and others, 'The Components of Sustainable Development - A Possible Approach' (2015) 26 Procedia Economics and Finance 806.

Fenhann J, *The Climate Initiatives Platform: Towards Greater Transparency in International Cooperative Climate Initiatives (ICIs)* TemaNord 2018:552 (Nordic Council of Ministers 2018).

Fernyhough J, 'Trade War Threatens Progress on Climate Change, Warns China' *Financial Review* (21 November 2019) <https://www.afr.com/companies/energy/trade-war-threatens-progress-on-climate-change-warns-china-20191120-p53c72> last accessed 20 April 2020.

Fransen T and Waskow D, 'Which Countries Will Strengthen Their National Climate Commitments (NDCs) by 2020?' (20 September 2019) <https://www.wri.org/blog/2019/09/which-countries-will-strengthen-their-national-climate-commitments-ndcs-2020> last accessed 30 April 2020.

Gladwell M, *What the Dog Saw: And Other Adventures* (Penguin 2010).

Griffin P, 'The Carbon Majors Database: CDP Carbon Majors Report 2017' (2017), Carbon Disclosure Project.

Hale T, 'How the UNFCCC Can Drive Climate Ambition in Advance of a Treaty: Record, Review, Reinforce, Recruit' (9 October 2013), University of Oxford.

Hale T, '"All Hands on Deck": The Paris Agreement and Nonstate Climate Action' (2016) 16(3) Global Environmental Politics 12.

Hale T, 'The Role of Sub-state and Non-state Actors in International Climate Processes' (Chatham House, The Royal Institute of International Affairs 2018).

Hale T and Roger C, 'Orchestration and Transnational Climate Governance' (2014) 9(1) The Review of International Organizations 59.

Halsnæs K and Shukla P, 'Sustainable Development as A Framework for Developing Country Participation in International Climate Change Policies' (2007) 13(2) Mitigation and Adaptation Strategies for Global Change 105.

Harrison N, *Enhancing Ambition through International Cooperative Initiatives* TemaNord 2014:518 (Nordic Council of Ministers 2014).

Hobbes T, *The English Works of Thomas Hobbes of Malmesbury (1839 - 1845)*: Now First Collected and Edited by Sir William Molesworth, *Bart* (1839-45).

Hook L, 'Climate Change: How China Moved from Leader to Laggard' *Financial Times* (25 November 2019) <https://www.ft.com/content/be1250c6-0c4d-11ea-b2d6-9bf4d1957a67> last accessed 20 April 2020.

Hook L and Wisniewska A, 'How Coronavirus Stalled Climate Change Momentum: Emissions have Fallen but the Pandemic will hit Policy Commitments as Nations Look to Kick-start their Economies' *Financial Times* (London, 14 April 2014) <https://www.ft.com/content/052923d2-78c2-11ea-af44-daa3def9ae03> last accessed 20 April 2020.

Hsu A, 'NAZCA: Track Climate Pledges of Cities and Companies' (2016) 532 Nature 303.

Hsu A and others, 'Bridging the Emissions Gap: The Role of Non-state and Subnational Actors' (Nairobi 2018), UNEP.

Incropera F P, *Climate Change: A Wicked Problem: Complexity and Uncertainty at the Intersection of Science, Economics, Politics and Human Behaviour* (Cambridge University Press 2016).

IRENA, 'Small Island Developing States: Renewable Ambition in Pursuit of Climate Change Adaptation' (10 December 2019) <https://www.irena.org/newsroom/articles/2019/Dec/SIDS-Renewable-Ambition-in-Pursuit-of-Climate-Change-Adaptation> accessed 30 April 2020.

Jetoo S, 'Stakeholder Engagement for Inclusive Climate Governance: The Case of the City of Turku' (2019) 11(21) Sustainability 1.

Ji Z, 'Enhancing Climate Mitigation Ambition Successively: The Drivers' in Stavins R N and Stowe R C (eds), The Paris Agreement and Beyond: International Climate Change Policy Post-2020 (Harvard Project on Climate Agreements 2016).

Kayla C, 'The Paris Agreement: Its Role in International Law and American Jurisprudence' (2018) 8(2) Notre Dame Journal of International & Comparative Law 107.

Kurukulasuriya L and Robinson N A, 'Training Manual on International Environmental Law' (Nairobi 2006), UNEP.
Kuyper J, Schroeder H and Linnér B-O, 'The Evolution of the UNFCCC' (2018) 43(1) Annual Review of Environment and Resources 343.
Kuyper J W, Linnér B-O and Schroeder H, 'Non-State Actors in Hybrid Global Climate Governance: Justice, Legitimacy, and Effectiveness in a Post-Paris Era' (2018) 9(1) Wiley Interdisciplinary Reviews: Climate Change e497.
Lélé SM, 'Sustainable Development: A Critical Review' (1991) 19(6) World Development 607.
Milman O, 'James Hansen, Father of Climate Change Awareness, Calls Paris Talks 'A Fraud'' *The Guardian* (London, 12 December 2015) <https://www.theguardian.com/environment/2015/dec/12/james-hansen-climate-change-paris-talks-fraud> last accessed 28 April 2020.
Mission Innovation, 'By the Numbers Infographic' <http://mission-innovation.net/wp-content/uploads/2019/07/MI-By-the-Numbers-infographic.pdf> last accessed 13 April 2020.
Mission Innovation, 'Overview' <http://mission-innovation.net/about-mi/overview/> last accessed 13 April 2014.
Najam A, Huq S and Sokona Y, 'Climate Negotiations Beyond Kyoto: Developing Countries Concerns and Interests' (2003) 3(3) Climate Policy 221.
Napoli C, 'Understanding Kyoto's Failure' (2012) 32(2) SAIS Review of International Affairs 183.
Nasiritousi N and Bäckstrand K, 'International Climate Politics in the Post-Paris Era' in Calmfors L and others (eds), Nordic Economic Policy Review 2019: Climate Policies in the Nordics (Nordic Council of Ministers 2019).
Ostrom E, *Understanding Institutional Diversity* (Princeton University Press 2005).
Payne R A 'The Global Politics of Climate Change' (2018) 37 Sustain 18.
Philibert C, 'International Energy Technology Collaboration and Climate Change Mitigation' (2004) OECD;IEA.
Phillips F-K, 'Participation of Non-party Stakeholders under the UNFCCC: Options for Future Engagement' (December 2018) CIGI Papers No. 205.
Pompeo MR, 'On the U.S Withdrawal from the Paris Agreement' (2019).
Rittel H W J and Webber M W, 'Dilemmas in a General Theory of Planning' (1973) 4(2) Policy Science 155.
Rockström J and others, 'A Roadmap for Rapid Decarbonization' (2017) 355(6331) Science 1269.
Roelfsema M and others, 'Climate Action Outside the UNFCCC: Assessment of the Impact of International Cooperative Initiatives on Greenhouse Gas Emissions' (2015), PBL Netherlands Environmental Assessment Agency.

Sachs NM, 'The Paris Agreement in the 2020s: Breakdown or Breakup?' (2019) 46(3) Ecology Law Quarterly 865.

Sandler T, *Global Collective Action* (Cambridge University Press 2004).

Seto KC and others, 'Human Settlements, Infrastructure, and Spatial Planning' in Edenhofer O and others (eds), *Climate Change 2014: Mitigation of Climate Change. Working Group III Contribution to the Fifth Assessment Report of the Intergovernmental Panel on Climate Change* (Cambridge University Press 2014).

The Climate Group, 'Global States and Regions Annual Disclosure: 2017 Update: How Over 100 States and Regions are Acting on Climate Change.' (2017) The Climate Group.

The Climate Group, 'Global States and Regions Annual Disclosure 2019: How States and Regions are Preparing for the Climate Decade' (2019), CDP and The Climate Group.

The Climate Group, 'RE100 Annual Report: Going 100% Renewable: How Committed Companies are Demanding a Faster Market Response' (2019), The Climate Group.

Tørstad V H, 'Participation, Ambition and Compliance: Can the Paris Agreement Solve the Effectiveness Trilemma?' (2020) 29(5) Environmental Politics 761.

Voigt C, *Sustainable Development as a Principle of International Law: Resolving Conflicts between Climate Measures and WTO Law* (Martinus Nijhoff Publishers 2009).

Widerberg O and Pattberg P, 'International Cooperative Initiatives in Global Climate Governance: Raising the Ambition Level or Delegitimizing the UNFCCC?' (2015) 6(1) Global Policy 45.

Yamamoto L and Esteban M, *Atoll Island States and International Law: Climate Change Displacement and Sovereignty* (Springer 2014).

Zhang Y-X and others, 'The Withdrawal of the U.S. from the Paris Agreement and Its impact on Global Climate Change Governance' (2017) 8(4) Advances in Climate Change Research 213.

CHAPTER 13

Indigenous Peoples and Local Communities' Participation Provisions in Negotiations on Conservation of Marine Areas Beyond National Jurisdiction

Violeta S. Radovich

1 Introduction

The objective of this chapter is to analyse Indigenous peoples and local communities' (IPLCs) participation provisions in the Draft Agreement on the conservation and sustainable use of marine biological diversity of areas beyond national jurisdiction (BBNJ)[1] to the United Nations Convention on the Law of the Sea (UNCLOS)[2] to provide an insight into whether they will lead to sustainability on the high seas and the Area.

This analysis will be led by a paradigm oriented towards putting the ocean centre stage, which includes incorporating IPLCs knowledge and participation as crucial elements, and by legal criteria defining participation as effective.

In addition to this, a comparison will be made between the participation standards established in the Aarhus Convention (AC),[3] the European Water Framework Directive (WFD)[4] and the Marine Strategy Framework Directive (MSFD).[5]

Finally, a comparison will be established with the participation standards contributions from the Human Rights Courts and Committees. Decisions of human rights bodies may be classified along a spectrum moving from the more

1 UNCLOS, Draft Agreement of an international legally binding instrument under the United Nations Convention on the Law of the Sea, <www.un.org/bbnj/sites/www.un.org.bbnj/files/revised_draft_text_a.conf_.232.2020.11_advance_unedited_version.pdf>, last accessed 17 August 2022.

2 UNCLOS entered into force 16 November 1994,1833 UNTS 397.

3 Aarhus Convention on Access to Information, Public Participation in Decision-Making and Access to Justice in Environmental Matters, entered into force 30 October 2001, 2161 UNTS 447.

4 Water Framework Directive (WFD) 2000/60/EC.

5 Marine Strategy Framework Directive (MSFD) 2008/56/EC.

© VIOLETA S. RADOVICH, 2023 | DOI:10.1163/9789004509382_015

general and less demanding forms of participation to procedural requirements that give IPLCs the ultimate power to decide on certain matters.

2 Regulating the High Seas and the Area through the Lens of Sustainability. Negotiations for a Binding Treaty for the Conservation of Biodiversity in Areas beyond National Jurisdiction

The current system of ocean governance has been challenged since 1992 when the UN Rio Declaration on Environment and Development (Rio Declaration),[6] adopted at the Conference on Environment and Development held in Rio de Janeiro, introduced the concept of sustainable development. Moreover, chapter 17 of the Agenda 21, adopted in the same Conference, emphasised the challenges and opportunities for the protection and sustainable development of the marine environment, integrated coastal zone management and the protection of biological resources.[7] Sustainable development goal 14, also adopted in the same Conference, mandates to conserve and sustainably use the oceans, seas and marine resources for sustainable development.[8] Recently, the Intergovernmental Oceanographic Commission, a body of the UN, declared the Oceanic Science Decade for Sustainable Development (2021–2030), a ten-year programme of joint action to advance research and technological innovation to comply with sustainable development goal 14.

The elaboration of many historical resource conservation schemes almost always included the participation of local stakeholders, such as Indigenous populations. Since the 1980s, these early manifestations of the connection between sustainability and participation have experienced a powerful renaissance with the international establishment of the principle of "sustainable development"[9] comprising the three pillars: economic development; environmental protection; and the protection of current and future generations.

Profs. Lohse and Peters state in their Deutsche Forschungsgemeinschaft project that contrary to their use in other disciplines, such as the social

6 UN, Rio Declaration on Environment and Development, Doc. A/CONF.151/26 (vol. I).

7 Report of the UN Conference on Environment and Development, 'Protection of the oceans, all kinds of seas, including enclosed and semi-enclosed seas, and coastal areas and the protection, rational use and development of their living resources', chapter 17, art 17.1, A/CONF.151/26 (Vol. II), 13 August 1992.

8 UNGA, '*Transforming our world: the 2030 Agenda for Sustainable Development*, 21 October 2015, A/RES/70/1, <www.refworld.org/docid/57b6e3e44.html>, last accessed 17 August 2022.

9 United Nations Environmental Programme, 'Report of the World Commission on Environment and Development – Our Common Future' (14 April 1987), para 27.

and political sciences,[10] in law the relationship between sustainability or sustainable development and participation has remained sketchy. Several questions remain and focus on how sustainabilty can be achieved and by which means of participation. It also remains unclear which procedures must be observed, and who must or should be considered participants. Moreover, does "sustainability" and "participation" describe particular substantive or procedural rules, standards, principles, programmes, or optimisation requirements and, under which circumstances may they be subject to enforcement? Is participation going beyond defence and consultation and leading to negotiation or co-decision? Finally, are participatory rights given to NGOs in the same manner as to individuals?[11] I aim to answer these questions in the present chapter in relation to the law of the high seas in the BBNJ Draft Agreement.

Covering three quarters of the earth's surface area, oceans are the world's largest ecosystem. BBNJ, including the high seas and the international seabed (the Area), comprise more than sixty percent of the ocean.[12] The legal framework for ocean governance in BBNJ does not operate in a void, however, it is largely fragmented and uncoordinated, resulting in a patchwork of regulatory schemes covering issue ranging from: protection of migratory birds; deep sea mining; the dumping of illegal waste from ships; and pollution from land-based sources. There are at least 190 multi- and bi-lateral agreements addressing a spectrum of issues affecting the ocean, not including other forms of global governance such as customary international law, working practice, or informal rules.[13]

In its Resolution 72/249 of 24 December 2017,[14] the UN General Assembly (UNGA) convened an Intergovernmental Conference (IGC) to consider the recommendations of the Preparatory Committee established by Resolution

10 Cf. especially: Virginie Barral, 'Sustainable Development in International Law: Nature and Operation of an Evolutive Legal Norm' (2012) European Journal of International Law 377; *Elinor Ostrom/Larry Schroeder/Susan Wynne, Institutional Incentives and Sustainable Development* (1993).

11 Eva J Lohse/Giulia Parola/Margherita Poto, 'Introductory remarks on the idea and the purpose of a German-Italian dialogue on participation in environmental decision making' in Eva J Lohse/Margherita Poto (eds), *Participatory Rights in the Environmental Decision-Making Process and the Implementation of the Aarhus Convention: a Comparative Perspective* (Dunker & Humblot 2015).

12 Elizabeth De Santo and others, 'Stuck in the middle with you (and not much time left): The third intergovernmental conference on biodiversity beyond national jurisdiction' (2020) Marine Policy 103957 117. See Art.1.4 Draft BBNJ Agreement.

13 Ibid.

14 UNGA on an International legally binding instrument under the United Nations Convention on the Law of the Sea on the conservation and sustainable use of marine biological diversity of areas beyond national jurisdiction, Res 72/249 (24 December 2017).

69/292 of 19 June 2015.[15] Further, it elaborated the text of an international legally binding instrument under UNCLOS on the conservation and sustainable use of BBNJ, with a view to developing the instrument as soon as possible. Resolution 69/292 creates an opportunity for a new and remarkable evolution of the Law of the Sea and provides evidence that the political momentum exists for negotiating an international legally binding instrument under UNCLOS on the conservation and sustainable use of marine biodiversity of BBNJ.[16]

In accordance with Resolution 72/249, the Conference held a three-day organisational meeting in New York, from 16 to 18 April 2018, to discuss organisational matters, including the process for the preparation of the zero draft of the instrument. The first session was convened from 4 to 17 September 2018, the second from 25 March to 5 April 2019 and the third from 19 to 30 August 2019. The fourth session was planned for March 2020, but was suspended because of the COVID pandemic. It was rescheduled on 16 to 27 August 2021, and suspended again due to the same reason.

The so-called Package 2011[17] identifies the following as the main substantive elements of the negotiation: first, marine genetic resources (MGRs), including questions on the sharing of benefits; second, measures such as area-based management tools, including marine protected areas (MPAs); third, environmental impact assessments (EIAs); and, fourth, capacity building and the transfer of marine technology. United Nations General Assembly (UNGA) Resolution 72/249 stressed the need for widest possible participation and the use of consensus-based decision-making.

The new BBNJ Agreement is intended to connect and coordinate fragmented governance institutions to ensure the conservation and sustainable use of marine biodiversity in BBNJ.[18] In this sense, the term 'integration' may be attributed to the following meaning in the third paragraph of UNCLOS Preamble: "Conscious that the problems of ocean space are closely interrelated and need to be considered as a whole."[19]

---

15 <https://sustainabledevelopment.un.org/index.php?page=view&type=111&nr=7897&menu=35> last accessed 20.10.2022.

16 Marta C Ribeiro, 'South Atlantic Perspectives on the Future International Legally Binding Instrument under the LOSC on Conservation and Sustainable Use of BBNJ' 32 (2017) The International Journal of Marine and Coastal Law 733.

17 UNGA, Res 69/292 (2015) para 2 (n 2).

18 Elisabeth Druel and Kristina M Gjerde, 'Sustaining marine life beyond boundaries: options for an implementing agreement for marine biodiversity beyond national jurisdiction under the United Nations Convention on the Law of the Sea' (2014) 49 Marine Policy 90.

19 Richard Barnes, 'The Law of the Sea and the Integrated Regulation of the Oceans' (2012) The International Journal of Marine and Coastal Law 27 (4) 860.

In addition to this, the Intergovernmental Science-Policy Platform on Biodiversity and Ecosystem Services (IPBES) last report in 2019 states that "integrative" governance shall be achieved in order to combat policy sectorial incoherence. Integrative governance is presented as one of the components to achieve "transformative" governance, along with informed, adaptative and inclusive governance.[20]

However, a "should not undermine" commitment has been consistently deployed throughout the four negotiation elements to argue that a new BBNJ instrument should not be empowered with any oversight or coordination functions in its relationship with existing institutions. This means that biodiversity conservation in BBNJ must be achieved without the treaty itself exerting any direct control over shipping or fishing activities.

IPLCs are the holders of a vast amount of traditional knowledge relating to the ocean and its resources.[21] However, IPLCs have generally been underrepresented in the debate about governance of BBNJ, as evidenced by the lists of participants in the intergovernmental meetings, although there are some regional exceptions within the context of the Convention on Biological Diversity (CBD). Nonetheless, IPLCs are custodians of many globally-significant migratory species that travel between coasts and high seas,[22] and are mentioned several times in the draft text of the Treaty.[23]

3 Towards an Ocean-centred System of Governance, Where IPLCs Should Have a Leading Role towards the Rights of Nature Perspective

Critical concerns have been raised regarding the adequacy of the current strategies offered by international law and the law of the sea regime for tackling climate change, and their integration and effectiveness in dealing with the challenges posed by environmental threats.[24] The ontology and the institu-

20 IPBES, *Global assessment report on biodiversity and ecosystem services of the Intergovernmental Science - Policy Platform on Biodiversity and Ecosystem Services*, chapter 6. E Brondizio and others (eds) (IPBES Secretariat 2019).

21 Clement Mulalap and others, 'Traditional knowledge and the BBNJ instrument' (2020) Marine Policy.

22 Marjo Vierros and others, 'Considering Indigenous Peoples and local communities in governance of the global ocean commons' (2020) 119 Marine Policy 104039.

23 Clement Mulalap and others, n 21, at 5.

24 Margherita Poto, 'The Law of the Sea and Its Institutions. Today's Hermeneutic Approach and Some Suggestions for an Ocean-Centred Governance Model' in Elise Johansen/ Signe V Busch/Ingvild UJakobsen (eds), *The Law of the Sea and Climate Change: Solutions and Constraints* (Cambridge University Press 2021).

tional framework of ocean governance should be reoriented and restructured towards a more effective ocean-centred system of governance.[25] The ocean shall be put at the centre of scene, restoring the connection between the seas and humanity. I have also proposed a similar approach in decided not to use the misleading word "offshore" when referring to exploration and exploitation of hydrocarbons at sea. Instead, I chose to use the word "marine", and call these structures, "sea or marine" platforms.[26] The use of the word "offshore" is at odds with the notions of sustainable development and the ecosystem approach.

The word "offshore" is traditionally used as an adjective to describe "away from or at a distance from the coast". It was adopted as a means of describing something that was the opposite of "onshore". However, in the context of installations, "offshore" identifies structures from a shore-based perspective and carries implications in the form of "non-shore" that do not adequately capture recent developments in seabed and subsoil exploration. For example, while exploration and exploitation initially took place in close proximity to the shore, over the last 80 years, exploration and exploitation have taken part in deeper waters. This has implications for environmental safety measures, which should be appropriate to evolving techniques; especially techniques deployed in deep water, which are subject to aggravating effects such as high water pressure. In reality, the structures in question are located in the marine, sea or ocean environment, rather than the "non-shore" environment.

This centrality contrasts with the regulatory approach of the law of the sea that emphasises the sovereign right of the state and state-like organisations towards the sea based on the presumption of the exploitable value of the world's oceans and seas.[27] When negotiated, the CBD was more oriented towards conservation than was the UNCLOS, which was oriented more towards resource exploration and exploitation.[28]

The conceptual framework of the law of the sea is based on the premise of the superiority of humans over nature. This has generated top-down regulatory patterns, with sovereign states at the top, and exploitable marine resources at the bottom. By contrast, integral and holistic views on the relationship between oceans and humans have recognised the oceans as an inseparable part of

25 Ibid.

26 Violeta Radovich, 'Governance of oil and gas exploration and exploitation at sea: towards coastal marine biodiversity preservation' in Ed Couzens, E/Alexander Paterson/Sophie Riley /Yanti Fristikawati(eds), *Protecting Forest and Marine Biodiversity: The Role of Law* (Edwar Elgar 2017).

27 Ibid.

28 Rüdiger Wolfrum/Nele Matz, 'The Interplay of the United Convention on the Law of the Sea and the Convention on Biological Diversity' (2000) 4 Max Planck Yearbook of United Nations Law 445.

existence. Examples of this vision may be found among Indigenous communities all over the world who acknowledge the unconditional value of water, independent of any economic appraisal. Coastal and marine people understand the oceans in terms of connections: between land and sea, earth and sky, day and night; between the spiritual and physical past, present and future; and between knowledge and practice, people and places.[29] In this sense, the IPBES Report[30] found that the loss of biodiversity and ecosystem function is much less pronounced on lands managed by IPLCs. In addition to this, UN's Agenda 21 acknowledges that over many generations, Indigenous peoples have developed a holistic traditional scientific knowledge of their lands, natural resources and environment.[31]

A re-reading of the concept of "institutions" shall include structures that are socially embedded, because they are generated by the interaction of all the actors beyond the states: collective organisations; individuals; and the ocean itself. This may pave the way for further reflection on the need to rethink the relationship between humanity and the sea in terms of connectivity, not mere superiority. This renewed definition not only expands the horizon of the actors involved and their mutual interactions, but also helps facilitate the integration of systems of laws that already focus on the connections that exist between peoples, knowledge, and ecosystems, such as the CBD.[32]

This approach supports a critical analysis of the system of the law of the sea in the context of interaction with climate change. Even though the issue of state sovereignty has been re-discussed in depth by new global actors like environmental NGOs and civil society, the regulation of the seas, when intersecting with the multi-actor-net of environmental governance, has remained a fine meshed system where non state actors have never served as decision makers. The response must involve recognising and developing the role of Indigenous peoples and marine communities as stewards of the ocean. UNCLOS Part XII provisions are linked to the Westphalian approach that gives precedence to the state action in any environmental decision. In other words, they are state-oriented. States are the sole actors with a major role in decision making.[33]

29 Margherita Poto (2021), n 24, at 5.

30 IPBES, 'Global assessment report of the Intergovernmental Science-Policy Platform on Biodiversity and Ecosystem Services;, S Díaz/J Settele/E. Brondízio/H T Ngo (eds) (IPBES Secretariat: 1753) <https://ipbes.net/global-assessment> last accessed 17 August 2018.

31 Paul Simon in Daniel Sitarz (ed), *Agenda 21: The Earth Summit Strategy to Save our Planet* 30 (1st Edn., 1993).

32 Margherita Poto (2021) n 24, at 5.

33 Margherita Poto (2021) n 24, at 5.

Globalisation and environmental challenges have offered great opportunities for re- conceptualising and re-orientating international law and the law of the sea regime, especially after the Rio Declaration. Gradually, the scope of ocean governance has moved beyond the need to regulate the seas at an inter-state affair, pushing the debate in the direction of defining the oceans as global commons.

Western systems of knowledge tend to delineate knowledge into areas such as "fisheries" or "management" or "species" while Indigenous knowledge is more circular and layered.[34] This is related to integrated ocean management approach as opposed to a sectorised one. The effect of globalisation on the domain of public law has contributed to changing perceptions of the relationships between actors and rules. Before the advent of globalisation, law was organised mainly within national boundaries.[35]

The opening towards a model of global governance marks a first step in the path towards a holistic approach, by strengthening the participation of non-state actors and by implementing a toolbox of rules that hold users accountable for damage caused to the environment. The centrality of the protection of the seas marks the second step, with the revitalisation of regenerative practices in Indigenous and local marine communities who have always understood the importance of paying central attention to the oceans.[36]

In recent years, for the most part in Latin America, Australia and New Zealand, there has been a shift from the anthropocentric approach of regulating natural resources to an ecocentric one. The first approach is well embedded in UNCLOS and the Rio Declaration where humans actions are recognised as the main centre of concern. Pursuant to the ecocentric shift, nature is conceived of as holding its own rights, rather than being an entitlement for human use.[37] The idea of human representatives providing a voice for nature is central to the idea of nature's rights. The development of rights of nature laws in Ecuador and Bolivia has applied the concept of *Buen Vivir,* the idea of living a good life, inspired by Indigenous communal societal goals. Ecuador and Bolivia also recognise the rights of *Pachamama*, Mother Earth.[38]

---

34 Melissa Nursey-Bray and Jacobson Chris, 'Which way?': The contribution of Indigenous marine governance' (2014) 6:1 Australian Journal of Maritime & Ocean Affairs 27.

35 Margherita Poto and Lara Fornabaio, 'Participation as the Essence of Good Governance: Some General Reflections and a Case Study on the Arctic Council' (2017) 8 Arctic Review on Law and Politics 139.

36 Margherita Poto (2021) n 24, at 5.

37 Elizabeth Macpherson, *Indigenous Water Rights in Law and Regulation* (Cambridge, 2019).

38 Maria V Berros, 'Defending Rivers: Vilcabamba in the South of Ecuador. Perspectives' (2017) Rachel Carson Center for Environment and Society Munich 37.

Proponents of the rights of nature focus on the need for natural resources to have standing before the courts in order for their rights to be protected. Most commonly, these declarations or the granting of legal personality has been related to rivers. Regulatory models that protect the rights of rivers have been largely driven, not by environmentalists, but by Indigenous and tribal communities, who claim distinct relationships with water based on their cosmovision of guardianship, symbiosis and respect, as opposed to western liberal utilitarianism.[39] As Māori legal scholar Linda Te Aho explains, "we see ourselves as direct descendants of our earth mother and sky father and consequently not only of the land but as the land."[40] Legal rights for rivers, at least when they directly involve Indigenous peoples, are an attempt to resolve historical and contemporary grievances about resource use and reconstitute governance arrangements. Therefore, I believe a next step in ocean regulation would be to grant them legal personality. In fact, the literature has proposed the establishment of a such new body, a "Council of Ocean Custodians" to provide a voice for the ocean areas beyond national jurisdiction (ABNJ).[41]

4 Environmental Participation in European Provisions

Three legal criteria will be employed as a reference to evaluate to what extent environmental participation has democratic features and/or contributes to the emergence of new forms of democracy.[42] These are: 1) the level of inclusiveness; 2) the influence of participatory experiences on final decisions; and 3) the level of accountability of final decision-makers with respect to the intermediate input provided by citizens during participatory processes.

Regarding the third criteria, as decisions taken by participatory instances are usually not mandatory, it is worth addressing the question of whether citizens have the means to check whether their opinions have been taken into account. Is there a way to sanction decision makers if they fail to take into account the result of participation? Because if not, participation is limited to exercising a

39 Elizabeth Macpherson (2021) n 37, at 7.

40 Linda Te Aho, 'Indigenous challenges to enhance freshwater governance and management in Aotearoa New Zealand- The Waikato River Settlement' (2009) 20(5–6) Journal of Water Law 285.

41 Harriet Harden-Davies and others, 'Rights of Nature: Perspectives for Global Ocean Stewardship' (2021) 122 Marine Policy 104059.

42 Federica Cittadino, 'Public Participation in the Water Framework Directive (WFD): A Contribution to Deliberative Democracy?' in Eva Lohse and Margherita Poto (eds.), *Best Practices for the protection of water by law* (Berliner Wissenschafts-Verlag 2017).

consultative role. Representative institutions shall be required to justify decisions not to include the results of public deliberation in final measures.[43]

Further development in the recognition of participatory rights in environmental decision-making is marked by the AC, which provides for free, prior and informed consent (FPIC) in the form of rights of access to information and participation in decision-making. More specifically, the AC has structured participation into three main pillars, dealing with: a) the right of access to information; b) the right to participate in decision-making; and c) the right of access to justice in environmental matters. AC in art 6.4. states that, "Each Party shall provide for early public participation, when all options are open and effective public participation can take place."

It should been analysed the extent to which the participatory mechanisms foreseen in the European WFD respond to the legal criteria employed. Public participation is foreseen under art 14 of the WFD, which reads as follows:

> Member States shall encourage the active involvement of all interested parties in the implementation of the directive in particular in the production, review and updating of the river basin management plans.

This provision contains at least two vague clauses whose content needs to be discussed in more detail, namely "active involvement" and "all interested parties".[44] In this respect, the Commission, in cooperation with the Member States, has elaborated a Common Implementation Strategy (CIS) for the WFD. Guidance document no 8 of the CIS[45] is specifically dedicated to public participation and thus may be used to interpret the above-mentioned open clause.

The CIS defines "active involvement" to be more than just consultation because it also implies participation in the whole planning process. More explicitly, public involvement is considered a "share in decision-making".[46] How is public involvement intended to be carried out in concrete terms?[47] Art 14 (2) provides some indication when it foresees that the public "has six months to comment in writing". Also, the CIS indicates some new legal tools, such as,

43 Ibid.

44 Federica Cittadino (2017) n 42, at 8.

45 CIS, Guidance document no 8 (2003) <https://circabc.europa.eu/sd/a/0fc804ff-5fe6-4874-8e0d-de3e47637a63/Guidance No 8 - Public participation (WG 2.9).pdf> last accessed 17 August 2022 p 12.

46 CIS, Guidance document no 8 (2003) <https://circabc.europa.eu/sd/a/0fc804ff-5fe6-4874-8e0d-de3e47637a63/Guidance No 8 - Public participation (WG 2.9).pdf> last accessed 17 August 2022, p 95.

47 Federica Cittadino (2017) n 42, at 8.

citizens' juries and creative sessions that are also discussed in the context of deliberative democracy. The former requires "randomly selected people, who represent a microcosm of their community [to discuss] a specific issue and make public their conclusions"[48] upon payment. The latter aims to develop common ground for the public involved and to understand and evaluate issues with the help of facilitators.[49]

The CIS of the WFD defines "interested parties" as "any person, group or organisation with an interest or "stake" in an issue, either because they will be directly affected or because they may have some influence on its outcome." Therefore, the WFD favours a broad notion of the public involvement because it is not only limited to the inclusion of affected parties, and is so broader than the AC.[50] In the AC, "The public concerned" means the public affected or likely to be affected by, or having an interest in, the environmental decision-making; for the purposes of this definition, non-governmental organisations promoting environmental protection and meeting any requirements under national law shall be deemed to have an interest (art 2.5), so it does not include individual people. The MSFD also provides for active involvement and participation of all interested parties, as does the WFD.

5 IPLCs Rights

The most commonly referred definition of Indigenous peoples at international level is in art 1 (1)(b) of the International Labour Organisation's (ILO) Convention concerning Indigenous and Tribal Peoples (ILO No 169),[51] which states that Indigenous peoples are:

> ... peoples in independent countries who are regarded as indigenous on account of their descent from populations which inhabited the country, or a geographical region to which the country belongs, at the time of conquest or colonisation or the establishment of present states boundaries and who, irrespective of their legal status, retain some or all of their own social, economic, cultural and political institutions.

48 CIS Guidance document no 8 (2003) <https://circabc.europa.eu/sd/a/0fc804ff-5fe6-4874-8e0d-de3e47637a63/Guidance No 8 - Public participation (WG 2.9).pdf> last accessed 17 August 2022, p 95.

49 CIS (2003), p 11.

50 Federica Cittadino (2017) n 42, at 8.

51 International Labour Organization Convention No 169 (27 June 1989) <https://www.ilo.org/dyn/normlex/en/f?p=NORMLEXPUB:55:0::NO::P55_TYPE,P55_LANG,P55_DOCUMENT,P55_NODE:REV,en,C169,/Document> last accessed 20.10.2022.

Several core international human rights treaties and their treaty bodies affirm the rights of Indigenous peoples to own, develop, control, and use their traditional territories and resources, as well as obligate States to ensure and protect those rights.[52] Additionally, various non-binding international instruments also acknowledge the crucial role that Indigenous peoples play in environmental management and decision-making, especially for the purposes of sustainable development.[53]

The acronym IPLCs encompasses not just indigenous peoples, but also local communities. Local communities, unlike Indigenous peoples, do not necessarily have a history of being invaded or colonised by external entities. However, like Indigenous peoples, local communities have cultural values, practices, and systems developed through multiple generations and poised to be passed to future generations. This is the approach taken in the CBD.[54]

As regards "traditional knowledge", the so-called CBD art 8(j) Working Group makes use of an informal working definition, as follows:

> Traditional knowledge refers to the knowledge, innovations and practices of indigenous and local communities around the world. Developed from experience gained over the centuries and adapted to the local culture and environment, traditional knowledge is transmitted orally from generation to generation. It tends to be collectively owned and takes the form of stories, songs, folklore, proverbs, cultural values, beliefs, rituals, community laws, local language, and agricultural practices, including the development of plant species and animal breeds. Sometimes it is referred to as an oral tradition for it is practiced, sung, danced, painted, carved, chanted and performed down through millennia. Traditional knowledge is mainly of a practical nature, particularly in such fields as agriculture, fisheries, health, horticulture, forestry and environmental management in general.[55]

52 See eg: UNGA, International Convention on the Elimination of All Forms of Racial Discrimination (1966); see also the provisions on economic self-determination for indigenous peoples in UNGA, International Covenant on Civil and Political Rights(1966) and International Covenant on Economic, Social, and Cultural Rights (1966).

53 See eg, UN Conference on the Human Environment(1972) Stockholm Declaration Principle 22; UN Conference on Environment and Development (1992) Rio Declaration on Environment and Development, Principle 22, UN Doc A/ CONF.151/26.

54 Clement Mulalap and others, n 21 at 5.

55 Secretariat of the Convention on Biological Diversity, Traditional Knowledge and the Convention on Biological Diversity, <www.cbd.int/doc/publications/8j-brochure-en.pdf> last accessed 17 August 2022.

Three major types of traditional knowledge may be mentioned: traditional knowledge based on the connectivity of species and marine processes (both active and passive) between ABNJs and coastal waters; traditional knowledge emerging from environmental management best practices in coastal waters that can be models for similar measures in ABNJs; and traditional knowledge derived from traditional instrument-free navigation between coastal communities and across ABNJs that is still utilised in voyaging in various parts of the world. The examples reveal, among other things, the interconnected nature of the natural environment (from highlands to shores to the deep ocean), a keen awareness among IPLCs of the need to balance sustainable use with ambitious conservation, the importance of involving all stakeholders (including IPLCs with relevant traditional knowledge) in environmental governance practices, the profound cultural and spiritual values IPLCs associate with the natural environment, and the necessity of interacting with the natural environment with caution and respect. As an example of the interconnected nature of the natural environment, it has been recently proved that rainfall causes microplastics in the ocean to be transported into the atmosphere.[56]

This body of knowledge and associated custodianship, particularly as relating to the ocean and its resources, predates the establishment of current national borders and continues to inform access and use of marine areas and resources throughout the world. As such, it has precedent and great relevance for consideration under the BBNJ instrument.[57]

Indigenous peoples' groups in the Arctic Council are granted the status of permanent participants, which has a number of consequences in terms of their involvement in any environmental decision which affects them. The reason for allowing this full engagement lies in the high level of consciousness of their connection with the land they live in. Arctic peoples consider themselves as a part of the whole with the natural resources with which they live, they self-identify with their natural environment and therefore they self-determine by participating in decisions that affect them.[58] In this way participation becomes transformative, since the empowerment of the parties so engaged leads to a transformation of the communities involved.[59]

56 Moritz Lehmann and others, 'Ejection of marine microplastics by raindrops: a computational and experimental study' (2021) Microplastics and Nanoplastics 1, 18.

57 Clement Mulalap and others, n 21 at 5.

58 Margherita Poto, 'Participatory rights of indigenous peoples: The virtuous example of the Arctic region' (2016) 2018 Environmental Law and Management 81.

59 Ibid.

6 Contributions of the CBD and the UN Framework Convention on Climate Change (UNFCCC) Regarding IPLCs Participation

6.1 Synergies from the UNFCCC

The world's oceans are affected by global warming, which leads to increases in temperatures, the generation of more severe storms, rising sea levels, coastal erosion and vertical stratification, to which the marine ecosystem is particularly sensitive. Moreover, ocean acidification is also on the increase, which may entail severe effects on marine animals.[60] Ocean acidification, along with climate change, are grounded reasons to propitiate a reduction in global CO_2 emissions. The ocean has a fundamental function in the carbon cycle, by absorbing approximately 0.5% of the CO_2 emitted to the atmosphere in the last 200 years.

In 2015, progress was made in the regulation of the climate change-ocean relationship, because for the first time the role of the ocean was mentioned in the Paris Agreement as a result of the N° 21 Convention of the Parties (COP) to the UNFCCC.[61]

As regards the UNFCCC, in the preamble to the Paris Agreement, Parties acknowledge that they "should", when taking action to address climate change, respect, promote, and consider their respective obligations on "The rights of indigenous peoples [and] local communities." Toward that end, per para 136 of the decision adopting the Paris Agreement, the Parties to the UNFCCC established in 2015 a Local Communities and Indigenous Peoples Platform (LCIPP).[62] In order to operationalise the LCIPP, Parties to the UNFCCC established the Facilitative Working Group for the LCIPP per para 3 of a 2018 decision, with membership comprising of an equal number of representatives from States and from Indigenous peoples organisations — a landmark achievement in international law and discourse with respect to participation of holders of traditional knowledge.[63,64]

60 IPCC Climate Change 2014: Synthesis Report. <https://www.ipcc.ch/site/assets/uploads/2018/05/SYR_AR5_FINAL_full_wcover.pdf> last accessed 17 August 2022.

61 UN, Paris Agreement (2015), entered into force 16 November 1994, Doc. FCCC/CP/2015/Add.1 Decision 1/CP 21.

62 UN Framework Convention on Climate Change, 21st Meeting of the Conference of the Parties, Decision 1/CP 21.

63 Clement Mulalap and others, n 21 at 5.

64 UN Framework Convention on Climate change, 24th meeting of the conference of the Parties, Decision 2/CP.24.

6.2 *Synergies from the CBD*

The Nagoya Protocol on Genetic Resources to the CBD[65] regulates the components of biodiversity in areas within national jurisdiction.[66] Many of the initiatives taken under the CBD are inspiring[67] and the geographical limitations of the CBD have not prevented the COPs debating, since 2004, issues concerning the conservation of ABNJ.[68] One concrete outcome of the initiatives taken, especially since 2008, is the work being done on the identification of ecologically or biologically significant marine areas (EBSAs).[69] In the EBSA process, CBD Contracting Parties hold regional workshops to identify maritime areas that meet the criteria for EBSA designation and lay the groundwork for future efforts by relevant and competent national, regional and international entities to impose special conservation and management measures on those areas.

In accordance with Decision XI/17 of the CBD Conference of the Parties, CBD Contracting Parties, other governments, competent intergovernmental organisations, and relevant IPLCs are invited to use guidance from the CBD on integrating traditional knowledge (with the approval and involvement of the holders of that knowledge) in any future descriptions of maritime areas qualifying as EBSAs as well as future conservation and management measures for those areas,[70] including extensive work done on the matter by the CBD

---

65 Nagoya Protocol on Access to Genetic Resources and the Fair and Equitable Sharing of Benefits Arising from their Utilization to the Convention on Biological Diversity (2010) UN Doc. UNEP/CBD/COP/DEC/X/1.

66 Article 4, CBD; Article 3, Nagoya Protocol.

67 For instance, acceptance of overarching principles, such as the precautionary approach and the ecosystem-based approach (Article 5 of the 1995 UN Fish Stocks Agreement); consultation processes and compatibility provisions in the case of transboundary impacts requiring EIA; review, monitoring, compliance and dispute settlement mechanisms; international minimum environmental standards; MPA definition and substantive criteria; benefit sharing mechanism with respect to genetic resources; institutional *governance*. In the case of networks of MPAs and other effective area-based conservation measures see the following decisions of the Conference of the Parties (COP) of CBD: COP 7-2004, Decision VII/30, Annex II, Target 1.1, and COP 10, Decision X/2 (*The Strategic Plan for Biodiversity 2011–2020 and the Aichi Biodiversity Targets*), Annex, IV, 13, Target 11. <www.cbd.int/cop/default.shtml> last accessed 17 August 2022.

68 See COP 7-2004, Decision VII/5, paragraphs 29–31, and subsequent decisions on marine and coastal biodiversity.

69 See COP 9-2008, Decision IX/20, paragraph 14; COP 10-2010, Decision X/29; and COP 11-2012, Decision XI/17. See also the EBSAs website: <www.cbd.int/ebsa/about?tab=relevantDecisions> last accessed 17 August 2022.

70 Decision adopted by the Conference of the Parties to the Convention on Biological Diversity at its eleventh session, held in Hyderabad, India, from 8 October to 19 October 2012, 24, UNEP/CBD/COP/DEC/XI/17 (Dec. 5, 2012).

Subsidiary Body on Scientific, Technical and Technological Advice (SBSTTA). Furthermore, in the same Decision, the CBD Conference of the Parties called for the development of training materials on the use of traditional knowledge to be included in the description and identification of EBSAs. A training manual on this topic was produced and presented to SBSTTA at its 20th meeting in 2016.[71,72] The CBD training manual refers to full, effective and meaningful participation, and states that there are several reasons why participation of IPLCs in the EBSA description process has been thus far challenging. Amongst these reasons are that providing full and effective participation is time consuming in that sufficient time will need to be scheduled for building relationships with communities, gaining prior informed consent, and collecting and applying traditional knowledge. Another reason is that many Indigenous peoples and local communities have limited resources for engaging in third party research projects or assessment work, providing traditional knowledge or travelling to workshops. Furthermore, communication barriers may arise from different languages spoken and styles of expression. From the above challenges, it becomes clear that simply inviting Indigenous peoples and local communities to participate in an EBSA workshop is not enough to achieve integration of traditional knowledge. This goal also requires that those compiling information related to the application of the EBSA criteria should actively arrange opportunities for meaningful IPLC participation.

Art 8(j) of the CBD obligates its Contracting Parties to "respect, preserve and maintain knowledge, innovations and practices of IPLCs embodying traditional lifestyles relevant for the conservation and sustainable use of biological diversity and promote their wider application with the approval and involvement of the holders of such knowledge, innovations and practices and encourage the equitable sharing of the benefits arising from the utilisation of such knowledge, innovations and practices." This art does not explicitly define traditional knowledge, but the so-called art 8(j) Working Group makes use of an informal working definition.[73]

Traditional knowledge and the rights of knowledge holders features prominently in another set of standards adopted by the CBD COP: "The Akwé: Kon Voluntary Guidelines for the Conduct of Cultural, Environmental and Social Impact Assessment regarding Developments Proposed to Take Place on, or which are Likely to Impact on, Sacred Sites and on Lands and Waters

71 UNEP/CBD/SBSTTA/20/INF/21: Training Manual on the Incorporation of Traditional Knowledge into the Description and Identification of EBSAs.

72 Clement Mulalap and others, n 21 at 5.

73 Clement Mulalap and others, n 21 at 5.

Traditionally Occupied or Used by Indigenous and Local Communities" (Akwé: Kon Voluntary Guidelines).[74] The Akwé: Kon Voluntary Guidelines, in building on art 8(j) of the CBD, aim to advise relevant entities on incorporating "cultural, environmental... and social considerations of IPLCs into new or existing impact-assessment procedures".

The international mandate for this endeavour is specified in many CBD COP decisions. Consistent with CBD art 8 (j) and Aichi Biodiversity Target 18 and together with decisions IX/20, X/29 and XI/17, COP called for a need to ensure the full, effective and meaningful participation of IPLCs and the integration of traditional knowledge into the EBSA description process.

In July 2021, the CBD released a draft of its newest ten-year global plan,[75] with non-binding duties for States. The fundamental difference between the biodiversity plan and the Paris Agreement is that binding commitments are a key component of the Paris Agreement. References to Indigenous participation and knowledge in the draft plan do not go much further than in the Aichi targets.[76]

In October 2021, representatives from nearly 200 countries met in Kunming, China in COP15 to finalise The Kunming Declaration and Framework.[77] The Declaration, as well as the IPBES last report acknowledge that IPLCs contribute to the conservation and sustainable use of biodiversity through the application of traditional knowledge, innovations and practices, and through their stewardship of biodiversity on their traditional lands and territories.

7 Contributions from Human Rights Law

The decisions of human rights bodies may be classified along a spectrum that goes from the more general and less demanding forms of participation to procedural requirements that give Indigenous peoples the ultimate power to

---

74 Decision adopted by the Conference of the Parties to the Convention on Biological Diversity at its seventh session, held in Kuala Lumpur, Malaysia, from 9 February to 20 February and 27 February 2004, Annex, UNEP/CBD/COP/DEC/VII/16 (13 Apr. 2004).

75 Convention on Biological Diversity, 'A new global framework for managing nature through 2030:firstdetaileddraftagreementdebuts' <www.cbd.int/article/draft-1-global-biodiversity-framework> last accessed 17 August 2022.

76 Convention on Biological Diversity, 'A new global framework for managing nature through 2030:firstdetaileddraftagreementdebuts' <www.cbd.int/article/draft-1-global-biodiversity-framework> last accessed 17 August 2021.

77 Kunming Declaration, <www.cbd.int/doc/c/df35/4b94/5e86e1ee09bc8c7d4b35aaf0/kunmingdeclaration-en.pdf> last accessed 17 August 2022.

decide on certain matters. Along this spectrum, four main types of participatory model that have been concretely applied by human rights bodies can be identified. These are: political rights; formal standards of participation; the paradigm of effective participation; and the FPIC.[78]

The first and lighter conceptualisation of participatory rights is one in which general political rights to participate democratically by the vote to influence public decision-making is deemed sufficient to satisfy the conditions for public participation in environmental matters. In its decision concerning the case *G. and E. v. Norway* of 1984, the European Commission of Human Rights has spelled out the criteria for this model of participation.[79] In the second strand of decisions, participatory rights are valued as a fundamental step in the fulfillment of other rights. However, the mechanism to assess whether the consultation of interested groups has occurred is merely formal, just the existence of a legal framework on consultation is considered sufficiently adequate to fulfill the procedural requirements of participation.

An example of this formal approach is the position adopted by the ILO supervisory mechanism in relation to the ILO No 169 on Indigenous and tribal peoples. Art 6 of the Convention establishes some requirements for consultation to take place. This must be done in good faith, should be culturally appropriate and should be carried out with the aim "of achieving agreement or consent". Although participation and consultation have been framed as the "cornerstone" of the ILO No. 169, the requirement of achieving consent has never been interpreted by the ILO Committee as implying an obligation to obtain consent before the initiation of any project. The Committee has concluded in two reports on Colombia adopted in 2001, that although the failure to consult with Indigenous people was in breach of ILO No. 169, consent is to be considered mainly as an objective of consultation, and does not represent a requirement in itself.[80] Moreover, analysis of the Committee usually stops at the acknowledgment that a legal framework on consultation has been adopted nationally, thus falling short of any consideration of the effectiveness of these

---

78 Federica Cittadino, 'The Public Interest to Environmental Protection and Indigenous Peoples' Rights: Procedural Rights to Participation and Substantive Guarantees' in Eva Lohse and Margherita Poto (eds), *Participatory Rights in the Environmental Decision-Making Process and the Implementation of the Aarhus Convention: a Comparative Perspective* (Duncker & Humblot 2015).

79 European Commission of Human Rights, *G. and E. v Norway*, Judgment (29 August 1990) Application no. 11701/85.

80 See Reports on Colombia: Central Unitary Workers' Union (CUT), Colombian Medical Trade Union Association, para 59; Central Unitary Workers' Union (CUT), para 77.

mechanisms.[81] A third tendency in the spectrum of international decisions on Indigenous rights is recognisable in the jurisprudence of the Human Rights Committee, which is the supervisory body of the International Covenant on Civil and Political Rights, and of the Inter-American Court of Human Rights, which oversees the correct application of the American Convention on Human Rights.

Regarding Indigenous participation in public decision-making affecting the environment, these bodies go beyond merely acknowledging the existence of participatory mechanisms to look at their effectiveness. The contribution of the Inter-American Court and Commission in the *Marie and Carrie Dann v. US and Sarayaku v. Ecuador* cases is significant in this respect.[82] Drawing from the *Saramaka v. Suriname* case, the Court requires States to carry out consultations "in accordance with (...) customs and traditions", thus operationalising the requirement of cultural appropriateness.[83] In the *Dann* case, this requirement translates into the need to ensure that the representatives of Indigenous peoples should have a clear mandate from the group affected and should be adequately involved in the decision-making process. The Commission in the Dann case also insisted on the need to ensure informed participation.

In the *Sarayaku case*, in responding to Ecuador's arguments that political participation of Indigenous peoples has been guaranteed by the State, the Court recalled the requirements elaborated in *Saramaka*, consultations must be in good faith, through culturally appropriate procedures and with the objective of reaching an agreement. Furthermore, IPLCs must be consulted, in accordance with their own traditions and at the early stages of a development or investment plan. Furthermore, the Court affirmed that the obligation to consult Indigenous peoples at any time their rights may be affected is a general obligation of international law that has been consolidated beyond treaty provisions.

The Court additionally emphasised the difference between consultation and participation, while concluding that both are mandatory requirements. It seems that while consultation is an *ad hoc* process that may be activated in cases where Indigenous rights are affected by particular decisions, participation requires well-established procedures that Indigenous peoples should have access to. The Court said that participatory requirements have become

81 Federica Cittadino (2015) n 78 at 17.

82 IACtHR, *Marie and Carrie Dann v United States*, Judgment, 27 December 2002, Report no.75/02 case no. 11.400; IACtHR, *the Kichwa Indigenous People of Sarayaku v. Ecuador*, Judgment, 27 June 2012, Report no.75/02 case no. 12.465.

83 IACtHR, *Saramaka v. Suriname*, Judgment, 28 November 2007, Series C No. 172.

obligatory for Ecuador since the entry into force of the ILO No. 169. In para 167 the Court said that the involvement of Indigenous people must occur in a timely manner, meaning from the very beginning of the decision-making process. Consultation must be conducted in good faith and with the aim of achieving an agreement. Consultation must be informed, which could also imply that an EIA should be carried out beforehand. The Court, therefore, derived participatory rights from an extensive interpretation of the American Convention in light of the ILO No. 169.[84]

At the far end of the participation spectrum, it is possible to recognise a fourth tendency in which consent, rather than being interpreted as a mere objective of consultation, becomes a requirement of effective participation. This trend is transversal to the decisions of several human rights bodies. In its General Recommendation No. 23 of 1997 on Indigenous peoples, the Committee on the Elimination of Racial Discrimination condemns the expropriation of traditional lands if obtained without FPIC of Indigenous peoples. This is the first, though implicit, international reference to consent as an essential component of Indigenous participation, it establishes the duty for States to obtain the meaningful consent of Indigenous peoples whenever Indigenous rights are affected.

Consent must be interpreted in a theological sense as a prerequisite for ensuring the very survival of Indigenous peoples. This often depends on the possibility for Indigenous groups to have access to traditional land and resources. In this sense, therefore, survival may be linked to a form of economic self-determination of Indigenous peoples. The Human Rights Committee has endorsed this approach in *Poma Poma v. Peru*[85] where it explicitly affirmed that for participation to be effective it requires not mere consultation but the FPIC of the members of the community.

The Saramaka decision was adopted a few months after the adoption of the UN Declaration on Indigenous Peoples. Participation has emerged as a collective interest, although in the AC it has often been conceptualised as a classical human right to be exercised by individuals or alternatively by a group of individuals sharing common interests. Since the decision of the Inter-American Court in *Mayagna* (Sumo) *Awas Tingi v. Nicaragua*,[86] Indigenous land rights have been conceived as collective rights, a communal form of property. This

84 Federica Cittadino (2015) n 78 at 17.

85 HRC, *Poma Poma v. Peru*, Judgment, Communication No. 1457/2006 UN Doc CCPR/C/95/D/1457/2006(27 March 2009).

86 IACtHR, *Case of the Mayagna Sumo Awas Tingi Community v Nicaragua*, Judgment, 31 August 2001, case No. 11, 577.

element is further confirmed by the UN Declaration on Indigenous Peoples, with the Preamble explicitly referring to collective rights in para 23. This is also confirmed by the fact that all Indigenous rights concerning land are granted to Indigenous peoples as such, as opposed to indigenous individuals.

As regards self-determination as a legitimating factor of Indigenous peoples' occupation of a certain land/landscape/territory, this implies that they do not have to provide evidence of being a part of an environmental non-governmental organisation (ENGO) in order to be entitled to participate in environmental decision-making. This is crucial, since participatory rights – seen as instrumental to legal standing in cases of liability – are usually granted to ENGOs on behalf of individuals who have suffered harm.[87] Therefore, the Indigenous peoples' participatory rights are not connected to any external recognition of their status, instead they are closely linked to the these peoples' self-determination and ultimately their discretionary power in evaluating whether they regard themselves as indigenous.

Judgment *Llaka Honhat against Argentina* issued in December 2020 by the Inter-American Court of Human Rights[88] mentions that FPIC and effective communication is needed. But, para 179 states that it may be pertinent – in relation to the right to consultation – to distinguish between the maintenance or improvement of existing infrastructure and the execution of new projects or public works. Furthermore, it adds that activities activities undertaken with the purpose of only maintaining or improving public works do not always require the intervention of prior consultation procedures. Siano and Clérico affirm that this distinction between maintenance of existing infrastructure and the execution of new projects may work contrary to the situation of this collective group in a state of structural inequality.[89]

8 Analysis of Participation Provisions in the BBNJ Draft

The current revised BBNJ draft text does not provide for any guidance on how holders of relevant traditional knowledge will be identified or designated or how to ensure that these holders are legitimate. This may be left to a later stage,

87 Margherita Poto (2016) n 58 at 13.

88 IACtHR, *Llaka Honhat Association (Our Land) v. Argentina*, Judgment, 6 February 2020, Series C No. 420.

89 Martín Aldao and Laura Clérico, 'El caso Lhaka Honhat vs. Argentina y las tendencias de su interamericanización' in E. Ferrer Mac-Gregor/Mariela Morales Antoniazzi/R. Flores Pantoja (coords), *Instituto de Estudios Constitucionales del Estado de Querétaro* (2021).

once the BBNJ instrument enters into force, perhaps through the work of a subsidiary body established by the COP to the BBNJ instrument under art 48 (4) (d). It is notable that the number of delegations that have voiced support in the IGC for substantive references to traditional knowledge and its holders has grown as the IGC has progressed, swelling beyond the initial Pacific Small Island Developing States, to gaining the support of the Group of 77 and China (representing over 130 developing countries), numerous developed countries, and observers. Indeed, there is currently no delegation calling for the universal deletion of references to traditional knowledge in the BBNJ instrument.[90]

An analysis of the BBNJ Treaty Draft[91] shows that in the Preamble an aspiration "to achieve universal participation" has been declared. In art 1 where the terms are defined, "Strategic environmental assessment" is said to include:

> the carrying out of public participation and consultations and the taking into account of the environmental report and the results of the public participation and consultations in a plan or programme.

This seems to include Cittadino's legal criteria 2 and 3.

Following this line of thought, art 34 in Section IV entitled "Environmental Impact Assessment" states that:

> States Parties shall ensure early notification to stakeholders about planned activities under their jurisdiction or control and effective, time-bound opportunities for stakeholder participation throughout the environmental impact assessment process, including through the submission of comments, before a decision is made as to whether to proceed with the activity.

Although the art states "before a decision is made as to whether to proceed with the activity", there is no direct reference to obtaining FPIC, which would be preferable, taking into account the decisions of the Inter-American Court of Human Rights and the four types of participatory models previously studied.

Section 2 art 34 enumerates stakeholders. All the Section is between brackets, which means that this is not the definite version. However, some possible stakeholders, such as IPLCs, scientists and affected parties remain between

90 Clement Mulalap and others n 21 at 5.

91 Available at <www.un.org/bbnj/node/391> last accessed 17 August 2022.

double brackets. The classical stakeholders – international organisations and NGOs – remain without double brackets:

> [2. Stakeholders in this process include potentially affected States, where those can be identified, [in particular adjacent coastal States] [, indigenous peoples and local communities with relevant traditional knowledge in adjacent coastal States,] relevant global, regional, subregional and sectoral bodies, non-governmental organisations, the general public, academia [, scientific experts] [, affected parties,] [adjacent communities and organisations that have special expertise or jurisdiction] [, interested and relevant stakeholders] [, and those with existing interests in an area].]

Of course, it would be essential that IPLCs be included as stakeholders for their rights to be totally guaranteed.

Section 3 art 34 then states that "Public notification and consultation shall be transparent and inclusive." A reference to "active involvement" as employed in the WFD and MSFD, which has proved to be effective, would be recommended.

In addition to this, in Part V, titled "Capacity building and transfer of marine technology", art 42 establishes that one of the objectives of this Part is to: "Enable inclusive and effective participation in the activities undertaken under this Agreement."

If we look up the words "traditional knowledge" in the Draft, art 5 which establishes the principles that the States Parties shall follow to achieve the objectives of this Agreement, states that, still in brackets, that one of the principles is:

> (i) The use of the best available [science] [scientific information and relevant traditional knowledge of indigenous peoples and local communities].

Art 10 bis states that traditional knowledge held by IPLCs associated with MGRs in areas beyond national jurisdiction shall only be accessed with the FPIC or approval and involvement of these IPLCs.

Moreover, art 16 under Part III titled "Measures such as area-based management tools, including marine protected areas" establishes as regards identification of MPAs that:

> Areas requiring protection through the establishment of area-based management tools, including marine protected areas, shall be identified

> on the basis of the best available [science] [scientific information and relevant traditional knowledge of indigenous peoples and local communities], the precautionary [approach] [principle] and an ecosystem approach.

As regards consultation on and assessment of MPAs proposals, art 18 states that consultations shall include IPLCs with relevant traditional knowledge, the scientific community, civil society and other relevant stakeholders.

In relation to EIAs, the relevant traditional knowledge of IPLCs may be used to define the scope of these impacts, as described by art 31 already between brackets. Art 32 imposes a duty to use the best available scientific information and relevant traditional knowledge of IPLCs when evaluating impacts in EIAs.

Art 49 provides for the creation of a Scientific and Technical Body:

> ... which shall be composed of experts, taking into account the need for multidisciplinary expertise [, including expertise in relevant traditional knowledge of indigenous peoples and local communities], gender balance and equitable geographical representation.

In order to achieve an effective participation of IPLCs in the topics governed by the BBNJ Agreement, it is essential that the brackets are eliminated and IPLCs become members of the Scientific and Technical Body.

9 Conclusions

In this chapter, an analysis was made of the provisions of the BBNJ Draft Agreement through the lenses of three legal criteria to evaluate participation: inclusiveness; the influence of participatory experiences on final decisions; and the level of accountability of final decision-makers. Moreover, provisions in the AC and the WFD and MSFD were also analysed.

A paradigm based on putting the ocean at center stage, which involves a protagonist role of the IPLCs has led this chapter. The goals of environmental participation are achieved when participation implies co-negotiation and co-decision making during the entire process of the environmental project at issue, not just consultation.

In particular, as regards IPLCs' participation, another classification concerning four types of participation within the human right law was explained. The requirement of IPLCs' FPIC before authorising an activity is the most demanding form of participation, which gives Indigenous peoples the ultimate say in decision making. FPIC should be taken into account in this Draft Agreement within the Law of the Sea, not only when IPLCs convey traditional knowledge, but also when they express their opinion in an EIA as stakeholders. IPLCs' participation as stakeholders in EIAs still remains between brackets in the Draft; these brackets should be eliminated in order to provide for their effective participation.

The active involvement of all affected parties established in the WFD and MSFD has been highlighted as efficient as regards environmental participation. The Draft mentions the adjectives "inclusive, transparent and effective". The "active involvement" as mentioned in the Directive should be included in the Draft.

Finally, the Draft provides for the creation of a Scientific and Technical Body, however, the participation of IPLCs in this Body remains between brackets. These brackets should be eliminated in order to guarantee an active involvement of IPLCs in the governance of conservation and sustainable use of BBNJ.

Acknowledgements

I acknowledge the Humboldt Centre at Bayreuth University for awarding me a fellowship and financing my research stage at Bayreuth hosted by Dr. Prof. Eva Lohse, one result of which is the writing of this chapter.

Bibliography

Aldao M and Clérico L, 'Igualdad multidemensional (redistribución/reconocimiento /partcipación) para revisitar la jurisprudencia de la Corte IDH sobre pueblos indígenas' in Ferrer Mac-Gregor E, Morales Antoniazzi M and Flores Pantoja R (eds), *El caso Lhaka Hohnat vs. Argentina y las tendencias de su interamericanización* (Instituto de Estudios Constitucionales del Estado de Querétaro 2021) 53–91.

Barnes R, 'The Law of the Sea and the Integrated Regulation of the Oceans' (2012) 27(4) The International Journal of Marine and Coastal Law 859.

Berros V, 'Defending Rivers: Vilcabamba in the South of Ecuador' (2017) 6 RCC Perspectives: Transformations in Environment and Society 37.

Cittadino F, 'Public Interest to Environmental Protection and Indigenous Peoples' Rights: Procedural Rights to Participation and Substantive Guarantees' in Lohse E and Poto M (eds), *Participatory Rights in the Environmental Decision-Making Process and the Implementation of the Aarhus Convention: A Comparative Perspective* (Duncker & Humblot 2015) 75–90.

Cittadino F, 'Public Participation in the Water Framework Directive (WFD): A Contribution to Deliberative Democracy?' in Lohse E and Poto M (eds), *Best Practices for the Protection of Water by Law* (Berliner Wissenschafts-Verlag 2017) 45–62.

De Santo E and others, 'Stuck in the Middle with You (and Not Much Time Left): The Third Intergovernmental Conference on Biodiversity Beyond National Jurisdiction' (2020) 117 Marine Policy 103957.

Druel E and Gjerde K M, 'Sustaining Marine Life Beyond Boundaries: Options for an Implementing Agreement for Marine Biodiversity Beyond National Jurisdiction Under the United Nations Convention on the Law of the Sea' (2014) 49 Marine Policy 90.

'*Global Assessment Report on Biodiversity and Ecosystem Services of the Intergovernmental Science – Policy Platform on Biodiversity and Ecosystem Services.*' Brondizio E and others (eds), Chapter 6 PBES Secretariat 2019.

Harden-Davies H and others, 'Rights of Nature: Perspectives for Global Ocean Stewardship' (2021) 122 Marine Policy 104059.

Lehmann M and others, 'Ejection of Marine Microplastics by Raindrops: a Computational and Experimental Study (2021) 1(18) Microplastics and Nanoplastics.

Lohse E, Parola G and Poto M, 'Introductory Remarks on the Idea and the Purpose of a German-Italian Dialogue on Participation in Environmental Decision Making' in Lohse E and Poto M (eds), *Participatory Rights in the Environmental Decision-Making Process and the Implementation of the Aarhus Convention: A Comparative Perspective* (Duncker & Humblot 2015) 9–14.

Macpherson E J, *Indigenous Water Rights in Law and Regulation* (Cambridge, 2019).

Mendenhall E and De Santo E, 'A Soft Treaty, Hard to Reach: The Second Inter-Governmental Conference for Biodiversity Beyond National Jurisdiction' (2019) 108 Marine Policy 103664.

Mulalap C Y and others, 'Traditional Knowledge and the BBNJ Instrument' (2020) 122 Marine Policy 104103.

Nursey-Bray M and Jacobson C, ''Which way?': The Contribution of Indigenous Marine Governance' (2014) 6(1) Australian Journal of Maritime & Ocean Affairs 27.

Poto M, 'Participatory Rights of Indigenous Peoples: The Virtuous Example of the Arctic Region' (2016) 28(2) Environmental Law and Management 81.

Poto M,' 'The Law of the Sea and Its Institutions: Today's Hermeneutic Approach and Some Suggestions for an Ocean-Centred Governance Model' in Johansen E, Busch S and Jakobsen I (eds), *The Law of the Sea and Climate Change: Solutions and Constraints* (Cambridge University Press 2020) 354–373.

Poto M and Fornabaio L, 'Participation as the Essence of Good Governance: Some General Reflections and a Case Study on the Arctic Council' (2017) 8 Arctic Review on Law and Politics 139.

Radovich V, 'Governance of Oil and Gas Exploration and Exploitation at Sea: Towards Coastal Marine Biodiversity Preservation' in Couzens E and others (eds), *Protecting Forest and Marine Biodiversity: The Role of Law* (Edward Elgar 2017) 227–250.

Ribeiro C M, 'South Atlantic Perspectives on the Future International Legally Binding Instrument under the LOSC on Conservation and Sustainable Use of BBNJ' (2017) 32(4) The International Journal of Marine and Coastal Law 733.

Te Aho L, 'Indigenous Challenges to Enhance Freshwater Governance and Management in Aotearoa New Zealand – The Waikato River Settlement' (2009) 20(5–6) Journal of Water Law 285.

Vierros M K and others, 'Considering Indigenous Peoples and Local Communities in Governance of the Global Ocean Commons' (2020) 119 Marine Policy 104039.

Wolfrum R and Matz N, 'The Interplay of the United Convention on the Law of the Sea and the Convention on Biological Diversity' (2000) 4 Max Planck Yearbook of United Nations Law 445.

CHAPTER 14

The Law of Multilateral Development Banks

Sustainability and Participation in International Development Finance

Michael Riegner

1 Introduction: Context and Argument

The current law of multilateral development finance contains relatively specific legal norms on sustainability and participation. These norms have developed incrementally since the 1990s in the internal administrative law of the multilateral development banks (MDBs), especially in environmental and social safeguard standards enforced by quasijudicial accountability mechanisms. The emergence, application and interrelationship of these standards is shaped by the institutional and geopolitical context in which the law of MDBs evolves.

In the institutional context, sustainability and participation standards function as conditionality on recipient states, reflecting the shifting balance between sovereignty, international public authority, and individual rights in global governance. The geopolitical context is marked by the asymmetric, triangular relationship between donor countries, MDBs, and recipient states, by increasing politicization and contestation of juridified global governance by civil society and rising powers, and by the shift towards a multipolar multilateralism, exemplified by counterinstitutionalizations like the Asian Infrastructure and Investment Bank (AIIB).[1]

In these contexts, sustainability and participation standards (SPS) respond to multiple concerns and serve multiple functions. For MDBs, they improve outcomes, provide legitimacy, attract funding, and highlight institutional expertise in increasingly competitive global financial markets. For donors, they satisfy domestic constituencies, exert leverage over recipients, diffuse norms and values, and help control international bureaucracies. For recipient governments, juridified SPS make conditionality more predictable, contribute to domestic capacity building, contain local resistance, and deflect criticism away from national governments. For projectaffected populations, they

1 On the changing contexts, see Philipp Dann and Michael Riegner, 'The World Bank's Environmental and Social Safeguards and the evolution of global order' (2019) 32(3) Leiden Journal of International Law 537.

provide additional avenues for legal contestation, internationalize local conflicts, and provide a focal point for transnational advocacy and solidarity.[2]

While these factors explain the popularity and proliferation of SPS over the past three decades, they should not belie serious problems in the MDBS' approach to sustainability and participation. This approach has long been based on functionalist and managerial logic, driven by faith in disinterested administration by bureaucratic experts objectively applying technical standards.[3] In this logic, participation is functionalized for, and ultimately subordinated to, a technically determined concept of sustainability that does not acknowledge the political tradeoffs it implies. Under this managerial conception, participation is thus unable to realize its emancipatory and legitimatory potential. To realize this potential, MDBS need to harness their expertise to enable inclusive, informed and contextsensitive decision-making in multilevel procedures.

To develop this argument, the chapter proceeds in four steps: It first analyses the legal evolution of sustainability (Section 2) and participation (Section 3), respectively, distinguishing different stages of development and conceptions. It then turns to the interrelationship of sustainability and participation (Section 4), discussing conflicts and contradictions, and the ways in which MDBS seek to reach convergence. The chapter concludes with some critical thoughts on the potential and future development of SPS in the law of MDBS (Section 5).

The focus will largely be on the World Bank Group,[4] whose system of safeguards and Inspection Panel have become a global model emulated by many other MDBS. In addition, the World Bank's SPS received a thorough overhaul in 2016 and thus represent the current legal state of the art. Consequently, while there is some variation compared to other MDBS, the Bank still serves as a good proxy for developments in the law of MDBS more generally.[5]

---

2 For an overview, see Giedre Jokubauskaite, 'The World Bank Environmental and Social Framework in a wider realm of public international law' (2019) 32(3) Leiden Journal of International Law 457.

3 On managerialism and functionalism, see generally Jan Klabbers, 'The Transformation of International Organizations Law' (2015) 26(1) The European Journal of International Law (EJIL) 9; Martti Koskenniemi, 'The Fate of Public International Law' (2007) 70 Modern Law Review 1.

4 This includes the International Bank for Reconstruction and Development IBRD, the International Development Association IDA, the International Finance Corporation IFC, the Multilateral Investment Guarantee Agency MIGA, and the International Centre for Settlement of Investment Disputes, cf. Maurizio Ragazzi, 'World Bank Group' [2014] *Max Planck encyclopedia of public international law*: MPEPIL online.

5 On harmonization and variation among MDBS SPS, see generally Makane M Mbengue and Stéphanie de Moerloose, 'Multilateral Development Banks and Sustainable Development: On

2 Sustainability as Procedural Risk Management

Sustainability has proliferated in international law since the 1990s and has become more inclusive as a legal concept in the process. Initially centred around ecological concerns and intergenerational justice, it has come to encompass aspects of social protection and the longterm viability of economic development.[6] This has blurred distinctions with other concepts, such as human and social rights and good governance. The UN's 2015 "Sustainable Development Goals" now list 17 goals and 169 targets, ranging from poverty reduction, health and education to environmental protection and climate change to sustainable cities and "peace, justice and strong institutions".[7] This inclusive approach has also been attractive to MDBs like the World Bank, which prefers to frame issues in terms of sustainability rather than as human rights concerns due to its nonpolitical mandate.[8] In the following analysis, "sustainability" thus refers to both literal uses of the term and a range of substantive concerns related to the ecological, social and economic longterm viability of projects and policies promoted by MDBs. The following subsections first trace the evolution of sustainability standards in MDB law (2.1.) and then analyse current conceptions of sustainability as risk management (2.2).

2.1 *Three Stages of Development*

Sustainability did not come naturally to the law of MDBs.[9] It emerged incrementally, in a process that can be divided into three stages: evolutive interpretation of economic mandates; emergence of enforceable safeguard policies in secondary law in the 1990s; and reformed, secondgeneration safeguards as the most recent step.

At the outset, the founding treaties of established MDBs conveyed an economic mandate to institutions that largely left social and ecological concerns

Emulation, Fragmentation and a Common Law of Sustainable Development' (2017) 10(2) Law and Development Review. By focusing on MDBs, this chapter thematically excludes the IMF, whose approach to sustainability is more focused on the long-term viability of public debt.

6 For an overview, see Virginie Barral, 'Sustainable Development in International Law: Nature and Operation of an Evolutive Legal Norm' (2012) 23(2) EJIL 377; Ulrich Beyerlin, 'Sustainable Development' [2013] *Max Planck encyclopedia of public international law*: MPEPIL online.

7 UNGA, Resolution adopted by the General Assembly on 25 September 2015, 'Transforming Our World: The 2030 Agenda for Sustainable Development', 21 October 21 UN Doc A/RES/70/1.

8 For an overview, see David Freestone, *The World Bank and sustainable development* (Martinus Nijhoff Publ 2013).

9 On the law of development cooperation in general, the law of the World Bank in particular, see Philipp Dann, *The Law of Development Cooperation* (Cambridge Univ. Pr. 2013).

to national law. The World Bank and IMF's Articles of Agreement of 1944 aim at economic development, promotion of trade and investment, and monetary stability, and they explicitly exclude noneconomic or "political" considerations from loan decisions.[10] The European Bank for Reconstruction and Development (EBRD), founded in 1991, is mandated to "foster the transition towards open market economies".[11] Only much later did "sustainable development" appear in the mandate provisions of MDBs, namely in the founding treaties of New Development Bank (NDB) and the Asian Infrastructure and Investment Bank (AIIB) founded in 2014 and 2015, respectively, by emerging powers like China and India.[12] Much earlier, however, sustainability appeared as an economic concern in the law of other MDBs. At the project or program level, legal requirements sought to ensure the longterm viability of an investment. At country level, they were concerned with the ability of the recipient to pay back the loan, which translated into increasingly complex debt sustainability assessments.[13] In contrast, social and ecological requirements, if any, were initially left to the law of the individual borrowing countries, which thus retained their sovereignty in this regard. This interpretation of mandates evolved first with regard to the substance of projects, which came to embrace "basic needs" and social issues like health and education especially during the 1970s.

During the 1980s and early 1990s, the second step involved the incremental juridification and centralization of sustainability standards in the secondary law of the MDBs.[14] Apart from the increasing recognition of sustainability in wider international law, a main reason for this change was increasing pressure

10 art I IBRD/IDA/IMF Articles of Agreement.

11 art I EBRD.

12 NDB art 1 The Bank shall mobilize resources for infrastructure and sustainable development projects in BRICS and other emerging economies and developing countries …; AIIB Article 1 Purpose 1. The purpose of the Bank shall be to: (i) foster sustainable economic development, create wealth and improve infrastructure connectivity in Asia by investing in infrastructure and other productive sectors; and (ii) promote regional cooperation and partnership …

13 Michael Riegner, 'Legal frameworks and general principles for indicators in sovereign debt restructuring' [2016] Yale Journal of International Law Online 141–175.

14 On the evolution see Laurence Boisson de Chazournes, 'Partnerships, Emulation, and Coordination Toward the Emergence of a Droit Commun in the Field of Development Finance' in Hassane Cissé, Daniel Bradlow and Benedict Kingsbury (eds), *International Financial Institutions and Global Legal Governance: The World Bank Legal Review Vol. 3* (World Bank 2012); Benedict Kingsbury, 'Operational Policies of International Institutions as Part of the Lawmaking Process' in Guy Goodwin-Gill and Stefan Talmon (eds), *The reality of international law: Essays in honour of Ian Brownlie* (1st edn. Clarendon 1999).

to address social and ecological degradation caused by MDBfunded "problem projects". A prominent example was the Narmada Dam in India, which displaced 140,000 people and is often cited as a turning point for the World Bank and the wider world of MDBs.[15] National law seemed inadequate to handle these cases, and civil society and Western donors pressured MDBs to incorporate social and environmental standards into their internal law. In response, they turned to a strategy of legal reform. The World Bank, in particular, decided to overhaul and formalize its policy framework.[16] Over time, a total of eleven social and environmental "safeguards" were enacted and provided protection against particular risks (e.g. resettlement) and for particular groups (e.g. indigenous people) or for specific resources (eg forests, natural habitats). Besides, an independent accountability mechanism, the Inspection Panel, was established to hear noncompliance claims by projectaffected individuals. This quasijudicial enforcement mechanism further hardened the standards.[17] Other MDBs emulated the World Bank's safeguards. By the 2000s, they had become the global standard for social and environmental sustainability in development finance. This left borrowing countries with little choice but to accept the standards, and safeguards even diffused into domestic law beyond MDB funded projects, especially with regard to sustainability standards.[18]

The third and current stage is marked by the World Bank's recent safeguards reform, which came into force in 2017. The reform consolidates the existing safeguards in a single "Environmental and Social Framework" (ESF) and seeks to strike a new balance between conflicting sustainability demands from donors, recipients and civil society. On one hand, the ESF broadens the notion of sustainability by introducing new standards on labour, biodiversity

---

15 Sreya Maitra, 'Development Induced Displacement: Issues of Compensation and Resettlement – Experiences from the Narmada Valley and Sardar Sarovar Project' (2009) 10(02) Japanese Journal of Political Science 191. Generally, Irene Hadiprayitno, *Hazard or right?* (Intersentia 2009).

16 On the Bank's internal system of legal instruments, see Dann, *supra* note 3, at 187–92; also, comparing World Bank Safeguards to legal instruments in other MDBs; Jochen von Bernstorff and Philipp Dann, *Reforming the World Bank's Safeguards* (2013), 10–16; OP/BP 4.00–4.37. In addition, there were two legal safeguard policies on transborder rivers and disputed territories that are not affected by the current reform.

17 On the legal nature of the safeguards, see Giedre Jokubauskaite, 'The Legal Nature of the World Bank Safeguards' (2018) 51(1) VRÜ/WCL 78; Daniel D Bradlow and Andria N Fourie, 'The Operational Policies of the World Bank and the International Finance Corporation' (2013) 10(1) International Organizations Law Review 3.

18 Susan Park, 'The World Bank Group: Championing Sustainable Development Norms?' (2007) 13(4) Global Governance 535.

and climate change demanded by many donors and civil society. On the other, the new framework expands the possibilities for using national law instead of international standards where this leads to similar outcomes. This "use of country systems" is a concession to borrowing countries, especially strong ones like China, India or South Africa, and restores some of their shrinking sovereignty in the field of sustainability standards. This tension between an expanding international concept of sustainability and a partial return to national sovereignty and recipient "ownership" defines the current law of MDBs.[19]

2.2 *Sustainability as Procedural Risk Management*

The current legal substance of sustainability in IFI law can be exemplified by a closer look at the World Bank's 2017 ESF. The framework begins with an overarching "Vision for Sustainable Development", which commits the Bank to "environmental sustainability" and recognizes that "social development and inclusion are critical for … achieving sustainable development".[20] These principles are then fleshed out in 120 pages of policies and standards. Their legal substance is characterized by three core elements: proceduralization; an emphasis on technical expertise; and a relationship with neighbouring regimes of international law characterized by institutional fragmentation and substantive integration.

Proceduralization is evident in the central role that environmental and social impact assessments play in the Bank's approach to sustainability. The requirement that borrowers assess, avoid and mitigate specific environmental and social risks is a decisive procedural conditionality in the project preparation phase. This procedural approach owes much to the influence of US-American administrative law.[21] Environmental impact assessments (EIAs) were first introduced in the early 1990s after US-American environmental activists successfully pressured US Congress to make US contributions to the World Bank dependent on the introduction of environmental impact assessments. After Congress thus passed the so-called 'Pelosi'-amendment to an appropriations bill (proposed by Democratic Representative Nancy Pelosi), the Bank duly enacted such a safeguard policy (Operational Policy 4.01), which largely

19 On the ESF reform, see Dann and Riegner (n 1); María V C Ormaza and Franz C Ebert, 'The World Bank, human rights, and organizational legitimacy strategies: The case of the 2016 Environmental and Social Framework' (2019) 32(3) Leiden Journal of International Law 483.

20 ESF, Vision, para 2 and 3.

21 See generally Richard B Stewart, 'U.S. Administrative Law: A Model for Global Administrative Law?' (2005) 68 Law and Contemporary Problems 63.

followed the model of the US-American National Environmental Policy Act (NEPA) of 1969.[22]

Over time, the number and type of risks included in these assessments has expanded considerably. Since 2017, the ESF requires a comprehensive assessment of environmental and social risks. Environmental and Social Standard (ESS) 1 on "Assessment and Management of Environmental and Social Risks and Impacts" requires borrowers to "to assess the environmental and social risks and impacts of the project throughout the project lifecycle" and prepare "an adequate, accurate, and objective evaluation and presentation of the risks and impacts, prepared by qualified and experienced persons."[23] This assessment covers concerns related to working conditions and labour, pollution prevention and climate change, community health and safety, land acquisition and involuntary resettlement, biodiversity, indigenous peoples and cultural heritage, all fleshed out in subsequent ESS 2–8. It is important to note, however, that the applicable standards rarely impose hard substantive limits but rather focus on management, mitigation and compensation of adverse impacts. The new standard on climate change, for instance, does not cap greenhouse gases but only requires borrowers to estimate and account for carbon emissions. Biodiversity losses deemed unavoidable can be offset by compensation measures. Expropriation and displacement of projectaffected people remain permissible as long as they are adequately resettled and compensated.[24]

Related to this procedural approach is a strong reliance on technical expertise in the application of standards and definition of environmental and social risk. This expertise is provided to a considerable extent by the Bank's own expert bureaucracy, especially its safeguards specialists.[25] This is part of a broader institutional strategy as "knowledge bank", which sees the institution's comparative advantage not in its financial resources but in its advisory and analytical services.[26] Besides, the Bank requires national governments

---

22 Susan Park, *World Bank Group interactions with environmentalists* (Manchester University Press 2010); Ian Bowles and Cyril Kormos, 'The American Campaign for Environmental Reforms at the World Bank' (1999) 23 Fletcher Forum of World Affairs Journal 211.

23 ESF), 'Environmental and Social Standard 1: Assessment and Management of Environmental and Social Risks and Impacts', paras 23, 25.

24 See especially ESF, ESS 3 'Resource Efficiency and Pollution Prevention and Management', 5 'Land Acquisition,'Restrictions on Land Use and Involuntary Resettlement', 6 'Biodiversity Conservation and Sustainable Management of Living Natural Resources'.

25 On the practical implementation, see Independent Evaluation Group (IEG) 'Safeguards and Sustainability Policies in a Changing World' (WBG, Washington D.C. 2010).

26 See generally Teresa Kramarz and Bessma Momani, 'The World Bank as Knowledge Bank: Analyzing the Limits of a Legitimate Global Knowledge Actor' (2013) 30(4) Review of Policy Research 409; and on the legal aspects in particular, see Michael Riegner, 'Towards

to "retain independent specialists to carry out the environmental and social assessment" where projects are classified as "high" or "substantial risk", or where governments have "limited capacity" on their own.[27] Private sector projects especially at the IFC also draw largely on private industry expertise.[28] Bank technical experts and external consultants play a crucial role in advising national governments in the process of project formulation, the conduct of impact assessments, and the design of mitigation plans.[29]

In contrast, there is no legal requirement for the involvement of other international institutions or specialized agencies with particular expertise, such as UNEP, ILO or UN human rights bodies. Their expertise would be relevant to Bank projects since the safeguards draw on, or refer to, neighbouring regimes for environmental or social protection, such as the biodiversity convention, ILO labour standards or the rights of indigenous peoples. The Bank, however, pursues an autonomous approach to sustainability that promotes integration of regimes at the level of substance but remains fragmented at the inter-institutional level.[30]

Taken together, these three elements define a managerial approach to sustainability focused on riskmanagement and the institutional autonomy of the MDBs. How sustainability is concretized in specific projects largely depends on the outcomes of internationalized procedures which draw heavily on the expertise of specialists in MDB bureaucracies and technical consultants who apply global industry standards. In substance, sustainability is defined in terms of "risk" for certain environmental and social goods, rather than by hard ceilings or caps on emissions or social impacts.[31] This "managerial sustainability" is both complemented and counter-balanced by the legal approach to participation.

an international institutional law of information' (2015) 12(1) International Organizations Law Review 50.

27 ESS 1, para 25.

28 Leonard Seabrooke and Ole J Sending, 'Contracting development: managerialism and consultants in intergovernmental organizations' (2020) 27(4) Review of International Political Economy 802.

29 See ESS 1, paras 23 et seq.

30 On integration and fragmentation with regard to labour and human rights, see Ormaza and Ebert (n 19).

31 On risk management from a human rights perspective, see Radu Mares, 'Securing human rights through riskmanagement methods: Breakthrough or misalignment?' (2019) 32(3) Leiden Journal of International Law 517.

3 Participation as Procedural Right

"Participation" has been part of MDB discourse since the 1970s but has taken the shape of legal rights only since the 1990s. "Participatory development" was introduced with the basic needs approach in the 1970s and gained new traction with the good governance agenda of the 1990s. It denotes a development strategy that is less "top down" and more "bottom up" and includes a greater number of actors in development planning and project design, ranging from MDBs and governments to NGOs, affected groups, the general public and the private sector.[32]

Conceptually, "participation" is at least as multivalent as sustainability, and it encompasses a range of legal and nonlegal practices, policies, procedures and development objectives.[33] It is thus important to distinguish participation *practices* that do not establish legal obligations, from participation *rights* that entail individual or collective legal entitlements to participate in specific MDB procedures and projects (subsection 3.1.). On this basis, it is possible to identify three models of participation rights in the law on MDBs (3.2.). Doctrinally, these rights include a range of entitlements, including rights to access to information, to a hearing, to consultation, or, rarely, to codecision.[34] Terminologically, the World Bank seems to have shifted from "participation" to "stakeholder engagement", which is also the technical term used in its secondary law and covers the rights described above.[35]

3.1 *Participation Practices vs Rights*

From a legal perspective, many if not most invocations of participation do not establish legal obligations on the part of the MDBs, or even grant individual

---

32 Giles Mohan and Kristian Stokke, 'Participatory development and empowerment' (2000) 21(2) Third World Quarterly 247; Giles Mohan, 'Participatory Development: From Epistemological Reversals to Active Citizenship' (2007) 1(4) Geography Compass 779.

33 For an overview of participation in international institutional law, see Jochen v Bernstorff, 'New Responses to the Legitimacy Crisis of International Institutions: The Role of 'Civil Society' and the Rise of the Principle of Participation of 'The Most Affected' in International Institutional Law' (2021) 32(1) EJIL 125.

34 For different types, see Sanae Fujita, *The World Bank, Asian Development Bank and Human Rights* (Elgar 2013); David Hunter, 'International Law and Public Participation in Policymaking at the International Financial Institutions' in Daniel D Bradlow and David B Hunter (eds), *International financial institutions and international law* (Kluwer Law International 2010); Dennis Dijkzeul, 'Programs and the problems of participation' in Dennis Dijkzeul and Yves Beigbeder (eds), *Rethinking international organizations: Pathologies and promise* (Berghahn Books 2003).

35 ESS 10 'Stakeholder Engagement and Information Disclosure'.

rights to participate in specific procedures or projects. The founding treaties of MDBs do not mention participation by individuals or project-affected groups. Since the 1990s, the turn to participation spurred a flurry of participation *practices and procedures* at MDBs, encompassing anything from information and transparency initiatives to opinion surveys and electronic "user feedback", public consultations and expert hearings as well as strengthening democratic procedures at the national level.[36] These procedural practices respond to multiple concerns ranging from institutional legitimacy to economic efficiency and control of corruption, and they are compatible with a range of political ideologies. In most cases, they are not enforceable legal requirements, as the Bank's Inspection Panel and comparable accountability mechanisms only have a mandate to review compliance with specific sources of secondary law, in the case of the World Bank the safeguard Operational Policies or now the ESF.

In the safeguards enshrined in secondary law of MDBs, participation has acquired a more specific and narrow meaning focused on enforceable legal rights to take part in concrete decision-making procedures.[37] They emerged in parallel with sustainability requirements in secondary law and are enforceable in the quasi-judicial proceedings at the Inspection Panel. Over time, we can distinguish three stages, or models, in the evolution of participation rights in the law of MDBs: a sovereignty-based model, a model based on affectedness and a cosmopolitan model.

3.2 *Three Models of Participation Rights*

The initial model of participation was sovereignty-based and channelled participation through national law and domestic representative processes. The founding treaties of MDBs reserve the right to propose projects to national governments and assign the competence to approve project proposals and secondary law to the political organs, like the Board of Directors of the World Bank. Primary law does not foresee the direct participation of citizens or project-affected groups in institutional decision-making procedures but assumes that national populations are represented by their diplomatic

36 For an overview, see eg World Bank, Ghazala Mansuri and Vijayendra Rao, *Localizing development* (World Bank 2013); World Bank, *Guidance Note on Multistakeholder Engagement*, June 2009, available at <https://documents1.worldbank.org/curated/en/319671468336604958/pdf/492200BR0SecM2101Official0Use0Only1.pdf> last accessed 3 August 2022.

37 For a general discussion of the theoretical background, see Francesca Bignami, 'Theories of civil society and Global Administrative Law: the case of the World Bank and international development' in Sabino Cassese (ed), *Research handbook on global administrative law* (Elgar 2016).

representatives in MDB organs. At this level, participation rights thus depend on national law, which may foresee the direct involvement of affected individuals in national administrative procedures and national processes of democratic decision-making and representation. Such participation rights, however, differ widely from country to country. They may be effective in democratic states with participatory procedures, as illustrated by the influence of civil society on the World Bank via US Congress.[38] Yet the US is in many ways an exceptional case, and in most other cases MDB decision-making remains dominated by executive actors, far removed from those affected by the decisions to fund a specific project.

The second model internationalizes participation rights based on affectedness by MDBfinanced projects. Secondary law thus requires borrowers to inform persons and populations affected by a proposed project and involve them in the process of assessment and decision-making. This model evolved partly in response to these legitimacy concerns, partly as a reaction to the dysfunctions and cognitive deficits of closed decision-making processes in complex environments. Beginning in the 1990s, the environmental and social safeguards also opened up administrative procedures to outside stakeholders and laid down specific rights to information, consultation and hearings of those affected by concrete projects. Following the Pelosi-amendment, the safeguards required not only the internal preparation of EIAs, but also their publication to enable affected populations to take note of and contest the assessments. After the Narmada dam disaster, the Bank enacted a safeguard policy on resettlement, which for the first time stipulated individual rights to a hearing for all affected, and for compensation of those subject to resettlement. Another safeguard introduced a requirement for free, prior and informed consultation of indigenous populations.[39] The ESF has introduced a separate standard, ESS 10 on "Stakeholder Engagement and Information Disclosure", which established a general right to "meaningful consultation" for all project-affected "stakeholders". Another standard, ESS7, even requires free, prior and informed *consent* from indigenous peoples if a project affects their land or results in their resettlement.[40]

38 Kristina Daugirdas, 'Congress Underestimated: The Case of the World Bank' (2013) 107(3) AJIL 517.

39 Kingsbury, n 14.

40 ESS 7 'Indigenous Peoples/Sub-Saharan African Historically Underserved Traditional Local Communities', paras 24 ff.; Margherita Brunori, 'Protecting access to land for indigenous and nonindigenous communities: A new page for the World Bank?' (2019) 32(3) Leiden Journal of International Law 501.

The decisive feature of all these rights is that they are enforceable in the Inspection Panel established by the Bank's Board of Executive Directors in 1993. After the so-called Wapenhans report had detailed enforcement gaps in the Bank's existing standards in the Narmada project, member states discussed different accountability mechanisms: European countries initially favoured a strengthened internal evaluation function, but eventually followed an American proposal for more legalized and adversarial control based on the American model of judicial review.[41] The Inspection Panel subsequently grew into a quasijudicial review institution effectuating participation rights and the Bank's environmental and social accountability towards external individuals.[42] Together, the safeguards and the Inspection Panel create a system of "simple" participation rights in international institutional law; "simple" here refers to the source and rank of the rights, which is (secondary) international institutional law, and not human rights law, sometimes conceived as a quasi"-constitutional" source of participation rights.[43] This system of enforcement now faces readjustment as the new ESF increasingly allows use of country-systems – a trend whose effect on MDB accountability mechanisms has yet to be ascertained.[44]

While the safeguards limit participation *ratione personae* to those affected by a concrete project, and *ratione materiae* to an individual administrative procedure, the third model goes beyond these limitations and relies on what some have called "cosmopolitan" rights.[45] These rights are embodied in regimes on access to information like the World Bank's "Access to Information Policy", enacted in 2010 and emulated by other MDBs. These legal instruments are

---

41 Susan Park, 'Accountability as justice for the Multilateral Development Banks? Borrower opposition and bank avoidance to US power and influence', (2017) 3 *Review of International Political Economy* 1.

42 Andria Naudé Fourie, *The World Bank Inspection Panel Casebook* (Eleven International Publishing 2014); Andria Naudé Fourie, *The World Bank Inspection Panel and quasijudicial oversight* (2009).

43 On this category of rights, see generally Anne Peters, *Beyond human rights* (English edition, Cambridge Univ. Pr. 2016).

44 For possible scenarios see Cristina Passoni, Ariel Rosenbaum and Eleanor Vermunt, 'Empowering the Inspection Panel - The Impact of the World Bank's Safeguards Review' (2015); International Organizations Clinic at NYU School of Law, Gráinne de Búrca and others, 'The Changing Role of the World Bank Inspection Panel' (2014); International Organizations Clinic at NYU School of Law <http://chrgj.org/wp-content/uploads/2014/10/ChangingRoleoftheWorldBankIP_IOClinic.pdf> last accessed 3 August 2022; Dann and Riegner n 1.

45 Philipp Dann, 'Der Zugang zu Dokumenten im Recht der Weltbank' (2011) 44(3) Die Verwaltung 313.

modelled on national freedom of information laws and grant any individual the right to access documents and electronic information held by the international institution which is not on a list of exceptions. These exceptions do not limit access by subject matter, eg to environmental information, but rather protect personal data or documents on internal deliberations. Most importantly, access rights entitle any individual worldwide, irrespective of personal affectedness, to request information and enforce access before a specialized enforcement mechanism, the independent Access to Information Appeals Board in the case of the World Bank. In that sense, they are cosmopolitan rights.[46]

Access rights do not convey any additional rights to hearings, consultations or codecision, but may enhance the effectiveness of already existing participation rights guaranteed in the safeguards or national law. They provide individuals, project affected people, NGOs and the general public with an opportunity for public scrutiny of IFI activities beyond concrete projects, including budget finance, structural adjustment programs, or internal lawmaking processes. Their main thrust is to decentralize control over information otherwise concentrated in the hands of international bureaucracies. In doing so, they provide one precondition for processes of opinion formation, public pressure, political contestation and democratic deliberation at the national and international level.[47]

Overall, the MDBs thus adopt a more individualized, juridified and information-based approach to generalized participation than the UN, which relies more on a formalized process of accreditation and participation of civil society organizations in their political organs. In both cases, the granting of legal participation rights responds to the perceived legitimacy crisis of international institutions, and they typically pursue two distinct and not always compatible rationales: functionalism and democratization.[48] These rationales also affect the relationship of participation rights to sustainability.

---

46 Michael Riegner, 'Towards an international institutional law of information' (n 26); Megan Donaldson and Benedict Kingsbury, 'Power and the Public: The Nature and Effects of Formal Transparency Policies in Global Governance Institutions' in Andrea Bianchi and Anne C Peters (eds), *Transparency in international law* (Cambridge Univ. Pr. 2013); in detail, Michael Riegner, *Informationsverwaltungsrecht internationaler Institutionen* (Mohr Siebeck 2017).

47 Michael Riegner, 'Access to information as a human right and constitutional guarantee. A comparative perspective' (2017) 50(4) VRÜ/WCL 332–366.

48 Bernstorff n 33.

4 Relating Sustainability and Participation: Conflicts and Convergence

The relationship between sustainability and participation in the law of MDBS is not straightforward. Conceptually, there is no necessary relationship between the two. Each can be conceived as an end in itself that is pursued independently of the other: sustainability seeks to limit negative externalities of projects and to ensure their ecological, social and economic viability in the long term, whereas participation can be understood as aiming to maximize individual and collective self-determination in the development process.[49] So defined, the relationship of the two implies a series of tensions, conflicts or even contradictions. The following subsections elaborate these conflicts (4.1.) and then analyse how the World Bank seeks to resolve these tensions and promote convergence between the two ideals (4.2.). The final subsection illustrates these approaches and reflects on whether climate finance presents a new paradigm, or rather a continuation of the old one.

4.1 *Conflicts*

Conflicts and contradictions between sustainability and participation appear both at the conceptual and practical level. If participation and sustainability are conceptualized as promoting distinct values, these values may come into conflict. Participation rights may be exercised in a manner that is incompatible with the long-term viability of a project or policy, or their exercise may prevent projects and policies that are necessary for a sustainability transformation. Individuals and affected groups can be assumed, in many cases at least, to exercise rights in their own interest, and not in the interest of larger collectives or an abstract notion of sustainability. In many MDB-funded projects, this goes beyond the ordinary and well-known "not in my backyard" (NIMBY) problem, as such projects tend to involve largescale infrastructure investments that may benefit populations as a whole but immediately destroy the livelihood, and at times even threaten the survival, of projectaffected people, as exemplified by largescale dam projects.[50]

To these intra-generational tradeoffs is added the presence-bias of participation rights: individual participation rights can by definition only be granted to present-day rightsholders, not future generations. If sustainability is also defined by a concern for future generations, participation does not necessarily help this cause. To the contrary, if one assumes that individuals exercise their

49 On this rationale of participation, see ibid.

50 See only Hadiprayitno, n 15.

rights primarily in a selfinterested way, participation may contradict the interests of future generations.[51] A renewable energy project that reduces carbon emissions but requires resettlement may be delayed or blocked by local resistance, thus increasing the risk of future damage due to global warming.

For this reason, the Bank's safeguards do not generally grant substantive veto rights to affected populations but privilege an autonomous, expert-driven definition of sustainability. Yet this approach points to tensions in the opposite direction: sustainability may conflict with, and limit, participation rights. If sustainability is understood in largely technical terms as a pre-defined notion concretized by experts, then this narrows the space for meaningful participation by affected citizens. It may exclude certain aspects of a project from the legitimate objects of participation, e.g. definition of the project goal: if a project goal is defined in such a way as to contribute to a certain aspect of sustainability, like reducing greenhouse gas emissions, this may insulate the formulation of the goal from change through participatory procedures. Or predefined notions of sustainability may impose certain mitigation practices to achieve emissions standards, while excluding others as legitimate objects of participation.

4.2 *Convergence*

In theory, there are two legal strategies to address the possible contradictions between sustainability and participation. A first strategy is to establish an instrumental, hierarchical relationship between the two, ie to conceptualise and implement one in a manner that serves the other; this effectively subordinates one ideal to the other. The other strategy is to establish an intrinsic relationship, i.e. to conceptualise participation and sustainability in a way that makes it possible to understand them as overlapping and mutually reinforcing. This effectively harmonizes the two and defines away possible contradictions at the conceptual level. In practice, these two strategies are not mutually exclusive, and the MDBs adopt both strategies to varying degrees and with varying outcomes.

On one hand, World Bank safeguards establish an instrumental relationship between the two concepts. This is most evident in the way participation rights are functionalized to serve the purposes of sustainability. Firstly, participation rights are instrumental in collecting and disseminating information to improve the basis for decision-making. Hearings and consultations broaden the sources of information the Bank can use and complement the knowledge produced

51 On this problem in general, see Emilie Gaillard, *Legal Actions for Future Generations* (Peter Lang 2020).

by environmental and social impact assessments. This functional approach is evident in the broad definition of "stakeholder", which goes beyond rights-holders whose subjective rights are interfered with.[52] Secondly, participation is also functionalized to improve implementation and monitor compliance. Consultations, access to information and complaints before the Inspection Panel provide avenues to make the safeguards more effective in the implementation phase by mobilizing individuals with a direct interest in compliance. This type of decentralized 'fire alarm' control, as opposed to centralized 'police patrol' enforcement by Bank management, can be seen as another element of US-American influence.[53] Thirdly, information and participation are designed to enhance the acceptance and perceived legitimacy of development projects, which usually involve tradeoffs and losses to some groups at the expense of others. Whether all these benefits of participation for sustainability actually materialize of course depends on a host of other factors, but the legal design clearly subscribes to this instrumental view that is consistent with the managerial approach inscribed in the Bank's DNA.[54]

While participation rights are thus designed in a way that potentially enhances sustainability, the reverse is not necessarily true. In this regard, one might point to the fact that the procedural approach to sustainability also implies procedural rights for stakeholders. After all, requirements for social and environmental sustainability have historically evolved in tandem with participation rights, and they have the same legal source in the safeguard policies. This, however, is not a necessary connection. In practice, the joint emergence of participatory procedures in the context of sustainability standards may have narrowed down the functions and potentials of participation rights from the outset. For instance, affected communities are not entitled to propose projects on their own, and meaningful consultations occur only after major parameters of project design have been determined by government and bank officials. Rather than aiming at emancipation of affected populations and at democratization of international institutions, the timing, intensity and subject-matter of participation are geared towards improving the output legitimacy

52 ESS 10, para 5.

53 On such a conception of administrative law, see Matthew D. McCubbins and Thomas Schwartz, 'Congressional Oversight Overlooked: Police Patrols versus Fire Alarms', (1984) 28 *American Journal of Political Science* 165.

54 For a detailed analysis of these functions of participation rights in World Bank law, see Michael Riegner, *Informationsverwaltungsrecht internationaler Institutionen* n 46, 353ff., 391ff.

of predefined projects, in terms of enhancing "development impact" and mitigating negative externalities.[55]

Functionalising participation for sustainability also contributes to an expertification and bureaucratization of the participation process. It establishes a dominant rationality that defines what valid knowledge is and that makes it difficult to introduce alternative epistemic conceptions into the process, such as those resulting from indigenous world views.[56] In this logic, participation only has value to the extent that it improves outcomes – and is thus replaceable if superior expertise or information is available from elsewhere, namely from international experts or consultants. Ultimately, this approach depoliticizes participation, does not empower citizens and fails to generate genuine input and throughput-legitimacy. If participation is understood as having emancipatory purposes, managerial sustainability contradicts this purpose.

On the other hand, one can also observe the emergence of an intrinsic relationship between sustainability and participation in MDB legal practice and discourse. In this regard, it can be argued that both ideals have their origin in a higher legal principle, namely sustainable development or human rights. Sustainable development is explicitly expressed as a legal principle only in the primary law of the new development banks, NDB and AIIB, but it can be read into older founding treaties by means of evolutive treaty interpretation. Conceptually, participation and sustainability then converge in a higher goal of sustainable development. This argumentative move is used as a discursive strategy to achieve universal consensus at a higher level of abstraction, as in the case of the UN Sustainable Development Goals, but it does not contribute much to addressing tradeoffs and distributive questions at the operational level in concrete projects and programs.[57]

A second line of argument seeks to achieve convergences by linking sustainability and participation with human rights: the former two then appear as components of the latter. To the extent that MDBs embrace human rights as part of their mandate, as the World Bank now does in its ESF Vision Statement, this strategy has increasingly been used at a discourse level, and to some extent

55 On functionalism and democratization as distinct rationales, see Bernstorff n 33.

56 Rachel Arsenault and others, 'Including Indigenous Knowledge Systems in Environmental Assessments: Restructuring the Process' (2019) 19(3) Global Environmental Politics 120.

57 Graham Long, 'The Idea of Universality in the Sustainable Development Goals' (2015) 29(02) Ethics & International Affairs 203; Norichika Kanie (ed), *Governing Through Goals: The Sustainable Development Goals and a New Governance Strategy in the 21st Century* (MIT Press 2017).

at the operational level.[58] It has been especially salient with regard to social sustainability, which is arguably achieved when basic social rights such as housing and health are realized in the longterm.[59] Development projects can contribute to the fulfilment of these rights, but they also risk disrupting them in the absence of social safeguards, for instance by driving forced displacement. One way of protecting the enjoyment of social rights to health, housing and work is thus to let rights-holders participate in decision-making processes affecting their rights. Here, participation is understood as a procedural component, a *status activus processualis,* of those rights whose substance defines the social dimension of sustainability.[60]

This argument applies not only to social rights, but also to individual rights related to a clean environment, where convergence has accelerated over the past few years. The European Court of Human Rights has interpreted the Convention as implying procedural environmental rights, the InterAmerican Court has fleshed out a right to environment, and the UN Human Rights Council has just recognized a universal human right to "a clean, healthy and sustainable environment".[61] If one subscribes to the view that human rights have constitutional features, they can be understood as constitutionalizing the administrative sustainability standards and participation rights enshrined in secondary institutional law, thus promoting convergence not only at a higher level of abstraction but also at a higher level of law.[62]

This human rights based, intrinsic approach also has its pitfalls. Many aspects of sustainability are ultimately regulatory questions, and reformulating regulatory problems in terms of human rights does not always have advantages: human rights tend to moralize complex issues and do not always have added value compared to differentiated administrative law solutions,

58 ESF Vision Statement, para. 3. Rechel Ball, 'Doing it Quietly': The World Bank's Engagement with Human Rights' (2008) 34(2) Monash University Law Review 331.

59 On the World Bank's tentative embrace of social rights (as opposed to civil and political rights), see ibid; Roberto Danino, 'The Legal Aspects of the World Bank's Work on Human Rights: Some preliminary Thoughts' in Philip Alston and Mary Robinson (eds), *Human rights and development: Towards mutual reinforcement* (Oxford Univ. Pr. 2005).

60 Cf. Michael Riegner, *Informationsverwaltungsrecht internationaler Institutionen* n 46, 278.

61 Birgit Peters, 'Unpacking the Diversity of Procedural Environmental Rights: The European Convention on Human Rights and the Aarhus Convention' (2018) 30(1) Journal of Environmental Law 1; Human Rights Council, Resolution 48/13 (2021). For a broad overview, see Anna Grear and Louis J Kotzé (eds), *Research handbook on human rights and the environment* (Elgar 2015).

62 See generally Anne Peters, 'Fragmentation and Constitutionalization' in Anne Orford and Florian Hoffmann (eds), *Oxford Handbook of the Theory of International Law* (Oxford Univ. Pr. 2016).

especially when different rights collide and must be balanced. Conversely, there is also the risk that excessive bureaucratisation of human rights will weaken the critical and emancipatory potential of universal rights. Constitutionalizing SPS by reference to human rights may thus simply shift the locus of expertise from one expert community to another, from environmental and social safeguard specialists to human rights experts, without empowering rights holders.[63] Ultimately, both managerial sustainability and human rights legalism risk obscuring distributive choices typically involved in development projects, rather than providing rational criteria for how to address the tradeoffs in practice.

5 Conclusion: Alternative Approaches and the Added Value of Administrative Law

At present, the law of MDBs adopts a managerial conception of sustainability which seeks to tame the excesses of capitalist industrialization through procedural standards and institutionalized expertise but does not question the economic model itself. In this conception, participation is functionalized for, and ultimately subordinated to, a technically determined concept of sustainability that does not acknowledge the political tradeoffs it implies. Under this managerial conception, participation is unable to realize its emancipatory and legitimatory potential.

At the same time, the existing legal regime in general, and the increasing incorporation of human rights in particular, also point to alternative understandings of sustainability and participation that problematize and re-configure the relationship of expertise, law and politics in multilevel development governance. Human rights based approaches can also provide a focal point for social protest, political mobilization, and for the contestation and renegotiation of notions of sustainability in development projects and processes – certainly an avenue for future research in the field.[64]

In that sense, constitutionalizing SPS by means of human rights does not necessarily replace politics, but can also complement and orient it in the

63 Cf. Martti Koskenniemi, 'Human Rights Mainstreaming as a Strategy for Institutional Power' (2010) 1(1) Humanity 47.

64 Regina Kreide, 'Between morality and law: In defense of a political conception of human rights' (2016) 12(1) Journal of International Political Theory 10. For a concrete case study, see Penelope Sanz and Robin Hansen, 'The Political Life of a Human Rights Impact Assessment: Canadian Mining in the Philippines' (2018) 7(1) Canadian Journal of Human Rights 97.

process of making the distributive choices involved in development projects, especially with respect to the inclusion of those who are excluded or underrepresented in political processes and public debate at national level. A politically grounded theory of human rights ultimately aims at a politicisation and democratization of those aspects of sustainability that involve major distributive choices, opening up the notion to deliberation while still ensuring an adequate role for expertise.

Concretely, this would require, for instance, procedural designs that improve the genuine coproduction of decision relevant knowledge between experts and affected populations.[65] Another approach might be to design participation procedures in a way that foster convergence between future-oriented sustainability and present day preferences, eg through rationalizing collective deliberation. Finally, the existing legal framework already provides hints towards alternative approaches that do not subordinate participation to sustainability: since 2017, the ESF recognizes the right of indigenous populations to free, prior and informed *consent* to development projects if they affect indigenous land or require resettlement.[66] This effectively gives indigenous populations a veto over certain kinds of development projects, and thus provides a legal opening for alternative visions – not only of sustainability but also of the economic system in which it operates.[67]

Such alternative procedural designs can be informed and induced by, but not necessarily deduced from, human rights guarantees: they require concretization and experimentation at the level of administrative law of international institutions. Here lies the added value of administrative standards below and beyond human rights, precisely because they deconstitutionalize individual entitlements and open them up to experimentation and democratic contestation.[68] In that vein, it can be argued that the process of law-making that

---

65 For practical examples, see Ida N S Djenontin and Alison M Meadow, 'The art of co-production of knowledge in environmental sciences and management: lessons from international practice' (2018) 61(6) Environmental Management 885.

66 ESS 7.

67 For a discussion, see Stéphanie de Moerloose, 'Indigenous Peoples' Free, Prior and Informed Consent (FPIC) and the World Bank Safeguards: Between Norm Emergence and Concept Appropriation' (2020) 53(3) WCL/VRÜ (Verfassung in Recht und Übersee) 223; Brunori n 40. On indigenous cosmologies, see eg Daniel Bonilla Maldonado, 'The Rights of Nature and a New Constitutional Environmental Law' in James R May and Erin Daly (eds), *Human rights and the environment: Legality, indivisibility, dignity and geography* (Elgar 2019); Louis Kotzé and Paola Villavicencio Calzadilla, 'Living in Harmony with Nature?' (2018) 7(3) TEL 397.

68 Michael Riegner, 'Deconstitutionalizing individual rights beyond the state?' (27 January 2016). Völkerrechtsblog, DOI 10.17176/20171005-172400 <http://voelkerrechtsblog.org/de

produced the World Bank's safeguards reform shows aspects of transnational deliberative democracy,[69] although that argument still struggles with the deep inequalities and less than open-ended nature of the entire process. Despite these challenges, MDBs have certain comparative advantages and expertise not just with respect to sustainability, but also with regard to designing procedures that enhance inclusive, informed and contextsensitive deliberation and decision-making in multilevel contexts. Whether this expertise is harnessed also of course depends on the quality of domestic democracy and deliberation, whose relationship to international law remains a persistent question for present and future research.[70]

References

Arsenault R and others, 'Including Indigenous Knowledge Systems in Environmental Assessments: Restructuring the Process' (2019) 19(3) Global Environmental Politics 120

Ball R, 'Doing it Quietly': The World Bank's Engagement with Human Rights' (2008) 34(2) Monash University Law Review 331

Barral V, 'Sustainable Development in International Law: Nature and Operation of an Evolutive Legal Norm' (2012) 23(2) European Journal of International Law 377

Beyerlin U, 'Sustainable Development' *Max Planck Encyclopedia of Public International Law* (Online, 2013) <https://opil.ouplaw.com/display/10.1093/law:epil/9780199231690/law-9780199231690-e1609?print=pdf> last accessed 25 February 2023.

Bignami F, 'Theories of Civil Society and Global Administrative Law: The Case of the World Bank and International Development' in Cassese S (ed), *Research Handbook on Global Administrative Law* (Edward Elgar 2016) 325–346

Boisson de Chazournes L, 'Partnerships, Emulation, and Coordination Toward the Emergence of a Droit Commun in the Field of Development Finance' in Cissé H, Bradlow D and Kingsbury B (eds), *The World Bank Legal Review Vol. 3: International Financial Institutions and Global Legal Governance* (Washington, World Bank 2011) 173–187

-constitutionalizing-individual-rights-beyond-the-state/> last accessed 3 August 2022.

69 Cf. Ruth Houghton, 'Looking at the World Bank's safeguard reform through the lens of deliberative democracy' (2019) 32(3) Leiden Journal of International Law 465.

70 Benedict Kingsbury, Megan Donaldson and Rodrigo Vallejo, 'Global Administrative Law and deliberative democracy' in Anne Orford and Florian Hoffmann (eds), *Oxford Handbook of the Theory of International Law* (Oxford Univ. Pr. 2016); Jan Klabbers and others, 'International Law and Democracy Revisited: Introduction to the Symposium' (2021) 32(1) EJIL 9.

Bonilla Maldonado D, 'The Rights of Nature and a New Constitutional Environmental Law' in May J R and Daly E (eds), *Human Rights and the Environment: Legality, Indivisibility, Dignity and Geography vol. 7* (Edward Elgar 2019) 310–322

Bowles I and Kormos C, 'The American Campaign for Environmental Reforms at the World Bank' (1999) 23(1) Fletcher Forum of World Affairs Journal 211

Bradlow D D and Fourie A N, 'The Operational Policies of the World Bank and the International Finance Corporation: Creating Law-Making and Law-Governed Institutions?' (2013) 10(1) International Organizations Law Review 3

Brunori M, 'Protecting Access to Land for Indigenous and Non-Indigenous Communities: A New Page for the World Bank?' (2019) 32(3) Leiden Journal of International Law 501

Dañino R, 'The Legal Aspects of the World Bank's Work on Human Rights: Some Preliminary Thoughts' in Alston P and Robinson M (eds), *Human Rights and Development: Towards Mutual Reinforcement* (Oxford University Press 2005) 509–524

Dann P, 'Der Zugang zu Dokumenten im Recht der Weltbank: Kosmopolitische Tendenzen im Internationalen Verwaltungsrecht' (2011) 44(3) Die Verwaltung 313

Dann P, *The Law of Development Cooperation: A Comparative Analysis of the World Bank, the EU and Germany* (Hammel A tr, Cambridge University Press 2013)

Dann P and Riegner M, 'The World Bank's Environmental and Social Safeguards and the Evolution of Global Order' (2019) 32(3) Leiden Journal of International Law 537

Daugirdas K, 'Congress Underestimated: The Case of the World Bank' (2013) 107(3) American Journal of International Law 517

de Búrca G and others, 'The Changing Role of the World Bank Inspection Panel: Responding to Contemporary Challenges at the World Bank' (2014) International Organizations Clinic at NYU School of Law <https://chrgj.org/wp-content/uploads/2014/09/ChangingRoleoftheWorldBankIP_IOClinic.pdf>

de Moerloose S, 'Indigenous Peoples' Free, Prior and Informed Consent (FPIC) and the World Bank Safeguards: Between Norm Emergence and Concept Appropriation' (2020) 53(3) Verfassung in Recht und Übersee/World Comparative Law 223

Dijkzeul D, 'Programs and the Problems of Participation' in Dijkzeul D and Beigbeder Y(eds), *Rethinking International Organizations* (Berghahn Books 2002) 197–233

Djenontin I N S and Meadow A M, 'The Art of Co-Production of Knowledge in Environmental Sciences and Management: Lessons from International Practice' (2018) 61(6) Environmental Management 885

Donaldson M and Kingsbury B, 'Power and the Public: The Nature and Effects of Formal Transparency Policies in Global Governance Institutions' in Bianchi A and Peters A C (eds), *Transparency in International Law* (Cambridge University Press 2013) 502–533

Freestone D, *The World Bank and Sustainable Development: Legal Essays* (Legal Aspects of Sustainable Development Vol 14 Leiden, Martinus Nijhoff 2013)

Fujita S, *The World Bank, Asian Development Bank and Human Rights: Developing Standards of Transparency, Participation and Accountability* (Edward Elgar 2013)

Gaillard E, *Legal Actions for Future Generations* (Générations Futures, Paix et Environnement / Future Generations, Peace and the Environment Series Vol 1, Peter Lang 2020)

Grear A and Kotzé L J (eds), *Research Handbook on Human Rights and the Environment* (Research Handbooks in Human Rights, Edward Elgar 2015)

Hadiprayitno I, *Hazard or Right?: The Dialectics of Development Practice and the Internationally Declared Right to Development, with Special Reference to Indonesia* (School of Human Rights Research Series Vol 31, Intersentia 2009)

Houghton R, 'Looking at the World Bank's Safeguard Reform Through the Lens of Deliberative Democracy' (2019) 32(3) Leiden Journal of International Law 465

Hunter D, 'International Law and Public Participation in Policy-Making at the International Financial Institutions' in Bradlow D D and Hunter D B (eds), *International Financial Institutions and International Law* (Kluwer Law International 2010) 199–238

IEG, 'Safeguards and Sustainability Policies in a Changing World: An Independent Evaluation of World Bank Group Experience' (IEG Study Series Washington, D.C. 2010) available at <http://documents.worldbank.org/curated/en/742801468177840668/Safeguards-and-sustainability-policies-in-a-changing-world-an-independent-evaluation-of-World-Bank-Group-experience>

Jokubauskaite G, 'The Legal Nature of the World Bank Safeguards' (2018) 51(1) Verfassung in Recht und Übersee/World Comparative Law 78

Jokubauskaite G, 'The World Bank Environmental and Social Framework in a Wider Realm of Public International Law' (2019) 32(3) Leiden Journal of International Law 457

Kanie N and Biermann F (eds), *Governing Through Goals: The Sustainable Development Goals as Governance Innovation* (MIT Press 2017)

Kingsbury B, 'Operational Policies of International Institutions as Part of the Law-making Process: The World Bank and Indigenous Peoples' in Goodwin-Gill G S and Talmon S (eds), *The Reality of International Law* (1st edn, Clarendon 1999) 323–342

Kingsbury B, Donaldson M and Vallejo R, 'Global Administrative Law and Deliberative Democracy' in Orford A and Hoffmann F (eds), *Oxford Handbook of the Theory of International Law* (Oxford University Press 2016) 526–542

Klabbers J, 'The Transformation of International Organizations Law' (2015) 26(1) European Journal of International Law 9

Klabbers J and others, 'International Law and Democracy Revisited: Introduction to the Symposium' (2021) 32(1) European Journal of International Law 9

Koskenniemi M, 'The Fate of Public International Law: Between Technique and Politics' (2007) 70(1) Modern Law Review 1

Koskenniemi M, 'Human Rights Mainstreaming as a Strategy for Institutional Power' (2010) 1(1) Humanity 47

Kotzé L and Villavicencio Calzadilla P, 'Living in Harmony with Nature? A Critical Appraisal of the Rights of Mother Earth in Bolivia' (2018) 7(3) Transnational Environmental Law 397

Kramarz T and Momani B, 'The World Bank as Knowledge Bank: Analyzing the Limits of a Legitimate Global Knowledge Actor' (2013) 30(4) Review of Policy Research 409

Kreide R, 'Between Morality and Law: In Defense of a Political Conception of Human Rights' (2016) 12(1) Journal of International Political Theory 10

Long G, 'The Idea of Universality in the Sustainable Development Goals' (2015) 29(2) Ethics & International Affairs 203

Maitra S, 'Development Induced Displacement: Issues of Compensation and Resettlement – Experiences from the Narmada Valley and Sardar Sarovar Project' (2009) 10(2) Japanese Journal of Political Science 191

Mares R, 'Securing Human Rights Through Risk-Management Methods: Breakthrough or Misalignment?' (2019) 32(3) Leiden Journal of International Law 517

Mbengue M M and de Moerloose S, 'Multilateral Development Banks and Sustainable Development: On Emulation, Fragmentation and a Common Law of Sustainable Development' (2017) 10(2) Law and Development Review 389

Mohan G, 'Participatory Development: From Epistemological Reversals to Active Citizenship' (2007) 1(4) Geography Compass 779

Mohan G and Stokke K, 'Participatory Development and Empowerment: the Dangers of Localism' (2000) 21(2) Third World Quarterly 247

Naudé Fourie A, *The World Bank Inspection Panel Casebook* (Eleven International Publishing 2014)

Ormaza M V C and Ebert F C, 'The World Bank, Human Rights, and Organizational Legitimacy Strategies: The Case of the 2016 Environmental and Social Framework' (2019) 32(3) Leiden Journal of International Law 483

Park S, 'The World Bank Group: Championing Sustainable Development Norms?' (2007) 13(4) Global Governance 535

Park S, *World Bank Group Interactions with Environmentalists: Changing International Organisation Identities* Issues in Environmental Politics (Manchester University Press 2010)

Passoni C, Rosenbaum A and Vermunt E, 'Empowering the Inspection Panel - The Impact of the World Bank's Safeguards Review' (2015) International Organizations Clinic at NYU School of Law <https://www.iilj.org/wp-content/uploads/2016/08/Empowering_the_Inspection_Panel_Web.pdf> last accessed 25 February 2023.

Peters A, *Beyond Human Rights: The Legal Status of the Individual in International Law* Cambridge Studies in International and Comparative Law Series Vol 126 (Huston J tr, Cambridge University Press 2016)

Peters A, 'Fragmentation and Constitutionalization' in Orford A and Hoffmann F (eds), *Oxford Handbook of the Theory of International Law* (Oxford University Press 2016) 1011–1032

Peters B, 'Unpacking the Diversity of Procedural Environmental Rights: The European Convention on Human Rights and the Aarhus Convention' (2018) 30(1) Journal of Environmental Law 1

Ragazzi M, 'World Bank Group' [2014] Max Planck Encyclopedia of Public International Law online <https://opil.ouplaw.com/display/10.1093/law:epil/9780199231690/law-9780199231690-e1982> last accessed 25 February 2023.

Riegner M, 'Towards an International Institutional Law of Information' (2015) 12(1) International Organizations Law Review 50

Riegner M, 'Legal Frameworks and General Principles for Indicators in Sovereign Debt Restructuring' [2016] Yale Journal of International Law Online 141–175

Riegner M, 'De-constitutionalizing Individual Rights Beyond the State?' (27 January 2016). Völkerrechtsblog, DOI 10.17176/20171005-172400 <http://voelkerrechtsblog.org/de-constitutionalizing-individual-rights-beyond-the-state/> last accessed 25 February 2023.

Riegner M, 'Access to Information as a Human Right and Constitutional Guarantee. A Comparative Perspective' (2017) 50(4) Verfassung und Recht in Übersee/World Comparative Law 332–366

Riegner M, *Informationsverwaltungsrecht internationaler Institutionen: Dargestellt am Entwicklungsverwaltungsrecht der Weltbank und Vereinten Nationen* (Mohr Siebeck 2017)

Sanz P and Hansen R, 'The Political Life of a Human Rights Impact Assessment: Canadian Mining in the Philippines' (2018) 7(1) Canadian Journal of Human Rights 97

Seabrooke L and Sending OJ, 'Contracting Development: Managerialism and Consultants in Intergovernmental Organizations' (2020) 27(4) Review of International Political Economy 802

Stewart RB, 'U.S. Administrative Law: A Model for Global Administrative Law?' (2005) 68(3/4) Law and Contemporary Problems 63

von Bernstorff J, 'New Responses to the Legitimacy Crisis of International Institutions: The Role of 'Civil Society' and the Rise of the Principle of Participation of 'The Most Affected' in International Institutional Law' (2021) 32(1) European Journal of International Law 125

World Bank, Mansuri G and Rao V, *Localizing Development: Does Participation Work?* (World Bank 2013)

CHAPTER 15

International Investment Law

The Anarchical Society Where Development and Sustainability Are Frenemies and Participation Plays Gooseberry

Paolo Turrini

1 Introduction

Discussing in a short chapter how Sustainable Development (SD) relates to international investment law is an almost herculean task. This is due both to the inextricable yet non-linear link between the two, which have multiple points of contact, and to the many doctrinal sources focusing on such a relationship, which can be studied from both a practical and legal perspective. The practical approach aims to understand the actual contribution of Foreign Direct Investment (FDI) and International Investment Agreements (IIAs) to SD (a role which is schematically outlined in Section 2). The legal approach questions how SD has been, and could be, factored into international investment law (a problem briefly addressed in Section 3). The first part of this chapter will show that, despite the fact that the economic literature does not unanimously confirm the positive role of FDI in fostering development and, also, of IIAs in promoting FDI, States are not demonstrating a true interest in properly redesigning this branch of law. The reform currently under consideration mainly deals with procedural questions, whereas the legal novelties of substantive nature scattered all over the investment regime tackle the issue of SD in an erratic manner. Something similar can be said with regard to public participation, which, also due to the legitimacy crisis that hit the investment system, has recently drawn the attention of scholars and international institutions (Section 4). How participation and SD can be best combined, however, is a problem that deserves greater consideration.

2 Investment (Treaties) and (Sustainable) Development

Although this chapter, and the book it is a part of, takes a legal perspective on the idea of SD, one cannot forget that reality takes precedence over legal fiction. Thus, if it were to be proven beyond doubt, for instance, that international investment law does not in fact further SD, or even just development, a legal analysis of how IIAs account for SD would be pointless. Of course, this requires that a definition of SD is decided upon beforehand (whereas the notions of development and economic development are slightly less problematic). Although empirical studies consider various parameters as proxies for sustainability, the aim of this section is simply to inform the reader about the existence of a host of analyses on the actual effects of IIAs. This issue is known by many legal scholars, who have also discussed it at times, but since it risks shaking the very foundations of the investment regime, lawyers usually avoid it. This is not a good reason, however, to ignore it when addressing the subject of SD, especially from a participation perspective: people taking part in decision-making should be acquainted with the literature on the consequences of IIAs in order to make informed choices.[1]

Despite the factual and sometimes law-grounded claim that the aim of IIAs is to protect investment, it can be maintained that this goal is of less importance than the attainment of socio-economic prosperity.[2] The latter view may be based on the preambles of some IIAs and that of the International Centre for Settlement of Investment Disputes (ICSID) Convention, which variously evoke the idea of development. The preamble of the ICSID Convention was also used to create the so-called *Salini* test,[3] which includes a 'contribution to the economic development of the host State' among the requirements aimed at establishing which investments are afforded protection through ICSID arbitral proceedings. However, the superficial analyses of this prerequisite carried out by arbitrators make clear how difficult its application is, because of the absence of an objective benchmark against which to assess whether an investment contributes to development and is thus worth being brought under the aegis of the ICSID Convention.[4]

1 The effect of this knowledge on people's attitudes towards FDI has been studied: Hye-Sung Kim and Youngchae Lee, 'The Effects of Environmental Costs on Public Support for Foreign Direct Investment: Differences Between the United States and India' in Cosimo Beverelli, Jürgen Kurtz and Damian Raess (eds), *International Trade, Investment, and the Sustainable Development Goals* (CUP 2020) 270.

2 Anne van Aaken and Tobias A Lehmann, 'Sustainable Development and International Investment Law: A Harmonious View from Economics' in Roberto Echandi and Pierre Sauvé (eds), *Prospects in International Investment Law and Policy: World Trade Forum* (CUP 2013) 330–31.

3 *Salini et al v Morocco*, ICSID Case No ARB/00/4, Decision on Jurisdiction, 23 July 2001, para 52. The test states that only transnational economic activities that entail (a) a contribution of money or assets, (b) a risk, (c) a certain duration and (d) a contribution to the host state's economy, can be deemed an "investment" and as such deserve the protection of international investment law.

4 Souvik Mukherjee and Nirmal Kanti Chakrabarti, 'Is "Contribution to the Host States Development" an Essential Criterion to Define Investment Under International Investment Law? A Search Through the Lens of Arbitral Awards' (2021) 42 Liverpool L Rev 429.

This is one of the reasons why arbitrators have engendered an inconsistent case law on the abovementioned requirement, which further exacerbated the unpredictability of investment protection,[5] and why all but a handful of IIAs do not incorporate the *Salini* test,[6] including the treaties of some prominent actors (although this is not enough to set aside the development requirement under the "double keyhole" condition).[7] However, legal qualifications apart, does FDI actually contribute to development?

Economists have long investigated this issue and arrived at no concrete answer. A recent literature review has stressed that few scholars doubt that 'there is a strong correlation between FDI and growth', although 'the direction of causality is less clear'.[8] This is due to the fact that certain conditions, relating to both the type of the investment and the domestic setting of the host country, are needed for FDI to unleash growth, so that one can assume that 'FDI inflows do not exert an independent influence on economic growth'.[9] States may enact policies that, according to some commentators, are key to success, including certain performance requirements. Governments can demand that corporations have a local investment partner (joint venture requirement), transfer their technologies to such a partner (technology transfer requirement) and buy inputs for their products in the host country (local contents

---

5 Alex Grabowski, 'The Definition of Investment Under the ICSID Convention: A Defense of *Salini*' (2014) 15 Chicago J Intl L 287. To avoid this problem, the author suggests to stick to the *Salini* requirements. *Contra*, van Aaken and Lehmann, n 2, who think SD considerations should be raised at the merit stage, not the jurisdiction phase (at 334–35), and Diane Desierto, 'Development as an International Right: Investment in the New Trade-Based IIAs' (2011) 3 Trade L & Development 296.

6 Ole Kristian Fauchald, 'International Investment Law in Support of the Right to Development?' (2021) 34 Leiden J Intl L 181, 189.

7 Gus Van Harten, 'The European Union's Emerging Approach to ISDS: A Review of the Canada-Europe CETA, Europe–Singapore FTA, and European-Vietnam FTA' (2016) 1 Bologna U L Rev 138, 153–54 (the European Union); Mukherjee and Chakrabarti, n 4, at 461 (the US in its model treaty, India in its actual agreements despite its model treaty).

8 Liesbeth Colen, Miet Maertens and Johan Swinnen, 'Foreign Direct Investment as an Engine for Economic Growth and Human Development: A Review of the Arguments and Empirical Evidence' in Olivier De Schutter, Johan Swinnen and Jan Wouters (eds), *Foreign Direct Investment and Human Development: The Law and Economics of International Investment Agreements* (Routledge 2013) 115. Reviews of relevant empirical studies are not uncommon and may address a number of issues, including those raised here. See eg Aaron Cosbey, *International Investment Agreements and Sustainable Development: Achieving the Millennium Development Goals* (Intl Institute Sustainable Development 2005).

9 Maria Carkovic and Ross Levine, 'Does Foreign Direct Investment Accelerate Economic Growth?' in Theodore H Moran, Edward M Graham and Magnus Blomström (eds), *Does Foreign Direct Investment Promote Development?* (Institute for Intl Economics 2005) 219.

requirement).[10] However, in order to ensure growth, positive factors must offset the negative ones. For instance, foreign companies do not always pay taxes in the host state (and they repatriate capital); they cannot pass their technical knowledge to the host economy if there are no local firms operating in the same sector; and host state companies may suffer a 'crowding out' effect in the credit market.[11]

It should also be noted at this point, that growth (meant as an increase in GDP) is not development, since the latter also entails a larger societal improvement capable of nurturing the former. Thus, development implies economic (eg distribution of wealth) as well as non-economic (eg human capital) aspects, even though no simple definition of it can be given.[12] Moreover, in this respect, too, scholars tend to think that the effects of investment are mixed and uncertain. Considering only a couple of economic parameters, it seems that, overall, investment may contribute to reducing poverty in the host country but, at the same time, it may increase inequality,[13] although high education levels and effective institutions may mitigate or even invert this latter outcome.[14]

However, even in those cases where true development is realised, it is necessary to consider at what cost this occurs. Is rampant growth, although beneficial to all population strata, worth defiling waters? Just as growth is not development, development cannot be equated to SD, which is usually intended as comprising social values such as human rights and a healthy environment from an intergenerational perspective. Again, experts are unable to reach unequivocal conclusions as to the role of investment, and studies show both positive and negative outcomes. For some, foreign investment facilitates the achievement of the United Nations Sustainable Development Goals (SDGs),

---

10 The catalogue of performance requirements is richer: International Institute for Sustainable Development, *Investment Treaties & Why They Matter to Sustainable Development: Questions & Answers* (Intl Institute Sustainable Development 2012) 27.

11 Ha-Joon Chang, *Economics: The User's Guide* (Pelican 2014) 427–29.

12 The idea of development can be split into multiple factors: eg Sumei Luo *et al*, 'Can FDI and ODI Two-Way Flows Improve the Quality of Economic Growth? Empirical Evidence from China' (2021) 53 Applied Economics 5028, analyses the quality of economic growth against the parameters of efficiency, stability and sustainability, the last one being made up only in part of environmental criteria.

13 Colen, Maertens and Swinnen, n 8.

14 Quoc Hoi Le *et al*, 'The Impact of Foreign Direct Investment on Income Inequality in Vietnam' (2021) 9 27 Economies 1. Incidentally, education and political institutions are also crucial factors in participatory processes.

except with regard to climate change,[15] whereas for others, it 'benefits the environment in wealthy countries … but degrades it in poor countries'.[16]

Let us posit, against part of the available evidence, that FDI promotes SD. Can we also say that IIAs promote FDI? Needless to say, inquiries are, in the aggregate, inconclusive. Econometric models detect a positive impact, no impact or even a negative impact of IIAs, depending on how the analyses are conducted.[17] Although some authors endorse the idea of a correlation between IIAs and FDI inflow, many others believe that the former's influence is marginal, and that investment treaties do not compensate for the lack of other requisites.[18] Among the variables to be considered – as suggested by a literature review finding a small role of IIAs and a major role of economic determinants – there are taxes, market size, GDP per capita, growth rate, labour cost, trade deficit, exchange rates, infrastructure, human capital, presence of investment promotion agencies, corruption and political stability.[19] As for the extractive sector, which is of paramount importance, unsurprisingly 'FDI is largely driven by geology'.[20] Equally obvious is the pivotal role played by an open trade and investment policy, that is, by guarantees for a frictionless flow of goods and

15 Viktoria Aust, Ana Isabel Morais and Inês Pinto, 'How Does Foreign Direct Investment Contribute to Sustainable Development Goals? Evidence from African Countries' (2020) 245 118823 J Cleaner Production 1.

16 Nadia Doytch and Merih Uctum, 'Globalization and the Environmental Impact of Sectoral FDI' (2016) 40 Economic Systems 582, 591. This cautions against drawing lessons from legal studies too swiftly, such as the one stating that, when it comes to arbitration, 'in environmental cases developing states seem to fare better than developed states' (Michael Faure and Wanli Ma, 'Investor-State Arbitration: Economic and Empirical Perspectives' (2020) 41 Michigan J Intl L 1, 47).

17 Joachim Pohl, 'Societal Benefits and Costs of International Investment Agreements: A Critical Review of Aspects and Available Empirical Evidence' (2018) OECD Working Papers on International Investment 2018/01, 16–31, <www.oecd-ilibrary.org/docserver/e5f85c3d-en.pdf> last accessed 31 March 2022.

18 Karl P Sauvant and Lisa E Sachs (eds), *The Effect of Treaties on Foreign Direct Investment: Bilateral Investment Treaties, Double Taxation Treaties, and Investment Flows* (OUP 2009) pt II (whose chapters are almost equally divided between supporters and critics of the causal relationship).

19 Liesbeth Colen, Miet Maertens and Johan Swinnen, 'Determinants of Foreign Direct Investment Flows to Developing Countries: The Role of International Investment Agreements' in De Schutter, Swinnen and Wouters (eds), n 8. Similar conclusions on the limited significance of BITs are in Josef C Brada, Zdenek Drabek and Ichiro Iwasaki, 'Does Investor Protection Increase Foreign Direct Investment? A Meta-Analysis' (2021) 35 J Economic Surveys 34.

20 Theodor H Moran, *Foreign Direct Investment and Development: The New Policy Agenda for Developing Countries and Economies in Transition* (Peterson Institute for Intl Economics 1998) 22.

capital. Given the focus of this chapter, it is worth noting that market liberalisation as a condition of credit by international financial institutions may be a problem if seen through the lens of participation, especially where democratic institutions are young and fragile.[21]

In light of the importance of internal factors, the difficulty of disentangling the effects of IIAs and of domestic reforms has been noted, so that polls would be a more trustworthy probing method.[22] Interestingly, the findings of the limited effect of investment treaties are usually confirmed through interviews with practitioners.[23] Moreover, the greater weight of domestic aspects is not at odds with the (seemingly substantiated) idea that IIAs lead to a boost of capital inflow only if they are complied with, that is, when a country is not challenged before arbitral panels. Conversely, FDI declines when a state is brought to ICSID and, even more so, when the dispute is lost by the government.[24] This can be explained with the hypothesis that IIAs primarily work as a proxy for governments' reliability in ensuring a favourable investment environment.

With few exceptions,[25] these studies do not consider the content of IIAs, only their being into force or concluded. Indeed, as we will see in Section 3, the true level of protection afforded by these agreements is hard to estimate. Therefore, one might argue that the actual provisions of an IIA do not significantly determine the magnitude of its contribution to capital influx. Somewhat ironically, the importance of such contribution may result in being inversely proportional to the spread of investment treaties: the more numerous they are, the less difference they make when all domestic factors – the economy, the legal and institutional framework – are roughly the same. The more successful (ie diffuse) IIAs are, the less successful (ie effective) they are. This provides ammunition against the multilateralisation and universalisation of the investment regime.

---

21 Daniel Kalderimis, 'IMF Conditionality as Investment Regulation: A Theoretical Analysis' (2004) 13 Soc & L Studies 103, 122–23.

22 Jason Yackee, 'Do BITs Really Work? Revisiting the Empirical Link Between Investment Treaties and Foreign Direct Investment' in Sauvant and Sachs (eds), n 18.

23 Lauge Skovgaard Poulsen, 'The Importance of BITs for Foreign Direct Investment and Political Risk Insurance: Revisiting the Evidence' in Karl P Sauvant (ed), *Yearbook on International Investment Law & Policy 2009–2010* (OUP 2010). Many other sources are quoted in Pohl, n 17, at 31–34.

24 Todd Allee and Clint Peinhardt, 'Contingent Credibility: The Impact of Investment Treaty Violations on Foreign Direct Investment' (2011) 65 Intl Org 401.

25 Jay Dixon and Paul Alexander Haslam, 'Does the Quality of Investment Protection Affect FDI Flows to Developing Countries? Evidence from Latin America' (2016) 39 World Economy 1080.

These issues, albeit known to many legal scholars, are by and large neglected in the debate on the reform of investment law, despite this field having been harshly criticised by states and academics alike in the last two decades. The current work on the investor–state dispute settlement system conducted by Working Group III (WGIII) of the United Nations Commission on International Trade Law (UNCITRAL) does not cover the potential uselessness of investment treaties in fostering SD, which might imply they could be disposed of. Of course, one could not expect WGIII to 'abolish' the bulk of international investment law. However, this could be a wasted opportunity to discuss a topic of utmost importance. As some representatives in WGIII noted, the fact that negative perceptions on the investment regime are not grounded in definitive empirical evidence should not hinder the needed reform.[26] In light of this, UNCITRAL would have been a proper forum to address these perceptions, maybe through a bottom-up approach with the involvement of the public, rather than the suggested top-down manner.[27]

3 The Investment Regime and Its Consequences on (the Idea of) Sustainable Development

In a well-contained legal regime, based on a single treaty or, at most, a limited set of harmoniously-designed instruments, looking into how SD is understood and pursued is relatively straightforward. This is the case, for example, of the other main branch of international economic law, that is, international trade law, which, despite some centrifugal tendencies, is quite solidly grounded in the few conventions establishing the World Trade Organisation. This system, in turn, has developed a fairly consistent case-law. Unfortunately, this is not the case of international investment law, which is exceptionally fragmented and can hardly be seen as a 'legal system' *stricto sensu* (Section 3.1). It is made up of countless agreements, whose interpretation is entrusted to arbitral panels that have often construed even identically-phrased provisions differently. This situation is not without consequences for our purposes. Here I stress three aspects. First, a decentralised regime is, in principle at least, ill-equipped in promoting communal values like SD (again, Section 3.1). Second, the lack of a common mechanism aimed at avoiding that investment protection comes

26 UNCITRAL, Report of Working Group III (Investor-State Dispute Settlement Reform) on the Work of its Thirty-fifth Session (New York, 23–27 April 2018), 14 May 2018, UN Doc A/CN.9/935, para 96.

27 Ibid para 95.

at the expense of SD has the effect of outsourcing this objective to individual states, which are free to choose, among many, the strategies they deem best-suited to promote SD (Section 3.2). Third, these strategies represent different means pointing at different aims, since, in the absence of a central law-making and adjudicatory authority, SD objectives are primarily those a state thinks they are. In such a scenario, the best way not to get lost in the maze of bilateral treaties is perhaps relying on 'big data' analyses by external observers: that is, reviewing how scholars and institutional actors categorise (their own understanding of) SD goals across a myriad of legal instruments (Section 3.3).

3.1 *Main Features of International Investment Law*

Some consequences for SD stem from the structure and content of the investment regime. As for the structure, the regime is mostly organised as a bundle of two-sided legal relations, taking the shape of Bilateral Investment Treaties (BITs). Their number now approaches 3,000 treaties, most of them still in force, and their content can be varied, despite similarities abound, with respect to both substantive and procedural provisions. The latter include reliance on a dispute settlement system with its fulcrum on investor-state arbitration managed by ICSID. An exception can be seen by Brazil's recent Cooperation and Investment Facilitation Agreements, which, albeit bilateral in nature, resort to classic state-state arbitration. In all such cases, one end of the bilateral relationship may be a multi-state subject, one example being the (not yet in force) 2020 Comprehensive Investment Agreement between China and the European Union (EU).

Further exceptions to the norm (ie BITs) can be isolated by looking at two parameters. First, content: some actors opt for concluding bilateral treaties encompassing a larger array of issues and including an investment chapter. These Free Trade Agreements (FTAs) are generally more 'structured' and thus the compliance mechanisms and bodies they set up may contribute to promoting SD more effectively than a simple BIT. Similarly, rules relevant to investment, and to SD, can be found in agreements primarily focusing on other themes. For instance, in matters of performance requirements, which are dealt with in a variety of ways in IIAs,[28] a key instrument is the Trade-Related Investment Measures Agreement, belonging to the World Trade Organisation galaxy. The second parameter is the number of parties: plurilateral agreements on investment are gaining momentum, like those in force among the members of

28 UNCTAD, *Foreign Direct Investment and Performance Requirements: New Evidence from Selected Countries* (United Nations 2003) 36 ff.

the Common Market for Eastern and Southern Africa and of the Association of Southeast Asian Nations.

Bilateral accords are still preponderant, though, which may have an effect on SD. One possible consequence regards the protection of common goods,[29] such as climate. FDI is likely to have a non-negligible role in bringing about climate change, but this problem is best tackled through concerted multilateral action, which cannot be adequately hosted in, and fully secured by, a multitude of BITs.[30] Indeed, a legal framework conceived as a cohesive system, rather than a loose set of distinct items, favours the design of rules and institutions aimed at coping with common problems. Thus, WGIII is now musing upon the establishment of an advisory centre for developing countries along the lines of the one existing in the field of trade law since 2001 (though not affiliated to the World Trade Organisation). However, the most far-reaching effect of the bilateral nature of the investment regime concerns the level of promotion of SD as opposed to investors' interests. Developing states usually have less bargaining leverage vis-à-vis capital-exporting powers and the former's *desiderata* do not always enter the final agreement; what is worse, these countries might not even be willing to enshrine SD-provisions in their BITs, since they might prefer to run a 'race to the bottom'.

The problem can be summarised as follows: since states are convinced they can attract a larger share of FDI if they promise more favourable investment conditions than those offered by competing countries, environmental and human rights standards will remain low. While the actual role of a fragmented system on the persistence of low standards can be debated,[31] as these can have a number of justifications, it seems safe to conclude that such a model does not provide a strong incentive to raise the standards. Remarkably, such an

---

29 Lise Johnson, Lisa Sachs and Nathan Lobel, 'Aligning International Investment Agreements with the Sustainable Development Goals' (2019) 58 Columbia J Transnational L 58, 116–18. See also Giorgio Sacerdoti, 'Investment Protection and Sustainable Development: Key Issues" in Steffen Hindelang and Markus Krajewski (eds), *Shifting Paradigms in International Investment Law: More Balanced, Less Isolated, Increasingly Diversified* (OUP 2016) 38 (but the example the author puts forth in the footnote sees the use of domestic resources, rather than their protection, as a common concern!).

30 Indeed, investors have already begun to challenge state measures aimed at tackling climate change: see Matteo Fermeglia *et al*, '"Investor-State Dispute Settlement" as a New Avenue for Climate Change Litigation'(Climate Law Blog, 2 June 2021) <http://blogs.law.columbia.edu/climatechange/2021/06/02/investor-state-dispute-settlement-as-a-new-avenue-for-climate-change-litigation> last accessed 31 March 2022.

31 Although the race-to-the-bottom hypothesis is dismissed by some scholars, others found support for it: see, in the field of labor laws, William W Olney, 'A Race to the Bottom? Employment Protection and Foreign Direct Investment' (2013) 91 J Intl Economics 191.

incentive would not necessarily stem from a uniform system (a multilateral investment agreement), should states merely be free to adopt high standards. As long as the so-called right to regulate remains a right as opposed to a duty, a centralised system could engender the same results as a fragmented one. Admittedly, freedom is key in a context where high standards have been rejected first and foremost by developing countries as a strategy of industrialised states to hinder the former's development, a strategy inspired by a questionable 'one-size-fits-all' approach, whereas SD should be pursued differently in different places. Again, this is worth emphasising in light of the focus of this chapter on participation, since the exogenous imposition of standards would narrow the scope of political self-determination of 'rule-taking' countries. A simple non-regression obligation would be more acceptable, provided that the degree of protection afforded by two distinct norms can be compared, which is not always the case. However, it could still be problematic from the standpoint of democracy: is a country not free to change its legislation so as to strike the best-suited balance between sustainability and development?

At any rate, currently, SD-related provisions are to be found in different sources.[32] IIAs do not generally provide for binding environmental and human rights standards, as they 'merely' set out investors' guarantees and, conversely, fence in the host states' room for manoeuver. Both types of rules, however, are capable of encroaching on SD.

On the one hand, standards of treatment of investors limit governmental leeway, to the effect that a non-justifiable breach of one such standard entails the state's duty to pay compensation to the investors. Practically all these norms have a bearing of some sort on SD,[33] be they general in character (such as the most-favoured-nation-treatment, the national-treatment, the fair-and-equitable-treatment and the full-security-and-protection standards) or more specific (like those ruling out restrictions on capital movements). Competition among investment-seeking states may take two paths: by including certain rules in an IIA or by phrasing them in a way more constraining for the state. Yet it must be said that, even if they have an identical wording, two provisions may still result in being construed differently by arbitrators. This is another significant outcome of the fragmentation of the investment regime, devoid of

32 As this chapter focuses on investment law, the sources addressed here do not include those rules primarily covering economic (eg trade and finance) or non-economic (eg labour and the environment) aspects, which are not investment, nor soft law instruments, which are not law. Nonetheless, one should be aware that these other sources – even the non-binding ones – may support SD and/or participatory practices in investment.

33 International Institute for Sustainable Development, n 10. See also below n 38.

any centralised judicial authority (even though WGIII is primarily working on this issue).

On the other hand, provisions preserving states' regulatory power and shielding non-discriminatory actions taken in the public interest against investors' entitlements also affect SD, this time, in a potentially positive way. Again, these safeguards may be formulated reductively by a government trying to secure a competitive advantage. In any case, irrespective of the language, and as already noted, it is up to states to exploit the leeway they are accorded and put it to good use.[34] Governments can do so not just through their own general laws, but also by enacting investment legislation[35] and concluding contracts[36] with investors. These are the other sources alluded to above that may explicitly, though not necessarily effectively, raise the issue of compliance with human rights, environmental standards and other SD-related norms (such as performance requirements, for instance the transfer of green technologies).

Having ascertained that most rules lying on the different planes of the multilayered investment regime are capable of having more or less immediate beneficial as well as adverse effects on SD, we should ask which are the possible strategies to pursue a reasonable equilibrium between sustainability and socio-economic progress.[37]

3.2 *Sustainable Development Strategies in International Investment Law*

Overall, the ways to promote SD through investment law can be traced back to three groups, which can roughly be said to be centered on the host state, the investor (or home state) and the investment.[38]

The first approach is quite obvious and consists of broadening governmental regulatory space, either by acting on the rules that carve out exceptions

34 As concluded by Lukas Stifter and August Reinisch, 'Expropriation in the Light of the UNCTAD Investment Policy Framework for Sustainable Development' in Hindelang and Krajewski (eds), n 29.

35 Fauchald, n 6, at 191–94.

36 Lorenzo Cotula, 'Rethinking Investment Contracts Through a Sustainable Development Lens' in Elena Blanco and Jona Razzaque (eds), *Natural Resources and the Green Economy: Redefining the Challenges for People, States and Corporations* (Brill | Nijhoff 2012).

37 UNCTAD has identified ten principles aimed at striking such a balance: UNCTAD, *Investment Policy Framework for Sustainable Development* (United Nations 2015) 30–36.

38 Albeit following a different categorisation, an analytical list of policy options is in ibid at 85, 91–121 (where the SD implications of each option are spelt out). Narrower in scope but discussed at length and accompanied by treaty practice are the ideas put forth in J Anthony VanDuzer, Penelope Simons and Graham Mayeda, *Integrating Sustainable Development into International Investment Agreements: A Guide for Developing Countries* (Commonwealth Secretariat 2012) 251–398.

ultimately based on the pursuit of public interest or the protection of the most vulnerable subjects such as workers or indigenous peoples, or by directly reducing the scope of the rights and privileges afforded to investors. These results, in turn, may be attained by different means. Some promises usually made to investors may be omitted from an IIA (or domestic investment law, or investor-state contract). Conversely, a clause may be included that allows the host state to take measures which have a legitimate SD-related aim. In multilateral IIAs, such commitments by the parties may be diversified and in tune with each state's individual stage of development.[39] Another option is the narrowing down of the scope of vaguely phrased provisions, which turns out to be an effective strategy in a field, such as that of investment law, where most protection standards are formulated as open-ended rules, perhaps as principles. Of course, exceptions to treatment standards, too, may be clarified so as to grant states non-easily-compressible room for maneuver. A third possibility is to pass through the interpretation rather than the reform of investment rules,[40] and more generally through judicial activity, for instance by avoiding that the reasonableness of the host state's conduct be assessed by resorting to a strict proportionality test.[41]

The second group of strategies stresses the duties of investors and the role of the home states in enforcing such duties or discharging their own responsibilities. The task of ensuring that investors comply with human rights and environmental standards rests primarily with the host state, which may be urged by an IIA to ratify treaties protecting such standards, although this has usually a simple hortatory value. These standards may also be included as investors' duties in IIAs or investor-state contracts, so that a breach arises not (only) from the violation of the host state's domestic laws but from the violation of the IIA or contract itself.[42] This would be conducive to arbitral claims where the investor is the defendant rather than the plaintiff. In the absence of similar clauses, one could maintain that investors' duties are set out directly

39 Desierto, n 5 (presenting the case of ASEAN).

40 Katharina Berner, 'Reconciling Investment Protection and Sustainable Development: A Plea for an Interpretative U-Turn' in Hindelang and Krajewski (eds), n 29. See also Sacerdoti, n 29, at 39 (who, however, thinks that BITs are not the main route to promote SD, as they are primarily aimed at protecting investment).

41 Federico Ortino, 'Investment Treaties, Sustainable Development and Reasonableness Review: A Case Against Strict Proportionality Balancing' (2017) 30 Leiden J Intl L 71. A similar position is taken by Roland Kläger, 'Revising Treatment Standards – Fair and Equitable Treatment in Light of Sustainable Development' in Hindelang and Krajewski (eds), n 29.

42 A similar effect is generated by the inclusion – which is common – in the treaty or contract of a provision demanding compliance with state law on the part of the investor. Of course, self-standing SD-related standards would afford greater flexibility.

by customary international law, perhaps a sort of international development law applicable to investors.[43] Nevertheless, enforcing them through investment arbitration would be hard for a series of reasons related to jurisdictional issues (eg demonstration of investors' consent to arbitration), the international subjectivity of natural and legal persons (in a context where corporations are usually seen as incapable of bearing real duties) and the relationship of investment rules with domestic law and international law at large (which is a major problem in light of the traditional uncertainty about the law applicable in investment arbitral proceedings).[44] It is unsurprising that claims against investors, or better, counterclaims, have rarely been successful.

As for the role of capital-exporting countries (home states), this could take the form of an improbable international law obligation not to act to the detriment of sustainability,[45] at least by way of due diligence, that is, by watching over the conduct of corporations abroad and possibly envisaging penalties for wrongdoers. A similar retributive but more plausible approach relies on the attachment of conditionalities to FTAs, whereby SD-related standards are upheld by the threat of lifting the benefits bargained with the counterpart. Viable options could also be the merger of SD considerations into the home state's decision-making process (what in the EU is known as the policy integration principle),[46] as well as the monitoring of policy outcomes, which may themselves be fed into the decision-making process. This is the so-called sustainability impact assessment, which is again regularly performed by the EU before concluding FTAs, and is crucial despite the uncertain calculation of such an impact. It is pointless to ask *in abstracto* if FTAs are beneficial or detrimental to SD, as this analysis must be conducted on a case-by-case basis and capture possible future scenarios in order to provide data for planning. Policymakers should know, *inter alia*, which sectors will be advantaged and those which will be impaired by the agreement; whether SD-oriented regulation in the capital-importing country will be more financially burdensome and politically costly following the liberalisation of investment and trade; and how

43 Daniel D Bradlow, 'Development Decision-Making and the Content of International Development Law' (2004) 27 Boston College Intl & Comp L Rev 195, 212 and 214–15.

44 Hege Elisabeth Kjos, *Applicable Law in Investor-State Arbitration* (OUP 2013).

45 Aaron Cosbey *et al*, *Investment and Sustainable Development: A Guide to the Use and Potential of International Investment Agreements* (Intl Institute Sustainable Development 2004), where an undefined duty to respect 'basic norms of sustainable development' is hypothesised, at 33.

46 Stephanie Schacherer, *Sustainable Development in EU Foreign Investment Law* (Brill | Nijhoff 2021).

many additional resources, made available through economic development, will be possible to invest in SD-related measures and technologies.

This brings us to the third approach to sustainability in investment law. Since investment may further as well as hinder SD, rules – at the international level but also at the domestic level of both the host state and the home state – should be designed to promote FDI that is beneficial to SD and discourage FDI that undermines it. In addition to the already mentioned sustainability impact assessment undertaken before concluding FTAs or during their implementation, home states could adopt a wide array of measures aimed at facilitating 'good' investment over 'bad' investment.[47] The host state, for its part, might refine the *Salini* test and refuse the entry of, or simply exclude from protection, certain investments: thus, the government might decide to target only those that are more problematic in light of SD (eg sector-specific restrictions or other limitations based on development priorities).[48] Conversely, SD-compatible FDI might be attracted into the host country by favourable legislation, which might entail the creation of SD-based special economic zones.[49] In addition, provisions for investment facilitation could be included in IIAs to attract 'recognized sustainable investors'.[50] However, the actions aimed at directing FDI towards the realisation of SD, also in light of the SDGs, are many more.[51]

3.3 *Looking for Sustainability in International Investment Law*

At this point, one might ask whether there is a definition of SD in international investment law. Apparently, although a number of IIAs refer to the concept, only a few attempt to explain it. For instance, the parties to the EU-Korea FTA unoriginally 'recognise that economic development, social development and environmental protection are interdependent and mutually reinforcing components of sustainable development'.[52] Even though the scope of the provision

47 An analytical list is provided by Karl P Sauvant and Evan Gabor, 'Facilitating Sustainable FDI for Sustainable Development in a WTO Investment Facilitation Framework: Four Concrete Proposals' (2021) 55 J World Trade 261, 283.

48 Fauchald, n 6, at 196.

49 UNCTAD, *World Investment Report 2019: Special Economic Zones* (United Nations 2019) 195–205.

50 Sauvant and Gabor, n 47, at 272–78.

51 This may entail mere promotion of investment in developing countries – the aim of Target 17.5 of SDGs – or, more specifically, investment in the goals themselves: see UNCTAD, *UNCTAD: Investing in Sustainable Development Goals* (United Nations 2015).

52 EU-Korea FTA, Art 13.1(2). This formula dates back at least to the 1995 Copenhagen Declaration on Social Development and now appears in several EU FTAs. A variant in a non-binding instrument can be found in Italy's 2020 Model BIT, speaking of SD 'in its economic, social and environmental dimensions' (Preamble). The definition stresses the

hosting the definition is limited to the trade relationship of the parties,[53] it cannot be excluded that such an article may have a larger interpretative value that also covers the investment parts of the treaty. Moreover, it is not that important that social and environmental conditions in a given country improve thanks to the 'strings' attached to trade rules rather than investment rules, as long as the effects are real. This must be remembered in light of the current spread of sophisticated, all-embracing FTAs.

At any rate, there are only a handful of similar provisions and these cannot be deemed to be representative of an entire branch of law, especially due to the fragmentation of the investment law regime, which hinders the emergence of a clear juridical idea of SD. This is also true when one tries to grasp the meaning of the notion by looking into either the context where SD is mentioned or the treaty part devoted to SD. The EU-CARIFORUM FTA is a good example of both cases. On the one hand, in its Preamble it states that the parties 'need to promote economic and social progress for their people in a manner consistent with sustainable development by respecting basic labour rights in line with the commitments they have undertaken within the International Labour Organisation and by protecting the environment in line with the 2002 Johannesburg Declaration':[54] the word 'by' indicates that labour rights and environmental protection are not by-products but an integral part of SD.[55] On the other hand, in an article named after SD, the parties express their understanding that this notion entails the 'commitment that: (a) the application of this Agreement shall fully take into account the human, cultural, economic, social, health and environmental best interests of their respective population and of future generations; (b) decision-taking methods shall embrace the fundamental principles of ownership, participation and dialogue', so that the parties 'agree to work cooperatively towards the realisation of a sustainable development centred on the human person, who is the main beneficiary of development'.[56]

interconnection and lack of hierarchy between what seem to be ends; the Trans-Pacific Partnership Agreement takes an analogous approach in speaking the language of means, claiming that SD can be attained "through mutually supportive trade and environmental policies and practices" (Preamble).

53 The same definition appears also in Sect IV, Art 1, of the abovementioned EU-China Comprehensive Investment Agreement, which is entirely devoted to investment. To my knowledge, this is one of the few IIAs mentioning "the welfare of [...] future generations".

54 EU-CARIFORUM Economic Partnership Agreement, Preamble.

55 But see the Preamble and Sect IV, Sub-Sect 2, Art 1, of the EU-China Comprehensive Investment Agreement, where SD and environmental and labour protection are "merely" juxtaposed, with no explicit causal implication.

56 Ibid, Art 3(2)–(3).

This locution draws near to being an open-ended definition of SD; however, such a choice is not particularly common, especially in IIAs that are not FTAs. Even the recent (2019) Model BIT of the Netherlands, for instance, in a section entirely devoted to SD, provides no definition. It simply restates the importance of maintaining high standards in labour and environmental matters and of complying with international obligations (in force for the parties) related to the protection of the environment, labour rights and human rights; it mentions the idea of corporate social responsibility as referred to the same fields; it invokes women's empowerment, but as a means to SD rather than an embodiment of it.[57]

The path followed by the abovementioned model agreement – ie the expression of some non-economic concerns and the specific ways to address them, in place of a general definition of SD – is very common in BITs, which are the backbone of the investment regime. Moreover, each BIT takes its own approach to the matter, by citing some issues and not others (the most common being human rights, labour, health, the environment and, to a lesser extent, corruption and transparency) and by devising some strategies and not others (non-relaxation of standards, *renvoi* to international obligations, well-defined power to regulate and so on). This is where treaty surveys come in useful. Indeed, scholars such as Chi,[58] Cordonier Segger,[59] Sauvant and Mann,[60] Fauchald,[61] Gordo, Pohl and Bouchard,[62] and institutions like the United Nations Conference on Trade and Development,[63] have tried to 'take photographs' of SD in IIAs, based on a variety of criteria. Their work is valuable for two reasons. First, it provides us with a rich statistical overview of the presence

57 Model BIT of The Netherlands, Arts 6–7.

58 Manjiao Chi, *Integrating Sustainable Development in International Investment Law: Normative Incompatibility, System Integration and Governance Implications* (Routledge 2018).

59 Marie-Claire Cordonnier Segger, *Crafting Trade and Investment Accords for Sustainable Development: Athena's Treaties* (OUP 2021) 341–96.

60 Karl P Sauvant and Howard Mann, 'Making FDI More Sustainable: Towards an Indicative List of FDI Sustainability Characteristics' (2019) 20 J World Investment & Trade 916.

61 Fauchald, n 6, at 191.

62 Kathryn Gordon, Joachim Pohl and Marie Bouchard, 'Investment Treaty Law, Sustainable Development and Responsible Business Conduct: A Fact Finding Survey' (2014) OECD Working Papers on International Investment 2014/01, <www.oecd-ilibrary.org/docserver/5jz0xvgx1zlt-en.pdf> last accessed 31 March 2022.

63 In its annual reports, UNCTAD regularly provides an overview of the 'reform-oriented provisions' in the IIAs concluded the year before, also stressing the most innovative features in state practice. At the time of writing, the most recent issue is UNCTAD, *World Investment Report 2020: International Production Beyond the Pandemic* (United Nations 2020). This body has also identified priority sectors for investment with respect to SD and a list of indicators of the impact of FDI on SD: UNCTAD, n 37, at 21 and 54, respectively.

of SD-related clauses in IIAs. Secondly and more important to our purposes, it allows us to open a window onto the multifarious components of SD according to states and, especially, academics and specialised bodies. In a fragmented context such as the one of investment law, SD is best spoken of as a 'narrative' or 'discourse', rather than as a coherent, circumscribed notion.

However, some caveats are due with regards to similar surveys. 'Big data' analyses do not always render properly the complexity of rules (two sentences formulated with almost identical language may conceal major differences as to their meaning), or the relevance of such rules, which might be somewhat superfluous because of their content (as when an IIA provision demands compliance with the host state's domestic law) or their container (as is the case for those new model BITs compiled by states that have ceased concluding such bilateral agreements).

More generally, one must remember that SD clauses may differ as to their bindingness, completeness,[64] enforceability and, ultimately, effectiveness.[65] Indeed, what counts is facts, not the law. For example, it is not a great relief to know that BITs have no significant adverse impact on domestic SD standards if, as it has been argued, these treaties worsen the actual conduct of investors on the field and therefore widen the gap between rules and practices.[66]

4 Participation in Investment Matters: A Door to Sustainability?

Many individuals take part in transboundary investment processes and are accorded a role by international investment law. However, by default only investors and "capital-friendly" parties enjoy such a role (Section 4.1), whereas the contribution of those affected by the investment, or of the population of the host state, is only occasionally sanctioned by law. In fact, it is believed by some that investment law diminishes the democratic potential of host states' politics by restricting the margins of political and legal self-determination of those states to a greater extent than it is usually done by international law,

64 Lorenzo Cotula, 'EU-China Comprehensive Agreement on Investment: An Appraisal of Its Sustainable Development Section' (2021) 6 Bus & Human Rights J 360, 364 (for a reference to labor rights).

65 Ibid at 365. A binding and enforceable provision might still be ineffective, perhaps due to power inequality.

66 Fangjin Ye, 'The Impact of Bilateral Investment Treaties (BITs) on Collective Labor Rights in Developing Countries' (2020) 15 Rev Intl Organizations 899. See also Ronald B Davies and Krishna Chaitanya Vadlamannati, 'A Race to the Bottom in Labor Standards? An Empirical Investigation' (2013) 103 J Development Economics 1.

due to the specificities of investment law (Section 4.2). This concern lies at the heart of today's legitimacy crisis of the investment regime and the ensuing attempts to reform it. However, little can be expected from these attempts, and other avenues must be explored so as to grant people that capacity to affect investment projects – by improving them or halting them – that is not always ensured through democratically elected bodies (ie the main door for participation). Involvement in the implementation of projects and in adjudication of disputes between state and investor are two such avenues. Other paths exist, but one must wonder whether all these means are capable of advancing the cause of SD (Section 4.3).

4.1 *The Protagonists on the Investment Stage*

Discourse on participation in investment matters cannot underestimate the fact that international investment law is one of the very few branches of international law where individuals play a prominent role. Of course, this is limited to the investor. In principle, the protection afforded by investment law, even the part that has attained customary status, can only be invoked by investors if a state has expressed its consent to arbitration through a BIT negotiated with the home state. Apparently, despite the huge number of existing treaties, only a small fraction of bilateral relations between countries (the host state and the home state) is covered.[67] Moreover, arbitral costs are extremely high and this cuts out other companies.

However, neither aspect is an insurmountable impediment, and both can be circumvented by means that increase the number of participants on the investors' side. On the one hand, the problem of high costs can be overcome through third-party funding, that is, the involvement of a subject extraneous to the dispute who financially supports the arbitration in order to obtain a share of the compensation eventually awarded (if any). As this practice may encourage specious litigation,[68] the WGIII is now considering how to regulate it. On the other hand, the issue of the lack of an IIA between the host state and the state of nationality of the investor can be bypassed by merely incorporating a new company – in fact, a subsidiary of the main investor – in a country that concluded an IIA with the host state (treaty shopping). In addition, multinational

67 Patrick Dumberry, 'The Legal Standing of Shareholders Before Arbitral Tribunals: Has Any Rule of Customary International Law Crystallised?' (2010) 18 Michigan State J Intl L 371 (of course, not all relations are equally important).

68 By the investor against the state. But, in principle, powerful states could sustain, both financially and legally, international claims by weak states against investors who incurred in violations of their obligations toward such states.

corporations can be complex juridical persons comprising a number of shareholders: investment tribunals have built up a case law that quite generously accords indirect shareholders the right to bring claims,[69] thus broadening the potential plaintiffs' basin indefinitely. This fact, also in light of the pivotal role played by shareholders in a company's decision-making, should be given consideration in the ongoing debate on sustainable corporate governance.

4.2 *Investment (Law) and Democracy*

If the investing company, its subsidiaries or otherwise controlled entities, its shareholders, as well as its funders, take part in investment litigation as 'representatives' of capital-exporting countries, who are the participants within FDI-importing countries? In general terms, international investment law does not recognise participatory rights (as opposed to a mere faculty) to people affected by investment projects or those acting on their behalf. This is a serious issue, since this branch of international law can, by design, reduce democratic spaces in the host state.

Indeed, many IIAs contain so-called stabilisation clauses,[70] that 'freeze' the laws of a host state throughout the duration of a contract with the investor (freezing clauses) or require the investor to comply with new laws but upon governmental compensation for the costs thus incurred (economic equilibrium clauses). As is evident, this can make changes in the domestic legislative framework very costly for the host state. Moreover, irrespective of this kind of clauses, a similar outcome may still stem from the abovementioned fair-and-equitable-treatment standard, which is included in all IIAs and may now have attained customary status. It requires the state to duly consider the investors' legitimate expectations,[71] which may be grounded on general regulations as well as on specific commitments undertaken by the government with the investors.[72] But, absent IIAs and thus in an even broader perspective,

69 Lukas Vanhonnaeker, *Shareholders' Claims for Reflective Loss in International Investment Law* (CUP 2020), especially ch 4.

70 See, with reference to SD, Jola Gjuzi, *Stabilization Clauses in International Investment Law: A Sustainable Development Approach* (Springer 2018).

71 Although expectations of economic gains can and should be discounted for the expectations of likely regulatory amendments, one cannot completely rule out the possibility of a risk-shifting effect, due to the use of an IIA as a sort of insurance for investors against a substantial legislative change, so that they do not feel pressured to comply in advance with future higher standards: Lise Johnson and Oleksandr Volkov, 'Investor-State Contracts, Host-State "Commitments" and the Myth of Stability in International Law' (2013) 24 American Rev Intl Arbitration 361.

72 This may result in different thresholds for establishing a breach: Sondra Faccio, 'The Assessment of the FET Standard Between Legitimate Expectations and Economic Impact

violation of contractual obligations owed to investors could result in a full compensation duty based on the *pacta sunt servanda* principle.[73]

It follows that the host state's legislature will not be free to amend the country's domestic laws – which include tax regulations –[74] without running the risk of being requested to pay significant sums as compensation for the investors' economic losses, which also cover those related to missed opportunities. Democracy might, therefore, suffer a condition known as 'regulatory chill', with law-making bodies being discouraged from enacting new rules promoting the public good and SD but prejudicing the investors' interests. In addition, the chilling effects may be protracted by the existence of a sunset clause, which prolongs the application of an IIA to investments made while the treaty was in force for some, even many, years after the host state's denunciation of the IIA. Although the anecdotal recounting of the existence of the regulatory chill has met with a few large-scale empirical studies downplaying the risk,[75] it seems wise to share the view taken by the OECD, which, while disproving the idea of the race to the bottom, admits that "[t]he possibility of a "regulatory chill" ... is harder to refute for the lack of a counterfactual scenario".[76]

In any case, international investment law can compress a country's political self-determination in other ways. For instance, a government could somewhat lose control of its own legislation during arbitration proceedings, should adjudicators decide to show little or no deference to the state's interpretation and application of its laws. Construing domestic rules as law or as facts and adopting a greater or smaller degree of judicial self-restraint in attributing a meaning to the defendant's laws when establishing eg whether the investor complied

in the Italian Solar Energy Investment Case Law' (2020) Zoom-in 71 Questions Intl L 3.

73 Jason Webb Yackee, '*Pacta Sunt Servanda* and State Promises to Foreign Investors Before Bilateral Investment Treaties: Myth and Reality' (2009) 32 Fordham Intl L J 1550 (who probes arbitral practice to argue against the possibility that breaches of contract can either be justified under international law, or give rise to milder compensation duties).

74 Sonia E Rolland, 'The Impact of Trade and Investment Treaties on Fiscal Resources and Taxation in Developing Countries' (2020) 21 Chicago J Intl L 48, 63–70.

75 Carolina Moehlecke, 'The Chilling Effect of International Investment Disputes: Limited Challenges to State Sovereignty' (2020) 64 Intl Studies Q 1; Tarald Laudal Berge and Axel Berger, 'Do Investor-State Dispute Settlement Cases Influence Domestic Environmental Regulation? The Role of Respondent State Bureaucratic Capacity' (2021) 12 J Intl Dispute Settlement 1 (the latter's generalisations have limits that the authors themselves recognise).

76 OECD, *Foreign Direct Investment for Development: Maximising Benefits, Minimising Costs* (OECD 2002) 20.

with such laws,[77] are actions that locate decision-making power mainly within or outside the state and its elected bodies.

Overall, the relationship between investment and democracy is complex and possibly negative.[78] Some empirical analyses find that, albeit democratic regimes protect property rights more firmly than autocratic countries (which of course is good in the eyes of investors), the former are also usually more likely to pay attention to the voice of the domestic industry and satisfy its requests to ensure economic equality of arms or even undercut competition against the 'invaders'.[79] Since foreign investors are more concerned with economic freedom than political freedom,[80] it follows that FDI does not necessarily flow towards more democratic states. As always, however, this kind of data-driven observations prove to be contentious, and other scholars have provided documentary evidence of a greater attractivity of democracies in terms of incoming FDI.[81] At any rate, the most interesting question inverts the perspective and asks not whether more democracy fosters FDI but, rather, whether FDI fosters democracy.[82]

Of course, given the fact that banning the inflow of foreign capital is undesirable for a country and perhaps even unfeasible, the rules on foreign investment should be devised so as to promote democracy rather than autocracy and corruption. This can be done in many ways. For instance, FDI in the primary sector (the extraction of natural resources), unlike investment in non-primary sectors (eg manufacturing), might exert a negative influence on democratic parameters in host countries and could thus be accorded a different

---

77 Jarrod Hepburn, *Domestic Law in International Investment Arbitration* (OUP 2017) ch 5.

78 Academic studies, like those quoted in the following, conceptualise "democracy" differently. Indeed, this many-sided notion should be broken down into its components. The question cannot be addressed in these pages, just like its problematisation – despite the latter's importance. For instance, can we say – with Antony Anghie, *Imperialism, Sovereignty and the Making of International Law* (CUP 2004) 253 – that 'governance is now designed to provide the political institutions that will enable the furtherance of globalization'? In other words, that domestic fora, as intended by the international community, are meant to advance economic interests rather than empower individuals and groups?

79 Quan Li and Adam Resnick, 'Reversal of Fortunes: Democratic Institutions and Foreign Direct Investment Inflows to Developing Countries' (2003) 57 Intl Org 175.

80 Aparna Mathura and Kartikeya Singh, 'Foreign Direct Investment, Corruption and Democracy' (2013) 45 Applied Economics 991.

81 Nathan M Jensen, 'Democratic Governance and Multinational Corporations: Political Regimes and Inflows of Foreign Direct Investment' (2003) 57 Intl Org 587.

82 On this see eg Roger Mongong Fon *et al*, 'Does Foreign Direct Investment Promote Institutional Development in Africa?' (2021) 30 101835 Intl Bus Rev 1.

treatment.[83] Similarly, different rules could be applied to investment projects arising out of contracts concluded with authoritarian regimes whose later fall made way for liberal governments. Currently, arbitrators do not usually take a more lenient approach when deciding cases on a breach of contract in transitional settings, so that investors' "claims may prevent incoming democratic regimes from pursuing their development priorities" and thus from becoming more politically stable.[84]

Another path for states is that of re-appropriating their power to confer meaning to IIAs, by expanding the possibility of issuing joint interpretations of such agreements, thus limiting the role of a supposedly unaccountable international judiciary. This hypothesis, however, is supportive of democracy only insofar as the interpretative power thus reconquered is not managed in an unaccountable manner by the government. Therefore, democratically elected bodies should be involved,[85] especially if they played a role in concluding the IIA, so that the meaning of it as understood by the executive is not seen by the parliament as an undue change in treaty arrangements. But, in more general terms, greater legitimacy requires larger participation, which includes non-state actors.

4.3 *Sustainable Development Through Public Participation*

As noted above, international investment law does not establish real participatory rights yet. This does not mean, however, that such rights are never provided for by other instruments such as investor-state contracts and domestic investment laws. Moreover, other branches of international law, such as environmental law[86] and human rights law,[87] may be used to prop up participation

83 Feng Sun, 'The Dual Political Effects of Foreign Direct Investment in Developing Countries' (2014) 48 J Developing Areas 107.

84 Jonathan Bonnitcha, 'Democracy, Development and Compensation Under Investment Treaties: The Case of Transition from Authoritarian Rule' in Stephan W Schill, Christian J Tams and Rainer Hofmann (eds), *International Investment Law and Development: Bridging the Gap* (Edward Elgar 2015) 288. But see also the subsequent chapter of the same book: Walid Ben Hamida, 'Investment Treaties and Democratic Transition: Does Investment Law Authorize not to Honor Contracts Concluded with Undemocratic Regimes?' in ibid.

85 A similar point is raised in Loris Marotti, 'L'interpretazione autentica dei trattati in materia di investimenti' (2018) 32 Diritto del commercio internazionale 651, 667.

86 Case T-9/19 *ClientEarth v European Investment Bank* (2021) General Court (Second Chamber, Extended Composition) (annulling a decision of the EIB that had rejected an application pursuant to the Aarhus Regulation for an internal review of a decision to finance a biomass power plant in Spain).

87 IACtHR, *Claude Reyes v Chile*, Judgment, 16 September 2006, Series C No 151 (recognising the right of an NGO to access information held by Chile's Foreign Investment Committee so as to exercise social control on a project for the exploitation of Río Cóndor).

in investment matters. The same is true for the internal procedures of the World Bank and other financial institutions at the regional level whose statutory aim is that of funding projects all over the world, although these codes of conduct also attracted criticisms.[88] Moreover, if we think that adding soft law has any sense, the list of investment-related tools where participation features prominently is even longer.[89]

Investment lawyers, at any rate, are now devoting increasing attention to the issue of participation.[90] They are considering how the public can be given the opportunity to have a say on investment issues, even if this, more often than not, takes the form of a faculty rather than an actual right. There are many possible avenues.

First, the public can be (and has been) asked to express their views on a number of instruments, binding or not. Some states consulted with their citizens before revising their model BITs: for instance, Norway (2008 and again 2015), India (2015), Morocco (2017), the Netherlands (2018) and, for its Cooperation and Investment Facilitation Agreements, Brazil (2021). Ecuador went a lot further when, in 2013, it set up its Citizens' Commission for a Comprehensive Audit of Investment Protection Treaties and of the International Arbitration System on Investments, comprising government officials, academics, lawyers and civil society groups, to assess whether the benefits of concluding IIAs were greater than the attached risks. The EU, for its part, in 2014 launched a wide-ranging consultation on investment protection and investor-to-state dispute settlement in the Transatlantic Trade and Investment Partnership Agreement, and in the same year the Union's civil society was again called upon to send comments in light of the 2015 revision of the Transparency Policy of the European Investment Bank. Similar initiatives have been recently taken at the international level in 2019 for the Hague Rules on Business and Human

88 Sanae Fujita, *The World Bank, Asian Development Bank and Human Rights: Developing Standards of Transparency, Participation and Accountability* (Edward Elgar 2013).

89 See eg Principle 9 of the 2014 Principles for Responsible Investment in Agriculture and Food Systems (known as the RAI Principles) by the Committee on World Food Security. On the issue of sources, see above n 32.

90 See, *inter alia*, Eric De Brabandere, Tarcisio Gazzini and Avidan Kent (eds), *Public Participation and Foreign Investment Law: From the Creation of Rights and Obligations to the Settlement of Disputes* (Brill | Nijhoff 2021); Farouk El-Hosseny, *Civil Society in Investment Treaty Arbitration: Status and Prospects* (Brill | Nijhoff 2018); Chrysoula Mavromati and Sarah Spottiswood, 'Voices That Shape Investment Treaties: Inside, Outside and Among States' in Catharine Titi (ed), *Public Actors in International Investment Law* (Springer 2021).

Rights Arbitration and in 2020 for the OECD paper on Business Responsibilities and Investment Treaties.

The interest elicited by these initiatives differed from case to case, but it was usually manifested by individual scholars, learned societies, networks of professionals and other well-organised groups more than by ordinary citizens. The same occurs with public participation in institutional (permanent or temporary) fora, like WGIII or the domestic advisory groups the EU has established under the SD chapters of its trade agreements, the latter comprising representatives of business, trade unions and NGOs.[91]

As is evident from the examples above, people can be involved in many decisions such as the drafting of a hard or soft law text, the choice of a stance in matters of investment policy and the implementation of IIAs.[92] However, the same can be replicated on a lesser scale, with the engagement of only a part of the population. Thus, for instance, those affected by an investment project could be allowed to voice their opinion in environmental impact assessments procedures[93] or even be granted the right to make that project conditional upon their free, prior and informed consent.[94] Both paths have been taken in practice, and the latter, in particular, is owed to indigenous peoples under human rights law.[95] The incorporation of the interests of affected communities into the investment contract between the state and the investor has also been carried out, albeit quite rarely, whereas the involvement of those communities as formal parties of the contract is, as of now, merely a doctrinal proposal.[96]

91 On the composition and work of such groups see Deborah Martens, Diana Potjomkina and Jan Orbie, 'Domestic Advisory Groups in EU Trade Agreements: Stuck at the Bottom or Moving up the Ladder?' (2020) Friedrich Ebert Stiftung, <https://library.fes.de/pdf-files/iez/17135.pdf> last accessed 31 March 2022.

92 Several channels for making one's voice heard at national and supranational level are discussed by Chrysoula Mavromati and Sarah Spottiswood, 'Public Participation in Investment Treaty Making' in Brabandere, Gazzini and Kent (eds), n 97.

93 David A Collins, 'Public Participation in Environmental Impact Assessments for Foreign Investment Projects: A Canadian Perspective' in Brabandere, Gazzini and Kent (eds), n 90.

94 Sam Szoke-Burke and Kaitlin Y Cordes, 'Mechanisms for Consultation and Free, Prior and Informed Consent in the Negotiation of Investment Contracts' (2020) 41 Northwestern J Intl L & Bus 49.

95 Some interesting cases are illustrated by Gloria M Alvarez and Ilias Kazeem, 'Measuring Public Participation in International Investment Treaty Law: A Study of the Latin American Extractive Industries' in Gloria M Alvarez, Mélanie Riofrio Piché and Felipe V Sperandio (eds), *International Arbitration in Latin America: Energy and Natural Resources Disputes* (Wolters Kluwer 2021).

96 Ibironke T Odumosu-Ayanu, 'Governments, Investors and Local Communities: Analysis of a Multi-Actor Investment Contract Framework' (2014) 15 Melbourne J Intl L 473.

Of course, civil society must have a role in the monitoring of the implementation of the investment contract, once concluded.

In addition to the participation in the creation of rules (of IIAs, contracts or other) and their actual operation 'on the ground', the option exists of public involvement in investment adjudication. This is perhaps the most common entry point for civil society into investment law. Indeed, as of today NGOs have been admitted innumerable times to arbitral proceedings as *amici curiae*,[97] who are allowed to put forth their remarks on the case even if they are not parties to the dispute. Again, the possibility for the representatives of affected population to directly submit claims against the state or the investor is still a doctrinal idea.[98] However, *amici curiae* are not usually permitted to access relevant documents.[99] Indeed, transparency is one of the most serious problems in investment law and policy. Many state-investor contracts are confidential, as is much investment-related information during proceedings. Arbitral awards may also be classified; a survey shows that, of the cases dealt with by ICSID panels between 1972 and 2012, about 40 per cent were kept secret.[100]

As can be seen, the means for a larger participation of the public are numerous. But do such means attain the goal of promoting SD? It goes without saying that the efficacy of the above-mentioned options can vary significantly. Much depends, and this is an aspect of utmost importance, on the kind of participating actors, who may not always be accountable to society at large.[101] Cooptation of representatives of trade unions or of the industry in monitoring bodies and advisory committees might forward sectoral interests rather than the collective good. Perhaps, this risk decreases slightly by organising consultations open to the general public, but this, in turn, would include people with no clear stakes in the matter at hand and who, moreover, would not necessarily foster SD or at least the 'sustainability' part of it.[102] To be honest, partisanship

97 Sondra Faccio, 'Public Participation in Arbitral Proceedings' in Brabandere, Gazzini and Kent (eds), n 90.

98 Stephan Schill, 'From Investor-State Dispute Settlement to a Multilateral Investment Court? Evaluating Options from an EU Law Perspective' in European Parliament (ed), *EU Investment Protection After the ECJ Opinion on Singapore: Questions of Competence and Coherence* (European Parliament 2019) 42.

99 This is deemed to be right by some commentators, as reported by James Harrison, 'Human Rights Arguments in *Amicus Curiae* Submissions: Promoting Social Justice?' in Pierre-Marie Dupuy, Francesco Francioni and Ernst-Ulrich Petersmann (eds), *Human Rights in International Investment Law and Arbitration* (OUP 2009) 406.

100 Faure and Ma, n 16, at 45.

101 Harrison, n 99, at 405–06.

102 Yulia Levashova, 'Role of Sustainable Development in Bilateral Investment Treaties: Recent Trends and Developments' (2011) 1 J Sustainable Finance & Investment 222, 226.

and promotion of non-sustainable causes cannot be ruled out even when participation is reserved to affected communities. In this case, however, their decisions enjoy greater legitimacy, grounded on those people being directly impacted by the consequences of an investment project.

One should also consider that, irrespective of the goal pursued, actual effects may not be those expected. For instance, the involvement of *amici curiae* in arbitral proceedings may render investment arbitration, which is based on privacy and party autonomy, less attractive.[103] This is not necessarily a problem, provided, on the one hand, that the alternative dispute settlement mechanism equally provides a means of publicity and participation and, on the other hand, that the reduced appeal of dispute settlement does not adversely impact on the attractivity of the country for FDI. Indeed, and more in general, a larger participation can lead to obstacles to investment plans, making the state a 'hostile business environment'.[104] The risk is that of having sustainability-oriented participation at the expense of development.

Open problems are also those related to the precise legal means and consequences of participation. As for the former, for each participatory channel more or less effective strategies can be followed. For example, *amici curiae* may hinge their comments on compliance with human rights and environmental law. However, this language may not be fruitful in terms of concrete results, as it is spoken with arbitrators who are better acquainted with the logic (and purposes) of investment law.[105] As for the latter, it must be noted that different consequences may be attached to the breach of participatory rights. Thus, for instance, investment lawyers must decide whether an investor who did not secure the free, prior and informed consent of affected communities should be punished by considering the contract as void, or merely by curtailing the damages awarded by the arbitral tribunal.[106] These are just some of the wide-ranging choices to be made to combine SD and participation.

---

103 Eugenia Levine, '*Amicus Curiae* in International Investment Arbitration: The Implications of an Increase in Third-Party Participation' (2011) 29 Berkeley J Intl L 200, 206; Harrison, n 99, 405.

104 Avidan Kent, Tarcisio Gazzini and Eric De Brabandere, 'Public Participation in International Investment Law: Setting the Scene' in Brabandere, Gazzini and Kent (eds), n 97, 7.

105 Harrison, n 99; Maxime Somda, 'Protecting Social Rights Using the Amicus Curiae Procedure in Investment Arbitration: A Smokescreen Against Third Parties?' (2019) 10 Investment Treaty News 14. Using the language of investment law could be a better argumentative strategy – which is consonant with the idea that such a branch of law should not be reformed but, rather, construed differently: see above Desierto n 5.

106 The latter solution is adopted by eg Philippe Sands in his interesting dissenting opinion attached to *Bear Creek Mining Corporation v Republic of Peru*, ICSID Case No ARB/14/21, Award, 30 November 2017.

5 Conclusion

Drawing conclusions on participation-driven SD in international investment law is as difficult as summarising how this legal field relates to such an intimately-connected notion as SD, and for the very same reasons. It is evident that the purpose of FDI is mainly economic, consisting of the financial gain of both the investor and the host country. Therefore, it is all too easy to see that (economic) development is a sort of "birthmark" for international investment law. Only in the new millennium, and particularly in the last decade, did lawyers discover the other side of SD and begin to seriously address the issue of sustainability. This academic attention has accompanied a process of partial renewal of international investment law that has seen the emergence of a new generation of IIAs attempting to strike a different balance between the interests of investors and those of capital-importing states. These latter interests, unlike the former, are not necessarily economic in character. However, the fact that these adjustments to the fissured building of investment law have stemmed from a legitimacy crisis that has little to do with the pursuit of SD, together with the primarily bilateral nature of investment law which hinders a systemic rethinking of the regime, explain why no clear understanding of the idea of SD has arisen so far. At any rate, this situation does not mean that states' practice cannot offer examples of legal strategies that can be resorted to with a view to fostering SD, nor has it prevented scholars from finding SD in a variety of diverse clauses contained in IIAs. These provisions also include those furthering participation of stakeholders, although the scholarly interest in this field seems to be even more recent. Many avenues for channelling public participation towards investment matters have been identified; now the challenge consists of comprehending whether, how and to what extent participation actually promotes SD.

Bibliography

Alvarez GM, and Kazeem I, 'Measuring Public Participation in International Investment Treaty Law: A Study of the Latin American Extractive Industries' in Alvarez GM, Riofrio Piché M, and Sperandio FV, (eds), *International Arbitration in Latin America: Energy and Natural Resources Disputes* (Wolters Kluwer 2021).

Anghie A, *Imperialism, Sovereignty and the Making of International Law* (CUP 2004).

Aust V, Morais AI, and Pinto I, 'How Does Foreign Direct Investment Contribute to Sustainable Development Goals? Evidence from African Countries' (2020) 245 118823 J Cleaner Production 1.

Ben Hamida W, 'Investment Treaties and Democratic Transition: Does Investment Law Authorize not to Honor Contracts Concluded with Undemocratic Regimes?' in Schill SW, Tams CJ, and Hofmann R, (eds), *International Investment Law and Development: Bridging the Gap* (Edward Elgar 2015).

Berner K, 'Reconciling Investment Protection and Sustainable Development: A Plea for an Interpretative U-Turn' in Steffen Hindelang and Markus Krajewski (eds), *Shifting Paradigms in International Investment Law: More Balanced, Less Isolated, Increasingly Diversified* (OUP 2016).

Bonnitcha J, 'Democracy, Development and Compensation Under Investment Treaties: The Case of Transition from Authoritarian Rule' in Schill SW, Tams CJ, and Hofmann R, (eds), *International Investment Law and Development: Bridging the Gap* (Edward Elgar 2015).

Brada JC, Zdenek D, and Ichiro I, 'Does Investor Protection Increase Foreign Direct Investment? A Meta-Analysis' (2021) 35 J Economic Surveys 34.

Bradlow DD, 'Development Decision-Making and the Content of International Development Law' (2004) 27 Boston College Intl & Comp L Rev 195.

Carkovic M, and Levine R, 'Does Foreign Direct Investment Accelerate Economic Growth?' in Moran TH, Graham EM, and Blomström M, (eds), *Does Foreign Direct Investment Promote Development?* (Institute for Intl Economics 2005).

Chang HJ, *Economics: The User's Guide* (Pelican 2014).

Chi M, *Integrating Sustainable Development in International Investment Law: Normative Incompatibility, System Integration and Governance Implications* (Routledge 2018).

Colen L, Maertens M, and Swinnen J, 'Foreign Direct Investment as an Engine for Economic Growth and Human Development: A Review of the Arguments and Empirical Evidence' in De Schutter O, Swinnen J, and Wouters J, (eds), *Foreign Direct Investment and Human Development: The Law and Economics of International Investment Agreements* (Routledge 2013).

Colen L, Maertens M, and Swinnen J, 'Determinants of Foreign Direct Investment Flows to Developing Countries: The Role of International Investment Agreements' in De Schutter O, Swinnen J, and Wouters J, (eds), Foreign Direct Investment and Human Development: The Law and Economics of International Investment Agreements (Routledge 2013).

Collins DA, 'Public Participation in Environmental Impact Assessments for Foreign Investment Projects: A Canadian Perspective' in De Brabandere E, Gazzini T,and Kent A, (eds), *Public Participation and Foreign Investment Law: From the Creation of Rights and Obligations to the Settlement of Disputes* (Brill | Nijhoff 2021).

Cordonnier Segger MC, *Crafting Trade and Investment Accords for Sustainable Development: Athena's Treaties* (OUP 2021).

Cosbey A, *et al*, *Investment and Sustainable Development: A Guide to the Use and Potential of International Investment Agreements* (Intl Institute Sustainable Development 2004).

Cosbey A, *International Investment Agreements and Sustainable Development: Achieving the Millennium Development Goals* (Intl Institute Sustainable Development 2005).

Cotula L, 'EU-China Comprehensive Agreement on Investment: An Appraisal of Its Sustainable Development Section' (2021) 6 Bus & Human Rights J 360.

Cotula L, 'Rethinking Investment Contracts Through a Sustainable Development Lens' in Blanco E, and Razzaque J, (eds), *Natural Resources and the Green Economy: Redefining the Challenges for People, States and Corporations* (Brill | Nijhoff 2012).

Davies RB, and Vadlamannati KC, 'A Race to the Bottom in Labor Standards? An Empirical Investigation' (2013) 103 J Development Economics 1.

De Brabandere E, Gazzini T, and Kent A, (eds), Public Participation and Foreign Investment Law: From the Creation of Rights and Obligations to the Settlement of Disputes (Brill | Nijhoff 2021).

De Schutter O, Swinnen J, and Jan Wouters (eds), Foreign Direct Investment and Human Development: The Law and Economics of International Investment Agreements (Routledge 2013).

Desierto D, 'Development as an International Right: Investment in the New Trade-Based IIAs' (2011) 3 Trade L & Development 296.

Dixon J, and Haslam PA, 'Does the Quality of Investment Protection Affect FDI Flows to Developing Countries? Evidence from Latin America' (2016) 39 World Economy 1080.

Doytch N, and Uctum M, 'Globalization and the Environmental Impact of Sectoral FDI' (2016) 40 Economic Systems 582.

Dumberry P, 'The Legal Standing of Shareholders Before Arbitral Tribunals: Has Any Rule of Customary International Law Crystallised?' (2010) 18 Michigan State J Intl L 371.

El-Hosseny F, *Civil Society in Investment Treaty Arbitration: Status and Prospects* (Brill | Nijhoff 2018).

Faccio S, 'Public Participation in Arbitral Proceedings' in De Brabandere E, Gazzini T, and Kent A, (eds), *Public Participation and Foreign Investment Law: From the Creation of Rights and Obligations to the Settlement of Disputes* (Brill | Nijhoff 2021).

Faccio S, 'The Assessment of the FET Standard Between Legitimate Expectations and Economic Impact in the Italian Solar Energy Investment Case Law' (2020) Zoom-in 71 Questions Intl L 3.

Fauchald OK, 'International Investment Law in Support of the Right to Development?' (2021) 34 Leiden J Intl L 181.

Faure M, and Wanli M, 'Investor-State Arbitration: Economic and Empirical Perspectives' (2020) 41 Michigan J Intl L 1.

Fermeglia M, *et al*, '"Investor-State Dispute Settlement" as a New Avenue for Climate Change Litigation', Climate Law Blog (2 June 2021) http://blogs.law.columbia.edu

/climatechange/2021/06/02/investor-state-dispute-settlement-as-a-new-avenue-for-climate-change-litigation.

Fujita S, *The World Bank, Asian Development Bank and Human Rights: Developing Standards of Transparency, Participation and Accountability* (Edward Elgar 2013).

Gjuzi J, *Stabilization Clauses in International Investment Law: A Sustainable Development Approach* (Springer 2018).

Gordon K, Pohl J, and Bouchard M, 'Investment Treaty Law, Sustainable Development and Responsible Business Conduct: A Fact Finding Survey' (2014) OECD Working Papers on International Investment 2014/01, www.oecd-ilibrary.org/docserver/5jz0xvgx1zlt-en.pdf.

Grabowski A, 'The Definition of Investment Under the ICSID Convention: A Defense of *Salini*' (2014) 15 Chicago J Intl L 287.

Harrison J, 'Human Rights Arguments in *Amicus Curiae* Submissions: Promoting Social Justice?' in Dupuy PM, Francioni F, and Petersmann EU, (eds), *Human Rights in International Investment Law and Arbitration* (OUP 2009).

Hepburn J, *Domestic Law in International Investment Arbitration* (OUP 2017).

International Institute for Sustainable Development, *Investment Treaties & Why They Matter to Sustainable Development: Questions & Answers* (Intl Institute Sustainable Development 2012).

Jensen NM, 'Democratic Governance and Multinational Corporations: Political Regimes and Inflows of Foreign Direct Investment' (2003) 57 Intl Org 587.

Johnson L, and Volkov O, 'Investor-State Contracts, Host-State "Commitments" and the Myth of Stability in International Law' (2013) 24 American Rev Intl Arbitration 361.

Johnson Lise, Sachs L, and Lobel N, 'Aligning International Investment Agreements with the Sustainable Development Goals' (2019) 58 Columbia J Transnational L 58.

Kalderimis D, 'IMF Conditionality as Investment Regulation: A Theoretical Analysis' (2004) 13 Soc & L Studies 103.

Kent A, Gazzini T, and De Brabandere E, 'Public Participation in International Investment Law: Setting the Scene' in De Brabandere E, Gazzini T, and Kent A, (eds), *Public Participation and Foreign Investment Law: From the Creation of Rights and Obligations to the Settlement of Disputes* (Brill | Nijhoff 2021).

Kim HS, and Lee Y, 'The Effects of Environmental Costs on Public Support for Foreign Direct Investment: Differences Between the United States and India' in Beverelli C, Kurtz J, and Raess D, (eds), *International Trade, Investment, and the Sustainable Development Goals* (CUP 2020).

Kjos HE, *Applicable Law in Investor-State Arbitration* (OUP 2013).

Kläger R, 'Revising Treatment Standards – Fair and Equitable Treatment in Light of Sustainable Development' in Hindelang S, and Krajewski M, (eds), *Shifting Paradigms in International Investment Law: More Balanced, Less Isolated, Increasingly Diversified* (OUP 2016).

Laudal Berge T, and Berger A, 'Do Investor-State Dispute Settlement Cases Influence Domestic Environmental Regulation? The Role of Respondent State Bureaucratic Capacity' (2021) 12 J Intl Dispute Settlement 1.

Le Quoc H, *et al*, 'The Impact of Foreign Direct Investment on Income Inequality in Vietnam' (2021) 9, 27 Economies 1.

Levashova Y, 'Role of Sustainable Development in Bilateral Investment Treaties: Recent Trends and Developments' (2011) 1(3–4) J Sustainable Finance & Investment 222.

Levine E, 'Amicus Curiae in International Investment Arbitration: The Implications of an Increase in Third-Party Participation' (2011) 29 Berkeley J Intl L 200.

Li Q, and Resnick A, 'Reversal of Fortunes: Democratic Institutions and Foreign Direct Investment Inflows to Developing Countries' (2003) 57 Intl Org 175.

Luo S, *et al*, 'Can FDI and ODI Two-Way Flows Improve the Quality of Economic Growth? Empirical Evidence from China' (2021) 53 Applied Economics 5028.

Marotti L, 'L'interpretazione autentica dei trattati in materia di investimenti' (2018) 32 Diritto del commercio internazionale 651.

Martens D, Potjomkina D, and Orbie J, 'Domestic Advisory Groups in EU Trade Agreements: Stuck at the Bottom or Moving up the Ladder?' (2020) Friedrich Ebert Stiftung, https://library.fes.de/pdf-files/iez/17135.pdf.

Mathura A, and Singh K, 'Foreign Direct Investment, Corruption and Democracy' (2013) 45 Applied Economics 991.

Mavromati C, and Spottiswood S, 'Public Participation in Investment Treaty Making' in De Brabandere E, Gazzini T, and Kent A, (eds), *Public Participation and Foreign Investment Law: From the Creation of Rights and Obligations to the Settlement of Disputes* (Brill | Nijhoff 2021).

Mavromati C, 'Voices That Shape Investment Treaties: Inside, Outside and Among States' in Catharine Titi (ed), *Public Actors in International Investment Law* (Springer 2021).

Moehlecke C, 'The Chilling Effect of International Investment Disputes: Limited Challenges to State Sovereignty' (2020) 64 Intl Studies Q 1.

Mongong Fon R, *et al*, 'Does Foreign Direct Investment Promote Institutional Development in Africa?' (2021) 30 101835 Intl Bus Rev 1.

Moran TH, *Foreign Direct Investment and Development: The New Policy Agenda for Developing Countries and Economies in Transition* (Institute for Intl Economics 1998).

Mukherjee S, and Chakrabarti NK, 'Is "Contribution to the Host States Development" an Essential Criterion to Define Investment Under International Investment Law? A Search Through the Lens of Arbitral Awards' (2021) 42 Liverpool L Rev 429.

Odumosu-Ayanu IT, 'Governments, Investors and Local Communities: Analysis of a Multi-Actor Investment Contract Framework' (2014) 15 Melbourne J Intl L 473.

OECD, *Foreign Direct Investment for Development: Maximising Benefits, Minimising Costs* (OECD 2002).

Olney WW, 'A Race to the Bottom? Employment Protection and Foreign Direct Investment' (2013) 91 J Intl Economics 191.

Ortino F, 'Investment Treaties, Sustainable Development and Reasonableness Review: A Case Against Strict Proportionality Balancing' (2017) 30 Leiden J Intl L 71.

Pohl J, 'Societal Benefits and Costs of International Investment Agreements: A Critical Review of Aspects and Available Empirical Evidence' (2018) OECD Working Papers on International Investment 2018/01, 16–31, www.oecd-ilibrary.org/docserver/e5f85c3d-en.pdf.

Rolland SE, 'The Impact of Trade and Investment Treaties on Fiscal Resources and Taxation in Developing Countries' (2020) 21 Chicago J Intl L 48.

Sacerdoti G, 'Investment Protection and Sustainable Development: Key Issues' in Hindelang S, and Krajewski M, (eds), *Shifting Paradigms in International Investment Law: More Balanced, Less Isolated, Increasingly Diversified* (OUP 2016).

Sauvant KP and Gabor E, 'Facilitating Sustainable FDI for Sustainable Development in a WTO Investment Facilitation Framework: Four Concrete Proposals' (2021) 55 J World Trade 261.

Sauvant KP and Mann H, 'Making FDI More Sustainable: Towards an Indicative List of FDI Sustainability Characteristics' (2019) 20 J World Investment & Trade 916.

Schacherer S, *Sustainable Development in EU Foreign Investment Law* (Brill | Nijhoff 2021).

Schill S, 'From Investor-State Dispute Settlement to a Multilateral Investment Court? Evaluating Options from an EU Law Perspective' in European Parliament (ed), *EU Investment Protection After the ECJ Opinion on Singapore: Questions of Competence and Coherence* (European Parliament 2019).

Skovgaard PL, 'The Importance of BITs for Foreign Direct Investment and Political Risk Insurance: Revisiting the Evidence' in Sauvant KP, (ed), *Yearbook on International Investment Law & Policy 2009–2010* (OUP 2010).

Stifter L, and Reinisch A, 'Expropriation in the Light of the UNCTAD Investment Policy Framework for Sustainable Development' in Hindelang S, and Krajewski M, (eds), Shifting Paradigms in International Investment Law: More Balanced, Less Isolated, Increasingly Diversified (OUP 2016).

Somda M, 'Protecting Social Rights Using the Amicus Curiae Procedure in Investment Arbitration: A Smokescreen Against Third Parties?' (2019) 10 Investment Treaty News 14.

Sun F, 'The Dual Political Effects of Foreign Direct Investment in Developing Countries' (2014) 48 J Developing Areas 107.

Szoke-Burke S, and Cordes KY, 'Mechanisms for Consultation and Free, Prior and Informed Consent in the Negotiation of Investment Contracts' (2020) 41 Northwestern J Intl L & Bus 49.

Todd A, and Peinhardt C, 'Contingent Credibility: The Impact of Investment Treaty Violations on Foreign Direct Investment' (2011) 65 Intl Org 401.

Van Aaken A, and Lehmann TA, 'Sustainable Development and International Investment Law: A Harmonious View from Economics' in Echandi R, and Sauvé P, (eds), *Prospects in International Investment Law and Policy: World Trade Forum* (CUP 2013).

Van Harten G, 'The European Union's Emerging Approach to ISDS: A Review of the Canada-Europe CETA, Europe–Singapore FTA, and European-Vietnam FTA' (2016) 1 Bologna U L Rev 138.

VanDuzer JA, Simons P, and Mayeda G, *Integrating Sustainable Development into International Investment Agreements: A Guide for Developing Countries* (Commonwealth Secretariat 2012).

Vanhonnaeker L, *Shareholders' Claims for Reflective Loss in International Investment Law* (CUP 2020).

Webb YJ, '*Pacta Sunt Servanda* and State Promises to Foreign Investors Before Bilateral Investment Treaties: Myth and Reality' (2009) 32 Fordham Intl L J 1550.

Webb YJ, 'Do BITs Really Work? Revisiting the Empirical Link Between Investment Treaties and Foreign Direct Investment' in Sauvant Karl P and Lisa E Sachs (eds), *The Effect of Treaties on Foreign Direct Investment: Bilateral Investment Treaties, Double Taxation Treaties, and Investment Flows* (OUP 2009).

Ye F, 'The Impact of Bilateral Investment Treaties (BITs) on Collective Labor Rights in Developing Countries' (2020) 15(4) Rev Intl Organizations 899.

Conclusions

Critical Reflections on the Epistemic Adequacy of the Western Legal Approach to Square the Circle and Grant a Common Future for All

Margherita Paola Poto

> We are in a giant car
> heading toward a brick wall
> and everyone's arguing
> where they are going to sit
> (DAVID SUZUKI)

1 Introduction

In the face of the planetary socio-ecological crises,[1] sustainability and participation have become prominent concepts guiding decision-making and regulatory reforms,[2] constantly invoked by scholars and policymakers as the environmental panacea.[3] Yet, the hope often associated with their effectiveness has been slipping away, indicating what appears to be a general insufficiency of their problem-solving power.

1 Here the term 'socio-ecological' is used in the way suggested by Elinor Ostrom, Marco A Janssen, John M Anderies 'Going beyond panaceas. *Proceedings of the National Academy of Sciences'* (2007) *104*(39), 15176–15178 to describe systems of human-environment interactions. For an updated report of the current multiple crises, see IPC, Summary for Policymakers (2022) <https://www.ipcc.ch/report/ar6/wg2/downloads/report/IPCC_AR6_WGII_SummaryForPolicymakers.pdf> last accessed 31 October 2022, in 'Climate Change 2022: Impacts, Adaptation, and Vulnerability. Contribution of Working Group II to the Sixth Assessment Report of the Intergovernmental Panel on Climate Change', Cambridge University Press.

2 James N Rosenau, 'Globalization and governance: sustainability between fragmentation and integration', (2017) in Governance and Sustainability, 20–38.

3 For a critical account of the prevalence of perceptions that panaceas can solve ecological disasters see fn 2 at 1. Critically, on participation as the panacea for environmental crisis, see also Stephen Morse, 'Post-sustainable Development' (2008) Sustainable Development 16, no. 5, 341: "[W]hile participation may provide the community with some control over the form of the process and its pace, it is still being 'acted upon' by an external body [...], and post-developmentalists argue that with this form of relationship the Western hegemony is entrenched, not weakened. [...] Unfortunately, participation is often assumed to be another word for 'panacea' [...].

DOI:10.1163/9789004509382_018

In the opinion of critical legal scholars, this inadequacy is rooted in their inherently anthropocentric matrix and features,[4] which continue to aggravate the disconnect between the ecosystems and the human attempt to regulate them.[5] In other words, as the rhetoric bedrocks of Western environmental law, sustainability and participation are concepts deeply embedded in the human centrality regarding questions of environmental significance,[6] where humans are immediate if not the exclusive ambit of concern.[7] In this framework, human interests take precedence and human responsibilities to non-human subjects are assessed based on the benefits that humans can derive from environmental protection.[8] This human supremacy encoded in the Western ethics and legal orders is vividly expressed in the words of Louis Kotze and Duncan French: 'In the Anthropocene, the anthropocentrism of law is considered to justify and promote ecological ravaging; aggravate the enclosure of the commons; justify and increase the dispossession of Indigenous peoples and other marginalised groups; perpetuate corporate neo-colonialism; and intensify the

4 Basil Bornemann, 'Environmental Governance in the Anthropocene: Challenges, Approaches and Critical Perspectives' in David Chandler, Franziska Müller, Delf Rothe (eds), *International Relations in the Anthropocene* (Palgrave Macmillan, 2021). The term 'Anthropocene' was coined by Paul J. Crutzen in 2002: Paul J. Crutzen 'The "anthropocene"', *Journal de Physique IV (Proceedings)*, *12*(10), 1–5. EDP sciences; Id, (2010); 'Anthropocene man' Nature, 467(7317), S10-S10; Id., (2006); 'The Anthropocene' in Eckart Ehlers, Thomas Krafft (eds), *Earth system science in the Anthropocene* (Springer,2006). Critically, on the need to rethink anthropocentrism as the cause of the environmental crisis Layna Droz 'Anthropocentrism as the scapegoat of the environmental crisis: a review' (2022) *Ethics in Science and Environmental Politics*, 22, 25.

5 Oran R Young, 'Institutional dynamics: resilience, vulnerability and adaptation in environmental and resource regimes' (2010) Global Environmental Change 20(3), 378; Oran R Young, *The institutional dimensions of environmental change: fit, interplay, and scale.* (MIT press, 2002); Carl Folke, Lowell Pritchard Jr., Fikret Berkes, Johan Colding, Uno Svedin, 'The problem of fit between ecosystems and institutions: ten years later' (2007) Ecology and society 12 (1).

6 Vito de Lucia, 'Competing narratives and complex genealogies: The ecosystem approach in international environmental law' (2015) Journal of Environmental Law, 27(1), 91–117; Helena Kopnina, Haydn Washington, Bron Taylor, John J Piccolo 'Anthropocentrism: More than just a misunderstood problem' (2018) Journal of Agricultural and Environmental Ethics 31(1), 109–127; Daniel Bodansky, Jutta Brunnee, Ellen Hey, 'International environmental law: Mapping the field' in Daniel Bodansky (ed) *The Oxford handbook of international environmental law* (Oxford University Press. 1080, 2012).

7 Vito de Lucia, 'Rethinking the Encounter Between Law and Nature in the Anthropocene: From Biopolitical Sovereignty to Wonder'(2020) Law and Critique 31(3), 329–349.

8 Satish C Shastri, 'Environmental ethics anthropocentric to eco-centric approach: a paradigm shift' (2013) Journal of the Indian Law Institute 55(4), 522.

asymmetrically distributed patterns of advantage and disadvantage that prevail in society, while deepening inter- and intra-species hierarchies'.[9]

Consequently, in perpetuating the paradigm of domination and sovereignty of humans over nature,[10] the attempts to achieve sustainability through participation within Western parameters are inadequate to address sustainability's main dimensions (economic, social, and environmental).[11] Human supremacy over nature informs the regulatory framework of environmental law and is drawn by modern science.[12] This reflects what Boaventura de Sousa Santos defines as 'the conversion of modern law into scientific statist law', which is a conversion that mimics 'the hegemonic rationality' of science and its 'central productive force'.[13] As Western science is based on the dogma of mastery of nature, acquired through the objectification of knowledge and manipulation of natural laws,[14] laws, similarly, manipulate social and ecological relations through categorisation of reality and the imposition of the sovereignty and dominion paradigms.[15]

Through a comprehensive mapping of the contributions in the book, I argue that sustainability and participation are over-exploited Western concepts that need to be rethought and re-cast in a hybridised scenario. To become effective factors of change in the socio-environmental crises of our time, Western legal

9 Louis J Kotze, Duncan French, 'The Anthropocentric Ontology of International Environmental Law and the Sustainable Development Goals: Towards an Ecocentric Rule of Law in the Anthropocene' (2018) Global Journal of Comparative Law 7, no. 1, 5.

10 On domination, sovereignty and governmentality see Michel Foucault, 'Power and strategies' in Colin Gordon (ed), *Power/Knowledge* (Pantheon Books, 1980); Michel Foucalt, 'The subject and power' in Hubert L Dreyfus, Paul Rabinow (eds)*: Beyond Structuralism and Hermeneutics* (University of Chicago Press; Id. (1991); Michel Foucault 'Governmentality' in Graham Burchell,, Colin Gordon, Peter Miller (eds) *The Foucault Effect: Studies in Governmentality* (Harvester Wheatsheaf, 1991).

11 For an analysis of the contradictions of, and therefore the challenges posed by sustainable development see Christiano Nogueira, 'Contradictions in the concept of sustainable development: An analysis in social, economic, and political contexts'(2019) Environmental Development, 30: 129.

12 In similar terms, Leslie Somonian, 'The critical intersection of environmental and social justice: a commentary' (2021) Global Health 17,30, talk about "dominance of the Eurocentric technoscientific epistemology". See also Dave Kendal, Christopher M Raymond, 'Understanding pathways to shifting people's values over time in the context of social–ecological systems' (2018) Sustain Sci.

13 Boaventura de Sousa Santos, 'Law: a map of misreading. Toward a postmodern conception of law' (1987) Journal of Law and Society, 279.

14 Luigi Pellizzoni, 'Towards a critical humanism. Ontological Politics in a Disposable World' in Luigi Pellizzoni (ed) *Ontological Politics in a Disposable World* (Routledge, 2015).

15 M. Foucault (1982). Michel Foucault, 'The subject and power' (1982) Critical inquiry, 8(4), 777.

paradigms must open up to pluralism, knowledge co-creation, and generally participatory approaches.[16]

Following a brief summary of the theme and scope of the book (section 2), the two interlaced concepts of sustainability through participation are analysed as a part of the multilevel or polycentric system of governance in which they are embedded (section 3). Three main features of polycentric governance (a plurality of actors, patterns of interaction, and overarching sets of rules) are regarded as the common threads in the chapters of this book. The analysis of the characteristics of polycentric governance provided in this chapter will show gaps and offer key insights for future research with the aim to improve the problem-solving power of the relationship between sustainability and participation (section 4)

2 Sustainability and Participation as Western Conceptualisations

Through the exploration and analysis of the different approaches to this book's main foundational question of whether sustainability can be achieved through participation, an internal contradiction in the relational dimension of the two concepts may be revealed. This revelation would demonstrate the difficulty of reconciling such a relationship and translating it into implementable policies.[17]

Sustainable development and sustainability stem from and are deeply embedded in Western legal constructions. As observed by Carmen G. Gonzales: 'Although its meaning is highly contested, sustainable development is widely recognized as one of the guiding principles of contemporary international law [...]'.[18] The Western origins of sustainable development appear problematic whereas 'the definition [provided by the Brundtland Commission] appeared to reconcile economic development and environmental protection without fundamentally challenging the growth-oriented development paradigm'.[19] As correctly pointed out by the author, the focus of the Brundtland Commission was to promote economic growth, in the first place, following the global North-Western model,

16 Andrea Cornwall, Deborah Eade, *Deconstructing development discourse: Buzzwords and fuzzwords* (Oxfam GB, 2010).

17 For this reason, sustainability and participation in the context of environmental governance have been defined as a 'wicked problem' by extensive sustainability science literature. For a reconstruction of this expression and the implication of the wickedness of sustainability through participation see Lael Parrott, 'The modelling spiral for solving 'wicked' environmental problems: Guidance for stakeholder involvement and collaborative model development' (2017) Methods in Ecology and Evolution 8.8: 1005.

18 Carmen G Gonzales, 'Bridging the North-South divide: International environmental law in the Anthropocene' (2015) Pace Envtl. L. Rev. 32, 407.

19 Ibid.

as the solution to poverty and inequality, rather than effectively being concerned with ecological sustenance that came into consideration in its merely instrumental function of supporting economic growth: 'Instead of encouraging the global North to reduce its ecological footprint in order to increase the living standards of the poor without exceeding biophysical limits, the Brundtland Commission extolled the benefits of international trade as the engine of economic growth and the solution to poverty and inequality'.[20]

As Gilbert Rist observes, '[t]he main contradiction, then, in the Report of the Brundtland Commission is that the growth policy supposed to reduce poverty and stabilize the ecosystem hardly differs at all from the policy which historically opened the gulf between rich and poor and placed the environment in danger'.[21] Instead of questioning the dominant development model that caused the major divide between the global north and the global south and provoked irreversible changes in the ecological system, sustainable development suggested upscaling the economic growth. Thus, sustainability and sustainable development served to promote the growth model that Heloise Weber defines as the 'market episteme',[22] which gives priority to highly contested neoliberal policies, promoting free-market capitalism,[23] 'implementing contentious policies which critics have shown to be highly exclusionary, unjust and therefore also not sustainable'[24] and ultimately causing those power asymmetries (exclusion, higher environmental risk, and disproportionate environmental exposures)[25] in environmental decision-making that participation tries to address.[26]

Therefore, the relationship between sustainability and participation is controversial[27] and, as pointed out by legal scholars advocating for critical

20 Ibid.

21 Gilbert Rist, 'Development as a buzzword' (2007) Development in practice, 17(4–5), 485.

22 Heloise Weber, 'Politics of 'Leaving No One Behind': Contesting the 2030 Sustainable Development Goals Agenda' (2017) Globalizations, 14:3, 399, in particular at page 410: "At its core, the 2030 SDG agenda is premised on the consolidation of the conditions of the 'market episteme' while attempting to mitigate against any challenges to this political project."

23 Ibid; Elena Danilova, 'Neoliberal Hegemony and Narratives of "Losers" and "Winners" in Post-Socialist Transformations' (2014) Journal of Narrative Theory, 44, no. 3, 442. For a thorough critical analysis of sustainable development see Juhani Koponen, 'Development: History and power of the concept' Forum for Development Studies Vol. 47, No. 1, 1..

24 Heloise Weber, n 22 at 4.

25 Vera Schattan P Coelho, Arilson Favareto, 'Questioning the relationship between participation and development: a case study of the Vale do Ribeira, Brazil' (2008) World Development, 36.12, 293

26 Nicholas Freudenberg, Manuel Pastor, Barbara Israel, 'Strengthening community capacity to participate in making decisions to reduce disproportionate environmental exposures' (2011) American Journal of Public Health, 101, 123.

27 Stephen R Dovers, John W Handmer, 'Contradictions in sustainability' (1993) vol 20 no 3 Environ Conserv 217.

approaches to sustainability[28] and by the contributors to this book, difficult to conciliate. Sustaining human development and guaranteeing that everybody participates in this endeavor is an undertaking dense with epistemological and material contradictions and oxymorons.[29] For this reason, how to effectively interlink sustainability and participation in ways that improve the environmental outcomes of public decision-making (by achieving social equality while protecting the environment simultaneously) is still an open question. However, the drastic shortcut could be boiled down to the conclusion that, within Western knowledge, the essence of a highly exclusionary human sustainability based on market epistemological premises and hegemonic rationality, inevitably hijacks participation.

Starting from the premise that sustainability and participation form a dichotomy that cannot be solved within a purely Western-centric context, it already dispenses from demonstrating that their relationship is successful at any cost. Acknowledging such difficulty helps to gather the threads of the discourse on the multiple applications of sustainability through participation, and their points of convergence and divergence, as showcased by the rich pool of contributions that compose this book.

Therefore, drawing insights from the previous chapters, this contribution first attempts to reconstruct the scenario in which the sustainability-participation relationship seems to be taking place, in what hereinafter is interchangeably referred to as the multilevel or polycentric governance system.[30] This is accomplished by focusing on three main features in the sustainability-participation relationship, then formulating a way forward for the Western neoliberal hegemony, and suggesting conceptual and methodological corrections to the framework.

By applying polycentric approaches to environmental governance[31] and suggesting improvements to the current relationship between sustainability

28 For an overview see Jeff Rose, Adrienne Cachelin, 'Critical sustainability: incorporating critical theories into contested sustainabilities' (2018) 8 J Environ Stud Sci 518.

29 Mary Menton, Carlos Larrea, Sara Latorre, Joan Martinez-Alier, Mika Peck, Leah Temper, Mariana Walter, 'Environmental justice and the SDGs: from synergies to gaps and contradictions' (2020) 15 Sustainability Science, 1621.

30 Elinor Ostrom, Michael Cox, 'Moving beyond panaceas: A multi-tiered diagnostic approach for social-ecological analysis' (2010) 37(4) Environmental Conservation 451.

31 Vincent Ostrom, Elinor Ostrom, 'Public Goods and Public Choices' in Michael, D McGinnis (ed) *Polycentricity and Local Public Economies: Readings from the Workshop in Political Theory and Policy Analysis* (The University of Michigan Press); Elinor Ostrom 'Coping with Tragedies of the Commons'(1999) 2 Annual Review of Political Science 493; Vincent Ostrom, 'Polycentricity (Part 1)' in Michael D McGinnis (ed) *Polycentricity and Local Public Economies: Readings from the Workshop. Political Theory and Policy Analysis* (The University of Michigan Press, 1999, 52–74). For a critical overview on multi-level governance see Pier D Tortola, 'Clarifying multilevel governance' (2017) 56(2) European Journal of Political Research 234.

and participation through decolonial and non-human centric approaches to law[32] this chapter explores how a multilevel polycentric governance system could be enhanced through deliberate processes of integration and co-creation of diverse epistemologies and non-human centric approaches to law.

3 Sustainability through Participation in Multilevel or Polycentric Governance

This book spans studies of sustainability through participation, looking at the historical and epistemological backgrounds of the two concepts (respectively, in Birgit Peters, and Paola Villavicencio-Calzadilla and Louis Kotze's analyses), through the national perspective level (Eva Julia Lohse, Daniele Brombal and Cristina Fraenkel-Haeberle), the EU thematic level (Matthias Valta, Julius Buckler, Giacomo Gattinara and Magnus Noll Ehlers) and the international thematic level (Federica Cittadino and Emma Mitrotta, Omondi R. Owino, Violeta Radovich, Michael Riegner, Angela Schwerdtfeger, Paolo Turrini, Matthias Uffer).

The result is a kaleidoscopic conceptual picture of the sustainability-participation relationship that in this section will be demonstrated via the filigree of the multilevel or polycentric[33] systems of governance[34] to identify common features, gaps, and possible solutions for strengthening the substrate in which sustainability and participation interact, thus, improving the relationship between the two.

As a premise to the analysis, the terms multilevel and polycentric encompass the complexity of layers and plurality of actors involved in environmental decision-making. In particular, the word 'multilevel' makes an explicit reference to the vertical or horizontal interactions between actors, while the adjective 'polycentric' emphasises the multiple centres of decision-making, each of them operating with some degree of autonomy, but hereinafter used interchangeably.[35]

---

32 Alice Benessia and others 'Hybridizing sustainability: towards a new praxis for the present human predicament' (2012) 7(1) Sustainability Science 75.

33 See Stephen R Dovers, John W Handmer, n 27 at 5.

34 Daniel H Cole, 'Advantages of a polycentric approach to climate change policy' (2015) 5(2) Nature Climate Change 114; Jens Newig, Oliver Fritsch, 'Environmental governance: participatory, multi-level – and effective?' (2009) 19(3) Environmental Policy and Governance 197.

35 Besides the studies already cited on polycentricity, on the definition of multi-level and polycentric see also Michael Roe, 'Multi-level and polycentric governance: effective policymaking for shipping' (2009) 36(1) Maritime Policy & Management 39.

The scholars invited to provide an analysis of sustainability through participation in their fields of expertise touched upon some of the basic conceptual elements of the polycentric governance system in which the sustainability-participation relationship is embedded. They approached their research using diverse methods, tools, substantive environmental issues, and geographic locations.

The collective result is that the chapters offer reflections on nature and the functioning of sustainability through participation in multilevel governance. Therefore, rather than summarising each chapter independently, I will focus on some key elements of the multilevel governance that emerge from the synoptic analysis of the different contributions.

The *leitmotif* that emerges is that, despite the promising environmental outcomes that a highly polycentric governance system is likely to yield when compared to monocentric governance,[36] it still requires a sustained commitment to overcome the limitations of a Western and anthropocentric knowledge system. For example, the analysis of Cristina Fraenkel-Haeberle reveals how the different levels, actors, networks, and agendas follow a structure informed by the EU subsidiarity principle, and therefore the multilevel governance the author refers to is deeply embedded in the Western paradigm. Highlighting the critical challenges of the multilevel framework, and following the historical pathway of sustainability through participation, Birgit Peters reflects on the limited role played by the eco-centric episteme in molding environmental governance. Along the same lines, Paola VillavicencioCalzadilla and Louis Kotze' develop their argumentation on the need to recenter the sustainability-participation narrative around nature, nature rights, and duties of guardianship. Also, Eva Julia Lohse emphasises the role that Indigenous peoples' cosmovisions play in strengthening Earth law and ecocentric perspectives.

Nested in this Western anthropocentric context, the three characteristics of polycentric governance systems (a plurality of actors, patterns of interactions, and an overarching set of rules)[37] reveal the gaps in the system but also the

36 Massimo Cattino, Diana Reckien, 'Does public participation lead to more ambitious and transformative local climate change planning?' (2021) 52 Current opinion in environmental sustainability 100

37 Mark Stephan, Graham Marshall,Michael McGinnis, 'An Introduction to Polycentricity and Governance' in Andreas Thiel, William A Blomquist and Dustin E Garrick (eds), *Governing Complexity* (New York: Cambridge University Press, 2019) identify eight characteristics in multilevel governance systems. In this chapter, I will focus on a few of them, and namely on the relevance of the characteristics n. 1 (Multiple decision centers); n. 4, 7, and 8 (Multiple processes of mutual adjustments among decision centers; Emergent

large future potential of polycentric systems to enable a relationship sustainability-participation more functional to address socio-ecological challenges.

The present analysis will focus on characteristics, gaps, and possible solutions. In the analysis of characteristics and gaps, I will observe how challenging it is for certain actors to be included, how a network or web-shaped structure[38] still subsides and hegemonic actors prevail, and how the overarching systems of rules need to be strengthened with knowledge pluralism and tackled with knowledge co-production approaches. These insights into the gaps will help identify possible ways forward and suggest developing hybridised solutions and the standardisation of participatory mechanisms that can secure a sustainable future for all.

4 The Good and the Bad in the Three Characteristics of Polycentric Governance

The first characteristic of polycentric environmental governance, where sustainability intersects participation, is the existence of multiple centres of decision-making, following what the doctrine calls the approach of a multiple and shared agency.[39]

A multiple and shared agency approach enhances the interaction in decision-making and, consequently, is expected to contribute to the development of complex adaptive social systems.[40] In this sense, a shared agency addresses the socio-ecological dimension of sustainability by improving the quality of the interactions and enriching the pool of environmental solutions that support social inclusion. In their study on social sustainability, Merlina Missimer *et al* point out how fostering complex adaptive social systems by broadening the spectrum of parties involved in decision-making, constitutes a strategic

---

patterns of behaviours; Combination of means of coordination); n. 6 (Overarching systems of rules).

38 Chenghui Tang, Jianmin Dou, 'Exploring the Polycentric Structure and Driving Mechanism of Urban Regions From the Perspective of Innovation Network' (2022) Frontiers in Physics 10: 855380.

39 Naim Kapucu, Brittany Haupt, Thomas Quint, Mostafizur Rahman, Murat Yuksel, 'Polycentric Governance and Decentralized Decision-Making for Pervasive Spectrum Sharing'(2021) International Journal of Public Administration, 1–10; Michael E Bratman, *Shared agency: A planning theory of acting together* (Oxford University Press 2013).

40 Fernando Tormos-Aponte, Gustavo A Garcia Lopez, 'Polycentric struggles: The experience of the global climate justice movement' (2018) 28(4) Environmental policy and governance 284.

approach to sustainability by enhancing trust, common meaning, diversity, capacity for learning and capacity for self-organisation, and ultimately by leading to adaptive and resilient environmental outcomes.[41] The participation of multiple actors in the design and implementation of environmental governance allows for greater complexity of understanding of socio-environmental issues, as well as for creating social cohesion and inclusion. As observed in the cited work of Kotze' and French,[42] often, because of social norms or lack of opportunities, the groups most affected by environmental impacts, such as women, Indigenous peoples, people with disabilities, and economically disadvantaged groups, possess limited agency in decision-making.[43] Thus, collective actions for sustainability have the potential to enhance the ability of these groups to act in concerted ways by engaging with inequities, dynamics of exclusion, and power asymmetries.

The first example of potential benefits for the environment deriving from a broadened spectrum of actors in the environmental decision-making process is offered in Cittadino and Mitrotta's chapter on the involvement of present and future generations in environmental justice (intergenerational justice). Supporting the need of broadening the spectrum of actors in polycentric governance, Radovich prospects the possibility of an expansion of actors in favour of Indigenous communities involved in a multi-actor environmental guardianship. In the same vein, Eva Julia Lohse underscores the need to decolonise sustainability through Indigenous participation; Villavicencio-Calzadilla and Kotzé consider that the system of nature rights and guardianship is the most meaningful way to facilitate effective environmental participation, Omondi R. Owino points out how the opening toward non-state actors in environmental decision-making had been encouraged also through Western-legal instruments, such as the Paris Agreement.

Moreover, Peters, Lohse, Schwerdtfeger, Gattinara and Nolls cite the 1998 Århus Convention (ÅC)[44] and 2018 Escazú Agreement (EA) for Latin America

41 Merlina Missimer, Karl-Henrik Robert, Göran I Broman, 'A strategic approach to social sustainability–Part 2: a principle-based definition' (2017) 140 Journal of Cleaner Production 42.

42 Louis J Kotze, Duncan French, 'Sustainable Development Goals' in Louis J Kotze, Duncan French (eds), Edward Elgar Publishing, (2018).

43 Dayna N Scott, Garance Malivel, 'Intergenerational Environmental Justice and the Climate Crisis: Thinking with and beyond the Charter' (2021) 17 Osgoode Legal Studies Research Paper Forthcoming, Journal of Law & Equality.

44 United Nations Economic Commission for Europe (UNECE), The Århus Convention: An Implementation Guide (2nd ed. 2014) available at <http://www.unece.org/fileadmin/DAM/env/pp/Publications/Aarhus_Implementation_Guide_interactive_eng.pdf> last accessed

and the Caribbean,[45] as two legal milestones that contributed to the development of environmental participatory rights. Both conventions bring forward the discourse of a plurality of actors in environmental decision-making. For instance, the ÅC captures all the parties potentially affected by environmental decisions (and especially e-NGOS), while the EA promotes the environmental defenders, carriers of nature-centred views. Passing the baton of environmental decision-making to the carriers of nature-centred views (and especially Indigenous peoples and vulnerable groups), the EA has catalysed the gradual recognition of non-human-centred epistemologies at the global level.[46]

The multi-actor feature of polycentric governance is not exempt from challenges. Already from the analysis of the different contributions, it is clear that, regardless of the new set of non-state actors, nation-states are still the key actors in climate governance.[47] Top-down approaches are still considered the most suitable forum for environmental and climate governance, based on the

---

31 October 2022. The literature on the ÅC is immense, see bibliography in Peters, 'The Historical Perspective', in this book, chapter b.(1), Lohse, 'Comparative Administrative Law Perspectives – Europe, Latin-America, Africa', in this book, chapter c.(1), and Schwerdtfeger, 'The Human Rights Dimension', in this book, chapter e.(1).

45 Regional Agreement on Access to Information, Public Participation and Justice in Environmental Matters in Latin America and the Caribbean, 4 March 2020, available at <https://treaties.un.org/doc/Treaties/2018/03/20180312%2003-04%20PM/CTC-XXVII-18.pdf> last accessed 31 October 2022. For updates on signature and ratification status see: <https://observatoriop10.cepal.org/en/treaties/regional-agreement-access-information-public-participation-and-justice-environmental> last accessed 31 October 2022. The EA is the first agreement of its kind because representatives of Indigenous groups and civil society organisations were engaged in the negotiations and included as beneficiaries of the Agreement provisions. One example among many was that of the participation of the organisation DAR (Derecho, Ambiente y Recursos Naturales) committed to building and strengthening environmental governance and promoting the exercise of human rights in the Amazon Basin. DAR focuses on issues of environmental policy and legislation, Indigenous peoples' rights, climate change and investment and good governance in the areas of infrastructure and extractive industries, see <https://civicus.org/index.php/media-resources/news/interviews/3728-escazu-the-work-of-civil-society-made-a-huge-difference> last accessed 31 October 2022.

46 Sofia Lopez-Cubillos and others, 'The landmark Escazú Agreement: An opportunity to integrate democracy, human rights, and transboundary conservation' (2021) Conservation Letters, e12838; Atilla Panovics, 'The Escazu Agreement and the Protection of Environmental Human Rights Defenders' (2021) Pecs Journal of International & Europe Law 23; Giada Ferucci, 'A Pioneering Platform: Strengthening Environmental Democracy and Justice in Latin America and the Caribbean' (2019) 20(5) Journal of Management Policy and Practice 10.

47 And usually, nation states from the Global North. See, for example, the studies in Shawkat Alam and others (eds) *International environmental law and the global south* (Cambridge University Press, 2015).

idea that only a cooperative effort between nation-states is the most appropriate way to tackle the global character of the socio-ecological crises.[48]

Even though bottom-up approaches to environmental governance are attempting to go beyond the idea of centralisation, following the logic and principle of subsidiarity (as highlighted in the analysis of Fraenkel-Haeberle),[49] the focus is still on nation-states in the international arena. Subsequently, this means that while the diversity of actors and subsidiary policy levels are increasingly being recognised in global politics, top-down and bottom-up approaches ruled by state law are still dominant in informing policy and research in environmental governance.

Among the critics of the actors' lack of diversity in environmental governance, Carmen G. Gonzalez points out how the expansion of actors, stemming from Western categories and institutions, is embedded in power relations and enables 'northern states and transnational corporations to evade responsibility for their abuse of nature and of vulnerable states and peoples'.[50] The solution, in the eyes of the scholar, is to:

> develop a non-Euro-centric [...] project, amplify the voices of grassroots environmental justice activists to influence the interpretation of environmental human rights law, and develop legal theories that challenge the systemic [...] violations of the global economic order rather than merely ameliorating its most egregious manifestations. [...] The local, not the global, it needs to be emphasized, remains the crucial site of struggle for the enunciation, implementation, and enjoyment and exercise of human rights.[51]

The second characteristic of polycentric governance relates to the types of interactions and behaviours that can happen among actors which help clarify some of the fundamental mechanisms that produce outcomes in polycentric systems. From the contributions, it emerges how the structure of complex polycentric approaches varies across legal orders and macro-level political

---

48 Marcel J Dorsch, Christian Flachsland, 'A Polycentric Approach to Global Climate Governance' Global Environmental Politics (2017) 17(2), 45.

49 Lena Bendlin, 'Local Governments in European Multi-Level Climate Governance' in Bendlin (ed) *Orchestrating Local Climate Policy in the European Union* (Springer VS, 2020).

50 Carmen G Gonzales, 'Environmental justice, human rights, and the global south' (2015) 13(1) Santa Clara Journal of International Law 151.

51 Ibid. See also Peter H Sand, 'Origin and History' (2021) 93(2) The Oxford Handbook of International Environmental Law 50.

institutions.[52] For example, the multi-actor interactions can range from conflict to cooperation, as respectively analysed in the studies of Buckler and Brombal, and might reveal a preference for anthropocentric approaches over eco-centric perspectives, as highlighted in Villavicencio-Calzadilla and Kotzé, Radovich, and Fraenkel-Haeberle's chapters.

The studies in this book align with the argumentation that in global environmental governance, power flows are not neatly structured, and are simultaneously subject to forces of fragmentation and aggregation. James N. Rosenau defines this process as 'governance of fragmentation'.[53] Martin Witte *et al* translate this concept into the vivid image of 'patchwork-quilt arrangements'[54] to describe the way authority is exerted in polycentric settings, partly following vertical hierarchical directions, partly horizontal and partly oblique links among overlapping vertical and horizontal interactions.[55] In addition to the unidirectional decision-making processes, be they vertical, horizontal, and intersectional between the two, in global environmental governance, the patchwork of arrangements develops along multidirectional paths (networked cooperation, side by side and Möbius strip or web).[56] This complicated matrix involves transnational corporations, international non-governmental organisations, e-NGOs, states, epistemic and Indigenous communities (represented, in Lohse and Radovich's works by the example of Indigenous peoples and local communities (IPLC)), transnational advocacy coalitions (as in the case of intergenerational justice movement analysed by Cittadino and Mitrotta).[57]

On the positive side, this complex system has the potential to prevent conflicts and foster cooperation, eventually helping to overcome the challenge of the perduring hegemony of state actors in power dynamics, enhance collaboration and offer alternatives to the hierarchical scales of global environmental

52 Ramiro Berardo, Mark Lubell, 'Understanding what shapes a polycentric governance system' (2016) 76.5 Public Administration Review, 738.

53 James N Rosenau, 'The governance of fragmegration: Neither a world republic nor a global interstate system'(2000) Studia Diplomatica 15.

54 Jan M Witte and others, 'Partnerships and networks in global environmental governance: Moving to the Next Stage'in Ulrich Petschow and others (eds) *Governance and Sustainability* (Routledge, 2017, 141–152).

55 Ibid.

56 Ibid. The Möbius strip, also called the twisted cylinder is a one-sided surface obtained by cutting a closed band into a single strip, giving one of the two ends thus produced a half twist, and then reattaching the two ends. See among others, E W Weisstein, Möbius strip (2001) <*https://mathworld.wolfram.com*> last accessed 31 October 2022.

57 For a complete overview of the interactions in global governance see James N Rosenau n 54, at 11.

governance.[58] It has been widely argued that interdisciplinary and multilevel cooperation among actors constitutes the breeding ground for exchanging experiences and mutual learning, ultimately leading to environmentally beneficial decisions, thanks to the knowledge exchange and brokerage towards solution-oriented approaches.[59]

Nevertheless, as in the case of the first characteristic, this complex matrix of power remains anchored in conventional political arenas and in the logic of nation-states' sovereignty.[60] In this regard, Michael Riegner prospects how the participation of Indigenous peoples—outside the hierarchical system where only state actors and local public entities participate—offers the possibility of legal alternative visions to sustainability.[61]

From this analysis, it is clear that the first two characteristics of polycentric governance call for new approaches and perspectives. For instance, drawn from Indigenous epistemologies, Kyle Whyte proposes the 'kincentric perspective'.[62] According to this reconstruction, human and non-human actors, following values of mutual responsibility, consent, and reciprocity, have the ability to effectively contribute to a system of environmental governance infused with qualities that replicate the patterns of kin relationships.[63] Through kin-centric

58 As defined by Harriet Bulkeley et al: "An epistemic community can be defined as a network of experts who share a common understanding of the scientific and political nature of a problem", Harriet Bulkeley and others, 'Environmental governance and transnational municipal networks in Europe' (2003) 5(3) Journal of Environmental Policy & Planning 235.

59 Laura Herzog, Karin Ingold und Edella Schlager,'Prescribed by law and therefore realized? Analyzing rules and their implied actor interactions as networks' (2021) 50 Policy studies journal 366; John S Dryzek, *The Politics of the Earth: Environmental Discourses* (OUP 2017); Margherita Paola Poto, Endalew Lifalem Enyew,'Nature Protection, Indigenous Rights and Climate Action', in Hans Christian Bugge (ed), *Klimarettsbok* (Universitetsforlaget 2021).

60 Margherita Paola Poto, *Environmental Law and Governance: The Helicoidal Pathway of Participation a study of a nature-based model inspired by the Arctic, the Ocean, and Indigenous Views* (Giappichelli 2022).

61 Bulkeley *et al*, n 59, at 12; Michele Betsill and Harriet Bulkeley, 'Transnational Networks and Global Environmental Governance: the Cities for Climate Protection program' (2004) 48 International Studies Quarterly 471.

62 Kyle Whyte, 'Too late for indigenous climate justice: Ecological and relational tipping points' (2019) 11 WIREs Climate Change 603.

63 And, especially in an Indigenous context, also past generations. See for example the Māori law (Part II of Te Awa Tupua (Whanganui River Claims Settlement) Act 2017, www.legislation.govt.nz/act/public/2017/0007/latest/whole.html last accessed 31 October 2022) on the Whanganui River, the living being that is also a living ancestor: the law defines the Te Awa Tupua as a living, actual ancestor that includes the various elements of nature and goes beyond the territorial delimitation of waters and land. Te Awa Tupua includes

perspectives, the Western anthropocentric scaffoldings can give way to more receptive conceptions of alterity, nature-centred views, and epistemic plurality. As Simone Bignall, Steve Hemming and Daryle Rigney put it:

> [T]hanks to the corresponding shift in ontology, posthuman justice is less concerned with securing rights for human subjects with full moral worth and more interested in advancing and protecting environmental diversity in communal life, as a constitutive source of human and nonhuman resilience and creativity.[64]

Furthermore, the need to overcome Western predominance emerges from the analysis of the third characteristic of polycentric governance, relating to the overarching set of rules and formal legal frameworks–legal principles, laws, and regulatory mechanisms that support the interaction among the diverse actors.

As repeatedly pointed out in this chapter and confirmed by the other contributions, the common umbrella of rules where sustainability crosses participation in environmental governance is predominantly infused with Western environmental law concepts.[65]

---

the main Whanganui River and its tributaries, from which two principal ancestors, the Paerangi and the Ruatipua, draw their life-force. It includes all the elements of nature, in their physical and metaphysical interconnections, from Mount Tongariro, where the Whanganui River has its source, to the Tasman Sea, where it has its estuary: Margherita Paola Poto 'Thinking about Ocean Governance: By Whom, for Whom?', in Vito De Lucia, Alex Oude Elferink and Lan Ngoc Nguyen (eds), *International Law and Marine Areas Beyond National Jurisdiction: Reflections on Justice, Space, Knowledge and Power* (Brill 2022); Matthias Kramm,'When a River Becomes a Person' (2020) 21 *Journal of Human Development and Capabilities*307.

64 Simone Bignall, Steve Hemming and Daryle Rigney, 'Three ecosophies for the Anthropocene: environmental governance, continental posthumanism and indigenous expressivism' (2016) 10 Deleuze Studies 455.

65 Ramiro Berardo and Mark Lubell, 'Understanding What Shapes a Polycentric Governance System' (2016) 76 PAR 738; Elinor Ostrom, 'Beyond Markets and States: Polycentric Governance of Complex Economic Systems' (2010) 100 American Economic Review 641; Krister Andersson and Elinor Ostrom, 'Analyzing decentralized resource regimes from a polycentric perspective' 41 Policy Sciences 71; Rolf Lidskog and Ingemar Elander, 'Addressing climate change democratically. Multi-level governance, transnational networks and governmental structures' (2010) 18 Sustainable Development 32; Katarina Eckerberg and Marko Joas, 'Multi-level Environmental Governance: a concept under stress?' (2004) 9 Local Environment 405.

The Western constructs[66] inform sets of rules where examples and applications of sustainability through participation unfold under fragmented and often uncoordinated regulatory systems, representing self-contained regimes and thematic fields of law (climate change, biodiversity, environmental crises, air, and land pollution, state aid, finances, and competition),[67] thus, evoking the image of the governance of fragmentation.[68]

---

66 As a specialized branch of law, Western environmental law has developed in two phases. The first phase, known as the 'classic phase', hinging on the Westphalian origins of international law characterised by the paradigm of state sovereignty, spans from the 1850s to the 1960s and is characterised by a utilitarian, anthropocentric rationale. The second phase, starting in the early 1970s, has seen the scope of environmental law broadening to the protection of the environment for future generations. As highlighted in many of the contributions to this book and especially in Birgit Peters' chapter, after the Stockholm Conference (1972), the first conference to comprehensively deal with environmental problems of broad international significance, environmental protection became firmly established as falling within the competence of the UN system. This institutional development was fostered by the creation, still in 1972, of UNEP through UNGA Res 2997 (XXVII) of 15 December 1972, following a recommendation for the creation of a permanent institutional arrangement for environmental protection and improvement within the UN system ([15 June 1972] A/CONF.48/14/REV.1, 29). Other milestones after of the Stockholm Conference were the United Nations (1972). *Action Plan for the Human Environment.* UN. (UN Doc A/CONF.48/14) and the Stockholm Declaration of the United Nations Conference on the Human Environment: United Nations. (1972). *Stockholm Declaration.* UN; and United nations. (2021). *Rio Declaration.* UN. See Marc Pallemaerts, 'International Environmental Law from Stockholm to Rio: Back to the Future?' (1992) 1 Review on European Community and International Environmental Law 254. Further steps were the World Summit on Sustainable Development 2002, 10 years after the first Earth Summit in Rio de Janeiro (<www.earthsummit2002.org/> last accessed 15 July 2022); the Agenda 2030 for Sustainable Development, adopted by all United Nations Member States in 2015 (<https://sdgs.un.org/2030agenda> last accessed 31 October 2022). In the same year, the Paris Agreement was adopted (<https://unfccc.int/process-and-meetings/the-paris-agreement/the-paris-agreement> last accessed 31 October 2022). For further references see Poto, n 61, at 12.

67 Harro van Asselt, *The Fragmentation of Global Climate Governance: Consequences and Management of Regime Interactions* (Edward Elgar Publishing 2014); Fariborz Zelli and Harro van Asselt, 'The Institutional Fragmentation of Global Environmental Governance: Causes, Consequences, and Responses: Introduction' (2013) 13 Global Environmental Politics 1; Fariborz Zelli, Frank Biermann, Philipp Pattberg and Harro van Asselt, 'The Consequences of a Fragmented Climate Governance Architecture: a Policy Appraisal', in Frank Biermann, Philipp Pattberg and Fariborz Zelli (eds), *Global Climate Governance Beyond 2012: Architecture, Agency and Adaptation* (CUP 2010); Harro van Asselt, 'Dealing with the fragmentation of global climate governance: legal and political approaches in interplay management' (2007) Global Governance Working Paper No. 30.

68 Rosenau, n 53, at 11.

A trend in research and policy-making to overcome such an impasse caused by the opposing forces of fragmentation and aggregation of Western rules suggests moving from conventional participatory rights and knowledge brokerage to environmental knowledge co-creation.[69]

In the academic literature, knowledge co-creation is defined as an emerging process. For example, in the field of Western law, a plurality of actors attempt to solve a shared problem, challenge, or task through a constructive exchange of different knowledge sets, values, expertise and competencies.[70]

Knowledge co-creation presents several advantages and ways forward to all the highlighted stalemates and open venues to consolidate sustainability and participation.

First, it captures the plurality of public and private actors aiming to solve public problems, challenges, and tasks. An innovative process emerges when a plurality of actors is collectively committed to solving shared problems by engaging in mutual, transformative learning, reciprocity and creativity, following kinship rather than market-oriented rules. Plural co-creation triggers a trust-building process where 'interactions enable co-creators to engage with and support other co-creators processes, creating a continuous feedback loop of knowledge integration, and drive knowledge integration into a never-ending spiral'.[71]

Second, knowledge co-creation allows a crucial shift in the critical register, as it comprises both poles of the binary (state sovereignty over nature and human-nature interconnected views), with no predominance of one over the other, showing a critique that is richer and more capable of capturing the competing narratives of environmental governance.[72]

Additionally, it provides an analytical framework that theorises how participation can effectively work in the decision-making processes of environmental

69 New modes of knowledge co-production are being negotiated and institutionalised by "Future Earth for Global Sustainability", a research programme launched at the United Nations Conference on Sustainable Development that took place in Rio de Janeiro, Brazil in June 2012. See more on this Sandra van der Hel, 'New science for global sustainability? The institutionalisation of knowledge co-production in Future Earth' (2016) 61 Environmental Science & Policy 165; Mark E Nissen, Nada Magdi and Kishore Sengupta, 'Integrated Analysis and Design of Knowledge Systems and Processes' (2000) 13 IRMJ 24.

70 Jacob Torfing, Asbjørn Røiseland and Eva Sørensen, 'Transforming the public sector into an arena for co-creation: Barriers, drivers, benefits, and ways forward' (2019) 51 Administration & Society 795.

71 Margherita Paola Poto, Environmental Law and Governance: The Helicoidal Pathway of Participation a study of a nature-based model inspired by the Arctic, the Ocean, and Indigenous Views (Giappichelli 2022).

72 Laura Kreiling and Carlonie Paunov, 'Knowledge co-creation in the 21st century: A cross-country experience-based policy report' (OECD Publishing 2021) OECD Science, Technology and Industry Policy Papers, No. 115.

governance, facilitating the exploration of how the law should allow the integration and co-evolution of Western and non-Western (e.g. Indigenous, local, traditional) views.[73]

Lastly, an institutional opening towards multiple knowledge systems enables the reading of environmental governance through the lens of the pluralism of environmental governance, and the diversity of approaches to sustainability. As observed by Ronald Ralf Becerra:

> legal pluralism favors the possibility to relax the concept of state sovereignty. [...] enshrined into the mechanisms of transnational legal systems and organizations that curtail and transform current powers and the constitutional sovereignty.[74]

In a dimension of legal pluralism, state sovereignty evolves according to the situation and social context, confirming how law and society are inseparable. The concept of evolving and dynamic sovereignty is crucial for environmental issues as it fosters the idea of adaptability to changes.[75] In this scenario, state sovereignty evolves into other concepts, such as stewardship and duty to protect, and is, thus, passed on to relevant actors to apply, create or orientate regulations, frameworks, and decision-making processes. These actors may include environmental organisations and Indigenous, traditional, and local communities.

The hybridisation of the polycentric governance scenario, in which the different applications of sustainability through participation are projected, shows the relevance of the commitment to developing integrated decision-making approaches. For instance, integrated decision-making enables integrated processes of co-designing policy and co-producing knowledge for addressing challenges for global sustainability and developing possible solutions.[76]

---

73 Dawn Martin-Hill,Colin M Gibson and Charles-François de Lannoy *et al,* 'Striving toward reconciliation through the co-creation of water research', in Miquel Sioui (ed), *Indigenous Water and Drought Management in a Changing World* (Elsevier 2022, vol 4).

74 Ronald Ralf Becerra, 'Legal Pluralism as a Theory for the Challenges on Environmental Health' (2019) 18 Opinión Jurídica 233. Pioneering on the role of legal pluralism to overcome state sovereignty is the work of Brian Z Tamanaha, 'Understanding Legal Pluralism: Past to Present, Local to Global' (2008) 30 Sydney Law Review 375. See also Nico Kirsch, 'The Pluralism of Global Administrative Law' (2008) 17 European Journal of International Law 247.

75 Becerra, n 74, at 15.

76 Wolfram Mauser and others 'Transdisciplinary global change research: the co-creation of knowledge for sustainability. 5 Current opinion in environmental sustainability' (2013) 420.

In this renewed sense, polycentric governance can play a key role in addressing socio-ecological development challenges. Thus, it can not only strengthen the processes of participation (and therefore contribute to inclusion, transparency, and good administration) but can encourage knowledge integration, co-design and co-creation, subsequently, providing a better understanding of the multiple drivers, interdependencies, and complexities of global sustainability challenges. Through the polycentric governance scenario, it is possible to reflect on ways of knowledge co-creation that better contributes to the development of robust policy solutions and their effective, equitable implementation. Consequently, within this understanding, the process of knowledge co-creation involves stakeholders, decision-makers, and the researcher community in a problem-oriented approach, driven by contexts of application, and starting with the joint framing of socio-ecological challenges, policy topics, and research questions. Co-creation upholds scientific integrity in reflexive learning processes that bring together different actors and knowledge practices. It builds on and supplements, traditional processes of disciplinary research by encouraging decision-making platforms where plurality-level dynamics are involved. This includes vertical, horizontal, networked, all-encompassing polycentric actors from central and local policymakers and decision-makers, e-NGOs, epistemic communities of researchers, and knowledge-keepers.

Consequently, hinging on the main teachings of polycentric governance and critically looking into the most advanced achievements in the environmental regulatory framework, this contribution suggests developing co-created approaches that go beyond the Western approaches by suggesting enhancements of Indigenous epistemologies, kinship perspectives applied to participatory dynamics as well as nature-based approaches. Such a perspective is expected to institutionalise effective counter-balances to the expansive dominion of some societal systems over others, especially of Western approaches over Indigenous and local communities.

A co-created approach to law based on integration, participation, and inclusiveness provides a platform to explore the integration of legal approaches and methods in the field of environmental decision-making and environmental protection.

Most importantly, a co-created approach to environmental law allows human and non-human-related challenges to be understood via a lens of an integral concept of ecology and health, of rights of the planet and its inhabitants, and of collective duties to respect both.[77]

77 Pope Francis, *Laudato Si: Encyclical letter on care of our common house*(Libreria Editrice Vaticana,2015); Eoin O'Neill, 'The Pope and the environment: Towards an integral

5 Conclusions

The variety of styles, epistemologies, experiences and legal systems explored in this collective work reflects the plurality of possibilities where sustainability and participation can interact. However, as repeatedly pointed out in this chapter, the interaction is fraught with challenges. Therefore, it is crucial to identify mechanisms that craft specific institutional arrangements for a polycentric governance scenario where sustainability through participation is enhanced. These mechanisms include but are not limited to, approaches of knowledge co-creation via the establishment of more inclusive networks that improve participation and, ultimately environmental governance.

Drawing on the conclusions from the cited work of Benessia et al.,[78] a hybridised scenario for sustainability rooted in participatory research tools could represent the way forward to the complex sustainability challenges. Essentially, participatory research prioritises local perspectives, values, needs, and knowledge through collaboration with community members throughout the entirety of the research process.[79] In this approach, research is not conducted *on* community members, but rather *with* them.[80]

---

ecology?'(2016) Environmental Politics 749; Ryszard Feliks Sadowski, 'The Concept of Integral Ecology in the Encyclical Laudato Si'(2016) Divyadaan Journal of Philosophy and Education 21; Fritjof Capra, Ugo Mattei, *The ecology of law: Toward a legal system in tune with nature and communit* (Berrett-Koehler Publishers, 2015); Giulia Sajeva, *When Rights Embrace Responsibilities: Biocultural Rights and the Conservation of Environment* (Oxford University Press, 2018); Michael E Zimmermann, 'Integral ecology: A perspectival, developmental, and coordinating approach to environmental problems' World Futures 50; Sean Esbjorn-Hargens, Michael E Zimmermann, *Integral ecology: Uniting multiple perspectives on the natural world* (Shambhala Publications, 2011).

78 Alice Benessia and others, n 32, at 6.

79 Laura Smith, Lisa Rosenzweig, Marjorie Schmidt, 'Best practices in the reporting of participatory action research: embracing both the forest and the trees' (2010) The Counseling Psychologist 1115. For the application of participatory research to the legal realm see: Jennifer Keahey 'Sustainable development and participatory action research: a systematic review' (2021) Systemic Practice and Action Research 291; Emily Houh, Kristin Kalsen, 'It's critical: Legal participatory action research' (2013) 19 Michigan Journal Race & Law 287; Davydd J Greenwood. William Foote Whyte, Ira Harkavy, 'Participatory action research as a process and as a goal' (1993) 46,2 Human Relations 175.

80 Sara Kindon, Rachel Pain, Mike Kesby, 'Participatory action research: Origins, approaches and methods' in Sara Kindon, Rachel Pain, Mike Kesby (eds), *Participatory action research approaches and methods* (Routledge, 2007); Mary Brydon-Miller, 'Education, research, and action theory and methods of participatory' in Tolman, D.L., & Brydon-Miller, M. (eds), *From subjects to subjectivities: A handbook of interpretive and participatory methods*, (New York University Press, 2001); Mary Brydon-Miller 'Participatory action research: Psychology and social change' (1997) 53(4) Journal of Social Issues, 657.

Moreover, it is worth highlighting that the borders of such a community extend to include students and learners in general, researchers, and representatives of local and Indigenous communities.[81]

Hence, cooperation becomes a driver of change with methodological, relational, and environmental implications since academic and community co-researchers 'implement the results in a way that will raise critical consciousness and promote change in the lives of those involved – changes that are in the direction and control of the participating group or community'.[82]

The analysis of participatory research opens venues to discuss the use of such a framework in the field of environmental law, including its relevance to decolonising approaches and overcoming the marginalisation of voices relevant to the environmental discourse. As observed by Lopez and recalled by Denzin and Lincoln, 'we are in the midst of a large-scale social movement of anticolonialism discourse' that calls for decolonization of research and engagement with Indigenous legal research to find solutions to the challenges of our time'.[83]

---

81 Community-based participatory research (CBPR) is mainly applied in health studies, where the major corpus of literature comes from and where it is possible to learn the constituent elements of this approach. In particular, when it comes to the identification of the community of interest, Karen Hacker observes that: "When embarking on a CBPR project, one of the first challenges is to define the community of interest. Who is the population of interest? What are the boundaries of their "community"? Is this a community that is geographically bounded (city, neighborhood, county) or one that is non geographically defined by a common culture (Latinos, African Americans) or condition (parents of children with special needs) or other shared concern? Are you planning to work with those directly impacted by the issue or with the organizations that represent or serve them? The CBPR approach is often used to examine issues for underserved populations, to give voice to their concerns and help identify their perspective on the problem. However one chooses to define "community," it remains the conceptual underpinning of CBPR, influencing who collaborates and participates, how sampling is conducted, where dissemination takes place, and, most importantly, how relevant the work is to the community of interest." See Karen A Hacker, *Community-based participatory research*, (Sage Publications, 2013).

82 Sean A Kidd, Michael J Kral, 'Practicing participatory action research' (2005) 52(2) Journal of Counseling Psychology 187; On the community of researchers and learners intended in a broad sense see also Michelle Pidgeon, 'More than a checklist: Meaningful Indigenous inclusion in higher education' (2016) 4(1) Social Inclusion 77.

83 Gerardo R Lopez, 'Reflections on epistemology and standpoint theories: A response to "A Māori approach to creating knowledge."' (1998) 11 International Journal of Qualitative Studies in Education 225; Norman K Denzin, Yvonna S Lincoln, 'Introduction: Critical Methodologies and Indigenous Inquiry' in Norman K Denzin and others (eds), *Handbook of critical and indigenous methodologies* (Sage Publications,2008).

Consequently, research with (human) participants develops as a system of interactions where researchers become parts of interconnected circles and relations that are connected and accountable to the researchers.[84] Continuing along this path, Fulvio Mazzocchi observes how:

> [...] it makes a big difference thinking of the world as made of 'relatives or 'peers' rather than 'resources' or mere 'experimental units'; and so, does the appreciation of nature as deserving respect, assuming that humans are (one of) their caretakers rather than the only owners or masters of the natural environment. By feeling that they belong to the earth and are part of it, people, subsequently, would treat it and behave accordingly. For instance, it would not make sense anymore to conceive nature as existing only to provide utility to humankind. Thus, rather than trying to dominate it or experiencing alienation, people would attempt to live in consonance with nature and the overall surrounding. Finally, it would be more easily recognized that nature plays an important role even in human well-being: environmental and social health are closely interlinked, that is, if one changes, the other does as well. Overall, the Indigenous view may lead us to recognize that a prerequisite for a more sustainable world is rebuilding an ecosophic awareness.[85]

Participated spaces for sustainability in a hybridised scenario could be one possible answer to the quest for a common future for all.

In revisiting David Suzuki's metaphor, cited in the *incipit* of this work, the hybridised scenario could help us realise how striking the resemblance is between sustainability and the trajectory of the car we are in, heading towards the brick wall, as well as between participation and the vain fight for the best place to sit:

> I used to say it's as if we're in a car heading toward a brick wall at 100 kilometres per hour, and everyone is arguing about where they want to sit rather than looking ahead, putting on the brakes and turning the wheel. I don't say that anymore because we're more like a Road Runner cartoon. Road Runner approaches the edge of a cliff, then stops suddenly

84 Bagele, Chilisa, *Indigenous Research Methodologies* (Sage Publications, 2019).

85 Fulvio Mazzocchi, 'A deeper meaning of sustainability: Insights from indigenous knowledge' (2020) 7(1) The Anthropocene Review 81; In the same vein see Diane Ruwhiu and others, 'Enhancing the sustainability science agenda through Indigenous methodology' (2021) Sustainability Science 1.

> or turns to avoid it. But Wile E. Coyote keeps charging straight ahead and goes over the edge. Wile E. has that moment of realization when he's suspended in air, looks down and sees he's gone too far, then plunges to the canyon bottom.[86]

Or, more cynically, the metaphor helps us realise that any scholarly attempt to square the circle and grant a common future for all comes down to one image: a considerable amount of chatter nicely put together to distract us from the iconic Wile E. Coyote's moment of realisation.

References

Alam S, Atapattu S, Gonzalez C, Razzaque J (eds.) *International environmental law and the global south* (Cambridge University Press 2015).

Andersson KP, Ostrom E, 'Analyzing decentralized resource regimes from a polycentric perspective'(2008) 41 Policy Sciences 71.

Becerra RR, 'Legal Pluralism as a Theory for the Challenges on Environmental Health' (2019) 18 Opinión Jurídica, 233.

Bendlin L, 'Local Governments in European Multi-Level Climate Governance' in Bendlin (ed.) *Orchestrating Local Climate Policy in the European Union* (Springer VS 2020).

Benessia A *et al*, 'Hybridizing sustainability: towards a new praxis for the present human predicament' (2012) 7 Sustainability Science75.

Berardo R and Lubell M, 'Understanding what shapes a polycentric governance system' (2016) 76 Public Administration Review 738.

Betsill MM and Harriet Bulkeley H, 'Transnational Networks and Global Environmental Governance: the Cities for Climate Protection program' (2004) 48 International Studies Quarterly 471.

Bignall S, Hemming S, Rigney D, 'Three ecosophies for the Anthropocene: environmental governance, continental posthumanism and Indigenous expressivism' (2016) 10 Deleuze Studies 455.

Bodansky D, Brunnee J and Hey E, 'International environmental law: Mapping the field' in Daniel Bodansky (ed), *The Oxford handbook of international environmental law* (Oxford University Press 2012).

Bornemann B, 'Environmental Governance in the Anthropocene: Challenges, Approaches and Critical Perspectives' in David Chandler, Franziska Müller and Delf Rothe (eds), *International Relations in the Anthropocene* (Palgrave Macmillan 2021).

86 David Suzuki, 'Stop fiddling when the planet burns' <https://davidsuzuki.org/story/stop-fiddling-while-the-planet-burns/> last accessed 31 October 2022.

Bratman ME, *Shared agency: A planning theory of acting together* (Oxford University Press 2013).

Bulkeley H, Davies A, Evans B and Gibbs D, 'Environmental governance and transnational municipal networks in Europe' (2003) 5 Journal of Environmental Policy & Planning 235.

Capra F and Mattei U, *The ecology of law: Toward a legal system in tune with nature and community* (Berrett-Koehler Publishers 2015).

Cattino M and Reckien D, 'Does public participation lead to more ambitious and transformative local climate change planning?' (2021) 52 Current opinion in environmental sustainability 100.

Chen T, Yang SO and Leo WWC, 'The beginning of value co-creation: understanding dynamics, efforts and betterment' (2017) 27 Journal of Service Theory and Practice 1145.

Chilisa B, *Indigenous Research Methodologies* (Sage Publications 2019).

Schattan V, Coelho P and Favareto A, 'Questioning the relationship between participation and development: a case study of the Vale do Ribeira, Brazil' (2008) 36 World Development 2937.

Cole DH, 'Advantages of a polycentric approach to climate change policy' (2015) 5 Nature Climate Change 114.

Cornwall A and Eade D, *Deconstructing development discourse: Buzzwords and fuzzwords* (Oxfam GB 2010).

Crutzen PJ, 'The "Anthropocene"'(2002) 12 Journal de Physique IV (Proceedings) 1.

Crutzen PJ, Crutzen, 'Anthropocene man' (2010) 467 Nature7317.

Danilova E, 'Neoliberal Hegemony and Narratives of "Losers" and "Winners" in Post-Socialist Transformations' (2014) 44 Journal of Narrative Theory 442.

De Lucia V, 'Competing narratives and complex genealogies: The ecosystem approach in international environmental law' (2015) 27 Journal of Environmental Law 91.

De Lucia V, 'Rethinking the Encounter Between Law and Nature in the Anthropocene: From Biopolitical Sovereignty to Wonder' (2020) 31 Law and Critique 329.

Denzin NK and Lincoln YS, 'Introduction: Critical Methodologies and Indigenous Inquiry' in Norman K Denzin, Yvonna S Lincoln and Linda Tuhiwai Smith (eds), *Handbook of critical and Indigenous methodologies* (Sage Publications 2008).

De Sousa Santos B, 'Law: a map of misreading. Toward a postmodern conception of law' (1987) 14 Journal of Law and Society 279.

Dorsch MJ and Flachsland C, 'A Polycentric Approach to Global Climate Governance' (2017) 17 Global Environmental Politics 45.

Dovers SR and Handmer JW, 'Contradictions in sustainability' (1993) 20 Environ Conserv 217.

Droz L, 'Anthropocentrism as the scapegoat of the environmental crisis: a review' (2022) 22 Ethics in Science and Environmental Politics 25.

Dryzek JS, *The Politics of the Earth. Environmental Discourses* (2nd edn, Oxford University Press 2005).
Eckerberg K and Joas M, 'Multi-level Environmental Governance: a concept under stress?' (2004) 9 Local Environment 405.
Esbjorn-Hargens S and Zimmermann ME, *Integral ecology: Uniting multiple perspectives on the natural world* (Shambhala Publications 2011).
Ferrucci G, 'A Pioneering Platform: Strengthening Environmental Democracy and Justice in Latin America and the Caribbean' (2019) 20 Journal of Management Policy and Practice 10.
Folke C *et al*, 'The problem of fit between ecosystems and institutions: ten years later' (2007) 12 Ecology and society 30.
Foucault M, 'Power and strategies' in Colin Gordon (ed), *Power/Knowledge* (Pantheon Books 1980).
Foucault M, 'The subject and power' in Hubert L Dreyfus, Paul Rabinow (eds), *Michel Foucault: Beyond Structuralism and Hermeneutics* (University of Chicago Press 1982).
Foucault M, 'The subject and power' (1982) 8 Critical inquiry 777.
Foucault M, 'Governmentality' in Graham Burchell, Colin Gordon and Peter Miller (eds), *The Foucault Effect: Studies in Governmentality* (Harvester Wheatsheaf 1991).
Freudenberg N, Pastor M and Israel B, 'Strengthening community capacity to participate in making decisions to reduce disproportionate environmental exposures' (2011) 101 American Journal of Public Health 123.
Gonzalez CG, 'Bridging the North-South divide: International environmental law in the Anthropocene' (2015) 32 Pace Environmental Law Review 407.
Gonzalez CG, 'Environmental justice, human rights, and the global south' (2015) 13 Santa Clara Journal of International Law 151.
Greenwood DJ, Whyte WF and Harkavy I, 'Participatory action research as a process and as a goal' (1993) 46 Human Relations175.
Hacker K 'Defining the community and power relationships' in Karen Hacker (ed), *Community-based participatory research* (Sage Publications 2013).
Herzog L, Ingold K and Schlager E, 'Prescribed by law and therefore realized? Analyzing rules and their implied actor interactions as networks' (2022) 50 Policy studies journal 366.
Houh E and Kalsen K, 'It's critical: Legal participatory action research' (2013) 19 Michigan Journal Race & Law 287.
IPCC, Summary for Policymakers [H.-O. Pörtner, D.C. Roberts, E.S. Poloczanska, K. Mintenbeck, M. Tignor, A. Alegría, M. Craig, S. Langsdorf, S. Löschke, V. Möller, A. Okem (eds)], in *Climate Change 2022: Impacts, Adaptation, and Vulnerability. Contribution of Working Group II to the Sixth Assessment Report of the Intergovernmental Panel on Climate Change* (Cambridge University Press 2022).

Kapucu N *et al*, 'Polycentric Governance and Decentralized Decision-Making for Pervasive Spectrum Sharing' (2021) International Journal of Public Administration 1.

Kidd SA and Kral, 'Practicing participatory action research' (2005) 52 Journal of Counseling Psychology187.

Keahey J, 'Sustainable development and participatory action research: a systematic review' (2021) 34 Systemic Practice and Action Research, 291.

Kendal D and Raymond CM, 'Understanding pathways to shifting people's values over time in the context of social–ecological systems.' (2019) 14 Sustainability Science 1333.

Kindon S, Pain R, and Kesby M, 'Participatory action research approaches and methods.' (2007) in *Connecting people, participation and place.* Abingdon: Routledge, 260.

Kopnina H, et al., 'Anthropocentrism: More than just a misunderstood problem.' (2018) 31Journal of Agricultural and Environmental Ethics 109.

Koponen J, 'Development: History and power of the concept.' *Forum for Development Studies*. Vol. 47. No. 1 (Routledge, 2020).

Kotzé LJ, and French D, 'The anthropocentric ontology of international environmental law and the Sustainable Development Goals: Towards an ecocentric rule of law in the Anthropocene.' (2018) 7 *Global Journal of Comparative Law*, 5.

Kreiling L, and Paunov C, Knowledge co-creation in the 21st century: A cross-country experience-based policy report. (OECD Publishing Paris 2021).

Krisch N, 'The pluralism of global administrative law.' (2006) 17 European Journal of International Law 247.

Lidskog R, and Elander I, 'Addressing climate change democratically. Multi-level governance, transnational networks and governmental structures.' (2010) 18 Sustainable Development 32.

Lopez GR, 'Reflections on epistemology and standpoint theories: A response to a Māori approach to creating knowledge' (1998) 11 International Journal of Qualitative Studies in Education 225.

López-Cubillos S, et al., 'The landmark Escazú Agreement: An opportunity to integrate democracy, human rights, and transboundary conservation.' (2022) 15 Conservation Letters e12838.

Martin-HillD, et al. 'Striving toward reconciliation through the co-creation of water research.' In *Current Directions in Water Scarcity Research.* Vol. 4. (Elsevier, 2022), 13.

MauserW, et al. 'Transdisciplinary global change research: the co-creation of knowledge for sustainability.' (2013) 5 Current opinion in environmental sustainability, 420.

Mazzocchi F, 'A deeper meaning of sustainability: Insights from indigenous knowledge.' (2020) 7 The Anthropocene Review 77.

Menton M, et al. 'Environmental justice and the SDGs: from synergies to gaps and contradictions' (2020) 15 Sustainability Science 1621.

Missimer M, Robèrt KH, and Broman G, 'A strategic approach to social sustainability–Part 1: exploring the social system.' (2017) 140 Journal of cleaner production 32.

Morse S, 'Post-sustainable development.' (2008) 16 Sustainable development 341.

Newig J, and Fritsch, O 'Environmental governance: participatory, multi-level–and effective?' (2009) 19 Environmental policy and governance 197.

Nissen M, Kamel M, and Sengupta K, 'Integrated analysis and design of knowledge systems and processes' (2000) 13 Information Resources Management Journal (IRMJ) 24.

Nogueira C, 'Contradictions in the concept of sustainable development: An analysis in social, economic, and political contexts.' (2019) 30 Environmental Development 129.

O'Neill E, 'The Pope and the environment: Towards an integral ecology?' (2016) 25 Environmental Politics 749.

Ostrom E, 'Beyond markets and states: polycentric governance of complex economic systems' (2010) 100 American Economic Review 641.

Ostrom E, 'Coping with Tragedies of the Commons' (1999) 2 Annual Review of Political Science 493.

Ostrom E, Cox M, 'Moving beyond panaceas: A multi-tiered diagnostic approach for social-ecological analysis' (2010) 37 Environmental Conservation 451.

Ostrom E, Janssen Marco A, and Anderies, JM 'Going beyond panaceas' (2017) 104 Proceedings of the National Academy of Sciences 15176.

Ostrom V, Ostrom E, Public Goods and Public Choices. In Michael, D., & McGinnis, A.A. (Eds). *Polycentricity and Local Public Economies: Readings from the Workshop in Political Theory and Policy Analysis* (The University of Michigan Press, 2019) 75.

Ostrom V, Polycentricity (Part 1). In McGinnis MD, M.D, and Arbor A, M.I. *Polycentricity and Local Public Economies: Readings from the Workshop. Political Theory and Policy Analysis,* (The University of Michigan Press, 2019) 52.

Pallemaerts M, 'International Environmental Law from Stockholm to Rio: Back to the Future?'(1992). 1 Review of European Community and International Environmental Law 254.

Pánovics A, 'The Escazú Agreement and the Protection of Environmental Human Rights Defenders' (2021) *Pecs J. Int'l & Eur. L.*, 23.

Parrott L, 'The modelling spiral for solving 'wicked' environmental problems: Guidance for stakeholder involvement and collaborative model development.' (2017) 8 Methods in Ecology and Evolution 1005.

Pellizzoni L, Ontological politics in a disposable world: the new mastery of nature (Routledge 2016).

Pope Francis Laudato Si': Encyclical letter on care of our common house (Libreria Editrice Vaticana 2015).

Poto MP, Environmental Law and Governance: The Helicoidal Pathway of Participation a study of a nature-based model inspired by the Arctic, the Ocean, and Indigenous Views (Giappichelli Torino, 2022), 1.

Poto MP, Thinking about Ocean Governance: by Whom and for Whom?, in Elferink, De Lucia, Nguyen (ed. by), *International Law and Marine Areas Beyond National Jurisdiction. Reflections on Justice, Space, Knowledge and Power* (Brill, 2022).

Poto MP, Enyew EL, Nature Protection, Indigenous Rights, and Climate Action. In Bugge, H.C. (Ed.). Klimarettsbok (Universitetsforlaget, Oslo, 2021), 155.

Rist G, 'Development as a buzzword' (2007) 17 Development in practice 485.

Roe M, 'Multi-level and polycentric governance: effective policymaking for shipping' (2009) 36 Maritime Policy & Management, 39.

Rose J, Cachelin A, 'Critical sustainability: incorporating critical theories into contested sustainabilities. (2018) 8 J Environ Stud Sci 518.

Rosenau JN, 'Globalisation and governance: sustainability between fragmentation and integration' (2017), Governance and Sustainability 20.

Rosenau JN, 'The governance of fragmegration: Neither a world republic nor a global interstate system' (2000), Studia Diplomatica, 15.

Ruwhiu D, et al, 'Enhancing the sustainability science agenda through Indigenous methodology' (2022) Sustainability Science, 1.

Sadowski RS, 'The Concept of Integral Ecology in the Encyclical Laudato Si (2016) 27 Divyadaan Journal of Philosophy and Education 21.

Sajeva G, When Rights Embrace Responsibilities: Biocultural Rights and the Conservation of Environment (Oxford University Press, 2018).

Sand PH, Origin and History *The Oxford Handbook of International Environmental Law* 93 (Oxford 2021), 50.

Scott DN, and Malivel G, 'Intergenerational Environmental Justice and the Climate Crisis: Thinking with and beyond the Charter.' (2021) 17 *Osgoode Legal Studies Research Paper, Journal of Law & Equality.*

Shastri SC, 'Environmental ethics anthropocentric to eco-centric approach: A paradigm shift.' (2013) Journal of the Indian Law Institute, 522.

Smith L, Rosenzweig L, and Schmidt M, Best practices in the reporting of participatory action research: embracing both the forest and the trees 1Ψ7, (2010) 38 The Counseling Psychologist 1115.

Solomonian L, and Ruggiero E, 'The critical intersection of environmental and social justice: a commentary' (2021) 17 Globalization and Health 1.

Stephan M, Marshall G, and McGinnis M, An introduction to polycentricity and governance' (2019) *Governing Complexity: Analyzing and Applying Polycentricity*, 21.

Suzuki D, Stop fiddling when the planet burns, (May 1st 2019), blogpost in https://davidsuzuki.org/story/stop-fiddling-while-the-planet-burns/, visited 19.07.2022.

Tamanaha BZ, 'Understanding legal pluralism: past to present, local to global' (2017), Legal Theory and the Social Sciences, 447.

Tang C, and Dou J, 'Exploring the Polycentric Structure and Driving Mechanism of Urban Regions From the Perspective of Innovation Network' (2022) 10 Frontiers in Physics 855380.

Torfing J, Sørensen E, and Røiseland A, 'Transforming the public sector into an arena for co-creation: Barriers, drivers, benefits, and ways forward.' (2019) 51 Administration & Society 795.

Tormos-Aponte F, and García-López GA, 'Polycentric struggles: The experience of the global climate justice movement' (2018) 28 Environmental Policy and Governance 284.

Tortola PD, 'Clarifying multilevel governance.' (2017) 56 European Journal of Political Research, 234.

Ven der Hel S, 'New science for global sustainability? The institutionalisation of knowledge co-production in Future Earth' (2016) 61 Environmental science & policy 165.

Van Asselt H, 'Dealing with the fragmentation of global climate governance: legal and political approaches in interplay management' (2007) 30 Global Governance Working Paper.

Van Asselt H, The fragmentation of global climate governance: Consequences and management of regime interactions. (Edward Elgar Publishing 2014).

Weber H, 'Politics of 'leaving no one behind': contesting the 2030 Sustainable Development Goals agenda' (2017) 14 Globalizations 399.

Weisstein EW, Möbius strip. *https://mathworld. wolfram. com/* (2021) accessed 15.07.2022.

White K, Too late for Indigenous climate justice: Ecological and relational tipping points' (2020) 11 Wiley Interdisciplinary Reviews: Climate Change e603.

Witte JM, Benner T, and Streck C, 'Partnerships and networks in global environmental governance: Moving to the next stage.' *Governance and Sustainability*. (Routledge, 2017) 141.

Young OR, 'Institutional dynamics: resilience, vulnerability and adaptation in environmental and resource regimes' (2010) 20 Global Environmental Change 378.

Young OR, Les Gasser, The institutional dimensions of environmental change: fit, interplay, and scale (MIT press 2002).

Zelli F, and Van Asselt H, 'Introduction: The institutional fragmentation of global environmental governance: Causes, consequences, and responses.' (2013) 13 Global environmental politics 1.

Zelli F, et al., The consequences of a fragmented climate governance architecture: a policy appraisal. In Biermann F., *Global Climate Governance Beyond 2012: Architecture, Agency and Adaptation*, 25 (Cambridge University Press 2010).

Zimmerman ME, 'Integral ecology: A perspectival, developmental, and coordinating approach to environmental problems' (2005), 61 World Future 1–2, 50–62.

Annex

Guiding Questions to Authors

1. Why is the question of sustainability through participation relevant in your individual issue area? Have sustainability and participation been legally recognised, are they merely policy guidelines, soft law, are they tools to further the implementation of norms and obligations, do they provide interpretive guidance?
2. What is sustainability and how would you describe the concept of sustainability in your issue area? You may refer to:
   a. What are legal documents that demand 'sustainable development' aiming for?
   b. Are there different meanings in international, supranational, and national legal documents?
   c. Are there empirical or theoretical parameters that can be used to pin down the concept?
   d. Does an interdisciplinary approach help to interpret the concept?
   e. How can it be differentiated from neighbouring concepts such as 'responsibility for future generations' or 'protection of natural resources'?
   f. Is sustainability per se linked to environmental protection or are there different concepts of sustainability depending on the area of research? If so, how does it relate to concepts in other disciplines (especially in economics and philosophy)? Are there further related concepts?
3. What is participation and how would you describe the concept of participation in your issue area?
   a. What are the legal documents that demand 'participation' aiming for?
   b. Are there different meanings in international, supranational, and national legal documents?
   c. Are there empirical or theoretical parameters that can be used to pin down the concept?
   d. Does an interdisciplinary approach help to define the concept?
4. Is participation used as a means to achieve sustainability in your issue area? If so, explain the connections between the two concepts. You may refer to:
   a. How are sustainability and participation interlinked?

b. What are the legal reasons for their interconnection, i.e. is the interconnection commended by higher-ranking norms, according to the hierarchy of laws in your issue area, etc.?

c. Which forms of participation in decision-making shall ensure sustainability or sustainable development in your issue area? In particular:
   - Which persons or groups are considered as rights-holders?
   - What are the actual legal obligations discussed under the concept of sustainability and participation?
   - How are the two concepts enforced?
   - If possible, refer to individual examples, answering those questions.

Index

If you have any questions regarding this title, please contact:

Koninklijke Brill BV
Plantijnstraat 2
2321 JC Leiden
Email: info@brill.com

Batch number: 10703835